YEARBOOK OF AMERICAN & CANADIAN CHURCHES 1994

Sixty-second issue   Annual

YEARBOOK OF AMERICAN & CANADIAN CHURCHES 1994

Edited by Kenneth B. Bedell

Prepared and edited for the Education, Communication and
Discipleship Unit of the National Council of the Churches of Christ
in the U.S.A. 475 Riverside Drive, New York, NY 10115-0050

Published and Distributed
by Abingdon Press
Nashville

Yearbook of American
and Canadian Churches
1994

Joan Brown Campbell
Publisher

J. Martin Bailey
Editorial Director

Printed in the United States of America

ISBN 0687-46650-4

ISSN 0195-9034

**Library of Congress catalog card number:
16-5726**

Kenneth Bedell
Editor

Leonard Wilson
Mary Jane Griffith
Kathryn H. Bedell
Production Assistants

Preparation of this Year-
book is an annual project of
the National Council of
Churches of Christ in the
United States of America.

This is the sixty-second
edition of a yearbook that was
first published in 1916. Previous editions have been enti-
tled, Federal Council
Yearbook (1916-1917),
Yearbook of the Churches
(1918-1925), The Handbook
of the Churches (1927), The
New Handbook of the
Churches (1928), Yearbook
of American Churches (1933-
1972) and Yearbook of
American and Canadian
Churches (1973-present).

Introduction

Latino/Hispanic Special Focus

The articles in this special section on Hispanic/Latino religiosity present a challenge to religious leaders to meet the needs of an important and growing portion of the population. Allan Deck concludes his article by pointing to the uncertainty of the future. He raises the possibility that Hispanics who have moved into evangelical churches may "return to Roman Catholicism or merge with a growing unchurched, secular mainstream." George Barna has studied trends and points out what will happen if current trends continue. Robert Pazmiño presents a very personal picture of how the future is being worked out. He talks about the need to recover "aspects of Hispanic language and culture which were decimated through decades of discriminatory practices." He also points to the need for this to "occur while actively participating in a wider society." The real challenge for current religious leadership is to open the door to ways that the Hispanic reality can enrich the religious experience of all Americans and at the same time be supportive of and encourage unique religious expressions among the diverse groups of people who call themselves Latinos.

This challenge is made more difficult by the complexity of the Hispanic community. One example of the difficulty of making generalizations about the Hispanic community in the United States is the language problem. Are we talking about Hispanics, Latinos, Chicanos . . . ? People have good reasons for using particular terms, but we are using Hispanic and Latino to mean the same thing. They describe a group of people who claim to have a cultural or historical connection. As Anthony Stevens-Arroyo points out in his article, 'Latino' is "an extremely important notion to produce political and social unity."

In the search for ways to meet the religious needs of Latinos, religious groups are blessed with the leadership coming from the Latino community. Articles in this section witness to some of the strong Latino leadership in the religious area.

Church Giving

The article on church giving challenges those who are concerned about the viability of religious institutions. As the editor of the *Yearbook*, I am particularly pleased to be able to share this information because it is based on the statistics that are published in the *Yearbook*. Each year we collect statistics from denominations and report them. This article is an example of the use of these statistics to help us better understand what is happening in religious organizations.

Who is Official?

Each year we attempt to make the *Yearbook* more useful. The listing of periodicals with each denomination is done to provide a connection between the denomination and periodicals. Some periodicals are written for people in a particular denomination or religious tradition, but the periodical is not actually 'officially' related to the denomination. This year we asked all the periodicals if they were 'official' or not. We also asked representatives of denominations to name their 'official' publications. The results were fascinating, but not very useful. For many editors the concept of 'official' was confusing. Sometimes a periodical is produced by a division of a denomination, but it does not represent the whole denomination. In a number of cases we received contradictory information from denominational representatives and periodical editors.

It soon became clear that a better method of describing periodicals needs to be devised. So for the present we list periodicals that have any connection to a particular denomination with the denomination listing and we list that denomination with the periodical. But the reader needs to be warned that the connection varies from periodical to periodical.

Ken Bedell
Editor

CONTENTS

I
THE CHURCH IN THE '90s: TRENDS AND DEVELOPMENTS

Trends in Latino Religion

Allan Figueroa Deck, S.J.
Hispanic Pastoral Programs
Loyola Marymount University
Los Angeles, California

Two trends in Latino religion are especially notable: 1) the ongoing success of evangelical and Pentecostal groups in attracting Latinos and 2) the growing diversity among Latinos themselves in terms of national origin, social class status, level of assimilation and English or Spanish language acquisition. This article briefly highlights these two important trends and tries to show how they may possibly be linked.

The more than 25 million Latinos in the United States are particularly suitable targets for outreach on the part of the churches and new religious movements. Latinos have a profound interest in religion in virtually all its manifestations, a quality that the first Christian missionaries noted almost 500 years ago. They are, moreover, an exceptionally youthful group, on the average 5-8 years younger than their Anglo counterparts.[1]

Mainline churches, both Protestant and Roman Catholic, have made significant attempts to reach out to them.[2] But the efforts of evangelical and Pentecostal Christians are especially noteworthy for their effectiveness.[3] This is reflected in the fact that today 70-75% of U.S. Hispanics surveyed identify themselves as Roman Catholics. This is down from more than 90% 25 years ago. The majority of Hispanics who have "defected" to other religions are

becoming evangelical Christians of one sort or another.[4]

MOVEMENT TOWARD EVANGELICAL/PENTECOSTAL CHRISTIANITY

Why are Hispanic Catholics moving out of their ancient Catholic tradition to become evangelical/Pentecostal Protestants? The literature suggest several reasons. First, the Roman Catholic Church does not have a ministerial structure that currently allows it to adequately *attend* to the huge number of baptized Hispanics. The dominant concept of ministry places great emphasis on *priestly office* seemingly at the expense of a *charismatic* approach to ministry. A charismatic approach would stress the baptismal call of the faithful and the corresponding need to identify gifts in the community and empower the faithful to assume responsibility for a wide range of ministries. The Second Vatican Council certainly encouraged such a movement, but it has not oc-

Allan Figueroa Deck, S.J., is the president of the National Catholic Council for Hispanic Ministry, Inc. His book, *The Second Wave: Hispanics Ministry and the Evangleization of Cultures* (Mahawan, NJ: Paulist Press, 1989) is a standard text on Hispanic Ministry in the Roman Catholic context.

curred as widely and rapidly as needed to keep pace with the Hispanic demographic explosion. Evangelical Christianity in contrast gives great importance to the recognition of gifts and the empowerment of the faithful to exercise them for the good of the church. This is seen especially in the creative and adaptable formation programs available for those who desire to serve in evangelical and Pentecostal communities. In contrast, Roman Catholicism offers fairly rigid, prolonged seminary, university and theologate formation programs that reasonably can touch only a handful of potential ministers.

The importance given to the reception of sacraments has also had a limiting effect on the Roman Catholic Church's outreach to Hispanics. Emphasis on sacraments over which only priests can preside coupled with the reluctance to empower laity to function as ministers creates a situation in which the ministry of the Word, especially engaging and effective preaching, becomes problematic. Yet the ministry of the Word, proclamation of the scriptures, bible study, biblically inspired prayer and powerful preaching are understandably put in second place as priests struggle to maintain a kind of "sacramental treadmill."

Evangelicals stress the identification and multiplication of ministers and the ministry of the Word. This allows them to be particularly effective within the context of the encounter and clash Hispanics are experiencing with regard to modern culture. Their Hispanic ways, among them their ancient Catholicism, does not seem quite adapted to the modern world, particularly to the United States experience.

What to do? A ministry focused on the discovery of the bible as providing rich and relevant guidelines for life in changed circumstances is especially effective. The large number of ministries allows the evangelicals to reach out to Hispanic Catholic parishes which are tending to become larger and larger and more impersonal despite some notable but still inadequate efforts to develop parish-based small ecclesial communities.

A second reason for the success of evangelical/Pentecostal outreach to Hispanics is the *continuity* between Hispanic popular Catholicism and evangelical Christianity. The continuity is found in the importance given affectivity in evangelical Christianity, especially Pentecostalism, on the one hand and in traditional, popular Hispanic Catholicism on the other. The dominant form of Catholicism in the United States is middle class and tends toward a *standardization* that finds the anomalies and idiosyncracies of the people's religion quite unfamiliar and suspect. While evangelicals often attack the symbolic, sacramental and ritualistic universe of popular Catholicism, they do provide what may be, at least for many, suitable substitutes: the discovery of the bible's rich imagery and symbolism and fire-in-the-belly preaching that speaks to Hispanics' true affective situation and needs. Mainline churches, Catholic or Protestant, with their middle class serenity, order and cool rationalism leave the struggling immigrants and the poor unimpressed.[5]

Related to the emphasis on emotions associated with evangelicalism is the role given to healing and to the miraculous. Those are prominent features of popular Hispanic Catholicism that are found as well in evangelicalism and Pentecostalism.

A third reason for the movement of Hispanic Catholics to evangelicalism is related to the efforts of Roman Catholic leaders to link faith with the struggle for justice. Hispanic popular religion was historically a vehicle for the expression of popular aspirations within an oppressive social and ecclesial context. To serve this function it had to develop *indirect*, symbolic ways to respond to and even sometimes protest against the harsh realities of life. The contemporary emphasis of progressive mainline Christians, Catholic and Protestants, on transformative action or "conscientization," had the unexpected effect of "blowing the cover," on the people's historic way of dealing with oppression.

Researcher Jorge E. Maldonado suggests that the Latin American masses find evangelical and Pentecostal Christianity more congenial in this regard since it plays down the *social implications* of faith and often, but not always, remains at the purely spiritual level. Maldonado believes that the movement of Latin Americans to evangelical and

Pentecostal Christianity is more significant than the movement of Catholics and mainline Protestants to politically committed ecclesial communities.[6] For the base ecclesial communities appear to be more political than religious. This is a turn-off for the struggling people who instinctively and for seemingly good reasons (such as preserving their lives) react against moving from *symbolic* to *overt* forms of resistance. If, as the Roman Catholic bishops say in their 1971 Roman Synod, "action on behalf of justice is a constitutive element of the preaching of the gospel," appropriate, effective ways must be found to establish that connection, ways that respect the people's reality.

DIVERSITY AMONG HISPANICS: BEYOND STEREOTYPES AND INADEQUATE ANALOGIES

A notable trend in Latino religion is a new awareness of this group's rich diversity. Concretely that means there is a growing recognition of the need to diversify or differentiate among ministries. For instance, evangelization may be conducted in Spanish, in English or even in a bilingual-bicultural fashion given the particular group's level of acculturation and language abilities. Social class awareness is also necessary. An undifferentiated "option for the poor" on the part of ministers can be interpreted in an exclusivist manner, leading some Hispanics who happen to be upwardly mobile to see themselves left out of the church's outreach and concerns.

Large migrations from the Dominican Republic to New York and even to places as remote as Alaska have dramatized the changing character of the Hispanic presence. No longer is it only a Southwestern phenomenon. Hispanics are found in virtually *every* section of the United States. The Mexican presence, for example, is growing in Florida. Nicaraguans and Salvadorans have moved into Miami by the thousands. Miami's "Little Havana" section, is now being called "Little Managua." While people of Mexican origin constitute the vast majority of Hispanics in the Los Angeles area, there are hundreds of thousands of Salvadorans, Guatemalans, and Hondurans in that city. Mexicans have overtaken Cubans as the dominant Hispanic group in Atlanta. Hispanics are penetrating such northern climes as Minnesota and Wisconsin.

The decade of the 1980's witnessed the rise of a diverse Hispanic presence in the United States. The word Hispanic or Latino was selected as an umbrella term. Outside the United States there are really no Hispanics or Latinos. The very use of these terms refers to the emergence in the United States of a new *consciousness*, perhaps more fragile than some imagine, that seeks to assert an underlying unity based upon Latin American roots, what some call the Hispanic Catholic ethos, the Spanish language and, in many cases, the unfinished struggle for socio-economic justice.

Related to the issue of the Hispanic communities' rich diversity is another question that researchers such as David Hayes-Bautista are highlighting: the inadequacy of the "urban underclass analogy" as applied to Hispanics. Hayes-Bautista is referring to the tendency to conceive of Hispanics in a one-dimensional manner, in terms of deficits or dysfunctions: socio-economic poverty, lack of schooling, social deviancies and addictions. Is this the only or even better way to approach these rich and diverse communities? Hayes-Bautista says no and goes on to show why in recent works such as *The Burden of Support* and *No Longer a Minority:Latinos and Social Policy in California*.[7] Hayes-Bautista points to a number of *positive traits* or strengths discovered in the most recent research: strong family orientation, high labor participation, low welfare dependency, strong health indicators and strong educational improvement.

The social science establishment has tended to view Hispanics as it has viewed African Americans. In doing so it has compounded the error. For the pan-racial or transracial character of Latino communities makes a racially-based analytical focus inappropriate. For Hispanics can be white, black, native American or even Asian.

Treating the Hispanics as a *racial* minority can obscure the considerable *mobility* that Hispanics have in comparison to African Americans who have continually experienced hypersegregation. While Hispanics often are segregated in urban *barrios,* they can and do move out. They can be found in a rich diversity of living contexts. This has not been the case for the vast majority of African American people in this country even today more than 40 years after the Brown vs. the Board of Education decision that inaugurated an intense period of "desegregation."

All of these factors point to the need to make many distinctions, to acknowledge the diversity of today's person of Latin American descent in the United States.

Churches are being forced to move beyond simple understandings to incorporate new data that speaks of a very *complex* socio-cultural pattern. The successes of evangelical Christians can perhaps be credited to their insight into this diversity and their willingness to experiment and to take risks in responding to that presence creatively and energetically.

Yet a word of caution is also in order. Diachronic studies of the movement of Hispanic evangelism and Pentecostalism are much needed. Is this a *permanent* change or is this movement simply a step in the modernization of United States Hispanics as David Martin suggests in his influential study of the phenomenon in Latin America?[8] If so, they will not remain in these evangelical churches for even a generation. Perhaps they will return to Roman Catholicism or merge with a growing unchurched, secular mainstream.

End Notes

1. For detailed Latino demographics see Joseph P. Fitzpatrick, S.J.,"The People: Demographic," in T. Howland Sanks and John A. Coleman, eds., *Reading the Signs of the Times.* Mahwah, NJ: Paulist Press, 1993, 27-29.

2. Two recent publications, one Protestant and the other Roman Catholic, outline the serious and significant outreach of those two mainline churches to the Latinos: Justo L. Gonzalez, general editor, *Each in Our Own Tongue: A History of Hispanic United Methodism,* Nashville: Abingdon, 1991; and Allan Figueroa Deck, S.J., *The Second Wave: Hispanic Ministry and the Evangelization of Cultures,* Mahwas, NJ: Paulist Press, 1989.

3. A forthcoming article of mine traces this development in some detail, "The Challenge of Evangelical/Pentecostal Christianity to Hispanic Catholicism in the United States" in Jay P. Dolan and Allan Figueroa Deck, S.J., eds., in the Notre Dame Study of Hispanic Catholics tentatively titled *Hispanic Catholics in the United States: Issues and Concerns,* Vol III, Notre Dame: University of Notre Dame Press, 1994. Also Sister Eleace King, I.H.M., ed., reports on the success of various evangelical and Pentecostal denominations in reaching immigrants, both Latinos and others in *Proselytism and Evangelization: An Exploratory Study,* Washington D.C.: CARA, Georgetown University, 1991.

4. Gerado Narin and Raymond J. Gamba, *Expectations and Experiences of Hispanic Catholics and Converts to Protestant Churches,* San Francisco: University of San Francisco Social Psychology Laboratory, 1990.

5. Roger Finke and Rodney Stark explain in considerable detail the movement of mainline churches away from the "unwashed masses" and the relationsip between this and the mainline Christianity's decline in the United States in *The Churching of America 1776-1990,* New Brunswick, NJ: Rutgers University Press, 1992.

6. Jorge E. Maldonado, "Building 'Fundamentalism' from the Family in Latin America," *Fundamentalisms and Society,* Martin Marty and R. Scott Appleby, eds., Chicago: University of Chicago Press, 1993, 214-239.

7. David Hayes-Bautista, *Burden of Support,* Palo Alto: Stanford University Press, 1988; and David Hayes-Bautista, Aida Hurtado, et. al., *No Longer a Minority,* Los Angeles: UCLA Chicano Studies Research Center, 1992.

8. David Martin, *Tongues of Fire: The Explosion of Protestantism in Latin America,* London: Basil Blackwell, 1990, 271ff.

How Latino/Hispanic Identity Becomes a Religious Reality

Anthony M. Stevens-Arroyo
Program for the Analysis of Religion Among Latinos
(PARAL), Bildner Center for Western Hemisphere Studies
New York City

Establishing the new field of study of Latino religion requires further attention to some basic issues. We may have let the good seed grow with the bad, but now we ought begin to separate wheat from tares. One issue we must answer to the satisfaction of social science is whether there is really such a thing as a Latino/Hispanic reality.

This question may be raised despite the well-rehearsed demographics that confirm a rapidly growing number of Spanish-speaking and Latin American origin people living in the United States. Depending on whose numbers you accept, there are between 24 and 28 million Latinos in the U.S. The conservative U.S. Bureau of the Census estimates that in the year 2013 there will be more Latinos than African Americans in the US making us the largest "minority" in the nation.

Through the dynamics of urban demographics, Latinos already outnumber African Americans in several regions of the country. So the future is already here. New York, Los Angeles and Miami are the model for demographic trend that will be national within twenty-five years.

Because of the traditional affiliation with Catholicism, no less than one out of every four Catholics today is Latino. We are more typical as United States' Catholics than are the Irish Americans. And in many dioceses, Latinos are an absolute majority of Catholics. The proportions in Protestantism are not quite the same, but they are growing, particularly in urban congregations. Within Pentecostalism, Latino congregations are rapidly multiplying with historic significance.

But does the demographic device of lumping together Spanish-speaking, Latin American born, Spanish-surnamed and Latin American origin peoples translate into a cohesive Latino/Hispanic reality? Is there such a thing as a Latino Group, or is this a misnomer for Mexican Americans, Mexicans, Chicanos, Puerto Ricans, Cuban Americans, etc. A recent national survey of political identification found, for instance, the respondents preferred the specific nationality name to a general designation like Latino or Hispanic.

But even if "Latino" is not a substitute for natial identity, it is an extremely important notion to produce political and social unity, much as "Jewish" unifies nationalities like Poles, Russians and Americans, as well as denominations like Hassids, Orthodox, Reform and non-believers alike. The Catholic church in particular has witnessed, over twenty-five years, interregional and interethnic cooperation on a grand scale under the aegis of Latino/Hispanic identity. Latino Catholics, for instance, have their own liturgical books and catechetical commission within the official church. And there are more Latino Catholics in the United States than in nearly 3/4 of the countries in Latin America.

In all denominations nationwide there is a veritable galaxy of church commissions, boards, committees and task forces united as Latino/Hispanic. Each of these entities influence not only policy but praxis. In retrospect, the churches have been more effective than university, political or educational

This article is excerpted from a presentation at the PARAL Symposium at Princeton University, April 19, 1993 agencies in fostering Latino unity. We owe a lot to our peers outside religion, but in creation of Latino unity, they can learn from us.

Given the relative weakness of institutionalized religion that struggles to finance parishes and schools, the cohesiveness of Latinos as a major constitu-ency of American religion is likely to increase, not diminish. Just as corporate America now emphasizes Latino marketing, the churches are going to have to work harder to enlist or keep Latino members. In the words of Ronald Hellman, Latino religion is a "growth industry."

Hispanic Membership in Several Denominations

The following statistics were supplied by officials in each denomination. Few denominations collect data on whether members consider themselves Hispanic or Latino. Various methods were used to establish these figures. The figure for the Roman Catholic Church is computed using the assumption that 70 percent of Hispanics living in the United States are Roman Catholic. Some denominations obtain estimates by totalling the membership in congregations that are Spanish speaking or have primarily Hispanic membership.

These figures represent estimates that officials of selected denominations have made of Hispanic participation.

American Baptist Churches USA	38,929
Brethren in Christ Church	700
Church of the Nazarene	15,203
Presbyterian Church (U.S.A.)	20,354
Roman Catholic Church	17,500,000
United Church of Christ	10,138
United Methodist Church	43,868

Values in Hispanic Culture: Double Dutch

Robert W. Pazmiño
Andover-Newton Theology School
Newton Centre, MA

As a North American Hispanic, I have been named a new breed of Hispanic. My ethnic roots are Ecuadorian in my father's lineage and Dutch and German from Pennsylvania in my mother's lineage. Because persons of German lineage in Pennsylvania are called Pennsylvania Dutch, my daughter names this strand of our family heritage from my mother's roots "Double Dutch."

It is an appropriate naming because double dutch is also the term for a rope game played with two jump ropes which are turned in tandem. My active daughter, Rebekah, enjoys this rope game which requires a unique combination of jumping coordination to successfully balance one's position between two ropes rotating in opposite directions and converging on the person whose turn it is to jump. Jumping rope in this way is both a risky and exhilarating activity. This image of jumping double dutch is appropriate for considering the status of minority persons in the United States within a dominant Anglo middle class ethos.

A person who is a North American-Hispanic is conscious of being at a point represented by the position of the hyphen in that term, the position of navigating and balancing the convergence of two cultures which rotate in distinct orbits and require careful coordination and balance. In our pluralistic society with various cultures converging, the image of jumping between two ropes provides insights for negotiating the interaction of elements in multicultural education. Yet this image is particularly helpful for the new breed Hispanic population which Virgilio Elizondo describes as *mestizaje*, the origination of a new people from two ethically disparate parent people.[1]

Like the rope game of double dutch, my life represents the tandem play of two cultures because I grew up in close association with my father's extended family and cultural roots due to a distancing and disassociation from my mother's family. Yet these extended family ties were immersed in the world of Anglo dominant local community and culture.

Elizondo vividly describes my status and that of others in relation to the experience of persons with mixed blood, not unlike the status of being a Galilean in first century Palestine. Like Galileans, new breed or new generation Hispanics are looked down upon by both Latin Americans for their cultural impurity, and by Anglos for their ethnic ties.

New breed Hispanics especially of the third and subsequent generations are Hispanic in their approach to life, but their first and dominant language is either English or "Spanglish" which is a mixture of English and Spanish. In most cases they are not at home in Anglo society and struggle with the status of being modern day Galileans.[2] Galilee at its best was a crossroads of cultures and people with an openness to each other, not unlike some small communities and associations in the city of my origin, New York.[3]

But Galilee at its worst resulted in the exclusion and division of those who were different, not unlike the experience of a vast majority of minority persons in the United States and some cultural groups in New York City. This experience of exclusion was heightened for me through my marriage to a woman who is of pure Puerto Rican decent.

Robert W. Pazmiño teaches religious education. This article is excerpted from his forthcoming book, *Latin American Journey: Insights for Christian Education in North America* (United Church Press).

I feel Puerto Rican as an adopted member of my wife's extended family and as a result of six years of ministry in a predominantly Puerto Rican church in East Harlem, New York. Being Puerto Rican and being Hispanic in that context requires nurture through a constant effort to reappropriate one's cultural heritage within a dominant culture that has generally sought to squelch it and assign it to an inferior status.

For those of new breed status who are second, third and subsequent generation Hispanics in the United States, the distinct challenge is to recover those aspects of Hispanic language and culture which were decimated through decades of discriminatory practices, components of which are ever present in individual and corporate life.

This recovery must occur while actively participating in a wider society which devalues this very renewal of Hispanic culture as evidenced through, for one example, the increased opposition to bilingual education. Such recovery confronts a variety of factors. One factor is the potential danger of further ghettoization where the maintenance of an ethnic enclave results in alienation from the wider society and an inability to impact upon that society in constructive ways. A second factor is the unwarranted perception by those in the wider society that the affirmation of one's ethnic identity inherently represents an immature longing for one's home group with the attending feelings of security and connection. A third factor is the complex of shifts in a multicultural global existence which necessitate interaction and dialogue on a daily basis across ethnic and cultural divisions. Additional factors can be cited, but the challenge remains to broaden our understanding for addressing such realities.

An image of double dutch distinct from the rope game and more in tune with the dominant North American culture is that of sharing equally the costs of one's outing with a date or friends. It is a multicultural model that assumes each contributing ethnic group can equally share their heritage and gain from that of others in a climate of mutual respect. To do otherwise is to deny the full implications of the gospel of Jesus Christ and to refuse to address the ethnocentrism resident in each of our lives.

End Notes

1. Virgil Elizondo, *Galilean Journey: The Mexican-American Promise* (Maryknoll, NY: Orbis, 1983).

2. Orlando Costas, "Evangelizing An Awakening Giant: Hispanics in the U.S.," in *Signs of the Kingdom in the Secular City*, Helen Ujvarosy, ed., (Chicago: Covenant, 1988), 57.

3. K. W. Clark, "Galilee," in *Interpreter's Dictionary of the Bible*, ed. George A. Buttrick (Nashville: Abingdon, 1962), 344-347

Perspective on the Spirituality of Hispanics in the United States

George Barna
President, Barna Research Group, Ltd.
Glendale, CA

The United States' population continues to grow—not so much because native-born Caucasian adults are having children, but due to immigration and the higher fertility rates of immigrant women. In 1960, just 3% of the nation's population was Hispanic. That proportion has tripled in the last three decades; today 9% of United States is Hispanic.[1]

An expanding Hispanic population has had a discernible effect on churches and religious institutions. Not only are there more Spanish-language congregations in the U.S. than ever, but we find a growing number of Protestant denominations aggressively seeking new ways to reach this burgeoning segment.

Beliefs

In most of our measures regarding matters of belief and religious practice, we find that Hispanic and non-Hispanic adults are similar. However, several key areas of distinction have emerged which set the two populations apart. Among the more important or intriguing of these differences are the following:

■ Hispanic adults are less likely than the typical American adult to attend a church service or to read the Bible outside of a church service during a typical week. At the same time, however, Hispanics are less likely than white or black adults to be unchurched. In other words, Hispanic adults do not attend church services as consistently as do other adults, but they are more likely to attend at least infrequently. Only one-fourth of Hispanic adults can be considered to be unchurched, compared to about one-third of other adults.[2]

■ Hispanic adults are less likely to be "born again" Christians. They are every bit as likely as other adults to say they have made a "personal commitment to

Jesus Christ that is still important in (their) life today" (an assertion made by two out of three Americans). However, they are less likely than others to say that they believe they will go to heaven when they die because they have "confessed (their) sins and have accepted Jesus Christ as (their) savior." In total, while 37% of Americans qualify as "born again Christians" under this two-part classification approach, just 22% of the Hispanic adults in the United States qualify. In fact, among Hispanics who say they have made a personal commitment to Christ, about one-third believe they will go to heaven because they have accepted Him as their savior and confessed their sins to Him; roughly one-third say they will live in heaven because of their good behavior during their life; and the remaining one-third state that they do not know what will happen to them after they die.[3]

■ Hispanics are more likely to believe that "if a person is generally good, or does enough good things for others during their life, they will earn a place in heaven." Half of Hispanics strongly agree with this sentiment, compared to one-third of all other adults. Other belief statements which reflect a "works theology" are also more widely embraced by Hispanics than by non-Hispanics.[4]

■ Hispanics are more likely than other adults to strongly concur with the notion that "Jesus Christ was crucified, died, rose from the dead, and is spiritually alive today." More than four out of five Hispanics (84%) strongly affirm this statement, compared to less than

George Barna is founder and president of Barna Research Group, Ltd., a full-service marketing research company located in Glendale, California. He is the author of *The Frog in the Kettle, User Friendly Churches* and *The Power of Vision.*

three-quarters of other Americans. They are also more likely than other adults to agree that "the bible is totally accurate in all that it teaches."[5]

■ Among most evangelical Christians, homosexual behavior is deemed unacceptable.[6] Hispanic adults have a different view, however. They are more likely than evangelicals and most other adults to decree that homosexuality is a private matter that is nobody's business. In fact, they are 48% more likely than all adults to strongly disagree that "homosexuality is immoral."[7]

Church Participation

While half of all adults associated with a church denomination say they are "very committed" to their denomination, less than one out of three Hispanics (31%) say they are very committed to their church. This is most prevalent among Hispanic Catholics.[8]

The gradual dissolution of the relationship between the Roman church and Hispanics can be witnessed in the rapid growth of Hispanics in Protestant churches, especially among the "charismatic" denominations; in the growing acceptance of Protestant doctrinal perspectives among Hispanics; and in the declining positive views possessed by Hispanic adults regarding the Catholic church.[9]

Among the great challenges to Protestantism, however, is the recognition that the worship and lifestyle patterns of Hispanics are different from those of the other population groups that have already been reached. New outreach strategies and church dynamics must be designed to address the unique religious views, life expectations and family practices of the Hispanics who have come to the United States.

Future

What does the future hold for Hispanics in the United States concerning their faith patterns? We anticipate the following during the coming decade:

■ Second and third generation Hispanics in the United States typically shed some of the traditions and cultural moorings of their parents. We expect a larger proportion of these culturally acclimated Hispanics to depart from the Catholic church and to participate instead in the life of Protestant churches.

■ Several thousand new churches will be planted specifically to address the needs and expectations of the Hispanic community. A significant proportion of these will be Spanish-language congregations, predominantly located in 16 key metropolitan areas of the nation.

■ Seminaries will see an increase in the number of Hispanic applicants for full-time ministry education as a result of the need for more Spanish-speaking ministers.

■ The dominant growth in the ranks of the nation's "born again" population will stem from conversions among the Hispanic population. Growth among the Caucasian population is expected to remain flat or to decline slightly.

■ Evangelistic events geared to penetrating the Hispanic community will become more prevalent as churches strive to reach out to this community. Because so many disenfranchised Hispanic Catholics are reluctant to make a direct leap from attending Catholic services to attending Protestant services, becoming acquainted with Protestant churches through "soft-sell" evangelistic events will be viewed by the host churches as a productive and effective means of reaching Hispanic families.

■ Suppliers of Christian education materials (e.g. Sunday school curriculum, small group guides) will identify the Hispanic market as a "growth" market for the late nineties.

■ Highly regarded Christian leaders from Central and South America will hold major "crusades" in the United States and experience great interest and results. This is a continuation of one of the trends of the nineties, in which Christian leaders from other nations become missionaries to the United States, reaching non-English speaking population groups which the indigenous church has failed to touch.

■ The Catholic church will make a concerted effort to strengthen its ties with Hispanic families by providing Spanish-language services, providing more opportunities to the laity for leadership within the church and importing priests from Spanish-speaking nations to reflect a sensitivity to, and familiarity with, native-land customs.

End Notes

1. 1992 Statistical Abstract of the United States, U.S. Dept. of Commerce, Bureau of the Census, U.S.G.P.O., Washington, D.C., 1993.

2. Absolute Confusion, George Barna, Regal Books, Ventura, CA, 1993.

3. OmniPoll 2-93, a nationwide probability survey of adults, N=1205, conducted by the Barna Research Group, Ltd., of Glendale, CA, during July-August, 1993.

4. Absolute Confusion, George Barna, Regal Books, Ventura, CA, 1993.

5. OmniPoll 2-93, conducted by the Barna Research Group, Ltd., July-August, 1993.

6. Absolute Confusion, George Barna, Regal Books, Ventura, CA, 1993.

7. Absolute Confusion, George Barna, Regal Books, Ventura, CA, 1993.

8. OmniPoll 2-93, conducted by the Barna Research Group, Ltd., July-August, 1993.

9. These figures are drawn from the combined data of two nationwide probability surveys of adults 18 or older: OmniPoll 1-93, conducted in January-February, 1993 and OmniPoll 2-93, conducted in July-August, 1993.

The State of Church Giving through 1991

John and Sylvia Ronsvalle
empty tomb, inc.
Champaign, Illinois

How does one measure the commitment of church members? This intriguing question has more than academic interest. In a society going through major culture shifts, as some assert the U.S. is, the level of support the church receives from its adherents is a telling indicator of how large a role the church will have in helping to define the values in an emerging new order.

In light of Jesus statement that where our treasure is there our hearts will be (Matt. 6:23), the level of financial support church members direct to their congregations, and how the congregations divide that support, can be a valuable indicator of commitment level. The amount of dollars donated indicates how much congregations and church structures have to spend. The percentage of income donated indicates how the member values the church in relationship to the member's total financial activity. In more worldly terms, what is the church's "market share" of its members' lives?

Data is available to measure church giving patterns over a 24-year period. *The State of Church Giving through 1991*[1] is the third and most recent update of an analysis of giving patterns in a defined set of Protestant denominations begun in 1988.[2] Of the original 31 Protestant denominations providing data to the *Yearbook of American and Canadian Churches* for 1968 and 1985, 28 continued to provide data that allowed the analysis to be updated through 1991. These denominations represented 30 million full or confirmed members and included communions across the theological spectrum of the Protestant church.

Constant dollar giving

Measuring giving in dollars provides information about how much the congregations and their related agencies had to spend over a period of time. Denominational data included in *The State of Church Giving* series was analyzed in terms of constant 1987 dollars. By using a deflator to factor inflation out of the current dollar contribution data, per member contributions in constant dollars were compared across various data years.

From this perspective, per member Total Contributions increased from $304.18 in 1968 to $359.04 in 1991. Of the $54.86 increase received by congregations, all of it was directed to Congregational Finances. This category increased from $240.03 in 1968 to $296.35 in 1991, an increase of $56.31.

In constant 1987 dollars, the per member contribution to Benevolences in 1991 was less than it was 24 years before, in 1968. Per member contributions to Benevolences in 1968 were $64.14 and had changed to $62.69 in 1991, a decrease of $1.45.[3]

Figure 1 presents per member giving to Congregational Finances and Benevolences in constant 1987 dollars for the period of 1968 through 1991. Changes in U.S. per capita (per person) income in constant 1987 dollars serves as the background in Figure 1.

Per member giving as a percentage of income

While dollars donated indicate how much the church had to spend, giving as a percentage of income reflects what portion of per capita income was being directed to the church rather than to other areas of members' lives. The

John and Sylvia Ronsvalle annually produce *A Report on the State of Church Giving*. They can be contacted at empty tomb, inc., P.O. Box 2404, Champaign, IL 61825-2404.

Figure 1: Per Member Giving in Constant 1987 dollars to Congregational Finances and Benevolences and U.S. Per Capita Disposable Personal Income, 1968-1991

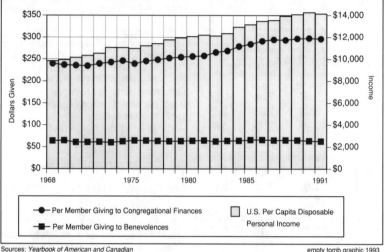

Sources: *Yearbook of American and Canadian Churches*, adjusted series; Bureau of Economic Analysis

empty tomb graphic 1993

analysis found that per member giving as a percentage of U. S. per capita disposable (after-tax) personal income declined between 1968 and 1985, and that this trend continued through 1991.

In 1968, per member giving as a percentage of income for a composite of the 31 denominations was 3.09%. By 1985, the level of giving had declined to 2.66%.

The downward trend continued through 1991, when the portion of income members contributed to their churches decreased to 2.54%. Using definitions outlined in the annual *Yearbook of American and Canadian Churches'* data request questionnaire, Total Contributions were divided into two subcategories. Congregational Finances refers to the internal operation of the congregation. Benevolences includes any activities beyond the local congregation, including denominational support, global missions, seminary support and contributions to agencies in the local community.

Of the two, Benevolences decreased proportionately faster than Congregational Finances. The percent change

from the 1968 base in giving as a percentage of income to Congregational Finances was -14% from 1968 to 1991, from 2.44% in 1968 to 2.10% in 1991. The percent change from the 1968 base in giving as a percentage of income to Benevolences was -32% in the same period, from 0.65% in 1968 to 0.44% in 1991

Table 1 presents the 1968-1991 levels of giving as a percentage of income to Total Contributions, Congregational Finances and Benevolences. Since the percent figures are rounded to the second decimal place, the bold type indicates a slight increase even if the percentage provided is the same numerical figure as the previous year.

Organizational Affiliation

Within the set of communions reporting data to the *Yearbook of American and Canadian Churches* for the 1968-1991 period, six were affiliated with the National Association of Evangelicals (NAE), and eight were members of the National Council of the Churches of Christ in the U.S.A. (NCC). Certainly

Table 1: Full or Confirmed Member Giving to Congregations as a Percentage of Income

Year	Total Contributions	Congregational Finances	Benevolences
1968	3.09	2.44	0.65
1969	3.03	2.38	0.65
1970	2.92	2.33	0.60
1971	2.86	2.27	0.59
1972	2.86	**2.28**	0.58
1973	2.74	2.20	0,54
1974	**2.80**	**2.23**	**0.57**
1975	2.77	2.19	**0.59**
1976	2.76	**2.19**	0.57
1977	2.74	2.18	0.56
1978	2.68	2.15	0.53
1979	2.66	2.13	0.53
1980	2.65	2.12	**0.53**
1981	2.64	2.11	0.53
1982	**2.70**	**2.19**	0.51
1983	2.69	2.18	**0.52**
1984	2.65	2.16	0.50
1985	**2.66**	**2.16**	**0.50**
1986	2.65	**2.16**	0.49
1987	**2.65**	**2.17**	0.48
1988	2.58	2.11	0.47
1989	2.57	2.11	0.46
1990	2.53	2.09	0.45
1991	**2.54**	**2.10**	0.44

Bold indicates years with increases

there are limitations to identifying the theological perspective of a denomination based solely on its affiliation with one of these two groups. However, for purposes of comparing giving patterns at the macro level, such organizational membership may suffice to identify a communion as "evangelical" or "mainline."

The hypothesis that evangelicals give a larger portion of their income to their churches proved to be true. During the entire period from 1968 through 1991, the denominations affiliated with the NAE received a larger contribution from their members than did the NCC denominations. This finding was true whether one considered giving as a percentage of income or giving in constant dollars.

However, when the change in giving as a percentage of income within each grouping was compared from 1968 to 1991, it became evident that per member contributions in the NAE-affiliated denominations were declining at a faster pace than those of the NCC-affiliated denominations.

In 1968, per member giving as a percentage of income in the NAE-affiliated denominations was 6.73%. By 1991, the level of giving had declined to 4.79%, a percent change from the 1968 base in giving as a percentage of income of -29%.

The NCC-affiliated denominations posted a 1968 level of giving as a percentage of income of 3.24% which decreased to 2.84% in 1991, a percent change from the 1968 base in giving as a percentage of income of -12%.

Similar trends were evident in both groups of denominations in terms of giving to Benevolences, whether in constant dollars or in giving as a percentage of income. Per member contributions to Benevolences were smaller in 1991 than in 1968.

In 1968, the NAE-affiliated denominations received 1.29% of income for Benevolences, which declined to 0.89% in 1991. In the NCC denominations, 0.62% was donated in 1968 and 0.40% in 1991.

Constant dollar contributions to Benevolences also declined. For the NAE-affiliated denominations, per member contributions to Benevolences declined from the 1968 level of $127.18 in constant 1987 dollars to the 1991 level of $126.29. The NCC-affiliated denominations experienced a decline from the 1968 level of per member contributions to Benevolences of $60.65 to $55.98 in 1991, also in constant 1987 dollars.

Although the NAE-affiliated denominations were receiving a lower per member contribution to Benevolences in 1991 than in 1968, their aggregate receipts increased as a function of a 50% increase in membership during the 1968 to 1991 period.

A loss of membership in the NCC-affiliated denominations between 1968 and 1991 combined with the decrease in per member giving to Benevolences to produce an aggregate Benevolences level 25% smaller in 1991 than in 1968.

Figure 2 presents giving as a percentage of income for both the NAE affiliated and NCC affiliated denominations, for the three categories of Total Contributions, Congregational Finances and Benevolences.

Conclusions

The State of Church Giving through 1991 explored patterns in church member giving for a defined set of Protestant denominations. The report found that giving as a percentage of income had declined in the categories of Total Contributions and in the two subcategories of Congregational Finances and Benevolences. Giving to Benevolences in constant 1987 dollars also decreased on a per member basis from 1968 to 1991.

Since giving as a percentage of income was decreasing between 1968 and 1991 across the theological spectrum, one conclusion seems inescapable: *something is happening to church members in the U.S.*

The trend for members to give a smaller portion of their incomes to their churches would indicate that the church is findings its members' attention, as evidenced by spending patterns, slowly turning elsewhere. This development is serious news.

Now is the time for the church to evaluate these findings. In light of this analysis, the church has a choice before it. Will leaders at all levels of the church do the hard work necessary to develop strategies that can reverse these trends? Or will the church tolerate a slow cooling of its members' affections, attempting to survive on less? The choice made will define whether the church becomes marginalized in an increasingly secular society or whether the church lives up to its potential as a faith community in a world of challenge.

TRENDS AND DEVELOPMENTS

Figure 2: Per Member Giving as a Percentage of Income to Total Contributions, Congregatinal Finances and Benevolence, for NAE and NCC Denominations, 1968, 1985 and 1991

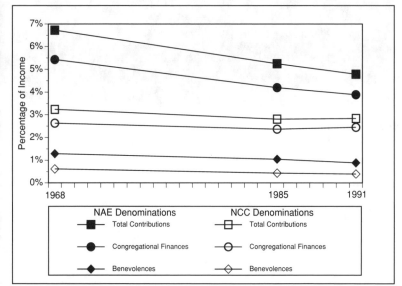

Sources: *Yearbook of American and Canadian Churches*, adjusted series; Bureau of Economic Analysis

empty tomb graphic 1993

End Notes

1. John Ronsvalle and Sylvia Ronsvalle, The State of Church Giving through 1991 (Champaign, IL: empty tomb, inc., 1993).

2. John Ronsvalle and Sylvia Ronsvalle, A Comparison of Church Member Giving with the Growth in United States Per Capita Income (Champaign, IL: empty tomb, inc., 1988).

3. Details in the text and Table 1 may not add to totals indicated due to rounding.

THE YEAR IN IMAGES

RNS PHOTO/Reuters

New Friends

President Bill Clinton presided over the first meeting of Yassir Arafat and Yitzhak Rabin. The leaders represented three different faith traditions. There was reason to hope that 1993 was the beginning of movement toward peace in the middle east.

II
DIRECTORIES

1. UNITED STATES COOPERATIVE ORGANIZATIONS, NATIONAL

The organizations listed in this section are cooperative religious organizations that are national in scope. All organizations are listed alphabetically including the National Council of the Churches of Christ in the USA.

American Bible Society

In 1816, pastors and laymen representing a variety of Christian denominations gathered in New York City to establish a truly interconfessional effort "to disseminate the Gospel of Christ throughout the habitable world." Since that time the American Bible Society (ABS) has continued to provide God's Word, without doctrinal note or comment, wherever it is needed and in the language and format the reader can most easily use and understand. The ABS is the servant of the denominations and local churches. It provides Scriptures at exceptionally low costs in various attractive formats for their use in outreach ministries here in the United States and all across the world.

Today the ABS has the endorsement of more than 100 denominations and agencies, and its board of managers is composed of distinguished clergy and laity drawn from these Christian groups.

Forty-eight years ago the American Bible Society played a leading role in the founding of the United Bible Societies, which are involved in Scripture translation, publication and distribution in more than 200 countries and territories around the world. The ABS contributes approximately 35 percent of the support provided by the UBS to those national Bible Societies financially unable to meet the total Scripture needs of people in their own countries.

The work of the ABS is supported through gifts from individuals, local churches, denominations and cooperating agencies. Their generosity made possible the distribution of 249,778,134 copies of the Scriptures during 1992, out of a total of 618,185,347 copies of the Scriptures distributed by all member societies of the UBS.

HEADQUARTERS

National Service Center, 1865 Broadway, New York, NY 10023 Tel. (212)408-1200
Media Contact, Dir., Pub. Rel., William P. Cedfeldt, Tel. (212)408-1419 Fax (212)408-1456

OFFICERS

Chpsn., James Wood
Vice-Chpsn., Mrs. Sally Shoemaker Robinson
Pres. & CEO, Dr. Eugene B. Habecker
Vice-Pres. for Natl. Programs, Maria I. Martinez
Vice-Pres. for Dev., Arthur Caccese
Vice-Pres. of Fin. & Treas., Daniel K. Scarberry
Departmental Heads: Natl Program Dev., Dir., Rev. Fred A. Allen; Translation & Scripture Res. Dev., Dir., Rev. Dr. David G. Burke; Volunteer Activities & Field Services, Dir., Dr. Haviland C. Houston; National Program Promotions, Dir., Jeanette Russo; Public Relations, Dir., William P. Cedfeldt; Human Resources, Dir., Robert P. Fichtel; National Program Services, Dir., Gary R. Ruth; Systems, Dir., George Balinski; Library & Archival Services., Dir., Dr. Peter Wosh

American Council of Christian Churches

Founded in 1941, The American Council of Christian Churches (ACCC) is comprised of major denominations—Asbury Bible Churches, Bible Presbyterian Church, Evangelical Methodist Church, Fellowship of Fundamental Bible Churches (formerly Bible Protestant), Free Presbyterian Church of North America, Fundamental Methodist Church, General Association of Regular Baptist Churches, Independent Baptist Fellowship of North America, Independent Churches Affiliated and Tioga River Christian Conference, along with hundreds of independent churches. The total membership nears 2 million. Each denomination retains its identity and full autonomy, but cannot be associated with the World Council of Churches, National Council of Churches or National Association of Evangelicals.

The ACCC is an agency for fellowship and cooperation among Bible-believing churches. Member churches believe in the inspiration and inerrancy of Scripture; the triune God; the virgin birth; substitutionary death and resurrection of Christ and His second coming; total depravity of man; salvation by grace through faith; and the necessity of maintaining the purity of the church in doctrine and life.

HEADQUARTERS

P.O. Box 19, Wallingford, PA 19086 Tel. (215)566-8154 Fax (215)892-0992
Media Contact, Exec. Dir., Dr. Ralph Colas

OFFICERS

Pres., Dr. E. Allen Griffith
Vice-Pres., Rev. Mark Franklin
Exec. Sec., Dr. Ralph Colas
Sec., Rev. David Natale
Treas., Mr. William H. Worrilow, Jr.
Commissions: Chaplaincy; Education; Laymen; Literature; Missions; Radio & Audio Visual; Relief; Youth

American Friends Service Committee

The American Friends Service Committee was founded in 1917 as a World War I Quaker effort to provide humanitarian assistance to civilians whose lives were devastated by violence. Since then, AFSC has evolved into a complex organization addressing an array of the most pressing issues before the human family.

AFSC's recent programs illustrate common themes that have emerged over nearly eight decades of multi-faceted Quaker witness to the dignity of all people. The AFSC works in 25 countries, aiding development and refugee relief, peace education and community organization. The AFSC sponsors seminars around the world to build better international understanding. Work within the U.S. includes conducting programs on problems of minority groups such as housing, employment and denial of legal rights. The AFSC maintains a Washington, D.C. office to present AFSC experience and perspectives to policymakers.

AFSC programs are multiracial, nondenominational and international. The programs illustrate the work for justice, peace and development which is based in timeless religious faith and the commitment of our predecessors in Quaker Service.

The AFSC is a co-recipient of the Nobel Peace Prize.

HEADQUARTERS
1501 Cherry St., Philadelphia, PA 19102 Tel. (215)241-7000 Fax (215)864-0104
Media Contact, Dir. of Information, Francine Cheeks

OFFICERS
Chpsn., Dulaney O. Bennett
Treas., Lois Forrest
Exec. Dir., Kara Newell

The American Theological Library Association, Inc.

The American Theological Library Association, Inc. (ATLA) is a special library association that works to improve theological and religious libraries and librarianship by providing continuing education, developing standards, promoting research and experimental projects, encouraging cooperative programs and publishing and disseminating research tools and aids. Founded in 1947, ATLA currently has a membership of over 180 institutions and 500 individuals.

HEADQUARTERS
820 Church St., Ste. 300, Evanston, IL 60201 Tel. (708)869-7788 Fax (708)869-8513
Media Contact, Dir. of Member Services

OFFICERS
Pres., Roger Loyd, Duke Divinity School Library, Duke University, Durham, NC 27706
Vice-Pres., Linda Corman, Trinity College Library, 6 Hoskin Ave., Toronto, ON M5S 1H8
Sec., David J. Wartluft, Krauth Mem. Library, Luth. Theol. Sem., 7301 Germantown Ave., Philadelphia, PA 19119-1794
Exec. Dir. & CEO, Albert E. Hurd

American Tract Society

The American Tract Society is a nonprofit, nonsectarian, interdenominational organization, instituted in 1825 through the merger of most of the then-existing tract societies. As one of the earliest religious publishing bodies in the United States, ATS has pioneered in the publishing of Christian books, booklets and leaflets. The volume of distribution has risen to more than 25 million pieces of literature annually.

HEADQUARTERS
P.O. Box 462008, Garland, TX 75046 Tel. (214)276-9408 Fax (214)272-9642
Media Contact, Dir. of Marketing, Perry Brown

OFFICERS
Chpsn., Stephen E. Slocum, Jr.
Vice-Chpsns.: Arthur J. Widman; Philip E. Worth
Sec., Edgar L. Bensen
Treas., Raymond P. Negris

The American Waldensian Society

The American Waldensian Society (AWS) promotes ministry linkages, broadly ecumenical, between U.S. churches and Waldensian (Reformed)-Methodist constituencies in Italy and Waldensian constituencies in Argentina-Uruguay. Founded in 1906, AWS aims to enlarge mission discovery and partnership among overseas Waldensian-Methodist forces and denominational forces in the U.S.

AWS is governed by a national ecumenical board, although it consults and collaborates closely with the three overseas Waldensian-Methodist boards. The Waldensian experience is the earliest continuing Protestant experience.

HEADQUARTERS
475 Riverside Dr., Rm. 1850, New York, NY 10115 Tel. (212)870-2671 Fax (212)870-2499
Media Contact, Exec. Dir., Rev. Frank G. Gibson, Jr.

OFFICERS
Pres., Rev. Laura R. Jervis
Vice-Pres., Rev. Gilbert W. Bowen, D.Min.
Sec., Kent Jackson
Treas., Lon Haines
Exec. Dir., Rev. Frank G. Gibson, Jr.

The Associated Church Press

The Associated Church Press was organized in 1916. Its member publications include major Protestant, Anglican and Orthodox groups in the U.S. and Canada. Some Roman Catholic publications and major ecumenical journals are also members. It is a professional Chrisitan journalistic association seeking to promote excellence among editors, recognize achievements and represent the interests of the religious press. It sponsors seminars, conventions, awards programs and workshops for editors, staff people and business managers.

HEADQUARTERS
Media Contact, Exec. Dir., Rev. John Stapert, P.O. Box 162, Ada, MI 49301-0162 Tel. (616)676-1017

OFFICERS
Pres., James Solheim, 815 Second Ave., New York, NY 10017
Exec. Dir., Rev. John Stapert, P.O. Box 162, Ada, MI 49301 Tel. (616)676-1190
Treas., Chris Woehr, P.O. Box 28001, Santa Ana, CA 92799

The Associated Gospel Churches

Organized in 1939, The Associated Gospel Churches (AGC) endorses chaplains primarily for Fundamental Independent Baptist Churches to the U.S. Armed Forces. The AGC has been recognized by the U.S. Department of Defense for more than 50 years as an Endorsing Agency, and it supports a strong national defense. The AGC also endorses VA chaplains, police, prison and civil air patrol chaplains.

The AGC provides fellowship and missionary support for Fundamental Independent Churches and represents their seminaries, colleges and Bible Institutes.

The AGC believes in the sovereignty of the local church, the historic doctrines of the Christian faith and the infallibility of the Bible. It practices separation from apostasy.

HEADQUARTERS

Media Contact, Acting Pres., George W. Baugham, D.D., AGC Admn. Ofc., P.O. Box 10777, Killeen, TX 76547 Tel. (817)539-4242

OFFICERS

Commission on Chaplains, Chpsn., Rev. Bob Ellis, 5000 Carney Rd., Pensacola, FL 32526-2516
Acting Pres & Vice-Chpsn., Comm. on Chaplains, George W. Baugham, D.D., AGC Admn. Ofc., P.O. Box 10777, Killeen, TX 76547 Tel. (817)539-4666 Fax (817)539-4242
Sec.-Treas., Mrs. Eva Baugham
Natl. Field Rep., Rev. Charles Flesher

Association for the Development of Religious Information Systems

The Association for the Development of Religious Information Systems (or Services) was established in 1971 to facilitate coordination and cooperation among information services that pertain to religion. Its goal is a worldwide network that is interdisciplinary, inter-faith and interdenominational to serve both administrative and research applications.

HEADQUARTERS

Media Contact, Coord., David O. Moberg, 7120 W. Dove Ct., Milwaukee, WI 53233-2766 Tel. (414)357-7247

Association of Catholic Diocesan Archivists

The Association of Catholic Diocesan Archivists, which began in 1979, has been committed to the active promotion of professionalism in the management of diocesan archives. The Association meets annually: in the even years it has its own summer conference, in the odd years it meets in conjunction with the Society of American Archivists. Publications include *Standards for Diocesan Archives*, *Access Policy for Diocesan Archives* and the quarterly *Bulletin*.

HEADQUARTERS

Archives & Records Center, 5150 Northwest Hwy., Chicago, IL 60630 Tel. (312)736-5150 Fax (312)736-0488
Media Contact, Ms. Nancy Sandleback

OFFICERS

Episcopal Mod., Archbishop of Chicago, Joseph Cardinal Bernardin
Pres., Mr. John J. Treanor
Vice-Pres., Msgr. Francis J. Weber, 15151 San Fernando Mission Blvd., Mission Hills, CA 91345 Tel. (818)365-1501
Sec.-Treas., Sr. Catherine Louise LaCoste, C.S.J., P.O. Box 85728, San Diego, CA 92186-5728 Tel. (619)574-6309
Bd. Members: Kinga Perzynska, P.O. Box 13327, Capital Station, Austin, TX 78711 Tel. (512)476-4888 Fax (512)476-3715; Ronald D. Patkus, 2121 Commonwealth Ave., Brighton, MA 03235 Tel. (617)254-0100; Johanna Mims, P.O. Box 36776, Charlotte, NC 28236 Tel. (704)377-6871; Marina Ochoa, 213 Cathedral Pl., Santa Fe, NM 87501 Tel. (505)983-3811 Fax (505)982-5619
Newsletter Editor, Nancy Sandleback

Association of Regional Religious Communicators (ARRC)

ARRC is a professional association of regional, ecumenical and interfaith communicators who work with local, state and regional religious agencies to fulfill their needs by providing occasional syndicated television and radio programs to members. ARRC also publishes the quarterly *ARRC Newsletter*. ARRC provides local representation on the Communication Commission of the National Council of Churches, before the Federal Communications Commission, and with the denominations. ARRC offers fellowship by participation at the annual convention of the North American Broadcast Section of the World Association for Christian Communication, by updating names and addresses of national and local communicators.

OFFICERS

Pres., Margaret Hoepfl, Ecumenical Communications of NW Ohio, 1102 Sandusky, Ste. M, Perrysburg, OH 43552 Tel. (419)874-3932

Association of Statisticians of American Religious Bodies

This Association was organized in 1934 and grew out of personal consultations held by representatives from *The Yearbook of American Churches, The National* (now *Official) Catholic Directory*, the Jewish Statistical Bureau, The Methodist (now The United Methodist), the Lutheran and the Presbyterian churches.

ASARB has a variety of purposes: to bring together those officially and professionally responsible for gathering, compiling, and publishing denominational statistics; to provide a forum for the exchange of ideas and sharing of problems in statistical methods and procedure; and to seek such standardization as may be possible in religious statistical data.

c\o American Baptist Churches, USA, P.O. Box 851, Valley Forge, PA 19082-0851 Tel. (610)768-2480 Fax (610)768-2470

Media Contact, Sec.-Treas., Dr. Norman M. Green, Jr.

OFFICERS

Pres., Dale E. Jones, Church of the Nazarene, 6401 The Paseo, Kansas City, MO 64131 Tel. (816)333-7000 Fax (816)333-1683

1st Vice-Pres., Lou McNeil, Glenmary Research Center, 750 Piedmont Ave. N.E., Atlanta, GA 30308 Tel. (404)876-6518 Fax (404)876-0604

2nd Vice-Pres., Ms. Greta Lauria, Presbyterian Church (USA), 100 Witherspoon St. #4420, Louisville, KY 40202-1396 Tel. (502)569-5360 Fax (502)569-8005

Sec.-Treas., Dr. Norman M. Green, Jr.

The Association of Theological Schools in the United States and Canada

The Association of Theological Schools is an association of schools which offer graduate professional degrees for church professions.

For information about enrollment in member schools see "Trends in Seminary Education" in the statistical section of this book. The member schools are all listed in sections 7 and 8.

HEADQUARTERS

10 Summit Park Drive, Pittsburgh, PA 15275-1103 Tel. (412)788-6505

Media Contact, Assoc. Dir., Gail Buchwalter King, Tel. (412)788-6510

OFFICERS

Pres., Robert E. Cooley, Gordon-Conwell Theological Seminary, South Hamilton, MA

Vice Pres., James H. Costen, Interdenominational Theological Center, Atlanta, GA

Secretary, Diane Kennedy, Aquinas Institute of Theology, St. Louis, MO

Treasurer, Anthony T. Ruger, Consultant, Wethersfield, CT

STAFF

Executive Director, James L. Waits

Associate Directors: Daniel O. Aleshire; Gail Buchwalter King

Campus Crusade for Christ International

Campus Crusade for Christ International is an interdenominational, evangelistic and discipleship ministry dedicated to helping fulfill the Great Commission through the multiplication strategy of win-build-send. Formed in 1951 on the campus of UCLA, the organization now includes 40 separate ministries reaching out to almost every segment of society. There are more than 40,000 full-time, trained associate and volunteer staff in 152 countries, with the numbers expanding almost daily. The NewLife 2000 (Reg) strategy to give every person on earth an opportunity to say "yes" to Jesus Christ by the year 2000 includes thousands of churches of all denominations and 350 mission groups.

HEADQUARTERS

100 Sunport La., Orlando, FL 32809 Tel. (407)826-2000 Fax (407)826-2120

Media Contact, Sid Wright

OFFICERS

Pres., William R. Bright

Exec. Vice-Pres., Stephen B. Douglass

Vice-Pres. of Admn. & Chief Fin. Officer, Kenneth P. Heckmann

Vice-Pres. of Intl. Ministries, Bailey E. Marks

CARA—Center for Applied Research in the Apostolate

CARA—the Center for Applied Research in the Apostolate is a not-for-profit research organization founded by a group of Roman Catholic laity, bishops, clergy and religious men and women on the premise that not only theological principles but also the findings of secular sciences, especially sociology and psychology, must be the basis for pastoral care.

CARA performs a wide range of studies and services including church management, religious life research and planning, church personnel, education, health care ministry, parish development. Since its roots are Roman Catholic, many of its studies are done for dioceses, religious orders, educational institutions, hospitals and social service agencies. Interdenominational studies are also performed.

HEADQUARTERS

Georgetown University, Washington, DC 20057-1033 Tel. (202)687-8080 Fax (202)687-8083

Media Contact, Gerald H. Early

STAFF

Exec. Dir., Gerald H. Early

Research Assoc.: Sr. Eleace King, Ed.D.; Joseph O'Hara, Ph.D.

Center for Parish Development

The Center for Parish Development is an ecumenical, non-profit research and development agency whose mission is to facilitate major and profound change in church organizations in today's post-Christendom era. Founded in 1968, the Center's goals are to develop an *ecclesial* paradigm (to challenge the current *privacy* and *societal* paradigms), to develop and test transformation theory and practice in church systems, to apply systems theory to the work of church transformation, and to contribute to the practical theology conversation.

The Center staff provides research, consulting and training resources for church organizations engaging in major change. The Center is governed by a 16-member Board of Directors.

HEADQUARTERS

5407 S. University Ave., Chicago, IL 60615 Tel. (312)752-1596

Media Contact, Exec. Dir., Paul M. Dietterich

OFFICERS

Chpsn., Eugene L. Delves, 9142 S. Winchester Ave., Chicago, IL 60620

Vice-Chpsn., Pastor Gordon Nusz, United Methodist Church, 111 E. Ridge St., Marquette, MI 49855

Sec., Raymond L. Alley, 5916 Cresthaven Ln, #527B, Toledo, OH 43614

Treas., Robert J. Schreiter, C.PP.S., Catholic Theological Union, 5401 S. Cornell Ave., Chicago, IL 60615

Past Chpsn., Anthony Shipley, The United Methodist Church, 475 Riverside Dr., Ste. 300, New York, NY 10115

Exec. Dir., Paul M. Dietterich

Chaplaincy of Full Gospel Churches

The Chaplaincy of Full Gospel Churches (CFGC) is a coalition of nondenominational churches united for the purpose of being represented in military and civilian chaplaincies. Since its inception in 1984, CFGC has grown rapidly and currently represents over 5.2 million American Christians.

Churches, fellowships and networks of churches which affirm the CFGC statement of faith that "Jesus is Savior, Lord and Baptizer in the Holy Spirit today, with signs, wonders and gifts following" may join the endorsing agency. CFGC represents its 101 members-networks before the Pentagon's Armed Forces Chaplains Board, the National Conference of Ministry to the Armed Forces, Endorsers Conference for Veterans Affairs Chaplaincy and other groups requiring professional chaplaincy endorsement.

HEADQUARTERS

2721 Whitewood Dr., Dallas, TX 75233-2713 Tel. (214)331-4373 Fax (214)333-4401

Media Contact, David B. Plummer

OFFICERS

Pres. & Dir., Rev. Jim Ammerman
Deputy Dir., Rev. Charlene Ammerman
Assoc. Dir., Chaplain David B. Plummer
Field Dir., Rev. Bob Elliott

Christian Endeavor International

Christian Endeavor is a Christ-centered, youth-oriented ministry which assists the local church in reaching young people with the gospel of Jesus Christ, discipling them in the Christian faith and equipping them for Christian ministry and service in their local church, community and world. It reaches across denominational, cultural, racial and geographical boundaries.

Christian Endeavor International produces materials for program enrichment, provides seminars for equipping youth leaders for effective ministry and holds conferences and conventions for Christian inspiration, spiritual growth and fellowship.

Organized in Portland, Me., in February 1881, there now are active Christian Endeavor groups in approximately 78 nations and island groups, totaling over 2 million members.

HEADQUARTERS

3575 Valley Rd., P.O. Box 820, Liberty Corner, NJ 07938-0820 Tel. (908)604-9440 Fax (908)604-6075

OFFICERS

Pres., Rev. Richard Cattermole
Exec. Dir., Rev. David G. Jackson

Christian Holiness Association

The Association is a coordinating agency of those religious bodies that hold the Wesleyan-Arminian theological view. It was organized in 1867.

HEADQUARTERS

CHA Center, P.O. Box 100, Wilmore, KY 40390 Tel. (606)858-4091

Media Contact, Ofc. Mgr., Patricia Walls

OFFICERS

Pres., Dr. O. D. Emery, High Point, NC
Exec. Dir., Burnis H. Bushong, Gas City, IN

AFFILIATED ORGANIZATIONS

Association of Evangelical Churches
Bible Holiness Movement
Brethren in Christ Church
Churches of Christ in Christian Union
Evangelical Christian Church
Evangelical Church of North America
Evangelical Friends Alliance
Evangelical Methodist Church
Free Methodist Church in North America
The Church of the Nazarene
The Salvation Army
The Salvation Army in Canada
United Brethren in Christ Church (Sandusky Conference)
The Wesleyan Church
Japan Immanuel Church

Christian Management Association

Christian Management Association is a member-based association devoted to educating, equipping and encouraging its members to improve their management skills. There are 61 local chapters and more than 3,500 members nationwide participating in strengthening, encouraging and challenging one another to perform the Lord's work with excellence and integrity.

As a nonprofit organization, CMA understands the complex and demanding needs of churches, parachurch organizations and other Christian ministries. CMA has resources and services to help with church management, planning, leading, fund raising, administration, data processing, finance, accounting and law.

Through seminars, books, tapes, newsletters, bi-monthly chapter meetings and much more, CMA strives in every way to live out its credo "Members Serving Members."

HEADQUARTERS

22632 Golden Springs, Ste. 390, Diamond Bar, CA 91765 Tel. (909)861-8861 Fax (909)860-8247

Media Contact, CEO, Sylvia Nash

OFFICERS

Chpsn. of the Bd., Commissioner James Osborne, The Salvation Army
Vice-Chpsn., Patrick Clements, Church Extension Plan, P.O. Box 12629, Salem, OR 97309
Treas., C. E. Crouse, Jr., Capin, Crouse & Company, 720 Executive Park Dr., Greenwood, IN 46143
Sec., Frederick Rudy, Good News Publishers, 1300 Crescent St., Wheaton, IL 60187
CEO, Sylvia Nash

A Christian Ministry in the National Parks

The Ministry is an independent ecumenical movement providing interdenominational religious services in 65 National Parks, Monuments and Recreation Areas. For 20 years it was administered by the National Council of Churches. On Jan. 1, 1972, it became an independent movement representing more than 40 denominations, 60 local park committees, more than 300 theological seminaries and 16 separate religious organizations. The program recruits and staffs 300 positions, winter and summer, in 65 areas.

HEADQUARTERS
222 1/2 E. 49th St., New York, NY 10017 Tel. (212) 758-3450

OFFICER
Dir., Dr. Warren W. Ost

Church Growth Center

The Church Growth Center is an interfaith, non-profit, professional organization of men and women who have the responsibility for promoting, planning and/or managing meetings, workshops, conferences and consultation services for churches, assemblies and other religious organizations.

Founded in 1978, the Church Growth Center ministry always strives toward bringing about the transformational change of the Christian Church toward the effective implementation of the Lord's Great Commission to make disciples of all peoples.

With focus on the Great Commission, today the Church Growth Center provides resources in the form of books, workshop materials and services which are used both nationally and internationally.

The Church Growth Center has conducted annual conferences and meetings that have gone to Africa, Cambodia, Japan, Korea and other locations.

HEADQUARTERS
1230 U. S. Highway Six, P.O. Box 145, Corunna, IN 46730 Tel. (219)281-2452 Fax (219)281-2167
Media Contact, Operations Mgr., Franklin L. Grepke

OFFICERS
Pres., Dr. Kent R. Hunter, D. Min.
Vice-Pres., Walter J. Kuleck, Ph.D., Cognitive Processes Inc., 3631 Fairmount Blvd., Cleveland, OH 44118
Sec.-Treas., Mr. Roger Miller, 1060 Park Dr., Turkey Lake, Lagrange, IN 46761

Church Women United

Church Women United in the U.S.A. is an ecumenical lay movement providing Protestant, Orthodox, Roman Catholic and other Christian women with programs and channels of involvement in church, civic and national affairs. CWU has 1,750 units formally organized in communities in all 50 states, greater Washington, D.C. and Puerto Rico.

HEADQUARTERS
475 Riverside Dr., Rm. 812, New York, NY 10115 Tel. (212)870-2347 Fax (212)870-2338

Other Offices: 777 United Nations Plz., New York, NY 10017 Tel. (212)661-3856; CWU Washington Ofc., 110 Maryland Ave. NE, Rm. 108, Washington, DC 20002 Tel. (202)544-8747

OFFICERS
Pres., Ann B. Garvin, New York, NY
1st Vice-Pres., Van Lynch, Indianapolis, IN
2nd Vice-Pres., Shirley Nilsson, Albuquerque, NM
Sec.-Treas., Rhoda Akiko Iyoya, Ogden, UT
Regional Coordinators: Central, Miriam Cline, Urbandale, IA; East Central, Helen Hokenson, Huntington Woods, MI; Mid-Atlantic, Hatti Hamilton, Philadelphia, PA; Northeast, Carolyn Hill-Jones, Ossining, NY; Northwest, Nadine Riley, Portland, OR; South Central, Marjorie Troeh, Independence, MO; Southeast, Gloria B. Montalvo, Cabo Rojo, PR; Southwest, Nancy Warner, Acampo, CA

CODEL—Coordination in Development

CODEL is a membership association of Orthodox, Protestant and Roman Catholic mission-sending agencies, communions and Christian organizations working together in international development. Founded in 1969, CODEL is committed to an ecumenical approach in the development process. The 40 U.S.-based member organizations combine expertise, funds, planning, project implementation and evaluation in a spirit of Christian unity working toward self-sufficiency of the poorest peoples and communities of the world.

There are more than 80 projects in 25 countries in health, agriculture, community development and informal education. Other CODEL programs include current issues, development education activities, environment and development projects and workshops.

HEADQUARTERS
475 Riverside Dr., Rm. 1842, New York, NY 10115 Tel. (212)870-3000 Fax (212)870-3545
Media Contact, Exec. Dir., Boyd Lowry

OFFICERS
Pres., V. Rev. John Lynch
1st Vice-Pres., Sr. Margaret Rogers
Sec., Mr. Kelly Miller
Treas., Rev. Theo Feldbrugge

STAFF
Exec. Dir., Rev. Boyd Lowry
Coord. for Africa, Dr. Caroline W. Njuki
Coord. for Asia & the Pacific, Dr. A. C. Bartholomew
Environment & Development, Sr. Mary Ann Smith
Ecumenical Relations/Development Educ., Rev. Nathan VanderWerf
Dir. for Admn., Lydia Rodriguez
Accountant, Florence Tees

Consultation on Church Union

Officially constituted in 1962, the Consultation on Church Union is a venture in reconciliation of nine American communions. It has been authorized to explore the formation of a united church, truly catholic, truly evangelical and truly reformed. In 1992 the participating churches were African Methodist Episcopal Church, African

Methodist Episcopal Zion Church, Christian Church (Disciples of Christ), Christian Methodist Episcopal Church, The Episcopal Church, International Council of Community Churches, Presbyterian Church (U.S.A.), United Church of Christ and The United Methodist Church.

The Plenary Assembly, which normally meets every four or five years, is composed of 10 delegates and 10 associate delegates from each of the participating churches. Included also are observer-consultants from more than 20 other churches, other union negotiations and conciliar bodies. The most recent Plenaries have been held in 1984 (Baltimore) and 1988 (New Orleans).

The Executive Committee is composed of the president, two representatives from each of the participating churches and the secretariat. The secretariat consists of the full-time executive staff of the Consultation, all of whom are based at the national office in Princeton, N.J. Various task groups are convened to fulfill certain assignments. In 1990 there were four task groups: Communications; Unity & Justice; Theology and Special Gifts. In addition there was an Editorial Board for the annual Lenten Booklet of devotional meditations.

HEADQUARTERS

151 Wall St., Princeton, NJ 08540 Tel. (609)921-7866 Fax (609)921-0471

OFFICERS

Gen. Sec., ——
Treas./Bus. Mgr., Christine V. Bilarczyk
Pres., Dr. Vivian U. Robinson, 125 Hernlen St., Augusta, GA 30901
Vice-Pres.: Bishop Vinton R. Anderson, P.O. Box 6416, St. Louis, MO 63107; Rev. Alice C. Cowan, Trinity Episcopal Church, Oxford, OH 45656
Sec., Mr. Abraham Wright, 1912-3 Rosemary Hills Dr., Silver Springs, MD 20910

REP. FROM PARTICIPATING CHURCHES

African Methodist Episcopal Church: Bishop Vinton R. Anderson, 4144 Lindell Blvd., Ste. 222, St. Louis, MO 63108; Bishop Marshall H. Strickland, 2000 Cedar Circle Dr., Baltimore, MD 21220
African Methodist Episcopal Zion Church: Bishop J. Clinton Hoggard, 1511 K. St. N.W., Ste. 1100, Washington, DC 20005; Bishop Cecil Bishop, 5401 Broadwater St., Temple Hill, MD 20748
Christian Church (Disciples of Christ): Rev. Dr. Paul A. Crow, Jr., P.O. Box 1986, Indianapolis, IN 46206; Rev. Dr. Albert M. Pennybacker, 120 E. Main St., Apt. 2101, Lexington, KY 40507
Christian Methodist Episcopal Church: Bishop Marshall Gilmore, 109 Holcomb Dr., Shreveport, LA 71103; Dr. Vivian U. Robinson, 1256 Hernlen St., Augusta, GA 30901
The Episcopal Church: Rt. Rev. William G. Burrill, 935 East Ave., Rochester, NY 14607; Rev. Alice C. Cowan, Holy Trinity Episcopal Church, Oxford, OH 45656
Intl. Council of Community Churches: Rev. Dr. Jeffrey R. Newhall, 7808 College Dr., Ste. 2-SE, Palos Hts., IL 60463; Mr. Abraham Wright, 1612-3 Rosemary Hills Dr., Silver Springs, MD 20910
Presbyterian Church (U.S.A.): Rev. Michael E. Livingston, CN-821, Princeton, NJ 08542; Rev. Lewis H. Lancaster, Jr., 100 Witherspoon St., Rm. 3418, Louisville, KY 40202

United Church of Christ: Rev. Clyde H. Miller, Jr., 175 S. Jasmine St., Denver, CO 80224; Rev. Dr. Thomas E. Dipko, 4041 N. High St., Ste. 301, Columbus, OH 43214
The United Methodist Church: Bishop William B. Grove, 234 Lark St., Albany, NY 12210; Rev. Dr. Larry D. Pickens, 5600 S. Indiana Ave., Chicago, IL 60649

Ecumenics International

Ecumenics International is a private, educational, not-for-profit corporation with prime interests in promoting interreligious, cross-cultural, multidisciplinary dialogue among national, regional and international organizations.

Founded in 1992, EI is the first Orthodox Christian-founded international academic research clearinghouse and representation forum on ecumenics. EI's international networking includes a non-bureaucratic structure, solely empowered by empowering people, void of high-tech programs and business complexes.

The General Secretariat, Board of Trustees and Executive Council oversee the EI University Project, networking universities and colleges towards upgrading curricula to the standards of ecumenics, and the EIUP Apprenticeship Opportunities Program, inviting people to study ecumenics through long-term academic internships. Also under the General Secretariat are EI Press and all EI Joint Working Programs.

HEADQUARTERS

P.O. Box 144, Sloatsburg, NY 10974-0144 Tel. (914)736-6307 Fax (914)736-6307
Media Contact, Communications Sec., Hamilton Martyr

OFFICERS

Sec.-Gen., Anastasios Zavales
Assoc. Sec.-Gen., Patrick John Farrell
Gen. Secretariat Intern, Christopher James Maresca
Research Foundation Sec., Joseph Brian MacMenamin
Representation Endowment Sec., George Enrique Bedoya

Evangelical Council for Financial Accountability

Founded in 1979, the Evangelical Council for Financial Accountability has the purpose of helping Christ-centered, evangelical, nonprofit organizations earn the public's trust through their ethical practices and financial accountability. ECFA assists its over 700 member organizations in making appropriate public disclosure of their financial practices and accomplishments, thus materially enhancing their credibility and support potential among present and prospective donors.

HEADQUARTERS

2411 Dulles Corner Park, Ste. 140, Herndon, VA 22071-3430 Tel. (703)713-1414 Fax (703)713-1133
P.O. Box 17456, Washington, DC 20041-0456
Media Contact, Pres., Clarence Reimer

OFFICERS

Pres., Clarence Reimer
Deputy Exec. Officer, Martha James
Dir. of Member Services, Lucinda McCord

Evangelical Press Association

The Evangelical Press Association is an organization of editors and publishers of Christian periodicals which seeks to promote the cause of Evangelical Christianity and enhance the influence of Christian journalism.

HEADQUARTERS
485 Panorama Rd., Earlysville, VA 22936 Tel. (804)973-5941 Fax (804)973-2710
Media Contact, Exec. Dir., Ronald Wilson

OFFICERS
Pres., Robert Ingram, Tabletalk Magazine, P.O. Box 7500, Orlando, FL 32854
Sec., Jonathan Singer, The Christian Jew Foundation, Box 470654, Charlotte, NC 28247-0654
Treas., W. Terry Whalin, Decision Magazine, 1300 Harmon Pl., Minneapolis, MN 55403
Exec. Dir., Ronald Wilson

Fellowship of Reconcilliation

The Fellowship of Reconciliation is an interfaith pacifist organization that has been working for peace and justice since 1915. The FOR has programs in the areas of international peace, social justice, and nonviolence education in an effort to respond creatively and compassionately to issues of violence and injustice.

HEADQUARTERS
Box 271, Nyack, NY 10960 Tel. (914)358-4601 Fax (914)358-4924
Media Contact, Ed. and Communications Dir., Richard Deats

OFFICERS
Chpsn., Natl. Council, Rebecca Dameron, 248 Oakridge Ave., SE, Atlanta, GA 30317-3319
Vice-Chpsn., Natl. Council, Scott Kennedy, 404 King St., Santa Cruz, CA 95060
Exec. Sec., Jo Becker

RELIGIOUS PEACE FELLOWSHIPS
Presbyterian Peace Fellowship
Jewish Peace Fellowship
Baptist Peace Fellowship of N. America
Buddhist Peace Fellowship
Sojourners Peace Ministry
NISBCO
Pax Christi USA
World Peacemakers
Church of God Peace Fellowship
Episcopal Peace Fellowship
Disciples Peace Fellowship
Methodist Peace Fellowship
Catholic Peace Fellowship
Lutheran Peace Fellowship
Unitarian Universalist Peace Fellowship
New Call to Peacemaking
Orthodox Peace Fellowship
United Church of Christ FOR
Brethren Peace Fellowship
Disciples Peace Fellowship
Hutterian Fellowship

Glenmary Research Center

The Research Center is a department of the Glenmary Home Missioners, a Catholic society of priests and brothers. The Center was established in 1966 to serve the rural research needs of the Catholic Church in the United States. Its research has led it to serve ecumenically a wide variety of church bodies. Local case studies as well as quantitative research is done to better understand the diversity of contexts in the rural sections of the country. The Center's statistical profiles of the nation's counties cover both urban and rural counties.

HEADQUARTERS
750 Piedmont Ave., NE, Atlanta, GA 30308 Tel. (404)876-6518
Media Contact, Lesilie Grant

OFFICERS
Pres., Rev. Robert A. Dalton, P.O. Box 465618, Cincinnati, OH 45246-5618
1st Vice-Pres., Rev. Gerald Dorn, P.O. Box 465618, Cincinnati, OH 45246-5618
2nd Vice-Pres., Bro. Terrence O'Rourke, P.O. Box 465618, Cincinnati, OH 45246-5618
Treas., Mr. Robert Knueven, P.O. Box 465618, Cincinnati, OH 45246-5618
Dir., Sr. Mary Priniski

Institutes of Religion and Health

The Institutes of Religion and Health is dedicated to helping people overcome emotional obstacles by joining mental health expertise with religious faith and values. Its Blanton-Peale Graduate Institute provides advanced training in marriage and family therapy, psychotherapy and pastoral care for ministers, rabbis, sisters, priests and other counselors. Its Blanton-Peale Counselor Centers provide counseling for individuals, couples, families and groups. IRH also offers a nationwide telephone support service for clergy and social service agencies and promotes interdisciplinary communication among theology, medicine and the behavioral sciences. IRH was founded in 1937 by Dr. Norman Vincent Peale and psychiatrist Smiley Blanton, M.D.

HEADQUARTERS
3 W. 29th St., New York, NY 10001 Tel. (212)725-7850 Fax (212)689-3212
Media Contact, Anne E. Impellizzeri

OFFICERS
Chpsn., Neal Gilliatt
Vice-Chpsn., Arthur Caliandro
Sec., E. Virgil Conway
Treas., Bruce Gregory
Pres. & CEO, Anne E. Impellizzeri

Interfaith Impact for Justice and Peace

Interfaith Impact for Justice and Peace is the religious community's united voice in Washington. It helps Protestant, Jewish, Muslim and Catholic national organizations have clout on Capitol Hill and brings grassroots groups and individual and congregational members to Washington and shows them how to turn their values into votes for justice and peace.

Interfaith Impact for Justice and Peace has established the following Advocacy Networks to advance the cause of justice and peace: Justice for Women; Health Care; Hunger and Poverty; International Justice and Peace; Civil and Human Rights. The Interfaith Impact Foundation provides an annual Legislative Briefing for their members.

Members receive the periodic Action alerts on initiatives, voting records, etc., and a free subscription to the Advocacy Networks of their choice.

HEADQUARTERS
110 Maryland Ave. N.E., Ste. 509, Washington, DC 20002 Tel. (202)543-2800 Fax (202)547-8107
Media Contact, Exec. Dir., James M. Bell

OFFICERS
Exec. Dir., Rev. James M. Bell
Chpsn. of Bd., Kay Dowhower, Evangelical Lutheran Church in America, Office for Governmental Affairs
Communications Director, Robert Greenwood, 110 Maryland Ave. NE, Washington, DC 20002 Tel. (202)543-2800 Fax (202)547-8107

MEMBERS
African Methodist Episcopal Church
African Methodist Episcopal Zion Church
Alliance of Baptists
American Baptist Churches, USA: Washington Office; World Relief Office
American Ethical Union
American Muslim Council
Center of Concern
Christian Methodist Episcopal (CME) Church
Christian Church (Disciples of Christ)
Church of the Brethren
Church Women United
Columban Fathers
Commission on Religion in Appalachia
Episcopal Church
Episcopal Urban Caucus
Evangelical Lutheran Church in America
Federation of Southern Cooperatives/LAF
Federation for Rural Empowerment
Graymoor Ecumenical and Interreligious Institute
Jesuit Social Ministries
Maryknoll Fathers and Brothers
Moravian Church in America
National Council of Churches of Christ: Church World Service; Washington Office
National Council of Jewish Women
NETWORK
Peoria Citizens Committee
Presbyterian Church (USA)
Progressive National Baptist Convention
Presbyterian Hunger Fund
Reformed Church in America
Rural Advancement Fund
Society of African Missions
Southwest Organizing Project
Southwest Voter Registration/Education Project
Toledo Metropolitan Ministries
Union of American Hebrew Congregations
Unitarian Universalist Association
Unitarian Universalist Service Committee
United Church of Christ: Bd. for Homeland Ministries; Bd. for World Ministries; Hunger Action Ofc.; Ofc. of Church in Society
United Methodist Church: Gen. Bd. of Church & Society; Gen. Bd. of Global Ministries Natl. Div.; Gen. Bd. of Global Ministries Women's Div.; Gen. Bd. of Global Ministries World Div.
Virginia Council of Churches
Western Organization of Resource Councils

International Christian Youth Exchange (ICYE)
ICYE sponsors the exchange of young people between nations as a means of international and ecumenical education in order to further commitment to and responsibility for reconciliation, justice and peace. Exchangees 16-30 years of age spend one year in another country and participate in family, school, church, voluntary service projects and community life. Short-term, ecumenical, international work camp experiences are also available for those 18-35 years of age.

The U.S. Committee works in cooperation with national committees in 28 other countries and the Federation of National Committees for ICYE, which has headquarters in Berlin, Germany. ICYE is one of the only two U.S. youth exchange programs operating in Africa.

Exchanges for American youth going abroad and for overseas youth coming to the United States are frequently sponsored by local churches and/or community groups. Participation is open to all regardless of religious affiliation. Denominational agencies who are sponsors of ICYE include: American Baptist Churches in the U.S.A.; Christian Church (Disciples of Christ); Church of the Brethren; Episcopal Church; Evangelical Lutheran Church in America; Presbyterian Church (U.S.A.); Reformed Church in America; United Church of Christ and The United Methodist Church. Collaborating organizations include the National Federation of Catholic Youth Ministry and the National Catholic Education Association. Scholarships covering part of the cost are provided by most sponsoring denominations.

HEADQUARTERS
134 W. 26th St., New York, NY 10001 Tel. (212)206-7307 Fax (212)633-9085
Media Contact, Heather Hutchens

OFFICERS
Exec. Dir., Ms. Andrea Spencer-Linzie

International Union of Gospel Missions
The International Union of Gospel Missions (IUGM) is an association of almost 250 rescue missions and other ministries that serve more than 7 million homeless and needy people in the inner cities of the U.S., Canada and overseas each year. Since 1913, IUGM member ministries have offered emergency food and shelter, youth and family services, prison and jail outreach, rehabilitation and specialized programs for the mentally ill, the elderly, the urban poor and street youth.

HEADQUARTERS
1045 Swift, N. Kansas City, MO 64116-4127 Tel. (816)471-8020 Fax (816)471-3718
Media Contact, Research Asst., Alice Young

OFFICERS
Exec. Dir., Rev. Stephen E. Burger
Pres., Rev. Kaleel Ellison
Vice-Pres., Mr. Richard McMillen
Sec.-Treas., Mr. Rick Alvis

Interreligious Foundation for Community Organization (IFCO)
IFCO is a national ecumenical agency created in 1966 by several Protestant, Roman Catholic and Jewish organizations, to be an interreligious, interracial agency for support of community organization and education in pursuit of social justice. Through IFCO, national and regional religious

bodies collaborate in development of social justice strategies and provide financial support and technical assistance to local, national and international social-justice projects.

IFCO serves as a bridge between the churches and communities and acts as a resource for ministers and congregations wishing to better understand and do more to advance the struggles of the poor and oppressed. IFCO conducts training workshops for community organizers and uses its vast national and international network of organizers, clergy and other professionals to act in the interest of justice.

HEADQUARTERS

402 W. 145th St., New York, NY 10031 Tel. (212)926-5757 Fax (212)926-5842
Media Contact, Dir. of Communications, Gail Walker

OFFICERS

Pres. & Dir., Community Dev., Natl. Min., Dr. Benjamin Greene, Jr., American Baptist Churches in the U.S.A.

Inter-Varsity Christian Fellowship of the U.S.A.

Inter-Varsity Christian Fellowship is a nonprofit, interdenominational student movement that ministers to college and university students and faculty in the United States. Inter-Varsity began in the United States when students at the University of Michigan invited C. Stacey Woods, then General Secretary of the Canadian movement, to help establish an Inter-Varsity chapter on their campus. Inter-Varsity Christian Fellowship-USA was incorporated two years later, in 1941.

Inter-Varsity's uniqueness as a campus ministry lies in the fact that it is student-initiated and student-led. Inter-Varsity strives to build collegiate fellowships that engage their campus with the gospel of Jesus Christ and develop disciples who live out biblical values. Inter-Varsity students and faculty are encouraged in evangelism, spiritual discipleship, serving the church, human relationships, righteousness, vocational stew- ardship and world evangelization. A triennial missions conference held in Urbana, Illinois, jointly sponsored with Inter-Varsity-Canada, has long been a launching point for missionary service.

HEADQUARTERS

6400 Schroeder Rd., P.O. Box 7895, Madison, WI 53707 Tel. (608)274-9001 Fax (608)274-7882
Media Contact, Dir. of Development Services, Carole Sharkey, P.O. Box 7895, Madison, WI 53707 Tel. (608)274-9001 Fax (608)274-7882

OFFICERS

Pres. & CEO, Stephen A. Hayner
Vice-Pres.: C. Barney Ford; Robert A. Fryling; Robert Peitscher; Samuel Barkat; Dan Harrison
Sec., H. Yvonne Vinkemulder
Treas., Thomas H. Witte
Bd. Chpsn., Karen Mains
Bd. Vice-Chpsn., Thomas Boyle

Laymen's National Bible Association, Inc.

The Laymen's National Bible Association, Inc. (LNBA) is an autonomous, interfaith organization of lay people who advocate regular Bible reading. LNBA sponsors National Bible Week (Thanksgiv-

ing week) each November. Program activities include public service advertising, distribution of nonsectarian literature and thousands of local Bible Week observances by secular and religious organizations. LNBA also urges constitutionally acceptable use of the Bible in public school classrooms. All support comes from individuals, corporations and foundations.

LNBA was founded in 1940 by a group of business and professional people. It publishes a quarterly newsletter and has the IRS nonprofit status of a 501(c)(3) educational association.

HEADQUARTERS

1865 Broadway, 12th floor, New York, NY 10023 Tel. (212)408-1390 Fax (212)408-1448
Media Contact, Exec. Dir., Thomas R. May

OFFICERS

Pres., Dr. Victor W. Eimicke
Chpsn., Kenneth S. Giniger
Vice-Pres.: Max Chopnick, Esq.; George Nichols
Treas., Henry W. Wyman
Sec., Stewart S. Furlong
Exec. Dir., Thomas R. May

The Liturgical Conference

Founded in 1940 by a group of Benedictines, the Liturgical Conference is an independent, ecumenical, international associ- ation of persons concerned about liturgical renewal and meaningful worship. The Liturgical Conference is known chiefly for its periodicals, books, materials and sponsorship of regional and local workshops on worship-related concerns in cooperation with various church groups.

HEADQUARTERS

8750 Georgia Ave., Ste. 123, Silver Spring, MD 20910-3621 Tel. (301)495-0885
Media Contact, Exec. Dir., Ralph R. Van Loon

OFFICERS

Pres., Shawn Madigan, CSJ
Vice-Pres., John B. Foley, SJ
Sec., Eleanor Bernstein, CSJ
Treas., Frank Senn
Exec. Dir., Ralph R. Van Loon

The Lord's Day Alliance of the United States

The Lord's Day Alliance of the United States, founded in 1888 in Washington, D.C., is the only national organization whose sole purpose is the preservation and cultivation of Sunday, the Lord's Day, as a day of rest and worship. The Alliance also seeks to safeguard a Day of Common Rest for all people regardless of their faith. Its Board of Managers is composed of representatives from 25 denominations.

It serves as an information bureau, publishes a magazine, *Sunday,* and furnishes speakers and a variety of materials such as pamphlets, a book, *The Lord's Day,* videos, posters, radio spot announcements, decals, cassettes, news releases, articles for magazines and television programs.

HEADQUARTERS

2930 Flowers Rd. S., Ste. 16, Atlanta, GA 30341 Tel. (404)936-5376 Fax (404)454-6081
Media Contact, Exec. Dir. & Ed., Dr. Jack P. Lowndes

Exec. Dir. & Ed., Dr. Jack P. Lowndes
Pres., Dr. Paul Craven, Jr.
Vice-Pres.: Donald R. Pepper; Roger A. Kvam; Timothy E. Bird; John H. Schaal; Faith Willard; W. David Sapp
Sec., Rev. Ernest A. Bergeson
Treas., Mr. E. Larry Eidson

Box 500, 21 S. 12th St., Akron, PA 17501 Tel. (717)859-1151 Fax (717)859-2171
Canadian Office, 134 Plaza Dr., Winnipeg, MB R3T 5K9 Tel. (204)261-6381 Fax (204)269-9875
Media Contact, Exec. Sec., John A. Lapp, P.O. Box 500, Akron, PA 17501 Tel. (717)859-1151 Fax (717)859-2171

OFFICERS

Exec. Secs.: Intl., John A. Lapp; Canada, John Dyck; U.S.A., Lynette Meck

Lutheran World Relief

Lutheran World Relief (LWR) is an overseas development and relief agency based in New York City which responds quickly to natural and man-made disasters and supports more than 160 long-range development projects in countries throughout Africa, Asia, the Middle East and Latin America.

Founded in 1945 to act in behalf of Lutherans in the United States, LWR has as its mission "to support the poor and oppressed of less-developed countries in their efforts to meet basic human needs and to participate with dignity and equity in the life of their communities; and to alleviate human suffering resulting from natural disaster, war, social conflict or poverty."

HEADQUARTERS

390 Park Ave. S., New York, NY 10016 Tel. (212)532-6350 Fax (212)213-6081
Media Contact, Larry M. Foreman

OFFICERS

Exec. Dir., Kathryn F. Wolford

The Mennonite Central Committee

The Mennonite Central Committee is the relief and service agency of North American Mennonite and Brethren in Christ Churches. Representatives from Mennonite and Brethren in Christ groups make up the MCC, which meets annually in February to review its program and to approve policies and budget. Founded in 1920, MCC administers and participates in programs of agricultural and economic development, education, health, self-help, relief, peace and disaster service. MCC has about 950 workers serving in 50 countries in Africa, Asia, Europe, Middle East and South, Central and North America.

MCC has service programs in North America that focus both on urban and rural poverty areas. Additionally there are North American programs focusing on such diverse matters as handicap concerns, community conciliation, employment creation and criminal justice issues. These programs are administered by two national bodies—MCC U.S. and MCC Canada.

Contributions from North American Mennonite and Brethren in Christ churches provide the largest part of MCC's support. Other sources of financial support include the contributed earnings of volunteers, grants from private and government agencies and contributions from Mennonite churches abroad. The total income in 1992, including material aid contributions amounted to $39,193,742.

MCC tries to strengthen local communities by working in cooperation with local churches or other community groups. Many personnel are placed with other agencies, including missions. Programs are planned with sensitivity to locally felt needs.

National Association of Ecumenical Staff

This is the successor organization to the Association of Council Secretaries which was founded in 1940. The name change was made in 1971.

NAES is an association of professional staff in ecumenical and interreligious services. It was established to provide creative relationships among them and to encourage mutual support and personal and professional growth. This is accomplished through training programs, through exchange and discussion of common concerns at conferences, and through the publication of the *Corletter*.

HEADQUARTERS

475 Riverside Dr., Rm. 868, New York, NY 10115 Tel. (212)870-2155 Fax (212)870-2158
Media Contact, Dir., Ecumenical Networks, Dr. Kathleen S. Hurty

OFFICERS

Pres., Ms. Dorothy F. Rose, Interreligious Council of Central NY, 910 Madison St., Syracuse, NY 18310 Tel. (315)476-2001
Vice-Pres., Rev. Robina Winbush, Church Women United, 475 Riverside Dr., Rm. 812, New York, NY 10115-0812 Tel. (212)870-3046
1994 Program Chpsn., Ms. Claudette Spence, 33-24 Parsons Blvd., Flushing, NY 11354 Tel. (718)463-0095
Sec., Ms. Janet Leng, Associated Min. of Tacoma/Pierce Co., 1224 South I St., Tacoma, WA 98405 Tel. (206)383-3056
Treas., Mr. Raymond S. Blanks, Ohio Council of Churches, 89 E. Wilson Bridge Rd., Columbus, OH 43085 Tel. (614)885-9590
Registrar, Rev. N. J. L'Heureux, Queens Fed. of Churches, 86-17 105th St., Richmond Hill, NY 11418 Tel. (718)847-6764

The National Association of Evangelicals

The National Association of Evangelicals is a voluntary fellowship of evangelical denominations, churches, schools, organizations and individuals. Its purpose is not to eliminate denominations, but to protect them; not to force individual churches into a mold of liberal or radical sameness, but to provide a means of cooperation in evangelical witness; not to do the work of the churches, but to stand for the right of churches to do their work as they feel called by God.

Based upon the affirmation of a common faith resting squarely in God's Word, the Bible, NAE provides evangelical identification for 50,000 churches from more than 77 denominations with a service constituency of more than 15 million through its commissions, affiliates and subsidiaries.

HEADQUARTERS

450 Gundersen Dr., Carol Stream, IL 60188 Tel. (708)665-0500 Fax (708)665-8575

Office of Public Affairs, 1023 15th St. N.W., Ste. 500, Washington, DC 20005 Tel. (202)789-1011 Fax (202)842-0392

Media Contact, Dir., Ofc. of Information, Donald R. Brown, P.O. Box 28, Wheaton, IL 60189 Tel. (708)665-0500 Fax (708)665-8575

OFFICERS

Pres., Dr. Don Argue, 910 Elliott Ave. S., Minneapolis, MN 55404

1st Vice-Pres., Dr. David Rambo, P.O. Box 35000, Colorado Springs, CO 80935

2nd Vice-Pres., Rev. Leonard J. Hofman, 2850 Kalamazoo Ave. SE, Grand Rapids, MI 49560

Sec., Dr. Jack Estep, P.O. Box 828, Wheaton, IL 60189

Treas., Mr. Paul Steiner, 1825 Florida Dr., Ft. Wayne, IN 46805

STAFF

Exec. Dir., Dr. Billy A. Melvin
Dir. of Field Services, Rev. Darrel L. Anderson
Dir. of Information, Rev. Donald R. Brown
Dir. of Business Admn., Darrell L. Fulton
Natl. Field Rep., Rev. David L. Melvin
Dir. of Public Affairs, Dr. Robert P. Dugan, Jr.
Public Policy Analyst, Rev. Richard Cizik
Counsel, Forest Montgomery, 1023 15th St., NW, Ste. 500, Washington, DC 20005 Tel. (202)789-1011

COMMISSIONS, AFFILIATES, AGENCIES

Commissions: Chaplains; Christian Higher Educ.; Churchmen; Evangelism & Home Mission; Hispanic; Natl. Christian Educ.; Social Action; Women's

Affiliates: Christian Stewardship Assoc.; Evangelical Child & Family; Evangelical Fellowship of Mission Agencies; National Assoc. of Christian Child & Family Agencies; National Religious Broadcasters

Subsidiary: World Relief Corp.

Service Agency: New Hope Family Services

MEMBER DENOMINATIONS

Advent Christian General Conference
Assemblies of God
Baptist General Conference
Brethren Church (Ashland, OH)
Brethren in Christ Church
Christian Catholic Church (Evang. Prot.)
Christian Church of North America
Christian and Missionary Alliance
Christian Reformed Church in N.A.
Christian Union
Church of God (Cleveland, TN)
Church of God of the Mountain Assembly
Church of the Nazarene
Church of the United Brethren in Christ
Churches of Christ in Christian Union
Classis Cascades (Reformed Church in America)
Conservative Baptist Assoc. of America
Conservative Congregational Christian Conf.
Conservative Lutheran Association
Elim Fellowship
Evangelical Christian Church
Evangelical Church of North America
Evangelical Congregational Church
Evangelical Free Church of America
Evangelical Friends Intl./North America
Evangelical Mennonite Church
Evangelical Methodist Church
Evangelical Presbyterian Church
Evangelistic Missionary Fellowship
Fellowship of Evangelical Bible Churches
Fire-Baptized Holiness Church of God of the Americas
Free Methodist Church of North America
General Association of General Baptists
Intl. Church of the Foursquare Gospel
Intl. Pentecostal Church of Christ
Intl. Pentecostal Holiness Church
Mennonite Brethren Churches, USA
Midwest Congregational Christian Fellowship
Missionary Church
Open Bible Standard Churches
Pentecostal Church of God
Pentecostal Free Will Baptist Church
Presbyterian Church in America
Primitive Methodist Church, USA
Reformed Church in America, Synods of Far West and Mid-America
Reformed Episcopal Church
Reformed Presbyterian Church of N.A.
Salvation Army
Wesleyan Church

The National Conference

The National Conference, founded in 1927 as the National Conference of Christians and Jews is a human relations organization dedicated to fighting bias, bigotry and racism in America. The National Conference promotes understanding and respect among all races, religions and cultures through advocacy, conflict resolution and education.

Primary program areas include interfaith and interracial dialogue, youth intercultural communications, training for the administration of justice and the building of community coalitions. The NCCJ has 6 regional offices staffed by approximately 240 people. Nearly 200 members comprise the National Board of Trustees and members from that group form the 22-member Executive Board. Each regional office has its own local board of trustees with a total of about 2,800. The National Board of Trustees meets once annually, the Executive Board at least three times annually.

HEADQUARTERS

71 Fifth Ave., New York, NY 10003 Tel. (212)206-0006 Fax (212)255-6177

Media Contact, Dir. of Communications, Christopher Bugbee

OFFICER

Acting Pres., Karl Berolzheimer

National Conference on Ministry to the Armed Forces

The Conference is an incorporated civilian agency. Representation in the Conference with all privileges of the same is open to all endorsing or certifying agencies or groups authorized to provide chaplains for any branch of the Armed Forces.

The purpose of this organization is to provide a means of dialogue to discuss concerns and objectives and, when agreed upon, to take action with the appropriate authority to support the spiritual ministry to and the moral welfare of Armed Forces personnel.

4141 N. Henderson Rd., Ste. 13, Arlington, VA 22203 Tel. (703)276-7905 Fax (703)276-7906
Media Contact, Clifford T. Weathers

STAFF

Coord., Clifford T. Weathers
Admn. Asst., Maureen Francis

OFFICERS

Chpsn., Lewis Burnett
Chpsn.-elect, Charles E. McMillan
Sec., Curt Bowers
Treas., William B. Leonard, Jr.
Committee Members: Catholic Rep., Msgr. John J. Glynn; Protestant Rep., Rev. Vincent McMenamy; Jewish Rep., Rabbi David Lapp; Orthodox Rep., Gregory Havrilak; Member-at-Large, Rev. Dr. James E. Townsend

National Council of the Churches of Christ in the U.S.A.

The National Council of the Churches of Christ in the U.S.A. is the preeminent expression in the United States of the movement toward Christian unity. The NCC's 32 member communions, including Protestant, Orthodox and Anglican church bodies, work together on a wide range of activities that further Christian unity, that witness to the faith and that serve people throughout the world. More than 48 million U.S. Christians belong to churches that hold Council membership. The Council was formed in 1950 in Cleveland, Ohio, by the action of representatives of the member churches and by the merger of 12 previously existing ecumenical agencies, each of which had a different program focus. The roots of some of these agencies go back to the 19th century.

HEADQUARTERS

475 Riverside Dr., New York, NY 10115. Tel. (212)870-2511
Media Contact, Dir. of News Services, Carol J. Fouke, 475 Riverside Dr., Rm. 850, New York, NY 10015, Tel. (212)870-2252, Fax (212)870-2030

GENERAL OFFICERS

Pres., Rev. Dr. Gordon L. Sommers
Gen. Sec., Rev. Dr. Joan B. Campbell
Pres.-Elect, Bishop Melvin G. Talbert
Immediate Past Pres., Rev. Dr. Syngman Rhee
Sec., Mary A. Love
Treas., Dr. Shirley M. Jones
Vice-Pres./Unit Chpsns.: Dr. William Watley (Unity & Relationships); Dr. Mary D. Matz (Educ., Communication & Discipleship); Rev. Benjamin F. Chavis, Jr. (Prophetic Justice); Dr. Belle Miller McMaster (Church World Service & Witness)

ELECTED STAFF

OFFICE OF THE GENERAL SECRETARY
Tel. (212)870-2141 Fax (212)870-2817
Gen. Sec., Rev. Dr. Joan B. Campbell
Deputy Gen. Sec., James A. Hamilton
Assoc. for Ecumenical Relations, Rev. Eileen W. Lindner
Assoc. for Inclusiveness & Justice, Lois M. Dauway
Assoc. for Public Witness, James A. Hamilton

Coord. for Governance Services, MelRose B. Corley
Washington, D.C.: Mailing Address, NCC, 110 Maryland Ave., NE, Washington, DC 20002. Tel. (202)544-2350; Fax (202)543-1297.
Dir. of the Washington Ofc., James A. Hamilton
Assoc. Dir., Mary Anderson Cooper

EDUCATION, COMMUNICATION AND DISCIPLESHIP
Tel. (212)870-2049 Fax (212)870-2030
Unit Dir./Assoc. Gen. Sec., Rev. J. Martin Bailey
Department of Communication
Dir., Rev. J. Martin Bailey
Dir., News Services, Carol J. Fouke
Dir., Electronic Media, Rev. David W. Pomeroy
Dir., Interpretation Resources, Sarah Vilankulu
Assoc. Dir., Electronic Media, Rev. Roy T. Lloyd
Ministries in Christian Education
Dir., Dorothy Savage
Education for Mission
Dir., Educ. for Mission/Friendship Press, Dr. Audrey A. Miller
Editor, Friendship Press, Margaret S. Larom
Audio-Visual Coord., Rev. David W. Pomeroy
Professional Church Leadership
Staff Assoc., Peggy L. Shriver
Women in Ministry, ——
Bible Translation and Utilization
Dir., Rev. Arthur O. Van Eck
Evangelization
Staff Assoc., ——
Worship
Staff Assoc., Rev. Herman E. Luben

CHURCH WORLD SERVICE AND WITNESS
Tel. (212)870-2257 Fax (212)870-2055
Unit Dir./Assoc. Gen. Sec., Rev. R. Lawrence Turnipseed
Dir., Finance Office, Howard Jost
Dir., Constituency Information and Development, Mel Lehman
Global Ecumenical Mission
Dir., Global Ecumenical Mission, ——
Dir., Agricultural Missions, Jun Atienza
Dir., World Community, ——
Dir., Global Educ., Loretta Whalen, 2115 N. Charles St., Baltimore, MD 21218. Tel. (410)727-6106
Dir., CWS/LWR Ofc. on Development Policy, Carol Capps, 110 Maryland Ave., NE, Suite 108, Washington, DC 20002. Tel. (202)543-6336
Dir., Disaster Response, Kenlynn Schroeder
Dir., Immigration & Refugee Program, Beth Ferris
Dir., Material Resources, Soon-Young Hahn
Dir., Leadership Development, John W. Backer
Dir., Overseas Personnel, Paul W. Yount, Jr.
Dir., Intl. Congregations & Lay Ministry, Arthur O. Bauer
Dir., Africa, Willis H. Logan
Dir., Caribbean & Latin America, Oscar Bolioli Fax: (212)870-3220
Dir., East Asia & the Pacific, Victor W. C. Hsu
Dir./Dir. China Program, Jean Woo
Dir., Japan North America Commission (JNAC), Patricia Patterson
Acting Dir., Europe/USSR, Kathy Todd
Dir., Middle East, ——
Interim Dir., Southern Asia, Perry Smith
Community Education and Fund Raising
Tel. (219)264-3102 Fax (219)262-0966
Dir., Community Educ. & Fund Raising, Rev. Mel H. Luetchens, P.O. Box 968, Elkhart, IN 46515

US COOPERATIVE ORGANIZATIONS

PROPHETIC JUSTICE

Tel (212)870-2491
Program Coord., Marilyn Winters
Program Dir., Racial Justice/Ecumenical Minority
Bail Bond Fund, Rev. Joseph E. Agne
Program Dir., Justice for Women, Ms. Karen Hessel
Project Dir., Ecumenical Child Health Project,
Rev. Sharon Keeling
Program Dir., Economic & Environmental Justice/Hunger Concerns, Dr. N. Jean Sindab
Religious & Civil Liberty Consultant, Rev. Dean
M. Kelley

Related Movements of Prophetic Justice

Council on Native American Ministries, Rev.
Lawrence Hart, RR#4 Box 230, Clinton, OK
73601. Tel. (405)323-624
Consilio Ecumenico Nacional de Ministerios Hispanos, German Acevedo-Delgado, P.O. Box
708, Perth Amboy, NJ 08862. Tel. (908)324-7969
Interfaith Center for Corporate Responsibility,
Timothy Smith, 475 Riverside Dr., New York,
NY 10115. Tel. (212)870-2293
Natl. Farm Worker Ministry, Sr. Patricia Drydyk,
O.S.F., 1337 W. Ohio, Chicago, IL 60622. Tel.
(312)829-6436
National Interreligious Task Force on Criminal
Justice, Rev. David Rogers, 1404 S. Charles St.,
Baltimore, MD 21230. Tel. (410)685-7845

UNITY AND RELATIONSHIPS

Tel. (212)870-2157 Fax (212)870-2158
Unit Dir./Assoc. Gen. Sec., Dr. Constance Tarasar.
Tel. (212)870-2923
Ecumenical Networks
Dir., Dr. Kathleen S. Hurty. Tel. (212)870-2155
Inter-Faith Relations
Christian-Jewish Concerns: Dir., Dr. Jay T. Rock.
Tel. (212)870-2560
Christian-Muslim Concerns: Dir., ——, 77 Sherman St., Hartford, CT 06105. Tel. (203)232-4451
Faith and Order
Interim Dir., Rev. Norman A. Hjelm. Tel.
(212)870-2569

FINANCE AND ADMINISTRATION

Tel. (212)870-2094 Fax (212)870-3112
Dir., Robert K. Soong
Financial Management
Controller, Leo Lamb
Deputy Controller, Marian Perdiz
Asst. Controller, William B. Price
Business Services
Dir., Phyllis Sharpe
Publication Services
Dir. Sean Grandits
Management Information Systems
Dir., Rev. Nelson Murphy
Office of Human Resources
Dir., Emilio F. Carrillo, Jr.
Dir. of Compensation & Benefits, Michael W.
Mazoki

CONSTITUENT BODIES OF THE NATIONAL COUNCIL (with membership dates)

African Methodist Episcopal Church (1950)
African Methodist Episcopal Zion Church (1950)
American Baptist Churches in the U.S.A. (1950)
The Antiochian Orthodox Christian Archdiocese
of North America (1966)
Armenian Church of America, Diocese of the
(1957)
Christian Church (Disciples of Christ) (1950)
Christian Methodist Episcopal Church (1950)
Church of the Brethren (1950)
The Coptic Orthodox Church (1978)
The Episcopal Church (1950)
Evangelical Lutheran Church in America (1950)
Friends United Meeting (1950)
Greek Orthodox Archdiocese of North & South
America (1952)
Hungarian Reformed Church in America (1957)
Intl. Council of Community Churches (1977)
Korean Presbyterian Church in America, Gen.
Assembly of the (1986)
Moravian Church in America (1950)
Natl. Baptist Convention of America (1950)
Natl. Baptist Convention, U.S.A., Inc. (1950)
Orthodox Church in America (1950)
Philadelphia Yearly Meeting of the Religious Society of Friends (1950)
Polish Natl. Catholic Church of America (1957)
Presbyterian Church (U.S.A.) (1950)
Progressive Natl. Baptist Convention, Inc. (1966)

Reformed Church in America (1950)
Russian Orthodox Church in the U.S.A., Patriarchal Parishes of the (1966)
Serbian Orthodox Church in the U.S.A. & Canada
(1957)
Swedenborgian Church (1966)
Syrian Orthodox Church of Antioch (1960)
Ukrainian Orthodox Church in America (1950)
United Church of Christ (1950)
The United Methodist Church (1950)

National Interfaith Coalition on Aging

The National Interfaith Coalition on Aging
(NICA), an affiliate of the National Council on
Aging, is composed of Protestant, Roman Catholic, Jewish and Orthodox national and regional
organizations and individuals concerned about the
needs of older people and the religious community's response to problems facing the aging population in the United States. NICA was organized in
1972 to address spiritual concerns of older adults
through religious sector action.

Primary objectives of NICA are: to enable religious organizations to serve older adults; to encourage religious communities to promote ministry by
and with older adults; to support religious workers
in aging in their many roles; to be a forum for
religious dialogue about aging; and to be an advocate for older adults' concerns.

NICA supports development of programs and
services for older people by religious organizations, agencies, judicatories and congregations;
develops and distributes resources that help
churches and synagogues develop services that
improve the quality of life of older people; convenes national and regional training conferences
for those who work with older adults; assists its
members in advocacy efforts on behalf of quality
of life for older people; maintains dialogue with the
Administration on Aging.

HEADQUARTERS

c/o NCOA, 409 Third St., SW, 2nd Floor, Washington, DC 20024 Tel. (202)479-6689 Fax
(202)479-0735
Media Contact, Chpsn., Communications Comm.,
Dr. A. Eugene Smiley, 644 Linn St., Ste. 1017,
Cincinnati, OH 45203 Tel. (513)721-4330

OFFICERS

Chpsn., Dr. Carol S. Pierskalla

Chpsn.-Elect, Elaine Tiller
Past Chpsn., Rev. Harry J. Ekstam
Sec., Mrs. Maj. Carolyn Peacock
Prog. Mgr., Rev. John F. Evans

National Interfaith Hospitality Networks

The National Interfaith Hospitality Networks is a non-profit organization which works with congregations to form Networks which provide shelter, meals and assistance to homeless families. The program mobilizes existing community resources: churches and synagogues for overnight lodging, congregations for volunteers, social service agencies for referrals and day programs. The Network also employs a director who provides assistance and advocacy to Network families as they seek housing and jobs.

NIHN provides technical assistance as well as videotapes, guides and manuals for successful programs.

HEADQUARTERS

120 Morris Ave., Summit, NJ 07901 Tel. (908)273-1100
Media Contact, Pres., Karen Olson

National Interreligious Service Board for Conscientious Objectors

NISBCO, formed in 1940, is a nonprofit service organization sponsored by more than thirty religious organizations. Its purpose is to defend and extend the rights of conscientious objectors to war and organized violence. NISBCO provides information on how to register for the draft and to document one's convictions and qualify as a conscientious objector, how to cope with penalties if one does not cooperate and how to qualify as a conscientious objector while in the Armed Forces. It also provides more general information and training for counselors and the public about conscientious objection, military service and the operation of the draft and possible programs for national service.

As a national resource center it also assists research in its area of interest including the peace witness of religious bodies. Its staff provides referral to local counselors and attorneys and professional support for them. Through publications and speaking, NISBCO encourages people to decide for themselves what they believe about participation in war and to act on the basis of the dictates of their own informed consciences.

HEADQUARTERS

1601 Connecticut Ave., NW, Ste. 750, Washington, DC 20009-1035 Tel. (202)483-4510 Fax (202)265-8022
Media Contact, Exec. Dir., L. William Yolton

OFFICERS

Exec. Dir., L. William Yolton
Chpsn., Rev. L. Robert McClean
Vice-Chpsn., Mary H. Miller
Sec., Rev. Titus M. Peachey

National Religious Broadcasters

National Religious Broadcasters is an association of more than 800 organizations which produce religious programs for radio and television or operate stations carrying predominately religious programs. NRB member organizations are responsible for more than 75 percent of all religious radio and television in the United States, reaching an average weekly audience of millions by radio and television.

Dedicated to the communication of the Gospel, NRB was founded in 1944 to safeguard free and complete access to the broadcast media. By encouraging the develop- ment of Christian programs and stations, NRB helps make it possible for millions to hear the good news of Jesus Christ through the electronic media.

HEADQUARTERS

7839 Ashton Ave., Manassas, VA 22110 Tel. (703)330-7000 Fax (703)330-7100
Media Contact, Pres., Brandt Gustavson

OFFICERS

Pres., Brandt Gustavson
Chpsn., David Clark, KMC Media, Dallas, TX
1st Vice-Pres., Robert Straton, Walter Bennett Communications, Ft. Washington, PA
2nd Vice-Pres., Sue Bahner, Cornerstone Group, Manlius, NY
Sec., Mike Trout, Focus on the Family, Colorado Springs, CO
Treas., Brian Erickson, Back to the Bible, Lincoln, NE
Dir. of PR, Ron J. Kopczick, NRB, 7839 Ashton Ave., Manassas, VA 22110 Tel. (703)330-7000 Fax (703)330-7100

National Woman's Christian Temperance Union

The National WCTU is a not-for-profit, nonpartisan, interdenominational organization dedicated to the education of our nation's citizens, especially children and teens, on the harmful effects of alcoholic beverages, other drugs and tobacco on the human body and the society in which we live. The WCTU believes in a strong family unit and, through legislation, education and prayer, works to strengthen and the home and family.

WCTU, which began in 1874 with the motto, "For God and Home and Every Land," is organized in 58 countries.

HEADQUARTERS

1730 Chicago Ave., Evanston, IL 60201 Tel. (708)864-1396
Media Contact, Michael C. Vitucci, Tel. (813)394-1343

OFFICERS

Pres., Rachel Kelly
Vice-Pres., Merry Lee Christy, Rt. 1, Box 26, Rivesville, WV 26588
Promotion Dir., Nancy Zabel
Treas., Marilyn Staples
Rec. Sec., Mildred Roland, 3802 Rolling Hill Ave. NW, Roanoke, VA 24017

MEMBER ORGANIZATIONS

Loyal Temperance Legion (LTL), for boys and girls ages 6-12
Yout Temperance Council (YTC), for teens through college age

North American Academy of Ecumenists

Organized in 1967, the stated purpose of the NAAE is "to inform, relate, and encourage men and women professionally engaged in the study, teaching, and other practice of ecumenism."

HEADQUARTERS

Namer Academy of Ecumenists, c/o Ecumenics International, P.O. Box 144, Sloatsburg, NY 10974 Tel. (914)736-6307 Fax (914)736-6307
Mailing Address, c/o Eugene Zoeller, 2001 Newburg Rd., Louisville, KY 40205
Media Contact, Anastasios Zavales, P.O. Box 144, Sloatsburg, NY 10974 Tel. (914)736-6307

OFFICERS

Pres., Dr. George Vandervelde, Institute for Christian Studies, 229 College At., Toronto, ON M5T 1R4 Tel. (416)979-2331
Vice-Pres., Donna Geernaert, 90 Parent Ave., Ottawa, ON K1N 7B1
Rec. Sec., Dr. Thomas Prinz, 1300 Collingwood Dr., Alexandria, VA 22308
Membership Sec. & Treas., Eugene Zoeller, 2001 Newburg Rd., Louisville, KY 40205

North American Baptist Fellowship

Organized in 1964, the North American Baptist Fellowship is a voluntary organization of Baptist Conventions in Canada and the United States, functioning as a regional body within the Baptist World Alliance. Its objectives are: (a) to promote fellowship and cooperation among Baptists in North America and (b) to further the aims and objectives of the Baptist World Alliance so far as these affect the life of the Baptist churches in North America. Its membership, however, is not identical with the North American membership of the Baptist World Alliance.

Church membership of the Fellowship bodies is more than 28 million.

The NABF assembles representatives of the member bodies once a year for exchange of information and views in such fields as evangelism and education, missions, stewardship promotion, lay activities and theological education. It conducts occasional consultations for denominational leaders on such subjects as church extension. It encourages cooperation at the city and county level where churches of more than one member group are located.

HEADQUARTERS

Baptist World Alliance Bldg., 6733 Curran St., McLean, VA 22101
Media Contact, Dr. Denton Lotz

OFFICERS

Pres., Dr. Harold Bennett, 202 Long Valley Rd., Brentwood, TN 37027
Vice-Pres., Dr. Ronald Mayforth, Box 851, Valley Forge, PA 19482-0851

MEMBER BODIES

American Baptist Churches in the USA
Baptist General Conference
Canadian Baptist Federation
General Association of General Baptists
National Baptist Convention of America
National Baptist Convention, USA, Inc.
Progressive National Baptist Convention, Inc.
Seventh Day Baptist General Conference

North American Baptist Conference
Southern Baptist Convention

North American Broadcast Section, World Association for Christian Communication

This group was created in 1970 to bring together those persons in Canada and the United States who have an interest in broadcasting from a Christian perspective.

An annual conference is held during the week after Thanksgiving in the United States that draws more than 200 persons from at least 25 communions.

HEADQUARTERS

1300 Mutual Building, Detroit, MI 48226 Tel. (313)962-0340

OFFICERS

Bus. Mgr., Rev. Edward Willingham

Parish Resource Center, Inc.

Parish Resource Center, Inc. promotes, establishes, nurtures and accredits local Affiliate Parish Resource Centers. Affiliate centers educate, equip and strengthen subscribing congregations of all faiths by providing professional consultants, resource materials and workshops. The Parish Resource Center was founded in 1976. In 1993, there were six free-standing affiliates located in Lancaster, Pa; Long Island, N.Y.; South Bend, Ind.; Denver, Colo.; Dayton, Ohio and New York City. These centers serve congregations from 39 faith traditions.

HEADQUARTERS

633 Community Way, Lancaster, PA 17603 Tel. (717)299-2223 Fax (717)299-7229
Media Contact, Exec. Dir., Dr. D. Douglas Whiting

OFFICERS

Pres., Richard G. Greiner, Esq.
Vice-Pres., Dr. James D. Glasse
Sec., Dr. Robert Webber
Treas., R. Leslie Ellis

Pentecostal Fellowship of North America

The fellowship was organized at Des Moines, Iowa, in October 1948 shortly after the first World Conference of Pentecostal Believers was held in Zurich, Switzerland, in May, 1947. The PFNA has the following objectives: 1) to provide a vehicle of expression and coordination of efforts in matters common to all member bodies including missionary and evangelistic effort; 2) to demonstrate to the world the essential unity of Spirit-baptized believers; 3) to provide services to its constituents to facilitate world evangelism; 4) to encourage the principles of community for the nurture of the body of Christ, endeavoring to keep the unity of the Spirit until we all come to the unity of the faith.

The PFNA has local chapters in communities where churches of the member groups are located and fellowship rallies are held. On the national level, representatives of the member bodies are assembled for studies and exchange of views in the fields of home missions, foreign missions and youth.

HEADQUARTERS

Media Contact, Chpsn., Rev. B. E. Underwood, P.O. Box 12609, Oklahoma City, OK 73157 Tel. (405)787-7110 Fax (405)789-3957

OFFICERS

Chpsn., Bishop B. E. Underwood
1st Vice-Chpsn., Ray E. Smith, 2020 Bell Ave., Des Moines, IA 50315
2nd Vice-Chpsn., Dr. John R. Holland, 1910 Sunset Blvd., Los Angeles, CA 90026
Sec., Rev. Joe Edmonson, 13334 E. 14th, Tulsa, OK 64802
Treas., Dr. James D. Gee, P.O. Box 850, Joplin, MO 64802
Custodial Sec., Wayne E. Warner, 1445 Boonville Ave., Springfield, MO 65802

MEMBER GROUPS

Anchor Bay Evangelistic Association
Apostolic Church of Canada
Assemblies of God
Christian Church of North America
Church of God
Church of God of Apostolic Faith
Church of God, Mountain Assembly
Congregational Holiness Church
Elim Fellowship
Free Gospel Church, Inc.
Karl Coke Evangelistic Assn.
International Church of the Foursquare Gospel
International Pentecostal Church of Christ
International Pentecostal Holiness Church
Italian Pentecostal Church of Canada
Open Bible Standard Churches, Inc.
Pentecostal Assemblies of Canada
Pentecostal Assemblies of Newfoundland
Pentecostal Church of God
Pentecostal Free-Will Baptist Church
Pentecostal Holiness Church of Canada

Project Equality, Inc.

Project Equality is a non-profit national interfaith program for affirmative action and equal employment opportunity.

Project Equality serves as a central agency to receive and validate the equal employment commitment of suppliers of goods and services to sponsoring organizations and participating institutions, congregations and individuals. Employers filing an accepted Annual Participation Report are included in the Project Equality "Buyer's Guide."

Workshops, training events and consultant services in affirmative action and equal employment practices in recruitment, selection, placement, transfer, promotion, discipline and discharge are also available to sponsors and participants.

HEADQUARTERS

Pres., 1020 E. 63rd St., Ste. 102, Kansas City, MO 64110 Tel. (816)361-9222 Fax (816)361-8997
Media Contact, Pres., Rev. Maurice E. Culver, 1020 E. 63rd St., Ste. 102, Kansas City, MO 64110 Tel. (816)361-9222 Fax (816)361-8997

OFFICERS

Chpsn., Emilio F. Carrillo, Dir. of Human Resources, Natl. Council of Churches
Vice-Chpsn., Dr. Lillian Anthony, Assoc. for Equal Employment Opportunity, Presbyterian Church (USA)
Sec., John Colon, Dir. of Human Resources, The Episcopal Church
Treas., Sister Christine Matthews, Adrian Dominican Sisters

Pres., Rev. Maurice E. Culver

SPONSORS/ENDORSING ORGANIZATIONS

American Baptist Churches in the U.S.A.
American Friends Service Committee
American Jewish Committee
Central Conference of American Rabbis
Christian Church (Disciples of Christ)
Church of the Brethren
Church Women United
Consultation on Church Union
The Episcopal Church
Evangelical Lutheran Church in America
National Association of Ecumenical Staff
National Association of Church Personnel Administration
National Catholic Conf. for Interracial Justice
National Council of Churches of Christ in the U.S.A.
National Education Association
Presbyterian Church (USA)
Progressive National Baptist Church
Reformed Church in America
Roman Catholic Dioceses & Religious Orders
Unitarian Universalist Association
Union of American Hebrew Congregations
United Church of Christ
United Methodist Assoc. of Health & Welfare Ministries
United Methodist Church
YWCA of the USA

Protestant Radio and Television Center, Inc.

The Protestant Radio and Television Center, Inc. (PRTVC) is an interdenominational organization dedicated to the purpose of creating, producing, marketing and distributing audio-visual products for the non-profit sector. Its primary constituency is religious, educational and service-oriented groups.

Chartered in 1949, PRTVC provides a state-of-the-art studio facility, professional staff and a talent pool for radio, TV, cassettes and other forms of media production.

Affiliate members include the Episcopal Church, Evangelical Lutheran Church in America, Presbyterian Church (U.S.A.), Agnes Scott College, Candler School of Theology, Emory University and Columbia Theological Seminary.

HEADQUARTERS

1727 Clifton Rd., NE, Atlanta, GA 30329 Tel. (404)634-3324 Fax (404)634-3326
Media Contact, Bill Bengtson

OFFICERS

Bd. Chpsn., Don Heald
Vice-Chpsn., Dr. Gerald Troutman
Treas., William W. Horlock
Pres., William W. Horlock
Sec., Betty Chilton

Religion In American Life, Inc.

Religion In American Life (RIAL) is a unique cooperative program of some 50 major national religious groups (Catholic, Eastern Orthodox, Jewish, Protestant, Muslim, etc.). It provides services for denominationally-supported, congregation-based outreach and growth projects such as the current *Invite a Friend* program. These projects are promoted through national advertising campaigns reaching the American public by the use of all media. The ad campaigns are produced by a volunteer agency with production/distribution and administration costs funded by denominations and business groups, as well as by individuals. Since 1949, RIAL ad campaign projects have been among the much coveted major campaigns of The Advertising Council. This results in as much as $20 million worth of time and space in a single year, contributed by media as a public service. Through RIAL, religious groups demonstrate respect for other traditions and the value of religious freedom. The RIAL program also includes seminars and symposia, research, leadership awards programs and the placement of worship directories in hotels, motels and public places throughout the nation.

HEADQUARTERS
2 Queenston Pl., Rm. 200, Princeton, NJ 08540 Tel. (609)921-3639 Fax (609)921-0551

EXECUTIVE COMMITTEE
Natl. Chpsn., O. Milton Gossett, Saatchi & Saatchi Worldwide
Chpsn. of Bd., Rabbi Joseph B. Glasser, (CCAR)
Vice-Chpsns.: Bishop Khajag Barsamian, Primate (Armenian Church of America); Rev. Bryant Kirkland, (Presbyterian Church, USA); Most Rev. William H. Keeler, (Archbishop of Baltimore); Rabbi Ronald B. Sobel, (Cong. Emanu-El of the City of N.Y.)
Sec., Beverly Campbell, (Church of Jesus Christ of LDS)
Treas., Francis J. Palamara

STAFF
Pres., Dr. Nicholas B. van Dvck
Exec. Asst., Sharon E. Lloyd
Worship Directory Mgr., Ms. Jane Kelly

Religion Newswriters Association
Founded in 1949, the RNA is a professional association of religion news editors and reporters on secular daily and weekly newspapers, news services and news magazines. It sponsors four annual contests for excellence in religion news coverage in the secular press. Annual meetings are held during a major religious convocation.

HEADQUARTERS
Media Contact, Newsletter Ed., Charles Austin, 634 Johnson Ct., Teaneck, NJ 07666 Tel. (201)641-6636 Fax (201)836-3497

OFFICERS
Pres., Jim Jones, Ft. Worth Star-Telegram, 400 W. 7th Street, Ft. Worth, TX 76102 Tel. (817)390-7707 Fax (817)390-7789
1st Vice-Pres., Richard Dujardin, Providence Journal-Bulletin, Providence, RI 02902
2nd Vice-Pres., Cecile Holmes White, Houston Chronicle, Houston, TX 77210
Sec., Joan Connell, Newhouse News Service, 2000 Pennsylvania Ave. NW, Washington, DC
Treas., Judith Weidman, Religious News Service, New York, NY 10101

Religious Conference Management Association, Inc.
The Religious Conference Management Association, Inc. (RCMA) is an interfaith, nonprofit,

professional organization of men and women who have responsibility for planning and/or managing meetings, seminars, conferences, conventions, assemblies or other gatherings for religious organizations.

Founded in 1972, RCMA is dedicated to promoting the highest professional performance by its members and associate members through the mutual exchange of ideas, techniques and methods.

Today RCMA has more than 1,800 members and associate members.

The association conducts an annual conference and exposition which provide a forum for its membership to gain increased knowledge in the arts and sciences of religious meeting planning and management.

HEADQUARTERS
One Hoosier Dome, Ste. 120, Indianapolis, IN 46225 Tel. (317)632-1888
Media Contact, Exec. Dir., DeWayne S. Woodring, Tel. (3317)632-1888

OFFICERS
Pres., Rainer B. Wilson, Sr., Church of Christ Holiness, U.S.A., 819 Hampton, Newport News, VA 23607
Vice-Pres., Rudy Becton, United Pentecostal Church Intl., 8855 Dunn Rd., Hazelwood, MO 63042
Sec.-Treas., Pat Mulloy, Tennessee Baptist Convention, P.O. Box 728, Brentwood, TN 37024-0728
Exec. Dir., DeWayne S. Woodring, Religious Conf. Mgt. Assoc., One Hoosier Dome, Ste. 120, Indianapolis, IN 46225

Religious News Service
Religious News Service is an interfaith news service marketed to daily newspapers and religious publications and agencies across the country.

Founded in 1933, RNS also sponsors research, fellowship and intern programs in support of religious journalism. Since 1991 RNS has been syndicated by the New York Times.

The service was founded and sponsored for 50 years by the National Conference of Christians and Jews. In 1983 it was taken over by the United Methodist Reporter, the flagship publication of an ecumenical publishing company in Dallas. RNS is editorially independent.

HEADQUARTERS
475 Riverside Dr., Ste. 1902, New York, NY 10115 Tel. (212)870-3311 Fax (212)870-3440
Media Contact, Exec. Ed., Judith Weidman

OFFICERS
Publisher, Ronald Patterson, P.O. Box 660275, Dallas, TX 75226 Tel. (214)630-6495 Fax (214)630-0079

The Religious Public Relations Council, Inc.
RPRC is an international, interfaith, interdisciplinary association of professional communicators who work for religious groups and causes. It was founded in 1929 and is the oldest non-profit professional public relations organization in the world. RPRC's 600 members include those who work in communications and related fields for church-related institutions, denominational agencies, non- and interdenominational organizations and communications firms who primarily serve relig-

ious organizations.

Members represent a wide range of faiths, including Presbyterian, Baptist, Methodist, Lutheran, Episcopalian, Mennonite, Roman Catholic, Seventh-day Adventist, Jewish, Salvation Army, Brethren, Bahá'í, Disciples, Latter-Day Saints and others.

On the national level, RPRC sponsors an annual three-day convention, and has published five editions of a *Religious Public Relations Handbook* for churches and church organizations, and a videostrip, *The Church at Jackrabbit Junction*. Members receive a quarterly newsletter (*Counselor*), and a quarterly digest of professional articles (*MediaKit*). RPRC also co-sponsors an annual national teleconference. There are 14 regional chapters.

RPRC administers the annual Wilbur Awards competition to recognize high quality coverage of religious values and issues in the public media. Wilbur winners include producers, reporters, editors and broadcasters nationwide. To recognize communications excellence within church communities, RPRC also sponsors the annual DeRose-Hinkhouse Awards for its own members.

In 1970,1980 and 1990, RPRC initiated a global Religious Communications Congress bringing together thousands of persons from western, eastern and third-world nations who are involved in communicating religious faith. Another Congress is planned for 2000.

HEADQUARTERS

357 Righters Mill Rd., P.O. Box 315, Gladwyne, PA 19035 Tel. (215)642-8895 Fax (215)896-8384

Media Contact, Robert Lear

OFFICERS

Pres., David B. Smith, Dir. Dev. & Public Relations, AMC, 1100 Rancho Conejo Blvd., Box O, Thousand Oaks, CA 91360 Tel. (805)373-7733 Fax (805)3733-7702

Vice-Pres., Rev. Daniel R. Gangler, Dir. of Communications, 2641 North 49th St., P.O. Box 4553, Lincoln, NE 68504 Tel. (402)464-5994 Fax j(402)466-7931

Exec. Dir., J. Ron Byler, RPRC, P.O. Box 315, Gladwyne, PA 19035

Standing Conference of Canonical Orthodox Bishops in the Americas

This body was established in 1960 to achieve cooperation among the various Eastern Orthodox Churches in the United States. The Conference is "a voluntary association of the Bishops in the Americas established to serve as an agency to centralize and coordinate the mission of the Church. It acts as a clearing house to focus the efforts of the Church on common concerns and to avoid duplication and overlapping of services and agencies. Special departments are devoted to campus work, Christian education, military and other chaplaincies, regional clergy fellowships, and ecumenical relations."

HEADQUARTERS

8-10 East 79th St., New York, NY 10021 Tel. (212)570-3500 Fax (212)861-2163

Media Contact, Ecumenical Officer, Rev. Dr. Milton B. Efthimiou, 10 E. 79th St., New York, NY 10021 Fax (212)861-2183

OFFICERS

Chpsn., Most Rev. Archbishop Iakovos
Vice Chpsn., Most Rev. Metropolitan Philip
Treas., Bishop Nicholas of Amissos
Sec., Most Rev. Metropolitan Joseph
Rec. Sec., V. Rev. Paul Schneirla

MEMBER CHURCHES

Albanian Orthodox Diocese of America
American Carpatho-Russian Orthodox Greek Catholic Ch.
Antiochian Orthodox Christian Archdiocese of All N.A.
Bulgarian Eastern Orthodox Church
Greek Orthodox Archdiocese of North & South America
Orthodox Church in America
Romanian Orthodox Church in America
Serbian Orthodox Church for the U.S.A. & Canada
Ukrainian Orthodox Church of America
Ukrainian Orthodox Church of Canada

T.H.E.O.S.

T.H.E.O.S. is a nonprofit, nondenominational self-help support network of men and women who provide emotional assistance to the widowed. Established in 1960, T.H.E.O.S. chapters hold monthly group meetings so that bereaved people can help themselves and others through the process of grieving. The organization also publishes a magazine called *Survivor's Outreach*, the brochure "What Do You Say to a Widowed Person?" and a grief bibliography. In addition, T.H.E.O.S. hosts an international annual conference.

T.H.E.O.S. is comprised of more than 500 volunteers throughout the United States and Canada. There are 120 T.H.E.O.S. chapters in North America.

HEADQUARTERS

1301 Clark Building, 717 Liberty Ave., Pittsburgh, PA 15222 Tel. (412)471-7779

Media Contact, Cathy Smith

OFFICERS

Pres., Barbara Moore
Sec., Janet Nataro
Public Educ. & Information Comm., Mimi Wilson

United Ministries in Higher Education

United Ministries in Higher Education embodies the covenant-based ministry coalition created more than thirty years ago and carries forward the work of United Campus Christian Fellowship, United Ministries in Education and Ministries in Public Education (K-12). UMHE works with churches and educational institutions as they seek to express their concern about the ways in which educating forces affect quality of life. UMHE focuses on the goals to design, manage, facilitate, nurture and participate in partnerships with regional and denominational organizations in support of ministry in higher education.

Current programs include mission and resource partnerships, campus ministry training for fundraising, AIDS prevention education, strategic conversations for developing models and planning strategies at the state and regional levels, training for new campus ministers and chaplains, personnel services, support and network for Christian student organizations.

Media Contact, Res. Sec., Linda Danby Freeman, 7407 Steele Creek Rd., Charlotte, NC 28217 Tel. (704)588-2182 Fax (704)588-3652

OFFICERS

Admn. Coord., Clyde O. Robinson, Jr., 7407 Steele Creek Rd., Charlotte, NC 28217 Tel. (704)588-2182 Fax (704)588-3652

Treas., Gary Harke, P. O. Box 386, Sun Prairie, WI 53590 Tel. (608)837-0537 Fax (608)825-6610

Personnel Service, Lawrence S. Steinmetz, 11780 Borman Dr., Ste. 100, St.Louis, MO 63146 Tel. (314)991-3000 Fax (314)993-9018

Resource Center, Linda Danby Freeman, 7407 Steele Creek Rd., Charlotte, NC 28217 Tel. (704)588-2182 Fax (704)588-3652

PARTICIPATING DENOMINATIONS

Christian Church (Disciples of Christ)
Church of the Brethren
Moravian Church (Northern Province)
Presbyterian Church (U.S.A.)
United Church of Christ

US COOPERATIVE ORGANIZATIONS

Vellore Christian Medical College Board (USA), Inc.

The Vellore Christian Medical College Board has been linked since 1900 to the vision of the young American medical doctor, Ida S. Scudder. Dr. Ida's dream initially was to ensure quality health care for women and children in India.

American women and men representing several church denominations wanted to be a part of Dr. Ida's dream and in 1916 recommended Vellore as the site for the proposed Missionary Medical College for Women. Since 1947 the Christian Medical College has admitted women and men. The hospital has a commitment to serve all regardless of ability to pay. The partnership between Vellore India and Vellore USA has continued uninterrupted to the present time.

HEADQUARTERS

475 Riverside Dr., Rm. 243, New York, NY 10115 Tel. (212)870-2640 Fax (212)870-2173
Media Contact, Exec. Dir., Linda L. Pierce

OFFICERS

Pres., Jane Cummings, 675 Upton Rd., NW, Atlanta, GA 30318
Vice-Pres., Alfred E. Berthold, 2452 Club Rd., Columbus, OH 43221
Sec., Sarla Lall, 475 Riverside Dr., Rm. 1540, New York, NY 10115
Treas., Anish Mathai, 235 W. 56th St., Apt. 25M, New York, NY 10115

The World Conference on Religion and Peace

The World Conference on Religion and Peace in the United States (WCRP/USA) provides a forum for the nation's religious bodies based upon respect for religious differences and the recognition that in today's world cooperation among religions offers an important opportunity to mobilize and coordinate the great capacities for constructive action inherent in religious communities.

WCRP/USA provides American religious bodies with opportunities for the following: to clarify their respective orientation to both national and international social concerns; to coordinate their efforts with other religious groups on behalf of widely-shared concerns; to design, undertake and evaluate joint action projects and to communicate and collaborate with similar national religious forums organized by WCRP around the world.

HEADQUARTERS

WCRP/USA OFFICE, 777 United Nations Plaza, New York, NY 10017 Tel. (212)687-2163 Fax (212)983-0566
Media Contact, Sec. Gen., Dr. William F. Vendley

OFFICERS

Pres., Ms. Mary Jane Patterson
Sec. Gen., Dr. William F. Vendley
Vice-Pres.: Dr. Viqar A. Hamdani; Ms. Judith M. Hertz; Rev. Malcolm R. Sutherland; Rev. Robert Smylie
Sec., Ms. Edna McCallion
Treas., Rev. Robert McClean
Officers *Ex Officio*: Intl. Pres., Mrs. Norma U. Levitt; Intl. Pres., Rt. Rev. Sir Paul Reeves
Exec. Comm. Officers: Dr. John Borelli; Edward Doty; Dr. Jane Evans; Ms. Betty Golumb; Dr. Anand Mohan; Sr. Mary Beth Reissen; Rev. Katsuji Suzuki

YMCA of the USA

The YMCA is one of the largest private voluntary organizations in the world, serving about 30 million people in more than 100 countries. In the Untied States, about 2,000 local branches, units, camps and centers annually serve almost 13 million people of all ages, races and abilities. About half of those served are female. No one is turned away because of an inability to pay.

The YMCA is best known for health and fitness. The Y teaches youngsters to swim, organizes youth basketball games and offers adult aerobics. But the Y represents more than fitness—it works to strengthen families and help people develop values and behavior that are consistent with Christian principles.

The Y offers hundreds of programs including day camp for children, child care, exercise for people with disabilities, teen clubs, environmental programs, substance abuse prevention, family nights, job training and many more programs from infant mortality prevention to overnight camping for seniors.

The kind of programs offered at a YMCA will vary; each is controlled by volunteer board members who make their own program, policy, and financial decisions based on the special needs of their community. In its own way, every Y promotes good health, strong families, confident youth, solid communities and a better world.

The YMCA was founded in London, England, in 1844 by George Williams and friends who lived and worked together as clerks. Their goal was to save other live-in clerks from the wicked life of the London streets. The first members were evangelical Protestants who prayed and studied the Bible as an alternative to vice. The Y has always been nonsectarian and today accepts those of all faiths at all levels of the organization.

HEADQUARTERS

101 N. Wacker Dr., Chicago, IL 60606 Tel. (312)977-0031 Fax (312)977-9063
Media Contact, Public Relations Assoc., Leslie Cohn

OFFICERS

Board Chpsn., E. H. Clark, Jr.

Exec. Dir., David R. Mercer
Public Relations Assoc., Leslie Cohn

Young Women's Christian Association of the United States

The YWCA of the U.S.A. is comprised of 425 affiliates in communities and on college campuses across the United States. It serves 2 million members and program participants. It seeks to empower women and girls to enable them, coming together across lines of age, race, religious belief, economic and occupational status to make a significant contribution to the elimination of racism and the achievement of peace, justice, freedom and dignity for all people. Its leadership is vested in a National Board, whose functions are to unite into an effective continuing organization the autonomous member Associations for furthering the purposes of the National Association and to participate in the work of the World YWCA.

HEADQUARTERS

726 Broadway, New York, NY 10003 Tel. (212)614-2700 Fax (212)677-9716

OFFICERS

Pres., Ann Stallard
Sec., Anne H. Perkins
Exec. Dir., Gwendolyn Calvert Baker

Youth for Christ/USA

Founded in 1945, the mission of YFC is to communicate the life-changing message of Jesus Christ to every young person.

Locally controlled YFC programs serve in 220 cities and metropolitan areas of the United States.

YFC's Campus Life Club program involves teens who attend approximately 1,365 high schools in the United States. YFC's staff now numbers approximately 1,000. In addition, nearly 10,000 part-time and volunteer staff supplement the full-time staff. Youth Guidance, a ministry for nonschool-oriented youth includes group homes, court referrals, institutional services and neighborhood ministries. The year-round conference and camping program involves approximately 35,000 young people each year. A family-oriented ministry designed to enrich individuals and church family education programs is carried on through Family Forum, a daily five-minute radio program on more than 300 stations. Independent, indigenous YFC organizations also work in 65 countries overseas.

HEADQUARTERS

U.S. Headquarters, P.O. Box 228822, Denver, CO 80222 Tel. (303)843-9000 Fax (303)843-9002
Canadian Organization, 220 Attwell Dr., Unit #1, Rexdale, ON M9W 5B2
Media Contact, Sr. Vice-Pres. - Admin. (COO), James Neal, Box 228822, Denver, CO 80222 Tel. (303)843-9000 Fax (303)843-9002

OFFICERS

United States, CEO, Roger Cross
Canada, Pres., ——
Intl. Organization: Singapore, Pres., Gerry Gallimore

2. CANADIAN COOPERATIVE ORGANIZATIONS, NATIONAL

In most cases the organizations listed here work on a national level and cooperate across denominational lines. Regional cooperative organizations in Canada are listed in section 6.

Aboriginal Rights Coalition (Project North)

ARC is a coalition for education and action on issues of Aboriginal justice in Canada. It works in partnership with native organizations and local network groups. The major focus is on the just settlement of Aboriginal land rights, impacts of major resource development, self-determination, and related military and environmental concerns.

HEADQUARTERS

151 Laurier E., Ottawa, ON K1N 6N8 Tel. (613)235-9956 Fax (613)235-1302
Media Contact, Exec. Dir., Lorna Schwartzentruber

OFFICERS

Co-Chpsns.: Lorraine Land; John Siebert
Exec. Dir., Lorna Schwartzentruber

MEMBER ORGANIZATIONS

Anglican Church of Canada
Canadian Conference of Catholic Bishops
Council of Christian Reformed Churches in Canada
Evangelical Lutheran Church in Canada
Mennonite Central Committee
Oblate Conference of Canada
Presbyterian Church of Canada
Religious Society of Friends (Quakers)
Society of Jesus (Jesuits)
United Church of Canada

Alliance For Life—Alliance Pour La Vie

Alliance For Life was incorporated in 1972 to promote the right to life from conception to natural death. A registered charity for the purpose of education, Alliance conducts research on all life issues: abortion, infanticide, euthanasia and more. Alliance publishes materials to disseminate the information gained through that research. Alliance has prepared a one-hour documentary on untimely pregnancy and maintains a toll-free line to counsel women with inconveniently timed pregnancies and to help others suffering from post-abortion syndrome.

Alliance is the umbrella organization for 245 pro-life organizations in Canada. Governed by a Board of Directors composed of representatives from all provinces, it holds annual conferences in alternating provinces. Conferences are open to the public.

In 1992, Alliance For Life was split to permit the establishment of Alliance Action, Inc., a non-profit, non-charitable entity which is mandated to do advocacy work which Alliance For Life cannot do as a charity. It is located at the same address and publishes *Pro Life News,* a monthly newsmaga-zine.

HEADQUARTERS

B1-90 Garry St., Winnipeg, MB R3C 4H1 Tel. (204)942-4772 Fax (204)943-9283
Media Contact, Exec. Dir., Anna M. Desilets

ALLIANCE FOR LIFE OFFICERS

Pres., Bernadette Mysko
1st Vice-Pres., Chuck Smith
2nd Vice-Pres., Denise Boutilier
Treas., Regina Weidinger
Sec., Betty Smith

ALLIANCE ACTION OFFICERS

Pres., Regina Weidinger
Dir., Ingrid Krueger
1st Vice-Pres., Bernadette Mysko
2nd Vice-Pres., Chuck Smith
Treas., Denise Boutilier
Sec., Betty Smith

Association of Canadian Bible Colleges

The Association brings into cooperative association Bible colleges in Canada that are evangelical in doctrine and whose objectives are similar. Services are provided to improve the quality of Bible college education in Canada and to further the interests of the Association by means of conferences, seminars, cooperative undertakings, information services, research, publications and other projects.

HEADQUARTERS

Box 173, Three Hills, AB T0M 2A0 Tel. (403)443-5511 Fax (403)443-5540
Media Contact, Pres., Dr. Paul Magnus

OFFICERS

Pres., Dr. Paul Magnus, Briercrest Bible College, 510 College Dr., Caronport, SK S0H 0S0 Tel. (306)756-3200 Fax (306)756-3366
Vice-Pres., Dr. James G. Richards, Western Pentecostal Bible College, Box 1700, Abbotsford, BC V2S 7E7 Tel. (604)853-7491 Fax (604)853-8951
Sec./Treas., Dr. Charlotte Kinvig Bates, Prairie Bible College, Box 173, Three Hills, AB T0M 2A0 Tel. (403)443-5511 Fax (403)443-5540
Members-at-Large: Rev. James Cianca, London Baptist Bible College, 30 Grand Ave., London, ON N6C 1K8 Tel. (519)434-6801; Dr. Arnold Friesen, Providence College, General Delivery, Otterburne, MB R0A 1G0 Tel. (204)433-7488 Fax (204)433-7158; Dr. Walter Unger, Columbia Bible College, 2940 Clearbrook Rd., Clearbrook, BC V2T 2Z8 Tel. (604)853-3358 Fax (604)853-3063

Canadian Association Pastoral Education/Association Canadienne Pour l'Éducation Pastorale

Canadian Association for Pastoral Education/Association Canadienne Pour l'Éducation Pastorale is an association committed to the professional education, certification and support of those endorsed by their faith communities in ministries of pastoral care, counselling and education.

HEADQUARTERS

Business Mgr., Verda Rochon, P.O. Box 96, Roxboro, QC H8Y 3E8

Canadian Bible Society

As early as 1804, the British and Foreign Bible Society was at work in Canada. The oldest Bible Society branch is at Truro, Nova Scotia, and has been functioning continually since 1810. In 1904, the various auxiliaries of the British and Foreign Bible Society joined to form the Canadian Bible Society.

The Canadian Bible Society has 16 district offices across Canada, each managed by a District Secretary. The Society holds an annual meeting consisting of one representative from each district, plus an Executive Committee whose members are appointed by the General Board.

Each year contributions, bequests and annuity income of $11 million come from Canadian supporters. Through the Canadian Bible Society's membership in the United Bible Societies' fellowship, nearly 80 million Bibles, Testaments and Portions were distributed globally in 1992. At least one book of the Bible is now available in over 2000 languages.

The Canadian Bible Society is nondenominational. Its mandate is to translate, publish and distribute the Scriptures, without note or comment, in languages that can be easily read and understood.

HEADQUARTERS

10 Carnforth Rd., Toronto, ON M4A 2S4 Tel. (416)757-4171 Fax (416)757-3376
Media Contact, Dir., Ministry Funding, Barbara Walkden

OFFICER

Gen. Sec., Dr. Floyd C. Babcock

Canadian Centre for Ecumenism

The Centre was founded in 1963 for the promotion of interdenominational dialogue in Montreal. It grew by stages to become a national, bilingual, ecumenical resource centre. The centre established an interchurch board of directors in 1976 and obtained a federal charter. Collaborating with the Canadian Council of Churches in work for Christian Unity, the Centre is an office related to the Canadian bishops and offers its services to other churches as well as other religions.

The Centre has three major areas of activity: education, dialogue and prayer/sharing of spiritual riches. Its quarterly magazine Ecumenism/Oecuménism is published in English and French and goes out to 44 countries. A specialized library is open to the public M-F, 9-5.

HEADQUARTERS

2065 Sherbrooke St. W, Montreal, QC H3H 1G6 Tel. (514)937-9176 Fax (514)935-5497
Media Contact, Bernice Baranowski

OFFICERS

Pres., Fr. Irénée Beaubien, S.J., 25 Jarry Street W, Montréal, QC H2P 1S6 Tel. (514)597-1468
Vice-Pres., Richard Bowie, 181 Morrison Ave., Mont Royal, QC H3R 1K5
Treas., George Cervinka, 3676 St. Hubert, Montréal, QC H2L 4A2 Tel. (514)877-3378 Fax (514)934-1200
Exec. Dir., Fr. Thomas Ryan, C.S.P.

Canadian Council of Christians and Jews

The Canadian Council of Christians and Jews builds bridges of understanding between Canadians. Its techniques of effecting social change are dialogue and education. The CCCJ believes that there exist in any community in Canada the reservoirs of good will, the mediating skills and the enlightened self-interest which make accommodation to change and the creation of social justice possible.

The CCCJ was established in Toronto in 1947 by a group of business, civic and religious leaders.

Its mandate is: "to promote justice, friendship, cooperation and understanding among people differing in race, religion or ethnic origins."

HEADQUARTERS

44 Victoria St., Ste. 600, Toronto, ON M5C 1Y2 Tel. (416)364-3101
Media Contacts: Exec. Dir., Elyse Graff; Pres., Ned Goodman, Tel. (416)365-5665

STAFF

Natl. Exec. Dir., Ms. Elyse Graff

The Canadian Council of Churches

The Canadian Council of Churches was organized in 1944. Its basic purpose is to provide the churches with an agency for conference and consultation and for such common planning and common action as they desire to undertake. It encourages ecumenical understanding and action throughout Canada through local councils of churches. It also relates to the World Council of Churches and other agencies serving the worldwide ecumenical movement.

The Council has a Triennial Assembly, a Governing Board which meets semiannually and an Executive Committee. Program is administered through three commissions—Faith and Witness, Justice and Peace and Ecumenical Education and Communication.

HEADQUARTERS

40 St. Clair Ave. E, Ste. 201, Toronto, ON M4T 1M9 Tel. (416)921-4152 Fax (416)921-7478
Media Contact, Education/Communication, James Hodgson

OFFICERS AND STAFF

Pres., The Very Rev. Bruce McLeod
Vice-Pres.: Anne Thomas; Rev. Joe Williams; Rev. Dr. Ronald Watts
Treas., Mr. John Hart
Gen. Sec., Rev. Clarke Raymond

Assoc. Sec.: Rev. Douglas duCharme; Mr. James Hodgson

AFFILIATED INSTITUTION

Canadian Churches' Forum for Global Min.: Co-Dirs. Patricia Talbot; Kevin Anderson, 11 Madison Ave., Toronto, ON M5R 2S2 Tel. (416)924-9351

MEMBERS

The Anglican Church of Canada
The Armenian Church of America—
 Diocese of Canada
Baptist Convention of Ontario and Quebec
British Methodist Episcopal Church*
Canadian Conference of Catholic Bishops*
Christian Church (Disciples of Christ)
Coptic Orthodox Church of Canada
Ethiopian Orthodox Church in Canada
Evangelical Lutheran Church in Canada
Greek Orthodox Diocese of
 Toronto (Canada)
Orthodox Church in America,
 Diocese of Canada
Polish National Catholic Church
Presbyterian Church in Canada
Reformed Church in America
Religious Society of Friends—
 Canada Yearly Meeting
Salvation Army—Canada and Bermuda
The Ukrainian Orthodox Church
The United Church of Canada
*Associate Member

Canadian Evangelical Theological Association

In May 1990, about 60 scholars, pastors and other interested persons met together in Toronto to form a new theological society. Arising out of the Canadian chapter of the Evangelical Theological Society, the new association established itself as a distinctly Canadian group with a new name. It sponsored its first conference as CETA in Kingston, Ontario, in May 1991.

CETA provides a forum for scholarly contributions to the renewal of theology and church in Canada. CETA seeks to promote theological work which is loyal to Christ and his Gospel, faithful to the primacy and authority of Scripture and responsive to the guiding force of the historic creeds and Protestant confessions of the Christian Church. In its newsletters and conferences, CETA seeks presentations that will speak to a general theologically-educated audience, rather than to specialists.

CETA has special interest in evangelical points of view upon and contributions to the wider conversations regarding religious studies and church life. Members therefore include pastors, students and other interested persons as well as professional academicians. CETA currently includes about 100 members, many of whom attend its annual conference in the early summer.

HEADQUARTERS

c/o John G. Stackhouse, Dept. of Religion, University of Manitoba, Winnipeg, MB R3T 5V5 Tel. (204)474-6277 Fax (204)275-5781
Media Contact, John G. Stackhouse

OFFICERS

Pres. & Western Rep., Dr. John G. Stackhouse, Jr.
Sec./Treas., Dr. Douglas Harink
Publications Coord., Mr. Bruce Guenther

Executive Members: Dr. Edith Humphrey; Dr. John Franklin; Dr. Barry Smith

Canadian Society of Biblical Studies/Société des Études Bibliques

The society was founded in 1933 to stimulate the critical investigation of classical biblical literature and related areas of research by exchange of scholarly research in published form and in public forum.

The CSBS/SEB has 283 members and meets annually in conjunction with the Learned Societies of Canada. Every year the Society publishes a Bulletin and is a member of the Canadian Corporation for the Study of Religion/Corporation Canadienne des Sciences Religieuses, which publishes *Studies in Religion/Sciences religieuses* quarterly.

HEADQUARTERS

Dept. of Religious Studies, Memorial University of Newfoundland, St. John's, NF A1C 5S7 Tel. (709)737-8166 Fax (709)737-4569
Media Contact, Exec. Sec., Dr. David J. Hawkin

OFFICERS

Pres., David Jobling, St. Andrew's College, 1121 College Dr., Saskatoon, SK S7N 0W3 Tel. (306)966-8978
Vice-Pres., Harold Remus, Dept. of Religion and Culture, Wilfrid Laurier University, Waterloo, ON N2L 3C5 Tel. (519)884-1970 Fax Tel Ext.2051
Sec., Dr. David J. Hawkin, Tel. (709)737-8173
Treas., Terry Donaldson, College of Emmanuel & St. Chad, 1337 College Dr., Saskatoon, SK S7N 0W6 Tel. (306)975-1050
Publications Coord., Lyle Eslinger, Dept. of Religious Studies, Univ. of Calgary, 2500 University Dr. NW, Calgary, AB T2N 1N4 Tel. (403)220-5886

Canadian Tract Society

The Canadian Tract Society was organized in 1970 as an independent distributor of Gospel leaflets to provide Canadian churches and individual Christians with quality materials proclaiming the Gospel through the printed page. It is affiliated with the American Tract Society, which encouraged its formation and assisted in its founding, and for whom it serves as an exclusive Canadian distributor. The CTS is a nonprofit international service ministry.

HEADQUARTERS

Box 2156, Brampton, ON L6T 3S4 Tel. (416)457-4559 Fax (416)457-4559
Media Contact, Mgr., Donna Croft

OFFICERS

Pres., Stanley D. Mackey
Sec., Robert J. Burns

The Church Army in Canada

The Church Army in Canada has been involved in evangelism and Christian social service since 1929.

HEADQUARTERS

397 Brunswick Ave., Toronto, ON M5R 2Z2 Tel. (416)924-9279
Media Contact, Dir., Capt. Walter W. Marshall

OFFICERS
Dir., Capt. Walter W. Marshall
Asst. Dir., Capt. R. Bruce Smith
Dir. of Training, Capt. Roy E. Dickson
Field Sec., Capt. Reed S. Fleming
Bd. Chmn., Ivor S. Joshua, C.A.

The Churches' Council on Theological Education in Canada: An Ecumenical Foundation

The Churches' Council (CCTE:EF) maintains an overview of theological education in Canada on behalf of its constituent churches and functions as a bridge between the schools of theology and the churches which they serve.

Founded in 1970 with a national and ecumenical mandate, the CCTE:EF provides resources for research into matters pertaining to theological education, opportunities for consultation and co-operation and a limited amount of funding in the form of grants for the furtherance of ecumenical theological education.

HEADQUARTERS
60 St. Clair Avenue E, Ste. 302, Toronto, ON M4T 1N5 Tel. (416)928-3223 Fax same
Media Contact, Exec. Dir., Dr. Thomas Harding

OFFICERS
Bd. of Dir., Chpsn., Dr. Howard M. Mills, The United Church of Canada, 85 St. Clair Ave. E., Toronto, ON M4T 1M8
Bd. of Dir., Vice-Chpsn., The Rev. Jean Armstrong, The Presbyterian Church in Canada, 50 Wynford Dr., Don Mills, ON M3C 1J7
Treas., Donald Hall, 80 Strathallan Blvd., Toronto, ON M5N 1S7
Exec. Dir., Dr. Thomas Harding

MEMBER ORGANIZATIONS
The General Synod of the Anglican Church of Canada
The Canadian Baptist Federation
The Evangelical Lutheran Church in Canada
The Presbyterian Church in Canada
The Canadian Conference of Catholic Bishops
The United Church of Canada

Concerns, Canada: a corporate division of Alcohol & Drug Concerns, Inc.

Concerns, Canada is a registered, non-profit, charitable organization that has been closely associated with the Christian Church throughout its long history. The organization's mandate is "to promote and encourage a positive lifestyle free from dependence upon alcohol, tobacco and other drugs."

The organization was granted a national charter in 1987, moving from an Ontario charter dating back to 1934. Among its services are: Toc Alpha (its youth wing for 14-to-24 year olds; PLUS (Positive Life-Using Skills), a teacher curriculum for grades 4 to 8; two Institutes on Addiction Studies; courses for clients of the Ontario Ministry of Corrections; and educational materials for target groups.

HEADQUARTERS
4500 Sheppard Ave. E, Ste. H, Agincourt, ON M1S 3R6
Media Contact, Exec. Dir., Rev. Karl N. Burden

OFFICERS
Pres., Linda Mills, 31 Sunnydene Cres., Toronto, ON M4N 3J5
Vice-Pres.: Keith Farraway, Douglas Dr., R.R. #2, Bracebridge, ON P1L 1W9; Mary Fleming, 177 Parkston Cr., Richmond Hill, ON L4C 4S2; Larry Gillians, P.O. Box 226, Newburgh, ON K0K 2S0
Treas., Jean Desgagne, Price Waterhouse, 1 First Canadian Pl., Ste. 3300, Toronto, ON M5X 1H7
Exec. Dir., Rev. Karl N. Burden

Ecumenical Coalition for Economic Justice (ECEJ)

Ecumenical Coalition for Economic Justice (ECEJ) is a national project of five Canadian churches (Anglican Church in Canada, Roman Catholic Church, Lutheran Church, Presbyterian Church and United Church of Canada) mandated to assist popular groups and progressive church organizations struggling for economic justice in Canada and the Third World. ECEJ pursues these objectives through research, popular education and political action. ECEJ is guided by an administrative committee composed of representatives from each of the sponsoring churches.

Research priorities for the next two years include international trade and trading agreements, women and economic justice, coalition building and social policy.

HEADQUARTERS
11 Madison Ave., Toronto, ON M5R 2S2 Tel. (416)921-4615 Fax (416)924-5356
Media Contact, Educ. & Communications, Jennifer Wershler-Henry

OFFICERS
Chpsn., David Pollock, Anglican Church of Canada

STAFF
Researcher, John Dillon
Women & Economic Justice, Programme Coord., Lorraine Michael
Education Programme Coord., Jennifer Wershler-Henry
Admn. Coord., Diana Gibbs

Evangelical Fellowship of Canada

The Fellowship was formed in 1964. There are 28 denominations, 115 organizations, 1025 local churches and 10,300 of individual members.

Its purposes are: "Fellowship in the gospel" (Phil. 1:5), "the defence and confirmation of the gospel" (Phil. 1:7) and "the furtherance of the gospel" (Phil. 1:12). The Fellowship believes the Holy Scriptures, as originally given, are infallible and that salvation through the Lord Jesus Christ is by faith apart from works.

In national and regional conventions the Fellowship urges Christians to live exemplary lives and to openly challenge the evils and injustices of society. It encourages cooperation with various agencies in Canada and overseas that are sensitive to social and spiritual needs.

CANADIAN COOPERATIVE ORGANIZATIONS

Office: 175 Riviera Dr., Markham, ON L3R 5J6 Tel. (416)479-5885 Fax (416)479-4742
Mailing Address: P.O. Box 8800, Stn. B, Willowdale, ON M2K 2R6
Media Contact, Exec. Dir., Dr. Brian C. Stiller

OFFICERS

Exec. Dir., Dr. Brian C. Stiller
Pres., Dr. Donald Jost
Vice-Pres., Major John Wilder
Treas., Rev. Grover Crosby
Sec., Mrs. Moira Brown
Past Pres., Dr. John Redekop
Committee Members-at-Large: Rev. David Collins; Dr. W. Harold Fuller; Mr. Donald Simmonds; Dr. Ken Birch; Dr. Arnold Cook; Rev. Abe Funk; Mrs. Marjorie Osborne; Mrs. Lynn Smith; Mrs. Linda Tripp; Rev. Andrew Wong
Social Action Commission, Co-Chpsns.: Dr. Paul Marshall; Mrs. Aileen VanGinkel
Task Force on Evangelism, Chpsn., Dr. William McRae
Task Force on the Family, Chpsn., Dr. Mavis Olesen

Interchurch Communications

Interchurch Communications is made up of the communication units of the Anglican Church of Canada, the Evangelical Lutheran Church in Canada, the Presbyterian Church in Canada, the Canadian Conference of Catholic Bishops (English Sector), and the United Church of Canada. ICC members collaborate on occasional video or print coproductions and on addressing public policy issues affecting religious communications.

HEADQUARTERS

315 Queen St., E., Toronto, ON M5A 1S7
Media Contact, Chpsn., Douglas Tindal, Anglican Church of Canada, 600 Jarvis St., Toronto, ON M4Y 2J6 Tel. (416)924-9199 Fax (416)968-7983

OFFICERS

Chpsn., Mr. Douglas Tindal, Anglican Church of Canada, 600 Jarvis St., Toronto, ON M4Y 2J6 Tel. (416)924-9199 Fax (416)968-7983
Vice-Chpsn., Rev. Randolph L. Naylor, United Church of Canada, 85 St. Clair Ave. E., Toronto, ON M4T 1M8 Tel. (416)925-4850 Fax (416)925-9692
Sec., Mr. Dennis Gruending, Canadian Conference of Catholic Bishops, 90 Parent Ave., Ottawa, ON K1N 7B1 Tel. (613)236-9461 Fax (613)236-8117

MEMBERS

Mr. Merv Campone, Evangelical Lutheran Church in Canada, 21415-76th Ave., RR #11, Langley, BC V3A 6Y3 Tel. (604)888-4562 Fax (604)888-3162
Rev. Glenn Cooper, Presbyterian Church in Canada, Box 1840, Pictou, NS B0K 1H0 Tel. (902)485-1561 Fax (902)485-1562
Rev. Rod Booth, United Church of Canada, 315 Queen St. E., Toronto, ON M5A 1S7 Tel. (416)366-9221 Fax (416)368-9774
Mr. James Hodgson, Canadian Council of Churches, 40 St. Clair Ave. E., Toronto, ON M4T 1M9 Tel. (416)921-4512 Fax (416)921-7478

Inter-Varsity Christian Fellowship of Canada

Inter-Varsity Christian Fellowship is a non-profit, interdenominational Canadian student movement centering on the witness to Jesus Christ in campus communities: universities, colleges and high schools and through a Canada-wide Pioneer Camping program. It also ministers to professionals and teachers through Nurses and Teachers' Christian Fellowship.

IVCF was officially formed in 1928-29 by the late Dr. Howard Guinness, whose arrival from Britain challenged students to follow the example of the British Inter-Varsity Fellowship by organizing themselves into prayer and Bible study fellowship groups. Inter-Varsity has always been a student-initiated movement, emphasizing and developing leadership on the campus to call Christians to outreach, challenging other students to a personal faith in Jesus Christ and studying the Bible as God's revealed truth within a fellowship of believers. A strong stress has been placed on missionary activity, and the triennial conference held at Urbana, Ill. (jointly sponsored by U.S. and Canadian IVCF) has been a means of challenging many young people to service in Christian vocation. Inter-Varsity works closely with and is a strong believer in the work of local and national churches.

HEADQUARTERS

Unit 17, 40 Vogell Rd., Richmond Hill, ON L4B 3N6 Tel. (905)884-6880 Fax (905)884-6550
Media Contact, Gen. Dir., James E. Berney

OFFICERS

Gen. Dir., James E. Berney

John Howard Society of Ontario

The John Howard Society of Ontario is a registered non-profit charitable organization providing services to individuals, families and groups at all stages in the youth and criminal justice system. The Society also provides community education on critical issues in the justice system and advocacy for reform of the justice system. The mandate of the Society is the prevention of crime through service, community education, advocacy and reform.

Founded in 1929, the Society has grown from a one-office service in Toronto to 17 local branches providing direct services in the major cities of Ontario and a provincial office providing justice policy analysis, advocacy for reform and support to branches.

HEADQUARTERS

6 Jackson Pl., Toronto, ON M6P 1T6 Tel. (416)604-8412 Fax (416)604-8948
Media Contact, Exec. Dir., Graham Stewart

OFFICERS

Pres., Angela Hildyard, Ofc. of Field Service & Research, 252 Bloor St. W, 12th Fl., Rm. 130, Toronto, ON M5S 1V6
Vice-Pres., Gerry Treble, 595 Trafalgar St., London, ON N5Z 1E6
Treas., Hugh Peacock, Ontario Labour Relations Board, 400 University Ave., 4th Fl., Toronto, ON M7A 1V4
Sec., Susan Reid-MacNevin, Dept. of Sociology, University of Guelph, Guelph, ON N1G 2W1
Exec. Dir., Graham Stewart

Oshawa
Hamilton
Kingston
London
Toronto
Collins Bay
St. Catherines
Ottawa
Brampton
Peterborough
Sarnia
Sault Ste. Marie
Sudbury
Thunder Bay
Lindsay
Waterloo
Windsor

John Milton Society for the Blind in Canada

The John Milton Society for the Blind in Canada is an interdenominational Christian charity whose mandate is producing Christian publications for Canadian adults or young people who are visually impaired or blind. As such, it produces *Insight*, a large-print magazine, *Insound*, a cassette magazine and *In Touch*, a braille magazine. The John Milton Society also features an audio cassette library called the *Library in Sound*, which contains Christian music, sermons, seasonal materials and workshops.

Founded in 1970, the Society is committed to seeing that visually-impaired people receive accessible Christian materials by mail.

HEADQUARTERS
40 St. Clair Ave. E., Ste. 202, Toronto, ON M4T 1M9 Tel. (416)960-3953
Media Contact, Debbie Wraith

OFFICERS
Pres., William Lawson, 65 Wynford Hghts. Cres., Apt. 1808, Don Mills, ON M3C 1L7
Vice-Pres., Miss Ruth Cowan, 267 Lawrence Ave. E., Toronto, ON M4N 1T6
Exec. Dir., Joanne Gunn

Lutheran Council in Canada

The Lutheran Council in Canada was organized in 1967 and is a cooperative agency of the Evangelical Lutheran Church in Canada and the Lutheran Church-Canada.

The Council's activities include communications, coordinative service and national liaison in social ministry, chaplaincy and scout activity.

HEADQUARTERS
1512 S. James St., Winnipeg, MB R3H 0L2 Tel. (204)786-6707 Fax (204)783-7548
Media Contact, Pres., Rev. Edwin Lehman, 200-1625 Dublin Ave., Winnipeg, MB R3H 0W3 Tel. (204)772-0676 Fax (204)772-1090

OFFICERS
Pres., Rev. Edwin Lehman
Sec., Rev. Lorraine Grislis
Treas., Mr. Stephen Klinck

Mennonite Central Committee Canada (MCCC)

Mennonite Central Committee Canada was or-ganized in 1964 to continue the work which several regional Canadian inter-Mennonite agencies had been doing in relief, service, immigration and peace. All but a few of the smaller Mennonite groups in Canada belong to MCC Canada.

MCCC is part of the binational Mennonite Central Committee (MCC) which has its headquarters in Akron, Pa. from where the overseas development and relief projects are administered. In 1993-93 MCCC's budget was $21,200,000, about 40 percent of the total MCC budget. There were 429 Canadians of a total of 953 MCC workers serving in North America and abroad during the same time period.

The MCC office in Winnipeg administers projects located in Canada. Domestic programs of Voluntary Service, Native Concerns, Peace and Social Concerns, Food Program, Employment Concerns, Ottawa Office, Victim/Offender Ministries, Mental Health and immigration are all part of MCC's Canadian ministry. Whenever it undertakes a project, MCCC attempts to relate to the church or churches in the area.

HEADQUARTERS
134 Plaza Dr., Winnipeg, MB R3T 5K9 Tel. (204)261-6381

OFFICER
Exec. Dir., John Dyck

Project Ploughshares

Founded in 1976, Project Ploughshares is an internationally recognized Canadian peace and justice organization sponsored by the Canadian Council of Churches with research, education and advocacy programs on the following issues: regional conflict and world order, militarism, international arms trade, disarmament, Canadian defense policy and Canadian military production and exports. The quarterly journal is the Ploughshares' *Monitor*. The Ploughshares' network includes national church and development agencies, affiliated community groups and 12,000 individual supporters.

Project Ploughshares operates under a voluntary Board of Directors that includes representatives from each of its sponsors and six members elected by its affiliated community groups.

HEADQUARTERS
Institute of Peace and Conflict Studies, Conrad Grebel College, Waterloo, ON N2L 3G6 Tel. (519)888-6541 Fax (519)885-0014
Media Contact, Research & Policy Dir., Ernie Regehr

OFFICERS
Chpsn., Leonard Johnson
Treas., Philip Creighton

SPONSORING ORGANIZATIONS
Anglican Church of Canada
Canadian Catholic Organization for Development & Peace
Canadian Unitarian Council
Canadian Friends Service Committee
Christian Church (Disciples of Christ) in Canada
Conrad Grebel College
CUSO
Inter-Pares
Evangelical Lutheran Church in Canada
Mennonite Central Committee Canada
Mennonite Conference of Eastern Canada
Oxfam Canada

Presbyterian Church in Canada
Union of Spiritual Communities in Christ (Doukhobors)
United Church of Canada
Voice of Women

Religious Television Associates

Religious Television Associates was formed in the early 1960s for the production units of the Anglican, Baptist, Presbyterian, Roman Catholic Churches and the United Church of Canada. In the intervening years, the Baptists have withdrawn and the Lutherans have come in. RTA provides an ecumenical umbrella for joint productions in broadcasting and development education. The directors are the heads of the Communications Departments participating in Interchurch Communications.

HEADQUARTERS

315 Queen St. East, Toronto, ON M5A 1S7 Tel. (416)366-9221 Fax (416)368-9774
Media Contact, Exec. Dir., Rod Booth

OFFICERS

Chpsn., Douglas Tindal, 600 Jarvis St., Toronto, ON M4Y 2J6
Sec., Dennis Gruending, 90 Parent Ave., Ottawa, ON K1N 7B1
Treas., Carolyn Pringle, 85 St. Clair Ave. E, Toronto, ON M4T 1M8

MEMBER ORGANIZATIONS

The Anglican Church of Canada
Canadian Conference of Catholic Bishops
The Canadian Council of Churches
The Evangelical Lutheran Church in Canada
The Presbyterian Church in Canada
The United Church of Canada

Scripture Union

Scripture Union is an international interdenominational missionary movement working in over 100 countries.
Scripture Union aims to work with the churches to make God's Good News known to children, young people and families and to encourage people of all ages to meet God daily through the Bible and prayer.
In Canada, a range of daily devotional booklets are offered on a no-charge basis to individuals from age four through adult.
A program of youth evangelism, including beach missions and community-based evangelistic holiday clubs, is also undertaken.

HEADQUARTERS

1885 Clements Rd., Unit 226, Pickering, OH L1W 3V4 Tel. (416)427-4957 Fax (416)427-0334

DIRECTORS

Dr. Emily Berkman, 217 Melrose Ave., Ottawa, ON K1Y 1V3
Alan Cairnie, R.R. #6, Renfrew, ON K7V 3Z9
Dr. Paul Pill, 5 Bendale Blvd., Scarborough, ON M1J 2B1
Ruth Russell, 14 Caronridge Cres., Agincourt, ON M1W 1L2
L. Claude Simmonds, Windfield Terr. E, Ste. 301, 1200 Don Mills Rd., Don Mills, ON M3B 3N8
Michael White, 251 Jefferson Sideroad, R.R. #1, Richmond Hill, ON L4C 4X7

Dr. Ruth Whitehead, 3002 Southmore Dr. E, Ottawa, ON K1V 6Z4
Rev. George Sinclair, 125 Victoria St., Eganville, ON K0J 1T0
Dr. Paul White, 21 Berkham Rd., Scarborough, ON M1H 2T1

Student Christian Movement of Canada

The Student Christian Movement of Canada was formed in 1921 from the student arm of the YMCA. It has its roots in the Social Gospel movements of the late 19th and early 20th centuries. Throughout its intellectual history, the SCM in Canada has sought to relate the Christian faith to the living realities of the social and political context of each student generation.
The present priorities are built around the need to form more and stronger critical Christian communities on Canadian campuses within which individuals may develop their social and political analyses, experience spiritual growth and fellowship and bring Christian ecumenical witness to the university.
The Student Christian Movement of Canada is affiliated with the World Student Christian Federation.

HEADQUARTERS

310 Danforth Ave., Ste. C3, Toronto, ON M4K 1N6 Tel. (416)463-4312
Media Contact, Gen. Sec., Bruce Gilbert

OFFICER

Gen. Sec., Bruce Gilbert

Taskforce on the Churches and Corporate Responsibility

The Taskforce on the Churches and Corporate Responsibility is a national ecumenical coalition of the major Christian churches in Canada founded in 1975 to assist its members in implementing policies adopted by them in the area of corporate social responsibility. Areas of special concern include human rights and aboriginal rights, environment, military exports and corporate governance. The Taskforce facilitates communication on these and other issues between church shareholders and other shareholders and corporate managers.

HEADQUARTERS

129 St. Clair Ave., W., Toronto, ON M4V 1N5 Tel. (416)923-1758 Fax (416)927-7554
Media Contact, Coord., Bill Davis, Tel. (416)923-1758 Fax (416)927-7554

OFFICERS

Coord., Bill Davis
Bd. Co-Chpsns.: David Hallman; Rev. David P. Frimmer
Treas., Mike Kelly
Chpsn., Corp. Governance Comm., Ann Stafford

MEMBERS

Anglican Church of Canada
Basilians
Canadian Conference of Catholic Bishops
Catholic Church Extension Society of Canada
Congregation of Notre Dame
Evangelical Lutheran Church in Canada
Grey Sisters of the Immaculate Conception
Jesuit Fathers of Upper Canada

Oblate Conference of Canada
Presbyterian Church in Canada
Redemptorist Fathers
Religious Hospitallers of St. Joseph
Scarboro Foreign Mission Society
Sisterhood of St. John the Divine
Sisters of Charity—Mount St. Vincent
Sisters of Charity of the Immaculate Conception
Sisters of the Holy Names of Jesus & Mary
Sisters of Mercy Generalate
Sisters of St. Joseph—Diocese of London
Sisters of St. Joseph—Toronto
Les Soeurs de Sainte-Anne
United Church of Canada
Ursulines of Chatham Union
Canadian University Service Overseas
Young Women's Christian Association

Ten Days for World Development

Supported by five of Canada's major Christian denominations and by the Canadian International Development Agency (CIDA), Ten Days is dedicated to helping people discover, examine and reflect on the ways global and domestic structures and policies promote and perpetuate poverty and injustice for the majority of the world's people. The program collaborates in defining goals and human values which insist that social structures respond justly to the needs of the poor and vulnerable. As it engages in action, it attempts to influence the policies and practice of Canadian churches, government, business, labour, education and the media.

HEADQUARTERS
85, St. Clair Ave. E., Toronto, ON M4T 1M8 Tel. (416)922-0591 Fax (416)922-1419
Media Contact, Natl. Coord., Dennis Howlett

STAFF
Natl. Coord., Dennis Howlett
Coord. for Leadership Dev. & Regional Communication, David Reid
Resource Coord., Debbie Culbertson
Admn. Asst., Ramya Hemachandra

MEMBER ORGANIZATIONS
Anglican Church of Canada
Canadian Cath. Orgn. for Dev. & Peace
Evangelical Lutheran Church in Canada
Presbyterian Church in Canada
United Church of Canada

Women's Interchurch Council of Canada

The council is an ecumenical movement through which Christians may express their unity by prayer, fellowship, study and action. The purpose is to enable Christian women across Canada to live in love and fellowship so that all people may find fullness of life in Christ. WICC sponsors the World Day of Prayer and the Fellowship of the Least Coin in Canada. Human rights projects are supported and ecumenical study kits produced. A newsletter is issued four times a year.

The council is affiliated with Ecumenical Decade for Churches in Solidarity with Women.

HEADQUARTERS
815 Danforth Ave., Ste 402, Toronto, ON M4J 1L2 Tel. (416)462-2528

Media Contact, Exec. Dir., Vivian Harrower, Fax (416)462-3915

OFFICERS
Pres., Diane Steffer
Exec. Dir., Vivian Harrower

World Vision Canada

World Vision Canada is a Christian humanitarian relief and development organization. Although its main international commitment is to translate child sponsorship into holistic, sustainable community development, World Vision also allocates resources to help Canada's poor and complement the mission of the church.

World Vision's Reception Centre assists government-sponsored refugees entering Canada. The NeighbourLink program mobilizes church volunteers to respond locally to people's needs. A quarterly publication, *Context*, provides data on the Canadian family to help churches effectively reach their communities. The development education program provides resources on development issues. During the annual 30-Hour Famine, people fast for 30 hours while discussing poverty and raising funds to support aid programs.

HEADQUARTERS
6630 Turner Valley Rd., Mississauga, ON L5N 2S4 Tel. (905)821-3030 Fax (905)821-1356
Media Contact, Senior Information Officer, Mr. Philip Maher, Tel. (905)567-2726

OFFICERS
Pres., J. Don Scott
Vice-Pres.: Intl. & Govt. Relations, Linda Tripp; Natl. Programs, Don Posterski; Donor Development, Dave Toycen; Fin. & Admin., Don Epp

Young Men's Christian Association in Canada

The YMCA began as a Christian association to help young men find healthy recreation and meditation, as well as opportunities for education, in the industrial slums of 19th century England. It came to Canada in 1851 with the same mission in mind for young men working in camps and on the railways.

Today, the YMCA maintains its original mission—helping individuals to grow and develop in spirit, mind and body—but attends to those needs for men and women of all ages and religious beliefs. The YMCA registers almost 1.5 million participants and 290,200 annual members in 69 autonomous associations representative of their communities.

The program of each association differs according to the needs of the community, but most offer one or more programs in each of the following categories: community support, housing and shelters, guidance and counselling, camping and outdoor education, leadership development, refugee and immigrant services, international development and education.

The YMCA encourages people of all ages, races, abilities, income and beliefs to mix in an environment which promotes balance in life, breaking down barriers and helping to create healthier communities.

HEADQUARTERS
2160 Yonge St., Toronto, ON M4S 2A9 Tel. (416)485-9447 Fax (416)485-8228

Media Contact, Dir., Communications, Donald S. McCuaig

OFFICERS

Chpsn., Betty Black
CEO, Sol Kasimer
Dir., Intl. Programs, Alan Hatton

Young Women's Christian Association of/du Canada

The YWCA of/du Canada is a national voluntary organization serving 44 YWCAs and YM-YWCAs across Canada. Dedicated to the development and improved status of women and their families, the YWCA is committed to service delivery and to being a source of public education on women's issues and an advocate of social change. Services provided by YWCAs and YM-YWCAs include adult education programs, residences and shelters, child care, fitness activities, wellness programs and international development education. As a member of the World YWCA, the YWCA of/du Canada is part of the largest women's organization in the world.

HEADQUARTERS

80 Gerrard St. E., Toronto, ON M5B 1G6 Tel. (416)593-9886 Fax (416)971-8084
Media Contact, CEO, Judith Wiley

OFFICERS

CEO, Judith Wiley
Pres., Dale Godsoe

Youth for Christ/Canada

Youth For Christ is an interdenominational organization founded in 1944 by Torrey Johnson. Under the leadership of YFC's 34 national board of directors, Youth For Christ/Canada cooperates with churches and serves as a mission agency reaching out to young people and their families through a variety of ministries.

YFC seeks to have maximum influence in a world of youth through high-interest activities and personal involvement. Individual attention is given to each teenager through small group involvement and counselling. These activities and relationships become vehicles for communicating the message of the Gospel.

HEADQUARTERS

220 Attwell Dr., #1, Rexdale, ON M9W 5B2 Tel. (416)674-0466 Fax (416)674-0616

OFFICERS

Vice-Pres., Ron Adams, 7115 Codlin Ave., Mississauga, ON L4T 2M3 Tel. (416)674-0466 Fax (416)674-0616
TYFC Exec. Dir., Paul Robertson, 58 Bridekirk Pl., Brampton, ON L6Y 2V8 Tel. (416)674-0466 Fax (416)674-0616
Natl. Min. Coord., John Wilkinson, 26 Lanewood Cres., Agincourt, ON M1W 1X1 Tel. (416)674-0466 Fax (416)674-0616

3. DENOMINATIONS IN THE UNITED STATES

The following lists were supplied by the denominations. They are printed in alphabetical order by the official name of the organization. A list of religious bodies by family group is found at the end of this section.

Information found in other places in this yearbook is not repeated. The denominational listing points you to additional information. Specifically, addresses and editor's names for periodicals are found in the listing of United States Periodicals. Also, statistical information is found in the statistical section.

When an organization supplied a headquarters address it is listed immediately following the description of the organization. This address, telephone number and fax number is not reprinted for entries that have exactly the same address and numbers. An address or telephone number is only printed when it is known to be different from the headquarters'. Individuals listed without an address can be contacted through the headquarters.

Denominations were asked to provide the name of a media contact. Many responded with a specific person that newspaper or other reporters can contact for official information. These people are listed with the headquarters address.

The organizations listed here represent the denominations to which the vast majority of church members in the United States belong. It does not include all religious bodies functioning in the United States. *The Encyclopedia of American Religions* (Gale Research Inc., P.O. Box 33477, Detroit MI 48232-5477) contains names and addresses of additional religious bodies.

Advent Christian Church

The Advent Christian Church is a conservative, evangelical denomination which grew out of the Millerite movement of the 1830s and 1840s. The members stress the authority of Scripture, justification by faith in Jesus Christ alone, the importance of evangelism and world missions and the soon visible return of Jesus Christ.

Organized in 1860, the Advent Christian Church maintains headquarters in Charlotte, N.C., with regional offices in Rochester, N. H., Augusta, Ga., Fort Worth, Tex., Lewiston, Idaho, and Lenoir, N.C. Missions are maintained in India, Nigeria, Japan, Malaysia, the Philippines, Mexico and Memphis, Tenn.

The Advent Christian Church maintains doctrinal distinctives in three areas: conditional immortality, the sleep of the dead until the return of Christ and belief that the kingdom of God will be established on earth made new by Jesus Christ.

HEADQUARTERS

P.O. Box 23152, Charlotte, NC 28227 Tel. (704)545-6161 Fax (704)573-0712
Media Contact, Exec. Vice-Pres., David E. Ross

OFFICERS

Pres., Rev. Glennon Balser, 6315 Studley Rd., Mechanicsville, VA 23111
Exec. Vice-Pres., David E. Ross
Sec., Rev. John Gallagher, P.O. Box 551, Presque Isle, ME 04769
Appalachian Vice-Pres., Rev. Marshall Tidwell, 1002 Grove Ave., SW, Lenoir, NC 28645
Central Vice-Pres., Rev. Clarence DuBois, 1401 Illinois Ave., Mendota, IL 61342
Eastern Vice-Pres., Rev. Tim Fox, RR 1 Box 3048, S. Paris, ME 04281
Southern Vice-Pres., Rev. Larry Withrow, 318 Crescent Dr., Clayton, NC 27520
Western Vice-Pres., Mr. Larry McIntyre, 1629 Jamie Cr., West Linn, OR 97068
The Woman's Home & Foreign Mission Soc., Pres., Mrs. Bea Moore, Rt. 8, Box 274, Loudon, NH 03301

PERIODICALS

Advent Christian News; The Advent Christian Witness; Insight; Maranatha

African Methodist Episcopal Church

This church began in 1787 in Philadelphia when persons in St. George's Methodist Episcopal Church withdrew as a protest against color segregation. In 1816 the denomination was started, led by Rev. Richard Allen who had been ordained deacon by Bishop Francis Asbury and was subsequently ordained elder and elected and consecrated bishop.

HEADQUARTERS

1134 11th St., NW, Washington, DC 20001
Media Contact, Bishop, Eighth District, Donald G. Ming, 2138 St. Bernard Ave., New Orleans, LA 70119 Tel. (504)948-4251

PERIODICALS

The Christian Recorder; A.M.E. Review; Journal of Christian Education; Secret Chamber; Women's Missionary Magazine; Voice of Missions

African Methodist Episcopal Zion Church

The A.M.E. Zion Church is an independent body, having withdrawn from the John Street Methodist Church of New York City in 1796. The first bishop was James Varick.

HEADQUARTERS

Dept. of Records & Research, P.O. Box 32843, Charlotte, NC 28232 Tel. (704)332-3851 Fax (704)333-1769
Media Contact, Gen. Sec.-Aud., Dr. W. Robert Johnson, III

OFFICERS

Senior Bishop, Bishop Ruben L. Speaks, 1238 Maxwell St., P.O. Box 986, Salisgury, NC 28144
Bd. of Bishops: Sec., Bishop Herman L. Anderson, 7013 Toby Ct., Charlotte, NC 28213; Asst. Sec.,

Bishop Marshall H. Strickland, 2000 Cedar Circle Dr., Baltimore, MD 21228; Treas., George W. Walker, Sr., 3654 Poplar Rd., Flossmoor, IL 60422

GENERAL OFFICERS AND DEPARTMENTS

Gen. Sec., Rev. W. Robert Johnson, III

Fin. Sec., Miss Madie L. Simpson, P.O. Box 31005, Charlotte, NC 28230 Tel. (704)333-4847 Fax (704)333-6517

A.M.E. Zion Publishing House: Gen. Mgr., Dr. Lem Long, Jr., P.O. Box 30714, Charlotte, NC 28230 Tel. (704)334-9596

Dept. of Overseas Missions: Sec.-Ed., Rev. Dr. Kermit J. DeGraffenreidt, 475 Riverside Dr., Rm. 1935, New York, NY 10115 Tel. (212)870-2952 Fax (212)870-2055

Dept. Brotherhood Pensions & Min. Relief: Sec.-Treas., Rev. David Miller, P.O. Box 34454, Charlotte, NC 28234-4454 Tel. (704)333-3779 Fax (704)333-3867

Christian Education Dept.: Sec., Rev. Raymon Hunt, P.O. Box 32305, Charlotte, NC 28231 Tel. (704)332-9323 Fax (704)332-9332

Dept. of Church School Literature: Ed., Ms. Mary A. Love, P.O. Box 31005, Charlotte, NC 28231 Tel. (704)332-1034 Fax (704)333-1769

Dept.of Church Extension & Home Missions: Sec.-Treas., Dr. Lem Long, Jr., P.O. Box 31005, Charlotte, NC 28231 Tel. (704)334-2519

Dept. of Evangelism: Dir., Dr. Norman H. Hicklin, P.O. Box 561071, Charlotte, NC 28256 Tel. (704)537-9247

Dir. of Public Affairs, Dr. Thaddeus Garrett, Jr., 1730 M St., NW, Ste. 808, Washington, DC 20036 Tel. (202)332-0200 Fax (202)872-0444

Dept. of Health & Social Concerns: Dir., Dr. James E. Milton, 910 Church St., Tuskegee, AL 36083 Tel. (205)727-4601

Judicial Council: Pres., Judge Adele M. Riley, 625 Ellsworth Dr., Dayton, OH 45426

BISHOPS

Piedmont: Bishop Ruben L. Speaks, 1238 Maxwell St., P.O. Box 986, Salisbury, NC 28144 Tel. (704)637-1471; Office, 217 W. Salisbury, Salisbury, NC 28144 Tel. (704)637-6018

Mid-Atlantic I: Bishop Cecil Bishop, 5401 Broadwater St., Temple Hills, MD 20748 Tel. (301)894-2165

North Eastern Region: Bishop George W. Walker, Sr., 3654 Poplar Rd., Flossmoor, IL 60422 Tel. (708)799-5599

Mid-Atlantic II: Bishop Milton A. Williams, 1015 Pineburr Rd., Jamestown, MC 27282 Tel. (919)454-4875; Office, P.O. Box 7441, Greensboro, NC 27417

Eastern West Africa: Bishop S. Chuka Ekemam, Sr., 98 Okigwe Rd., P.O. Box 1149, Owerri, W. Africa, Tel. 083-232-271; Office, Tel. 083-232-271 Fax 234-83-232-271

South Atlantic: Bishop George E. Battle, Jr., 8233 Charles Crawford La., Charlotte, NC 28213 Tel. (704)547-7405; Office, P.O. Box 26396, Charlotte, NC 28221-6396 Tel. (704)332-7600 Fax (704)343-3743

Southwestern Delta: Bishop Joseph Johnson, 4 Russwood Cove, Little Rock, AK 72211; Mailing Address, P.O. Box 56058, Little Rock, AR 72215 Tel. (501)228-9711

Cahaba: Bishop Richard K. Thompson, 1420 Missouri Ave. NW, P.O. Box 55458, Washington, DC 20040 Tel. (202)723-8993

Mid-West: Bishop Enoch B. Rochester, 32 Trebling, Willingboro, NJ 08046 Tel. (609)871-2759 Fax (800)243-LOVE

Western West Africa: Bishop Marshall H. Strickland, 2000 Cedar Circle Dr., Baltimore, MD 21228 Tel. (410)744-7330; Office, Tel. (410)764-0876

Western: Bishop Clarence Carr, 2600 Normandy Dr., Greendale, MO 63121 Tel. (314)727-2931; Office, Tel. (314)727-2940

PERIODICALS

Star of Zion; Quarterly Review; Missionary Seer; Church School Herald

Albanian Orthodox Archdiocese in America

The Albanian Orthodox Church in America traces its origins to the groups of Albanian immigrants which first arrived in the United States in 1886, seeking religious, cultural and economic freedoms denied them in the homeland.

In 1908 in Boston, the Rev. Fan Stylian Noli (later Archbishop) served the first liturgy in the Albanian language in 500 years, to which Orthodox Albanians rallied, forming their own diocese in 1919. Parishes began to spring up throughout New England and the Mid-Atlantic and Great Lakes states. In 1922, clergy from the United States traveled to Albania to proclaim the self-governance of the Orthodox Church in the homeland at the Congress of Berat.

In 1971 the Albanian Archdiocese sought and gained union with the Orthodox Church in America, expressing the desire to expand the Orthodox witness to America at large, giving it an indigenous character. The Albanian Archdiocese remains vigilant for its brothers and sisters in the homeland and serves as an important resource for human rights issues and Albanian affairs, in addition to its programs for youth, theological education, vocational interest programs and retreats for young adults and women.

HEADQUARTERS

523 E. Broadway, S. Boston, MA 02127

Media Contact, Sec., Ms. Dorothy Adams, Tel. (617)268-1275 Fax (617)268-3184

Albanian Orthodox Diocese of America

This Diocese was organized in 1950 as a canonical body administering to the Albanian faithful. It is under the ecclesiastical jurisdiction of the Ecumenical Patriarchate of Constantinople (Istanbul).

HEADQUARTERS

6455 Silver Dawn La., Las Vegas, NV 89118-1186 Tel. (702)221-8245

Media Contact, Vicar General, The Rev. Ik. Ilia Katre

OFFICER

Vicar General, The Rev. Ik. Ilia Katre

Allegheny Wesleyan Methodist Connection (Original Allegheny Conference)

This body was formed in 1968 by members of the Allegheny Conference (located in eastern Ohio and western Pennsylvania) of the Wesleyan Methodist Church, which merged in 1966 with the Pilgrim Holiness Church to form The Wesleyan Church.

The Allegheny Wesleyan Methodist Connection is composed of persons "having the form and seeking the power of godliness, united in order to pray together, to receive the word of exhortation, and to watch over one another in love, that they may help each other to work out their salvation." There is a strong commitment to congregational government and to holiness of heart and life. There is a strong thrust in church extension within the United States and in missions worldwide.

HEADQUARTERS

1827 Allen Dr., Salem, OH 44460 Tel. (216)337-9376

Media Contact, Pres., Rev. John Englant

OFFICERS

Pres., Rev. John Englant
Vice-Pres., Rev. William Cope, 1231 Conser Dr., Salem, OH 44460
Sec., Rev. W. H. Cornell, Box 266, Sagamore, PA 16250
Treas., Mr. Clair Taylor, 858 E. Philadelphia Ave., Youngstown, OH 44502

PERIODICAL

The Allegheny Wesleyan Methodist

Amana Church Society

The Amana Church Society was founded by a God-fearing, God-loving and pioneering group not associated with any other church or organization. It had its beginning as the Community of True Inspiration in 1714 in the province of Hesse, Germany. The members were much persecuted in Germany because of their belief in the "power of divine inspiration," because they would not send their children to the 10 established schools and because they were pacifistic.

The Community of True Inspiration had its humble beginning under the inspired leadership of Eberhard Ludwig Gruber and Johann Friedrich Rock. Beginning in 1842, Christian Metz, while divinely inspired, led the community to the West and the New World, where they established the Ebenezer Community near Buffalo, N.Y. Because of deterring and worldly influences, the Ebenezer lands were abandoned in 1854. The Amana Colonies were founded in Iowa in 1855.

The Amana Church Society does no proselyting or missionary work. It believes in a peaceful, quiet, "brotherly" way of life. Although many of the stricter church rules have been relaxed over the years, the Amana Church Society maintains its simple, unostentatious churches and rituals. There have been no divinely inspired leaders since the demise of Barbara Landman in 1883, but the faith is still paramount in divine revelation of the Word of God through God's chosen representatives, and the testimonies of the aforementioned religious leaders are read in all the regular services. This small group over the years attests to a faith in God that makes the term *Amana* meaningful—"as a rock" or "to remain faithful."

HEADQUARTERS

P.O. Box 103, Middle, IA 52307

OFFICERS

Pres., Kirk Setzer, Amana, IA 52203
Vice-Pres., Steward Geiger, Cedar Rapids, IA 52203
Sec., Martin Roemig, Amana, IA 52203
Treas., Ivan Reihmann, Middle, IA 52307

The American Association of Lutheran Churches

This church body was constituted on Nov. 7, 1987. The AALC was formed by laity and pastors of the former American Lutheran Church in America who held to a high view of Scripture (inerrancy and infallibility). This church body also emphasizes the primacy of evangelism and world missions and the authority and autonomy of the local congregation.

Congregations of the AALC are distributed throughout the continental United States from Long Island, N.Y., to Los Angeles. The primary decision-making body is the General Convention, to which each congregation has proportionate representation.

HEADQUARTERS

The AALC National Office, 17800 Lyndale Ave. S., Ste. 120, Minneapolis, MN 55420 Tel. (612)884-7784
Mailing Address, P.O. Box 17097, Minneapolis, MN 55417
The AALC Regional Office, 2211 Maynard St., Waterloo, IA 50701 Tel. (319)232-3971
Media Contact, Admn. Coord., Dick Day, P.O. Box 416, Waterloo, IA 50704 Tel. (319)232-3971

OFFICERS

Presiding Pastor, Dr. Duane R. Lindberg, P.O. Box 416, Waterloo, IA 50701 Tel. (319)232-3971
Asst. Presiding Pastor, Rev. Robert Dennis, 2961 Yellowtail Dr., Los Anamitos, CA 90720 Tel. (310)597-6507
Sec., Rev. Daniel W. Selbo, 8701 Elk Grove-Florin Rd., Elk Grove, CA 95624 Tel. (916)689-7300
Treas., Rev. James E. Minor, P.O. Box 193, Church Rd., Rowland, PA 18457 Tel. (717)685-4350
Admn. Coord., Pastor Dick Day, P.O. Box 416, Waterloo, IA 50704 Tel. (319)232-3971

PERIODICAL

The Evangel

The American Baptist Association

The American Baptist Association (ABA) is an international fellowship of independent Baptist churches voluntarily cooperating in missionary, evangelistic, benevolent and Christian education activities throughout the world. Its beginnings can be traced to the landmark movement of the 1850s. Led by James R. Graves and J. M. Pendleton, a significant number of Baptist churches in the South, claiming a New Testament heritage, rejected as extrascriptural the policies of the newly formed Southern Baptist Convention (SBC). Because they strongly advocated church equality, many of these churches continued doing mission and benevolent work apart from the SBC, electing to work through local associations. Meeting in Texarkana, Tex., in 1924, messengers from the various churches effectively merged two of these major associations, the Baptist Missionary Association of Texas and the General Association, forming the American Baptist Association.

Since 1924, mission efforts have been supported in Canada, Mexico, Central and South America, Australia, Africa, Europe, Asia, India, New Zealand, Korea and Japan. An even more successful domestic mission effort has changed the ABA from a predominantly rural southern organization to one with churches in 45 states.

Through its publishing arm in Texarkana, the ABA publishes literature and books numbering into the thousands. Major seminaries include the Missionary Baptist Seminary, founded by Dr. Ben M. Bogard in Little Rock, Ark., Texas Baptist Seminary, Henderson, Tex., Oklahoma Missionary Baptist College in Marlow, Okla., and Florida Baptist Schools in Lakeland, Fla.

While no person may speak for the churches of the ABA, all accept the Bible as the inerrant Word of God. They believe Christ was the virgin-born Son of God, that God is a triune God, that the only church is the local congregation of scripturally baptized believers and that the work of the church is to spread the gospel.

HEADQUARTERS

4605 N. State Line Ave., Texarkana, TX 75503 Tel. (903)792-2783
Media Contact, Public Rel. Dir., Wayne Sewell, P.O. Box 1828, Texarkana, AR 75504-1828 Tel. (903)792-2783

OFFICERS

Pres., J. O. Phillips, P.O. Box 561, Mauldin, SC 29662
Vice-Pres.: James F. Homes, 109 Tanglewood Dr., North Little Rock, AR 72118; Art Richardson, 457 Mark Ave., Shafter, CA 93263; Marlin Gipson, 1526 N. Mulberry Ave., Panama City, FL 32405
Rec. Clks.: Larry Clements, P.O. Box 234, Monticello, AR 71655; Gene Smith, 5201 Summerhille Rd., #509, Texarkana, TX 75503
Publications: Ed.-in-Chief, Bill Johnson, P.O. Box 502, Texarkana, AR 75504; Bus. Mgr., Tom Sannes, Box 1828, Texarkana, AR 75501
Meeting Arrangements, Dir., Edgar N. Sutton, P.O. Box 240, Alexandria, AR 72002
Sec.-Treas., D. S. Madden, P.O. Box 1050, Texarkana, TX 75504

American Baptist Churches in the U.S.A.

Originally known as the Northern Baptist Convention, this body of Baptist churches changed the name to American Baptist Convention in 1950 with a commitment to "hold the name in trust for all Christians of like faith and mind who desire to bear witness to the historical Baptist convictions in a framework of cooperative Protestantism."

In 1972 American Baptist Churches in the U.S.A. was adopted as the new name. Although national missionary organizational developments began in 1814 with the establishment of the American Baptist Foreign Mission Society and continued with the organization of the American Baptist Publication Society in 1824 and the American Baptist Home Mission Society in 1832, the general denominational body was not formed until 1907. American Baptist work at the local level dates back to the organization by Roger Williams of the First Baptist Church in Providence, R. I. in 1638.

HEADQUARTERS

P.O. Box 851, Valley Forge, PA 19482 Tel. (215)768-2000 Fax (215)768-2275
Media Contact, Dir., ABC News Service, Richard W. Schramm, Tel. (215)768-2077 Fax (215)768-2320

OFFICERS

Pres., Hector M. Gonzales
Vice-Pres., Carole H. Penfield
Budget Review Officer, Anne J. Mills
Gen. Sec., Daniel E. Weiss
Assoc. Gen. Sec.-Treas., Cheryl H. Wade

REGIONAL ORGANIZATIONS

Central Region, ABC of, Fred W. Thompson, Box 4105, Topeka, KS 66614-4105
Chicago, ABC of Metro, (Interim), Millie B. Myren, 28 E. Jackson Blvd., Ste. 210, Chicago, IL 60604-2207
Cleveland Baptist Assoc., Dennis E. Norris, 1836 Euclid Ave., Ste. 603, Cleveland, OH 44115-2234
Connecticut, ABC of, Lowell H. Fewster, 100 Bloomfield Ave., Hartford, CT 06105-1097
Dakotas, ABC of, Ronald E. Cowles, 1524 S. Summit Ave., Sioux Falls, SD 57105-1697
District of Columbia Bapt. Conv., W. Jere Allen, 1628 16th St., NW, Washington, DC 20009-3099
Great Rivers Region, ABC of the, Malcolm G. Shotwell, P.O. Box 3786, Springfield, IL 62708-3786
Indiana, ABC of, L. Eugene Ton, 1650 N. Delaware St., Indianapolis, IN 46202-2493
Indianapolis, ABC of Greater, Larry D. Sayre, 1350 N. Delaware St., Indianapolis, IN 46202-2493
Los Angeles Bapt. City Mission Soc., Emory C. Campbell, 1212 Wilshire Blvd., Ste. 201, Los Angeles, CA 90017-1902
Maine, ABC of, Gary G. Johnson, P.O. Box 667, Augusta, ME 04332-0667
Massachusetts, ABC of, Linda C. Spoolstra, 20 Milton St., Dedham, MA 02026-2967
Metropolitan New York, ABC of, James D. Stallings, 475 Riverside Dr., Rm. 432, New York, NY 10115-0432
Michigan, ABC of, Robert E. Shaw, 4578 S. Hagadorn Rd., East Lansing, MI 48823-5355
Mid-America Baptist Churches, Telfer L. Epp, Ste. 15, 2400 86th St., Des Moines, IA 50322-4380
Nebraska, ABC of, Dennis D. Hatfield, 6404 Maple St., Omaha, NE 68104-4079
New Jersey, ABC of, A. Roy Medley, 161 Freeway Dr. E., East Orange, NJ 07018-4099
New York State, ABC of, William A. Carlson, 5842 Heritage Landing Dr., East Syracuse, NY 13057-9359
Northwest, ABC of, Gaylord L. Hasselblad, 321 First Ave. W., Seattle, WA 98119-4103
Ohio, ABC of, Robert A. Fisher, P.O. Box 376, Granville, OH 43023-0376
Oregon, ABC of, James T. Ledbetter, 0245 SW Bancroft St., Ste. G, Portland, OR 97201-4270
Pacific Southwest, ABC of the, John J. Jackson, 970 Village Oaks Dr., Covina, CA 91724-3679
Pennsylvania & Delaware, ABC of, Richard E. Rusbuldt, P.O. Box 851, Valley Forge, PA 19482-0851
Philadelphia Baptist Assoc., Larry K. Waltz, 100 N. 17th St., Philadelphia, PA 19103-2736

Pittsburgh Baptist Assoc., Clayton R. Woodbury, 1620 Allegheny Bldg., 429 Forbes Ave., Pittsburgh, PA 15219-1627

Puerto Rico, Baptist Churches of, E. Yamina Apolinaris, Mayaguez #21, Hato Rey, PR 00917

Rhode Island, ABC of, Donald H. Crosby, 734 Hope St., Providence, RI 02906-3535

Rochester/Genessee Region, ABC of, Carrol A. Turner, 151 Brooks Ave., Rochester, NY 14619-2454

Rocky Mountains, ABC of, Louise B. Barger, 1344 Pennsylvania St., Denver, CO 80203-2499

South, ABC of the, Walter L. Parrish, II, 525 Main St., Ste. 105, Laurel, MD 20707-4995

Vermont/New Hampshire, ABC of, Robert W. Williams, P.O. Box 796, Concord, NH 03302-0796

West, ABC of the, Robert D. Rasmussen, P.O. Box 23204, Oakland, CA 94623-0204

West Virginia Baptist Convention, Lloyd D. Hamblin, Jr., P.O. Box 1019, Parkersburg, WV 26102-1019

Wisconsin, ABC of, George E. Daniels, 15330 W. Watertown Plank Rd., Elm Grove, WI 53122-2391

BOARDS

Bd. of Educational Ministries: Exec. Dir., Jean B. Kim; Pres., Margaret C. Susman

American Baptist Assembly: Green Lake, WI 54941; Pres., Paul W. LaDue; Chpsn., J. Ralph Beaty

American Baptist Historical Society: 1106 S. Goodman St., Rochester, NY 14620; or P.O. Box 851, Valley Forge, PA 19482-0851; Admn./Archivist, Beverly C. Carlson; Pres., John F. Mandt

American Baptist Men: Exec. Dir., Richard S. McPhee; Pres., Richard A. Renquest

American Baptist Women's Ministries: Exec. Dir. (Interim), Louise M. Jensen; Pres., Ruth Housam

Commission on the Ministry: Exec. Dir., Craig A. Collemer

Bd. of Intl. Ministries: Exec. Dir., John A. Sundquist; Pres., Michael A. Buckles

Bd. of Natl. Ministries: Exec. Dir., Aidsand F. Wright-Riggins; Pres., G. Elaine Smith

Ministers & Missionaries Benefit Bd.: Exec. Dir., Gordon E. Smith; Pres., John W. Reed, 475 Riverside Dr., New York, NY 10115

Minister Council: Dir. (Interim), J. Eugene Wright; Pres., Milton P. Ryder

PERIODICALS

Baptist Leader; The Secret Place; American Baptist Quarterly; American Baptists in Mission

The American Carpatho-Russian Orthodox Greek Catholic Church

The American Carpatho-Russian Orthodox Greek Catholic Church is a self-governing diocese that is in communion with the Ecumenical Patriarchate of Constantinople. The late Patriarch Benjamin I, in an official Patriarchal Document dated Sept. 19, 1938, canonized the Diocese in the name of the Orthodox Church of Christ.

HEADQUARTERS

312 Garfield St., Johnstown, PA 15906 Tel. (814)536-4207

Media Contact, Chancellor, V. Rev. Msgr. Frank P. Miloro, Tel. (814)539-8086 Fax (814)536-4699

OFFICERS

Bishop, Rt. Bishop Nicholas Smisko

Vicar General, V. Rev. Msgr. John Yurcisin, 249 Butler Ave., Johnstown, PA 15906

Chancellor, V. Rev. Msgr. Frank P. Miloro

Treas., V. Rev. Msgr. Ronald A. Hazuda, 115 East Ave., Erie, PA 16503

PERIODICAL

Cerkovnyj Vistnik—Church Messenger

American Evangelical Christian Churches

Founded in 1944, the AECC is composed of individual ministers and churches who are united in accepting "Seven Articles of Faith." These seven articles are: the Bible as the written word of God; the Virgin birth; the deity of Jesus Christ; Salvation through the atonement; guidance of our life through prayer; the return of the Saviour; the establishment of the Millenial Kingdom.

The organization offers credentials (licenses and ordinations) to those who accept the Seven Articles and who put unity in Christ above individual interpretations and are approved by A.E.C.C.

A.E.C.C. seeks to promote the gospel through its ministers, churches and missionary activities.

Churches operate independently with all decisions concerning local government left to the individual churches.

The organization also has ministers in Canada.

HEADQUARTERS

64 South St., Indianapolis, IN 46227 Tel. (317)784-9726

Media Contact, Natl. Mod., Dr. Ben Morgan, Tel. (317)784-9726

OFFICERS

Mod., Dr. Ben Morgan

Exec. Dir., Dr. David I. Moshier, 900 S. Washington St., Ste. 205, Falls Church, VA 22046-4020 Tel. (703)671-9219

Sec., Dr. Charles Wasielewski, Box 51, Barton, NY 13734 Tel. (607)565-4074

Treas., Dr. S. Omar Overly, 2481 Red Rock Blvd., Grove City, OH 43123-1154 Tel. (614)871-0710

REGIONAL MODERATORS

California: Rev. Richard Cuthbert, 1195 Via Seville, Cathedral City, CA 92234 Tel. (619)321-6682

Carolinas-Georgia: Rev. Larry Walker, P.O. Box 1165, Lillington, NC 27546 Tel. (919)893-9529

Chesapeake: Rev. James J. Mulcahey, Jr., 661 San Juan Ct., Lusby, MD 20657 Tel. (410)326-3574

Florida: Rev. Otis Osborne, 1421 Roseland Ave., Sebring, FL 33870 Tel. (813)382-4462

Indiana: Rev. Gene McClain, Box 337, Morgantown, IN 46160 Tel. (812)597-5021

Inter-Continental: Dr. David I. Moshier, 3686 King St., #150, Alexandria, VA 22302-1906 Tel. (703)671-9219

Maryland: Dr. Kenneth White, 701 Spruce St., Hagerstown, MD 21740 Tel. (301)790-3923

Michigan: Rev. Arthur Mirek, Box 361, Hazel Park, MI 48030 Tel. (313)754-8838

Mid-West: Rev. Charles Clark, P.O. Box 121, Pleasant Hill, IL 62366 Tel. (217)734-9431

New England: Rev. Paul Gilbert, 190 Warwick Rd., Melrose, MA 02176 Tel. (617)979-0056

New York: Rev. Kenneth DeHond, 6 Sodus Mobile Home Park, Sodus, NY 14551 Tel. (315)483-9179

US RELIGIOUS BODIES

Ohio: Dr. S. Omar Overly, 2481 Red Rock Blvd., Grove City, OH 43123-1154 Tel. (614)871-0710
Pennsylvania: Rev. Wesley Kuntz, 34 Catherine Ave., Latrobe, PA 15650 Tel. (412)537-5630

American Rescue Workers

This group was founded in 1884 by Thomas Moore as The Salvation Army. Soon after, a dispute with William Booth's Salvation Army forced a name change in 1890 to the American Salvation Army. In 1913 the current name, American Rescue Workers, was adopted.

It is a national religious social service agency which operates on a quasimilitary basis. Membership includes officers (clergy), soldiers/adherents (laity), members of various activity groups and volunteers who serve as advisors, associates and committed participants in ARW service functions.

The American Rescue Workers, founded in 1884, is an evangelical part of the Universal Christian Church.

The motivation of the organization is the love of God. Its message is based on the Bible. This is expressed by its spiritual Ministry, the purposes of which are to preach the gospel of Jesus Christ and to meet human needs in his name without discrimination.

HEADQUARTERS
2827 Frankford Ave., P.O. Box 4766, Philadelphia, PA 19134 Tel. (215)739-6524
Washington, DC Capital Area Office, 716 Ritchie Rd., Capitol Heights, MD 20743 Tel. (301)336-6200
National Field Office, 1209 Hamilton Blvd., Hagerstown, MD 21742 Tel. (301)797-0061
Media Contact, Natl. Communication Sec., Col. Robert N. Coles, Natl. Field Ofc., Fax (301)797-1480

OFFICERS
Commander-In-Chief & Pres. of Corp., General Paul E. Martin
Chief of Staff, Col. Claude S. Astin, Jr.
Natl. Bd. Pres., Col. George B Gossett
Special Services/Aide-de-Camp, Col. Robert N. Coles, Natl. Field Ofc.
Natl. Chief Sec., Col. Joyce Gossett

PERIODICAL
The Rescue Herald

The Anglican Orthodox Church

This body was founded on Nov. 16, 1963, in Statesville, N. C., by the Most Rev. James P. Dees. The church holds to the Thirty-Nine Articles of Religion, the 1928 Book of Common Prayer, the King James Version of the Bible and basic Anglican traditions and church government. It upholds biblical morality and emphasizes the fundamental doctrines of the virgin birth, the incarnation, the atoning sacrifice of the cross, the Trinity, the resurrection, the second coming, salvation by faith alone and the divinity of Christ.

Branches of the worldwide Orthodox Anglican Communion are located in South India, Madagascar, Pakistan, Liberia, Nigeria, the Philippines, the Fiji Islands, South Africa, Kenya and Colombia.

The entire membership totals over 300,000.

An active program of Christian education is promoted both in the United States and on a worldwide basis. This includes but is not limited to

weekly Sunday School Bible study classes and weekday youth clubs.

The Anglican Orthodox Church operates Cranmer Seminary in Statesville, North Carolina, to train men for holy orders.

HEADQUARTERS
P.O. Box 128, Statesville, NC 28677 Tel. (704)873-8365
Media Contact, Admn. Asst., Mrs. Betty Hoffman

OFFICER
Presiding Bishop, The Most Rev. George C. Schneller, 323 Walnut St., P.O. Box 128, Statesville, NC 28677 Tel. (704)873-8365

PERIODICAL
The News

The Antiochian Orthodox Christian Archdiocese of North America

The spiritual needs of Antiochian faithful in North America were first served through the Syro-Arabian Mission of the Russian Orthodox Church in 1892. In 1895, the Syrian Orthodox Benevolent Society was organized by Antiochian immigrants in New York City. Raphael Hawaweeny, a young Damascene clergyman serving as professor of Arabic language at the Orthodox theological academy in Kazan, Russia, came to New York to organize the first Arabic- language parish in North America in 1896, after being canonically received under the omophorion of the head of the Russian Church in North America. Saint Nicholas Cathedral, now located at 355 State St. in Brooklyn, is considered the "mother parish" of the Archdiocese.

On March 12, 1904, Hawaweeny became the first Orthodox bishop to be consecrated in North America. He traveled throughout the continent and established new parishes. The unity of Orthodoxy in the New World, including the Syrian Greek Orthodox community, was ruptured after the death of Bishop Raphael in 1915 and by the Bolshevik revolution in Russia and the First World War. Unity returned in 1975 when Metropolitan Philip Saliba, of the Antiochian Archdiocese of New York, and Metropolitan Michael Shaheen of the Antiochian archdiocese of Toledo, Ohio, signed the Articles of Reunification, ratified by the Holy Synod of the Patriarchate. Saliba was recognized as the Metropolitan Primate and Shaheen as Auxiliary Archbishop. A second auxiliary to the Metropolitan, Bishop Antoun Khouri, was consecrated at Brooklyn's Saint Nicholas Cathedral, in 1983. A third auxiliary, Bishop Basil Essey, was consecrated at Wichita's St. George Cathedral, in 1992.

The Archdiocesan Board of Trustees (consisting of 50 elected and appointed clergy and lay members) and the Metropolitan's Advisory Council (consisting of clergy and lay representatives from each parish and mission) meet regularly to assist the Primate in the administration of the Archdiocese.

HEADQUARTERS
358 Mountain Rd., Englewood, NJ 07631 Tel. (201)871-1355 Fax (201)871-7954
Media Contact, Vicar, The V. Rev. George S. Corey, 52 78th St., Brooklyn, NY 11209 Tel. (718)748-7940 Fax (718)855-3608

OFFICERS
Primate, Metropolitan Philip Saliba

Auxiliary, Bishop Antoun Khouri
Auxiliary, Bishop Basil Essey

PERIODICALS
The Word; Again

Apostolic Catholic Assyrian Church of the East, North American Dioceses

The Holy Apostolic Catholic Assyrian Church of the East is the ancient Christian church that developed within the Persian Empire from the day of Pentecost. The Apostolic traditions testify that the Church of the East was established by Sts. Peter, Thomas, Thaddaeus and Bartholomew from among the Twelve and by the labors of Mar Mari and Aggai of the Seventy. The Church grew and developed carrying the Christian gospel into the whole of Asia and islands of the Pacific. Prior to the Great Persecution at the hands of Tamer'leng the Mongol, it is said to have been the largest Christian church in the world.

The doctrinal identity of the church is that of the Apostles. The church stresses two natures and two Qnume in the One Person, Perfect God-Perfect man. The church gives witness to the original Nicene Creed, the Ecumenical Councils of Nicea and Constantinople and the church fathers of that era. Since God is revealed as Trinity, the appellation "Mother of God" is rejected for the Ever Virgin Blessed Mary Mother of Christ, we declare that she is Mother of Emmanuel, God with us!

The church has maintained a line of Catholicos Patriarchs from the time of the Holy Apostles until this present time. Today the present occupant of the Apostolic Throne is His Holiness Mar Dinkha IV, 120th successor to the See of Selucia Ctestiphon.

HEADQUARTERS

Catholicos Patriarch, His Holiness Mar Dinkha, IV, Metropolitanate Residence, The Assyrian Church of the East, Baghdad, Iraq
Media Contact, Chancellor to the Bishop, The Rev. Chancellor C. H. Klutz, 7201 N. Ashland, Chicago, IL 60626 Tel. (312)465-4777 Fax (312)465-0776

BISHOPS

Diocese Eastern USA: His Grace Bishop Mar Aprim Khamis, 8908 Birch Ave., Morton Grove, IL 60053 Tel. (312)465-4777 Fax (708)966-0012
Diocese Western USA: His Grace Bishop Mar Bawai Soro, St. Joseph Cathedral, 680 Minnesota Ave., San Jose, CA 95125 Tel. (408)286-7377 Fax (408)286-1236
Diocese of Canada: His Grace Bishop Mar Emmanuel Joseph, St. Mary Cathedral, 57 Apted Ave., Weston, ON M9L 2P2 Tel. (416)744-9311

PERIODICAL

Qala min M'Dinkha (Voice from the East)

Apostolic Christian Church (Nazarene)

This body was formed in America by an immigration from various European nations, from a movement begun by Rev. S. H. Froehlich, a Swiss pastor, whose followers are still found in Switzerland and Central Europe.

HEADQUARTERS

Apostolic Christian Church Foundation, 1135 Sholey Rd., Richmond, VA 23231 Tel. (804)222-1943 Fax (804)222-1943
Media Contact, Exec. Dir., James Hodges

OFFICERS

Exec. Dir., James Hodges

Apostolic Christian Churches of America

The Apostolic Christian Church of America was founded in the early 1830s in Switzerland by Samuel Froehlich, a young divinity student who had experienced a religious conversion based on the pattern found in the New Testament. The church, known then as Evangelical Baptist, spread to surrounding countries. A Froehlich associate, Elder Benedict Weyeneth, established the church's first American congregation in 1847 in upstate New York. In America, where the highest concentration today is in the Midwest farm belt, the church became known as Apostolic Christian.

Church doctrine is based on a literal interpretation of the Bible, the infallible Word of God. The church believes that a true faith in Christ's redemptive work at Calvary is manifested by a sincere repentance and conversion. Members strive for sanctification and separation from worldliness as a consequence of salvation, not as a means to obtain it. Security in Christ is believed to be conditional based on faithfulness. Uniform observance of scriptural standards of holiness are stressed. Holy Communion is confined to members of the church. Male members are willing to serve in the military, but do not bear arms. The holy kiss is practiced and women wear head coverings during prayer and worship.

Doctrinal authority rests with a council of elders, each of whom serves as a local elder (bishop). Both elders and ministers are chosen from local congregations, do not attend seminary and serve without compensation. Sermons are delivered extemporaneously as led by the Holy Spirit, using the Bible as a text.

HEADQUARTERS

3420 N. Sheridan Rd., Peoria, IL 61604
Media Contact, Sec., Dale R. Eisenmann, 6913 Wilmette, Darien, IL 60561 Tel. (708)969-7021

OFFICERS

Sec., Elder (Bishop) Dale R. Eisenmann, 6913 Wilmette, Darien, IL 60561 Tel. (708)969-7021

PERIODICAL

The Silver Lining

Apostolic Faith Mission Church of God

The Apostolic Faith Mission Church of God was founded and organized July 10, 1906, by Bishop F. W. Williams in Mobile, Ala.

Bishop Williams was saved and filled with the Holy Ghost at a revival in Los Angeles under Elder W. J. Seymour of The Divine Apostolic Faith Movement. After being called into the ministry, Bishop Williams went out to preach the gospel in Mississippi, then moved on to Mobile.

On Oct. 9, 1915, the Apostolic Faith Mission Church of God was incorporated in Mobile under Bishop Williams, who was also the general overseer of this church.

Ward's Temple, 806 Muscogee Rd., Cantonment, FL 32533

Media Contact, Natl. Sunday School Supt., Elder Thomas Brooks, 3298 Toney Dr., Decatur, GA 30032 Tel. (404)284-7596

OFFICERS

Bd. of Bishops: Presiding Bishop, Donice Brown, 2265 Welcome Cir., Cantonment, FL 32533 Tel. (904)968-5225; Billy Carter; J. L. Smiley; T. L. Frye; D. Brown; T. C. Tolbert; James Truss

NATIONAL DEPARTMENTS

Missionary Dept., Pres., Sarah Ward, Cantonment, FL

Youth Dept., Pres., W. J. Wills, Lincoln, AL

Sunday School Dept., Supt., Thomas Brooks, Decatur, GA

Mother Dept., Pres., Mother Juanita Phillips, Birmingham, AL

INTERNATIONAL DEPARTMENTS

Morobia, Liberia, Bishop Beter T. Nelson, Box 3646, Bush Rhode Islane, Morobia, Liberia

Apostolic Faith Mission of Portland, Oregon

The Apostolic Faith Mission of Portland, Oregon, was founded in 1907. It had its beginning in the Latter Rain outpouring on Azusa Street in Los Angeles in 1906.

Some of the main doctrines are justification by faith; spiritual new birth, as Jesus told Nicodemus and as Martin Luther proclaimed in the Great Reformation; sanctification, a second definite work of grace; the Wesleyan teaching of holiness; the baptism of the Holy Ghost as experienced on the Day of Pentecost and again poured out at the beginning of the Latter Rain revival in Los Angeles.

Mrs. Florence L. Crawford, who had received the baptism of the Holy Ghost in Los Angeles, brought this Latter Rain message to Portland on Christmas Day 1906. It has spread to the world by means of literature which is still published and mailed everywhere without a subscription price. Collections are never taken in the meetings and the public is not asked for money.

Camp meetings have been held annually in Portland, Ore., since 1907, with delegations coming from around the world.

Missionaries from the Portland headquarters have established churches in Korea, Japan, the Philippines and many countries in Africa.

HEADQUARTERS

6615 SE 52nd Ave., Portland, OR 97206 Tel. (503)777-1741 Fax (503)777-1743

Media Contact, Gen. Overseer, Dwight L. Baltzell

OFFICER

Gen. Overseer, Rev. Dwight L. Baltzell

PERIODICAL

The Light of Hope

Apostolic Lutheran Church of America

Organized in 1872 as the Solomon Korteniemi Lutheran Society, this Finnish body was incorporated in 1929 as the Finnish Apostolic Lutheran Church in America and changed its name to Apostolic Lutheran Church of America in 1962.

This body stresses preaching the Word of God. There is an absence of liturgy and formalism in worship. A seminary education is not required of pastors. Being called by God to preach the Word is the chief requirement for clergy and laity.

The church stresses personal absolution and forgiveness of sins, as practiced by Martin Luther, and the importance of bringing converts into God's kingdom.

HEADQUARTERS

Rt. 1 Box 462, Houghton, MI 49931 Tel. (906)482-8269

Media Contact, Sec., James Johnson

OFFICERS

Pres., Earl Kaurala, Rt. 1, Box 303, Houghton, MI 49931

Sec., James Johnson

Treas., Richard Sakrisson, 7606 NE Vancouver Mall Dr., #14, Vancouver, WA 98662

PERIODICAL

Christian Monthly

Apostolic Overcoming Holy Church of God, Inc.

The Right Reverend William Thomas Phillips (1893-1973) was thoroughly convinced in 1912 that Holiness was a system through which God wanted him to serve. In 1916 he was led to Mobile, Ala., where he organized the Ethiopian Overcoming Holy Church of God. In April 1941 the church was incorporated in Alabama under its present title.

Each congregation manages its own affairs, united under districts governed by overseers and diocesan bishops and assisted by an executive board comprised of bishops, ministers, laymen and the National Secretary. The General Assembly convenes annually.

The church's chief objective is to enlighten people of God's holy Word and to be a blessing to every nation. The main purpose of this church is to ordain elders, appoint pastors and send out divinely called missionaries and teachers. This church enforces all ordinances enacted by Jesus Christ. The church believes in water baptism (Acts 2:38, 8:12, and 10:47), administers the Lord's Supper, observes the washing of feet (John 13:4-7), believes that Jesus Christ shed his blood to sanctify the people and cleanse them from all sin and believes in the resurrection of the dead and the second coming of Christ.

HEADQUARTERS

1120 N. 24th St., Birmingham, AL 35234

Media Contact, Natl. Exec. Sec., Juanita R. Arrington, Tel. (205)324-2202

OFFICERS

Senior Bishop & Exec. Head, Rt. Rev. Jasper Roby

Associate Bishops: G. W. Ayers, 2257 St. Stephens Rd., Mobile, AL 36617; L. M. Bell, 2000 Pio Nono Ave., Macon, GA 31206; Gabriel Crutcher, 526 E. Bethune St., Detroit, MI 48202; John Mathews, 12 College St., Dayton, OH 45407; Bishop Joe Bennett, 15718 Drexel Ave., Dalton, IL 60419

Exec. Sec., Mrs. Juanita R. Arrington

The People's Mouthpiece

Armenian Apostolic Church of America

Widespread movement of the Armenian people over the centuries caused the development of two seats of religious jurisdiction of the Armenian Apostolic Church in the World: the See of Etchmiadzin, in Armenia, and the See of Cilicia, in Lebanon.

In America, the Armenian Church functioned under the jurisdiction of the Etchmiadzin See from 1887 to 1933, when a division occurred within the American diocese over the condition of the church in Soviet Armenia. One group chose to remain independent until 1957, when the Holy See of Cilicia agreed to accept them under its jurisdiction.

Despite the existence of two dioceses in North America, the Armenian Church has always functioned as one church in dogma and liturgy.

HEADQUARTERS

Eastern Prelacy, 138 E. 39th St., New York, NY 10016 Tel. (212)689-7810 Fax (212)689-7168

Western Prelacy, 4401 Russel Ave., Los Angeles, CA 90027 Tel. (213)663-8273 Fax (213)663-0438

Media Contact, Exec. Dir., Vasken Ghougassian

OFFICERS

Eastern Prelacy, Prelate, Archbishop Mesrob Ashjian

Eastern Prelacy, Chpsn., Nazareth Emlikian

Eastern Prelacy, Exec. Dir., Vasken Ghougassian

Western Prelacy, Prelate, Archbishop Datev Sarkissian, 4401 Russell Ave., Los Angeles, CA 90027 Fax (213)663-0428

Western Prelacy, Chpsn., Khajag Dikidjian

DEPARTMENTS

AREC, Armenian Religious Educ. Council, Exec. Coord., Deacon Shant Kazanjian

ANEC, Armenian Natl. Educ. Council, Exec. Coord., Hourig Sahagian-Papazian

PERIODICAL

Outreach

Assemblies of God

From a few hundred delegates at its founding convention in 1914 at Hot Springs, Ark., the Assemblies of God has become one of the largest church groups in the modern Pentecostal movement worldwide. Through-out its existence it has emphasized the power of the Holy Spirit to change lives and the participation of all members in the work of the church.

The revival that led to the formation of the Assemblies of God and numerous other church groups early in the 20th century began during times of intense prayer and Bible study. Believers in the United States and around the world received spiritual experiences like those described in the Book of Acts. Accompanied by baptism in the Holy Spirit and its initial physical evidence of "speaking in tongues," or a language unknown to the person, their experiences were associated with the coming of the Holy Spirit at Pentecost (Acts 2), so participants were called Pentecostals.

The church also believes that the Bible is God's infallible Word to man, that salvation is available only through Jesus Christ, that divine healing is made possible through Christ's suffering and that Christ will return again for those who love him. In recent years, this Pentecostal revival has spilled over into almost every denomination in a new wave of revival sometimes called the charismatic renewal.

Assemblies of God leaders credit their church's rapid and continuing growth to its acceptance of the New Testament as a model for the present-day church. Aggressive evangelism and missionary zeal at home and abroad characterize the denomination.

Assemblies of God believers observe two ordinances—water baptism by immersion and the Lord's Supper, or Holy Communion. The church is trinitarian, holding that God exists in three persons: Father, Son and Holy Spirit.

HEADQUARTERS

1445 Boonville Ave., Springfield, MO 65802 Tel. (417)862-2781 Fax (417)862-8558

Media Contact, Sec. of Information, Juleen Turnage

EXECUTIVE PRESBYTERY

Gen. Supt., Thomas E. Trask

Asst. Supt., Charles T. Crabtree

Gen. Sec., George O. Wood

Gen. Treas., James E. Bridges

Foreign Missions, Exec. Dir., Loren O. Triplett

Home Missions, Exec. Dir., Charles Hackett

Great Lakes, Robert K. Schmidgall, P.O. Box 296-1155, Aurora Ave., Naperville, IL 60540

Gulf, Phillip Wannenmacher, 1301 N. Boonville, Springfield, MO 65802

North Central, David Argue, P.O. Box 22178, Lincoln, NE 68542

Northeast, Almon Bartholomew, P.O. Box 39, Liverpool, NY 13088

Northwest, R. L. Brandt, 1702 Colton Blvd., Billings, MT 59102

South Central, Armon Newburn, P.O. Box 13179, Oklahoma City, OK 73113

Southeast, Ronald McManus, 3730 University Pkwy., Winston-Salem, NC 27106

Southwest, Glen D. Cole, 9470 Micron Rd., Sacramento, CA 95827

INTERNATIONAL HEADQUARTERS

Gen. Supt.'s Office Administration, Gen. Supt., Thomas E. Trask

Gen. Sec.'s Office Administration, Gen. Sec., George O. Wood

Division of the Treasury, Gen. Treas., James E. Bridges

Division of Christian Education, Natl. Dir., David Torgerson

Division of Christian Higher Education, Natl. Dir., David Bundrick

Division of Church Ministries, Natl. Dir., Terry Raburn

Division of Foreign Missions, Exec. Dir., Loren O. Triplett

Division of Home Missions, Exec. Dir., Charles Hackett

Div. of Publication, Gospel Publishing House, Natl. Dir., Joseph Kilpatrick

PERIODICALS

Advance; At Ease; Caring; High Adventure; Memos: A Magazine for Missionettes Leaders; Mountain Movers; Paraclete; Pentecostal Evangel; Christian Education Counselor; Woman's Touch; Heritage; On Course

Assemblies of God International Fellowship (Independent/Not Affiliated)

April 9, 1906 is the date commonly accepted by Pentecostals as the 20th-century outpouring of God's spirit in America, which began in a humble gospel mission at 312 Azusa Street in Los Angeles.

This spirit movement spread across the United States and gave birth to the Independent Assemblies of God (Scandinavian). Early pioneers instrumental in guiding and shaping the fellowship of ministers and churches into a nucleus of independent churches included Pastor B. M. Johnson, founder of Lakeview Gospel Church in 1911; Rev. A. A. Holmgren, a Baptist minister who received his baptism of the Holy Spirit in the early Chicago outpourings, was publisher of *Sanningens Vittne*, a voice of the Scandinavian Independent Assemblies of God and also served as secretary of the fellowship for many years; Gunnar Wingren, missionary pioneer in Brazil; and Arthur F. Johnson, who served for many years as chairman of the Scandinavian Assemblies.

In 1935, the Scandinavian group dissolved its incorporation and united with the Independent Assemblies of God of the U.S. and Canada which by majority vote of members formed a new corporation in 1986, Assemblies of God International Fellowship (Independent/Not Affiliated).

HEADQUARTERS
8504 Commerce Ave., San Diego, CA 92121 Tel. (619)530-1727 Fax (619)530-1543
Media Contact, Exec. Dir. & Ed., Rev. T. A. Lanes

OFFICERS
Exec. Dir., Rev. T. A. Lanes
Vice-Pres., Rev. Winston Mattsson-Boze
Sec., Rev. Clair Hutchins
Treas., Dr. Joseph Bohac
Canada, Sec., Harry Nunn, Sr., 15 White Crest Ct., St. Catherines, ON 62N 6Y1

PERIODICAL
The Fellowship Magazine

Associate Reformed Presbyterian Church (General Synod)

The Associate Reformed Presbyterian Church (General Synod) stems from the 1782 merger of Associate Presbyterians and Reformed Presbyterians. In 1822, the Synod of the Carolinas broke with the Associate Reformed Church (which eventually became part of the United Presbyterian Church of North America).

The story of the Synod of the Carolinas began with the Seceder Church, formed in Scotland in 1733 and representing a break from the established Church of Scotland. Seceders, in America called Associate Presbyterians, settled in South Carolina following the Revolutionary War. They were joined by a few Covenanter congregations which, along with the Seceders, had protested Scotland's established church. The Covenanters took their name from the Solemn League and Covenant of 1643, the guiding document of Scotch Presbyterians. In 1790, some Seceders and Covenanters formed the Presbytery of the Carolinas and Georgia at Long Cane, S.C. Thomas Clark and John Boyse led in the formation of this presbytery, a unit within the Associate Reformed Presbyterian Church. The presbytery represented the southern segment of that church.

In 1822 the southern church became independent of the northern Associate Reformed Presbyterian Church and formed the Associate Reformed Presbyterian Church of the South. "Of the South" was dropped in 1858 when the northern group joined the United Presbyterian Church and "General Synod" was added in 1935. The General Synod is the denomination's highest court; it is composed of all the teaching elders and at least one ruling elder from each congregation.

Doctrinally, the church holds to the Westminster Confession of Faith. Liturgically, the synod has been distinguished by its exclusive use of psalmody; in 1946 this practice became optional.

HEADQUARTERS
Associate Reformed Presbyterian Center, One Cleveland St., Greenville, SC 29601 Tel. (803)232-8297
Media Contact, Principal Clk., Rev. C. Ronald Beard, D.D., 3132 Grace Hill Rd., Columbia, SC 29204 Tel. (803)787-6370

OFFICERS
Mod., Rev. Harry T. Schutte, D.D., 520 Holiday Rd., Gastonia, NC 28054
Principal Clk., Rev. C. Ronald Beard, D.D., 3132 Grace Hill Rd., Columbia, SC 29204

AGENCIES AND INSTITUTIONS
Ofc. of Admn. Services, Dir., Mr. Ed Hogan
Assoc. Reformed Presb. Foundation, Inc.
Assoc. Reformed Presb. Retirement Plan
Ofc. Of Christian Education, Dir., Rev. J. B. Hendrick, D. Min.
Ofc. of Church Extension, Dir., Rev. James T. Corbitt
Ofc. of Synod's Treasurer, Mr. Guy H. Smith, III
Ofc. of Secretary of World Witness, Exec. Sec., John E. Mariner, Tel. (803)233-5226
Bonclarken Assembly, Dir., Mr. James T. Brice, 500 Pine St., Flat Rock, NC 28731 Tel. (704)692-2223
Erskine College, Pres., James W. Strobel, Ph.D., Due West, SC 29639 Tel. (803)379-8759
Erskine Theological Seminary, Dean, Rev. Randall R. Ruble, Ph.D., Due West, SC 26939 Tel. (803)379-8885

PERIODICALS
The Associate Reformed Presbyterian; The Adult Quarterly

The Association of Free Lutheran Congregations

The Association of Free Lutheran Congregations, rooted in the Scandinavian revival movements, was organized in 1962 by a Lutheran Free Church remnant which rejected merger with The American Lutheran Church. The original 42 congregations were joined by other like-minded conservative Lutherans, especially from the former Evangelical Lutheran Church and the Suomi Synod. There has been more than a fivefold increase in the number of congregations. Congregations subscribe to the Apostles', Nicene and Athanasian creeds; Luther's Small Catechism; and the Unaltered Augsburg Confession. The Fundamental Principles and Rules for Work (1897) declare that the local congregation is the right form of the kingdom of God on earth, subject to no authority but the Word and the Spirit of God.

Distinctive emphases are: (1) the infallibility and inerrancy of Holy Scriptures as the Word of God; (2) congregational polity; (3) the spiritual unity of all believers, resulting in fellowship and cooperation transcending denominational lines; (4) evangelical outreach, calling all to enter a personal relationship with Jesus Christ; (5) a wholesome Lutheran pietism that proclaims the Lordship of Jesus Christ in all areas of life and results in believers becoming the salt and light in their communities; (6) a conservative stance on current social issues.

A two-year Bible school and a theological seminary are in suburban Minneapolis. Support is channeled to churches in Brazil, Mexico, Canada and India.

HEADQUARTERS

3110 E. Medicine Lake Blvd., Minneapolis, MN 55441 Tel. (612)545-5631 Fax (612)545-0079
Media Contact, Pres., Rev. Robert L. Lee

OFFICERS

Pres., Rev. Robert L. Lee
Sec., Rev. Bruce Dalager, 2708 Olive, Grand Forks, ND 58201

PERIODICAL

The Lutheran Ambassador

Baptist Bible Fellowship International

Organized on May 24, 1950 in Fort Worth, Tex., the Baptist Bible Fellowship was founded by about 100 pastors and lay people who had grown disenchanted with the policies and leadership of the World Fundamental Baptist Missionary Fellowship, an outgrowth of the Baptist Bible Union formed in Kansas City in 1923 by fundamentalist leaders from the Southern Baptist, Northern Baptist and Canadian Baptist Conventions. The BBF elected W. E. Dowell as its first president and established offices and a three-year (now four-year with a graduate school) Baptist Bible College.

The BBF statement of faith was essentially that of the Baptist Bible Union, adopted in 1923, a variation of the New Hampshire Confession of Faith. It presents an infallible Bible, belief in the substitutionary death of Christ, his physical resurrection and his premillennial return to earth. It advocates local church autonomy and strong pastoral leadership and maintains that the fundamental basis of fellowship is a missionary outreach. The BBF vigorously stresses evangelism and the international missions office reports 791 adult missionaries working on 86 fields throughout the world in 1992.

There are BBF-related churches in every state of the United States, with special strength in the upper South, the Great Lakes region, southern states west of the Mississippi, Kansas and California. There are six related colleges and one graduate school or seminary.

A Committee of Forty-Five, elected by pastors and churches within the states, sits as a representative body, meeting in three subcommittees, each chaired by one of the principal officers: an administration committee chaired by the president, a missions committee chaired by a vice-president and an education committee chaired by a vice-president.

HEADQUARTERS

Baptist Bible Fellowship Missions Bldg., 720 E. Kearney St., Springfield, MO 65803 Tel. (417)862-5001 Fax (417)865-0794
Mailing Address, P.O. Box 191, Springfield, MO 65801
Media Contact, Mission Dir., Dr. Bob Baird, P.O. Box 191, Springfield, MO 65801

OFFICERS

Pres., Parker Dailey, Blue Ridge Baptist Temple, 10306 Blue Ridge Blvd., Kansas City, MO 64134
First Vice-Pres., Jack Baskin, Western Hills Baptist Church, 700 Mars Hill Rd., NW, Kennesaw, GA 30144
Second Vice-Pres., Don Elmore, Temple Baptist Church, P.O. Box 292, Springdale, AR 72764
Sec., K. B. Murray, Millington Street Baptist Church, Box 524, Winfield, KS 67156
Treas., Billy Hamm, Mountain States Baptist Church, 8333 Acoma Way, Denver, CO 80221
Mission Dir., Dr. Bob Baird, P.O. Box 191, Springfield, MO 65801

PERIODICALS

The Baptist Bible Tribune; The Preacher

Baptist General Conference

The Baptist General Conference, rooted in the pietistic movement of Sweden during the 19th century, traces its history to Aug. 13, 1852. On that day a small group of believers at Rock Island, Ill., under the leadership of Gustaf Palmquist, organized the first Swedish Baptist Church in America. Swedish Baptist churches flourished in the upper Midwest and Northeast, and by 1879, when the first annual meeting was held in Village Creek, Iowa, 65 churches had been organized, stretching from Maine to the Dakotas and south to Kansas and Missouri.

By 1871, John Alexis Edgren, an immigrant sea captain and pastor in Chicago, had begun the first publication and a theological seminary. The Conference grew to 324 churches and nearly 26,000 members by 1902. There were 40,000 members in 1945 and 135,000 in 1991.

Many churches began as Sunday schools. The seminary evolved into Bethel, a four-year liberal arts college with 1,800 students, and theological seminaries in Arden Hills, Minn. and San Diego, California.

Missions and the planting of churches have been main objectives both in America and overseas. Today churches have been established in the United States, Canada and Mexico, as well as a dozen countries overseas. In 1985 the churches of Canada founded an autonomous denomination, The Baptist General Conference of Canada.

The Baptist General Conference is a member of the Baptist World Alliance, the Baptist Joint Committee on Public Affairs and the National Association of Evangelicals. It is characterized by the balancing of a conservative doctrine with an irenic and cooperative spirit. Its basic objective is to seek the fulfillment of the Great Commission and the Great Commandment.

HEADQUARTERS

2002 S. Arlington Heights Rd., Arlington Heights, IL 60005 Tel. (708)228-0200 Fax (708)228-5376
Media Contact, Exec. Vice-Pres., C. Herbert Hage

US RELIGIOUS BODIES

Pres. & Chief Exec. Officer, Dr. Robert S. Ricker

Business & Planning, Vice-Pres., Rev. C. Herbert Hage

Bd. of Home Missions, Exec. Dir., Dr. John C. Dickau

Bd. of World Missions, Exec. Dir., Rev. Herbert Skoglund

Bd. of Regents: Bethel College & Seminary, Pres., Dr. George K. Brushaber, 3900 Bethel Dr., St. Paul, MN 55112

PERIODICAL
The Standard

Baptist Missionary Association of America

A group of regular Baptist churches organized in associational capacity in May, 1950, in Little Rock, Ark., as the North American Baptist Association. The name changed in 1969 to Baptist Missionary Association of America. There are several state and numerous local associations of cooperating churches. In theology, these churches are evangelical, missionary, fundamental and for the most part premillennial.

HEADQUARTERS
9219 Sibly Hole Rd., Little Rock, AR Tel. (501)455-4977 Fax (501)455-5008

Mailing Address, P.O. Box 193920, Little Rock, AR 72219-3920

Media Contact, Dir. of Baptist News Service, James C. Blaylock, P.O. Box 97, Jacksonville, TX 75766 Tel. (903)586-2501 Fax (903)586-0378

OFFICERS
Pres., James V. Schoenrock, 611 Butler St., Springhill, LA 71075

Vice-Pres.: Grady L. Higgs, P.O. Box 34, Jacksonville, TX 75766; Stephen Howell, 4226 Hwy 15 N, Laurel, MS 39440

Rec. Sec.: Rev. Ralph Cottrell, P.O. Box 1203, Van, TX 75790; Gene Elrod, 1077 Toltec St., Camden, AR 71701; G. H. Gordon, 3202 W. 7th St., Hattiesburg, MS 39401

DEPARTMENTS
Missions: Gen. Sec., Rev. F. Donald Collins, P.O. Box 193920, Little Rock, AR 72219-3920

Publications: Ed.-in-Chief, Rev. James L. Silvey, 1319 Magnolia, Texarkana, TX 75501

Christian Education: Bapt. Missionary Assoc. Theological Sem., Pres., Dr. Philip R. Bryan, Seminary Heights, 1530 E. Pine St., Jacksonville, TX 75766

Baptist News Service: Dir., Rev. James C. Blaylock, P.O. Box 97, Jacksonville, TX 75766

Life Word Broadcast Ministries: Dir., Rev. George Reddin, P.O. Box 6, Conway, AR 72032

Armed Forces Chaplaincy: Exec. Dir., William Charles Pruitt, Jr., P.O. Box 912, Jacksonville, TX 75766

BMAA Dept. of Church Ministries: Bobby Tucker, P.O. Box 3376, Texarkana, TX 75504

Daniel Springs Encampment: James Speer, P.O. Box 310, Gary, TX 75643

Ministers Benefit Dept.: James A. Henry, 4001 Jefferson St., Texarkana, AR 75501

OTHER ORGANIZATIONS
Baptist Missionary Assoc. Brotherhood: Pres., Thomas Monroe, Rt. 4, Box 585, Carthage, TX 75633

National Women's Missionary Auxiliary: Pres., Mrs. James V. Schoenrock, 611 Butler St., Springhill, LA 71075

PERIODICALS
The Gleaner; Baptist Progress; Baptist Trumpet; Baptist Herald; The Advocate; Midwest Missionary Baptist; Northwest Profile

Beachy Amish Mennonite Churches

The Beachy Amish Mennonite Church was established in 1927 in Somerset County, Pa. following a division in the Amish Mennonite Church in that area. As congregations in other locations joined the movement, they were identified by the same name. There are currently 87 churches in the United States, 8 in Canada and 17 in other countres. Total membership is 7,459, according to the 1993 Mennonite Yearbook.

Beachy Churches believe in one God eternally existent in three persons (Father, Son and Holy Spirit); that Jesus Christ is the one and only way to salvation; that the Bible is God's infallible Word to us, by which all will be judged; that heaven is the eternal abode of the redeemed in Christ; and that the wicked and unbelieving will endure hell eternally.

Evangelical mission boards sponsor missions in Central and South America and in Kenya, Africa.

The Mission Interests Committee, founded in 1953 for evangelism and other Christian services, sponsors homes for handicapped youth and elderly people, mission outreaches among the Indians in Canada and a mission outreach in Europe.

HEADQUARTERS
Media Contact, Ervin N. Hershberger, Rt. 1, Box 176, Meyersdale, PA 15552 Tel. (814)662-2483

ORGANIZATIONS
Amish Mennonite Aid: Sec.-Treas., Noah J. Beachy, 9650 Iams Rd., Plain City, OH 43064 Tel. (614)873-8140

Mission Interests Committee: Sec.-Treas., Melvin Gingerich, 42555 900W, Topeka, IN 46571 Tel. (219)593-9090

Choice Books of Northern Virginia: Supervisor, Simon Schrock, 4614 Holly Ave., Fairfax, VA 22030 Tel. (703)830-2800

Calvary Bible School: HC 61, Box 202, Calico Rock, AR 72519 Tel. (501)297-8658; Sec.-Treas., Elmer Gingerich, HC 74, Box 282, Mountain View, AR 72560 Tel. (501)296-8764

PERIODICAL
The Calvary Messenger

Berean Fundamental Church

Founded 1932 in North Platte, Neb., this body emphasizes conservative Protestant doctrines.

HEADQUARTERS
6400 S. 70th St., Lincoln, NE 68516 Tel. (402)483-6512 Fax (402)483-6642

Media Contact, Pres., Pastor Doug Shada

OFFICERS
Pres., Doug Shada

The Bible Church of Christ, Inc.

The Bible Church of Christ was founded on March 1, 1961 by Bishop Roy Bryant, Sr. Since that time, the Church has grown to include congregations in the United States, Africa and India. The church is trinitarian and accepts the Bible as the divinely inspired Word of God. Its doctrine includes miracles of healing and the baptism of the Holy Ghost.

HEADQUARTERS
1358 Morris Ave., Bronx, NY 10456 Tel. (718)588-2284
Media Contact, Pres., Bishop Roy Bryant, Sr.

OFFICERS
Pres., Bishop Roy Bryant, Sr., 3033 Gunther Ave., Bronx, NY 10469 Tel. (718)379-8080
Vice-Pres., Bishop Roy Bryant, Jr., 34 Tuxedo Rd., Montclair, NJ 07042 Tel. (201)746-0063
Sec., Sissieretta Bryant
Treas., Elder Artie Burney

EXECUTIVE TRUSTEE BOARD
Chpsn., Leon T. Mims
Vice-Chpsn., Evangelist Peggy Rawls, 100 W. 2nd St., Mount Vernon, NY 10550 Tel. (914)664-4602

OTHER ORGANIZATIONS
Foreign Missions: Pres., Elder Diane Cooper
Home Missions: Pres., Evangelist Eleanor Samuel
Sunday Schools: Gen. Supt., Elder Diane Cooper
Evangelism: Natl. Pres., Evangelist Gloria Gray
Youth: Pres., Deacon Tommy Robinson
Minister of Music: Leon T. Mims; Asst., Ray Brown
Minister of Education, Gloria Pratt
Prison Ministry Team: Pres., Evangelist Marvin Lowe
Presiding Elders: Delaware, Elder Roland Miflin, Diamond Acre, Dagsboro, DE 19939; North Carolina, Elder George Houston; Adm., Elder Larry Bryant, West Johnson Rd., Clinton, NC 28328; Monticello, Elder Jesse Alston, 104 Waverly Ave., Monticello, NY 12701; Mount Vernon, Elder Artie Burney, Sr., 100 W. 2nd St., Mount Vernon, NY 10550; Bronx, Elder Anita Robinson; Annex, Elder Betty Gilliard, 1069 Morris Ave., Bronx, NY 10456
Bible School: Pres., Dr. Roy Bryant, Sr.
Bookstore: Mgr., Elder Elizabeth Johnson, Tel. (718)293-1928

PERIODICAL
The Voice

Bible Way Church of Our Lord Jesus Christ World Wide, Inc.

This body was organized in 1957 in the Pentecostal tradition for the purpose of accelerating evangelistic and foreign missionary commitment and to effect a greater degree of collective leadership than leaders found in the body in which they had previously participated.

The doctrine is the same as that of the Church of Our Lord Jesus Christ of the Apostolic Faith, Inc., of which some of the churches and clergy were formerly members.

This organization has churches and missions in Africa, England, Guyana, Trinidad and Jamaica, and churches in 25 states in America. The Bible Way Church is involved in humanitarian as well as evangelical outreach with concerns for urban housing and education and economic development.

HEADQUARTERS
4949 Two-Notch Rd., Columbia, SC 29204 Tel. (803)691-0622 Fax (803)691-0583
Media Contact, Exec. Admn., Rose English, Tel. (800)432-5612

OFFICERS
Presiding Bishop, Bishop Lawrence G. Campbell
Gen. Sec., Bishop Edward Williams, 5118 Clarendon Rd., Brooklyn, NY 11226 Tel. (718)451-1238

Brethren Church (Ashland, Oh.)

The Brethren Church (Ashland, Ohio) was organized by progressive-minded German Baptist Brethren in 1883. They reaffirmed the teaching of the original founder of the Brethren movement, Alexander Mack, and returned to congregational government.

HEADQUARTERS
524 College Ave., Ashland, OH 44805 Tel. (419)289-1708 Fax (419)281-0450
Media Contact, Dir. of Brethren Church Ministries, Ronald W. Waters

GENERAL ORGANIZATIONS
Dir. of Pastoral Ministries, Rev. David Cooksey
Dir. of Brethren Church Ministries, Rev. Ronald W. Waters
Ed. of Publications, Rev. Richard C. Winfield
Conf. Mod. (1994-1995), Rev. Reilly Smith

BOARD
The Missionary Bd., Exec. Dir., Rev. James R. Black
Dir. of Home Missions, Rev. Russell Gordon

PERIODICAL
The Brethren Evangelist

Brethren in Christ Church

The Brethren in Christ Church was founded in Lancaster County, Pa. in about the year 1778 and was an outgrowth of the religious awakening which occurred in that area during the latter part of the 18th century. This group became known as "River Brethren" because of their original location near the Susquehanna River. The name "Brethren in Christ" was officially adopted in 1863. In theology they have accents of the Pietist, Anabaptist, Wesleyan and Evangelical movements.

HEADQUARTERS
General Church Office, P.O. Box 290, Grantham, PA 17027-0290 Tel. (717)697-2634 Fax (717)697-7714
Media Contact, Mod., Harvey R. Sider, Tel. (717)697-2634 Fax (717)697-7714

OFFICERS
Mod., Rev. Harvey R. Sider, P.O. Box 290, Grantham, PA 17027 Tel. (717)697-2634 Fax (717)697-7714
Dir. of Bishops, Dr. John A. Byers
Gen. Sec., Dr. R. Donald Shafer
Dir. of Finance, Harold D. Chubb

OTHER ORGANIZATIONS

Bd. of Administration: Mod. & Chair, Rev. Harvey R. Sider

Bd. of Brotherhood Concerns: Admn. Dir., Dr. R. Donald Shafer; Chpsn., Dr. Samuel Brubaker, 307 N. Main St., 155 S. Popular St., Arcanum, OH 45304

Bd. for Congregational Life: Admn. Dir., Dr. John A. Byers; Chpsn., Martha Starr, Lancaster Brethren in Christ Church, 1865 Fruitville Pike, Lancaster, PA 17601

Bd. of Dir.: Chpsn., Dr. Mark Garis, 504 Swartley Rd., Hatfield, PA 19440

Bd. for Evangelism & Church Planting: Chpsn., Douglas P. Sider, 142 Streb Cresc., Saskatoon, SK S7M 4T8; Dir. of Bishops, John A. Byers

Bd. for Media Ministries: Chpsn., Emerson C. Frey, Box 317, Owlbridge Rd., Millersville, PA 17551; Exec. Dir., Roger Williams, P.O. Box 189, Nappanee, IN 46550

Bd. for Ministry & Doctrine: Chpsn., James D. Ernst, 1865 Fruitville Pike, Lancaster, PA 17601

Bd. for World Missions: Chpsn., Lowell D. Mann, 8 W. Bainbridge St., Elizabethtown, PA 17022 Fax (717)653-6911; Dir., Rev. Jack McClane, P.O. Box 390, Grantham, PA 17027-0390

Commission on Christian Educ. Lit.: Chpsn., Gwen White, 230 Philadelphia Ave., Waynesboro, PA 17268

Jacob Engle Foundation Bd. of Dir.: Chpsn., Dr. Donald R. Zook

Pension Fund Trustees: Chpsn., Donald R. Zook

Bd. for Stewardship Services: Chpsn., Charles F. Frey, 259 Willow Valley Dr., Lancaster, PA 17602

Publishing House: Exec. Dir., Roger Williams, Evangel Press, P.O. Box 189, Nappannee, IN 46550

PERIODICAL

Evangelical Visitor

Bulgarian Eastern Orthodox Church

Bulgarian immigration to the United States and Canada started around the turn of the century, and the first Bulgarian Orthodox church was built in 1907 in Madison, Ill. In 1938, the Holy Synod of the Bulgarian E. O. Church established the diocese in New York as an Episcopate, and Bishop Andrey was sent as diocesan Bishop. In 1947, the diocese was officially incorporated in New York and Bishop Andrey became the first elected Metropolitan.

In 1969 the Bulgarian Eastern Orthodox Church was divided into the Diocese of New York (incorporated Bulgarian Eastern Orthodox Church—Diocese of America, North and South, and Australia) and the Diocese of Akron (incorporated American Bulgarian Eastern Orthodox Diocese of Akron, Ohio). In 1989 both Dioceses were united into one Bulgarian Eastern-Orthodox Diocese in the USA, Canada and Australia.

HEADQUARTERS

Holy Metropolia, 550 A West 50th St., New York, NY 10019 Tel. (212)246-4608
Media Contact, Metropolitan Joseph Bosakov

OFFICER

Metropolitan Joseph Bosakov

Christ Catholic Church

The church is a catholic communion established in 1968 to minister to the growing number of people who seek an experiential relationship with God and who desire to make a total commitment of their lives to God. The church is catholic in faith and tradition and its orders are recognized as valid by catholics of every tradition. The Christ Catholic Church is working to bring together various branches of Old Catholicism into one united church. Participating cathedrals, churches and missions are located in several states and Canadian provinces.

HEADQUARTERS

5165 Palmer Ave., Niagara Falls, ON L2G 1Y4 Tel. (416)354-2329 Fax (416)354-9934
Media Contact, Suffragen Bishop, The Most Rev. Karl Pruter, P.O. Box 98, Highlandville, MO 65669 Tel. (417)587-3951

OFFICERS

Archbishop, The Most Rev. Donald W. Mullan

PERIODICALS

St. Willibrord Journal; St. Luke Magazine

Christadelphians

The Christadelphians are a body of people who believe the Bible to be the divinely inspired word of God, written by "Holy men who spoke as they were moved by the Holy Spirit" (II Peter 1:21). They also believe in the return of Christ to earth to establish the Kingdom of God; in the resurrection of those dead, at the return of Christ, who come into relation to Christ in conformity with his instructions, to be judged as to worthiness for eternal life; in opposition to war; in spiritual rebirth requiring belief and immersion in the name of Jesus; and in a godly walk in this life.

The denomination was organized in 1844 by a medical doctor, John Thomas, who came to the United States from England in 1832, having survived a near shipwreck in a violent storm. This experience affected him profoundly, and he vowed to devote his life to a search for the truth of God and a future hope from the Bible.

HEADQUARTERS

Media Contact, Trustee, Norman D. Zilmer, Christadelphian Action Society, 1000 Mohawk Dr., Elgin, IL 60120-3148 Tel. (708)741-5253

LEADERS

Co-Ministers: Norman Fadelle, 815 Chippewa Dr., Elgin, IL 60120-4016; Norman D. Zilmer, 1000 Mohawk Dr., Elgin, IL 60120-3148

PERIODICALS

Christadelphian Tidings; Christadelphian Watchman; Christadelphian Advocate

The Christian and Missionary Alliance

The Christian and Missionary Alliance was formed in 1897.

The church resulted from the merger of two organizations begun in 1887 by Dr. Albert B. Simpson, The Christian Alliance and the Evangelical Missionary Alliance. The Christian and Missionary Alliance is an evangelical church which stresses the sufficiency of Jesus—Savior, Sanctifier, Healer and Coming King—and has earned a worldwide reputation for its missionary accomplishments. The Canadian districts became autonomous in 1981 and formed The Christian and Missionary Alliance in Canada.

HEADQUARTERS

P.O. Box 35000, Colorado Springs, CO 80935-3500 Tel. (719)599-5999 Fax (719)593-8692

OFFICERS

Pres., Rev. David Rambo, PhD
Vice-Pres., Rev. Paul F. Bubna, DD
Sec., Rev. R. H. Mangham, DD
Vice-Pres. for Fin./Treas., Mr. D. A. Wheeland, CPA
Vice-Pres. for Church Ministries, Rev. R. W. Bailey, DD
Vice-Pres. for Overseas Ministries, Rev. P. N. Nanfelt
Vice-Pres. for Gen. Services, Rev. J. A. Davey

BOARD OF MANAGERS

Chpsn., Rev. Paul L. Alford, LLD, DD
Vice-Chpsn., Mr. F. S. Jennings

DISTRICT SUPERINTENDENTS

Central: Rev. Howard D. Bowers, 1218 High St., Wadsworth, OH 44281 Tel. (216)336-2911 Fax (216)334-3702
Central Pacific: Rev. D. Duane Adamson, 3824 Buell St., Suite A, Oakland, CA 94619 Tel. (510)530-5410 Fax (510)530-1369
Eastern: Rev. Randall B. Corbin, DMin., 1 Sherwood Dr., Mechanicsburg, PA 17055 Tel. (717)766-0261 Fax (717)766-0486
Great Lakes: Rev. Dahl B. Seckinger, 2250 Huron Pkwy, Ann Arbor, MI 48104 Tel. (313)677-8555 Fax (313)677-0087
Metropolitan: Rev. Paul B. Hazlett, 349 Watchung Ave., N. Plainfield, NJ 07060 Tel. (908)668-8421 Fax (908)757-6299
Mid-Atlantic: Rev. C. E. Mock, 7100 Roslyn Ave., Rockville, MD 20855 Tel. (301)258-0035 Fax (301)258-1021
Midwest: Rev. Gerald R. Mapstone, 260 Glen Ellyn Rd., Bloomingdale, IL 60108 Tel. (708)893-1355 Fax (708)893-1027
New England: Rev. Cornelius W. Clarke, 34 Central St., S. Easton, MA 02375 Tel. (508)238-3820 Fax (508-238-2361
Northeastern: Rev. Woodford C. Stemple, Jr., 6275 Pillmore Dr., Rome, NY 13440 Tel. (315)336-4720 Fax (315)336-4720
Northwestern: Rev. Gary M. Benedict, 1813 N. Lexington Ave., St. Paul, MN 55113 Tel. (612)489-1391 Fax (612)489-8535
Ohio Valley: Rev. David F. Presher, 4050 Executive Park Dr., Ste. 402, Cincinnati, OH 45241 Tel. (513)733-4833
Pacific Northwest: Rev. R. H. Mangham, DD, P.O. Box 1030, Canby, OR 97013 Tel. (503)226-2238 Fax (503)263-8052
Puerto Rico: Rev. Jorge Cuevas, P.O. Box 51394, Levittown, PR 00950 Tel. (809)261-0101 Fax (809)261-0107

Rocky Mountain: Rev. Harvey A. Town, LLD, 1215 24th W., Ste. 210, Billings, MT 59102 Tel. (406)656-4233 Fax (406)656-5502
South Atlantic: Rev. Gordon G. Copeland, 10801 Johnston Rd., Ste. 125, Charlotte, NC 28226 Tel. (704)543-0470 Fax (704)543-0215
South Pacific: Rev. Bill J. Vaughn, 4130 Adams St., Ste. A, Riverside, CA 92506 Tel. (909)351-0111 Fax (909)351-0146
Southeastern: Rev. Mark T. O'Farrell, P.O. Box 720430, Orlando, FL 32872 Tel. (407)823-9662 Fax (407)823-9668
Southern: Rev. Garfield G. Powell, 8420 Division Ave., Birmingham, AL 35206 Tel. (205)836-7048 Fax (205)836-7168
Southwestern: Rev. Loren G. Calkins, DMin., 5600 E. Loop 820 S., Fort Worth, TX 76119 Tel. (817)561-0879 Fax (817)572-4131
Western: Rev. Fred G. King, 1301 S. 119th St., Omaha, NE 68144 Tel. (402)330-1888 Fax (402)330-7213
Western Great Lakes: Rev. John W. Fogal, W6107 Aerotech Dr., Appleton, WI 54915 Tel. (414)734-1123
Western Pennsylvania: Rev. D. Paul McGarvey, P.O. Box 429, Punxsutawney, PA 15767 Tel. (814)938-6920 Fax (814)938-7528

INTERCULTURAL MINISTRIES DISTRICTS

Cambodian: Supt., Rev. Joseph S. Kong, 1616 S. Palmetto Ave., Ontario, CA 91762 Tel. (909)988-9434 Fax (909)395-0572
Dega: c/o Rev. A. E. Hall, P.O. Box 35000, Colorado Springs, CO 80935
Haitian: Dir., Rev. Paul V. Lehman, 21 College Ave., Nyack, NY 10960 Tel. (914)353-7305
Hmong: Supt., Rev. Timothy Teng Vang, P.O. Box 219, Brighton, CO 80601 Tel. (303)659-1538 Fax (303)659-2171
Jewish: Missionary, Rev. Abraham Sandler, 9820 Woodfern Rd., Philadelphia, PA 19115 Tel. (215)676-9089
Korean: Supt., Rev. Gil Kim, 2175 Lemoine Ave., Rm. 304, Fort Lee, NJ 07024 Tel. (201)461-5755 Fax (201)461-5756
Lao: Dir., Mr. Sisouphanh Ratthahao, 459 Addison St., Elgin, IL 60120 Tel. (708)741-3871
Native American: Dir., Rev. Stephen Wood, 5664 Corinth Dr., Colorado Springs, CO 80918 Tel. (719)531-7823
Spanish Central: Supt., Rev. Kenneth N. Brisco, 260 Glen Ellyn Rd., Bloomingdale, IL 60108 Tel. (708)924-7171 Fax (708)893-1027
Spanish Eastern: Supt., Rev. Carlos Santiago, 6220 S. Orange Blossom Tr., Ste. 136, Orlando, FL 32809 Tel. (407)855-5942
Spanish Western: Dir., Rev. Angel V. Ortiz, 334 Springtree Pl., Escondido, CA 92026-1417 Tel. (619)489-4835 Fax (619)747-9887
Vietnamese: Supt., Rev. Tai Anh Nguyen, 1681 W. Broadway, Anaheim, CA 92802 Tel. (714)491-8007

NATIONAL ASSOCIATIONS

Black Ministries Consultation: c/o Div. of Church Ministries, P.O. Box 35000, Colorado Springs, CO 80935
Chinese Association of the C&MA: c/o Rev. Peter Chu, 14209 Secluded La., Gaithersburg, MD 20878 Tel. (301)294-8067
Filipino Association of the C&MA: c/o Rev. Hernan C. Pada, 5662 Cathy La., Cypress, CA 90630 Tel. (714)761-9287

US RELIGIOUS BODIES

Alliance Life

Christian Brethren (also known as Plymouth Brethren)

The Christian Brethren began in the 1820s as an orthodox and evangelical movement in the British Isles and is now worldwide. Congregations are usually called "assemblies." The name Plymouth Brethren was given by others because the group in Plymouth, England, was a large congregation. In recent years the term Christian Brethren has replaced Plymouth Brethren for the "open" branch of the movement in Canada and British Commonwealth countries and to some extent in the United States.

The unwillingness to establish a denominational structure makes the autonomy of local congregations an important feature of the movement. Other features are weekly observance of the Lord's Supper and adherence to the doctrinal position of conservative, evangelical Christianity.

In the 1840s the movement divided. The "exclusive" branch, led by John Darby, stressed the interdependency of congregations. Since disciplinary decisions were held to be binding on all assemblies, exclusives had subdivided into seven or eight main groups by the end of the century. Since 1925 a trend toward reunification has reduced that number to three or four. United States congregations number approximately 300, with an estimated 19,000 members.

The "open" branch of the movement, stressing evangelism and foreign missions, now has about 850 U.S. congregations, with an estimated 79,000 members. Following the leadership of George Muller in rejecting the "exclusive" principle of binding discipline, this branch has escaped large-scale division.

HEADQUARTERS
Media Contact, Ed. Asst., Naomi Bauman, P.O. Box 190, Wheaton, IL 60189 Tel. (708)653-6573 Fax (708)653-6595

CORRESPONDENT
Interest Ministries, Pres., Bruce R. McNicol, P.O. Box 190, Wheaton, IL 60189 Tel. (708)653-6573 Fax (708)653-6595

OTHER ORGANIZATIONS
Christian Missions in Many Lands, Box 13, Spring Lake, NJ 07762

Stewards Foundation, 218 W. Willow, Wheaton, IL 60187

International Teams, Box 203, Prospect Heights, IL 60070

Emmaus Bible College, 2570 Asbury Rd., Dubuque, IA 52001

Stewards Canada, 9 Horner Ct., Richmond Hill, ON L4C 4Y8

Stewards Ministries, 1655 N. Arlington Hts. Rd., Arlington Hts., IL 60004

Vision Ontario, P.O. Box 28032, Waterloo, ON N2L 6J8

PERIODICAL
Interest

Christian Catholic Church (Evangelical-Protestant)

This church was founded by the Rev. John Alexander Dowie on Feb. 22, 1896 at Chicago, Ill. In 1901 the church opened its headquarters in Zion, Ill. Theologically, the church is rooted in evangelical orthodoxy. The Scriptures are accepted as the rule of faith and practice. Other doctrines call for belief in the necessity of repentance for sin and personal trust in Christ for salvation, baptism by triune immersion and tithing as a practical method of Christian stewardship. The church teaches the Second Coming of Christ.

The Christian Catholic Church is a denominational member of The National Association of Evangelicals. It has work in 8 other nations in addition to the United States. Branch ministries are found in Michigan City, Ind., Phoenix, Ariz., Tonalea, Ariz. and Lindenhurst, Ill.

HEADQUARTERS
2500 Dowie Memorial Dr., Zion, IL 60099 Tel. (708)746-1411 Fax (708)746-1452

Media Contact, Senior Pastor & Gen. Overseer

OFFICER
Gen. Overseer, Roger W. Ottersen

PERIODICAL
Leaves of Healing

Christian Church (Disciples of Christ)

Born on the American frontier in the early 1800s as a movement to unify Christians, this body drew its major inspiration from Thomas and Alexander Campbell in western Pennsylvania and Barton W. Stone in Kentucky. Developing separately, the "Disciples," under Alexander Campbell, and the "Christians," led by Stone, united in 1832 in Lexington, Ky.

The Christian Church (Disciples of Christ) is marked by informality, openness, individualism and diversity. The Disciples claim no official doctrine or dogma. Membership is granted after a simple statement of belief in Jesus Christ and baptism by immersion—although most congregations accept transfers baptized by other forms in other denominations. The Lord's Supper—generally called Communion—is open to Christians of all persuasions. The practice is weekly Communion, although no church law insists upon it.

Thoroughly ecumenical, the Disciples helped organize the National and World Councils of Churches. The church is a member of the Consultation on Church Union. The Disciples and the United Church of Christ have declared themselves to be in "full communion" through the General Assembly and General Synod of the two churches. Official theological conversations have been going on since 1967 directly with the Roman Catholic Church, and since 1987 with the Russian Orthodox Church.

Disciples have vigorously supported world and national programs of education, agricultural assistance, urban reconciliation, care of mentally retarded, family planning and aid to victims of war and calamity. Operating ecumenically, Disciples personnel or funds work in more than 100 countries outside North America.

Three levels of church polity (general, regional and congregational) operate as equals, managing their own finances, property and program, with strong but voluntary ties to one another.

Local congregations own their property and control their budgets and program. A General Assembly meets every two years and has voting representation from each congregation.

HEADQUARTERS
222 S. Downey Ave., P.O. Box 1986, Indianapolis, IN 46206-1986 Tel. (317)353-1491 Fax (800)458-3318

Media Contact, Dir. of News & Information, Cliff Willis

OFFICERS
Gen. Minister & Pres., Richard L. Hamm
Mod., D. Duane Cummins, Bethany College, Bethany, WV 26032
1st Vice-Mod., Cynthia L. Hale, Ray of Hope Christian Church, 3936 Rainbow Dr., Decatur, GA 30034
2nd Vice-Mod., Joyce Blair, 107 Post Wood Pl., Nashville, TN 37205

GENERAL OFFICERS
Gen. Minister & Pres., Richard L. Hamm
Dep. Gen. Min./Vice-Pres. for Communication, Claudia E. Grant
Dep. Gen. Min./Vice-Pres. for Admn., Donald B. Manworren
Dep. Gen. Min./Vice-Pres. for Inclusive Ministries, John R. Foulkes

ADMINISTRATIVE UNITS
Bd. of Church Extension: Pres., Harold R. Watkins, 110 S. Downey Ave., Box 7030, Indianapolis, IN 46207-7030 Tel. (317)356-6333
Christian Bd. of Pub. (Chalice Press): Pres., James C. Suggs, Box 179, 1316 Convention Plaza Dr., St. Louis, MO 63166-0179 Tel. (314)231-8500 Fax (314)231-8524
Christian Church Foundation, Inc.: Pres., James P. Johnson
Church Finance Council, Inc.: Pres., Robert K. Welsh
Council on Christian Unity, Inc.: Pres., Paul A. Crow, Jr.
Disciples of Christ Historical Society: Pres., James M. Seale, 1101 19th Ave. S., Nashville, TN 37212-2196 Tel. (615)327-1444
Division of Higher Education: Pres., James I. Spainhower, 11780 Borman Dr., Ste. 100, St. Louis, MO 63146-4159 Tel. (314)991-3000 Fax (314)993-9018
Division of Homeland Ministries: Pres., Ann Updegraff Spleth
Division of Overseas Ministries: Pres., Pat Tucker Spier
National Benevolent Association: Pres., Richard R. Lance, 11780 Borman Dr., Ste. 200, St. Louis, MO 63146-4157 Tel. (314)993-9000 Fax (314)993-9018
Pension Fund: Pres., Lester D. Palmer, 200 Barrister Bldg., 155 E. Market St., Indianapolis, IN 46204-3215 Tel. (317)634-4504 Fax (317)634-4071

REGIONAL UNITS OF THE CHURCH
Alabama-Northwest Florida: Regional Minister, Carl R. Flock, 1336 Mont-gomery Hwy. S., Birmingham, AL 35216-2799 Tel. (205)823-5647
Arizona: Regional Minister, Gail F. Davis, 4423 N. 24th St., Ste 700, Phoenix, AZ 85016-5544 Tel. (602)468-3815
Arkansas: Exec. Minister, W. Chris Hobgood, 6100 Queensboro Dr., P.O. Box 191057, Little Rock, AR 72219-1057 Tel. (501)562-6053

California North-Nevada: Regional Minister/Pres., Richard Lauer, 111-A Fairmount Ave., Oakland, CA 94611-5918 Tel. (510)839-3550
Canada: Exec. Minister, Robert W. Steffer, 128 Woolwich St., Ste. 202, P.O. Box 64, Guelph, ON N1H 6J6 Tel. (519)823-5190
Capital Area: Regional Minister, ——, 8901 Connecticut Ave., Chevy Chase, MD 20815-6700 Tel. (301)654-7794
Central Rocky Mountain Region: Exec. Regional Minister, William E. Crowl, 2080 Kline Ct., Lakewood, CO 80215 Tel. (303)274-8567
Florida: Regional Minister, Jimmie L. Gentle, 924 N. Magnolia, Ste. 200, Orlando, FL 32803 Tel. (407)843-4652
Georgia: Regional Minister, David L. Alexander, 2370 Vineville Ave., Macon, GA 31204-3163 Tel. (912)743-8649
Idaho-South: Regional Minister, Larry Crist, 4900 No. Five Mile Rd., Boise, ID 83704-1826 Tel. (208)322-0538
Illinois-Wisconsin: Regional Minister/Pres., Nathan S. Smith, 1011 N. Main St., Bloomington, IL 61701-1797 Tel. (309)828-6293
Indiana: Regional Minister, C. Edward Weisheimer, 1100 W. 42nd St., Indianapolis, IN 46208-3375 Tel. (317)926-6051
Kansas: Regional Minister/Pres., Ralph L. Smith, 2914 S.W. MacVicar Ave., Topeka, KS 66611-1787 Tel. (913)266-2914
Kansas City (Greater): Regional Minister/Pres., David C. Downing, 5700 Broadmoor, Ste 408, Mission, KS 66202-2405 Tel. (913)432-1414
Kentucky: Gen. Minister, A. Guy Waldrop, 1125 Red Mile Rd., Lexington, KY 40504-2660 Tel. (606)233-1391
Louisiana: Regional Minister, Bill R. Boswell, 3524 Holloway Prairie Rd., Pineville, LA 71360-9998 Tel. (318)443-0304
Michigan: Regional Minister, Morris Finch, Jr., 2820 Covington Ct., Lansing, MI 48912-4830 Tel. (517)372-3220
Mid-America Region: Regional Minister, Stephen V. Cranford, Hwy. 54 W., Box 104298, Jefferson City, MO 65110-4298 Tel. (314)636-8149
Mississippi: Regional Minister, William E. McKnight, 1619 N. West St., P.O. Box 4832, Jackson, MS 39296-4832 Tel. (601)352-6774
Montana: Regional Minister, Karen Frank-Plumlee, 1019 Central Ave., Great Falls, MT 59401-3784 Tel. (406)452-7404
Nebraska: Regional Minister, N. Dwain Acker, 1268 S. 20th St., Lincoln, NE 68502-1699 Tel. (402)476-0359
North Carolina: Regional Minister, Larry Gibbons, 509 N.E. Lee St., Box 1568, Wilson, NC 27894 Tel. (919)291-4047
Northeastern Region: Regional Minister, Charles F. Lamb, 1272 Delaware Ave., Buffalo, NY 14209-1531 Tel. (716)882-4793
Northwest Region: Regional Minister/Pres., Robert Clarke Brock, 6558-35th Ave. SW, Seattle, WA 98126-2899 Tel. (206)938-1008
Ohio: Regional Pastor/Pres., Howard M. Ratcliff, 38007 Butternut Ridge Rd., P.O. Box 299, Elyria, OH 44036-0299 Tel. (216)458-5112
Oklahoma: Exec. Regional Minister, Thomas R. Jewell, 301 N.W. 36th St., Oklahoma City, OK 73118-8699 Tel. (405)528-3577
Oregon: Regional Minister, Mark K. Reid, 0245 S.W. Bancroft St., Suite F, Portland, OR 97201-4267 Tel. (503)226-7648

Pacific Southwest Region: Acting Regional Minister, John D. Wolfersberger, 1755 N. Park Ave., Pomona, CA 91768 Tel. (909)620-5503

Pennsylvania: Regional Minister, Dwight L. French, 670 Rodi Rd., Pittsburgh, PA 15235-4524 Tel. (412)731-7000

South Carolina: Regional Minister, ——-, 1098 E. Montague Ave., North Charleston, SC 29406 Tel. (803)554-6886

Southwest Region: Regional Minister, M. Margaret Harrison, 3209 S. University Dr., Fort Worth, TX 76109-2239 Tel. (817)926-4687

Tennessee: Interim Regional Ministers/Pres., Howard B. Goodrich, Jr.; Darlene B. Goodrich, 3700 Richland Ave., Nashville, TN 37205-2499 Tel. (615)269-3409

Upper Midwest Region: Regional Minister/Pres., Richard L. Guentert, 3300 University Ave., Box 1024, Des Moines, IA 50311 Tel. (515)255-3168

Utah: Exec. Regional Minister, William E. Crowl, 2080 Kline Ct., Lakewood, CO 80215 Tel. (303)274-8567

Virginia: Regional Minister, R. Woods Kent, 518 Brevard St., Lynchburg, VA 24501 Tel. (804)846-3400

West Virginia: Regional Minister, William B. Allen, Rt. 5, Box 167, Parkersburg, WV 26101-9576 Tel. (304)428-1681

PERIODICALS

The Disciple; Vanguard; Mid-Stream: An Ecumenical Journal

Christian Church of North America, General Council

Originally known as the Italian Christian Church, its first General Council was held in 1927 at Niagara Falls, N.Y. This body was incorporated in 1948 at Pittsburgh, Pa., and is described as Pentecostal but does not engage in the "the excesses tolerated or practiced among some churches using the same name."

The movement recognizes two ordinances—baptism and the Lord's Supper. Its moral code is conservative and its teaching is orthodox. Members are exhorted to pursue a life of personal holiness, setting an example to others. A conservative position is held in regard to marriage and divorce. The governmental form is, by and large, congregational. District and National officiaries, however, are referred to as Presbyteries led by Overseers.

The group functions in cooperative fellowship with the Italian Pentecostal Church of Canada and the Evangelical Christian Churches—Assemblies of God in Italy. It is an affiliate member of the Pentecostal Fellowship of North America and of the National Association of Evangelicals.

HEADQUARTERS

1294 Rutledge Rd., Transfer, PA 16154-9005 Tel. (412)962-3501 Fax (412)962-1766

Media Contact, Ofc. of Gen. Sec./Treas.

OFFICERS

Executive Bd., Gen. Overseer, Rev. David Farina, 41 Sherbrooke Rd., Trenton, NJ 08638

Exec. Vice-Pres., Rev. Andrew Farina, 3 Alhambra Pl., Greenville, PA 16125

Asst. Gen. Overseers: Rev. James Demola, P.O. Box 157, Mullica Hill, NJ 08062; Rev. Anthony Freni, 10 Elkway Ave., Norwood, MA 02062; Rev. Charles Gay, 26 Delafield Dr., Albany, NY 12205; Rev. Michael Marino, 25595 Chardon Rd., Richmond Heights, OH 44143; Rev. Raymond Patronelli, 6203 Kelly Rd., Plant City, FL 33565

Gen. Sec.-Treas., ——-

DEPARTMENTS

Benevolence, Rev. Eugene DeMarco, 155 Scott St., New Brighton, PA 15066

Church Growth & Media Ministries, Rev. Carmine Reigle, P.O. Box 644, Niles, OH 44446

Finance, ——-

Faith, Order & Credentials, Rev. Andrew Farina, 3 Alhambra Pl., Greenville, PA 16125

Missions, Rev. John DelTurco, P.O. Box 1198, Hermitage, PA 16148

Publications & Promotion, Rev. John Tedesco, 1188 Heron Rd., Cherry Hill, NJ 08003

Youth, Education & Sunday School, Rev. Lou Fortunato, Jr., 248 Curry Pl., Youngs-town, OH 44504

PERIODICAL

Vista

Christian Churches and Churches of Christ

The fellowship, whose churches were always strictly congregational in polity, has its origin in the American movement to "restore the New Testament church in doctrine, ordinances and life" initiated by Thomas and Alexander Campbell, Walter Scott and Barton W. Stone in the early 19th century.

HEADQUARTERS

Media Contact, No. American Christian Convention Dir., Rod Huron, 4210 Bridgetown Rd., Box 11326, Cincinnati, OH 45211 Tel. (513)598-6222 Fax (513)598-6471

CONVENTIONS

North American Christian Convention: Dir., Rod Huron, 4210 Bridgetown Rd., Box 11326, Cincinnati, OH 45211 Tel. (513)598-6222; NACC Mailing Address, Box 39456, Cincinnati, OH 45239

National Missionary Convention, Coord., Walter Birney, Box 11, Copeland, KS 67837 Tel. (316)668-5250

Eastern Christian Convention, Kenneth Meade, 5300 Norbeck Rd., Rockville, MD 20853 Tel. (301)460-3550

PERIODICALS

Christian Standard; Restoration Herald; Horizons; The Lookout

The Christian Congregation, Inc.

The Christian Congregation is a denominational evangelistic association that originated in 1798 and was active on the frontier in areas adjacent to the Ohio River. The church was an unincorporated organization until 1887. At that time a group of ministers who desired closer cooperation formally constituted the church. The charter was revised in 1898 and again in 1970.

Governmental polity basically is congregational. Local units are semi-autonomous. Doctrinal positions, strongly biblical, are essentially universalist in the sense that ethical principles, which motivate us to creative activism, transcend national boundaries and racial barriers. A central tenet, John 13:34-35, translates to such respect for sanctity of life that abortions on demand, capital punishment and all warfare are vigorously opposed. All wars are considered unjust and obsolete as a means of resolving disputes.

Early leaders were John Chapman, John L. Puckett and Isaac V. Smith. Bishop O. J. Read was chief administrative and ecclesiastic officer for 40 years until 1961. Rev. Dr. Ora Wilbert Eads has been general superintendent since 1961. Ministerial affiliation for independent clergymen is provided.

HEADQUARTERS
804 W. Hemlock St., LaFollette, TN 37766
Media Contact, Gen. Supt., Rev. Ora W. Eads, D.D., Tel. (615)562-8511

OFFICER
Gen. Supt., Rev. Ora W. Eads, D.D.

Christian Methodist Episcopal Church
In 1870 the General Conference of the Methodist Episcopal Church, South, approved the request of its colored membership for the formation of their conferences into a separate ecclesiastical body, which became the Colored Methodist Episcopal Church.

At its General Conference in Memphis, Tenn., May 1954, it was overwhelmingly voted to change the name of the Colored Methodist Episcopal Church to the Christian Methodist Episcopal Church. This became the official name on Jan. 3, 1956.

HEADQUARTERS
First Memphis Plaza, 4466 Elvis Presley Blvd., Memphis, TN 38116
Media Contact, Exec. Sec., Dr. W. Clyde Williams, 201 Ashby St., N.W., Ste. 312, Atlanta, GA 30314 Tel. (404)522-2736 Fax (404)522-2736

OFFICERS
Exec. Sec., Dr. W. Clyde Williams, 201 Ashby St., NW, Suite 312, Atlanta, GA 30314 Tel. (404)522-2736
Sec. Gen. Conf., Rev. Edgar L. Wade, P.O. Box 3403, Memphis, TN 38103

OTHER ORGANIZATIONS
Christian Education: Gen. Sec., Dr. Ronald M. Cunningham, 4466 Elvis Presley Blvd., Ste. 214, Box 193, Memphis, TN 38116-7100 Tel. (901)345-0580
Lay Ministry: Gen. Sec., Dr. I. Carlton Faulk, 1222 Rose St., Berkeley, CA 94702 Tel. (415)655-4106
Evangelism, Missions & Human Concerns: Gen. Sec., Rev. Raymond F. Williams, 909 Shanon Bradley Rd., Gastonia, NC 28052 Tel. (704)867-8119
Finance: Sec., Mr. Joseph C. Neal, Jr., P.O. Box 75085, Los Angeles, CA 90075 Tel. (213)233-5050
Publications: Gen. Sec., Rev. William George, 4466 Elvis Presley Blvd., Memphis, TN 38116 Tel. (901)345-0580
Personnel Services: Gen. Sec., Dr. N. Charles Thomas, P.O. Box 74, Memphis, TN 39101 Tel. (901)345-0580
Women's Missionary Council: Pres., Dr. Sylvia M. Faulk, 623 San Fernando Ave., Berkeley, CA 94707 Tel. (415)526-5536

BISHOPS
First District: Bishop William H. Graves, 564 Frank Ave., Memphis, TN 38101 Tel. (901)947-6180
Second District: Bishop Othal H. Lakey, 6322 Elwynne Dr., Cincinnati, OH 45236 Tel. (513)984-6825
Third District: Bishop Dotcy I. Isom, Jr., 11470 Northway Dr., St. Louis, MO 63136 Tel. (314)381-3111
Fourth District: Bishop Marshall Gilmore, 109 Holcomb Dr., Shreveport, LA 71103 Tel. (318)222-6284
Fifth District: Bishop Richard O. Bass, 308 10th Ave. W., Birmingham, AL 35204 Tel. (205)252-3541
Sixth District: Bishop Joseph C. Coles, Jr., 2780 Collier Dr., Atlanta, GA 30018 Tel. (404)794-0096
Seventh District: Bishop Oree Broomfield, Sr., 6524 16th St., N.W., Washington, DC 20012 Tel. (202)723-2660
Eighth District: Bishop C. D. Coleman, Sr., 2330 Sutter St., Dallas, TX 75216 Tel. (214)942-5781
Ninth District: Bishop E. Lynn Brown, P.O. Box 11276, Los Angeles, CA 90011 Tel. (213)216-9278
Tenth District: Bishop Nathaniel L. Linsey, P.O. Box 170127, Atlanta, GA 30317
Retired: Bishop Henry C. Bunton, 853 East Dempster Ave., Memphis, TN 38106; Bishop Chester A. Kirkendoll, 10 Hurtland, Jackson, TN 38305

PERIODICALS
The Christian Index; The Missionary Messenger

Christian Nation Church U.S.A.
Organized in 1895, at Marion, Ohio, as a group of "equality evangelists," who later formed the Christian Nation Church, this church is Wesleyan and Arminian in doctrine, emphasizes the premillenial coming of Christ, is semi-congregational in government and emphasizes evangelism. It was reincorporated as the Christian Nation Church U.S.A. in 1961.

HEADQUARTERS
Media Contact, Gen. Overseer, Rev. Ronald Justice, 11245 St. Rt. 669 NE, Roseville, OH 43777 Tel. (614)982-7827

OFFICERS
Gen. Overseer, Rev. Ronald Justice
Asst. Overseer, Rev. Jim Brown, RR #2, 6943 NE Park St., New Lexington, OH 43764
Exec. Sec., Rev. Carl M. Eisenhart, 10303 Murdock-Cozaddale Rd., Goshen, OH 45122 Tel. (513)677-8274

Christian Reformed Church in North America
The Christian Reformed Church represents the historic faith of Protestantism. Founded in the United States in 1857 and active in Canada since 1908, it asserts its belief in the Bible as the inspired Word of God, and is creedally united in the Belgic Confession (1561), the Heidelberg Catechism (1563), and the Canons of Dort (1618-19).

HEADQUARTERS

2850 Kalamazoo Ave., SE, Grand Rapids, MI 49560 Tel. (616)246-0744 Fax (616)246-0834
Media Contact, Gen. Sec., Leonard J. Hofman

OFFICERS

Gen. Sec., Rev. Leonard J. Hofman
Exec. Dir. of Ministries, Dr. Peter Borgdorff
Financial Coord., Harry J. Vander Meer

OTHER ORGANIZATIONS

The Back to God Hour: Dir. of Ministries, Dr. Joel H. Nederhood, International Headquarters, 6555 W. College Dr., Palos Heights, IL 60463
Christian Reformed Home Missions: Dir., Rev. John A. Rozeboom
Christian Reformed World Missions, US: Dir., Rev. William Van Tol
Christian Ref. World Missions, Canada: Dir., Albert Karsten, 3475 Mainway, P.O. Box 5070, Burlington, ON L7R 3Y8
Christian Reformed World Relief, US: Dir., John De Haan
Christian Reformed World Relief, Canada: Dir., Ray Elgersma, 3475 Mainway, P.O. Box 5070, Burlington, ON L7R 3Y8
CRC Publications: Dir., Gary Mulder
Ministers' Pension Fund: Admn., Dr. Ray Vander Weele

PERIODICAL

The Banner

Christian Union

Organized in 1864 in Columbus, Ohio, the Christian Union stresses the oneness of the Church with Christ as its only head. The Bible is the only rule of faith and practice and good fruits the only condition of fellowship. Each local church governs itself.

HEADQUARTERS

c/o Christian Union Bible College, P.O. Box 27, Greenfield, OH 45123 Tel. (513)981-2897
Media Contact, Pres., Dr. Joseph Harr, 3025 Converse-Roselm Rd., Grover Hill, OH 45849 Tel. (419)587-3226

OFFICERS

Pres., Dr. Joseph Harr

Church of the Brethren

German pietists-anabaptists founded the Church of the Brethren in 1708 under Alexander Mack in Schwarzenau, Germany. They entered the colonies in 1719 and settled at Germantown, Pa. They have no other creed than the New Testament, hold to principles of nonviolence, temperance and volunteerism and emphasize religion in daily life.

HEADQUARTERS

Church of the Brethren General Offices, 1451 Dundee Ave., Elgin, IL 60120 Tel. (708)742-5100 Fax (708)742-6103
New Windsor Service Center, P.O. Box 188, New Windsor, MD 21776 Tel. (301)635-6464 Fax (301)635-8789
Washington Office, 110 Maryland Ave. NE, Box 50, Washington, DC 20002 Tel. (202)546-3202 Fax (202)544-5852
Media Contact, Dir. of Interpretation, Howard Royer, Elgin Ofc.

OFFICERS

Mod., Earl K. Ziegler

Mod.-Elect, Judy Mills Reimer
Sec., Anne M. Myers

GENERAL BOARD STAFF

Ofc. of Gen. Sec.: Gen. Sec., Donald E. Miller

ADMINISTRATIVE COUNCIL

Treasurer's Ofc.: Treas., Darryl K. Deardorff
General Services Commission: Assoc. Gen. Sec./Exec. of Comm., Dale E. Minnich
Parish Ministries Commission: Assoc. Gen. Sec./Exec. of Comm., Glenn F. Timmons
World Ministries Commission: Assoc. Gen. Sec./Exec. of Comm., Joan G. Deeter
Annual Conference: Mgr., Duane Steiner; Treas., Darryl K. Deardorff
Brethren Benefit Trust: Exec. Sec., Wilfred E. Nolen

PERIODICAL

Messenger

Church of Christ

Joseph Smith and five others organized the Church of Christ on April 6, 1830 at Fayette, N.Y. In 1864 this body was directed by revelation through Granville Hedrick to return in 1867 to Independence, Mo. to the "consecrated land" dedicated by Joseph Smith. They did so and purchased the temple lot dedicated in 1831.

HEADQUARTERS

Temple Lot, P.O. Box 472, Independence, MO 64051 Tel. (816)833-3995
Media Contact, Gen. Church Rep., William A. Sheldon

PERIODICAL

Zion's Advocate

Church of Christ, Scientist

The Christian Science Church was founded by New England religious leader Mary Baker Eddy in 1879 "to commemorate the word and works of our Master (Christ Jesus), which should reinstate primitive Christianity and its lost element of healing." In 1892 the church was reorganized and established as The First Church of Christ, Scientist, in Boston, also called The Mother Church, with local branch churches around the world, of which there are nearly 2,700 in 68 countries today.

The church is administered by a five-member board of directors in Boston. Local churches govern themselves democratically. Since the church has no clergy, services are conducted by laypersons elected to serve as Readers. There are also about 3,000 Christian Science practitioners who devote their full time to healing through prayer.

Organizations within the church include the Board of Education, the Board of Lectureship, the Committee on Publication and the Christian Science Publishing Society.

HEADQUARTERS

The First Church of Christ, Scientist, 175 Huntington Ave., Boston, MA 02115
Media Contact, Mgr., Comm. on Publication, M. Victor Westberg, Tel. (617)450-3301 Fax (617)450-3325

OFFICERS

Bd. of Dirs.: Chpsn., Virginia S. Harris; Richard C. Bergenheim; Olga M. Chaffee; Al M. Carnesciali; John Lewis Selover

Pres., K. Dieter Förster
Treas., John Lewis Selover
Clk., Olga M. Chaffee
First Reader, Howard E. Johnson
Second Reader, Margaret Rogers

PERIODICALS

The Christian Science Monitor; The Christian Science Journal; Christian Science Sentinel; The Herald of Christian Science; Christian Science Quarterly

Church of Daniel's Band

The Church of Daniels's Band is Methodist in form and evangelistic in spirit. It was organized in Michigan in 1893.

HEADQUARTERS

Media Contact, Sec.-Treas., Rev. Wesley Hoggard, 2960 Croll Rd., Beaverton, MI 48612 Tel. (517)435-3649

OFFICERS

Pres., Rev. Jim Seaman, Adams St., Coleman, MI 48618 Tel. (517)465-6059
Vice-Pres., Rev. Wesley A. Hoggard, 605 N. 5th St., Coleman, MI 48618
Sec.-Treas., Rev. Wesley J. Hoggard, 2960 Croll Rd., Beaverton, MI 48612

The Church of God

The Church of God, from which many groups of the Pentecostal and Holiness Movement stemmed, was inaugurated by Bishop A. J. Tomlinson, who served as General Overseer from 1903 to 1943. The church is episcopal in administration and evangelical in doctrines of justification by faith, sanctification as a second work of grace and baptism of the Holy Ghost. Believers speak with other tongues and participate in miracles of healing. Bishop Homer A. Tomlinson served as General Overseer from 1943 to 1968 and Bishop Voy M. Bullen has been the General Overseer since 1968.

HEADQUARTERS

Box 13036, 1207 Willow Brook, Apt. #2, Huntsville, AL 35802 Tel. (205)881-9629
Media Contact, Gen. Overseer, Voy M. Bullen

OFFICERS

Gen. Overseer & Bishop, Voy M. Bullen
Gen. Sec.-Treas., Marie Powell

CHURCH AUXILIARIES

Assembly Band Movement, Gen. Sec., Bishop Bill Kinslaw
Women's Missionary Band, Gen. Sec., Maxine McKenzie
Theocratic Bands, Gen. Sec., Rev. Ted Carr
Victory Leader's Band, Youth, Gen. Sec., Larry Meadows
Admn. for Highway & Hedge Campaign, Earnest Hoover
Sunday School, Gen. Sec., Judy Foskey

PERIODICAL

The Church of God Quarterly; COG Newsletter

Church of God (Anderson, Ind.)

The Church of God (Anderson, Ind.) began in 1881 when Daniel S. Warner and several associates felt constrained to forsake all denominational hierarchies and formal creeds, trusting solely in the Holy Spirit as their overseer and the Bible as their statement of belief. These people saw themselves at the forefront of a movement to restore unity and holiness to the church, not to establish another denomination, but to promote primary allegiance to Jesus Christ so as to transcend denominational loyalties.

Deeply influenced by Wesleyan theology and Pietism, the Church of God has emphasized conversion, holiness and attention to the Bible. Worship services tend to be informal, accentuating expository preaching and robust singing.

There is no formal membership. Persons are assumed to be members on the basis of witness to a conversion experience and evidence that supports such witness. The absence of formal membership is also consistent with the church's understanding of how Christian unity is to be achieved—that is, by preferring the label Christian before all others.

The Church of God is congregational in its government. Each local congregation is autonomous and may call any recognized Church of God minister to be its pastor and may retain him or her as long as is mutually pleasing. Ministers are ordained and disciplined by state or provincial assemblies made up predominantly of ministers. National program boards serve the church through coordinated ministries and resource materials.

There are Church of God congregations in 83 foreign countries, most of which are resourced by one or more missionaries. There are slightly more Church of God adherents overseas than in North America. The heaviest concentration is in the nation of Kenya.

HEADQUARTERS

Box 2420, Anderson, IN 46018 Tel. (317)642-0256
Media Contact, Gen. Sec., Leadership Council, Edward L. Foggs

LEADERSHIP COUNCIL

Gen. Sec., Edward L. Foggs
Assoc. Gen. Sec., David L. Lawson
Church Service, Exec. Dir., Keith Huttenlocker
World Service, Exec. Dir., James Williams

OTHER ORGANIZATIONS

Bd. of Christian Education, Exec. Dir., Sherrill D. Hayes, Box 2458, Anderson, IN 46018
Bd. of Church Extension & Home Missions, Pres., J. Perry Grubbs, Box 2069, Anderson, IN 46018
Foreign Missionary Bd., Pres., Norman S. Patton, Box 2498, Anderson, IN 46018
Women of the Church of God, Exec. Sec.-Treas., Doris Dale, Box 2328, Anderson, IN 46018
Bd. of Pensions, Exec. Sec.-Treas., Jeffrey A. Jenness, Box 2299, Anderson, IN 46018
Mass Communications Bd., Exec. Sec.-Treas., Dwight L. Dye, Box 2007, Anderson, IN 46018
Warner Press, Inc., Pres., Robert G. Rist, Box 2499, Anderson, IN 46018

PERIODICALS

Vital Christianity; Church of God Missions

Church of God by Faith, Inc.

Founded 1914, in Jacksonville Heights, Fla., by Elder John Bright, this church believes the word of God as interpreted by Jesus Christ to be the only hope of salvation and Jesus Christ the only mediator for people.

3220 Haines St., P.O. Box 3746, Jacksonville, FL 32206 Tel. (904)353-5111 Fax (904)355-8582
Media Contact, Ofc. Mgr., Sarah E. Lundy

OFFICERS
Bishop Emeritus, W. W. Matthews, P.O. Box 907, Ozark, AL 36360
Bishop, James E. McKnight, P.O. Box 121, Gainesville, FL 32601
Treas., Elder Theodore Brown, 93 Girard Pl., Newark, NJ 07108
Ruling Elders: Elder John Robinson, 300 Essex Dr., Ft. Pierce, FL 33450; Elder D. C. Rourk, 207 Chestnut Hill Dr., Rochester, NY 14617
Exec. Sec., Elder George Matthews, 8834 Camphor Dr., Jacksonville, FL 32208

Church of God (Cleveland, Tenn.)

America's oldest Pentecostal Church began in 1886 as an outgrowth of the holiness revival under the name Christian Union. Reorganized in 1902 as the Holiness Church, in 1907 the church adopted the name Church of God. Its doctrine is fundamental and Pentecostal; it maintains a centralized form of government and an evangelistic and missionary program.

HEADQUARTERS
P.O. Box 2430, Cleveland, TN 37320 Tel. (615)472-3361 Fax (615)478-7052
Media Contact, Dir. of Publ. Relations, Michael L. Baker, Tel. (615)478-7112 Fax (615)478-7066

EXECUTIVES
Gen. Overseer, R. Lamar Vest
Asst. Gen. Overseers: Robert White; John D. Nichols; Ray H. Hughes
Gen. Sec.-Treas., Robert E. Fisher

DEPARTMENTS
Black Evangelism, Dir., Joseph E. Jackson
Business & Records, Dir., Julian B. Robinson
Evangelism & Home Missions, Dir., Bill F. Sheeks
Ladies Ministries, Dir., Mrs. Rebecca Jenkins
Lay Ministries, Dir., Leonard Albert
Media Ministries, Dir., Robert E. Fisher
Ministerial Dev., Dir., Larry G. Hess
Pension & Legal Services, Dir., O. Wayne Chambers
Publications, Dir., Donald T. Pemberton
Public Relations, Dir., Michael L. Baker
Stewardship, Dir., Al Taylor
World Missions, Dir., Roland Vaughan
Youth & Christian Educ., Dir., T. David Sustar
Benevolence, Dir., B. J. Moffett
Computer Info. Serv., Dir., Timothy D. O'Neal
Cross-Cultural Min., Dir., Billy J. Rayburn
Hispanic Min., Dir., Esdras Betancourt
Chaplains Commission, Dir., Robert D. Crick
Ministerial Care, Dir., Sam Crisp
Ministry to the Military, Dir., John D. Nichols
Music Min., Dir., Delton Alford

PERIODICAL
Church of God Evangel

Church of God General Conference (Oregon, IL and Morrow, GA)

This church is the outgrowth of several independent local groups of similar faith. Some were in existence as early as 1800, and others date their beginnings to the arrival of British immigrants around 1847. Many local churches carried the name Church of God of the Abrahamic Faith.

State and district conferences of these groups were formed as an expression of mutual cooperation. A national organization was instituted at Philadelphia in 1888. Because of strong convictions on the questions of congregational rights and authority, however, it ceased to function until 1921, when the present General Conference was formed at Waterloo, Iowa.

The Bible is accepted as the supreme standard of faith. Adventist in viewpoint, the second (premillenial) coming of Christ is strongly emphasized. The church teaches that the kingdom of God will be literal, beginning in Jerusalem at the time of the return of Christ and extending to all nations. Emphasis is placed on the oneness of God and the Sonship of Christ, that Jesus did not pre-exist prior to his birth in Bethlehem and that the Holy Spirit is the power and influence of God. Membership is dependent on faith, repentance and baptism by immersion.

The work of the General Conference is carried on under the direction of the board of directors. With a congregational church government, the General Conference exists primarily as a means of mutual cooperation and for the development of yearly projects and enterprises.

The headquarters and Bible College were moved to Morrow, Ga. in 1991.

HEADQUARTERS
P.O. Box 100,000, Morrow, GA 30260 Tel. (404)362-0052 Fax (404)362-9307
Media Contact, Pres., David Krogh

OFFICERS
Chpsn., Pastor Stephen Bolhous, 9 Pancake La., Fonthill, ON L0S 1E2
Vice-Chpsn., Joe James, 100 Buck Dr., Piedmont, SC 29673
Pres., David Krogh, Georgia Ofc.
Sec., Pastor Gary Burnham, 14419 Turin Lane, Centreville, VA 22020
Treas., Frank Johnson, Rt. 2, Box 211, Hector, MN 55342

OTHER ORGANIZATIONS
Bus. Admn., Controller, Terri Tschaenn, Georgia Ofc.
Atlanta Bible College, Pres., David Krogh, Georgia Ofc.

PERIODICALS
The Restitution Herald; Church of God Progress Journal

The Church Of God In Christ

The Church of God in Christ was founded in 1907 in Memphis, Tenn., and was organized by Bishop Charles Harrison Mason, a former Baptist minister who pioneered the embryonic stages of the Holiness movement beginning in 1895 in Mississippi.

Its founder organized four major departments between 1910-1916: the Women's Department, the Sunday School, Young Peoples Willing Workers and Home and Foreign Mission.

The Church is trinitarian and teaches the infallibility of scripture, the need for regeneration and subsequent baptism of the Holy Ghost. It emphasizes holiness as God's standard for Christian conduct. It recognizes as ordinances Holy Communion, Water Baptism and Feet Washing. Its governmental structure is basically episcopal with the General Assembly being the Legislative body.

HEADQUARTERS

Mason Temple, 939 Mason St., Memphis, TN 38126

World Headquarters, 272 S. Main St., Memphis, TN 38103 Tel. (901)578-3800

Mailing Address, P.O. Box 320, Memphis, TN 38101

The Mother Church, Pentecostal Institutional, 229 S. Danny Thomas Blvd., Memphis, TN 38126 Tel. (901)527-9202

Media Contact, Dr. David Hall, Tel. (901)578-3814

GENERAL OFFICES

Office of the Presiding Bishop: Presiding Bishop, Rt. Rev. L. H. Ford, Tel. (901)578-3838; Exec. Sec., Elder A. Z. Hall, Jr.

Office of the General Secretary: Gen. Sec., Bishop W. W. Hamilton, (901)521-1163

PERIODICALS

Whole Truth; Y.P.W.W. Topics; The Pentecostal Interpreter; The Voice of Missions

Church of God in Christ, International

The Church of God in Christ, International was organized in 1969 in Kansas City, Mo., by 14 bishops of the Church of God in Christ of Memphis, Tenn. The doctrine is the same, but the separation came because of disagreement over polity and governmental authority. The Church is Wesleyan in theology (two works of grace) but stresses the experience of full baptism of the Holy Ghost with the initial evidence of speaking with other tongues as the spirit gives utterance.

HEADQUARTERS

170 Adelphi St., Brooklyn, NY 11205 Tel. (718)625-9175

Media Contact, Natl. Sec., Rev. Sis. Sharon R. Dunn

OFFICERS

Presiding Bishop, The Most Rev. Carl E. Williams, Sr.

Vice-Presiding Bishop, Rt. Rev. J. P. Lucas, 90 Holland St., Newark, NJ 07103

Sec.-Gen., Rev. William Hines

Exec. Admn., Horace K. Williams, Word of God Center, Newark, NJ

Women's Dept., Natl. Supervisor, Dr. Louise Norris, 360 Colorado Ave., Bridgeport, CT 06605

Youth Dept., Pres., Evangelist Joyce Taylor, 137-17 135th Ave., S., Ozone Park, NY 11420

Music Dept., Pres., Rev. Carl E. Williams, Jr.

Bd. of Bishops, Chpsn., Bishop J. C. White, 360 Colorado Ave., Bridgeport, CT 06605

Natl. Dir. of Public Relations, Rev. William A. Hines, 187 St. Marks Ave., #1-R, Brooklyn, NY 11238

Church of God in Christ, Mennonite

The Church of God in Christ, Mennonite was organized in Ohio in 1859 by the evangelist-reformer John Holdeman. The church unites with the faith of the Waldenses, Anabaptists and other such groups. Emphasis is placed on obedience to the teachings of the Bible, including the doctrine of the new birth and spiritual life, noninvolvement in government or the military, head-coverings for the women, beards for the men and separation from the world shown by simplicity in clothing, homes, possessions and life-style. The church has a worldwide membership of about 15,000, most of them in the United States and Canada.

HEADQUARTERS

P.O. Box 313, 420 N. Wedel Ave., Moundridge, KS 67107 Tel. (316)345-2532 Fax (316)345-2582

Media Contact, Dale Koehn, P.O. Box 230, Moundridge, KS 67107 Tel. (316)345-2532 Fax (316)345-2582

PERIODICAL

Messenger of Truth

Church of God, Mountain Assembly, Inc.

The church was formed in 1895 and organized in 1906 by J. H. Parks, S. N. Bryant, Tom Moses and Andrew Silcox.

HEADQUARTERS

110 S. Florence Ave., P.O. Box 157, Jellico, TN 37762 Tel. (615)784-8260

Media Contact, Gen. Sec.-Treas., Rev. James Kilgore

OFFICERS

Gen. Overseer, Rev. Jasper Walden

Asst. Gen. Overseer/World Missions Dir., Rev. Cecil Johnson

Gen. Sec.-Treas., Rev. James Kilgore, Box 157, Jellico, TN 37762

Youth Ministries & Camp Dir., Rev. Rick Massingill

PERIODICAL

The Gospel Herald

Church of God of Prophecy

The Church of God of Prophecy is one of the churches that grew out of the work of A. J. Tomlinson in the first half of this century. It was named in 1952, but historically shares the traditions of the holiness classical pentecostal church, the Church of God (Cleveland, TN).

At the death of A. J. Tomlinson in 1943, M. A. Tomlinson was named overseer and served until 1990. He emphasized unity and fellowship that is not limited socially, racially or nationally. The present general overseer, Billy D. Murray, Sr. is committed to promoting Christian unity and moving forward with world-wide evangelism.

The official teachings include special emphasis on sanctification, the doctrine of Spirit-baptism and belief that tongues-speech is an initial evidence. The church teaches an imminence-oriented eschatology that involves a premillennial return of the risen Jesus which itself will be preceded by a series of events; a call for the sanctity of the home which includes denial of a multiple marriage; practice of water baptism by immersion, the Lord's Supper and washing of the saints' feet; total abstinence from intoxicating beverages and tobacco; a concern for moderation in all dimensions of life; and an appreciation for various gifts of the Holy Spirit.

The Church is racially integrated on all levels and various leadership positions are occupied by women. The Church's history includes a strong emphasis on youth ministries, national and international missions and various parochial educational ministries.

HEADQUARTERS

P.O. Box 2910, Cleveland, TN 37320-2910
Media Contact, Perry Gillum, Tel. (615)559-5336
Fax (615)559-5338

OFFICERS

Gen. Overseer, Bishop Billy Murray, Sr.
Gen. Overseer, Emeritus, Bishop Milton A. Tomlinson
Admn. Asst.: Perry Gillum; E. L. Jones; Jose A. Reyes, Sr.
Admn. Committee: Billy Murray; Perry Gillum; E. L. Jones; D. Elwood Matthews; Jose A. Reyes, Sr.; Jerlena Riley; Adrian Varlack

GENERAL STAFF

Center for Biblical Leadership, Educ. Dept., Oswill Williams
Communications Bus. Mgr., Thomas Duncan
Communications Min. (English), D. Elwood Matthews
Communications Min. (Spanish), Jose A. Reyes, Sr.
Evangelism Dir., D. Elwood Matthews
Fin. Dir., Jerlena Riley
Genl. Ofc. Mgr./Personnel Dir., Perry Gillum
Ministerial Aid Dir., E. L. Jones
Women's Ministries, Cathy Payne
World Language Dir., Henry O'Neal
World Missions Dir., Adrian Varlack
Youth & Children's Ministries, William M. Wilson

PERIODICALS

White Wing Messenger; Victory (Youth Magazine)

The Church of God (Seventh Day), Denver, Colo.

The Church of God (Seventh Day) began in southwestern Michigan in 1858, when a group of Sabbath-keepers led by Gilbert Cranmer refused to give endorsement to the visions and writings of Ellen G. White, a principal in the formation of the Seventh-Day Adventist Church. Another branch of Sabbath-keepers, which developed near Cedar Rapids, Iowa, in 1860, joined the Michigan church in 1863 to publish a paper called *The Hope of Israel*, the predecessor to the *Bible Advocate*, the church's present publication. As membership grew and spread into Missouri and Nebraska, it organized the General Conference of the Church of God in 1884. The words "Seventh Day" were added to its name in 1923. The headquarters of the church was in Stanberry, Mo., from 1888 until 1950, when it moved to Denver.

The church observes the seventh day as the Sabbath. It believes in the imminent, personal and visible return of Jesus; that the dead are in an unconscious state awaiting to be resurrected, the righteous to immortality and the wicked to extinction by fire; and that the earth will be the eternal abode of the righteous. It observes two ordinances: baptism by immersion and an annual Communion service accompanied by foot washing.

HEADQUARTERS

330 W. 152nd Ave., P.O. Box 33677, Denver, CO 80233 Tel. (303)452-7973 Fax (303)452-0657
Media Contact, Pres., Calvin Burrell

OFFICERS

Chpsn., Calvin Burrell
Sec.-Treas., Jayne Kuryluk
Spring Vale Academy, Dir., Richard Weidenheft
Youth Agency, Dir., John & Ruth Tivald
Bible Advocate Press, Dir., Roy Marrs
Women's Assoc., Pres., Mrs. Emogene Coulter
Summit School of Theology, Dir., Jerry Griffin
Missions Abroad, Dir., Victor Burford

PERIODICAL

The Bible Advocate

Church of God (Which He Purchased with His Own Blood)

This body was organized in 1953 in Oklahoma City, Okla., by William Jordan Fizer after his excommunication from the Church of the Living God (C.W.F.F.) over doctrinal disagreements relating to the Lord's Supper. The first annual convention was held in Oklahoma City, Nov. 19-21, 1954.

The church believes that water is not the element to be used in the Lord's Supper, observed every Sunday, but rather grape juice or wine and unleavened bread.

Its doctrine holds that the Holy Ghost is given to those who obey the Lord. Feet washing is observed as an act of humility and not the condition of salvation. Baptism must be administered in the name of the Father, Son and Holy Ghost. The Church of God believes it is the Body of Christ, and because of scriptural doctrine and practice, that it is the church organized by Jesus Christ. The members are urged to lead consecrated lives unspotted from the world. Tobacco and strong drinks are condemned. Divine healing is an article of faith, but not to the exclusion of doctors.

HEADQUARTERS

1628 N.E. 50th, Oklahoma City, OK 73111 Tel. (405)427-8264
Media Contact, Chief Bishop, William J. Fizer, 1907 N.E. Grand Blvd., Oklahoma City, OK 73111 Tel. (405)427-2166

OFFICERS

Chief Bishop, William J. Fizer
Gen. Sec.-Treas., Evang. Alsie M. Fizer
Vice-Chief Bishop, George Hill, 1109 N.W. 74, Lawton, OK 73505 Tel. (405)536-4941
Overseers: J. W. Johnson, 12837 E. Carver, Spencer, OK 73084 Tel. (405)769-4691; Rueben Tyson, 1628 NE 50th, Oklahoma City, OK Tel. (405)427-8264; M. Roberson, P.O. Box 71, Mounds, OK 74047 Tel. (918)827-6694; Thomas R. Smith, P.O. Box 27431, Tucson, AZ 85726 Tel. (602)624-0138; DeWayne Cobbs, 1325 Seminary Dr., Fort Worth, TX Tel. (817)922-0663
Overseas Bishops: M. Okon, P.O. Box 1710 Uyo, Akwa Ibom State, Nigeria, W. Africa; E. Akpan, P.O. Box 34, Ikot Okoro, Akwa Ibom State, Nigeria, W. Africa; Xavier G. Prado, P.O. Box 81529, 8000 Davao City, Philippines

The Church of Illumination

The Church of Illumination was organized in 1908 for the express purpose of establishing congregations at large, offering a spiritual, esoteric, philosophic interpretation of the vital biblical teachings, thereby satisfying the inner spiritual

70

needs of those seeking spiritual truth, yet permitting them to remain in, or return to, their former church membership.

HEADQUARTERS

Beverly Hall, 5966 Clymer Rd., Quakertown, PA 18951 Tel. (800)779-3796

Media Contact, Dir. General, Gerald E. Poesnecker, P.O. Box 220, Quakertown, PA 18951 Tel. (215)536-7048 Fax (215)529-9034

OFFICERS

Dir.-General, Gerald E. Poesnecker, P.O. Box 220, Quakertown, PA 18951

The Church of Jesus Christ (Bickertonites)

This church was organized in 1862 at Green Oak, Pa., by William Bickerton, who obeyed the Restored Gospel under Sidney Rigdon's following in 1845.

HEADQUARTERS

Sixth & Lincoln Sts., Monongahela, PA 15063 Tel. (412)258-3066

Media Contact, Exec. Sec., John Manes, 2007 Cutter Dr., McKees Rocks, PA 15136 Tel. (412)771-4513

OFFICERS

Pres., Dominic Thomas, 6010 Barrie, Dearborn, MI 48126

First Counselor, Paul Palmieri, 319 Pine Dr., Aliquippa, PA 15001

Second Counselor, Robert Watson, Star Rt. 5, Box 36, Gallup, NM 87301

Exec. Sec., John Manes, 2007 Cutter Dr., McKees Rocks, PA 15136 Tel. (412)771-4513

PERIODICAL

The Gospel News

The Church of Jesus Christ of Latter-day Saints

This church was organized April 6, 1830, at Fayette, N.Y., by Joseph Smith. Members believe Joseph Smith was divinely directed to restore the gospel to the earth, and that through him the keys to the Aaronic and Melchizedek priesthoods and temple work also were restored. Members believe that both the Bible and the Book of Mormon (a record of the Lord's dealings with His people on the American continent 600 B.C. - 421 A.D.) are scripture. Membership is worldwide, approaching nine million in 1993.

In addition to the First Presidency, the governing bodies of the church include the Quorum of the Twelve Apostles, the Presidency of the Seventy, the First Quorum of the Seventy, the Second Quorum of the Seventy and the Presiding Bishopric.

HEADQUARTERS

50 East North Temple St., Salt Lake City, UT 84150 Tel. (801)240-1000 Fax (801)240-1167

Media Contact, Dir., Media Relations, Don LeFevre, Tel. (801)240-4377 Fax (801)240-1167

OFFICERS

Pres., Ezra Taft Benson

1st Counselor, Gordon B. Hinckley

2nd Counselor, Thomas S. Monson

Council of the Twelve Apostles: Pres., Howard W. Hunter; Boyd K. Packer; Marvin J. Ashton; L. Tom Perry; David B. Haight; James E. Faust; Neal A. Maxwell; Russell M. Nelson; Dallin H. Oaks; M. Russell Ballard; Joseph B. Wirthlin; Richard G. Scott

AUXILIARY ORGANIZATIONS

Sunday Schools, Gen. Pres., Merlin R. Lybbert

Relief Society, Gen. Pres., Elaine Jack

Young Women, Gen. Pres., Janette C. Hales

Young Men, Gen. Pres., Jack H. Goaslind

Primary, Gen. Pres., Michaelene P. Grassli

PERIODICALS

The Ensign; The New Era; The Friend

Church of the Living God (Motto: Christian Workers for Fellowship)

The Church of the Living God was founded by William Christian in April 1889 at Caine Creek, Ark. It was the first black church in America without Anglo-Saxon roots and not begun by white missionaries.

Christian was born a slave in Mississippi on Nov. 10, 1856, and grew up uneducated. In 1875 he united with the Missionary Baptist Church and began to preach. In 1888 he left the Baptist Church and began what was known as Christian Friendship Work. Believing himself to have been inspired by the Spirit of God through divine revelation and close study of the Scriptures, he was led to the truth that the Bible refers to the church as The Church of the Living God (I Tim. 3:15).

The church believes in the infallibility of the Scriptures, is Trinitarian and believes there are three sacraments ordained by Christ: baptism (by immersion), the Lord's Supper (unleavened bread and water) and foot washing.

The Church of the Living God, C.W.F.F., believes in holiness as a gift of God subsequent to the New Birth and manifested only by a changed life acceptable to the Lord.

HEADQUARTERS

430 Forest Ave., Cincinnati, OH 45229 Tel. (513)569-5660

Media Contact, Chief Bishop, W. E. Crumes

OFFICERS

Executive Board: Chief Bishop, W. E. Crumes; Vice-Chief Bishop, Alonza Ponder, 5609 N. Terry, Oklahoma City, OK 73111; Exec. Sec., Bishop C. A. Lewis, 1360 N. Boston, Tulsa, OK 73111; Gen. Sec., Elder Milton S. Herring, Los Angeles, CA; Gen. Treas., Elder Harry Hendricks, Milwaukee, WI; Bishop E. L. Bowie, 2037 N.E. 18th St., Oklahoma City, OK 73111; Chaplain, Bishop E. A. Morgan, 735 S. Oakland Dr., Decatur, IL 62525; Bishop L. A. Crawford, 3711 Biglow, Dallas, TX 74216; Bishop A. R. Powell, 8557 S. Wabash, Chicago, IL 60619; Bishop Jeff Ruffin, Phoenix, AZ; Aux. Bishop, R. S. Morgan, 4508 N. Indiana, Oklahoma City, OK 73118; Overseer, S. E. Shannon, 1034 S. King Hwy., St. Louis, MO 63110

NATIONAL DEPARTMENTS

Convention Planning Committee

Young People's Progressive Union

Christian Education Dept.

Sunday School Dept.

Natl. Evangelist Bd.

Natl. Nurses Guild

Natl. Women's Work Dept.

Natl. Music Dept.

The Gospel Truth

Church of the Lutheran Brethren of America

The Church of the Lutheran Brethren of America was organized in December 1900. Five independent Lutheran congregations met together in Milwaukee, Wisc., and adopted a constitution patterned very closely on that of the Lutheran Free Church of Norway.

The spiritual awakening in the Midwest during the 1890s crystallized into convictions that led to the formation of a new church body. Chief among the concerns were church membership practices, observance of Holy Communion, confirmation practices and local church government.

The Church of the Lutheran Brethren practices a simple order of worship with the sermon as the primary part of the worship service. It believes that personal profession of faith is the primary criterion for membership in the congregation. The Communion service is reserved for those who profess faith in Christ as savior. Each congregation is autonomous and the synod serves the congregations in advisory and cooperative capacities.

The synod supports a world mission program in Cameroon, Chad, Japan and Taiwan. Approximately 40 percent of the synodical budget is earmarked for world missions. A growing home mission ministry is planting new congregations in the United States and Canada. Affiliate organizations operate several retirement/nursing homes, conference and retreat centers.

HEADQUARTERS

1007 Westside Dr., Box 655, Fergus Falls, MN 56538 Tel. (218)739-3336 Fax (218)739-5514
Media Contact, Pres., Rev. Robert M. Overgaard

OFFICERS

Pres., Rev. Robert M. Overgaard, Sr.
Vice-Pres., Rev. David Rinden
Sec., Rev. Richard Vettrus, 707 Crestview Dr., West Union, IA 52175
Exec. Dir. of Finance, Mr. Bradley Martinson
Lutheran Brethren Schools, Pres., Rev. Joel Egge, Lutheran Brethren Schools, Box 317, Fergus Falls, MN 56538
World Missions, Exec. Dir., Rev. Jarle Olson
Home Missions, Exec. Dir., Rev. John Westby
Church Services, Exec. Dir., Rev. David Rinden
Youth Ministries, Exec. Dir., ———-

PERIODICAL

Faith & Fellowship

Church of the Lutheran Confession

The Church of the Lutheran Confession held its constituting convention in Watertown, S.D., in August of 1960. The Church of the Lutheran Confession was begun by people and congregations who withdrew from church bodies that made up what was then known as the Synodical Conference over the issue of unionism. Following such passages as I Corinthians 1:10 and Romans 16:17-18, the Church of the Lutheran Confession holds the conviction that mutual agreement with the doctrines of Scripture is essential and necessary before exercise of church fellowship is appropriate.

Members of the Church of the Lutheran Confession uncompromisingly believe the Holy Scriptures to be divinely inspired and therefore inerrant. They subscribe to the historic Lutheran Confessions as found in the Book of Concord of 1580 because they are a correct exposition of Scripture.

The Church of the Lutheran Confession exists to proclaim, preserve and spread the saving truth of the gospel of Jesus Christ, so that the redeemed of God may learn to know Jesus Christ as their Lord and Savior and follow him through this life to the life to come.

HEADQUARTERS

460 75th Ave., NE, Minneapolis, MN 55432 Tel. (612)784-8784
Media Contact, Pres., Daniel Fleischer

OFFICERS

Pres., Rev. Daniel Fleischer
Vice-Pres., Rev. Elton Hallauer, 608 1st St., Hancock, MN 56244
Mod., Prof. Ronald Roehl, 515 Ingram Dr. W., Eau Claire, WI 54701
Sec., Rev. Paul Nolting, 626 N. Landing Rd., Rochester, NY 14625
Treas., Lowell Moen, 3455 Jill Ave., Eau Claire, WI 54701
Archivist-Historian, John Lau
Statistician, Harvey Callies

PERIODICALS

The Lutheran Spokesman; Journal of Theology

Church of the Nazarene

The Church of the Nazarene resulted from the merger of three independent holiness groups. The Association of Pentecostal Churches in America, located principally in New York and New England, joined at Chicago in 1907 with a California body called the Church of the Nazarene and formed the the Pentecostal Church of the Nazarene. The southern group, known as the Holiness Church of Christ, united with this Pentecostal Church of the Nazarene at Pilot Point, Tex., in 1908. In 1919 the word Pentecostal was dropped from the name. Principal leaders in the organization were Phineas Bresee, William Howard Hoople, H. F. Reynolds and C. B. Jernigan. The first Church of the Nazarene in Canada was organized in November 1902 by Dr. H. F. Reynolds in Oxford, Nova Scotia.

The Church of the Nazarene emphasizes the doctrine of entire sanctification on the proclamation of Christian Holiness. It stresses the importance of a devout and holy life and a positive witness before the world by the power of the Holy Spirit. The church feels that caring is a way of life.

Nazarene government is representative, a studied compromise between episcopacy and congregationalism. Quadrennially, the various districts elect delegates to a general assembly at which six general superintendents are elected.

The international denomination has 10 liberal arts colleges, two graduate seminaries, 16 seminaries and 24 Bible colleges. The church maintains missionaries in 109 countries. World services include medical, educational and religious ministries. Books, periodicals and other Christian literature are published at the Nazarene Publishing House.

The church is a member of the Christian Holiness Association and the National Association of Evangelicals.

6401 The Paseo, Kansas City, MO 64131 Tel. (816)333-7000 Fax (816)333-1748
Media Contact, Gen. Sec., Dr. Jack Stone, Tel. (816)333-7000, Ext. 2366

OFFICERS

Gen. Supts.: Jerald Johnson; John A. Knight; James H. Diehl; William J. Prince; Donald D. Owens; Paul Cunningham
Gen. Sec., Jack Stone
Gen. Treas., Norman O. Miller

OTHER ORGANIZATIONS

General Bd.: Sec., Jack Stone; Treas., Norman O. Miller
Church Growth Div., Dir., Bill Sullivan
Chaplaincy Min., Dir., Curt Bowers
Church Ext. Min., Dir., Mike Estep
Evangelism Min., Dir., Bill Sullivan
Pastoral Min., Dir., Wilbur Brannon
Communications Div., Dir., Paul Skiles
Media Services, Dir., David Anderson
Publications Intl., Dir., Ray Hendrix
Fin. Div., Dir., D. Moody Gunter
Planned Giving, Dir., Martin Butler
Pensions & Benefits Services, Dir., Don Walter
Stewardship Services, Dir., D. Moody Gunter
Sunday School Min. Div., Dir., Phil Riley
Adult Min., Dir., Randy Cloud
Children's Min., Dir., Miriam Hall
NYI Min., Dir., Fred Fullerton
World Mission Div., Dir., Robert H. Scott
Missionary Min., Dir., John Smee
Fin. Services, Dir., Dennis Berard
Nazarene World Missionary Soc., Dir., Nina Gunter
Intl. Bd. of Educ., Ed. Commissioner, Stephen Nease

PERIODICALS

Herald of Holiness; World Mission; Preacher's Magazine; Crosswalk

Church of Our Lord Jesus Christ of the Apostolic Faith, Inc.

This church body was founded by Bishop R.C. Lawson in Columbus, Ohio, and moved to New York City in 1919. It is founded upon the teachings of the apostles and prophets, Jesus Christ being its chief cornerstone.

HEADQUARTERS

2081 Adam Clayton Powell Jr. Blvd., New York, NY 10027 Tel. (212)866-1700
Media Contact, Exec. Sec., Bishop T. E. Woolfolk, P.O. Box 119, Oxford, NC 27565 Tel. (919)693-9449 Fax (919)693-6115

OFFICERS

Board of Apostles: Pres., Bishop William L. Bonner; Chief Apostle, Bishop J. P. Steadman; Bishop Frank S. Solomon; Bishop Henry A. Ross, Sr.; Bishop Matthew A. Norwood; Bishop Gentle L. Groover; Bishop Wilbur L. Jones
Bd. of Bishops, Chmn., Bishop James I. Clark, Jr.
Bd. of Presbyters, Pres., Elder Michael A. Dixon
Exec. Secretariat, Sec., Bishop T. E. Woolfolk
Natl. Rec. Sec., Bishop Fred Rubin, Sr. (J.B.)
Natl. Fin. Sec., Bishop Clarence Groover
Natl. Corr. Sec., Bishop Raymond J. Keith, Jr. (J.B.)
Natl Treas., Bishop Thomas J. Richardson, (H.B.)

Churches of Christ

Churches of Christ are autonomous congregations whose members appeal to the Bible alone to determine matters of faith and practice. There are no central offices or officers. Publications and institutions related to the churches are either under local congregational control or independent of any one congregation.

Churches of Christ shared a common fellowship in the 19th century with the Christian Churches/Churches of Christ and the Christian Church (Disciples of Christ). Fellowship was gradually estranged following the Civil War due to theistic evolution, higher critical theories and centralization of church-wide activities through a missionary society.

Members of Churches of Christ believe in the inspiration of the Scriptures, the divinity of Jesus Christ and immersion into Christ for the remission of sins. The New Testament pattern is followed in worship and church organization.

HEADQUARTERS

Media Contact, Ed., Gospel Advocate, Dr. F. Furman Kearley, P.O. Box 726, Kosciusko, MO 39090

PERIODICALS

Action; Wineskins; Image; Christian Bible Teacher; The Christian Chronicle; The Christian Echo; Firm Foundation; Gospel Advocate; Guardian of Truth; Power for Today; Restoration Quarterly; 21st Century Christian; Upreach; Rocky Mountain Christian; Gospel Tidings; The Spiritual Sword

Churches of Christ in Christian Union

Organized in 1909 at Washington Court House, Ohio, as the Churches of Christ in Christian Union, this body believes in the new birth and the baptism of the Holy Spirit for believers. It is Wesleyan, with an evangelistic and missionary emphasis.

The Reformed Methodist Church merged with the Churches of Christ in Christian Union in 1952.

HEADQUARTERS

1426 Lancaster Pike, Box 30, Circleville, OH 43113 Tel. (614)474-8856 Fax (614)477-7766
Media Contact, Gen. Supt., Daniel L. Tipton

OFFICERS

Gen. Supt., Dr. Daniel L. Tipton
Asst. Gen. Supt., Rev. David Dean
Gen. Treas., Beverly R. Salley
Gen. Bd. of Trustees: Chpsn., Dr. Daniel L. Tipton; Vice-Chpsn., Rev. David Dean
District Superintendents: West Central District, Rev. Ron Reese; South Central District, Rev. Jack Norman; Northeast District, Rev. Art Penird, Rt. 2, P.O. Box 790, Port Crane, NY 13833

PERIODICAL

Advocate

Churches of God, General Conference

The Churches of God, General Conference had its beginnings in Harrisburg, Pa., in 1825.

John Winebrenner, recognized founder of the Church of God movement, was an ordained minister of the German Reformed Church. His experience-centered form of Christianity, particularly the "new measures" he used to promote it, his close connection with the local Methodists, his "experience and conference meetings" in the church and his "social prayer meetings" in parishioners' homes resulted in differences of opinion and the establishment of new congregations. Extensive revivals, camp meetings and mission endeavors led to the organization of additional congregations across central Pennsylvania and westward through Ohio, Indiana, Illinois and Iowa.

In 1830 the first system of cooperation between local churches was initiated as an "eldership" in eastern Pennsylvania. The organization of other elderships followed. General Eldership was organized in 1845, and in 1974 the official name of the denomination was changed from General Eldership of the Churches of God in North America to its present name.

The Churches of God, General Conference, is composed of 16 conferences in the United States. The polity of the church is presbyterial in form. The church has mission ministries in the southwest among native Americans and is extensively involved in church planting and whole life ministries in Bangladesh, Haiti and India.

The General Conference convenes in business session triennially. An Administrative Council composed of 16 regional representatives is responsible for the administration and ministries of the church between sessions of the General Conference.

HEADQUARTERS

Legal Headquarters, United Church Center, Rm. 213, 900 S. Arlington Ave., Harrisburg, PA 17109 Tel. (717)652-0255

Administrative Offices, General Conf. Dir., Dr. David E. Draper, 700 E. Melrose Ave., P.O. Box 926, Findlay, OH 45839 Tel. (419)424-1961

Media Contact, Exec. Sec., Roberta G. Bakies, P.O. Box 926, Findlay, OH 45840 Tel. (419)424-1961 Fax (419)424-3343

OFFICERS

Pres., Pastor George Reser, 506 N. Main St., Columbia City, IN 46725 Tel. (219)248-2482

Journalizing Sec., Dr. C. Darrell Prichard, 700 E. Melrose Ave., P.O. Box 1132, Findlay, OH 45839 Tel. (419)423-7694

Treas., Mr. Robert E. Stephenson, 700 E. Melrose Ave., P.O. Box 926, Findlay, OH 45839 Tel. (419)424-1961

DEPARTMENTS

Church Publications, Mrs. Linda M. Draper
Cross-Cultural Ministries, Mr. Travis C. Perry
Pensions, Dr. Royal P. Kear
Curriculum, Mrs. Evelyn J. Sloat
Church Renewal, Pastor Jim G. Martin
Chruch Planting, James W. Moss, Sr.
Youth & Family Life, Mrs. Susan L. Calloway
Fin., Mr. Robert E. Stephenson

PERIODICALS

The Church Advocate; The Workman; The Gem

Congregational Holiness Church

This body was organized in 1921 and embraces the doctrine of Holiness and Pentecost. It carries on mission work in Mexico, Honduras, Costa Rica, Cuba, Brazil, Guatemala, India, Nicaragua and El Salvador.

HEADQUARTERS

3888 Fayetteville Hwy., Griffin, GA 30223 Tel. (404)228-4833 Fax (404)228-1177
Media Contact, Gen. Supt., Bishop Chet Smith

EXECUTIVE BOARD

Gen. Supt., Bishop Chet Smith
1st Asst. Gen. Supt., Rev. William L. Lewis
2nd Asst. Gen. Supt., Rev. Wayne Hicks

PERIODICAL

The Gospel Messenger

Conservative Baptist Association of America

The Conservative Baptist Association of America was organized May 17, 1947 at Atlantic City, N.J. The Old and New Testaments are regarded as the divinely inspired Word of God and are therefore infallible and of supreme authority. Each local church is independent, autonomous and free from ecclesiastical or political authority.

CBA provides wide-ranging support to its affiliate churches and individuals. CBA offers personnel to assist churches in areas such as growth, conflict resolution and financial analysis. The association supports its clergy with medical insurance programs, retirement planning, referrals for new places of ministry and spiritual counseling. The Conservative Baptist Women's Ministries assists women in the church to be effective in their personal growth and leadership.

Each June or July there is a national meeting giving members an opportunity for fellowship, inspiration and motivation.

HEADQUARTERS

25W560 Geneva Rd., P.O. Box 66, Wheaton, IL 60189 Tel. (708)653-5350 Fax (708)653-5387
Media Contact, Gen. Dir., Dr. Dennis N. Baker

OTHER ORGANIZATIONS

Conservative Baptist Foreign Mission Soc., Gen. Dir., Dr. Hans Finzel, Box 5, Wheaton, IL 60189
Conservative Baptist Home Mission Soc., Gen. Dir., Dr. Jack Estep, Box 828, Wheaton, IL 60189
Conservative Baptist Higher Ed. Council, Dr. James Sweeney, Denver Conservative Baptist Seminary, P.O. Box 10,000, Denver, CO 80210

PERIODICALS

Spectrum; Front Line

Conservative Congregational Christian Conference

In the 1930s, evangelicals within the Congregational Christian Churches felt a definite need for fellowship and service. By 1945, this loose association crystallized into the Conservative Congregational Christian Fellowship, committed to maintaining a faithful, biblical witness.

In 1948 in Chicago, the Conservative Congregational Christian Conference was established to provide a continuing fellowship for evangelical churches and ministers on the national level. In recent years, many churches have joined the Conference from backgrounds other than Congregational. These Community or Bible Churches are truly congregational in polity and thoroughly evangelical in conviction. The CCCC welcomes all evangelical churches that are, in fact, congregational. The CCCC believes in the necessity of a regenerate membership, the authority of the Holy Scriptures, the Lordship of Jesus Christ, the autonomy of the local church and the universal fellowship of all Christians.

The Conservative Congregational Christian Conference is a member of the World Evangelical Congregational Fellowship (formed in 1986 in London, England) and the National Association of Evangelicals.

HEADQUARTERS
7582 Currell Blvd., Ste. #108, St. Paul, MN 55125 Tel. (612)739-1474
Media Contact, Conf. Min., Rev. Clifford R. Christensen

OFFICERS
Pres., Rev. Donald Eyler, 620 High Ave., Hillsboro, WI 54634
Vice-Pres., Rev. Clarence Schultz, 7023 Pershing Blvd., Kenosha, WI 53142-1723
Conf. Min., Rev. Clifford R. Christensen, 57 Kipling St., St. Paul, MN 55519 Tel. (612)735-8898
Controller, Mr. Leslie Pierce, 5220 E. 105th St. S., Tulsa, OK 74137
Treas., Rev. John D. Nygren, 579 Sterling St., Maplewood, MN 55119
Rec. Sec., Rev. Larry E. Scovil, 317 W. 40th St., Scottsbluff, NE 69361
Editor, Mrs. Wanda Evans, 4072 Clifton Ridge, Highland, MI 48357
Historian, Rev. Milton Reimer, P.O. Box 4456, Lynchburg, VA 24502

PERIODICAL
Foresee

Conservative Lutheran Association
The Conservative Lutheran Association (CLA) was originally named Lutheran's Alert National (LAN) when it was founded in 1965 by 10 conservative Lutheran pastors and laymen meeting in Cedar Rapids, Iowa. Its purpose was to help preserve from erosion the basic doctrines of Christian theology, including the inerrancy of Holy Scripture. The group grew to a worldwide constituency, similarly concerned with maintaining the doctrinal integrity of the Bible and the Lutheran Confessions.

HEADQUARTERS
3504 N. Pearl St., P.O. Box 7186, Tacoma, WA 98407 Tel. (800)228-4650 Fax (206)759-1790
Media Contact, Pres., The Rev. Dr. R. H. Redal

OFFICERS
Pres., Rev. Dr. R. H. Redal, 409 Tacoma Ave. N., Tacoma, WA 98403 Tel. (206)383-5528
Vice-Pres., Rev. P. J. Moore, 420 Fernhill La., Anaheim, CA 92807 Tel. (714)637-8370
Sec., Rev. Greg DeVore, 4349 Via Del Obispo, Yorba Linda, CA 92686 Tel. (714)693-0712
Treas., Mr. Wayne Brooks, 33838 Pacific Hwy. S., Federal Way, WA 98003 Tel. (206)927-0651
Faith Seminary, Dean, The Rev. Dr. Michael J. Adams

Coptic Orthodox Church
This body is part of the ancient Coptic Orthodox Church of Egypt which is currently headed by His Holiness Pope Shenouda III, 116th Successor to St. Mark the Apostle. Egyptian immigrants have organized many parishes in the United States. Copts exist outside Egypt in Ethiopia, Europe, Asia, Australia, Canada and the United States. The total world Coptic community is estimated at 27 million. The church is in full communion with the other members of The Oriental Orthodox Church Family, The Syrian Orthodox Church, Armenian Orthodox Church, Ethiopian Orthodox Church, the Syrian Orthodox Church in India and the Eritrean Orthodox Church.

CORRESPONDENT
Archpriest, V. Rev. Fr. Gabriel Avdelsayed, PhD, 427 West Side Ave., Jersey City, NJ 07304 Tel. (201)333-0004 Fax (201)333-0502

Cumberland Presbyterian Church
The Cumberland Presbyterian Church was organized in Dickson County, Tenn., on Feb. 4, 1810. It was an outgrowth of the Great Revival of 1800 on the Kentucky and Tennessee frontier. The founders were Finis Ewing, Samuel King and Samuel McAdow, ministers in the Presbyterian Church who rejected the doctrine of election and reprobation as taught in the Westminster Confession of Faith.

By 1813, the Cumberland Presbytery had grown to encompass three presbyteries, which constituted a synod. This synod met at the Beech Church in Sumner County, Tenn., and formulated a "Brief Statement" which set forth the points in which Cumberland Presbyterians dissented from the Westminster Confession. These points are:

1. That there are no eternal reprobates;
2. That Christ died not for some, but for all people;
3. That all those dying in infancy are saved through Christ and the sanctification of the Spirit;

4. That the Spirit of God operates on the world, or as coextensively as Christ has made atonement, in such a manner as to leave everyone inexcusable.

From its birth in 1810, the Cumberland Presbyterian Church grew to a membership of 200,000 at the turn of the century. In 1906 the church voted to merge with the then-Presbyterian Church. Those who dissented from the merger became the nucleus of the continuing Cumberland Presbyterian Church.

HEADQUARTERS
1978 Union Ave., Memphis, TN 38104 Tel. (901)276-4572 Fax (901)276-4578
Media Contact, Stated Clk., Rev. Robert D. Prosser

OFFICERS
Mod., Dr. Robert M. Shelton, 7920 Rockwood La. #226, Austin, TX 78758
Stated Clk., Rev. Robert D. Prosser
General Assembly Council, Pres., Rev. E. G. Sims, 1410 Golf Club La., Clarksville, TN 37040

INSTITUTIONS
Cumberland Presbyterian Children's Home, Exec. Dir., Dr. Marvin E. Leslie, Drawer G, Denton, TX 76202 Tel. (817)382-5112 Fax (817)387-0821
Cumberland Presbyterian Center

BOARDS
Bd. of Christian Education, Exec. Dir., Ms. Claudette Pickle
Bd. of Missions, Exec. Dir., Rev. Jack Barker

Bd. of Finance, Exec. Sec., Rev. Richard Magrill

PERIODICALS

The Cumberland Presbyterian; The Missionary Messenger

Cumberland Presbyterian Church in America

This church, originally known as the Colored Cumberland Presbyterian Church, was formed in May 1874. In May 1869, at the General Assembly meeting in Murfreesboro, Tenn., Moses Weir of the black delegation sucessfully appealed for help in organizing a separate African church so that: blacks could learn self-reliance and independence; they could have more financial assistance; they could minister more effectively among blacks; and they could worship close to the altar, not in the balconies. He requested that the Cumberland Presbyterian Church organize blacks into presbyteries and synods, develop schools to train black clergy, grant loans to assist blacks to secure hymnbooks, Bibles and church buildings and establish a separate General Assembly.

In 1874 the first General Assembly of the Colored Cumberland Presbyterian Church met in Nashville. The moderator was Rev. P. Price and the stated clerk was Elder John Humphrey.

The denomination's General Assembly, the national governing body, is organized around its three program boards and agencies: Finance, Publication and Christian Education, and Missions and Evangelism. Other agencies of the General Assembly are under these three program boards.

The church has four synods (Alabama, Kentucky, Tennessee and Texas), 15 presbyteries and 153 congregations. The CPC extends as far north as Cleveland, Ohio, and Chicago, as far west as Marshalltown, Iowa, and Dallas, Tex., and as far south as Selma, Ala.

HEADQUARTERS

Media Contact, Stated Clk., Rev. Dr. Robert Stanley Wood, 226 Church St., Huntsville, AL 35801 Tel. (205)536-7481 Fax (205)536-7482

OFFICERS

Mod., Rev. Joel P. Rice, 6951 Clearglenn, Dallas, TX 75232

Stated Clk., Rev. Dr. Robert Stanley Wood, 226 Church St., Huntsville, AL 35801 Tel. (205)536-7481

SYNODS

Alabama, Stated Clk., Arthur Hinton, 511 10th Ave. N.W., Aliceville, AL 35442

Kentucky, Stated Clk., Mary Martha Daniels, 8548 Rhodes Ave., Chicago, IL 60619

Tennessee, Stated Clk., Elder Clarence Norman, 145 Jones St., Huntington, TN 38334

Texas, Stated Clk., Arthur King, 2435 Kristen, Dallas, TX 75216

PERIODICAL

The Cumberland Flag

Diocese of the Armenian Church of America

The Armenian Apostolic Church was founded at the foot of the biblical mountain of Ararat in the ancient land of Armenia, where two of Christ's Holy Apostles, Saints Thaddeus and Bartholomew, preached Christianity. In A.D. 301

the historic Mother Church of Etchmiadzin was founded by Saint Gregory the Illuminator, the first Catholicos of All Armenians. This cathedral still stands and serves as the center of the Armenian Church. A branch of this Church was established in North America in 1889 and the first Armenian Diocese was set up in 1898 by the then-Catholicos of All Armenians, Mgrditch Khrimian (Hairig). Armenian immigrants built the first Armenian church in the new world in Worcester, Mass., under the jurisdiction of Holy Etchmiadzin.

In 1927, the churches and the parishes in California were formed into a Western Diocese and the parishes in Canada formed their own diocese in 1984. Other centers of major significance of the Armenian Apostolic Church are the Catholicate of Cilicia, now located in Lebanon, the Armenian Patriarchate of Jerusalem and the Armenian Patriarchate of Constantinople.

HEADQUARTERS

Eastern Diocese: 630 Second Ave., New York, NY 10016-4885 Tel. (212)686-0710 Fax (212)779-3558

Western Diocese: 1201 N. Vine St., Hollywood, CA 90038 Tel. (213)466-5265

Canadian Diocese: 615 Stuart Ave., Outremont, QC H2V 3H2 Tel. (514)276-9479 Fax (514)276-9960

Media Contact, Dir., Zohrab Information Ctr., V. Rev. Fr. Krikor Maksoudian, Eastern Diocese

OFFICERS

Eastern Diocese

Primate, Archbishop Khajag Barsamian, Eastern Diocese Ofc.

Vicar Gen., V. Rev. Fr. Haigazoun Najarian, Eastern Diocese Ofc.

Chancellor, Rev. Fr. Garabed Kochakian

Diocesan Council, Chpsn., Vincent Gurahian, Macauley Rd., RFD 2, Katonah, NY 10536

Western Diocese

Primate, His Em. Archbishop Vatche Hovsepian, Western Diocese Ofc.

Diocesan Council, Chpsn., The Rev. Fr. Vartkes Barsam, St. Mary Armenian Church, P.O. Box 367, Yettem, CA 93670

Diocesan Council, Sec., Armen Hampar, 6134 Pat Ave., Woodland Hills, CA 91367

Canadian Diocese

Primate, His Em. Archbishop Hovnan Derderian

PERIODICALS

The Armenian Church; The Mother Church

Elim Fellowship

The Elim Fellowship, a Pentecostal Body established in 1947, is an outgrowth of the Elim Missionary Assemblies formed in 1933.

It is an association of churches, ministers and missionaries seeking to serve the whole Body of Christ. It is of Pentecostal conviction and charismatic orientation, providing ministerial credentials and counsel and encouraging fellowship among local churches. Elim Fellowship sponsors leadership seminars at home and abroad and serves as a transdenominational agency sending long-term, short-term and tent-making missionaries to work with national movements.

HEADQUARTERS

7245 College St., Lima, NY 14485 Tel. (716)582-2790 Fax (716)624-1229

Media Contact, Gen. Sec., Chester Gretz

OFFICERS

Gen. Overseer, L. Dayton Reynolds
Asst. Gen. Overseer, Bernard J. Evans
Gen. Sec., Chester Gretz
Gen. Treas., Kenneth Beukema

PERIODICAL

Elim Herald

Episcopal Church

The Episcopal Church entered the colonies with the earliest settlers at Jamestown, Va., in 1607 as the Church of England. After the American Revolution, it became autonomous in 1789 as The Protestant Episcopal Church in the United States of America. (The Episcopal Church became the official alternate name in 1967.) Samuel Seabury of Connecticut was elected the first bishop and consecrated in Aberdeen by bishops of the Scottish Episcopal Church in 1784.

In organizing as an independent body, The Episcopal Church created a bicameral legislature, the General Convention, modeled after the new U.S. Congress. It comprises a House of Bishops and a House of Clerical and Lay Deputies and meets every three years. A 38-member Executive Council, which meets three times a year, is the interim governing body. An elected presiding bishop serves as Primate and Chief Pastor.

After severe setbacks in the years immediately following the Revolution because of its association with the British Crown and the fact that a number of its clergy and members were Loyalists, the church soon established its own identity and sense of mission. It sent missionaries into the newly settled territories of the United States, establishing dioceses from coast to coast, and also undertook substantial missionary work in Africa, Latin America and the Far East. Today, the overseas dioceses are developing into independent provinces of the Anglican Communion, the worldwide fellowship of churches in communion with the Church of England and the Archbishop of Canterbury.

The beliefs and practices of The Episcopal Church, like those of other Anglican churches, are both Catholic and Reformed, with bishops in the apostolic succession and the historic creeds of Christendom regarded as essential elements of faith and order, along with the primary authority of Holy Scripture and the two chief sacraments of Baptism and Eucharist.

EPISCOPAL CHURCH CENTER

815 Second Ave., New York, NY 10017 Tel. (212)867-8400 Fax (212)949-8059
Media Contact, News Dir., James Solheim

OFFICERS

Presiding Bishop & Primate, The Most Rev. Edmond L. Browning
House of Deputies: Pres., Mrs. Pamela Chinnis
Treas., Mrs. Ellen Cooke
Sec., The Rev. Donald A. Nickerson, Jr.

OFFICE OF THE PRESIDING BISHOP

Presiding Bishop, The Most Rev. Edmond L. Browning
Deputy for Admn., The Rev. Richard Chang
Information Officer, Barbara Braver
Exec. Dir., Office of Pastoral Dev., The Rt. Rev. Harold Hopkins, Jr.
Suffragan Bishop for the Armed Forces, The Rt. Rev. Charles L. Keyser
Suffragan Bishop for American Churches in Europe, The Rt. Rev. Jeffrey Rowthorn

Prof. Ministry Dev., The Rev. John Docker

ADMINISTRATIVE AND FINANCIAL GROUP

Treas. & Senior Exec., Mrs. Ellen Cooke
Asst. Treas., J. Thompson Hiller
Business Systems, Barbara Kelleher Bunten
Contracts & Services, Robert E. Brown
Episcopal Parish Services, James Vest
Human Resources, John Colon

PROGRAM GROUP

Senior Exec., Diane Porter

ADVOCACY, WITNESS AND JUSTICE

Exec., Diane Porter
Asiamerica Ministry, The Rev. Winston Ching
Hispanic Ministry, The Rev. Herbert Arrunategui
Jubilee Ministry, Ntsiki Kabane-Langford
Native American Ministry, Owanah Anderson
Peace & Justice Ministry, The Rev. Brian Grieves
Rural & Small Town Ministry, The Rev. Allen Brown
Washington Ofc.: The Rev. Robert Brooks; Dr. Betty Coats
Episcopal Migration Ministry, The Rev. Canon Burgess Carr
AIDS Ministry, The Rev. Randolph Frew

COMMUNICATION

Exec., Sonia Francis
Electronic Media, The Rev. Clement Lee
Publications, Frank Tedeschi
News Dir., James Solheim
Episcopal Life, Jerrold Hames
Interpretation, John Ratti
Art Dir., Rochelle Arthur

EDUCATION, EVANGELISM & MINISTRY DEV.

Exec., The Rev. David Perry
Children's Ministry, The Rev. Howard Williams
Youth Ministry, The Rev. Sheryl Kujawa
Evangelism, The Rev. A. Wayne Schwab
Liturgy & Music, The Rev. Clayton Morris
Adult Education, Leadership Dev., The Rev. Linda Grenz

PARTNERSHIPS

Exec., The Rev. Patrick Mauney
Ecumenical Officer, The Rev. William Norgren
Mission Personnel, Dorothy Gist
Africa, R. Nathaniel Porter
East Asia, Pacific & Middle East, The Rev. Mark Harris
Latin America & the Caribbean, The Rev. Ricardo Potter
Women in Mission & Ministry, Ann Smith

PLANNING AND DEVELOPMENT GROUP

Senior Exec. & Deputy for PBFWR, Barry Menuez
Exec., The Rev. Bill Carradine
Development, Timothy Holder
Grants Dir., Nancy Marvel
Planning Officer, Vernon Hazelwood
Stewardship, Laura Wright
Planned Giving, Frederick Osborn

RELATED AGENCIES

Church Pension Group, Alan Blanshard
Episcopal Church Foundation, William Andersen
Archives, Mark Duffy

BISHOPS IN THE U.S.A.

C, Coadjutor; S, Suffragan; A Assistant
Address: Right Reverend

Headquarters Staff: Presiding Bishop & Primate, The Most Rev. Edmond L. Browning; Pastoral Dev., Rt. Rev. Harold Hopkins; S. Bishop for Chaplaincies to Military\Prisons\Hosp., Rt. Rev. Charles L. Keyser

Alabama: Robert O. Miller, 521 N. 20th St., Birmingham, AL 35203

Alaska: Steve Charleston, Box 441, Fairbanks, AK 99707

Albany: David S. Ball, 62 S. Swan St., Albany, NY 12210

Arizona: Joseph T. Heistand; Robert Shahan, (C), P.O. Box 13647, Phoenix, AZ 85002

Arkansas: Larry Maze; Herbert Donovan, Jr., P.O. Box 164668, Little Rock, AR 72216

Atlanta: Frank Kellog Allan, 2744 Peachtree Rd. N.W., Atlanta, GA 30305

Bethlehem: J. Mark Dyer, 333 Wyandotte St., Bethlehem, PA 18015

California: William E. Swing, 1055 Taylor St., San Francisco, CA 94108

Central Florida: John H. Howe, 1017 E. Robinson St., Orlando, FL 32801

Central Gulf Coast: Charles F. Duvall, 201 North Baylen, Pensacola, FL 32591-3330

Central New York: David B. Joslin, 310 Montgomery St., Syracuse, NY 13203

Central Pennsylvania: Charlie F. McNutt, P.O. Box W, Harrisburg, PA 17108

Chicago: Frank T. Griswold, III; William Wiedrich, (S), 65 E. Huron St., Chicago, IL 60611

Colorado: William J. Winterrond, 1300 Washington St., Denver, CO 80203

Connecticut: Arthur E. Walmsley; Clarence N. Coleridge, (C), 1335 Asylum Ave., Hartford, CT 06105

Dallas: James Stanton, 1630 Garrett St., Dallas, TX 75206

Delaware: Calvin C. Tennis, 2020 Tatnall St., Wilmington, DE 19802

East Carolina: B. Sidney Sanders, P.O. Box 1336, Kinston, NC 28501

East Tennessee: William E. Sanders; Robert Tharp, (C), 401 Cumberland Ave., Knoxville, TN 37902-2302

Eastern Oregon: Rustin R. Kimsey, P.O. Box 620, The Dalles, OR 97058

Easton: Martin G. Townshend, P.O. Box 1027, Easton, MD 21601

Eau Claire: William C. Wantland, 510 S. Farwell St., Eau Claire, WI 54701

El Camino Real: Richard Shimpfky, P.O. Box 1093, Monterey, CA 93940

Florida: Frank S. Cerveny, 325 Market St., Jacksonville, FL 32202

Fond du Lac: William L. Stevens, P.O. Box 149, Fond du Lac, WI 54935

Fort Worth: Clarence Cullam Pope, Jr.; Jack Iker, (C), 7300 Ridgelea Pl., Ste. 1100, Fort Worth, TX 76116

Georgia: Harry W. Shipps, 611 East Bay St., Savannah, GA 31401

Hawaii: Donald P. Hart, Queen Emma Square, Honolulu, HI 93813

Idaho: John S. Thornton, IV, Box 936, Boise, ID 83701

Indianapolis: Edward W. Jones, 1100 W. 42nd St., Indianapolis, IN 46208

Iowa: C. Christopher Epting, 225 37th St., Des Moines, IA 50312

Kansas: William E. Smalley, Bethany Place, Topeka, KS 66612

Kentucky: David B. Reed, 421 S. 2nd St., Louisville, KY 40202

Lexington: Don A. Wimberly, P.O. Box 610, Lexington, KY 40586

Long Island: Orris G. Walker, 36 Cathedral Ave., Garden City, NY 11530

Los Angeles: Federick H. Borsch; Chester Talton, (S), P.O. Box 2164, Los Angeles, CA 90051-2145

Louisiana: James Barrow Brown, 1623 7th St., New Orleans, LA 70115

Maine: Edward C. Chalfant, 143 State St., Portland, ME 04101

Maryland: A. Theodore Eastman; Charles L. Longest, (S), 4 E. University Blvd., Baltimore, MD 21218

Massachusetts: David Elliott Johnson; Barbara Harris, (S), 138 Tremont St., Boston, MA 02111

Michigan: R. Stewart Wood; Harry Irving Mayson, (S), 4800 Woodward Ave., Detroit, MI 48201

Milwaukee: Roger J. White, 804 E. Juneau Ave., Milwaukee, WI 53202

Minnesota: James Jelinek; Sanford Hampton, (S), 309 Clinton Ave., Minneapolis, MN 55403

Mississippi: Duncan M. Gray, Jr.; Alfred Marble, Jr., (S), P.O. Box 2307, Jackson, MS 39225-3107

Missouri: Hays Rockwell, 1210 Locust St., St. Louis, MO 63103

Montana: Charles I. Jones, 515 North Park Ave., Helena, MT 59601

Nebraska: James E. Krotz, 200 N. 62nd St., Omaha, NE 68132

Nevada: Stewart C. Zabriski, 2930 W. 7th St., Reno, NV 89503

New Hampshire: Douglas E. Theuner, 63 Green St., Concord, NH 03301

New Jersey: G. P. Mellick Belshaw; Joe M. Dees, (C), 808 W. State St., Trenton, NJ 08618

New York: Richard F. Grein; Walter D. Dennis, (S), 1047 Amsterdam Ave., New York, NY 10025

Newark: John Shelby Spong; Jack McKelvey, (S), 24 Rector St., Newark, NJ 07102

North Carolina: Robert W. Estill; Frank H. Vest, Jr., (S), 201 St. Alban's, P.O. Box 17025, Raleigh, NC 27609

North Dakota: Andrew H. Fairfield, P.O. Box 10337, Fargo, ND 58106

Northern California: Jerry A. Lamb, 1322 27th St., P.O. Box 131268, Sacramento, CA 95816

Northern Indiana: Frank C. Gray, 117 N. Lafayette Blvd., South Bend, IN 46601

Northern Michigan: Thomas K. Ray, 131 E. Ridge St., Marquette, MI 49855

Northwest Texas: Sam Byron Hulsey, 1802 Broadway, P.O. Box 1067, Lubbock, TX 79408

Northwestern Pennsylvania: Robert D. Rowley, 145 W. 6th St., Erie, PA 16501

Ohio: James R. Moodey; Arthur B. Williams, (S), 2230 Euclid Ave., Cleveland, OH 44115

Oklahoma: Robert M. Moody; William J. Cox, (A), 924 N. Robinson, Oklahoma City, OK 73102

Olympia: Vincent W. Warner, 1551 Tenth Ave. E., Seattle, WA 98102

Oregon: Robert Louis Ladehoff, P.O. Box 467, Portland, OR 97034

Pennsylvania: Allan C. Bartlett; Franklin D. Turner, (S), 240 South 4th St., Philadelphia, PA 19106

Pittsburgh: Alden M. Hathaway, 325 Oliver Ave., Pittsburgh, PA 15222

Quincy: Edward H. MacBurney, 3601 N. North St., Peoria, IL 61604

Rhode Island: George Hunt, 275 N. Main St., Providence, RI 02903

Rio Grande: Terence Kelshaw, 4304 Carlisle NE, Albuquerque, NM 87107

Rochester: William G. Burrill, Jr., 935 East Ave., Rochester, NY 14607

San Diego: Gethin B. Hughes, St. Paul's Church, 2728 6th Ave., San Diego, CA 92103

San Joaquin: David Schofield, 4159 East Dakota, Fresno, CA 93726

South Carolina: Edward L. Salmon; G. Edward Haynesworth, (A), P.O. Box 20127, Charleston, SC 29413-0127

South Dakota: ———, 200 W. 18th St., P.O. Box 517, Sioux Falls, SD 57101

Southeast Florida: Calvin O. Schofield, Jr., 525 NE 15 St., Miami, FL 33132

Southern Ohio: Herbert Thompson, Jr., 412 Sycamore St., Cincinnati, OH 45202

Southern Virginia: Frank H. Vest, 600 Talbot Hill Rd., Norfolk, VA 23505

Southwest Florida: Rogers S. Harris, P.O. Box 491, St. Petersburg, FL 33731

Southwestern Virginia: A. Heath Light, P.O. Box 2068, Roanoke, VA 24009

Spokane: Frank J. Terry, 245 E. 13th Ave., Spokane, WA 99202

Springfield: Donald M. Hulstrand; Peter H. Beckwith, 821 S. 2nd St., Springfield, IL 62704

Tennessee: Bertram M. Herlong, One LeFleur Bldg., Ste. 100, 50 Vantage Way, Nashville, TN 37228

Texas: Maurice M. Benitez; Claude E. Payne, (C); Anselmo Carroll, (A), 3023 W. Alabama St., Houston, TX 77098

Upper South Carolina: William A. Beckhan, (S), P.O. Box 1789, Columbia, SC 29202

Utah: George E. Bates, 231 E. First St. S., Salt Lake City, UT 84111

Vermont: Mary Adelia McLeod, Rock Point, Burlington, VT 05401

Virginia: Peter J. Lee; Frank C. Matthews, (S); David H. Lewis, Jr., (S), 110 W. Franklin St., Richmond, VA 23220

Washington: Ronald Haines; Jane H. Dixon, (S), Mt. St. Alban, Washington, DC 20016

West Missouri: John Buchanan, P.O. Box 413227, P.O. Box 23216, Kansas City, MO 64141

West Tennessee: Alex D. Dickson; James M. Coleman, (C), 692 Poplar Ave., Memphis, TN 38105

West Texas: John H. McNaughton; Earl N. MacArthur, (S), P.O. Box 6885, San Antonio, TX 78209

West Virginia: Robert P. Atkinson; William Franklin Carr, (S), 1608 Virginia St. E., Charleston, WV 25311

Western Kansas: John F. Ashby, 142 S. 8th St., P.O. Box 1383, Salina, KS 67401

Western Louisiana: Robert J. Hargrove, P.O. Box 2031, Alexandria, LA 71309

Western Massachusetts: Robert S. Denig, 37 Chestnut St., Springfield, MA 01103

Western Michigan: Edward L. Lee, Jr., 2600 Vincent Ave., Kalamazoo, MI 49001

Western New York: David C. Bowman, 1114 Delaware Ave., Buffalo, NY 14209

Western North Carolina: William G. Weinhauer, P.O. Box 369, Black Mountain, NC 28711

Wyoming: Bob Gordon Jones, 104 W. 4th St., Box 1007, Laramie, WY 82070

Am. Churches in Europe—Jurisdiction: Jeffrey Rowthorn, The American Cathedral, 23 Avenue Georges V, 75008, Paris, France

Navajoland Area Mission: Steven Plummer, P.O. Box 720, Farmington, NM 47401

The Estonian Evangelical Lutheran Church

For information on the Estonian Evangelical Lutheran Church (EELC), please see the listing in Chapter 4, "Religious Bodies in Canada."

HEADQUARTERS

383 Jarvis St., Toronto, ON M5B 2C7

The Evangelical Church

The Evangelical Church was born June 4, 1968 in Portland, Ore., when 46 congregations and about 80 ministers, under the leadership of V. A. Ballantyne and George Millen, met in an organizing session. Within two weeks a group of about 20 churches and 30 ministers from the Evangelical United Brethren and Methodist churches in Montana and North Dakota became a part of the new church. Richard Kienitz and Robert Strutz were the superintendents.

Under the leadership of Superintendent Robert Trosen, the former Holiness Methodist Church became a part of the Evangelical Church in 1969, bringing its membership and a flourishing mission field in Bolivia. The Wesleyan Covenant Church joined in 1977, with its missionary work in Mexico, in Brownsville, Tex. and among the Navahos in New Mexico.

The Evangelical Church in Canada, where T. J. Jesske was superintendent, became an autonomous organization on June 5, 1970. In 1982, after years of discussions with the Evangelical Church of North America, a founding General Convention was held at Billings, Mont., where the two churches united. In 1993 the Canadian conference merged with the Canadian portion of the Missionary Church to form the Evangelical Missionary Church. The new group maintains close ties with their American counterparts. Currently there are nearly 150 U.S. congregations of the Evangelical Church.

The following guide the life, program and devotion of this church: faithful, biblical and sensible preaching and teaching of those truths proclaimed by scholars of the Wesleyan-Arminian viewpoint; an itinerant system which reckons with the rights of individuals and the desires of the congregation; local ownership of all church properties and assets.

The church is officially affiliated with the Christian Holiness Association, the National Association of Evangelicals, Wycliffe Bible Translators, World Gospel Mission and OMS International. The denom- ination has more than 150 missionaries.

HEADQUARTERS

Media Contact, Gen. Supt., John F. Sills, 3000 Market St. NE, Ste. 528, Salem, OR 97301 Tel. (503)371-4818 Fax (503)375-9646

OFFICERS

Gen. Supt., Rev. John F. Sills
Dir. of Missions, Rev. Duane Erickson

PERIODICALS

Share; The Challenge

The Evangelical Church Alliance

The Evangelical Church Alliance was incorporated in 1928 in Missouri as The World's Faith Missionary Association and was later known as The Fundamental Ministerial Association. The title Evangelical Church Alliance was adopted in 1958.

ECA licenses and ordains ministers who are qualified and provides them with credentials from a recognized ecclesiastical body; provides through the Bible Extension Institute courses of study to those who have not had seminary or Bible school training; provides an organization for autonomous churches so they may have communion and association with one another; provides an organization for autonomous churches so they may have communion and association with one another; provides an organization where members can find companionship through correspondence, Regional Conventions and General Conventions; and cooperates with churches in finding new pastors when vacancies occur in their pulpits.

ECA is an interdenominational, nonsectarian, Evangelical organization. There are 1882 ordained and licensed clergy members.

HEADQUARTERS

205 W. Broadway St., P.O. Box 9, Bradley, IL 60915 Tel. (815)937-0720 Fax (815)937-0001
Media Contact, Exec. Dir., Rev. George L. Miller

OFFICERS

Exec. Dir., Rev. George L. Miller
Pres., Dr. Sterling L. Cauble, Sunman Bible Church, P.O. Box 216, Sunman, IN 47041
1st Vice-Pres., Rev. Richard J. Sydnes, P.O. Box 355, Des Moines, IA 50302
2nd Vice-Pres., Dr. Allen A. Hammond, 1921 Ohio St., Bluefield, WV 24701

The Evangelical Congregational Church

This denomination had its beginning in the movement known as the Evangelical Association, organized by Jacob Albright in the early nineteenth century. A division which occurred in 1891 in the Evangelical Association resulted in the organization of the United Evangelical Church in 1894. An attempt to heal this division was made in 1922, but a portion of the United Evangelical Church was not satisfied with the plan of merger and remained apart, taking the above name in 1928. This denomination is Arminian in doctrine, evangelistic in spirit and Methodistic in church government, with congregational ownership of local church property.

Congregations are located from New Jersey to Illinois. A denominational center, a retirement village and a seminary are located in Myerstown, Pa. Three summer youth camps and four camp meetings continue evangelistic outreach. A worldwide missions movement includes conferences in North East India, Liberia, Mexico and Japan. The denomination is a member of National Association of Evangelicals.

HEADQUARTERS

Evangelical Congregational Church Center, 100 W. Park Ave., P.O. Box 186, Myerstown, PA 17067 Tel. (717)866-7581 Fax (717)866-7581
Media Contact, Bishop, Rev. Richard W. Kohl, Tel. (717)-866-7581

OFFICERS

Presiding Bishop, Rev. Richard W. Kohl
1st Vice-Chpsn., Rev. Robert W. Daneker, Sr., 122 S. Emerson St., Allentown, PA 18104
Sec., Rev. Robert J. Stahl, RD 2, Box 1468, Schuylkill Haven, PA 17972

Asst. Sec.: Rev. Gregory Dimick, Hatfield, PA; Rev. Richard Reigle, Dixon, IL
Treas., Martha Metz
E.C.C. Retirement Village, Supt., Rev. Franklin H. Schock, Fax (717)866-6448
Evangelical School of Theology, Acting Pres., Dr. Kirby N. Keller, Fax (717)866-4667

OTHER ORGANIZATIONS

Administrative Council: Chpsn., Bishop Richard W. Kohl; Vice-Chpsn., Rev. Robert W. Daneker; Treas., Martha Metz
Div. of Evangelism & Spiritual Care, Chpsn., Bishop Richard W. Kohl
Div. of Church Ministries & Services, Chpsn., Rev. Keith R. Miller
Div. of Missions, Chpsn., Rev. David G. Hornberger
Bd. of Pensions: Pres., Mr. Homer Luckenbill, Jr., Pine Grove, PA; Sec., Dr. James D. Yoder, Myerstown, PA 17067

The Evangelical Covenant Church

The Evangelical Covenant Church has its roots in historic Christianity as it emerged during the Protestant Reformation, in the biblical instruction of the Lutheran State Church of Sweden and in the great spiritual awakenings of the 19th century.

The Covenant Church adheres to the affirmations of the Protestant Reformation regarding the Holy Scriptures, believing that the Old and the New Testament are the Word of God and the only perfect rule for faith, doctrine and conduct. It has traditionally valued the historic confessions of the Christian church, particularly the Apostles' Creed, while at the same time emphasizing the sovereignty of the Word over all creedal interpretations. It has especially cherished the pietistic restatement of the doctrine of justification by faith as basic to its dual task of evangelism and Christian nurture. It recognizes the New Testament emphasis upon personal faith in Jesus Christ as Savior and Lord, the reality of a fellowship of believers which acknowledges but transcends theological differences and the belief in baptism and the Lord's Supper as divinely ordained sacraments of the church.

While the denomination has traditionally practiced the baptism of infants, in conformity with its principle of freedom it has given room to divergent views. The principle of personal freedom, so highly esteemed by the Covenant, is to be distinguished from the individualism that disregards the centrality of the Word of God and the mutual responsibilities and disciplines of the spiritual community.

HEADQUARTERS

5101 N. Francisco Ave., Chicago, IL 60625 Tel. (312)784-3000 Fax (312)784-4366
Media Contact, Pres., Paul E. Larsen

OFFICERS

Pres., Dr. Paul E. Larsen

PERIODICALS

Covenant Companion; Covenant Quarterly; Covenant Home Altar

The Evangelical Free Church of America

In October 1884, 27 representatives from Swedish churches met in Boone, Iowa, to establish the Swedish Evangelical Free Church. In the fall of that same year, two Norwegian-Danish groups began worship and fellowship (in Boston and in Tacoma) and by 1912 had established the Norwegian-Danish Evangelical Free Church Association. These two denominations, representing 275 congregations, came together at a merger conference in 1950.

The Evangelical Free Church is an association of local, autonomous churches across the United States and Canada, blended together by common principles, policies and practices. A 12-point statement addresses the major doctrines but also provides for differences of understanding on minor issues of faith and practice.

Overseas outreach includes 450 missionaries serving in 21 countries.

HEADQUARTERS

901 East 78th St., Minneapolis, MN 55420-1300 Tel. (612)854-1300 Fax (612)853-8488
Media Contact, Dir. of Communications, Mr. Timothy Addington

OFFICERS

Pres., Dr. Paul Cedar
Exec. Vice-Pres., Rev. William Hamel
Mod., Rev. Joseph Bubar, Jr., 3936 CTH "B", LaCrosse, WI 54601
Vice-Mod., Mr. Ronald Aucutt, 3417 Silver Maple Pl., Falls Church, VA 22042
Sec., Dr. Roland Peterson, 235 Craigbrook Way, NE, Fridley, MN 55432
Vice-Sec., Rev. William S. Wick, 92 South Main, Northfield, VT 05663
Chief Fin. Ofc., Mr. Robert Peterson, 901 E. 78th St., Minneapolis, MN 55420-1300
Fin. Sec., Mr. James Hagman, 1895 Hampshire La., Golden Valley, MN 55427
Exec. Dir., Evangelical Free Church Mission, Dr. Ben Swatsky
Exec. Dir. of Church Ministries, Rev. Bill Hull

PERIODICAL

Evangelical Beacon

Evangelical Friends International—North America Region

The organization restructured from Evangelical Friends Alliance in 1990 to become internationalized for the benefit of its world-wide contacts. The North America Region continues to function within the United States as EFA formerly did. The organization represents one corporate step of denominational unity, brought about as a result of several movements of spiritual renewal within the Society of Friends. These movements are: (1) the general evangelical renewal within Christianity, (2) the new scholarly recognition of the evangelical nature of 17th-century Quakerism, and (3) EFA, which was formed in 1965.

The EFA is conservative in theology and makes use of local pastors. Sunday morning worship includes singing, Scripture reading, a period of open worship and a sermon by the pastor.

HEADQUARTERS

393 S. Vaughn Way, Aurora, CO 80012 Tel. (303)363-0116 Fax (303)363-0116
Media Contact, Regional Dir., Stanley Perisho

YEARLY MEETINGS

Evangelical Friends Church, Eastern Region, Ron Johnson, 5350 Broadmoor Cir., N.W., Canton, OH 44709 Tel. (216)493-1660 Fax (216)493-0852
Rocky Mountain YM, John Brawner, 3350 Reed St., Wheat Ridge, CO 80033 Tel. (303)238-5200 Fax (303)766-9609
Mid-America YM, Roscoe Townsend, 2018 Maple, Wichita, KS 67213 Tel. (316)267-0391 Fax (316)263-1092
Northwest YM, Mark Ankeny, 200 N. Meridian St., Newberg, OR 97132 Tel. (503)538-9419 Fax (503)538-7033
Alaska YM, P.O. Box 687, Kotebue, AK 99752 Tel. (907)442-3906

PERIODICAL

Evangelical Friend

Evangelical Lutheran Church in America

The Evangelical Lutheran Church in America (ELCA) was organized April 30-May 3, 1987, in Columbus, Ohio, bringing together the 2.3 million-member American Lutheran Church, the 2.9 million-member Lutheran Church in America, and the 100,000-member Association of Evangelical Lutheran Churches.

The ELCA is, through its predecessors, the oldest of the major U.S. Lutheran churches. In the mid-17th century, a Dutch Lutheran congregation was formed in New Amsterdam (now New York). Other early congregations were begun by German and Scandinavian immigrants to Delaware, Pennsylvania, New York and the Carolinas.

The first Lutheran association of congregations, the Pennsylvania Ministerium, was organized in 1748 under Henry Melchior Muhlenberg. Numerous Lutheran organizations were formed as immigration continued and the United States grew.

In 1960, the American Lutheran Church (ALC) was created through a merger of an earlier American Lutheran Church, formed in 1930, the Evangelical Lutheran Church, begun in 1917, and the United Evangelical Lutheran Church in America. In 1963 the Lutheran Free Church merged with the ALC.

In 1962, the Lutheran Church in America (LCA) was formed by a merger of the United Lutheran Church, formed in 1918, with the Augustana Lutheran Church, begun in 1860, the American Evangelical Lutheran Church, founded in 1872, and the Finnish Lutheran Church or Suomi Synod, founded in 1891.

The Association of Evangelical Lutheran Churches arose in 1976 from a doctrinal split with the Lutheran Church-Missouri Synod.

The ELCA, through its predecessor church bodies, was a founding member of the Lutheran World Federation, the World Council of Churches, and the National Council of the Churches of Christ in the USA.

The church is divided into 65 geographical areas or synods. These 65 synods are grouped into nine regions for mission, joint programs and service.

HEADQUARTERS

8765 W. Higgins Rd., Chicago, IL 60631 Tel. (312)380-2700
Media Contact, Dir. for News, Ann E. Haften, Tel. (312)380-2957 Fax (312)380-1465

81

OFFICERS

Bishop, The Rev. Dr. Herbert W. Chilstrom
Sec., The Rev. Dr. Lowell G. Almen
Treas., Richard L. McAuliffe
Vice-Pres., Kathy J. Magnus
Exec. for Admn., Rev. Dr. Robert N. Bacher
Office of the Bishop: Exec. Asst. for Federal Chaplaincies, Rev. Lloyd W. Lyngdal; Exec. Assts., Lita B. Johnson; Rev. Dr. Craig Lewis; Rev. Lee S. Thoni

DIVISIONS

Div. for Congregational Min.: Exec. Dir., Revs. Mark R. & Mary Ann Moller-Gunderson; Bd. Chpsn., Jim Myers; Lutheran Youth Organization, Pres., Tim Seitz
Div. for Higher Educ. & Schools: Exec. Dir., Rev. Dr. W. Robert Sorensen; Bd. Chpsn., Rev. Stephen P. Bauman
Div. for Global Mission: Exec. Dir., Rev. Dr. Mark W. Thomsen; Bd. Chpsn., Marjorie J. Carlson
Div. for Ministry: Exec. Dir., Rev. Dr. Joseph M. Wagner; Bd. Chpsn., Marybeth A. Peterson
Div. for Outreach: Exec. Dir., Rev. Dr. Malcolm L. Minnick, Jr.; Bd. Chpsn., Susan C. Barnard
Div. for Church in Society: Exec. Dir., Rev. Charles S. Miller; Chpsn., Ingrid Christiansen

COMMISSIONS

Comm. for Multicultural Ministries: Exec. Dir., Rev. Fred E.N. Rajan; Chpsn., Rev. Dr. Edmond Yee
Comm. for Women: Exec. Dir., Joanne Chadwick; Chpsn., Audrey R. Mortensen

CHURCHWIDE UNITS

Conference of Bishops: Interim Dir., Rev. Harold R. Lohr; Chpsn., Rev. Dr. Kenneth H. Sauer
ELCA Foundation: Exec. Dir., Rev. Dr. Harvey A. Stegemoeller; Bd. Chpsn., William R. Halling
ELCA Publishing House: Exec. Dir., Gary J. N. Aamodt; Bd. Chpsn., Rev. Dr. David L. Tiede
ELCA Bd. of Pensions: Exec. Dir., John G. Kapanke; Bd. Chpsn, Mildred M. Berg
Women of the ELCA: Exec. Dir., Charlotte E. Fiechter; Bd. Chpsn., Janet Peterson

DEPARTMENTS

Dept. for Communication, Dir., Rev. Eric C. Shafer
Dept. for Ecumenical Affairs, Dir., Rev. Dr. William G. Rusch
Dept. for Human Resources, Dr., Rev. A. C. Stein
Dept. for Research & Evaluation, Dir., Kenneth W. Inskeep
Dept. for Synodical Relations, Dir., Rev. Harold R. Lohr

SYNODICAL BISHOPS

Region 1
Alaska, Rev. Donald D. Parsons, 1836 W. Northern Lights Blvd., Anchorage, AK 99517-3342 Tel. (907)272-8899
Northwest Washington, Rev. Dr. Lowell E. Knutson, 5519 Pinney Ave. N, Seattle, WA 98103-5899 Tel. (206)783-9292
Southwestern Washington, Rev. David C. Wold, 420 121st St., S., Tacoma, WA 98444-5218 Tel. (206)535-8300
Eastern Washington-Idaho, Rev. Robert M. Keller, 314 South Spruce St., Ste. A, Spokane, WA 99204-1098 Tel. (509)838-9871
Oregon, Rev. Paul R. Swanson, 2801 N. Gantenbein Ave., Portland, OR 97227-1674 Tel. (503)280-4191

Montana, Rev. Dr. Mark R. Ramseth, 2415 13th Ave. S., Great Falls, MT 59405-5199 Tel. (406)453-1461
Regional Coord., Ronald L. Coen, Region 1, 766-B John St., Seattle, WA 98109-5186 Tel. (206)624-0093

Region 2
Sierra Pacific, Rev. Lyle G. Miller, 401 Roland Way, #215, Oakland, CA 94621-2011 Tel. (510)430-0500
Southern California (West), Rev. J. Roger Anderson, 1340 S. Bonnie Brae St., Los Angeles, CA 90006-5416 Tel. (213)387-8183
Pacifica, Rev. Robert L. Miller, 23655 Via Del Rio, Ste. B, Yorba Linda, CA 92687-2718 Tel. (714)692-2791
Grand Canyon, Rev. Dr. Howard E. Wennes, 4423 N. 24th St., Ste. 400, Phoenix, AZ 85016-5544 Tel. (602)957-3223
Rocky Mountain, Rev. Elwin D. Farwell, 7000 Broadway Ofc. Bldg., Ste. 401, 7000 N. Broadway, Denver, CO 80211-2907 Tel. (303)427-7553
Regional Coord., Rev. James E. Miley, Region 2, 2700 Chandler, Ste. A6, Las Vegas, NV 89120-4029 Tel. (702)798-3980

Region 3
Western North Dakota, Rev. Robert D. Lynne, 721 Memorial Way, P.O. Box 370, Bismarck, ND 58502-3070 Tel. (701)223-5312
Eastern North Dakota, Rev. Richard J. Foss, 1703 32nd Ave., S., Fargo, ND 58103-5936 Tel. (701)232-3381
South Dakota, Rev. Norman D. Eitrheim, Augustana College, Sioux Falls, SD 57197-0001 Tel. (605)336-4011
Northwestern Minnesota, Rev. Dr. Arthur V. Rimmereid, Concordia College, Moorhead, MN 56561-0001 Tel. (218)299-3019
Northeastern Minnesota, Rev. Roger L. Munson, 3900 London Rd., Duluth, MN 55804-2241 Tel. (218)525-1947
Southwestern Minnesota, Rev. Charles D. Anderson, 175 E. Bridge St., P.O. Box 277, Redwood Falls, MN 56283-0277 Tel. (507)637-3904
Minneapolis Area, Rev. David W. Olson, 122 W. Franklin Ave., Rm. 600, Minneapolis, MN 55404-2474 Tel. (612)870-3610
Saint Paul Area, Rev. Lowell O. Erdahl, 105 W. University Ave., St. Paul, MN 55103-2094 Tel. (612)224-4313
Southeastern Minnesota, Rev. Glenn W. Nycklemoe, Assisi Heights, 1001-14 St. NW, P.O. Box 4900, Rochester, MN 55903-4900 Tel. (507)280-9457
Regional Coord., Ms. Shirley A. Teig, Region 3, Bockman Hall, 2481 Como Ave., W. St. Paul, MN 55108 Tel. (612)649-0454

Region 4
Nebraska, Rev. Dr. Richard N. Jessen, 4980 S. 118th St., Ste. D, Omaha, NE 68137-2220 Tel. (402)896-5311
Central States, Rev. Dr. Charles H. Maahs, 6400 Glenwood, Ste. 210, Shawnee Mission, KS 66202-4021 Tel. (913)362-0733
Arkansas-Oklahoma, Rev. Dr. Robert H. Studtmann, 4803 S. Lewis Ave., Tulsa, OK 74105-5199 Tel. (918)747-8517
Northern Texas-Northern Louisiana, Rev. Mark B. Herbener, 1230 Riverbend Dr., Ste. 105, P.O. Box 560587, Dallas, TX 75356-0587 Tel. (214)637-6865

Southwestern Texas, Rev. Henry Schulte, Jr., 1800 Northeast Loop 410, Ste. 202, P.O. Box 171270, San Antonio, TX 78217-8270 Tel. (210)824-0068

Texas-Louisiana Gulf Coast, Rev. Paul J. Blom, 12707 N. Freeway, #580, Houston, TX 77060-1239 Tel. (713)873-5665

Regional Coord., Rev. Roger J. Gieschen, Region 4, 6901 W. 63rd St., Rm. 205, Overland Park, KS 66202 Tel. (913)831-3727

Region 5

Metropolitan Chicago, Rev. Sherman G. Hicks, 18 S. Michigan Ave., Rm. 605, Chicago, IL 60603-3283 Tel. (312)346-3150

Northern Illinois, Rev. Ronald K. Hasley, 103 W. State St., Rockford, IL 61101-1105 Tel. (815)964-9934

Central/Southern Illinois, Rev. Dr. John P. Kaitschuk, 1201 Veterans Pkwy., Ste. D, Springfield, IL 62704-6321 Tel. (217)546-7915

Southeastern Iowa, Rev. Dr. Paul M. Werger, 2635 Northgate Dr., P.O. Box 3167, Iowa City, IA 52244-3167 Tel. (319)388-1273

Western Iowa, Rev. Curtis H. Miller, 318 E. Fifth St., P.O. Box 1145, Storm Lake, IA 50588-2312 Tel. (712)732-4968

Northeastern Iowa, Rev. Steven L. Ullestad, 201-20th St. SW, P.O. Box 804, Waverly, IA 50677-0804 Tel. (319)352-1414

Northern Great Lakes, Rev. Dale R. Skogman, 1029 N. Third St., Marquette, MI 49855-3588 Tel. (906)228-2300

Northwest Synod of Wisconsin, Rev. Gerhard I. Knutson, 12 W. Marshall St., P.O. Box 730, Rice Lake, WI 54868-0730 Tel. (715)234-3373

East-Central Synod of Wisconsin, Rev. Dr. Robert H. Herder, 16 Tri-Park Way, Appleton, WI 54914-1658 Tel. (414)734-5381

Greater Milwaukee, Rev. Peter Rogness, 1212 S. Layton Blvd., Milwaukee, WI 53215-1653 Tel. (414)671-1212

South-Central Synod of Wisconsin, Rev. Dr. Jon S. Enslin, 2705 Packers Ave., Madison, WI 53704-3085 Tel. (608)249-4848

LaCrosse Area, Rev. April Ulring Larson, 2350 S. Ave., Ste. 106, LaCrosse, WI 54601-6272 Tel. (608)788-5000

Regional Coord., Rev. Edward F. Weiskotten, Region 5, 333 Wartburg Pl., Dubuque, IA 52003-7797 Tel. (319)589-0312

Region 6

Southeast Michigan, Rev. J. Philip Wahl, 19711 Greenfield Rd., Detroit, MI 48235-2097 Tel. (313)837-3522

North/West Lower Michigan, Rev. Dr. Reginald H. Holle, 801 S. Waverly Rd., Ste. 201, Lansing, MI 48917-4254 Tel. (517)321-5066

Indiana-Kentucky, Rev. Dr. Ralph A. Kempski, 911 E. 86th St., Ste. 200, Indianapolis, IN 46260-1840 Tel. (317)846-4026

Northwestern Ohio, Rev. James A. Rave, 621 Bright Rd., Findlay, OH 45840-6987 Tel. (419)423-3664

Northeastern Ohio, Rev. Dr. Robert W. Kelley, 282 W. Bowery, 3rd Fl., Akron, OH 44307-2598 Tel. (216)253-1500

Southern Ohio, Rev. Dr. Kenneth H. Sauer, 57 E. Main St., Columbus, OH 43215-7102 Tel. (614)464-3532

Regional Coord., Rev. Hermann J. Kuhlmann, 6100 Channingway Blvd., Ste. 503, Columbus, OH 43232 Tel. (614)759-9090

Region 7

New Jersey, Rev. E. Leroy Riley, Jr., 1930 State Hwy. 33, Trenton, NJ 08690-1714 Tel. (609)586-6800

New England, Rev. Robert L. Isaksen, 90 Madison St., Ste. 303, Worcester, MA 01608-2030 Tel. (508)791-1530

Metropolitan New York, Rev. James E. Sudbrock, 390 Park Ave., S., 7th Floor, New York, NY 10016-8803 Tel. (212)532-6350

Upstate New York, Rev. Dr. Lee M. Miller, 3049 E. Genesee St., Syracuse, NY 13224 Tel. (315)446-2502

Northeastern Pennsylvania, Rev. Dr. Harold S. Weiss, 4865 Hamilton Blvd., Wescosville, PA 18106-9705 Tel. (215)395-6891

Southeastern Pennsylvania, Rev. Michael G. Merkel, 4700 Wissahickon Ave., Philadelphia, PA 19144-4248 Tel. (215)438-0600

Slovak Zion, Rev. Juan Cobrda, 8340 N. Oleander, Niles, IL 60648-2552 Tel. (312)545-7300

Regional Coord., Rev. George E. Handley, Region 7, Hagan Hall, 7301 Germantown Ave., Philadelphia, PA 19119 Tel. (215)248-4616

Region 8

Northwestern Pennsylvania, Rev. Paull E. Spring, Rte. 257, Salina Rd., P.O. Box 338, Seneca, PA 16346-0338 Tel. (814)677-5706

Southwestern Pennsylvania, Rev. Donald J. McCoid, 9625 Perry Hwy., Pittsburgh, PA 15237-5590 Tel. (412)367-8222

Allegheny, Rev. Gregory R. Pile, 701 Quail Ave., Altoona, PA 16602-3010 Tel. (814)942-1042

Lower Susquehanna, Rev. Dr. Guy S. Edmiston, Jr., 900 S. Arlington Ave., Rm. 208, Harrisburg, PA 17109-5031 Tel. (717)652-1852

Upper Susquehanna, Rev. Dr. A. Donald Main, Rt. 192 & Reitz Blvd., P.O. Box 36, Lewisburg, PA 17837-0036 Tel. (717)524-9778

Delaware-Maryland, Rev. Dr. George P. Mocko, 7604 York Rd., Baltimore, MD 21204-7570 Tel. (410)825-9520

Metropolitan Washington, D.C., Rev. Dr. E. Harold Jansen, 224 E. Capitol St., Washington, DC 20003-1036 Tel. (202)543-8610

West Virginia-Western Maryland, Rev. L. Alexander Black, The Atrium, Ste. 100, 503 Morgantown Avenue, Fairmont, WV 26554-4374 Tel. (304)363-4030

Regional Coord., Dir., Rev. Phillip C. Huber, Lutheran Theological Sem. at Gettysburg, 61 NW Confederate Ave., Gettysburg, PA 17325-1795 Tel. (717)334-6286

Region 9

Virginia, Rev. Richard F. Bansemer, Roanoke College, Bittle Hall, P.O. Drawer 70, Salem, VA 24153-3794 Tel. (703)389-1000

North Carolina, Rev. Dr. Mark W. Menees, 1988 Lutheran Synod Dr., Salisbury, NC 28144-4480 Tel. (704)633-4861

South Carolina, Rev. Dr. James S. Aull, 1003 Richland St., P.O. Box 43, Columbia, SC 29202-0043 Tel. (803)765-0590

Southeastern, Rev. Dr. Harold C. Skillrud, 756 W. Peachtree St. NW, Atlanta, GA 30308-1188 Tel. (404)873-1977

Florida-Bahamas, Rev. Lavern G. Franzen, 3838 W. Cypress St., Tampa, FL 33607-4897 Tel. (813)876-7660

Caribbean, Rev. Gregory J. Villalón, P.O. Box 14426, Barrio-Obrero Station, Santurce, PR 00916-4426 Tel. (809)727-6015

Regional Coord., Dr. Dorothy L. Jeffcoat, Region 9, 4201 N. Main St., Columbia, SC 29203 Tel. (803)754-2879

PERIODICALS
The Lutheran; Currents in Theology and Mission

Evangelical Lutheran Synod

The Evangelical Lutheran Synod had its beginning among the Norwegian settlers who brought with them their Lutheran heritage. The Synod was organized in 1853. It was reorganized in 1918 by those who desired to adhere to the synod's principles not only in word but also in deed.

The Synod owns and operates Bethany Lutheran College and Bethany Lutheran Theological Seminary. It has congregations in 18 states and maintains foreign missions in Peru, Chile, Czechoslovakia and Ukraine. It operates a seminary in Lima, Peru.

HEADQUARTERS
The Evangelical Lutheran Synod, 447 N. Division St., Mankato, MN 56001
Media Contact, Pres., Rev. George Orvick, Tel. (507)388-4868 Fax (507)625-1849

OFFICERS
Pres., Rev. George Orvick, 447 Division St., Mankato, MN 56001 Tel. (507)388-4868 Fax (507)625-1849
Sec., Rev. Alf Merseth, 106 13th St. S., Northwood, IA 50459
Treas., Mr. LeRoy W. Meyer, 1038 S. Lewis Ave., Lombard, IL 60148

OTHER ORGANIZATIONS
Lutheran Synod Book Co., Bethany Lutheran College, Mankato, MN 56001

PERIODICALS
Lutheran Sentinel; Lutheran Synod Quarterly

Evangelical Mennonite Church

The Evangelical Mennonite Church is an American denomination in the European free church tradition, tracing its heritage to the Reformation period of the 16th century. The Swiss Brethren of that time believed that salvation could come only by repentance for sins and faith in Jesus Christ; that baptism was only for believers; and that the church should be separate from controls of the state. Their enemies called them Anabaptists, since they insisted on rebaptizing believers who had been baptized as infants. As the Anabaptist movement spread to other countries, Menno Simons became its principal leader. In time his followers were called Mennonites.

In 1693 a Mennonite minister, Jacob Amman, insisted that the church should adopt a more conservative position on dress and style of living and should more rigidly enforce the "ban" — the church's method of disciplining disobedient members. Amman's insistence finally resulted in a division within the South German Mennonite groups; his followers became known as the Amish.

Migrations to America, involving both Mennonites and Amish, took place in the 1700s and 1800s, for both religious and economic reasons.

The Evangelical Mennonite Church was formed in 1866 out of a spiritual awakening among the Amish in Indiana. It was first known as the Egly Amish, after its founder Bishop Henry Egly.

Bishop Egly emphasized regeneration, separation and nonconformity to the world. His willingness to rebaptize anyone who had been baptized without repentance created a split in his church, prompting him to gather a new congregation in 1866. The conference, which has met annually since 1895, united a number of other congregations of like mind. This group became The Defenseless Mennonite Church in 1898 and has been known as the Evangelical Mennonite Church since 1948.

HEADQUARTERS
1420 Kerrway Ct., Fort Wayne, IN 46805 Tel. (219)423-3649 Fax (219)420-1905
Media Contact, Admn. Asst., Diane Rodocker

OFFICERS
Pres., Rev. Donald W. Roth
Chpsn., Rev. Roger Andrews, 11275 Eckel Junction Rd., Perrysburg, OH 43551
Vice-Chpsn., Rev. Scott Wagoner, Box 160, Grabill, IN 46741
Sec., Jerry Lugbill, 320 Short-Buehrer Rd., Archbold, OH 43502
Treas., Alan L. Rupp, 5724 Spring Oak Ct., Ft. Wayne, IN 46845

PERIODICAL
EMC Today

Evangelical Methodist Church

The Evangelical Methodist Church was organized in 1946 at Memphis, Tenn., largely as a movement of people who opposed modern liberalism and wished for a return to the historic Wesleyan position. In 1960, it merged with the Evangel Church (formerly Evangelistic Tabernacles) and with the People's Methodist Church in 1962.

HEADQUARTERS
3000 West Kellogg, Wichita, KS 67213 Tel. (316)943-3278
Media Contact, Gen. Conf. Sec.-Treas., Vernon W. Perkins, Fax (316)943-5939

OFFICERS
Gen. Supt., Rev. Clyde Zehr
Gen. Conf. Sec.-Treas., Rev. Vernon W. Perkins

Evangelical Presbyterian Church

The Evangelical Presbyterian Church (EPC), established in March 1981, is a conservative denomination of 9 geographic presbyteries — 8 in the United States and one in Argentina. From its inception with 12 churches, the EPC has grown to 180 churches with a membership of over 56,000.

Planted firmly within the historic Reformed tradition, evangelical in spirit, the EPC places high priority on church planting and development along with world missions. Forty-two missionaries serve the church's mission.

Based on the truth of Scripture and adhering to the Westminster Confession of Faith plus its Book of Order, the denomination is committed to the "essentials of the faith." The historic motto "In essentials, unity; in nonessentials, liberty; in all things charity" catches the irenic spirit of the EPC, along with the Ephesians theme, "truth in love."

The Evangelical Presbyterian Church is a member of the World Alliance of Reformed Churches, National Association of Evangelicals, World

Evangelical Fellowship and the Evangelical Council for Financial Accountability. Observers annually attend the North American Presbyterian and Reformed Council (NAPARC).

HEADQUARTERS

Office of the General Assembly, 29140 Buckingham Ave., Ste. 5, Livonia, MI 48154 Tel. (313)261-2001 Fax (313)261-3282

Media Contact, Stated Clk., Dr. L. Edward Davis, 29140 Buckingham Ave., Ste. 5, Livonia, MI 48154 Tel. (313)261-2001 Fax (313)261-3282

OFFICERS

Mod., Dr. Graham Smith, Faith Presbyterian Church, 6076-B Franconia Ad., Alexandria, VA 22310

Administration Committee, Chpsn., Mr. John Adamson, Second Presbyterian Church, 4055 Poplar Ave., Memphis, TN 38111

Stated Clk., Dr. L. Edward Davis

PERMANENT COMMITTEES

Committee on Admn., Chpsn., Mr. John Adamson, Second Presbyterian Church, 4055 Poplar, Memphis, TN 38111

Committee on Church Development, Chpsn., Rev. Lee Kizer, Harvest Church, P.O. Box 9175, Asheville, NC 28815

Committee on World Outreach, Chpsn., Dr. Perry Mobley, World Presbyterian Church, 1700 Farmington Rd., Livonia, MI 48154

Committee on Fraternal Relations

Committee on Ministerial Vocation, Chpsn., Rev. Malcolm Brown, Evangelical Presbyterian Ch., 29140 Buckingham Ave., Ste. 5, Livonia, MI 48154

Comm. on Christian Educ. & Publ.

Committee on Women's Ministries, Chpsn., Ms. Susan Nash, Second Presbyterian Church, 4055 Poplar Ave., Memphis, TN 38111

Committee on Theology, Chpsn., Mr. Philip Tiews, Covenant Presbyterian Church, P.O. Box 7087, Ann Arbor, MI 48107

Committee on Youth Ministries, Chpsn., Rev. Gary Koerth, Tabernacle Presbyterian Church, 2342 S. Raccoon Rd., Youngs-town, OH 44515

PRESBYTERIES

Central South, Stated Clk., Rev. Michael Swain, First Presbyterian Church, P.O. Box 366, West Point, MS 39773

East, Stated Clk., Mr. Richard Bingham, 95 Prospect Ave., Maybrook, NY 12543

Florida, Stated Clk., Rev. Robert Garment, Trinity EPC, 5150 Oleander, Ft. Pierce, FL 34982

Mid-America, Stated Clk., Mr. Kenneth Breckner, 7500 Wydown Blvd., St. Louis, MO 64105

Mid-Atlantic, Stated Clk., Mr. Llew Fischer, 3164 Golf Colony Dr., Salem, VA 24153

Midwest, Stated Clk., Mr. Robert Sanborn

Southeast, Stated Clk., Rev. Sam Harris, Valleybrook Presbyterian Church, 6001 Hixson Pike, Hixson, TX 37343

West, Stated Clk., Mr. Claude Russell, Faith Presbyterian Church, 11373 E. Alameda Ave., Aurora, CO 80012

St. Andrews, Stated Clk., Mr. Freddie Berk, Iglesia Presbiteriana San Andres, Peru 352, 1067 Buenos Aires, Argentina

Fellowship of Evangelical Bible Churches

Formerly known as Evangelical Mennonite

Brethren, this body emanates from the Russian immigration of Mennonites into the United States, 1873-74. Established with the emphasis on true repentance, conversion and a committed life to Jesus as Savior and Lord, the conference was founded in 1889 under the leadership of Isaac Peters and Aaron Wall. The founding churches were located in Mountain Lake, Minn., and in Henderson and Janzen, Neb. The conference has since grown to a fellowship of 36 churches with approximately 4,400 members in Argentina, Canada, Paraguay and the United States.

Foreign missions have been a vital ingredient of the total ministry. Today missions constitute about 75 percent of the total annual budget, with one missionary for every 30 members in the home churches. The conference does not develop and administer foreign mission fields of its own, but actively participates with existing evangelical "faith" mission societies. The conference has representation on several mission boards and has missionaries serving under approximately 32 different agencies around the world.

The church is holding fast to the inerrancy of Scripture, the Deity of Christ and the need for spiritual regeneration of man from his sinful natural state by faith in the death, burial and resurrection of Jesus Christ as payment for sin. Members look forward to the imminent return of Jesus Christ and retain a sense of urgency to share the gospel with those who have never heard of God's redeeming love.

HEADQUARTERS

5800 S. 14th St., Omaha, NE 68107 Tel. (402)731-4780 Fax (402)731-1173

Admn. Sec., Robert L. Frey, 5800 S. 14th St., Omaha, NE 68107 Tel. (402)731-4780 Fax (402)731-1173

OFFICERS

Pres., Rev. Melvin Epp, RR 1, Wymark, SK S0N 2Y0 Tel. (306)773-6845

PERIODICAL

Gospel Tidings

Fellowship of Fundamental Bible Churches

This body was called the Bible Protestant Church until 1985. The FFBC is a fellowship of fundamental Bible-believing local autonomous churches which believe in an inerrant and infallible Bible. The FFBC is dispensational as related to the study of the Scriptures, espouses the pre-Tribulation Rapture and is premillenial. It is evangelistic and missions-oriented. It regards itself as separatistic in areas of personal life and ecclesiastical association and believes that baptism by immersion most adequately symbolizes the truth of death and resurrection with Christ.

The Fellowship of Fundamental Bible Churches relates historically to the Eastern Conference of the Methodist Protestant Church, which changed its name to Bible Protestant Church at the 2nd Annual Session, held in Westville, N.J., Sept. 26-30, 1940.

HEADQUARTERS

P.O. Box 43, Glassboro, NJ 08028

Media Contact, Natl. Rep., Rev. Harold E. Haines, Tel. (609)881-5516

Pres., Rev. Mark Franklin, RD 1 Box 300, Monroeville, NJ 08343 Tel. (609)881-0057

Vice-Pres., Rev. Edmund Cotton, P.O. Box 31, Cassville, PA 16623 Tel. (814)448-3394

Sec., Rev. A. Glenn Doughty, 134 Delsea Dr., Westville, NJ 08093 Tel. (609)456-3791

Asst. Sec., Rev. Albert Martin, 195 East Front St., Atco, NJ 08004 Tel. (609)767-9376

Treas., Mr. William Rainey, RD 1 Box 302, Monroeville, NJ 08343 Tel. (609)881-4790

Stat. Sec., Rev. James Korth, 237 W. Main St., Moorestown, NJ 08057 Tel. (609)235-8077

Natl. Rep., Rev. Howard E. Haines, Tel. (609)881-5516

Fellowship of Grace Brethren Churches

A division occurred in the Church of the Brethren in 1882 on the question of the legislative authority of the annual meeting. It resulted in the establishment of the Brethren Church under a legal charter requiring congregational government. This body divided in 1939 with the Grace Brethren establishing headquarters at Winona Lake, Ind., and the Brethren Church at Ashland, Ohio.

HEADQUARTERS

Media Contact, Fellowship Coord., Rev. Charles Ashman, P.O. Box 386, Winona Lake, IN 46590 Tel. (219)269-1269

OFFICERS

Mod., Robert Fetterhoff, 912 Douglas Dr., Wooster, OH 44691

Mod.-Elect, Ed Lewis, P.O. Box 365, Winona Lake, IN 46590

2nd Mod.-Elect, Steve Peters, 600 S. Main St., West Milton, OH 45383

Fellowship Coord., Charles Ashman, P.O. Box 386, Winona Lake, IN 46590 Tel. (219)267-5566

Sec., Greg Howell, 129 NW Second St., Goldendale, WA 98620

Treas., Steve Poppenfoose, R. 1, Box 425A, Warsaw, IN 46580

OTHER BOARDS

Grace Brethren Foreign Missions, Exec. Dir., Rev. Tom Julien, P.O. Box 588, Winona Lake, IN 46590

Grace Brethren Home Missions, Exec. Dir., Larry Chamberlain, P.O. Box 587, Winona Lake, IN 46590

Grace Schools, Acting Pres., Ronald E. Manahan, 200 Seminary Dr., Winona Lake, IN 46590 Tel. (210)372-5100

Brethren Missionary Herald Co., Pub. & Gen. Mgr., Jeffry Carroll, P.O. Box 544, Winona Lake, IN 46590

Women's Missionary Council, Pres., Mrs. Geneva Ixman, 2244 Fernwood Dr., Colorado Springs, CO 80910

CE National, Exec. Dir., Rev. Ed Lewis, P.O. Box 365, Winona Lake, IN 46590

Grace Brethren Men & Boys, Exec. Dir., Rev. Ed Jackson, c/o Grace Brethren Church of Columbus, 6675 Worthington-Galena Rd., Worthington, OH 43085

Brethren Evangelistic Ministries, Dir., Ron Thompson, 3580 Robin Hood Cir., Roanoke, VA 24019

Brethren Navajo Ministries, Dir., Steve Galegor, Counselor, NM 87018

Grace Village Retirement Community, Exec. Dir., Scott Pucket, P.O. Box 337, Winona Lake, IN 46590

PERIODICAL

Brethren Missionary Herald

The Fire Baptized Holiness Church (Wesleyan)

This church came into being about 1890 as the result of definite preaching on the doctrine of holiness in some Methodist churches in southeastern Kansas. It became known as The Southeast Kansas Fire Baptized Holiness Association. The name was changed in 1945 to The Fire Baptized Holiness Church. It is entirely Wesleyan in doctrine, episcopal in church organization and intensive in evangelistic zeal.

HEADQUARTERS

600 College Ave., Independence, KS 67301 Tel. (316)331-3049

Media Contact, Gen. Supt., Gerald Broadaway

OFFICERS

Gen. Supt., Gerald Broadaway

Gen. Sec., Wayne Knipmeyer, Box 457, South Pekin, IL 61564

Gen. Treas., Victor White, 709 N. 13th, Independence, KS 67301

PERIODICALS

The Flaming Sword; John Three Sixteen

Free Christian Zion Church of Christ

This church was organized in 1905 at Redemption, Ark., by a company of African-American ministers associated with various denominations. Its polity is in general accord with that of Methodist bodies.

HEADQUARTERS

1315 S. Hutchinson St., Nashville, AR 71852 Tel. (501)845-4933

Media Contact, Gen. Sec., Shirlie Cheatham

OFFICER

Chief Pastor, Willie Benson, Jr.

Free Methodist Church of North America

The Free Methodist Church was organized in 1860 in Western New York by ministers and laymen who had called the Methodist Episcopal Church to return to what they considered the original doctrines and lifestyle of Methodism. The issues included human freedom (anti-slavery), freedom and simplicity in worship, free seats so that the poor would not be discriminated against and freedom from secret oaths (societies) so the truth might be spoken freely at all times. The founders emphasized the teaching of the entire sanctification of life by means of grace through faith.

The denomination continues to be true to its founding principles. It communicates the gospel and its power to all people without discrimination through strong missionary, evangelistic and educational programs. Six colleges, a Bible college and numerous overseas schools train the youth of the church to serve in lay and ministerial roles.

Its members covenant to maintain simplicity in

life and worship, daily devotion to Christ and responsible stewardship of time, talent and finance.

HEADQUARTERS

World Ministries Center: 770 N. High School Rd., Indianapolis, IN 46214 Tel. (317)244-3660 Fax (317)244-1247

Mailing Address, P.O. Box 535002, Indianapolis, IN 46253 Tel. (800)342-5531

Media Contact, Yearbook Ed., P.O. Box 535002, Indianapolis, IN 46253

OFFICERS

Bishops: Gerald E. Bates; David M. Foster; Bya'ene Akulu Ilangyi; Noah Nzeyimana; Daniel Ward; Richard D. Snyder; Luis Uanela Nhaphale

Gen. Conf. Sec., Melvin J. Spencer

Admn. & Finance, Gen. Dir., Gary M. Kilgore

Christian Educ., Gen. Dir., Daniel L. Riemenschneider

Evangelism & Church Growth, Gen. Dir., Raymond W. Ellis

Free Methodist Publishing House, Gen. Dir., John E. Van Valin

Higher Education, Gen. Sec., Bruce L. Kline

Light & Life Magazine, Ed., Robert B. Haslam

Light & Life Men Intl., Exec. Dir., Lucien E. Behar

Free Methodist Foundation, Stanley B. Thompson

Women's Ministries Intl., Pres., Mrs. Carollyn Ellis

World Missions, Gen. Dir., M. Doane Bonney

PERIODICAL

Light and Life Magazine

Friends General Conference

Friends General Conference is an association of yearly meetings within the Religious Society of Friends, open to all Friends meetings which wish to be actively associated with its programs and services. It was organized in 1900, bringing together four associations, including the First-day School Conference (1868) and the Friends Union for Philanthropic Labor (1882).

Friends General Conference is primarily a service organization and has no authority over its constituent meetings. Its purpose is to nurture the Religious Society of Friends by developing and providing resources and opportunities for spiritual growth. A Central Committee, to which constituent yearly meetings name appointees approximately in proportion to membership, or its Executive Committee is responsible for the direction of FGC's year-round services.

There are seven standing program committees: Advancement & Outreach, Christian & Interfaith Relations, Long Range Conference Planning, Ministry & Nurture, Publications & Distribution, Religious Education and Friends Meeting House Fund.

HEADQUARTERS

1216 Arch St., 2B, Philadelphia, PA 19107 Tel. (215)561-1700

Media Contact, Gen. Sec., Bruce Birchard

OFFICERS

Gen. Sec., Bruce Birchard

Clk., Tyla Ann Burger

Treas., David Miller

YEARLY MEETINGS

Philadelphia, Arthur Larrabee, 1515 Cherry St., Philadelphia, PA 19102

Lake Erie, Patricia Campbell, 710 Indianola Ave., Ann Arbor, MI 48105 Tel. (313)668-8865

*New England, Elizabeth Cazden, 118 Walnut St., Manchester, NH 03014 Tel. (603)622-9835

*New York, George Rubin, 545 Rockland St., Westbury, NY 11590 Tel. (516)977-9665

*Baltimore, Miriam D. Green, 316 Rossiter Ave., Baltimore, MD 21212 Tel. (410)435-2528

*Canadian, Elaine Bishop, Box 5333, Peace River, AB T85 I9R Tel. (403)629-3745

Illinois, Jerry Nurenberg, 60255 Myrtle Rd., South Bend, IN 46614 Tel. (219)232-5729

Ohio Valley, Ellen Armontine Hodge, 4240 Cornelius Ave., Indianapolis, IN 46208 Tel. (612)879-2835

South Central, Dan O'Brien, 1007 NW 32nd St., Oklahoma City, OK 73118 Tel. (405)521-8720

*Southeastern, Ken Leibman, 4545 Highway 346, Archer, FL 32618 Tel. (904)495-9482

Northern, Jim Greenley, 1909 Vilas Ave., Madison, WI 53711 Tel. (608)251-0372

Piedmont FF, Ralph McCracken, 913 Ridgecrest Dr., Greensboro, NC 27410-3237 Tel. (919)292-8631

Southern Appalachian YM & Assoc., Peggy Bonnington, 408 West Coy Cir., Clarksville, TN 37043 Tel. (615)647-9284

Central Alaska, Jan Pohl, P.O. Box 22316, Juneau, AK 99802

* also affiliated with Friends United Meeting

PERIODICAL

Friends Journal

Friends United Meeting

Friends United Meeting was organized in 1902 (the name was changed in 1963 from the Five Years Meeting of Friends) as a loose confederation of North American yearly meetings to facilitate a united Quaker witness in missions, peace work and Christian education.

Today Friends United Meeting is comprised of 18 member yearly meetings (12 North American plus Cuba, East Africa, East Africa Yearly Meeting (South), Elgon Religious Society of Friends, Nairobi and Jamaica yearly meetings) representing about half the Friends in the world. FUM's current work includes programs of mission and service and congregational renewal. FUM publishes Christian education curriculum, books of Quaker history and religious thought and a magazine, *Quaker Life*.

HEADQUARTERS

101 Quaker Hill Dr., Richmond, IN 47374 Tel. (317)962-7573 Fax (317)966-1293

Media Contact, Gen. Sec., Johan Maurer

OFFICERS

Presiding Clk., Harold Smuck

Treas., Ann Kendall

Gen. Sec., Johan Maurer

DEPARTMENTS

World Ministries Commission, Assoc. Sec., Bill Wagoner

Meeting Ministries Commission, Assoc. Sec., Mary Glenn Hadley

Quaker Hill Bookstore, Mgr., Dick Talbot

Friends United Press, Ed., Ardith Talbot

Nebraska, Dean Young, 253 S. Lorraine, Wichita, KS 67211

*New England, Elizabeth Cazden, 118 Walnut St., Manchester, NH 03104 Tel. (603)622-9835

*New York, George Rubin, 545 Rockland St., Westbury, NY 11590 Tel. (516)997-9665

*Baltimore, Miriam D. Green, 316 Rossiter Ave., Baltimore, MD 21212

Iowa, Stan Bauer, 52473 Norwegian Church Rd., Lavalle, WI 53941

Western, Lester Paulsen, 2025 Redfern Dr., Indianapolis, IN 46227

North Carolina, Carter Pike, RR 5, Box 96, Asheboro, NC 27203

Indiana, Don Garner, 471 W 1125 S, Fairmont, IN 46928

Wilmington, Rudy Haag, P.O. Box 19, Cuba, OH 45114

Cuba, Maulio Ajo Berencen, Libertad 114, c/o Argamente & Garayalde, Holguin 80100, Holguin, Cuba

*Canadian, Elaine Bishop, Box 5333, Peace River, AB T8S 1R9

Jamaica, Angela Johnson, 4 Worthington Ave., Kingston 5, Jamaica, W.I.

*Southeastern, Ken Leibman, 15413 SW 107th St., Archer, FL 32618 Tel. (904)495-9482

East Africa, James Ashihunde, P.O. Box 1510, Kakamega, Kenya

East Africa (South), Joseph Kisia, P.O. Box 160, Vihiga, Kenya

Nairobi, Stanley Ndezwa, P.O. Box 377, Nakuru, Kenya

Elgon Religious Society of Friends, Elisha Wakube, P.O. Box 98, Kimilili, Kenya, East Africa

* also affiliated with Friends Gen. Conference

PERIODICAL

Quaker Life

Full Gospel Assemblies International

The Full Gospel Assemblies International was founded in 1962 under the leadership of Dr. Charles Elwood Strauser. The roots of Full Gospel Assemblies may be traced to 1947 with the beginning of the Full Gospel Church of Coatesville, Pennsylvania. As an Assemblies of God Pentecostal church, the Full Gospel Church of Coatesville was active in evangelization and educational ministries to the community. In service to the ministers and students of the Full Gospel Church ministries, the Full Gospel Trinity Ministerial Fellowship was formed in 1962, later changing name to Full Gospel Assemblies International.

Retaining its original doctrine and faith, Full Gospel Assemblies is trinitarian and believes in the Bible as God's infallible Word to all people, in baptism in the Holy Spirit according to Acts 2, in divine healing made possible by the sufferings of our Lord Jesus Christ and in the imminent return of Christ for those who love him.

The body of Full Gospel Assemblies is an evangelical missionary fellowship sponsoring ministry at home and abroad, composed of self governing ministries and churches. Congregations, affiliate ministries and clerical bodies are located throughout the United States and 27 countries of the world.

HEADQUARTERS

P.O. Box 1230, Coatesville, PA 19320 Tel. (215)857-2357

OFFICERS

Pres., Dr. AnnaMae Strauser

Executive Officers: Paul Bryson, Jr.; Betty Stewart; Carol Strauser

National Ministers Council: Chpsn., Simeon Strauser, Sadsburyville, PA; Rev. Marilyn Allen, Colorado Springs, CO; Pastor Donald Campbell, Mt. Morris, PA; Pastor Richard Hartman, Harrisburg, PA; Pastor David Treat, Bloomington, IN; Pastor J. Victor Fisk, Apollo, PA; Pastor James Scott, Mad River, CA; Rev. Harold Oswold, Rochester, NY; Pastor Shirley Carozzolo, Tonawanda, NY

PERIODICALS

Pentecost Today; Full Gospel Ministries Mission Outreach Report

Full Gospel Fellowship of Churches and Ministers International

In the early 1960s a conviction grew in the hearts of many ministers that there should be closer fellowship between the people of God who believed in the apostolic ministry. At the same time, many independent churches were experiencing serious difficulties in receiving authority from the IRS to give governmentally accepted tax-exempt receipts for donations.

In September 1962 a group of ministers met in Dallas, Tex., to form a Fellowship to give expression to the essential unity of the Body of Christ under the leadership of the Holy Spirit—a unity that goes beyond individuals, churches or organizations. This was not a movement to build another denomination, but rather an effort to join ministers, churches and ministry organizations of like mind across denominational lines.

To provide opportunities for fellowship and to support the objectives and goals of local and national ministries: regional conventions and an annual international convention are held.

HEADQUARTERS

4325 W. Ledbetter Dr., Dallas, TX 75233 Tel. (214)339-1200 Fax (214)337-1865

Media Contact, Exec. Sec., Dr. Chester P. Jenkins

OFFICERS

Pres., Dr. Don Arnold, P.O. Box 324, Gadsden, AL 35901

1st Vice-Pres., Dr. Ray Chamberlain, P.O. Box 986, Salisbury, MD 21801

Sec., Dr. Chester P. Jenkins

Treas., Rev. S. K. Biffle, 3833 Westerville Rd., Columbus, OH 43224

Ofc. Sec., Mrs. Anne Rasmussen

Vice-Pres. at Large: Rev. Maurice Hart, P.O. Box 4316, Omaha, NE 68104; Rev. Don Westbrook, 3518 Rose of Sharon Rd., Durham, NC 27705

REGIONAL VICE-PRESIDENTS

Southeast, Rev. Gene Evans, P.O. Box 813, Douglasville, GA 30133

South Central, Rev. Robert J. Miller, P.O. Box 10621, Killeen, TX 76547

Southwest, Rev. Don Shepherd, 631 Southgate Rd., Sacramento, CA 95815

Northeast, Rev. Roy C. Smith, P.O. Box 193, Shrewsbury, PA 17361

North Central, Rev. Raymond Rothwell, P.O. Box 367, Eaton, OH 45320

Northwest, Rev. Ralph Trask, 3212 Hyacinth NE, Salem, OR 97303

Exec. Sec., Dr. Chester P. Jenkins
Chmn. of Evangelism, Dr. Marty Tharp
Past Pres., Dr. James Helton

PERIODICAL

Fellowship Tidings

Fundamental Methodist Church, Inc.

This group traces its origin through the Methodist Protestant Church. It withdrew from The Methodist Church and organized on Aug. 27, 1942.

HEADQUARTERS

1034 N. Broadway, Springfield, MO 65802
Media Contact, Dist. Supt., Pastor Ronnie Fieker, 425 W. Wishart, Monett, MO 65708 Tel. (417)235-3168

OFFICERS

Treas., Mr. Everett Etheridge, 3844 W. Dover, Springfield, MO 65802 Tel. (417)865-4438
Sec., Mrs. Betty Nicholson, Rt. 2, Box 397, Ash Grove, MO 65604 Tel. (417)672-2268
Dist. Supt., Rev. Ronnie Fieker, 425 W. Wishart, Monett, MO 65708 Tel. (417)235-3168

General Assembly of the Korean Presbyterian Church in America

This body came into official existence in the United States in 1976 and is currently an ethnic church, using the Korean language.

HEADQUARTERS

P.O. Box 457, Morganville, NJ 07951 Tel. (908)591-2771 Fax (908)591-2260
Media Contact, Gen. Sec., Rev. John Woo

OFFICERS

Mod., Rev. Do Seuk Kim, 909 N. Alexandria Ave., Los Angeles, CA 90029 Tel. (213)662-1838 Fax (213)409-0465
Vice-Mod., Rev. Chang Kil Kim, 15 N. Browning Ave., Tenafly, NJ 07670 Tel. (201)816-0268 Fax (201)944-0109
Stated Clk., Rev. Sang Koo Kim, 5777 Los Arcos Way, Buena Park, CA 90620 Tel. (714)826-5714 Fax (714)680-6418
Treas., Eld. Won K. Baik, 6355 Edsall Rd., Alexandria, VA 22312 Tel. (703)354-7468

STAFF

Intl. Mission Dept., Chpsn., Rev. Hee Min Park, 4529 Frederick Ave., La Crescenta, CA 91214 Tel. (818)248-1496 Fax (818)227-0718
Gen. Sec., Rev. Nicholas C. Chun, 1251 Crenshaw Blvd., Los Angeles, CA 90019 Tel. (213)857-0361

General Association of General Baptists

Similar in doctrine to those General Baptists organized in England in the early 17th century, the first General Baptist churches were organized on the Midwest frontier following the Second Great Awakening. The first church was established by the Rev. Benoni Stinson, in 1823 at Evansville, Ind.

Stinson's major theological emphasis was general atonement — "Christ tasted death for every man." The group also allows for the possibility of apostasy. It practices open communion and believer's baptism by immersion.

Called "liberal" Baptists because of their emphasis on the freedom of man, General Baptists organized a General Association in 1870 and invited other "liberal" Baptists (e.g., "free will" and Separate Baptists) to participate.

The policy-setting body is composed of delegates from local General Baptist churches and associations. Each local church is autonomous but belongs to an association. The group currently consists of more than 60 associations in 16 states, as well as several associations in the Philippines, Guam, Saipan, Jamaica and India. Ministers and deacons are ordained by a presbytery.

A number of boards continue a variety of missions, schools and other support ministries. General Baptists belong to the Baptist World Alliance, the North American Baptist Fellowship and the National Association of Evangelicals.

HEADQUARTERS

100 Stinson Dr., Poplar Bluff, MO 63901 Tel. (314)785-7746 Fax (314)785-0564
Media Contact, Exec. Dir., Rev. Dwight Chapman

OFFICER

Exec. Dir., Rev. Dwight Chapman

PERIODICALS

General Baptist Messenger; Capsule; Voice; The Wave

General Association of Regular Baptist Churches

This association was founded in May, 1932, in Chicago by a group of churches which had withdrawn from the Northern Baptist Convention (now the American Baptist Churches in the U.S.A.) because of doctrinal differences. Its Confession of Faith, which it requires all churches to subscribe to, is essentially the old, historic New Hampshire Confession of Faith with a premillennial ending applied to the last article.

HEADQUARTERS

1300 N. Meacham Rd., Schaumburg, IL 60173 Tel. (708)843-1600 Fax (708)843-3757
Media Contact, Dr. Paul N. Tassell

OFFICERS

Chpsn., Dr. Daniel E. Gelatt
Vice-Chpsn., Dr. Paul Dixon
Treas., Vernon D. Miller
Sec., Rev. David Gower
Natl. Rep., Dr. Paul N. Tassell

PERIODICAL

Baptist Bulletin

General Church of the New Jerusalem

The General Church of the New Jerusalem is the result of a reorganization in 1897 of the General Church of The Advent of the Lord. It stresses the full acceptance of the doctrines contained in the theological writings of Emanuel Swedenborg.

HEADQUARTERS

Bryn Athyn, PA 19009 Tel. (215)947-4200
Media Contact, Ed., Church Journal, Donald L. Rose, Tel. (215)947-6812 Fax (215)947-3078

Presiding Bishop, Rt. Rev. P. M. Buss
Sec., Rev. Louis D. Synnestvedt
Treas., Neil M. Buss

PERIODICAL

New Church Life

The General Conference of Mennonite Brethren Churches

A small group, requesting that closer attention be given to prayer, Bible study and a consistent life-style, withdrew from the larger Mennonite Church in the Ukraine in 1860. Anabaptist in origin, the group was influenced by Lutheran pietists and Baptist teachings and adopted a quasi-congregational form of church government. In 1874 and years following, small groups of these German-speaking Mennonites left Russia, settled in Kansas and then spread to the Midwest west of the Mississippi and into Canada. Some years later the movement spread to California and the West Coast. In 1960, the Krimmer Mennonite Brethren Conference merged with this body.

Today the General Conference of Mennonite Brethren Churches conducts services in many European languages as well as in Vietnamese, Mandarin and Hindi. It works with other denominations in missionary and development projects in 25 countries outside North America.

HEADQUARTERS

4812 E. Butler Ave., Fresno, CA 93727 Tel. (209)251-8681 Fax (209)251-7212
Media Contact, Exec. Sec., Marvin Hein

OFFICERS

Mod., Edmund Janzen, 4935 E. Heaton, Fresno, CA 93727
Asst. Mod., Harry Heidebrecht, 2285 Clearbrook Rd., Clearbrook, BC V2T 2X4
Sec., John E. Toews, 4884 E. Butler Ave., Fresno, CA 93727
Exec. Sec., Marvin Hein

PERIODICAL

Christian Leader

General Conference of the Evangelical Baptist Church, Inc.

This denomination is an Arminian, Wesleyan, premillennial group whose form of government is congregational.

It was organized in 1935 and was formerly known as the Church of the Full Gospel, Inc.

HEADQUARTERS

1601 E. Rose St., Goldsboro, NC 27530 Tel. (919)734-2482

OFFICERS

Pres., Rev. David J. Crawford, 101 William Dr., Goldsboro, NC 27530 Tel. (919)734-2482
1st Vice-Pres., Dr. Harry E. Jones, 3741 Sunset Ave., Westridge Village, Apt. B-1, Rocky Mount, NC 27801 Tel. (919)443-1239
2nd Vice-Pres., Rev. George C. Wallace, 909 W. Walnut St., Chanute, KS 66720 Tel. (316)431-0706
Sec.-Treas., Mrs. Evelyn Crawford, 101 William Dr., Goldsboro, NC 27530 Tel. (919)734-2482

Dir. of Evangelism, Rev. B. L. Proctor, Rt. 3, Box 442, Nashville, NC 27856 Tel. (919)459-2063
Dir. of Women's Work, ——
Dir. of Youth Work, Rev. Ralph Jarrell, P.O. Box 1112, Burgaw, NC 28425 Tel. (919)259-9329

Grace Gospel Fellowship

The Grace Gospel Fellowship was organized in 1944 by a group of pastors who held to a dispensational interpretation of Scripture. Most had ministries in the Midwest. Two prominent leaders were J. C. O'Hair of Chicago and Charles Baker of Milwaukee. Subsequent to 1945, a Bible Institute was founded (now Grace Bible College of Grand Rapids, Mich.), and a previously organized foreign mission (now Grace Ministries International of Grand Rapids) was affiliated with the group. Churches have now been established in most sections of the country.

The body has remained a fellowship, each church being autonomous in polity. All support for its college, mission and headquarters is on a contributory basis.

The binding force of the Fellowship has been the members' doctrinal position. They believe in the Deity and Saviorship of Jesus Christ and subscribe to the inerrant authority of Scripture. Their method of biblical interpretation is dispensational, with emphasis on the distinctive revelation to and the ministry of the apostle Paul.

HEADQUARTERS

Media Contact, Pres., Roger G. Anderson, 2125 Martindale SW, P.O. Box 9432, Grand Rapids, MI 49509 Tel. (616)245-0100 Fax (616)241-2542

OFFICERS

Pres., Roger G. Anderson

OTHER ORGANIZATIONS

Grace Bible College, Pres., Rev. E. Bruce Kemper, 1011 Aldon St. SW, Grand Rapids, MI 49509
Grace Ministries Intl., Exec. Dir., Dr. Samuel Vinton, 2125 Martindale Ave. SW, Grand Rapids, MI 49509
Missionary Literature Distributors, Dir., Mrs. Betty Strelow, 7514 Humbert Rd., Godfrey, IL 62305
Prison Mission Association, Gen. Dir., Mr. Vern Bigelow, P.O. Box 1587, Port Orchard, WA 98366-0140
Grace Publications Inc., Exec. Dir., Roger G. Anderson, 2125 Martindale Ave. SW, Grand Rapids, MI 49509
Bible Doctrines to Live By, Exec. Dir., Lee Homoki, P.O. Box 2351, Grand Rapids, MI 49501

PERIODICAL

Truth

Greek Orthodox Archdiocese of North and South America

The Greek Orthodox Archdiocese of North and South America is under the jurisdiction of the Ecumenical Patriarchate of Constantinople in Istanbul. It was chartered in 1922 by the State of New York and has parishes in the United States, Canada and Central and South America. The first Greek Orthodox Church was founded in New Orleans in 1864.

8-10 E. 79th St., New York, NY 10021 Tel.
(212)570-3500 Fax (212)861-2183
Media Contact, News Media Liaison, Jim Golding,
Tel. (212)628-2590 Fax (212)570-4005

ARCHDIOCESAN COUNCIL

Chpsn., Archbishop Iakovos
Vice-Chpsn., Metropolitan Silas of New Jersey
Pres., Andrew A. Athens, Chicago, IL
1st Vice-Pres., George Chimples, Cleveland, OH
2nd Vice-Pres., Nicholas Paul
3rd Vice-Pres., Alexandras Zynnis
Sec., Peter T. Kourides
Treas., Peter Dion, New York, NY
Theodore Prounis, New York, NY

SYNOD OF BISHOPS

Chpsn., His Eminence Archbishop Iakovos
New Jersey, His Excellency Metropolitan Silas, 8
East 79th St., New York, NY 10021
Chicago, His Grace Bishop Iakovos, Forty East
Burton Pl., Chicago, IL 60610
Detroit, His Grace Bishop Timothy, 19504 Ren-
frew, Detroit, MI 48211
Toronto, His Grace Bishop Sotirios, 40 Donlands
Ave., Toronto, ON M4J 3N6
San Francisco, His Grace Bishop Anthony, 372
Santa Clara Ave., San Francisco, CA 94127
Pittsburgh, His Grace Bishop Maximos, 5201
Ellsworth Ave., Pittsburgh, PA 15232
Buenos Aires, His Grace Bishop Gennadios,
Avenida Figueroa Alcorta 3187, Buenos Aires,
Argentina
Boston, His Grace Bishop Methodios, 162 God-
dard Ave., Brookline, MA 02146
Atlanta, His Grace Bishop Philip, 6 W. Druid Hills,
Ste. 620, Atlanta, GA 30329
Denver, His Grace Bishop Isaiah, 10225 E. Gill Pl.,
Denver, CO 80231
Assistant Bishops to Archbishop Iakovos: His
Grace Bishop Philotheos, of Meloa; Chancellor,
Rev. Germanos Stavropoulos; His Grace Bishop
Alexios, of Troas, Chorepiscopos of Astoria,
27-09 Crescent St., Astoria, NY 11102

ARCHDIOCESAN DEPARTMENTS

Rel. Educ., 50 Goddard Ave., Brookline, MA
02146
Go Telecom, 27-09 Crescent St., Astoria, NY
11102
Archives Logos, Mission Center, P.O. Box 4319,
St. Augustine, FL 32085
Youth Ministry & Camping
Economic Development
Church & Society
Ecumenical Ofc.
Stewardship
Registry
Ionian Village
Communications

ORGANIZATIONS

Ladies Philoptochos Society, 345 E. 74th St., New
York, NY 10021
Greek Orthodox Young Adult League (GOYAL)
Order of St. Andrew the Apostle
Archdiocesan Presbyters' Council
National Sisterhood of Presbyteres
Natl. Forum of Greek Orthodox Church Musicians,
1700 N. Walnut St., Bloomington, IN 47401

PERIODICAL

The Orthodox Observer

The Holiness Church of God, Inc.

The Holiness Church of God was established at
Madison, N.C., in 1920 and incorporated at Winston-Salem, N.C in 1928.

OFFICERS

Pres., Bishop B. McKinney, 602 E. Elm St., Graham, NC 27253 Tel. (919)116-4787

Holy Ukrainian Autocephalic Orthodox Church in Exile

This church was organized in a parish in New
York in 1951 by Ukrainian laymen and clergy who
settled in the Western Hemisphere after World War
II. In 1954 two bishops, immigrants from Europe,
met with clergy and laymen and formally organized the religious body.

HEADQUARTERS

103 Evergreen St., W. Babylon, NY 11704

OFFICER

Admn., Rt. Rev. Serhij K. Pastukhiv, Tel.
(516)669-7402

House of God, Which is the Church of the Living God, the Pillar and Ground of the Truth, Inc.

This body, founded by Mary L. Tate in 1919, is
episcopally organized.

HEADQUARTERS

58 Thompson St., Philadelphia, PA 19131
Media Contact, Sec., Rose Canon, 515 S. 57th St.,
Philadelphia, PA 19143 Tel. (215)474-8913

OFFICER

Bishop, Raymond W. White, 6107 Cobbs Creek
Pkwy., Philadelphia, PA 19143 Tel. (215)748-
6338

Hungarian Reformed Church in America

A Hungarian Reformed Church was organized in
New York in 1904 in connection with the Reformed Church of Hungary. In 1922, the Church in
Hungary transferred most of its congregations in
the United States to the Reformed Church in the
U.S. Some, however, preferred to continue as an
autonomous, self-supporting American denomination, and these formed the Free Magyar Reformed Church in America. This group changed its
name in 1958 to Hungarian Reformed Church in
America.

This church is a member of the World Alliance
of Reformed Churches, Presbyterian and Congregational, the World Council of Churches and the
National Council of Churches of Christ. It is deeply
involved in the Roman Catholic, Presbyterian Reformed Consultation, of which Dr. Andrew Harsanyi was co-chairman for 12 years.

HEADQUARTERS

Bishop's Office, P.O. Box D, Hopatcong, NJ
07843 Tel. (201)398-2764
Media Contact, Bishop, Dr. Andrew Harsanyi

OFFICERS

Bishop, Rt. Rev. Dr. Andrew Harsanyi

Chief Lay-Curator, Prof. Stephen Szabo, 464 Forest Ave., Paramus, NJ 07652
Gen. Sec. (Clergy), Rt. Rev. Paul A. Mezö, 8 Dunthorne Ct., Toronto, ON M1B 2S9
Gen Sec. (Lay), Zoltan Ambrus, 3358 Maple Dr., Allen Park, MI 48122
Eastern Classis, Dean (Senior of the Deans, Chair in Bishop's absence), The V. Rev. Stefan M. Torok, 331 Kirkland Pl., Perth Amboy, NJ 08861
New York Classis, Dean, The V. Rev. Alex Forro, 13 Grove St., Poughkeepsie, NY 12601
Western Classis, Dean, The V. Rev. Andor Demeter, 3921 W. Christy Dr., Phoenix, AZ 85029

PERIODICAL

Magyar Egyhaz

Hutterian Brethren

Small groups of Hutterites derive their names from Jacob Hutter, a 16th-century Anabaptist who taught true discipleship after accepting Jesus and advocated communal ownership of property and was burned as a heretic in Austria in 1536.

Many believers are of German descent and still use their native tongue at home and in church. Much of the denominational literature is produced in German and English. "Colonies" share property, practice non-resistance, dress differently, refuse to participate in politics and operate their own schools. There are 375 colonies with 40,000 members in North America.

Each congregation conducts its own youth work through Sunday school. Until age 15, children attend German school after attending public school. All youth ages 15 to 20 must attend Sunday school. They are baptized upon confession of faith, around age 20.

HEADQUARTERS

Media Contact, Paul S. Gross, Rt. 1, Box 6E, Reardon, WA 99029 Tel. (509)299-5400 Fax (509)299-3099

OFFICERS

Vice-Pres., Rev. Joseph Hofer, P.O. Box 159, Sunburst, MT 59482 Tel. (406)937-3045
Hutterite Bishop, Rev. John Wipf, P.O. Box 1509, Rosetown, SK S0L 2V0 Tel. (306)882-3112

Independent Fundamental Churches of America

This group of churches was organized in 1930 at Cicero, Ill., by representatives of the American Council of Undenominational Churches and representatives of various independent churches. The founding churches and members had separated themselves from various denominational affiliations.

The IFCA provides a way for independent churches and ministers to unite in close fellowship and cooperation, in defense of the fundamental teachings of Scripture and in the proclamation of the gospel of God's grace.

HEADQUARTERS

3520 Fairlanes, Grandville, MI 49468 Tel. (616)531-1840 Fax (616)531-1814
Mailing Address, P.O. Box 810, Grandville, MI 49418
Media Contact, Natl. Exec. Dir., Dr. Richard Gregory, Tel. (513)531-1840

OFFICERS

Natl. Exec. Dir., Dr. Richard Gregory, 2684 Meadow Ridge Dr., Byron Center, MI 49315 Tel. (616)878-1285
Pres., Dr. David L. Meschke, 6763 S. High St., Littleton, CO 80122 Tel. (303)794-0095
1st Vice-Pres., Rev. Donald Fredericks, 3224 North Patterson Blvd., Flagstaff, AZ 86004-2009 Tel. (602)526-1493
2nd Vice-Pres., Dr. William A. BeVier, 4149 Nancy Pl., Shoreview, MN 55126-6411 Tel. (612)631-5228

PERIODICAL

The Voice

International Church of the Foursquare Gospel

Founded by Aimee Semple McPherson in 1927, the International Church of the Foursquare Gospel proclaims the message of Jesus Christ the Savior, Healer, Baptizer with the Holy Spirit and Soon-coming King. Headquartered in Los Angeles, this evangelistic missionary body of believers consists of nearly 1,609 churches in the United States and Canada.

The International Church of the Foursquare Gospel is incorporated in the state of California and governed by a Board of Directors who direct its corporate affairs. A Foursquare Cabinet, consisting of the Corporate Officers, Board of Directors and District Supervisors of the various districts of the Foursquare Church in the United States and other elected or appointed members, serves in an advisory capacity to the President and the Board of Directors.

Each local Foursquare Church is a subordinate unit of the International Church of the Foursquare Gospel. The pastor of the church is appointed by the Board of Directors and is responsible for the spiritual and physical welfare of the church. To assist and advise the pastor, a church council is elected by the local church members.

Foursquare Churches seek to build strong believers through Christian education, Christian day schools, youth camping and ministry, Foursquare Women International who support and encourage Foursquare missionaries abroad, radio and television ministries, the *Foursquare World Advance Magazine* and 167 Bible Colleges worldwide.

Worldwide missions remains the focus of the Foursquare Gospel Church with nearly 26,925 churches, 19,606 national Foursquare pastors/leaders and 1,743,117 members and adherents in 78 countries around the globe. The Church is affiliated with the Pentecostal Fellowship of North America, National Association of Evangelicals and the World Pentecostal Fellowship.

HEADQUARTERS

1910 W. Sunset Blvd., Ste. 200, Los Angeles, CA 90026 Tel. (213)484-2400 Fax (213)413-3824
Media Contact, Editor, Dr. Ron Williams, Fax (213)484-8401

CORPORATE OFFICERS

Pres., Dr. John R. Holland
Pres. Emeritus, Dr. Rolf K. McPherson
Vice-Pres., Dr. J. Eugene Kurtz
Gen. Supt., Dr. J. Eugene Kurtz
Dir. of Missions Intl., Dr. Don McGregor
Sec., Dr. John W. Bowers
Treas., Rev. Virginia Cravens
Exec. Sec., Rev. James Rogers

Bd. of Directors: Dr. John R. Holland; Dr. Don McGregor; Dr. Paul Risser; Rev. Ralph Torres; Rev. Naomi Beard; Dr. John W. Bowers; Dr. Harold Helms; Dr. J. Eugene Kurtz; Dr. Ron Williams; Dr. Howard P. Courtney, Sr.; Rev. Loren Edwards; Mr. Douglas L. Slaybaugh

District Supervisors: Eastern, Rev. Dewey Morrow; Great Lakes, Rev. Fred Parker; Midwest, Dr. Glenn Metzler; Northwest, Dr. Cliff Hanes; South Central, Dr. Sidney Westbrook; Southeast, Rev. Glenn Burris, Jr.; Southern California, Rev. Don Long; Southwest, Rev. John Watson; Western, Dr. Fred Wymore

Foursquare Cabinet: Composed of Bd. of Directors; District Supervisors; Dr. Ron Mehl; Rev. Charles Aldridge; Rev. Tom Ferguson; Rev. Ken Wold, Jr.; Dr. Daniel Brown; Rev. David Holland; Corporate Officers

SUPPORT MINISTRIES

Natl. Dept. of Youth, Natl. Youth Minister, Rev. Gregg Johnson

Natl. Dept. of Chr. Educ. & Publications, Dir., Rev. Rick Wulfestieg

Foursquare Women International, Dir., Rev. Beverly Brafford

PERIODICALS

Foursquare World Advance; VIP Communique

International Council of Community Churches

This body is a fellowship of locally autonomous, ecumenically minded, congregationally governed, non-creedal Churches. The Council came into being in 1950 as the union of two former councils of community churches, one formed of black churches known as the Biennial Council of Community Churches and the other of white churches known as the National Council of Community Churches.

HEADQUARTERS

19115 S. LaGrange Rd., Ste. C, Mokena, IL 60448 Tel. (708)479-8400 Fax (708)479-8402

Media Contact, Exec. Dir., Dr. Jeffrey R. Newhall

OFFICERS

Pres., Orsey Malone
Vice-Pres., Ronald Miller
Sec., Abraham Wright
Treas., Martha Nolan
Exec. Dir., Dr. Jeffrey R. Newhall

OTHER ORGANIZATIONS

Commission on Church Relations
Commission on Ecumenical Relations
Commission on Clergy Relations
Commission on Laity Relations
Commission on Faith & Order
Commission on Social Concerns
Commission on Missions
Commission on Informational Services
Women's Christian Fellowship, Pres., Carolyn Ford
Samaritans (Men's Fellowship), Pres., J. Edward Jones
Young Adult Fellowship, Pres., Sandra Woodard
Youth Fellowship, Pres., Peter Singley

PERIODICALS

The Christian Community; The Pastor's Journal

The International Pentecostal Church of Christ

At a General Conference held at London, Ohio, Aug. 10, 1976, the International Pentecostal Assemblies and the Pentecostal Church of Christ consolidated into one body, taking the name International Pentecostal Church of Christ.

The International Pentecostal Assemblies was the successor of the Association of Pentecostal Assemblies and the International Pentecostal Missionary Union. The Pentecostal Church of Christ was founded by John Stroup of Flatwoods, Ky., on May 10, 1917 and was incorporated at Portsmouth, Ohio, in 1927. The International Pentecostal Church of Christ is an active member of the Pentecostal Fellowship of North America, as well as a member of the National Association of Evangelicals.

The priorities of the International Pentecostal Church of Christ are to be an agency of God for evangelizing the world, to be a corporate body in which people may worship God and to be a channel of God's purpose to build a body of saints being perfected in the image of His Son.

The Annual Conference is held each year during the first full week of August in London, Ohio.

HEADQUARTERS

2245 St. Rt. 42 SW, P.O. Box 439, London, OH 43140 Tel. (614)852-0348 Fax Same

Media Contact, Gen. Overseer, Clyde M. Hughes

EXECUTIVE COMMITTEE

Gen. Overseer, Clyde M. Hughes, P.O. Box 439, London, OH 43140 Tel. (614)852-0348

Asst. Gen. Overseer, Wells T. Bloomfield, P.O. Box 439, London, OH 43140 Tel. (614)852-0448

Gen. Sec., Rev. Thomas Dooley, 3200 Dueber Ave. S.W., Canton, OH 44706 Tel. (216)484-6053

Gen. Treas., Rev. Clifford A. Edwards, P.O. Box 18145, Atlanta, GA 30316 Tel. (404)627-2681

Dir. of Global Missions, Dr. James B. Keiller, P.O. Box 18145, Atlanta, GA 30316 Tel. (404)627-2681

DISTRICT OVERSEERS

Blue Ridge District, Robert Culler, Rt. 2, Box 12, Pinnacle, NC 27043 Tel. (919)368-2540

Central District, Ervin Hargrave, 2279 Seminole Ave., Springfield, OH 45506 Tel. (513)323-6433

Mid-Eastern District, Robert Cannon, Box 9056, Richmond, VA 23225 Tel. (804)233-1027

Mountain District, Jerry L. Castle, Rt. 276, Box 377, Paintsville, KY 41240 Tel. (606)789-5598

New River District, Calvin Weikel, Rt. 2, Box 300, Ronceverte, WV 24970 Tel. (304)647-4301

North Central District, David West, 9977 M-46, Lakeview, MI 48850 Tel. (517)352-8161

North Eastern District, Thomas Dillow, P.O. Box 7, Millville, WV 25432 Tel. (304)725-0587

South Eastern District, Dexter Keith, 881 Berne St. SE, Atlanta, GA 30316 Tel. (404)622-2795

Tri-State District, J. W. Ferguson, 9724 US Rt. 60, Ashland, KY 41102 Tel. (606)928-6651

OTHER ORGANIZATIONS

Beulah Heights Bible College, Pres., Samuel R. Chand, 892 Berne St., Atlanta, GA 31306 Tel. (404)627-2681

Ladies Auxiliary, Gen. Pres., Janice Boyce, 121 W. Hunters Tr., Elizabeth City, NC 27909 Tel. (919)338-3003

Locust Grove Rest Home, Dir., Frank Myers, Rt. 3, Box 175, Harpers Ferry, WV 25425 Tel. (304)535-6355

Pentecostal Ambassadors, Gen. Pres., Asa Lowe, 3153 Old Carolina Rd., Virginia Beach, VA 23457 Tel. (404)421-3773

Sunday School Dept., P.O. Box 439, London, OH 43140 Tel. (614)852-0348

PERIODICALS

The Bridegroom's Messenger; Pentecostal Leader

International Pentecostal Holiness Church

This body grew out of the National Holiness Association movement of the last century, with roots in Methodism. Beginning in the South and Midwest, the church represents the merger of the Fire-Baptized Holiness Church founded by B. H. Irwin in Iowa in 1895; the Pentecostal Holiness Church founded by A. B. Crumpler in Goldsboro, N.C., in 1898; and the Tabernacle Pentecostal Church founded by N. J. Holmes in 1898.

All three bodies joined the ranks of the pentecostal movement as a result of the Azusa Street revival in Los Angeles in 1906 and a 1907 pentecostal revival in Dunn, N.C., conducted by G. B. Cashwell, who had visited Azusa Street. In 1911 the Fire-Baptized and Pentecostal Holiness bodies merged in Falcon, N.C., to form the present church; the Tabernacle Pentecostal Church was added in 1915 in Canon, Ga.

The church stresses the new birth, the Wesleyan experience of entire sanctification, the pentecostal baptism in the Holy Spirit, evidenced by speaking in tongues, divine healing and the premillennial second coming of Christ.

HEADQUARTERS

P.O. Box 12609, Oklahoma City, OK 73157 Tel. (405)787-7110 Fax (405)789-3957

Media Contact, Admn. Asst.

OFFICERS

Gen. Supt., Bishop B. E. Underwood
Vice Chpsn./Asst. Gen. Supt., Rev. James Leggett
Asst. Gen. Supt., Rev. Jesse Simmons
Asst. Gen. Supt., Rev. Paul Howell
Gen. Sec.-Treas., Rev. Donald Duncan

OTHER ORGANIZATIONS

The Publishing House (Advocate Press), Gen. Admn., Greg Hearn, Franklin Springs, GA 30639

Gen. Woman's Ministries, Pres., Mrs. Doris Moore

Gen. Men's Ministries, Natl. Dir., Col. Jack Kelley, P.O. Box 53307, Fayetteville, NC 28305

PERIODICALS

The International Pentecostal Holiness Advocate; Helping Hand; Witness; Worldorama

Israelite House of David

The Israelite House of David, commonly called House of David, was established in 1903 in Benton Harbor, Mich., by Brother Benjamin after he had preached the Life of the Body without going to the grave, while traveling for seven years throughout a number of mid-American states.

This denomination is a Christian Association following Jesus' teachings (I Tim. 1:16) and the first born among many brethren (Rom. 8:29). The House of David is an Apostolic order (Acts 2 & 4).

Refer to Deuteronomy 7:6-7. The followers believe Brother Benjamin to have been the voice of the seventh angel referred to in Revelation 10:7, Malachi 3:1 and Job 33:23-25. His writings seek to explain the way for the elect to receive the Life of the Body (Hosea 13:14, Isaiah 38:18, I Thess. 5:23, Matt. 7:14, Titus 1:2, II Tim. 1:10, John 10:10, 27, 28).

The church expects to gather the 12 tribes of Israel (Jer. 31:1, Ezek. 20:34, 34:13, 14 and Hosea 1:11), which will be carried over into the millennium day of rest, 1,000 years (Rev. 20:1, 2 and 21:2, 4 and Isaiah 11:6-9, 35:1, 55:13, 54:13). Israel will be gathered from both Jew and Gentile.

The church uses the King James version of the Bible and the Apocrypha.

HEADQUARTERS

P.O. Box 1067, Benton Harbor, MI 49023 Tel. (616)926-6695 Fax (616)429-5594

Media Contact, Pillar & Sec., H. Thomas Dewhirst, Tel. (616)429-5594

OFFICERS

Chpsn. of Bd., Lloyd H. Dalager
Pillar & Sec., H. Thomas Dewhirst

PERIODICAL

Shiloh's Messenger of Wisdom

Jehovah's Witnesses

Modern-day Jehovah's Witnesses began in the early 1870s when Charles Taze Russell was the leader of a Bible study group in Allegheny City, Pa. In July 1879, the first issue of *Zion's Watch Tower and Herald of Christ's Presence* (now called *The Watchtower*) appeared. In 1884 Zion's Watch Tower Tract Society was incorporated, later changed to Watch Tower Bible and Tract Society. Congregations spread into other states and followers witnessed from house to house.

By 1913, printed sermons were in four languages in 3,000 newspapers in the United States, Canada and Europe. Books, booklets and tracts had been distributed by the hundreds of millions. In 1931 the name Jehovah's Witnesses, based on Isaiah 43:10-12, was adopted.

During the 1930s and 1940s Jehovah's Witnesses fought many court cases in the interest of preserving freedom of speech, press, assembly and worship. They have won a total of 43 cases before the Supreme Court.

The Watchtower Bible School of Gilead was established in 1943 for training missionaries. Since then the Witnesses have grown to 4.5 million in 229 countries (1992).

Jehovah's Witnesses believe in one almighty God, Jehovah; that Christ is God's Son, the first of God's creations and subject to Jehovah; that Christ's human life was paid as a ransom for obedient humans; and that Jehovah has assigned Christ a heavenly Kingdom to rule in righteousness over the earth. 144,000 individuals will rule with Christ over an unnumbered great crowd who will receive salvation into an earth cleansed of evil. (Rev. 7:9,10; 14:1-5). These, along with the resurrected dead, will transform the earth into a global Edenic paradise.

HEADQUARTERS

25 Columbia Heights, Brooklyn, NY 11201 Tel. (718)625-3600

Media Contact, Information Desk, Robert P. Johnson

Pres., Milton G. Henschel

Awake!; The Watchtower

Kodesh Church of Immanuel

The Kodesh Church of Immanuel was founded in 1929 and incorporated in April 1930 by Rev. Frank Russell Killingsworth and 120 laymen, some of whom were former members of the African Methodist Episcopal Zion Church. On Jan. 22, 1934, the Christian Tabernacle Union, a body of fundamental believers with headquarters in Pittsburgh, merged with the Kodesh Church of Immanuel.

The Hebrew word "Kodesh" means "sanctified, holy"; and Immanuel is a title of the Messiah which means "God with us." The church is composed of a sanctified, Spirit-filled constituency, an interracial body of believers whose teachings are Wesleyan and Arminian.

HEADQUARTERS

2601 Centre Ave., Pittsburgh, PA 15219
Media Contact, Supv. Elder, Dr. Kenneth O. Barbour, 932 Logan Rd., Bethel Park, PA 15102 Tel. (412)833-1351

OFFICERS

Supervising Elder, Dr. Kenneth O. Barbour

The Latvian Evangelical Lutheran Church in America

This body was organized into a denomination on Aug. 22, 1975 after having existed as the Federation of Latvian Evangelical Lutheran Churches in America since 1955. This church is a regional constituent part of the Lutheran Church of Latvia in Exile, a member of the Lutheran World Federation and the World Council of Churches.

The Latvian Evangelical Lutheran Church in America works to foster religious life, traditions and customs in its congregations in harmony with the Holy Scriptures, the Apostles', Nicean and Athanasian Creeds, the unaltered Augsburg Confession, Martin Luther's Small and Large Catechisms and other documents of the Book of Concord.

The LELCA is ordered by its Synod (General Assembly), executive board, auditing committee and district conferences.

HEADQUARTERS

6551 West Montrose Ave., Chicago, IL 60634 Tel. (312)725-3820 Fax (312)725-3835
Media Contact, Pres., Rev. Vilis Varsbergs

OFFICERS

Pres., Rev. Uldis Cepure, 2140 Okla Dr., Golden Valley, MN 55427 Tel. (612)546-3712
Vice-Pres., Rev. Maris Kirsons, 171 Erskin Ave. #1101, Toronto, ON M4P 1Y8 Tel. (416)486-3910
2nd Vice-Pres., Aivrs Ronis, 449 S. 40th St., Lincoln, NE 68510 Tel. (402)489-2776
Sec., Ansis Abele, 25182 Northrup Dr., Laguna Beach, CA 92653 Tel. (714)830-9712
Treas., Mr. Alfreds Trautmanis, 103 Rose St., Freeport, NY 11520 Tel. (516)623-2646

PERIODICAL

Cela Biedrs

The Liberal Catholic Church—Province of the United States of America

The Liberal Catholic Church was founded Feb. 13, 1916 as a reorganization of the Old Catholic Church in Great Britain with the Rt. Rev. James I. Wedgwood as the first Presiding Bishop. The first ordination of a priest in the United States was Fr. Charles Hampton, later a Bishop. The first Regionary Bishop for the American Province was the Rt. Rev. Irving S. Cooper (1919-1935).

HEADQUARTERS

Pres., Rt. Rev. Lawrence J. Smith, 9740 S. Avers Ave., Evergreen Park, IL 60642 Tel. (708)424-6548

OFFICERS

Pres. & Regionary Bishop, The Rt. Rev. Lawrence J. Smith
Vice-Pres., Rev. Alfred Strauss, 5954 SE 22nd Ave., Portland, OR 97202 Tel. (503)238-5713
Sec. (Provincial), Rev. Lloyd Worley, 1232 24th Avenue Ct., Greeley, CO 80631 Tel. (303)356-3002
Provost, The V. Rev. William Holme, P.O. Box 7042, Rochester, MN 55903
Treas., Rev. Lloyd Worley

BISHOPS

Regionary Bishop for the American Province, The Rt. Rev. Lawrence J. Smith
Aux. Bishops of the American Province: Rt. Rev. Dr. Robert S. McGinnis, Jr., 2204 Armond Blvd., Destrehan, LA 70065; Rt. Rev. Joseph L. Tisch, P.O. Box 1117, Melbourne, FL 32901; Rt. Rev. Dr. Hein VanBeusekom, 12 Krotona Hill, Ojai, CA 93023; Rt. Rev. Ruben Cabigting, P.O. Box 270, Wheaton, IL 60189

PERIODICAL

Ubique

Liberty Baptist Fellowship

The Liberty Baptist Fellowship consists of independent Baptist churches and pastors organized for the purpose of planting indigenous local New Testament churches in North America. The Fellowship is in general accord with the doctrines and philosophy of the Independent Baptist movement.

HEADQUARTERS

Candler's Mountain Rd., Lynchburg, VA 24506 Tel. (804)582-2410
Media Contact, Pres., Dr. Danny Lovett, P.O. Box 368, Madison Heights, VA 24572 Tel. (804)582-2410

OFFICERS

Natl. Chmn.: Jerry Falwell; A. Pierre Guillermin
Pres., Dr. Danny Lovett
Exec. Sec., Herb Fitzpatrick
LBF Endorsing Agent, Rev. Lew A. Weider
Natl. Comm.: Pres., Dr. Danny Lovett; John Cartwright; Johnny Basham; Herb Fitzpatrick; Lindsay Howan; Frank Lacey; Allen McFarland; Steve Reynolds; David Rhodenhizer; Daren Ritchey; Gary Roy; George Sweet

The Lutheran Church—Missouri Synod

The Lutheran Church—Missouri Synod, began in the state of Missouri in 1847.

It has more than 6,000 congregations in the United States and works in 42 other countries. It has 2.6 million members worldwide and is the second-largest Lutheran denomination in North America.

Christian education is offered for all ages. The North American congregations operate the largest elementary and secondary school systems of any Protestant denomination in the nation, and 12,260 students are enrolled in 12 LCMS institutions of higher learning.

Traditional beliefs concerning the authority and interpretation of Scripture are important. The synod is known for mass-media outreach through "The Lutheran Hour" on radio, "This Is The Life" dramas on television, and the products of Concordia Publishing House, the third-largest Protestant publisher, whose Arch Books children's series has sold more than 55 million copies.

An extensive Braille volunteer network of more than 1,000 volunteers in 40 work centers makes devotional materials for the blind; 54 of the 85 deaf congregations affiliated with U.S. denominations are LCMS; and many denominations use the Bible lessons prepared for developmentally disabled persons.

The involvement of women is high, although they do not occupy clergy positions. Serving as teachers, deaconesses and social workers, women comprise approximately 48 percent of total professional workers.

The members' responsibility for congregational leadership is a distinctive characteristic of the synod. Power is vested in voters' assemblies, generally comprised of adults of voting age. Synod decision making is given to the delegates at national and regional conventions, where the franchise is equally divided between lay and pastoral representatives.

HEADQUARTERS

The Lutheran Church—Missouri Synod, International Center, 1333 S. Kirkwood Rd., St. Louis, MO 63122-7295

Media Contact, Dir., News & Information, Rev. David Mahsman, Tel. (314)965-9000 Fax (314)965-3396

OFFICERS

Pres., Dr. A.L. Barry
1st Vice-Pres., Dr. August T. Mennicke
2nd Vice-Pres., Dr. Robert King
3rd Vice-Pres., Dr. Eugene Bunkowske
4th Vice-Pres., Dr. Robert C. Sauer
5th Vice-Pres., Dr. Walter A. Maier
Sec., Dr. Walter L. Rosin
Treas., Dr. Norman Sell
Admn. Officer of Bd. of Dir., Dr. John P. Schuelke
Dir. of Personnel, Mr. Gary Mittendorf
Bd. of Directors: Dr. Karl L. Barth, Milwaukee, WI; Rev. Richard L. Thompson, Billings, MT; Donald Brosz, Laramie, WY; John L. Daniel, Emmaus, PA; Ernest Garbe, Dietirich, IL; Oscar H. Hanson, Lafayette, CA; ; Mr. Robert W. Hirsch, Yankton, SC; Dr. Florence Montz, Bismarck, ND; Dr. Harold M. Olsen, Springfield, IL; Mr. Lester W. Schultz, Russellville, AR; Mr. Gilbert E. LaHaine, Lansing, MI; Dr. Donald Snyder, Henrietta, NY

BOARDS AND COMMISSIONS

Communication Services, Exec. Dir., Rev. Paul Devantier
Evangelism Services, Exec. Dir., Rev. Lyle Muller
Mission Services, Exec. Dir., Dr. Glenn O'Shoney
Parish Services, Exec. Dir., Dr. H. James Boldt
Higher Education Services, Exec. Dir., Dr. William F. Meyer
Youth Services, Exec. Dir., Mr. LeRoy Wilke
Human Care Ministries, Exec. Dir., Rev. Richard L. Krenzke
Worker Benefit Plans, Admn., Mr. Earl E. Haake
Lutheran Church Ext. Fund-Missouri Synod, Pres., Mr. Arthur C. Haake
Min. to the Armed Forces Standing Comm., Exec. Dir., Rev. James Shaw
Dept. of Stewardship, Acting Dir., Rev. John Meyer

ORGANIZATIONS

Concordia Publishing House, Pres./CEO, John Gerber, 3558 S. Jefferson Ave., St. Louis, MO 63118-3968
Concordia Historical Institute, Dir., Dr. August R. Suelflow, Concordia Seminary, 801 De Mun Ave., St. Louis, MO 63105
Intl. Lutheran Laymen's League, Exec. Dir., Mr. Laurence E. Lumpe, 2185 Hampton Ave., St. Louis, MO 63139-2983
KFUO Radio, Exec. Dir., Rev. Paul Devantier, 85 Founders Ln., St. Louis, MO 63105
Intl. Lutheran Women's Missionary League, Pres., Mrs. Ida Mall, 3558 S. Jefferson Ave., St. Louis, MO 63118-3910

PERIODICALS

The Lutheran Witness; Reporter

Mennonite Church

The Mennonite Church in North America traces its beginnings to the Protestant Reformation. Conrad Grebel, Georg Blaurock and a small band of radical believers baptized one another in Zurich, Switzerland, on Jan. 21, 1525. First nicknamed Anabaptists (Rebaptizers) by their opponents, they preferred the term Brothers and Sisters in Christ. They later took their name from the Dutch priest Menno Simons, who joined the movement in 1536.

The Mennonites' refusal to conform to majesterial decrees, including bearing of arms and the swearing of oaths, attracted fierce animosity. Thousands were martyred for their beliefs in nearly a century of persecution. They moved to many places, including the United States and Canada, where some arrived as early as 1683.

North American Mennonites began their first home mission program in Chicago, Ill., in 1893 and their first overseas mission program in India in 1899. Since the 1920s the church has established extensive emergency relief and development services in conjunction with its mission program.

Mennonites hold that the Word of God is central and that new life in Christ is available to all who believe. Adult "Believers" baptism is practiced, symbolizing a conscious decision to follow Christ. Mennonites take seriously Christ's command to witness in word and deed. They stress that Christians need the support of a faith community for encouragement and growth. They view the teachings of Jesus as directly applicable to their lives. Mennonites generally refuse to serve in the military or to use violent resistance.

The largest body of Mennonites in North America, the Mennonite Church is a member of the Mennonite and Brethren in Christ World Conference, a worldwide fellowship, and the Mennonite Central Committee, an international relief and service agency. Individuals and program agencies participate in a variety of ecumenical activities at various levels of church life.

HEADQUARTERS
421 S. Second St., Ste. 600, Elkhart, IN 46516 Tel. (219)294-7131
Media Contact, Churchwide Communications Dir., John Bender, Fax (219)293-3977

OFFICER
Mod., Donella Clemens

OTHER ORGANIZATIONS
Gen. Bd., Gen. Sec., James M. Lapp
Historical Cmte., Dir., Levi Miller, 1700 S. Main, Goshen, IN 46526 Tel. (219)535-7477
Council on Faith, Life & Strategy, Staff, Miriam Book
Bd. of Congregational Min., Exec. Sec., Everett Thomas, Box 1245, Elkhart, IN 46515 Tel. (219)294-7523
Bd. of Educ., Exec. Sec., Albert Meyer, Box 1142, Elkhart, IN 46515 Tel. (219)294-7523
Bd. of Missions, Pres., Stanley W. Green, Box 370, Elkhart, IN 46515 Tel. (219)294-7523
Mutual Aid Bd., Pres., Howard Brenneman, 1110 North Main, P.O. Box 483, Goshen, IN 46526 Tel. (219)533-9511
Mennonite Publication Bd., Publisher, J. Robert Ramer, 616 Walnut Ave., Scottdale, PA 15683 Tel. (412)887-8500

PERIODICALS
Gospel Herald; Christian Living; Builder; Mennonite Historical Bulletin; Mennonite Quarterly Review; Purpose; On the Line; Story Friends; Voice

Mennonite Church, The General Conference
The General Conference Mennonite Church was formed in 1860, uniting Mennonites throughout the United States who were interested in doing missionary work together. Today 60,000 Christians in 363 congregations try to follow the way of Jesus in their daily lives.

The conference consists of people of many ethnic backgrounds — Swiss and German, Russian and Dutch, African-American, Hispanic, Chinese, Vietnamese and Laotian. Some native Americans in both Canada and the United States also relate to the conference.

The basic belief and practice of the conference come from the life and teachings of Jesus Christ, the early church of the New Testament and the Anabaptists of the 16th-century Reformation. Thus the conference seeks to be evangelical, guided by the Bible, led by the Holy Spirit and supported by a praying, discerning community of believers in congregations and fellowships. Peace, or shalom, is at the very heart of members, who seek to be peacemakers in everyday life.

The goals of the conference are to evangelize, teach and practice biblical principles, train and develop leaders and work for Christian unity.

HEADQUARTERS
722 Main, Newton, KS 67114 Tel. (316)283-5100 Fax (316)283-0454

Media Contact, Communications Dir., David Linscheid

OFFICERS
Mod., Darrell Fast, 328 E. 2nd St., Newton, KS 67114
Asst. Mod., Bernie Wiebe, 46 Belair Rd., Winnipeg, MB R3T 0S2
Sec., Anita Penner, 33304 Century Cres., Abbotsford, BC V2S 5V5
Gen. Sec., Vern Preheim

OTHER ORGANIZATIONS
Commission on Home Ministries, Exec., Lois Barrett
Commission on Overseas Mission, Exec. Sec., Erwin Rempel
Women in Mission, Coord., Susan Jantzen
Commission on Education, Exec. Sec., Norma Johnson
Div. of General Services: Bus. Mgr., Ted Stuckey; Planned Giving Dir., Gary Franz; Communications Dir., David Linscheid
Mennonite Men, Coord., Heinz Janzen
Faith & Life Press, Mgr., Dietrich Rempel
Committee on Ministry, Dir. of Ministerial Leadership, John A. Esau

PERIODICALS
Being In Touch; The Mennonite; Window to Mission

The Metropolitan Church Association, Inc.
Organized after a revival movement in Chicago in 1894 as the Metropolitan Holiness Church, this organization was chartered as the Metropolitan Church Association in 1899. It has Wesleyan _theology.

HEADQUARTERS
323 Broad St., Lake Geneva, WI 53147 Tel. (414)248-6786
Media Contact, Pres., Rev. Warren W. Bitzer

OFFICERS
Pres., Rev. Warren W. Bitzer
Vice-Pres. & Sec., Elbert L. Ison
Treas., Gertrude J. Puckhaber

PERIODICAL
The Burning Bush

The Missionary Church
The Missionary Church was formed in 1969 through a merger of the United Missionary Church (organized in 1883) and the Missionary Church Association (founded in 1898). It is evangelical and conservative with a strong emphasis on missionary work and church planting.

There are three levels of church government with local, district and general conferences. There are 10 church districts in the United States. The general conference meets every two years. The denomination operates one college in the United States.

HEADQUARTERS
3811 Vanguard Dr., P.O. Box 9127, Ft. Wayne, IN 46899-9127 Tel. (219)747-2027 Fax (219)747-5331
Publishing Headquarters, Bethel Publishing Co., 1819 S. Main St., Elkhart, IN 46516 Tel. (219)293-8585

Media Contact, Pres., Dr. John P. Moran

OFFICERS

Pres., Dr. John P. Moran
Vice-Pres., Rev. William Hossler
Sec., Rev. Dave Engbrecht
Treas., Mr. Milt Gerber
Asst. to the Pres., Rev. Robert Ransom
Overseas Ministries (World Partners): Dir., Rev. Charles Carpenter; Dir. of Mission Ministries, Rev. David Mann
Services Dir., Mr. David von Gunten
Bethel Publishing Co., Exec. Dir., Rev. Richard Oltz
Stewardship, Dir., Rev. Ken Stucky
Youth Dir., Mr. Eric Liechty
Children's Dir., Dr. Neil McFarlane
Adult Dir., Dr. Duane Beals
Senior Adult Ministry Dir., Dr. Charles Pureton
Missionary Men Liaison, Rev. Bob Ransom
Missionary Women Intl., Pres., Mrs. Opal Speicher
Investment Foundation, Mr. Bob Henschen

PERIODICALS

Emphasis on Faith and Living; Ministry Today; World Partners; Priority

Moravian Church in America (Unitas Fratrum)

In 1735 German Moravian missionaries of the pre-Reformation faith of Jan Hus came to Georgia, in 1740 to Pennsylvania, and in 1753 to North Carolina. They established the American Moravian Church, which is broadly evangelical, ecumenical, liturgical, "conferential" in form of government and with an episcopacy as a spiritual office.

HEADQUARTERS

See Provincial addresses
Media Contact, Editor, *The Moravian*, The Rev. Hermann I. Weinlick, Tel. (610)867-7566 Fax (610)866-9223

NORTHERN PROVINCE

1021 Center St., P.O. Box 1245, Bethlehem, PA 18016-1245 Tel. (610)867-7566 Fax (610)866-9223

PROVINCIAL ELDERS' CONFERENCE

Pres., Rev. Dr. Gordon L. Sommers
Vice-Pres./Sec. (Eastern Dist.), The Rev. David L. Wickmann
Vice-Pres. (Western Dist.), Rev. R. Burke Johnson, P.O. Box 386, Sun Prairie, WI 53590 Fax (608)825-6610
Treas., John F. Ziegler, 1021 Center St., P.O. Box 1245, Bethlehem, PA 18016

SOUTHERN PROVINCE

459 S. Church St., Winston-Salem, NC 27108 Tel. (910)725-5811 Fax (910)725-1893

PROVINCIAL ELDERS' CONFERENCE

Pres., Rev. Dr. Graham H. Rights
Vice-Pres./Asst. to Pres., The Rev. William H. McElveen
Sec., Richard R. Bovender
Treas., Ronald R. Hendrix, Drawer O, Salem Station, Winston-Salem, NC 27108

ALASKA PROVINCE

P.O. Box 545, Bethel, AK 99559

OFFICERS

Pres., The Rev. John P. Andrew
Vice-Pres., The Rev. David Paul
Sec., Ferdinand Sharp
Treas., Juanita Asicksik
Dir. of Theological Education, Rev. Dr. Kurt H. Vitt

PERIODICAL

The Moravian

National Association of Congregational Christian Churches

This association was organized in 1955 in Detroit, Mich., by delegates from Congregational Christian Churches committed to continuing the congregational way of faith and order in church life. Participation by member churches is voluntary.

HEADQUARTERS

P.O. Box 1620, Oak Creek, WI 53154 Tel. (414)764-1620 Fax (414)764-0319
Media Contact, Exec. Sec., Michael S. Robertson, 8473 So. Howell Ave., Oak Creek, WI 53154 Tel. (414)764-1620 Fax (414)764-0319

OFFICERS

Mod., William Ahrens
Exec. Sec., Michael S. Robertson, 8473 South Howell Ave., Oak Creek, WI 53154
Assoc. Exec. Secs.: Rev. Dr. Michael Halcomb; Rev. Dr. Harry W. Clark

PERIODICAL

The Congregationalist

National Association of Free Will Baptists

This evangelical group of Arminian Baptists was organized by Paul Palmer in 1727 at Chowan, N.C. Another movement (teaching the same doctrines of free grace, free salvation and free will) was organized June 30, 1780, in New Durham, N.H., but there was no connection with the southern organization except for a fraternal relationship.

The northern line expanded more rapidly and extended into the West and Southwest. This body merged with the Northern Baptist Convention Oct. 5, 1911, but a remnant of churches reorganized into the Cooperative General Association of Free Will Baptists Dec. 28, 1916, at Pattonsburg, Mo.

Churches in the southern line were organized into various conferences from the beginning and finally united in one General Conference in 1921.

Representatives of the Cooperative General Association and the General Conference joined Nov. 5, 1935 to form the National Association of Free Will Baptists.

HEADQUARTERS

5233 Mt. View Rd., Antioch, TN 37013-2306 Tel. (615)731-6812 Fax (615)731-0049
Mailing Address, P.O. Box 5002, Antioch, TN 37011-5002
Media Contact, Exec. Sec., Melvin Worthington

OFFICERS

Exec. Sec., Dr. Melvin Worthington
Mod., Rev. Ralph Hampton, P.O. Box 50117, Nashville, TN 37205

DENOMINATIONAL AGENCIES

Free Will Baptist Foundation, Exec. Sec., William Evans
Free Will Baptist Bible College, Pres., Dr. Tom Malone
Foreign Missions Dept., Dir., Rev. R. Eugene Waddell
Home Missions Dept., Dir., Rev. Roy Thomas
Bd. of Retirement, Dir., Rev. William Evans
Historical Commission, Chpsn., Dr. Mary R. Wisehart
Commission for Theological Integrity, Chpsn., Rev. Leroy Forlines, P.O. Box 50117, Nashville, TN 37205
Music Commission, Chpsn., Vernon Whaley, P.O. Box 50117, Nashville, TN 37205
Radio & Television Commission, Chpsn., Bob Shockey, P.O. Box 50117, Nashville, TN 37205
Sunday School & Church Training Dept., Dir., Dr. Roger Reeds
Women Nationally Active for Christ, Exec. Sec., Dr. Mary R. Wisehart
Master's Men Dept., Dir., Mr. James Vallance

PERIODICALS

A Magazine for Christian Men Attack; Contact; Free Will Bible College Bulletin; Co-Laborer; Free Will Baptist Gem; Heartbeat; Mission Grams

National Baptist Convention of America, Inc.

The National Baptist Convention of America, Inc., was organized in 1880 following a dispute over control of the publishing board in which another Convention was organized. Membership of the churches is largely African-American.

HEADQUARTERS

Media Contact, Liaison Officer, Dr. Richard A. Rollins, 777 S. R.L. Thornton Fwy., Ste. 205, Dallas, TX 75203 Tel. (214)946-8913 Fax (214)946-9619

OFFICER

Pres., Dr. E. Edward Jones, 1540 Pierre Ave., Shreveport, LA 71103 Tel. (318)221-3701 Fax (318)222-7512

PERIODICAL

NBCA Lantern

National Baptist Convention, U.S.A., Inc.

The older and parent convention of black Baptists, this body is to be distinguished from the National Baptist Convention of America.

HEADQUARTERS

1700 Baptist World Center Dr., Nashville, TN 37207 Tel. (615)228-6292 Fax (615)226-5935
Media Contact, Gen. Sec., W. Franklyn Richardson, 52 S. 6th Ave., Mt. Vernon, NY 10550 Tel. (914)664-2676 Fax (914)664-2833

OFFICERS

Pres., Dr. T. J. Jemison, 356 East Boulevard, Baton Rouge, LA 70802 Tel. (504) 383-5401
Gen. Sec., Dr. W. Franklyn Richardson, 52 South 6th Ave., Mt. Vernon, NY 10550 Tel. (914) 664-2676

Vice-Pres.-at-large, Dr. C. A. W. Clark, 3110 Bonnie View Rd., Dallas, TX 75216 Tel. (214)375-6982
Treas., Dr. Isaac Green, 3068 Iowa St., Pittsburgh, PA 15219 Tel. (412)556-1437
Vice-Pres.: Dr. David Matthews, P.O. Box 627, Indianola, MS; Dr. P. J. James, 1104 E. Cherry St., Blytheville, AZ 72315; Dr. Henry L. Lyons; Dr. E. Victor Hill, 1300-08 East 50th St., Los Angeles, CA 90011; Dr. Allen Stanley, 2165 Fifth Ave., Troy, NY 12182
Asst. Sec.: Dr. B. J. Whipper, Sr., 15 Ninth St., Charleston, SC 29403; Rev. Otis B. Smith, P.O. Box 544, Tuscaloosa, AL 35404; Dr. Roger P. Derricotte, 539 Roseville Ave., Newark, NJ 07107; Dr. McKinley Dukes, 4223 S. Benton, Kansas City, MO 64130
Stat., Rev. H. L. Harvey, Jr., 3212 Reading Rd., Cincinnati, OH 45229
Hist., Dr. Clarence Wagner, 500 Myrtle St., Gainesville, GA 30501 Tel. (404)536-8474

OFFICERS OF BOARDS

Foreign Mission Bd., Sec., Dr. William J. Harvey, 701 S. 19th St. Philadelphia, PA 19146
Home Mission Bd., Exec. Sec., Dr. Jerry Moore, 1612 Buchanan St. N.W., Washington, DC 20011
Sunday School Publishing Bd., Exec. Dir., Mrs. C. N. Adkins, 330 Charlotte Ave., Nashville, TN 37201
Education Bd., Chpsn., Dr. J. Parrish Wilson, 114 S. 22nd St., Saginaw, MI 48601
Evangelism Bd., Dr. Manuel Scott, 2600 S. Marsalis Ave., Dallas, TX 75216
Laymen's Movement, Pres., Mr. Walter Cade, 1421 North 13th St., Kansas City, KS 66102
Woman's Auxiliary Convention, Pres., Mrs. Mary O. Ross, 584 Arden Pk., Detroit, MI 48202
Congress of Christian Education, Dr. A. Lincoln James, Sr., 5302 S. Michigan Ave., Chicago, IL 60615 Tel. (312)373-3188

PERIODICAL

Mission Herald

National Missionary Baptist Convention of America

The National Missionary Baptist Convention of America was organized in 1988 as a separate entity from the National Baptist Convention of America, Inc., after a dispute over control of the convention's publishing efforts. The new organization intended to remain committed to the National Baptist Sunday Church School and Baptist Training Union Congress and the National Baptist Publishing Board.

The purpose of the National Missionary Baptist Convention of America is to serve as an agency of Christian education, church extension and missionary efforts. It seeks to maintain and safeguard full religious liberty and engage in social and economic development.

HEADQUARTERS

6717 Centennial Blvd., Nashville, TN 37209 Tel. (615)350-8000

OFFICER

Gen. Sec., Dr. S. J. Gilbert, Sr., 902 W. 8th St., Houston, TX 77007 Tel. (713)869-9171 Fax (713)869-0902

99

National Organization of the New Apostolic Church of North America

This body is a variant of the Catholic Apostolic Church which began in England in 1830. The New Apostolic Church distinguished itself from the parent body in 1863 by recognizing a succession of Apostles.

HEADQUARTERS

3753 N. Troy St., Chicago, IL 60618
Media Contact, Sec. & Treas., Ellen E. Eckhardt, Tel. (312)539-3652 Fax (312)478-6691

OFFICERS

Pres., Rev. Michael Kraus, 267 Lincoln Rd., Waterloo, ON
First Vice-Pres., Rev. John W. Fendt, 36 Colony La., Manhasset, NY 11030
Second Vice-Pres., Rev. Erwin Wagner, 330 Arlene Pl., Waterloo, ON
Treas. & Sec., Ellen E. Eckhardt, 6380 N. Indian Rd., Chicago, IL 60646
Asst. Sec., Rev. William K. Schmeerbauch, 5516 Pine Wood Forest, St. Louis, MO 63128

National Primitive Baptist Convention, Inc.

Throughout the years of slavery and the Civil War, the Negro population of the South worshipped with the white population in their various churches. At the time of emancipation, their white brethren helped them to establish their own churches, granting them letters of fellowship, ordaining their deacons and ministers and helping them in other ways.

The doctrine and polity of this body are quite similar to that of white Primitive Baptists, except that they are "opposed to all forms of church organization"; yet there are local associations and a national convention, organized in 1907.

Each church is independent and receives and controls its own membership. This body was formerly known as Colored Primitive Baptists.

HEADQUARTERS

P.O. Box 2355, Tallahassee, FL 32316 Tel. (904)22-5218

OFFICER

Natl. Convention, Pres., Elder F. L. Livingston, 1334 Carson St., Dallas, TX 75216 Tel. (214)946-4650

National Spiritualist Association of Churches

This organization is made up of believers that Spiritualism is a science, philosophy and religion based upon the demonstrated facts of communication between this world and the next.

HEADQUARTERS

Media Contact, Publ. Rel. Dir., Rev. Brenda Wittich, 3903 Connecticut St., St. Louis, MO 63116 Tel. (314)773-0106

OFFICERS

Pres., Rev. Joseph H. Merrill, 13 Cleveland Ave., Lily Dale, NY 14752
Vice-Pres., Rev. Brenda Wittich, 3903 Connecticut St., St. Louis, MO 63116

Sec., Rev. Sharon L. Snowman, P.O. Box 217, Lily Dale, NY 14752 Tel. (716)595-2000 Fax (716)595-2020
Treas., Rev. Alfred A. Conner, 293 Jersey St., San Francisco, CA 94114

OTHER ORGANIZATIONS

Bureau of Educ., Supt., Rev. Joseph Sax, Morris Pratt Institute, 11811 Watertown Plank Rd., Milwaukee, WI 53226
Bureau of Public Relations, Rev. Brenda Wittich, 3903 Connecticut St., St. Louis, MO 63116
The Stow Memorial Foundation, Sec., Rev. Sharon L. Snowman, P.O. Box 217, Lily Dale, NY 14752 Tel. (716)595-2000 Fax (716)595-2020
Spiritualist Benevolent Society, Inc., P.O. Box 217, Lily Dale, NY 14752

PERIODICAL

The National Spiritualist Summit

Netherlands Reformed Congregations

The Netherlands Reformed Congregations organized denominationally in 1907. In the Netherlands, the so-called Churches Under the Cross (established in 1839, after breaking away from the 1834 Secession congregations) and the so-called Ledeboerian churches (established in 1841 under the leadership of the Rev. Ledeboer, who seceded from the Reformed State Church), united in 1907 under the leadership of the then 25-year-old Rev. G. H. Kersten, to form the Netherlands Reformed Congregations. Many of the North American congregations left the Christian Reformed Church to join the Netherlands Reformed Congregations after the Kuyperian presupposed regeneration doctrine began making inroads.

All Netherlands Reformed Congregations, office-bearers and members subscribe to three Reformed Forms of Unity: The Belgic Confession of Faith (by DeBres), the Heidelberg Catechism (by Ursinus and Olevianus) and the Canons of Dort. Both the Belgic Confession and the Canons of Dort are read regularly at worship services, and the Heidelberg Catechism is preached weekly, except on church feast days.

HEADQUARTERS

Media Contact, Synodical Clk., Dr. Joel R. Beeke, 2115 Romence Ave., N.E., Grand Rapids, MI 49503 Tel. (616)459-6565 Fax (616)459-7709

OFFICER

Clk. of Synod, Dr. Joel R. Beeke, 2115 Romence Ave. N.E., Grand Rapids, MI 49503

OTHER ORGANIZATION

Netherlands Reformed Book and Publishing, 1020 N. Main Ave., Sioux Center, IA 51250

PERIODICAL

The Banner of Truth

North American Baptist Conference

The North American Baptist Conference was begun by immigrants from Germany. The first church was organized by the Rev. Konrad Fleischmann in Philadelphia in 1843. In 1865 delegates of the churches met in Wilmot, Ont., and organized the North American Baptist Conference. Today only a few churches still use the German language, mostly in a bilingual setting.

The Conference meets in general session once every three years for fellowship, inspiration and to conduct the business of the Conference through elected delegates from the local churches. The General Council, composed of representatives of the various Associations and Conference organizations and departments, meets annually to determine the annual budget and programs for the Conference and its departments and agencies. The General Council also makes recommendations to the Triennial Conference on policies, long-range plans and election of certain personnel, boards and committees.

Approximately 80 missionaries serve in Cameroon, Nigeria, West Africa, Japan, Brazil, Eastern Europe, Mexico and the Philippines, as well as among various ethnic groups throughout the United States and Canada.

Nine homes for the aged are affiliated with the Conference and ten camps are operated on the association level.

HEADQUARTERS
1 S. 210 Summit Ave., Oakbrook Terrace, IL 60181 Tel. (708)495-2000 Fax (708)495-3301
Media Contact, Development Dir., Dr. Lewis Petrie

OFFICERS
Mod., Mr. Richard Russell
Vice-Mod., Rev. Ron Norman
Exec. Dir., Dr. John Binder
Treas., Mr. Jackie Loewer

OTHER ORGANIZATIONS
Missions Dept., Dir., Dr. Herman Effa
Church Min. Dept., Dir., Dr. Ronald Mayforth
Management Services Dept., Dir., Mr. Ron Salzman
Church Extension Investors Fund, Dir., Mr. Robert Mayforth

PERIODICALS
Baptist Herald; Moments With God

North American Old Roman Catholic Church
The North American Old Roman Catholic Church can be traced back to the early 1700s to the Ultrajectine Tradition when the Church in Holland experienced a truly catholic reform. The Church came to the United States and Mexico in its present form in the early part of this century.

English and Latin pre-Vatican II masses are celebrated. The Baltimore Catechism is used in all CCD and adult classes. The Pontificale Romanum is used for consecration and other episcopal and liturgical functions. This church recognizes the authority of the See of St. Peter.

The sacraments and holy orders of the Old Roman Catholic Church are universally accepted as valid.

HEADQUARTERS
4200 N. Kedvale Ave., Chicago, IL 60641 Tel. (312)685-0461
Media Contact, Presiding Archbishop, Most Rev. Theodore J. Rematt, SGS

OFFICER
Archbishop, Most Rev. Theodore J. Rematt

PERIODICAL
The North American Catholic

North American Old Roman Catholic Church (Archdiocese of New York)
This body is identical with the Roman Catholic Church in faith but differs from it in discipline and worship. The Mass is offered with the appropriate rite either in Latin or in the vernacular. All other sacraments are taken from the Roman Pontifical. This jurisdiction allows for married clergy.

PRIMATIAL HEADQUARTERS
Box 021647 GPO, Brooklyn, NY 11202-0036 Tel. (718)855-0600
Media Contact, Chancellor, Rev. Albert J. Berube

OFFICERS
Primate, The Most Rev. Herve L. Quessy
Chancellor, Most Rev. Albert J. Berube
Diocese of New York: Ordinary, Most Rev. Albert J. Berube
Diocese of Montreal & French Canada: Ordinary, Most Rev. Herve L. Quessy

Old German Baptist Brethren
This group separated from the Church of the Brethren (formerly German Baptist Brethren) in 1881 as a protest against a liberalizing tendency.

HEADQUARTERS
Media Contact, Vindicator Ofc. Ed., Elder M. Keith Skiles, 1876 Beamsville-Union City Rd., Union City, OH Tel. (513)968-3877

OFFICERS
Foreman, Elder Clement Skiles, Rt. 1, Box 140, Bringhurst, IN 46913 Tel. (219)967-3367
Reading Clk., Elder Herman Shuman, Rt. 4, Box 301, Pendleton, IN 46064
Writing Clk., Elder Carl Bowman, 4065 State Rt. 48, Covington, OH 45318 Tel. (513)473-2729

PERIODICAL
The Vindicator

Old Order Amish Church
The congregations of this Old Order Amish group have no annual conference. They worship in private homes. They adhere to the older forms of worship and attire. This body has bishops, ministers and deacons.

INFORMATION
Der Neue Amerikanische Calendar, c/o Raber's Book Store, 2467 C R 600, Baltic, OH 43804
Telephone Contact, LeRoy Beachy, Beachy Amish Mennonite Church, 4324 SR 39, Millersburg, OH 44654 Tel. (216)893-2883

Old Order (Wisler) Mennonite Church
This body arose from a separation of Mennonites dated 1872, under Jacob Wisler, in opposition to what were thought to be innovations.

The group is in the Eastern United States and Canada. Each state, or district, has its own organization and holds a yearly conference.

HEADQUARTERS
Media Contact, Amos B. Hoover, 376 N. Muddy Creek Rd., Denver, PA 17517 Tel. (717)484-4849 Fax (717)484-1042

Open Bible Standard Churches, Inc.

Open Bible Standard Churches originated from two revival movements: Bible Standard Conference, founded in Eugene, Ore., under the leadership of Fred L. Hornshuh in 1919, and Open Bible Evangelistic Association, founded in Des Moines, Iowa, under the leadership of John R. Richey in 1932.

Similar in doctrine and government, the two groups amalgamated on July 26, 1935 as "Open Bible Standard Churches, Inc." with headquarters in Des Moines, Iowa.

The original group of 210 ministers has enlarged to incorporate over 1,586 ministers and 861 churches in 30 countries. The first missionary left for India in 1926. The church now ministers in Asia, Africa, South America, Europe, Canada, Mexico and the Caribbean Islands.

Historical roots of the parent groups reach back to the outpouring of the Holy Spirit in 1906 at Azusa Street Mission in Los Angeles and to the full gospel movement in the Midwest. Both groups were organized under the impetus of pentecostal revival. Simple faith, freedom from fanaticism, emphasis on evangelism and missions and free fellowship with other groups were characteristics of the growing organizations.

The highest governing body of Open Bible Standard Churches meets biennially and is composed of all ministers and one voting delegate per 100 members from each church. A National Board of Directors, elected by the national and regional conferences, conducts the business of the organization. Official Bible College is Eugene Bible College in Oregon.

Open Bible Standard Churches is a charter member of the National Association of Evangelicals and of the Pentecostal Fellowship of North America. It is a member of the Pentecostal World Conference.

HEADQUARTERS
2020 Bell Ave., Des Moines, IA 50315 Tel. (515)288-6761 Fax (515)288-2510
Media Contact, Exec. Dir., Communications & Resources, Randall A. Bach, Tel. (515)288-6761 Fax (515)288-5200

OFFICERS
Pres., Ray E. Smith
Sec.-Treas., Patrick L. Bowlin
Dir. of Intl. Min., Paul V. Canfield

PERIODICALS
Message of the Open Bible; World Vision

The (Original) Church of God, Inc.

This body was organized in 1886 as the first church in the United States to take the name "The Church of God." In 1917 a difference of opinion led this particular group to include the word (Original) in its name. It is a holiness body and believes in the whole Bible, rightly divided, using the New Testament as its rule and government.

HEADQUARTERS
P.O. Box 3086, Chattanooga, TN 37404 Tel. (615)629-4505
Media Contact, Gen. Overseer, Rev. Johnny Albertson, 2214 E. 17th St., Chattanooga, TN 37404 Tel. (615)629-4505

OFFICERS
Gen. Overseer, Rev. Johnny Albertson
Asst. Gen. Overseer, Rev. Alton Evans
Sec.-Treas., Michael B. Mitchell

PERIODICAL
The Messenger

The Orthodox Church in America

The Russian Orthodox Greek Catholic Church of America entered Alaska in 1794 before its purchase by the United States in 1867. Its canonical status of independence (autocephaly) was granted by its Mother Church, the Russian Orthodox Church, on April 10, 1970, and it is now known as The Orthodox Church in America.

HEADQUARTERS
P.O. Box 675, Syosset, NY 11791 Tel. (516)922-0550 Fax (516) 922-0954
Media Contact, Dir. of Communications, Rev. Gregory Havrilak

OFFICERS
Primate, Archbishop of Washington, Metropolitan of All America & Canada, The Most Blessed Theodosius
Chancellor, V. Rev. Robert S. Kondratick, Fax (516)922-0954

SYNOD
Chpsn., His Beatitude Theodosius
Archbishop of New York, The Most Rev. Peter, 33 Hewitt Ave., Bronxville, NY 10708
Archbishop of Pittsburgh & Western PA, The Most Rev. Kyrill, P.O. Box R, Wexford, PA 15090
Archbishop of Dallas, The Rt. Rev. Dmitri, 4112 Throckmorton, Dallas, TX 75219
Bishop of Philadelphia, The Rt. Rev. Herman, St. Tikhon's Monastery, South Canaan, PA 18459
Bishop of Sitka, The Rt. Rev. Gregory, St. Michael's Cathedral, Box 697, Sitka, AK 99835
Bishop of Detroit, The Rt. Rev. Nathaniel, 2522 Grey Tower Rd., Jackson, MI 49201
Bishop of Hartford, The Rt. Rev. Job, 6 Clark Rd., Cumberland, RI 02864
Bishop of San Francisco, The Rt. Rev. Tikhon, 649 North Robinson St., Los Angeles, CA 90026
Bishop of Ottawa and Canada, The Rt. Rev. Seraphim, RR 5, Box 179, Spencerville, ON K0E 1X0 Tel. (613)925-5226
Auxiliary Bishop, Titular Bishop of Bethesda, The Rt. Rev. Mark, 9511 Sun Pointe Dr., Boynton Beach, FL 33437

PERIODICAL
The Orthodox Church

The Orthodox Presbyterian Church

On June 11, 1936, certain ministers, elders and lay members of the Presbyterian Church in the U.S.A. withdrew from that body to form a new denomination. Under the leadership of the late Rev. J. Gresham Machen, noted conservative New Testament scholar, the new church determined to continue to uphold the Westminster Confession of Faith as traditionally understood by Presbyterians and to engage in proclamation of the gospel at home and abroad.

The church has grown modestly over the years and suffered early defections, most notably one in

1937 that resulted in the formation of the Bible Presbyterian Church under the leadership of Dr. Carl McIntire. It now has congregations throughout the states of the continental United States.

The denomination is a member of the North American Presbyterian and Reformed Council and the International Council of Reformed Churches.

HEADQUARTERS
303 Horsham Rd., Ste. G, Horsham, PA 19044 Tel. (215)956-0123 Fax (215)957-6286
Media Contact, Stated Clerk, The Rev. Donald J. Duff

OFFICERS
Mod., Rev. Donald M. Poundstone, 624 N.E. 63rd Ave., Portland, OR 97213 Tel. (503)253-0695
Stated Clk., Rev. Donald J. Duff

PERIODICAL
New Horizons in the Orthodox Presbyterian Church

Patriarchal Parishes of the Russian Orthodox Church in the U.S.A.

This group of parishes is under the direct jurisdiction of the Patriarch of Moscow and All Russia, His Holiness Aleksy II, in the person of a Vicar Bishop, His Grace Paul, Bishop of Zaraisk.

HEADQUARTERS
St. Nicholas Cathedral, 15 E. 97th St., New York, NY 10029 Tel. (212)831-6294 Fax (212)427-5003
Media Contact, Sec. to the Bishop, Deacon Vladimir Tyschuk, Tel. (212)289-1915

PERIODICAL
One Church

Pentecostal Assemblies of the World, Inc.

This organization is an interracial Pentecostal holiness of the Apostolic Faith, believing in repentance, baptism in Jesus's name and being filled with the Holy Ghost, with the evidence of speaking in tongues. It originated in the early part of the century in the Middle West has spread throughout the country.

HEADQUARTERS
3939 Meadows Dr., Indianapolis, IN 46205 Tel. (317)547-9541
Media Contact, Admin., John E. Hampton, Fax (317)543-0512

OFFICERS
Presiding Bishop, Paul A. Bowers
Asst. Presiding Bishop, David Ellis
Bishops: Arthus Brazier; George Brooks; Ramsey Butler; Morris Golder; Francis L. Smith; Brooker T. Jones; C. R. Lee; Robert McMurray; Philip L. Scott; William L. Smith; Samuel A. Layne; Freeman M. Thomas; James E. Tyson; Charles Davis; Willie Burrell; Harry Herman; Jeremiah Reed; Jeron Johnson; Clifton Jones; Robert Wauls; Ronald L. Young; Henry L. Johnson; Leodis Warren; Thomas J. Weeks; Eugene Redd; Thomas W. Weeks, Sr.; Willard Saunders; Davis L. Ellis; Earl Parchia; Vanuel C. Little; Norman Wagner; George Austin; Benjamin A. Pitt; Markose Thopil; John K. Cole; Peter Warkie; Norman Walters; Alphonso Scott;

David Dawkins
Gen. Sec, Suffragan Bishop Richard Young
Gen. Treas., Elder James Loving
Asst. Treas., Suffragan Bishop Willie Ellis

PERIODICAL
Christian Outlook

Pentecostal Church of God

Growing out of the pentecostal revival at the turn of the century, the Pentecostal Church of God was organized in Chicago on Dec. 30, 1919, as the Pentecostal Assemblies of the U.S.A. The name was changed to Pentecostal Church of God in 1922; in 1934 it was changed again to The Pentecostal Church of God of America, Inc.; and finally the name became the Pentecostal Church of God (Inc.) in 1979.

The International Headquarters was moved from Chicago to Ottumwa, Iowa, in 1927, then to Kansas City, Mo., in 1933 and finally to Joplin, Mo., in 1951.

The denomination is evangelical and pentecostal in doctrine and practice. Active membership in the National Association of Evangelicals and the Pentecostal Fellowship of North America is maintained.

The church is Trinitarian in doctrine and teaches the absolute inerrancy of the Scripture from Genesis to Revelation. Among its cardinal beliefs are the doctrines of salvation, which includes regeneration; divine healing, as provided for in the atonement; the baptism in the Holy Ghost, with the initial physical evidence of speaking in tongues; and the premillennial second coming of Christ.

HEADQUARTERS
4901 Pennsylvania, P.O. Box 850, Joplin, MO 64802 Tel. (417)624-7050 Fax (417)624-7102
Media Contact, Gen. Sec., Dr. Ronald R. Minor

OFFICERS
Gen. Supt., Dr. James D. Gee
Gen. Sec., Dr. Ronald R. Minor

OTHER GENERAL EXECUTIVES
Dir. of World Missions, Rev. Charles R. Mosier
Dir. of Indian Missions, Dr. C. Don Burke
Gen. PYPA Pres., Rev. R. Edward Vansell
Dir. of Home Missions/Evangelism, Dr. H. O. Wilson

ASSISTANT GENERAL SUPERINTENDENTS
Northwestern Division, Rev. Robert L. McGee
Southwestern Division, Dr. Norman D. Fortenberry
North Central Division, Rev. Freddy A. Burcham
South Central Division, Rev. E. L. Redding
Northeastern Division, Rev. Thomas E. Branham
Southeastern Division, Rev. James F. Richter

OTHER DEPARTMENTAL OFFICERS
Bus. Mgr., Rev. George Gilmore
Gen. PLA Dir., Mrs. Diana L. Gee
Christian Educ., Dir., Ms. Billie Blevins

PERIODICAL
The Pentecostal Messenger

Pentecostal Fire-Baptized Holiness Church

Organized in 1918, this group consolidated with the Pentecostal Free Will Baptists in 1919. It maintains rigid discipline over members.

Dry Fork, VA 24549 Tel. (804)724-4879
Media Contact, Gen. Mod., Steve E. Johnson

OFFICERS

Gen. Treas., Kenwin N. Johnson, P.O. Box 1528,
Laurinburg, NC 28352 Tel. (919)276-1295
Gen. Sec., W. H. Preskitt, Sr., Rt. 1, Box 169,
Wetumpka, AL 36092 Tel. (205)567-6565
Gen. Mod., Steve E. Johnson
Gen. Supt. Mission Bd., Jerry Powell, Rt. 1, Box
384, Chadourn, NC 28431

PERIODICAL

Faith and Truth

The Pentecostal Free Will Baptist Church, Inc.

The Cape Fear Conference of Free Will Baptists,
organized in 1855, merged in 1959 with The Wilmington Conference and The New River Conference of Free Will Baptists and was renamed the
Pentecostal Free Will Baptist Church, Inc. The
doctrines include regeneration, sanctification, the
Pentecostal baptism of the Holy Ghost, the Second
Coming of Christ and divine healing.

HEADQUARTERS

P.O. Box 1568, Dunn, NC 28335 Tel. (910)892-
4161
Media Contact, Genl. Supt., Don Sauls

OFFICERS

Gen. Supt., Dr. Don Sauls
Asst. Gen. Supt., Dr. W. L. Ellis
Gen. Sec., Rev. J. T. Hammond
Gen. Treas., Dr. W. L. Ellis
World Witness Dir., Rev. David Taylor
Christian Ed. Dir., Rev. J. T. Hammond
Gen. Services Dir., Chuch Hardison
Ministerial Council Dir., Rev. Preston Heath
Ladies' Auxiliary Dir., Mrs. Dollie Davis
Heritage Bible College, Pres., Dr. W. L. Ellis
Crusader Youth Camp, Dir., Rev. J. T. Hammond

OTHER ORGANIZATIONS

Heritage Bible College, P.O. Box 1628, Dunn, NC
28335 Tel. (910)892-4268
Crusader Youth Camp
Mutual Benefit Assoc.
Blessings Bookstore, 1006 W. Cumberland St.,
Dunn, NC 28334 Tel. (910)892-2401
Cape Fear Christian Academy, Rt 1 Box 139,
Erwin, NC 28339 Tel. (910)897-5423

PERIODICAL

The Messenger

Pillar of Fire

The Pillar of Fire was founded by Alma Bridwell
White in Denver on Dec. 29, 1901 as the Pentecostal Union. In 1917, the name was changed to Pillar
of Fire. Alma White was born in Kentucky in 1862
and taught school in Montana where she met her
husband, Kent White, a Methodist minister, who
was a University student in Denver.

Because of Alma White's evangelistic endeav-
ors, she was frowned upon by her superiors, which
eventually necessitated her withdrawing from
Methodist Church supervision. She was ordained
as Bishop and her work spread to many states, to
England, and since her death to Liberia, West
Africa, Malawi, East Africa, Yugoslavia, Spain,
India and the Philippines.

The Pillar of Fire organization has a college and
two seminaries stressing Biblical studies. It operates eight separate schools for young people. The
church continues to keep in mind the founder's
goals and purposes.

HEADQUARTERS

Zarephath, NJ 08890 Tel. (201)356-0102
Western Headquarters, 1302 Sherman St., Denver,
CO 80203 Tel. (303)427-5462 Fax (908)271-
1968
Media Contact, 1st Vice Pres., Robert B. Dallen-
bach, Tel. (303)427-5462 Fax (303)429-0910

OFFICERS

Pres. & Gen. Supt., Bishop Donald J. Wolfram
1st Vice-Pres. & Asst. Supt., Bishop Robert B.
Dallenbach
2nd Vice-Pres./Sec.-Treas., Lois R. Stewart
Trustees: Kenneth Cope; Elsworth N. Bradford; S.
Rea Crawford; June Blue

PERIODICAL

Pillar of Fire

Polish National Catholic Church of America

After a number of attempts to resolve differences
regarding the role of the laity in parish administration in the Roman Catholic Church in Scranton,
Pa., this Church was organized in 1897. With the
consecration to the episcopacy of the Most Rev. F.
Hodur, this Church became a member of the Old
Catholic Union of Utrecht in 1907.

HEADQUARTERS

Office of the Prime Bishop, 1002 Pittston Ave.,
Scranton, PA 18505 Tel. (717)346-9131
Media Contact, Prime Bishop, Most Rev. John F.
Swantek, Fax (717)346-2188

OFFICERS

Prime Bishop, Most Rev. John F. Swantek, 115
Lake Scranton Rd., Scranton, PA 18505
Central Diocese: Bishop, Rt. Rev. Anthony M.
Rysz, 529 E. Locust St., Scranton, PA 18505
Eastern Diocese: Bishop, Rt. Rev. Thomas J. J.
Gnat, 166 Pearl St., Manchester, NH 03104
Buffalo-Pittsburgh Diocese: Bishop, Rt. Rev.
Thaddeus S. Peplowski, 216 Sobieski St., Buf-
falo, NY 14211
Western Diocese: Bishop, Rt. Rev. Joseph K.
Zawistowski, Chancery, 5201 Hazelwood Ct.,
South Bend, IN 46619; Auxiliary Bishop, Rt.
Rev. Robert M. Nemkovich
Canadian Diocese: Bishop, Rt. Rev. Joseph P.
Tomczyk, 182 Cowan Ave., Toronto, ON M6K
2N6
Ecumenical Officer, V. Rev. Stanley Skrzypek,
206 Main Street, New York Mills, NY 13416 Tel.
(315)736-9757

PERIODICALS

God's Field; Polka

Presbyterian Church in America

The Presbyterian Church in America has a strong
commitment to evangelism, to missionary work at
home and abroad and to Christian education.

Organized in December 1973, this church was
first known as the National Presbyterian Church
but changed its name in 1974 to Presbyterian
Church in America (PCA).

The PCA made a firm commitment on the doctrinal standards which had been significant in presbyterianism since 1645, namely the Westminster Confession of Faith and Catechisms. These doctrinal standards express the distinctives of the Calvinistic or Reformed tradition.

The PCA maintains the historic polity of Presbyterian governance, namely rule by presbyters (or elders) and the graded courts which are the session governing the local church. The presbytery is responsible for regional matters and the general assembly for national matters. The PCA has taken seriously the position of the parity of elders, making a distinction between the two classes of elders, teaching and ruling.

In 1982, the Reformed Presbyterian Church, Evangelical Synod (RPCES) joined the PCA. It brought with it a tradition that had antecedents in Colonial America. It also included Covenant College in Lookout Mountain, Ga., and Covenant Theological Seminary in St. Louis, both of which are national denominational institutions of the PCA.

HEADQUARTERS

1852 Century Pl., Atlanta, GA 30345 Tel. (404)320-3366 Fax (404)329-1275
Media Contact, Ed., Rev. Robert G. Sweet, Tel. (404)320-3388 Fax (404)329-1280

OFFICERS

Mod., Mr. G. Richard Hostetter, Chattanooga, TN
Stated Clk., Dr. Paul R. Gilchrist, 1852 Century Pl., Ste. 190, Atlanta, GA 30345 Tel. (404)320-3366

PERMANENT COMMITTEES

Admn., Dr. Paul R. Gilchrist, 1852 Century Pl., Ste. 190, Atlanta, GA 30345 Tel. (404)320-3366 Fax (404)329-1275
Christian Educ. & Publ., Dr. Charles Dunahoo, Tel. (404)320-3388
Mission to North America, Rev. Terry Gyger, 1852 Century Pl., Ste. 205, Atlanta, GA 30345 Tel. (404)320-3330
Mission to the World, Rev. John E. Kyle, 1852 Century Pl., Ste. 201, Atlanta, GA 30345 Tel. (404)320-3373

PERIODICAL

Messenger

Presbyterian Church (U.S.A.)

The Presbyterian Church (U.S.A.) was organized June 10, 1983, when the Presbyterian Church in the United States and the United Presbyterian Church in the United States of America united in Atlanta. The union healed a major division which began with the Civil War when Presbyterians in the South withdrew from the Presbyterian Church in the United States of America to form the Presbyterian Church in the Confederate States.

The United Presbyterian Church in the United States of America had been created by the 1958 union of the Presbyterian Church in the United States of America and the United Presbyterian Church of North America. Of those two uniting bodies, the Presbyterian Church in the U.S.A. dated from the first Presbytery organized in Philadelphia, about 1706. The United Presbyterian Church of North America was formed in 1858, when the Associate Reformed Presbyterian Church and the Associate Presbyterian Church united.

Strongly ecumenical in outlook, the Presbyterian Church (U.S.A.) is the result of at least 10 different denominational mergers over the last 250 years. A restructure, adopted by the General Assembly meeting in June 1993, has been implemented. The Presbyterian Church (U.S.A.) dedicated its new headquarters in Louisville, Ky. in 1988.

HEADQUARTERS

100 Witherspoon St., Louisville, KY 40202 Tel. (502)569-5000 Fax (502)569-5018
Media Contact, Mgr., Ofc. of News Service, Marj Carpenter, Tel. (502)569-5519 Fax (502)569-8039

OFFICERS

Mod., David Dobler
Vice-Mod., Margaret Peery
Stated Clk., James E. Andrews
Assoc. Stated Clk., Catherine M. Phillippe

THE OFFICE OF THE GENERAL ASSEMBLY

Tel. (502)569-5360 Fax (502)569-8005
Stated Clk., James E. Andrews
Dept. of the Stated Clerk: Dir., Juanita H. Granady
Dept. of Administration: Dir., J. Scott Schaefer
Dept. of Constitutional Services: Dir., C. Fred Jenkins
Dept. of Governing Body: Ecumenical & Agency Rel., Dir., Gene Turner
Dept. of Assembly Services: Dir., Catherine M. Phillippe; Mgr. for Assembly Arrangements, Kerry Clements
Dept. of Hist., Philadelphia: 425 Lombard St., Philadelphia, PA 19147 Tel. (215)627-1852 Fax (215)627-0509; Dir., Frederick J. Heuser, Jr
Dept. of Hist., Montreat: P.O. Box 847, Montreat, NC 28757 Tel. (704)669-7061; Deputy Dir. of Prog., Michelle Francis

GENERAL ASSEMBLY COUNCIL

Office of the Exec. Dir., James Brown, Fax (502)569-8080
Assoc., Operations, Frank Diaz

DIVISIONS

Worldwide Ministries, Clifton Kirkpatrick
Congregational Ministries, John Coffin
National Ministries, Mary Ann Lundy
Treas., G. A. Goff
Bd. of Pensions, Pres., John Detterick, 215 Arch St., Philadelphia, PA 19107 Tel. 215)574-5200

PRESBYTERIAN CHURCH (U.S.A.) FOUNDATION

Ofc., 200 E. Twelfth St., Jeffersonville, IN 47130 Tel. (812)288-8841 Fax (502)569-5980
Chpsn. of the Bd., Frank Deming
Pres., Larry Carr

SYNOD EXECUTIVES

Alaska-Northwest, David C. Meekhof, 233 6th Ave. N., Ste. 100, Seattle, WA 98109-5000 Tel. (206)448-6403
Covenant, Rev. Lowell Sims, 6172 Bush Blvd., Ste. 3000, Columbus, OH 43229-2564 Tel. (614)436-3310
Lakes & Prairies, Rev. Robert T. Cuthill, 8012 Cedar Ave. S., Bloomington, MN 55425-1204 Tel. (612)854-0144
Lincoln Trails, Rev. Verne E. Sindlinger, 1100 W. 42nd St., Indianapolis, IN 46208-3381 Tel. (317)923-3681
Living Waters, Rev. J. Harold Jackson, P.O. Box 290275, Nashville, TN 37229-0275 Tel. (615)370-4008

Mid-America, Rev. John L. Williams, 6400 Glenwood, Ste. 111, Overland Park, KS 66202-4072 Tel. (913)384-3020

Mid-Atlantic, Carroll D. Jenkins, P.O. Box 27026, Richmond, VA 23261-7026 Tel. (804)342-0016

Northeast, —— 3049 E. Genesee St., Syracuse, NY 13224-1644 Tel. (315)446-5990

Pacific, Rev. Philip H. Young, P.O. Box 1810, San Anselmo, CA 94960-7091 Tel. (415)258-0333

Puerto Rico, Rev. Harry Fred Del Valle, Medical Center Plaza, Oficina 216, Mayaguez, PR 00708 Tel. (809)832-8375

Rocky Mountains, Ramona McKee, 7000 N. Broadway, Suite 410, Denver, CO 80221-2475 Tel. (303)428-0523

South Atlantic, Rev. John Niles Bartholomew, Interstate North Office Center, 435 Clark Rd., Ste. 404, Jacksonville, FL 32218-5574 Tel. (904)764-5644

Southern California, Hawaii, Rev. Rafael J. Aragon, 1501 Wilshire Blvd., Los Angeles, CA 90017-2293 Tel. (213)483-3840

Southwest, Rev. Gary Skinner, 4423 N. 24th St., Ste. 800, Phoenix, AZ 85016-5544 Tel. (602)468-3800

Sun, Rev. William J. Fogelman, 920 S. 135 E, Denton, TX 76205-7898 Tel. (817)382-9656

Trinity, Rev. Thomas M. Johnston, Jr., 3040 Market St., Camp Hill, PA 17011-4599 Tel. (717)737-0421

PERIODICALS

American Presbyterians: Journal of Presbyterian History; Church & Society Magazine; Horizons; Monday Morning; Presbyterian Survey; These Days; Presbyterian Outlook

Primitive Advent Christian Church

This body split from the Advent Christian Church. All its churches are in West Virginia. The Primitive Advent Christian Church believes that the Bible is the only rule of faith and practice and that Christian character is the only test of fellowship and communion. The church agrees with Christian fidelity and meekness; exercises mutual watch and care; counsels, admonishes, or reproves as duty may require and receives the same from each other as becomes the household of faith. Primitive Advent Christians do not believe in taking up arms.

The church believes that three ordinances are set forth by the Bible to be observed by the Christian church: (1) baptism by immersion; (2) the Lord's Supper, by partaking of unleavened bread and wine; (3) feet washing, to be observed by the saints' washing of one another's feet.

HEADQUARTERS

Media Contact, Sec.-Treas., Hugh W. Good, 395 Frame Rd., Elkview, WV 25071 Tel. (304)965-1550

OFFICERS

Pres., Herbert Newhouse, 7632 Hughart Dr., Sissionville, WV 25320 Tel. (304)984-9277

Vice-Pres., Roger Hammons, 273 Frame Rd., Elkview, WV 25071 Tel. (304)965-6247

Sec. & Treas., Hugh W. Good, 395 Frame Rd., Elkview, WV 25071 Tel. (304)965-1550

Primitive Baptists

This large group of Baptists, located throughout the United States, opposes all centralization and modern missionary societies. They preach salvation by grace alone.

HEADQUARTERS

Cayce Publ. Co., S. Second St., P.O. Box 38, Thornton, AR 71766 Tel. (501)352-3694

Media Contact, Elder W. H. Cayce

OFFICERS

Elder W. H. Cayce

Elder Lasserre Bradley, Jr., Box 17037, Cincinnati, OH 45217 Tel. (513)821-7289

Elder S. T. Tolley, P.O. Box 68, Atwood, TN 38220 Tel. (901)662-7417

Elder Hartsel Cayce

PERIODICALS

Baptist Witness; The Christian Baptist; Primitive Baptist; For the Poor

Primitive Methodist Church in the U.S.A.

Hugh Bourne and William Clowes, local preachers in the Wesleyan Church in England, organized a daylong meeting at Mow Cop in Staffordshire on May 31, 1807, after Lorenzo Dow, a Methodist preacher from America, told them of American camp meetings. Thousands attended and many were converted but the Methodist church, founded by the open-air preacher John Wesley, refused to accept the converts and reprimanded the preachers.

After waiting for two years for a favorable action by the Wesleyan Society, Bourne and Clowes established The Society of the Primitive Methodists. This was not a schism, Bourne said, for "we did not take one from them ... it now appeared to be the will of God that we fear of God." Primitive Methodist missionaries were sent to New York in 1829. An American conference was established in 1840.

Missionary efforts reach into Guatemala, Spain and other countries. The denomination joins in federation with the Evangelical Congregational Church, the United Brethren in Christ Church and the Southern Methodist Church and is a member of the National Association of Evangelicals.

The church believes the Bible is the only true rule of faith and practice, the inspired Word of God. It believes in one Triune God, the Deity of Jesus Christ, the Deity and personality of the Holy Spirit, the innocence of Adam and Eve, the Fall of the human race, the necessity of repentance, justification by faith of all who believe, regeneration witnessed by the Holy Spirit, sanctification by the Holy Spirit, the second coming of the Lord Jesus Christ, the resurrection of the dead and conscious future existence of all people and future judgments with eternal rewards and punishments.

HEADQUARTERS

Media Contact, Exec. Dir., Rev. William H. Fudge, 1045 Laurel Run Rd., Wilkes-Barre, PA 18702 Tel. (717)472-3436 Fax (717)472-9283

OFFICERS

Pres., Dr. K. Gene Carroll, 223 Austin Ave., Wilkes-Barre, PA 18702

Exec. Dir., Rev. William H. Fudge, 1045 Laurel Run Rd., Wilkes-Barre, PA 18702 Fax (717)472-9283

Treas., Mr. Raymond Baldwin, 11012 Langton Arms Ct., Oakton, VA 22124

Gen. Sec., Rev. Reginald H. Thomas, 110 Pittston Blvd., Wilkes-Barre, PA 18702 Tel. (717)823-3425

Progressive National Baptist Convention, Inc.

This body held its organizational meeting in Cincinnati in November, 1961. Subsequent regional sessions were followed by the first annual session in Philadelphia in 1962.

HEADQUARTERS

601 50th Street, N.E., Washington, DC 20019 Tel. (202)396-0558 Fax (202)398-4998
Media Contact, Gen. Sec., Rev. Tyrone S. Pitts

OFFICERS

Pres., Dr. Charles G. Adams, Hartford Memorial Baptist Church, 18900 James Couzens Hwy., Detroit, MI 48235

The Protes'tant Conference (Lutheran), Inc.

The Conference came into being in 1927 as the result of expulsions of pastors and teachers from the Wisconsin Evangelical Lutheran Synod (WELS). The underlying cause which ignited the suspensions was a rebellion against what was labeled The Wauwatosa Theology, so named after the location of the Wisconsin Synod seminary at that time and the fresh approach to Scripture study there by the faculty. This approach sought to overcome the habits of dogmatism. Chiefly responsible for this renewal was Professor John Philipp Koehler.

The Conference was formed as the result of these suspensions, which were to be followed by other suspensions. To give testimony to the issues at operation in this controversy and in particular to bear witness to the grace of the Wauwatosa Theology, the Conference has published *Faith-Life* since 1928. The congregations are chiefly in Wisconsin. The Conference has no official officers. Chief in influence have been Professor J. P. Koehler (1859-1951); his son Karl Koehler (1885-1948), who was the chief architect of *Faith-Life* with its Policy and Purpose; and Paul Hensel (1888-1977) who displayed the Wauwatosa Theology in his writings and commentary.

OFFICERS

Recording Sec., Pastor Gerald Hinz, P.O. Box 86, Shiocton, WI 54170 Tel. (414)986-3918
Fin. Sec.-Treas., Michael Meler, 1023 Colan Blvd., Rice Lake, WI 54868

PERIODICAL

Faith-Life

Protestant Reformed Churches in America

The Protestant Reformed Churches in America were organized in 1926 as a result of doctrinal disagreement relating to such matters as world conformity, problems of higher criticism and God's grace that pervaded the Christian Reformed Church in the early 1920s.

After the passage of the formula on Three Points of Common Grace by the Synod of the Christian Reformed Church in 1924, and during the resulting storm of controversy, three clergy and those in their congregations who agreed with them were ex-

pelled from the Christian Reformed Church. These clergy were Herman Hoeksema of the Eastern Ave. Christian Reformed Church in Grand Rapids, Mich., George Ophoff, pastor of the Hope congregation in Riverbend, Mich., and Henry Danhof in Kalamazoo, Mich.

In March 1925, the consistories of these congregations signed an Act of Agreement and adopted the temporary name of "Protesting Christian Reformed Churches." The break was made final following the Synod of the Christian Reformed Church of 1926.

The Protestant Reformed Churches in America hold to the doctrinal tenets of Calvinism, the Belgic Confession, the Heidelberg Catechism and the Canons of Dordrecht.

HEADQUARTERS

16515 South Park Ave., South Holland, IL 60473 Tel. (708)333-1314
Media Contact, Stat. Clk., Rev. M. Joostens, 2016 Tekonsha, S.E., Grand Rapids, MI 49506 Tel. (616)247-0638

OFFICER

Stat. Clk., Rev. M. Joostens

Reformed Church in America

The Reformed Church in America was established in 1628 by the earliest settlers of New York. It is the oldest Protestant denomination with a continuous ministry in North America. Until 1867 it was known as the Reformed Protestant Dutch Church.

The first ordained minister, Domine Jonas Michaelius, arrived in New Amsterdam from The Netherlands in 1628. Throughout the colonial period, the Reformed Church lived under the authority of the Classis of Amsterdam. Its churches were clustered in New York and New Jersey. Under the leadership of Rev. John Livingston, it became a denomination independent of the authority of the Classis of Amsterdam in 1776. Its geographical base was broadened in the 19th century by the immigration of Reformed Dutch and German settlers in the midwestern United States. The Reformed Church now spans the United States and Canada.

The Reformed Church accepts as its standards of faith the Heidelberg Catechism, Belgic Confession and Canons of Dort. It has a rich heritage of world mission activity. It claims to be loyal to reformed tradition which emphasizes obedience to God in all aspects of life.

Although the Reformed Church in America has worked in close cooperation with other churches, it has never entered into merger with any other denomination. It is a member of the World Alliance of Reformed Churches, the World Council of Churches and the National Council of the Churches of Christ in the United States of America.

HEADQUARTERS

475 Riverside Dr., New York, NY 10115 Tel. (212)870-2841 Fax (212)870-2499
Media Contact, Dir., Stewardship & Communications Services, E. Wayne Antworth, Tel. (212)870-2954

OFFICERS AND STAFF OF GENERAL SYNOD

Pres., Warren D. Burgess, 475 Riverside Dr., Rm. 1814, New York, NY 10115
Gen. Sec., Edwin G. Mulder

Bd. of Dir., Pres., Gerald Verbridge, 475 Riverside Dr., Rm. 1814, New York, NY 10115
Bd. of Pensions: Pres., Denneth Weller; Sec., Edwin G. Mulder
General Synod Council: Mod., Beth E. Marcus, 475 Riverside Dr., Rm. 1812, New York, NY 10115
Ofc. of Ministry & Personnel Services, Dir., Alvin J. Poppen
Ofc. of Finance, Treas., Andrew Lee
Ofc. of Stewardship & Comm. Services, Dir., E. Wayne Antworth
Reformed Church Women, Exec. Dir., Diana Paulsen
African-American Council, Exec. Dir., John David Cato
Council for Hispanic Ministries, Natl. Sec., Johnny Alicea-Baez
American Indian Council, Natl. Sec., Kenneth W. Mallory
Council for Pacific/Asian-American Min., Natl. Sec., Ella Campbell

The Church Herald

Reformed Church in the United States

Lacking pastors, early German Reformed immigrants to the American colonies were led in worship by "readers." One reader, schoolmaster John Philip Boehm, organized the first congregations near Philadelphia in 1725. A Swiss pastor, Michael Schlatter, was sent by the Dutch Reformed Church in 1746. Strong ties with the Netherlands existed until the formation of the Synod of the Reformed High German Church in 1793.

The Eureka Classis, organized in North and South Dakota in 1910 and strongly influenced by the writings of H. Kohlbruegge, P. Geyser and J. Stark, refused to become part of the 1934 merger of the Reformed Church with the Evangelical Synod of North America, holding that it sacrificed the Reformed heritage. (The merged Evangelical and Reformed Church became part of the United Church of Christ in 1957.) Under the leadership of pastors W. Grossmann and W. J. Krieger, the Eureka Classis in 1942 incorporated as the continuing Reformed Church in the United States.

The growing Eureka Classis dissolved in 1986 to form a Synod with four regional classes. An heir to the Reformation theology of Zwingli and Calvin, the Heidelberg Catechism of 1563 is used as the confessional standard of the church. The Bible is strictly held to be the inerrant, infallible Word of God.

The RCUS supports Westminster Theological Seminary in Escondido, Calif., and Dordt College and Mid-America Reformed Seminary in Iowa. The RCUS is the official sponsor to the Reformed Confessing Church of Zaire.

HEADQUARTERS
Media Contact, Stated Clk., Rev. Frank Walker, 927 E. Graceway Dr., Napoleon, OH 43545 Tel. (419)599-2266

OFFICERS
Pres., Rev. Vernon Pollema, 235 James Street, Shafter, CA 93263
Vice-Pres., Rev. Paul Treick, 1515 Carlton Ave., Modesto, CA 95350 Tel. (209)526-0637

Stated Clk., Rev. Frank Walker, 927 E. Graceway Dr., Napoleon, OH 43545 Tel. (419)599-2266
Treas., Mr. Clayton Greimon, RR 3, Garner, IA 50438

Reformed Herald

Reformed Episcopal Church

The Reformed Episcopal Church was founded Dec. 2, 1873 in New York City by Bishop George D. Cummins, an assistant bishop in the Protestant Episcopal Church from 1866 until 1873. Cummins and other evangelical Episcopalians viewed with alarm the influence of the Oxford Movement in the Protestant Episcopal Church, for the interest it stimulated in Roman Catholic ritual and doctrine and for intolerance it bred toward evangelical Protestant doctrine.

Throughout the late 1860s, evangelicals and ritualists clashed over ceremonies and vestments, exchanges of pulpits with clergy of other denominations, the meaning of critical passages in the Book of Common Prayer, interpretation of the sacraments and validity of the Apostolic Succession.

In October, 1873, other bishops publicly attacked Cummins in the church newspapers for participating in an ecumenical Communion service sponsored by the Evangelical Alliance. Cummins resigned and drafted a call to Episcopalians to organize a new Episcopal Church for the "purpose of restoring the old paths of their fathers." On Dec. 2, 1873, a *Declaration of Principles* was adopted and Dr. Charles E. Cheney was elected bishop to serve with Cummins. The Second General Council, meeting in May 1874 in New York City, approved a *Constitution and Canons* and a slightly amended version of the *Book of Common Prayer*. In 1875, the Third General Council adopted a set of *Thirty-Five Articles*.

Cummins died in 1876. The church had grown to nine jurisdictions in the United States and Canada at that time. Substantial growth ceased after 1900. The church now comprises three synods (New York-Philadelphia, Chicago, Charleston-Atlanta-Charlotte) and a missionary jurisdiction of the West. The Reformed Episcopal Church is a member of the National Association of Evangelicals.

HEADQUARTERS
Diocese of the Southeast, 705 S. Main St., Summerville, SC 29483 Tel. (803)873-3451
Media Contact, Bishop Sanco K. Rembert, P.O. Box 20068, Charleston, SC 29413 Tel. (803)723-5500

OFFICERS
Pres. & Presiding Bishop, Rev. Franklin H. Sellers, Sr., 1629 W. 99th St., Chicago, IL 60643
Vice-Pres., Bishop Sanco K. Rembert, P.O. Box 20068, Charleston, SC 29413
Sec., Rev. Willie J. Hill, Jr., 271 W. Tulpehocken St., Philadelphia, PA 19144
Treas., Mr. William B. Schimpf, 67 Westaway Lane, Warrington, PA 18976

Reformed Mennonite Church

This is a small group of people who were organized into church fellowship by John Herr and others. They adhere to the doctrine and principles of love as taught in the New Testament and practiced by true Christians in all ages since the church was established on the day of Pentecost.

HEADQUARTERS

Lancaster County only, Reformed Mennonite Church, 602 Strasburg Pike, Lancaster, PA 17602

Media Contact, Bishop, Glenn M. Gross, Tel. (717)697-4623

OFFICER

Bishop Glenn M. Gross, 906 Grantham Rd., Mechanicsburg, PA 17055

Reformed Methodist Union Episcopal Church

The Reformed Methodist Union Episcopal church was formed after a group of ministers withdrew from the African Methodist Episcopal Church following a dispute over the election of ministerial delegates to the General Conference.

These ministers organized the Reformed Methodist Union church during a four-day meeting beginning on Jan. 22, 1885 at Hills Chapel (now known as Mt. Hermon RMUE church), in Charleston, S.C. The Rev. William E. Johnson was elected president of the new church. Following the death of Rev. Johnson in 1896, it was decided that the church would conform to regular American Methodism (the Episcopacy). The first Bishop, Edward Russell Middleton, was elected, and "Episcopal" was added to the name of the church. Bishop Middleton was consecrated on Dec. 5, 1896, by Bishop P. F. Stephens of the Reformed Episcopal Church.

HEADQUARTERS

1136 Brody Ave., Charleston, SC 29407

OFFICERS

Bishop, Rt. Rev. Leroy Gethers, Tel. (803) 766-3534

Asst. Bishop, Rt. Rev. Gary M. DeVoe, Jr.

Reformed Presbyterian Church of North America

Also known as the Church of the Covenanters, this church's origin dates back to the Reformation days of Scotland when the Covenanters signed their "Covenants" in resistance to the king and the Roman Church in the enforcement of state church practices. The Church in America has signed two "Covenants" in particular, those of 1871 and 1954.

HEADQUARTERS

Media Contact, Stated Clk., Louis D. Hutmire, 7408 Penn Ave., Pittsburgh, PA 15208 Tel. (412)731-1177 Fax (412)731-8861

OFFICERS

Mod., Rev. J. Paul McCracken, 617 Salano Dr., Colorado Springs, CO 80906 Tel. (719)471-2417

Clk., J. Bruce Martin, 1328 Goodin Dr., Clay Center, KS 67432 Tel. (913)632-5861

Asst. Clk., Jerrold S. Milroy, 14103 W. 62nd Terr., Shawnee, KS 66216 Tel. (913)631-9380

Stated Clk., Louis D. Hutmire, 7408 Penn Ave., Pittsburgh, PA 15208 Tel. (412)731-1177

PERIODICAL

The Covenanter Witness

Reformed Zion Union Apostolic Church

This group was organized in 1869 at Boyd-ton,

Va., by Elder James R. Howell of New York, a minister of the A.M.E. Zion Church, with doctrines of the Methodist Episcopal Church.

OFFICER

Exec. Brd., Chair, Rev. Hilman Wright, Tel. (804)447-3988

Sec., Joseph Russell, Tel. (804)634-4520

Religious Society of Friends (Conservative)

These Friends mark their present identity from separations occurring by regions at different times from 1845 to 1904. They hold to a minimum of organizational structure. Their meetings for worship, which are unprogrammed and based on silent, expectant waiting upon the Lord, demonstrate the belief that all individuals may commune directly with God and may share equally in local ministry.

They continue to stress the importance of the Living Christ and the experience of the Holy Spirit working with power in the lives of individuals who obey it.

YEARLY MEETINGS

North Carolina YM, George Stabler, 788 W. 52nd St., Norfolk, VA 23508

Iowa YM: Martha Davis, 678 38th St., Des Moines, IA 50312; Bill Deutsch

Ohio YM, Susan S. Smith, RD #4 Box 288, Harrisonburg, VA 22801

Religious Society of Friends (Unaffiliated Meetings)

Though all groups of Friends acknowledge the same historical roots, 19th-century divisions in theology and experience led to some of the current organizational groupings. Many newer yearly meetings, often marked by spontaneity, variety and experimentation and hoping for renewed Quaker unity, have chosen not to identify with past divisions by affiliating in traditional ways with the larger organizations within the Society. Some of these unaffiliated groups have begun within the past 25 years.

HEADQUARTERS

Friends World Committee for Consulation, Section of the Americas, 1506 Race St., Philadelphia, PA 19102 Tel. (215)241-7250 Fax (215)241-7285

Media Contact, Exec. Sec., Asia Bennett

UNAFFILIATED YEARLY MEETINGS

Amigos Central de Bolivia, Casilla 11070, La Paz, Bolivia

Amigos de Santidad de Bolivia, Casilla 992, La Paz, Bolivia

Central Yearly Meeting, 109 West Berry St., Alexandria, IN 46001

Iglesia Evangelica Amigos, Apartado 235, Santa Rosa de Capan, Honduras

Iglesia Nacional Evangelica de Los Amigos-Bolivia, Casilla 8385, La Paz, Bolivia

Iglesia Nacional Evangelica de Los Amigos-Peru, Apartado 369, Puno, Peru

El Salvador Yearly Meeting, Calle Roosevelt, Km. 4.5, #60, Soyapango, San Salvador, El Salvador

Guatemala Yearly Meeting, Apartado 8, Chiquimula, Guatemala

Reorganized Church of Jesus Christ of Latter Day Saints

This church was founded April 6, 1830, by Joseph Smith, Jr., and reorganized under the leadership of the founder's son, Joseph Smith III, in 1860. The church, with headquarters in Independence, Mo., is established in 36 countries in addition to the United States and Canada. A biennial world conference is held in Independence, Mo. The current president is Wallace B. Smith, great-grandson of the original founder. The church has a world-wide membership of approximately 245,000.

HEADQUARTERS

World Headquarters, P.O. Box 1059, Independence, MO 64051 Tel. (816)833-1000 Fax (816)521-3096

Media Contact, Publ. Rel. Commissioner, Stephanie Kelley

OFFICERS

First Presidency: Wallace B. Smith; Counselor, Howard S. Sheehy, Jr.; Counselor, W. Grant McMurray

Council of 12 Apostles, Pres., Geoffrey F. Spencer

Presiding Bishopric: Presiding Bishop, Norman E. Swails; Counselor, Larry R. Norris; Counselor, Dennis D. Piepergerdes

Presiding Evangelist, Paul W. Booth

World Church Sec., A. Bruce Lindgren

Public Relations, Stephanie Kelley

PERIODICALS

Saints Herald; Restoration Witness

The Roman Catholic Church

The largest single body of Christians in the United States, the Roman Catholic Church, is under the spiritual leadership of His Holiness the Pope. Its establishment in America dates back to the priests who accompanied Columbus on his second voyage to the New World. A settlement, later discontinued, was made at St. Augustine, Fla. The continuous history of this Church in the Colonies began at St. Mary's in Maryland, in 1634.

(The following information has been furnished by the editor of The Official Catholic Directory, published by P. J. Kenedy & Sons, 3004 Glenview Rd., Wilmette, IL 60091. Reference to this complete volume will provide additional information.)

INTERNATIONAL ORGANIZATION

His Holiness the Pope, Bishop of Rome, Vicar of Jesus Christ, Supreme Pontiff of the Catholic Church.

Pope John Paul II, Karol Wojtyla (born May 18, 1920; installed Oct. 22, 1978)

APOSTOLIC PRO NUNCIO TO THE UNITED STATES

Archbishop Agostino Cacciavillan, 3339 Massachusetts Ave., N.W., Washington, DC 20008. Tel. (202)333-7121

U.S. ORGANIZATION

National Conference of Catholic Bishops, 3211 Fourth St., Washington, DC 20017. Tel. (202)541-3000

The National Conference of Catholic Bishops (NCCB) is a canonical entity operating in accordance with the Vatican II Decree, Christus Dominus. Its purpose is to foster the Church's mission to mankind by providing the Bishops of this country with an opportunity to exchange views and insights of prudence and experience and to exercise in a joint manner their pastoral office.

OFFICERS

Pres., Archbishop William H. Keeler
Vice-Pres., Archbishop Anthony M. Pilla
Treas., Archbishop Daniel W. Kucera
Sec., Bishop Robert F. Sanchez

NCCB GENERAL SECRETARIAT

Gen. Sec., Rev. Msgr. Robert N. Lynch
Assoc. Gen. Sec., Francis X. Doyle, Sr. Sharon A. Euart, R.S.M., Rev. Dennis M. Schnurr, Rev. Kenneth F. Jenkins
Sec. for Communication, Richard W. Daw

NCCB COMMITTEES

Administrative Committee: Chmn., Archbishop William H. Keeler

Executive Committee: Chmn., Archbishop William H. Keeler

Committee on Budget and Finance: Chmn., Archbishop Daniel W. Kucera, O.S.B.

Committee on Personnel: Chmn., Archbishop Anthony M. Pilla

Committee on Priorities and Plans: Chmn., Archbishop William H. Keeler

American Board of Catholic Missions: Chmn., Bishop J. Keith Symons

American College Louvain: Chmn., Bishop Daniel P. Reilly

Bishop's Welfare Emergency Relief: Chmn., Archbishop William H. Keller

African American Catholics: Chmn., Bishop J. Terry Steib, S.V.D.

Boundaries of Dioceses and Provinces: Chmn., William H. Keeler

Canonical Affairs: Chmn., Anthony Cardinal Bevilacqua

Church in Latin America: Chmn., Bishop Arthur N. Tafoya

Doctrine: Chmn., Bishop Alfred C. Hughes

Ecumenical and Interreligious Affairs: Chmn., Archbishop Rembert G. Weakland, O.S.B.

Evangelization: Chmn., Bishop William R. Houck

Hispanic Affairs: Chmn., Bishop Enrique San Pedro, S.J.

Laity: Chmn. Bishop Robert F. Morneau

Liturgy: Chmn., Bishop Wilton D. Gregory

Marriage and Family Life: Chmn., Joseph Cardinal Bernardin

Migration: Chmn., Archbishop Theodore E. McCarrick

Missions: Chmn., Bishop Edmond Carmody

North American College Rome: Chmn., Bishop Edward M. Egan

Pastoral Practices: Chmn., Bishop Emil A. Wcela

Permanent Diaconate: Chmn., Bishop Dale J. Melczek

Priestly Formation: Chmn., Archbishop Daniel M. Buechlein, O.S.B.

Priestly Life and Ministry: Chmn., Bishop Robert H. Brom

Pro-Life Activities: Chmn., Roger Cardinal Mahony

Religious Life and Ministry: Chmn., Bishop Carlos A. Sevilla, S.J.

Science and Human Values: Chmn., Bishop William B. Friend

Selection of Bishops: Chmn., Archbishop William H. Keeler

Vocations: Chmn. Bishop Robert J. Carlson
Women in Society and in the Church: Chmn.,
Bishop John J. Snyder

United States Catholic Conference, 3211 Fourth
St., Washington, DC 20017, Tel. (202)541-3000

The United States Catholic Conference (USCC)
is a civil entity of the American Catholic Bishops
assisting them in their service to the Church in this
country by uniting the people of God where voluntary, collective action on a broad diocesan level is
needed. The USCC provides an organizational
structure and the resources needed to insure coordination, cooperation and assistance in the public,
educational and social concerns of the church at the
national, regional, state and, as appropriate, diocesan levels.

OFFICERS
Pres., Archbishop William H. Keeler
Vice-Pres., Anthony M. Pilla
Treas., Archbishop Daniel W. Kucera, O.S.B.
Sec., Archbishop Robert F. Sanchez

GENERAL SECRETARIAT
Gen. Sec., Rev. Msgr. Robert N. Lynch
Assoc. Gen. Sec., Mr. Francis X. Doyle, Sr. Sharon
A. Euart, R.S.M., Rev. Dennis M. Schnurr,
Rev.,Kenneth R. Jenkins
Sec. for Communications, Richard W. Daw

USCC COMMITTEES AND DEPARTMENTS
Administrative Board: Chmn., Archbishop Wil-
liam H. Keeler
Executive Committee: Chmn., Archbishop Wil-
liam H. Keeler
Committee on Budget and Finance: Chmn., Arch-
bishop Daniel W. Kucera, O.S.B.
Committee on Personnel: Chmn., Bishop Anthony
M. Pilla
Committee on Priorities and Plans: Chmn., Arch-
bishop William H. Keeler
Campaign for Human Development: Chmn.,
Bishop James H. Garland
Committee on Communications: Chmn., Bishop
Raymond J. Boland
Committee on Education: Chmn., Bishop John J.
Leibrecht
Committee of Bishops and Catholic College and
University Presidents: Chmn., Bishop John J.
Leibrecht
Advisory Committee on Public Policy and Catho-
lic Schools: Chmn., Bishop John J. Leibrecht
Ex Corde Ecclesiae: Chmn., Bishop John J. Lei-
brecht
Sapientia Christiana: Chmn., Bishop John P. Boles
USCC Department of Education: Sec., Sr. Lourdes
Sheehan, R.S.M.
Committee on Domestic Policy: Chmn., Bishop
John H. Ricard, S.S.J.
Committee on International Policy: Chmn., Arch-
bishop John R. Roach
Department of Social Development and World
Peace: Sec., John L. Carr
Office of Domestic Social Development: Dir.,
Nancy Wisdo
Office of International Justice and Peace: Dir.,
Rev. Drew Christiansen, S.J.
U.S. Catholic Bishops' National Advisory Coun-
cil: Chmn. Rev. Kenneth G. Morman

RELATED ORGANIZATIONS

U.S.CATHOLIC BISHOPS' NATIONAL ADVISORY COUNCIL
Chmn., Elizabeth Habergerger

NATIONAL ORGANIZATIONS
Catholic Charities,-USA Exec. Dir., Rev. Thomas
J. Harvey, 1319 F St., N.W., Washington, DC
20004
Conference of Major Religious Superiors of Men,
Men's Institutes of the United States, Inc., Exec.
Dir., Rev. Roland Faley, T.O.R., 8808 Cameron
St., Silver Spring, MD 20910. Tel. (301)588-
4030
Leadership Conference of Women Religious,
Exec. Dir., Sr. Janet Roesener, C.S.J., 8808
Cameron St., Silver Spring, MD 20910. Tel.
(301)588-4955
National Catholic Educational Association, Pres.,
Sr. Catherine McNamee, 1077 30th St., N.W.,
Suite 100, Washington, DC 20007. Tel.
(202)337-6232
National Council of Catholic Laity, Pres., Thomas
Simmons, 5664 Midforest Ln., Cincinnati, OH
45231. Tel. (513)922-2495
National Council of Catholic Women, Pres., Bev-
erly Medved; Exec. Adm., Annette Kane, 1275
K. St., NW, Washington, DC 20005. Tel.
(202)682- 0334
National Office for Black Catholics, The Paulist
Center, 3025 4th St., N.E., Washington, D.C.
20017. Tel. (202)635-1778

CATHOLIC ORGANIZATIONS WITH INDIVIDUAL I.R.S. RULINGS
Canon Law Society of America, Exec. Coord.,
Rev. Edward Pfnausch, Catholic University,
Washington, DC 20064. Tel. (202)269-3491
National Institute for the Word of God, Exec. Dir.,
Rev. John Burke, O. P., 487 Michigan Ave., NE,
Washington, DC 20017. Tel. (202)529-0001

ARCHDIOCESES AND DIOCESES
There follows an alphabetical listing of Archdio-
ceses and Dioceses of The Roman Catholic
Church. Each Archdiocese or Diocese contains the
following information in sequence: Name of in-
cumbent Bishop; name of Auxiliary Bishop or
Bishops, and the Chancellor or Vicar General of the
Archdiocese or Diocese, or just the address and
telephone number of the chancery office.
Cardinals are addressed as His Eminence and
Archbishops and Bishops as Most Reverend.
Albany, Bishop Howard J. Hubbard; Chancellor,
Rev. Randall P. Patterson. Chancery Office,
Pastoral Center, 40 N. Main Ave., Albany, NY
12203. Tel. (518)453-6600. Fax (518)453-6793
Diocese of Alexandria, Bishop Sam G. Jacobs;
Chancellor, Rev. Msgr. Joseph M. Susi. Chan-
cery Office, 4400 Coliseum Blvd., P.O. Box
7417, Alexandria, LA 71306. Tel. (318)445-
2401
Allentown, Bishop Thomas J. Welsh; Chancellor,
Rev. Msgr. Joseph M. Whalen. Chancery Office,
202 N. 17th St., P.O. Box F, Allentown, PA
18105. Tel. (215)437-0755
Altoona-Johnstown, Bishop Joseph V. Adamec;
Chancellor, Rev. Dennis P. Boggs. Chancery
Office, 126 Logan Blvd., Hollidaysburg, PA
16648. Tel. (814)695-5579. Fax (814)695-8894
Amarillo, Bishop Leroy T. Matthiesen; Chancellor, Sr. Christine Jensen. Chancery Office, 1800
N. Spring St., P.O. Box 5644, Amarillo, TX
79117. Tel.(806)383-2243. Fax (806)383-8452

Archdiocese of Anchorage, Archbishop Francis T. Hurley; Chancellor, 225 Cordova St., P.O. Box 102239, Anchorage, AK 99510. Tel. (907)258-7898. Fax (905)279-3885

Arlington, Bishop John R. Keating; Chancellor, Rev. Robert J. Rippy. Chancery, Ste. 704, 200 N. Glebe Rd., Arlington, VA 22203. Tel. (703)841-2500. (703)524-5028

Archdiocese of Atlanta, Vacant See; Chancellor, Rev. Donald A. Kenny. Chancery Office, 680 W. Peachtree St., N.W., Atlanta, GA 30308. Tel. (404)888-7844

Austin, Bishop John E. McCarthy; Vicar General, Rev. Msgr. Edward C. Matocha. Chancery Office, N. Congress and 16th, P.O. Box 13327 Capital Sta. Austin, TX 78711. Tel. (512)476-4888. Fax (512)469-9537

Baker, Bishop Thomas J. Connolly; Chancellor, Rev. Charles T. Grant. Chancery Office, 911 S.E. Armour, Bend, OR 97702, P.O. Box 5999, Bend, OR 97708. Tel. (503)388-4004

Archdiocese of Baltimore, Archbishop William H. Keeler; Auxiliary Bishops: John H. Ricard, P. Francis Murphy, William C. Newman. Chancery Office, 320 Cathedral St., Baltimore, MD 21201. Tel. (410)547-5446

Baton Rouge, Vacant See; Chancellor, Rev. Msgr. Robert Berggreen. Chancery Office, 1800 S. Acadian Thruway, P.O. Box 2028, Baton Rouge, LA 70821. Tel. (504)387-0561. Fax (504)336-8789

Beaumont, Bishop Bernard J. Ganter; Chancellor Rev. Bennie J. Patillo. Chancery Office, 703 Archie St., P.O. Box 3948, Beaumont, TX 77704. Tel. (409)838-0451. Fax (409)838-4511.

Belleville, Bishop James P. Keleher; Chancellor, Rev. Msgr. Bernard O. Sullivan. Chancery Office, 222 S. Third St., Belleville IL 62220. Tel. (618)277-8181. Fax (618)277-0387

Biloxi, Bishop Joseph L. Howze; Chancellor, Rev. Msgr. Andrew Murray. Chancery Office, 120 Reynoir St., P.O. Box 1189, Biloxi, MS 39533. Tel. (601)374-0222. Fax (601)435-7949

Birmingham, Bishop Raymond J. Boland; Chancellor, Rev. Paul L. Rohling. Chancery Office, 8131 Fourth Ave. S., P.O. Box 12047, Birmingham, AL 35202. Tel. (205)833-0175. Fax (205)836-1910

Bismarck, Bishop John F. Kinney, Chancellor, Sr. Joanne Graham. Chancery Office, 420 Raymond St., Box 1575, Bismarck, ND 58502. Tel. (701)223-1347. Fax (701)223-3693

Boise, Bishop Tod D. Brown; Chancellor, Deacon James Bowen; Chancery Office, Box 769, 303 Federal Way, Boise, ID 83701. Tel. (208)342-1311. Fax (208)342-0224

Archdiocese of Boston, Archbishop Bernard Cardinal Law; Auxiliary Bishops: Lawrence J. Riley, John J. Mulcahy, Daniel A. Hart, Alfred C. Hughes, Roberto O. Gonzalez, John P. Boles, John R. McNamara; Chancellor, Gerald T. Reilly. Chancery Office, 2121 Commonwealth Ave., Brighton, MA 02135. Tel. (617)254-0100. Fax (617)787-8144, 783-5642

Bridgeport, Bishop Edward M. Egan; Chancellor, Rev. Msgr. Thomas J. Driscoll. Chancery Office, 238 Jewett Ave., Bridgeport CT 06606. Tel. (203)372-4301. Fax (203)371-8698

Brooklyn, Bishop Thomas V. Daily; Auxiliary Bishops: Joseph M. Sullivan, Rene A. Valero; Chancellor, Rev. Msgr. Otto L. Garcia. Chancery Office, 75 Greene Ave., Box C, Brooklyn, NY 11202. Tel. (718)399-5900. Fax (718)399-5934

Brooklyn, St. Maron of, Bishop Francis M. Zayek; Auxiliary Bishop John G. Chedid; Chancellor, Chorbishop John D. Faris. Chancery Office, 8120 15th Ave., Brooklyn, NY 11228. Tel. (718)259-9200. Fax (718)259-8968

Brownsville, Bishop Enrique San Pedro; Chancellor, Sr. Esther Dunegan. Chancery, P.O. Box 2279, Brownsville, TX 78522. Tel. (210)542-2501. Fax (210)542-6751.

Buffalo, Bishop Edward D. Head; Auxiliary Bishop Edward M. Grosz; Chancellor, Rev. Msgr. Robert J. Cunningham. Chancery Office, 795 Main St., Buffalo, NY 14203. Tel. (716)847-5500. Fax (716)847-5557

Burlington, Bishop Kenneth A. Angell; Chancellor, Rev. Jay C. Haskin. Chancery Office, 351 North Ave., Burlington, VT 05401. Tel. (802)658-6110. Fax (802)658-0436

Camden, Bishop James T. McHugh; Auxiliary Bishop James L. Schad; Chancellor, Rev. Msgr. Joseph W. Pokusa. Chancery Office, 1845 Haddon Ave., P.O. Box 709, Camden, NJ 08101. Tel. (609)756-7900. Fax (609)963-2655

Canton, Romanian Diocese of, Bishop Louis Puscas, 1121 44th St., NE, Canton, OH 44714, Tel. (216)492-4086

Charleston, Bishop David B. Thompson; Vicar General, Rev. Msgr. Thomas R. Duffy; Chancellor for Administration, Miss Cleo C. Cantey. Chancery Office, 119 Broad St., P.O. Box 818, Charleston, SC 29402. Tel. (803)723-3488. Fax (803)724- 6387

Charlotte, Bishop John F. Donoghue; Chancellor, Rev. John J. McSweeney. Chancery Office P.O. Box 36776, Charlotte, NC 28236. Tel. (704)377-6871. Fax (704)358-1208

Cheyenne, Bishop Joseph H. Hart; Chancellor, Rev. Carl Beavers. Chancery Office, 2121 Capitol Ave., Box 426, Cheyenne, WY 82003. Tel. (307)638-1530. Fax (307)637-7936

Archdiocese of Chicago, Archbishop Joseph Cardinal Bernardin; Auxiliary Bishops: Bishop Alfred L. Abramowicz, Bishop Wilton D. Gregory, Bishop Timothy J. Lyne, Bishop Placido Rodriquez, Bishop Thad J. Jakubowski; Bishop John R. Gorman, Raymond E. Goedert; Chancellor, Rev. Thomas J. Paprocki. Chancery Office, 155 E. Superior Ave., P.O. Box 1979, Chicago, IL 60611. Tel. (312)751- 7999

Chicago, St. Nicholas for Ukrainians, Bishop Innocent Lotocky; Chancellor, Sonia Ann Peczeniuk. Chancery Office, 2245 W. Rice St., Chicago, IL 60622. Tel. (312)276-5080. Fax (312)276-6799

Archdiocese of Cincinnati, Archbishop Daniel E. Pilarczyk; Chancellor, Rev. R. Daniel Conlon. Chancery Office, 6616 Beechmont Ave., Cincinnati, OH 45230. Tel. (513)231-0810

Cleveland, Bishop Anthony M. Pilla; Auxiliary Bishops: Bishop A. Edward Pevec, Bishop A. James Quinn; Chancellor, Rev. Ralph E. Wiatrowski. Chancery Office, 350 Chancery Bldg., Cathedral Square, 1027 Superior Ave., Cleveland, OH 44114. Tel. (216)696-6525

Colorado Springs, Bishop Richard C. Hanifen; Chancellor, Rev. George V. Fagan. Chancery Office, 29 West Kiowa St., Colorado Springs, CO 80903. Tel. (719)636-2345

Columbus, Bishop James A. Griffin; Chancellor, Rev. Joseph M. Hendricks. Chancery Office, 198 E. Broad St., Columbus, OH 43215. Tel. (614)224-2251. Fax (614)224-6306

Corpus Christi, Bishop Rene H. Gracida; Chancellor, Deacon Roy M. Grassedonio. Chancery Office, 620 Lipan St., P.O. Box 2620, Corpus Christi, TX 78403. Tel. (512)882-6191. Fax (512)882-1018

Covington, Bishop William A. Hughes; Chancellor, Rev. Roger L. Kriege. Chancery Office, The Catholic Center, P. O. Box 18548 Erlanger, KY 41018. Tel. (606)283-6210. Fax (606)283- 6334

Crookston, Bishop Victor Balke; Chancellor, Very Rev. Michael Patnode. Chancery Office, 1200 Memorial Dr., P.O. Box 610, Crookston, MN 56716. Tel. (218) 281-4533. Fax (218)281- 3328

Dallas, Bishop Charles V. Grahmann; Chancellor, Rev. Ramon Alvarez. Chancery Office, 3725 Blackburn, P.O. Box 190507, Dallas, TX 75219. Tel. (214) 528-2240. Fax (214)526- 1743

Davenport, Bishop Gerald Francis O'Keefe; Chancellor, Rev. Msgr. Leo J. Feeney. Chancery Office, 2706 N. Gaines St., Davenport, IA 52804. Tel. (319)324-1911. Fax (319)324- 5842

Archdiocese of Denver, Archbishop J. Francis Stafford; Chancellor, Sr. Rosemary Wilcox. Chancery Office, 200 Josephine St., Denver, CO 80206. Tel. (303) 388-4411. Fax (303)388-0517

Des Moines, Bishop William H. Bullock; Chancellor, Lawrence Breheny. Chancery Office, 818 5th Ave., P.O. Box 1816, Des Moines, IA 50306. Tel. (515)243-7653. Fax (515)283- 1982

Archdiocese of Detroit, Archbishop Adam J. Maida; Auxiliary Bishops: Moses B. Anderson, Thomas J. Gumbleton, Bishop Dale J. Melczek, Walter J. Schoenherr. Chancery Office, 1234 Washington Blvd., Detroit, MI 48226. Tel. (313) 237-5800

Dodge City, Bishop Stanley G. Schlarman; Chancellor, Rev. David H., Kraus. Chancery Office, 910 Central Ave., P.O. Box 137, Dodge City, KS 67801. Tel. (316) 227-1500. Fax (316)227- 1570

Archdiocese of Dubuque, Archbishop Daniel W. Kucera; Auxiliary Bishop William E. Franklin; Chancellor, Sr. Mary Kevin Gallagher, P.O. Box 479, Dubuque IA 52004. Tel. (319) 556-2580. Fax (319)588-0557

Duluth, Bishop Roger L. Schwietz; Chancellor, Rev. Dale Nau, Chancery Office, 2803 E. 4th St., Duluth, MN 55812. Tel. (218)727-6861. Fax (218)724-1056

El Paso, Bishop Raymundo J. Pena; Chancellor, Rev. John Telles. Chancery Office, 499 St. Matthews, El Paso, TX 79907. Tel. (915)595-5000. Fax (915)595-5095

Erie, Bishop Donald W. Trautman; Chancellor, Rev. Msgr. Lawrence E. Brandt. Chancery Office, P.O. Box 10397, Erie, PA 16514. Tel. (814)824-1135. Fax (814)824-1128

Evansville, Bishop Gerald A. Gettelfinger; Chancellor, Sr. Louise Bond. Chancery Office, 4200 N. Kentucky Ave., P.O. Box 4169, Evansville, IN 47724. Tel. (812)424-5536. Fax (812)421- 1334

Fairbanks, Bishop Michael Kaniecki; Chancellor, Sr. Marilyn Marx. Chancery Office, 1316 Peger Rd., Fairbanks, AK 99709. Tel. (907) 474-0753.

Fall River, Bishop Sean P. O'Malley; Chancellor, Rev. Msgr. John J. Oliveira. Chancery Office, 47 Underwood St., Box 2577, Fall River, MA 02722. Tel. (508) 675- 1311. Fax (508)679-9220

Fargo, Bishop James S. Sullivan; Chancellor, Rev. T. William Coyle. Chancery Office, 1310 Broadway, P.O. Box 1750, Fargo, ND 58107. Tel. (701)235-6429. (701)235-0296

Fort Wayne-South Bend, Bishop John M. D'Arcy; Auxiliary Bishop John R. Sheets. Chancellor, Rev. Msgr. J. William Lester. Chancery Office, 1103 S. Calhoun St., P.O. Box 390. Fort Wayne, IN 46801. Tel. (219)422-4611. Fax (219)423- 3382

Fort Worth, Bishop Joseph P. Delaney; Chancellor, Rev. Robert W. Wilson. Chancery Office, 800 W. Loop 820 South, Fort Worth TX 76108. Tel. (817)560-3300

Fresno, Bishop John T. Steinbock; Chancellor, Rev. Perry Kavookjian. Chancery Office, P.O. Box 1668, 1550 N. Fresno St., Fresno, CA 93717. Tel. (209)488-7400. Fax (209)488-7444

Gallup, Bishop Donald E. Pelotte; Chancellor, Br. Duane Torisky. Chancery Office, 711 S. Puerco Dr., P.O. Box 1338, Gallup, NM 87301. Tel. (505)863-4406. Fax (505)722-9131

Galveston-Houston, Bishop Joseph A. Fiorenza; Auxiliary Bishops: Bishop Curtis J. Guillory, James A. Tamayo; Chancellor, Rev. Msgr. Daniel Scheel. Chancery Office, 1700 San Jacinto St., Houston, TX 77002, P.O. Box 907, Houston, TX 77001. Tel. (713)659-5461. Fax (713)759-9151

Gary, Bishop Norbert F. Gaughan; Chancellor, Rev. Richard A. Emerson. Chancery Office, 9292 Broadway, Merrillville, IN 46410. Tel. (219)769-9292. Fax (219)738-9034

Gaylord, Bishop Patrick R. Cooney; Vicar Gen., Raymond C. Mulka. Chancery Office, 1665 West M-32, Gaylord, MI 49735. Tel. (517)732-5147. Fax (517)732-1706

Grand Island, Bishop Lawrence J. McNamara; Chancellor, Rev. Richard L. Piontkowski. Chancery Office, 311 W. 17th St., P.O. Box 996, Grand Island, NE 68802. Tel. (308)382-6565

Grand Rapids, Bishop Robert J. Rose; Auxiliary Bishop Joseph McKinney; Chancellor, Sr. Patrice Konwinski. Chancery Office, 660 Burton St. S.E., Grand Rapids, MI 49507. Tel. (616)243-0491. Fax (616)243- 4910

Great Falls-Billings, Bishop Anthony M. Milone; Chancellor, Rev. Martin J. Burke. Chancery Office, 121 23rd St. S., P.O. Box 1399, Great Falls, MT 59403. Tel. (406)727-6683. Fax (406)454- 3480

Green Bay, Bishop Robert J. Banks; Auxiliary Bishop Robert F. Morneau; Chancellor, Sr. Ann F. Rehrauer. Chancery Office, Box 20366, Green Bay, WI 54305. Tel. (414)435-4406. Fax (414)435-1330

Greensburg, Bishop Anthony G. Bosco; Chancellor, Rev. Lawrence T. Persico. Chancery Office, 723 E. Pittsburgh St., Greensburg, PA 15601. Tel. (412)837-0901. Fax (412)837-0857

Harrisburg, Bishop Nicholas C. Dattilo; Chancellor, Carol Houghton. Chancery Office, P.O. Box 2557, Harrisburg, PA 17105. Tel. (717)657-4804

Archdiocese of Hartford, Archbishop Daniel A. Cronin; Auxiliary Bishops Peter A. Rosazza, Bishop Paul S. Loverde; Chancellor, Sr. Helen Margaret Feeney. Chancery Office, 134 Farmington Ave., Hartford, CT 06105. Tel. (203) 527-4201. Fax (203)244-2056

Helena, Bishop Elden F. Curtiss; Chancellor, Rev. John W. Robertson. Chancery Office, 515 N. Ewing, P.O. Box 1729, Helena, MT 59624. Tel. (406)442-5820. Fax (406)442-5191

Honolulu, Bishop Joseph A. Ferrario; Chancellor, Sr. Grace Dorothy Lim. Chancery Office, 1184 Bishop St., Honolulu, HI 96813. Tel. (808)533-1791. Fax (808)521-8428

Houma-Thibodaux, Bishop Warren L. Boudreaux; Chancellor, Rev. Msgr. James B. Songy. Chancery Office, P.O. Box 9077, Houma, LA 70361. Tel. (504)868-7720. Fax (504)868-7727

Archdiocese of Indianapolis, Archbishop Daniel M. Buechlein; Chancellor, Suzanne L. Magnant. Chancery Office, 1400 N. Meridian St., P.O. Box 1410, Indianapolis, IN 46206. Tel. (317)236-1400. Fax (317)236-1406

Jackson, Bishop William R. Houck; Chancellor, Rev. Francis J. Cosgrove. Chancery Office, 237 E. Amite St., P.O. Box 2248, Jackson, MS 39225. Tel. (601)969-1880. Fax (601)960-8455

Jefferson City, Bishop Michael F. McAuliffe; Chancellor, Sr. Mary Margaret Johanning. Chancery Office, 605 Clark Ave., P.O. Box 417, Jefferson City, MO 65101. Tel. (314)635-9127. Fax (314)635-2286

Joliet, Bishop Joseph L. Imesch; Auxiliary Bishop Roger L. Kaffer; Chancellor, Sr. Judith Davies. Chancery Office, 425 Summit St., Joliet, IL 60435. Tel. (815) 722-6606. Fax (815)722-6602

Juneau, Bishop Michael H. Kenny; Vicar General, Rev. Msgr. James F. Miller. Chancery Office, 419 6th St., #200, Juneau, AK 99801. Tel. (907)586-2227

Kalamazoo, Bishop Paul V. Donovan; Chancellor, Rev. Msgr. Dell F. Stewart. Chancery Office, P.O. Box 949, 215 N. Westnedge Ave., P.O. Box 949, Kalamazoo, MI 49005. Tel. (616)349-8714. Fax (616)349-6440

Archdiocese of Kansas City in Kansas, Archbishop Ignatius J. Strecker; Auxiliary Bishop Marion F. Forst; Chancellor, Rev. Msgr. William T. Curtin. Chancery Office, 12615 Parallel, KS 66109, Tel. (913)721-1570

Kansas City-St. Joseph, Bishop John J. Sullivan; Chancellor, Rev. Richard F. Carney. Chancery Office, P.O. Box 419037, Kansas City, MO 64141. Tel. (816)756-1850. (816)756-0878

Knoxville, Bishop Anthony J. O'Connell; Chancellor, Rev. F. Xavier Mankel. Chancery Office, 417 Erin Dr., P.O. Box 11127, Knoxville, TN 37939. Tel. (615)584-3307.

La Crosse, Bishop John J. Paul; Chancellor, Rev. Michael J. Gorman. Chancery Office. 3710 East Ave., P.O. Box 4004, La Crosse, WI 54602. Tel. (608)788-7700. Fax (608)788-8413

Lafayette in Indiana, Bishop William L. Higi; Chancellor, Rev. Robert L. Sell. Chancery Office, P. O. Box 260, Lafayette, IN 47902. Tel. (317) 742-0275. Fax (317)742-7513

Lafayette, Bishop Harry J. Flynn; Chancellor, Sr. Joanna Valoni. Chancery Office, Diocesan Office Bldg., 1408 Carmel Ave., Lafayette, LA 70501. Tel. (318)261-5500

Lake Charles, Bishop Jude Speyrer; Chancellor Deacon George Stearns. Chancery Office, 414 Iris St., P.O. Box 3223, Lake Charles, LA 70602. Tel. (318)439-7404. (318)439-7413

Lansing, Bishop Kenneth J. Povish; Chancellor, Rev. James A. Murray. Chancery Office, 300 W. Ottawa, Lansing, MI 48933. Tel. (517)342-2440. Fax (517)342-2515

Las Cruces, Bishop Ricardo Ramirez; Chancellor, Sr. Mary Ellen Quinn. Chancery Office, 1280 Med Park Dr., Las Cruces, NM 88005. Tel. (505)523-7577. Fax (505)524-3874

Lexington, Bishop James K. Williams; Chancellor, Sr. Mary Kevan Seibert. Chancery Office, 1310 Leestown Rd., P.O. Box 12350, Lexington, KY 40582. Tel. (606)253-1993. Fax (606)254-6284

Lincoln, Fabian W. Bruskewitz; Chancellor, Rev. Timothy J. Thorburn. Chancery Office, 3400 Sheridan Blvd., Lincoln, NE 68506, P.O. Box 80328, Lincoln, NE 68501. Tel. (402)488-0921

Little Rock, Bishop Andrew J. McDonald; Chancellor, Francis I. Malone. Chancery Office, 2415 N. Tyler St., P.O. Box 7239, Little Rock, AR 72217. Tel. (501) 664-0340

Archdiocese of Los Angeles, Archbishop Roger Cardinal Mahony; Auxiliary Bishops: Juan Arzube, John J. Ward, Carl Fisher, Armando Ochoa, Stephen E. Blaire; Chancellor, Bishop Stephen E. Blaire. Chancery Office, 1531 W. Ninth St., Los Angeles, CA 90015. Tel. (213) 251-3200. Fax (213)251-2607

Archdiocese of Louisville, Archbishop Thomas C. Kelly; Auxiliary Bishop Charles G. Maloney; Chancellor, Very Rev. Bernard J. Breen. Chancery Office, 212 E. College St., P.O. Box 1073, Louisville, KY 40201. Tel. (502)585-3291

Lubbock, Bishop Michael Sheehan; Chancellor, Sr. Elena Gonzalez. Chancery Office. 4620 4th St., Lubbock, TX 79416, P.O. Box 98700, Lubbock, TX 79499- 8700. Tel. (806)792-3943. Fax (806)792-8109

Madison, Vacant see; Auxiliary Bishop George O. Wirz; Chancellor, Rev. Joseph P. Higgins. Chancery Office, 15 E. Wilson St., Box 111, Madison, WI 53701. Tel. (608)256-2677

Manchester, Bishop Leo E. O'Neil; Chancellor Rev. Msgr. Francis J. Christian. Chancery Office, 153 Ash St., P.O. Box 310, Manchester, NH 03105. Tel. (603)669-3100. Fax (603)669-0377

Marquette, Bishop James H. Garland; Chancellor, Rev. Peter Oberto. Chancery Office, 444 S. Fourth St., P.O. Box 550, Marquette, MI 49855. Tel. (906)225-1141. Fax (906)225-0437

Memphis, Vacant See; Chancellor, Rev. Robert D. Ponticello. Chancery Office, 1325 Jefferson Ave., P.O. Box 41679, Memphis, TN 38174. Tel. (901)722- 4700. Fax (901)722-4769

Metuchen, Bishop Edward T. Hughes; Chancellor, Sr. M. Michaelita Wiechetek. Chancery Office, P.O. Box 191, Metuchen, NJ 08840. Tel. (908)283-3800. Fax (908)283-2012

Archdiocese of Miami, Archbishop Edward A. McCarthy; Auxiliary Bishop Agustin A. Roman; Chancellor, Very Rev. Gerard T. LaCerra. Chancery Office, 9401 Biscayne Blvd., Miami Shores, FL 33138. Tel. (305)757-6241. Fax (305)754-1797.

Archdiocese for the Military Services, Bishop Joseph T. Dimino; Auxiliary Bishops: Francis X. Roque, John G. Nolan, Joseph J. Madera, John J. Glynn; Chancellor, Bishop John J. Glynn. Chancery Office, 962 Wayne Ave., Silver Spring, MD 20910. Tel. (301)495-4100. Fax (301)589-3774

Archdiocese of Milwaukee, Archbishop Rembert G. Weakland, Auxiliary Bishop Richard J. Sklba; Chancellor, Rev. Ralph C. Gross. Chancery Office, 3501 S. Lake Dr., P.O. Box 07912, Milwaukee, WI 53207. Tel. (414)769-3340. Fax (414)769-3408

Archdiocese of Mobile, Archbishop Oscar H. Lipscomb; Chancellor, Very Rev. G. Warren Wall. Chancery Office, 400 Government St., P.O. Box 1966, Mobile, AL 36633. Tel. (205)434-1585. Fax (205) 434-1588

Monterey, Bishop Sylvester D. Ryan; Chancellor, Rev. Charles G. Fatooh. Chancery Office, 580 Fremont St., P.O. Box 2048, Monterey, CA 93942. Tel. (408)373-4345. Fax (408)373-1175

114

Nashville, Bishop Edward U. Kmiec, Chancellor, Rev. J. Patrick Connor. Chancery Office, 2400 21st Ave., S., Nashville, TN 37212. Tel. (615)383-6393. Fax (615)292- 8411

Archdiocese of Newark, Archbishop Theodore E. McCarrick; Auxiliary Bishops: David Arias, Joseph Francis, Robert F. Garner, Dominic A. Marconi, Michael A. Salterelli; Chancellor, Sr. Thomas Mary Salerno. Chancery Office, 31 Mulberry St., Newark, NJ 07102. Tel. (201)596-4000. Fax (201)596-3763

Archdiocese of New Orleans, Archbishop Francis B. Schulte; Auxiliary Bishops: Robert W. Muench; Dominic Carmon; Chancellor, Rev. Msgr. Thomas J. Rodi. Chancery Office, 7887 Walmsley Ave., New Orleans, LA 70125. Tel. (504)861-9521. Fax (504)866-2906

Newton, Melkite Diocese of, Vacant See, Auxiliary Bishops: John A. Elya, Nicholas J. Samra. Chancellor, Very Rev. James E. King. Chancery Office, 19 Dartmouth St., West Newton, MA 02165. Tel. (617)969-8957

New Ulm, Bishop Raymond A. Lucker; Chancellor, Rev. Dennis C. Labat. Chancery Office, 1400 Sixth North St., New Ulm, MN 56073. Tel. (507)359-2966

Archdiocese of New York, Archbishop John Cardinal O'Connor; Auxiliary Bishops: Patrick V. Ahern, Francis Garmendia, James P. Mahoney, Emerson J. Moore, Austin B. Vaughan, Anthony F. Mestice, William J. McCormack, Patrick J. Sheridan; Chancellor, Rev. Msgr. Henry J. Mansell. Chancery Office, 1011 First Ave., New York, NY 10022. Tel. (212)371-1000. Fax (212)319-8265

Norwich, Bishop Daniel P. Reilly; Chancellor, Rev. Msgr. Robert L. Brown. Chancery Office, 201 Broadway, P.O. Box 587, Norwich, CT 06360. Tel. (203)887-9294. Fax (203)886-1670

Oakland, Bishop John S. Cummins; Chancellor, Rev. Raymond Breton. Chancery Office, 2900 Lakeshore Ave., Oakland, CA 94610. Tel. (415)893-4711. Fax (415)893-0945

Ogdensburg, Bishop Stanislaus J. Brzana; Chancellor, Rev. Robert H. Aucoin. Chancery Office, P.O. Box 369, 622 Washington St., Ogdensburg, NY 13669. Tel. (315)393-2920

Archdiocese of Oklahoma City, Archbishop Eusebius J. Beltran, Chancellor, Rev. John A. Steichen. Chancery Office, 7501 Northwest Expressway, P.O. Box 32180, Oklahoma City, OK 73123. Tel. (405)721-5651. Fax (405)721-5210

Archdiocese of Omaha, Archbishop Daniel E. Sheehan; Chancellor, Rev. Eldon J. McKamy. Chancery Office, 100 N. 62nd St., Omaha, NE 68132. Tel. (402)558-3100

Orange, Bishop Norman F. McFarland; Auxiliary Bishop Michael P. Driscoll; Chancellor, Rev. John Urell. Chancery Office, 2811 E. Villa Real Dr., Orange, CA 92667. Tel. (714)974-7120

Orlando, Bishop Norbert M. Dorsey; Chancellor, Sr. Lucy Vazquez. Chancery Office, 421 E. Robinson, P.O. Box 1800, Orlando, FL 32802. Tel. (305)425-3556. Fax (407)649-7846

Owensboro, Bishop John J. McRaith; Chancellor, Sr. Joseph Angela Boone. Chancery Office, 600 Locust St., Owensboro, KY 42301. Tel. (502)683-1545. Fax (502)683-6883

Palm Beach, Bishop J. Keith Symons; Chancellor, Rev. Charles Hawkins. Chancery Office, 9995 N. Military Tr., Palm Beach Gardens, FL 33410. Tel. (407)775-9500. Fax (407)775-9556

Parma, Byzantine Eparchy of, Bishop Andrew Pataki; Chancellor, Rev. Emil Masich. Chancery Office, 1900 Carlton Rd., Parma, OH 44134. Tel. (216)741-8773. Fax (216)741-9356

Parma, Ukrainian Diocese of St. Joseph in, Bishop Robert M. Moskal; Chancellor, Rev. Msgr. Thomas A. Sayuk. Chancery Office 5720 State Rd., P.O. Box 347180, Parma, OH 44134. Tel. (216)888-1522. Fax (216)888-3477

Passaic, Byzantine Diocese of, Bishop Michael J. Dudick; Chancellor, Rev. Msgr. Raymond Misulich. Chancery Office, 445 Lackawanna Ave., West Paterson, NJ 07424. Tel. (201)890-7777. Fax (201)890- 7175

Paterson, Bishop Frank J. Rodimer; Chancellor, Rev. Msgr. Herbert K. Tillyer. Chancery Office, 777 Valley Rd., Clifton, NJ 07013. Tel. (201)777-8818. Fax (201)777-8976

Pensacola-Tallahassee, Bishop John M. Smith; Chancellor, Rev. Msgr. James Amos. Chancery Office, 11 N. B St., Pensacola, FL 32501, P.O. Drawer 17329, Pensacola, FL 32522. Tel. (904)432-1515. Fax (904)469-8176

Peoria, Bishop John J. Myers; Chancellor, Rev. James F. Campbell. Chancery Office, P.O. Box 1406, 607 NE Madison Ave., Peoria, IL 61655. Tel. (309)671-1550. Fax (309)671-5079

Archdiocese of Philadelphia, Archbishop Anthony Cardinal Bevilacqua; Auxiliary Bishops: Louis A. DeSimone, Martin N. Lohmuller; Chancellor, Rev. Steven J. Harris. Chancery Office, 222 N. 17th St. Philadelphia, PA 19103. Tel. (215)587-4538

Archdiocese of Philadelphia, Ukrainian, Archbishop Stephen Sulyk; Auxiliary Bishop Walter Paska; Chancellor, Sr. Thomas Hrynewich. Chancery Office, 827 N. Franklin St., Philadelphia, PA 19123. Tel. (215)627-0143. Fax (215)627-0377

Phoenix, Bishop Thomas J. O'Brien; Chancellor, Marge Injasoulian. Chancery Office, 400 E. Monroe St., Phoenix, AZ 85004. Tel. (602)257-0030. Fax (602)258-3425

Pittsburgh, Bishop Donald W. Wuerl; Auxiliary Bishops: John B. McDowell, William J. Winter; Chancellor, Rev. Lawrence A. DiNardo. Chancery Office, 111 Blvd. of Allies, Pittsburgh, PA 15222. Tel. (412)456-3000

Archdiocese of Pittsburgh, Byzantine, Archbishop Thomas V. Dolinay; Auxiliary Bishop John M. Bilock; Chancellor. Rev. Msgr. Raymond Balta. Chancery Office, 925 Liberty Ave., Pittsburgh, PA 15214. Tel. (412)281-1000. Fax (412)281-0388

Portland, Bishop Joseph J. Gerry; Auxiliary Bishop Amedee Proulx; Co-Chancellors, Rev. Michael J. Henchal, Sr. Rita-Mae Bissonnette. Chancery Office, 510 Ocean Ave., P.O. Box 11559, Portland, ME 04104-7559. Tel. (207)773-6471. Fax (207)773-0182

Archdiocese of Portland in Oregon, Archbishop William J. Levada; Auxiliary Bishop Kenneth Steiner; Chancellor, Mary Jo Tully. Chancery Office, 2838 E. Burnside St., Portland, OR 97214-1895. Tel. (503)234-5334. Fax (503)234-2545

Providence, Bishop Louis E. Gelineau; Chancellor, Rev. Msgr. William I. Varsanyi. Chancery Office, 1 Cathedral Sq., Providence, RI 02903-3695. Tel. (401)278-4500. Fax (401)278-4548

Pueblo, Bishop Arthur N. Tafoya; Vicar General, Rev. Edward H. Nunez. Chancery Office, 1001 N. Grand Ave., Pueblo, CO 81003. Tel. (303)544-9861

Raleigh, Bishop F. Joseph Gossman; Chancellor, John P. Reidy. Chancery Office, 300 Cardinal Gibbons Dr., Raleigh, NC 27606. Tel. (919)821-9703. Fax (919)821-9705

Rapid City, Bishop Charles J. Chaput; Chancellor, Sr. M. Celine Erk. Chancery Office, 606 Cathedral Dr., P.O. Box 678, Rapid City, SD 57709. Tel. (605)343-3541. Fax (605)345-7985

Reno-Las Vegas, Bishop Daniel F. Walsh; Chancellor-North, Rev. Anthony Vercellone, Jr.; Chancellor-South, Rev. Patrick Leary. Chancery Office, 336 E. Desert Inn Rd., Las Vegas, NV 89109, P.O. Box 18316, Las Vegas, NV 89114-8316. Tel. (702)735-3500. Fax (702)873-4946

Richmond, Bishop Walter F. Sullivan; Auxiliary Bishop David E. Foley; Chancellor, Bishop David E. Foley. Chancery Office, 811 Cathedral Pl., Richmond, VA 23220-4898. Tel. (804)359-5661. Fax 358-9159

Rochester, Bishop Matthew H. Clark; Chancellor, Rev. Kevin E. McKenna. Chancery Office, 1150 Buffalo Rd., Rochester, NY 14624-1890. Tel. (716)328-3210. Fax (716)328-3149

Rockford, Bishop Arthur J. O'Neill; Chancellor, V. Rev. Charles W. McNamee. Chancery Office, 1245 N. Court St., Rockford, IL 61103 Tel. (815)962-3709. Fax (815)968-2824

Rockville Centre, Bishop John R. McGann; Auxiliary Bishops: James J. Daly, Alfred J. Markiewicz, Emil A. Wcela, John C. Dunne; Chancellor, Rev. Msgr. John A. Alesandro. Chancery Office, 50 N. Park Ave. Rockville Centre, NY 11570. Tel. (516)678-5800. Fax (516)678-1786

Sacramento, Bishop Francis A. Quinn; Chancellor, Sr. Bridget Mary Flynn. Chancery Office, 1119 K St., P.O. Box 1706, Sacramento, CA 95812-1706. Tel. (916)443-1996 Fax (916)446-6990

Saginaw, Bishop Kenneth E. Untener; Chancellor, Rev. Msgr. Thomas P. Schroeder. Chancery Office, 5800 Weiss St., Saginaw, MI 48603. Tel. (517)799-7910. Fax (517)797-6670

St. Augustine, Bishop John J. Snyder; Chancellor, Rev. Keith R. Brennan. Chancery Office, 11625 Old St. Augustine Rd., Jacksonville, FL 32241, P.O. Box 24000, Jacksonville, FL 32241-3200. Tel. (904)262-3200. Fax (904)262-0698

St. Cloud, Bishop Jerome Hanus; Chancellor, Rev. Severin Schwieters. Chancery Office, P.O. Box 1248, 214 Third Ave. S., St. Cloud, MN 56302. Tel. (612)251-2340

Archdiocese of St. Louis, Vacant See; Auxiliary Bishops: Edward J. O'Donnell, J. Terry Steib, Paul A. Zipfel; Chancellor, Rev. George J. Lucas. Chancery Office, 4445 Lindell Blvd., St. Louis, MO 63108. Tel. (314)533-1887. Fax (314)533-1887 (Station 212)

Archdiocese of St. Paul and Minneapolis, Archbishop John R. Roach; Auxiliary Bishops: Robert J. Carlson, Joseph J. Charron, Lawrence H. Welsh; Chancellor, William S. Fallon. Chancery Office, 226 Summit Ave., St. Paul, MN 55102. Tel. (612)291-4400. Fax (612)290-1629

St. Petersburg, Bishop John C. Favalora; Chancellor, V. Rev. Robert Sherman. Chancery Office, 6363 9th Ave. N., St. Petersburg, FL 33710, P.O. Box 40200, St. Petersburg, FL 33743-0200. Tel. (813)344-1611. Fax (813)345-2143

Salina, Bishop George K. Fitzsimons; Chancellor, Rev. Msgr. James E. Hake. Chancery Office, 103 N. 9th, P.O. Box 980, Salina, KS 67402. Tel. (913)827-8746. Fax (913)827-8746

Salt Lake City, Bishop William K. Weigand; Chancellor, Deacon Silvio Mayo. Chancery Office, 27 C. St., Salt Lake City, UT 84103. Tel. (801)328-8641. Fax (801)328-9680

San Angelo, Bishop Michael Pfeifer; Chancellor, Rev. Msgr. Larry J. Droll. Chancery Office, 804 Ford, Box 1829, San Angelo, TX 76902. Tel. (915)653-2466

Archdiocese of San Antonio, Archbishop Patrick F. Flores; Auxiliary Bishops: Bernard F. Popp, Joseph A. Galante; Chancellor, Rev. Msgr. Patrick J. Murray. Chancery Office, 2718 W. Woodlawn Ave., P.O. Box 28410, San Antonio, TX 78228. Tel. (512)734-2620. Fax (512)734-0231

San Bernardino, Bishop Phillip F. Straling; Auxiliary Bishop, Gerald R. Barnes, Chancellor, Rev. Donald Webber, Auxiliary Bishop Gerald R. Barnes. Chancery Office, 1450 North D St., San Bernardino, CA 92405 Tel. (714)384-8200. Fax (714)884-4890

San Diego, Bishop Robert H. Brom; Auxiliary Bishop Gilbert E. Chavez; Chancellor, Rev. Msgr. Daniel J. Dillabough. Chancery Office, Alcala Park, San Diego, CA 92110, P.O. Box 85728, San Diego, CA 92186-5728. Tel. (619)574-6300. Fax (619)574-0962

Archdiocese of San Francisco, Archbishop John R. Quinn; Auxiliary Bishops: Carlos A. Sevilla, Patrick J. McGrath; Chancellor, Sr. Mary B. Flaherty. Chancery Office, 445 Church St., San Francisco, CA 94114. Tel. (415)565-3600. Fax (415)565-3633

San Jose, Bishop Pierre DuMaine; Chancellor, Sr. Patricia Marie Mulpeters. Chancery Office, 900 Lafayette St., Ste. 301, San Jose, CA 95050-4966. Tel. (408)983-0100. Fax (408)983-0295

Archdiocese of Santa Fe, Archbishop Robert F. Sanchez; Chancellor, Rev. Ronald Wolf. Chancery Office, 4000 St. Joseph Pl., NW, Albuquerque, NM 87120. Tel. (505)831-8100

Santa Rosa, Bishop Patrick G. Zieman; Chancellor, Rev. Msgr. James E. Pulskamp. Chancery Office, 547 B St., P.O. Box 1297, Santa Rosa, CA 95402. Tel. (707)545-7610. Fax (707)542-9702

Savannah, Bishop Raymond W. Lessard; Chancellor, Rev. Jeremiah J. McCarthy. Chancery Office, 601 E. Liberty St., Savannah, GA 31401-5196. Tel. (912)238-2320 (912)238-2335

Scranton, Bishop James C. Timlin; Auxiliary Bishop Francis X. DiLorenzo; Chancellor, Rev. Msgr. Neil J. Van Loon. Chancery Office, 300 Wyoming Ave., Scranton, PA 18503. Tel. (717)346-8910

Archdiocese of Seattle, Archbishop Thomas J. Murphy; Chancellor, V. Rev. George L. Thomas. Chancery Office, 910 Marion St., Seattle, WA 98104. Tel. (206)382-4560. Fax (206)382-4840

Shreveport, Bishop William B. Friend; Chancellor, Sr. Margaret Daues. Chancery Office, 2500 Line Ave., Shreveport, LA 71104. Tel. (318)222-2006. Fax (318)222-2080

Sioux City, Bishop Lawrence D. Soens; Chancellor, Rev. Kevin C. McCoy. Chancery Office, 1821 Jackson St., P.O. Box 3379, Sioux City, IA 51102. Tel. (712)255-7933. Fax (712)255-3994

Sioux Falls, Bishop Paul V. Dudley; Chancellor, Rev. Gregory Tschakert. Chancery Office, 609 W. 5th St., Box 5033, Sioux Falls, SD 57117. Tel. (605)334-9861. Fax (605)334-2092

Spokane, Bishop William Skylstad; Chancellor, Rev. Mark Pautler. Chancery Office, 1023 W. Riverside Ave., P.O. Box 1453, Spokane, WA 99210-1453. Tel. (509)456-7100

Springfield-Cape Girardeau, Bishop John J. Leibrecht; Chancellor, Rev. Msgr. Thomas E. Reidy. Chancery Office, 601 S. Jefferson, Springfield, MO 65806-3143. Tel. (417)866-0841. Fax (417)866-1140

Springfield in Illinois, Bishop Daniel L. Ryan; Vicar Gen., V. Rev. John Renken. Chancery Office, 1615 W. Washington, P.O. Box 3187, Springfield, IL 62708-3187. Tel. (217)698-8500. Fax (217)698-8620

Springfield in Massachusetts, Bishop John A. Marshall; Auxiliary Bishop Thomas L. Dupre; Chancellor, Bishop Thomas L. Dupre. Chancery Office, 76 Elliot St., Springfield, MA 01105, P.O. Box 1730, Springfield, MA 01101. Tel. (413)732-3175. Fax (413)737-2337

Stamford, Ukrainian, Bishop Basil H. Losten; Chancellor, Rt. Rev. Mitred Matthew Berko. Chancery Office, 161 Glenbrook Rd., Stamford, CT 06902-3092. Tel. (203)324-7698. Fax (203)967-9948

Steubenville, Bishop Gilbert I. Sheldon; Chancellor, Linda A. Nichols. Chancery Office, 422 Washington St., P.O. Box 969, Steubenville, OH 43952. Tel. (614)282-3631. Fax (614)282-3327

Stockton, Bishop Donald W. Montrose; Chancellor, Rev. Richard J. Ryan. Chancery Office, 1105 N. Lincoln St., Stockton, CA 95203, P.O. Box 4237, Stockton, CA 95204-0237. Tel. (209)466-0636. Fax (209)941-9722

Superior, Bishop Raphael M. Fliss; Chancellor, Rev. James F. Tobolski. Chancery Office, 1201 Hughitt Ave., Box 969, Superior, WI 54880. Tel. (715)392-2937

Syracuse, Bishop Joseph T. O'Keefe; Auxiliary Bishop Thomas J. Costello; Co-Chancellors, Rev. David W. Barry, Rev. Richard M. Kopp. Chancery Office, 240 E. Onondaga St., Syracuse, NY 13202, P.O. Box 511, Syracuse, NY 13201. Tel. (315)422-7203. Fax (315)478-4619

Toledo, Bishop James R. Hoffman; Auxiliary Bishop Robert W. Donnelly. Chancery Office, 1933 Spielbush, Toledo, OH 43696, P.O. Box 985, Toledo, OH 43624. Tel. (419)244-6711. Fax (419)244- 4791

Trenton, Bishop John C. Reiss; Chancellor, Rev. Msgr. William F. Fitzgerald. Chancery Office, 701 Lawrenceville Rd., P.O. Box 5309, Trenton, NJ 08638. Tel. (609)882-7125. Fax (609)771-6793

Tucson, Bishop Manuel D. Moreno; Chancellor, Rev. John F. Allt. Chancery Office, 192 S. Stone Ave., Box 31, Tucson, AZ 85702. Tel. (602)792-3410

Tulsa, Vacant See; Chancellor, Rev. Patrick J. Gaalaas. Chancery Office, 820 S. Boulder St., Tulsa, OK 74119, P.O. Box 2009, Tulsa, OK 74101. Tel. (918)587-3115. Fax (918)587-6692

Tyler, Bishop Edmond Carmody; Chancellor, Rev. Gavin Vaverek. Chancery Office, 1920 Sybil Ln., Tyler, TX 75703. Tel. (214)534-1077. Fax (903)534-1370

Van Nuys Eparchy, Byzantine Rite, Bishop George M. Kuzma; Chancellor, Rev. Wesley Izer. Chancery Office, 18024 Parthenia St., Northridge, CA 91325. Tel. (818)701-6114. Fax (818)701-6116

Venice, Bishop John J. Nevins; Chancellor, V. Rev. Jerome A. Carosella. Chancery Office, 1000 Pinebrook Rd., Venice, FL 34292, P.O. Box 2006, Venice, FL 34284. Tel. (813) 484-9543. Fax (813)484-1121

Victoria, Bishop David E. Fellhauer; Chancellor, Rev. Msgr. Thomas C. McLaughlin. Chancery Office, 1505 E. Mesquite Lane, P.O. Box 4708, Victoria, TX 77903. Tel. (512)573-0828. Fax (512)573-5725

Archdiocese of Washington, Archbishop James Cardinal Hickey; Auxiliary Bishops: Alvaro Corrada, Leonard J. Oliver, William C. Curlin; Chancellor, Rev. William J. Kane. Chancery Office, 5001 Eastern Ave., P.O. Box 29260, NW, Washington, DC 20017. Tel. (301)853-3800. Fax (301)853-3246

Wheeling-Charleston, Bishop Bernard W. Schmitt; Chancellor, Rev. Robert C. Nash. Chancery Office, 1300 Byron St., P.O. Box 230, Wheeling, WV 26003. Tel. (304) 233-0880. Fax (304)233-0890

Wichita, Bishop Eugene J. Gerber; Chancellor, Rev. Robert E. Hemberger. Chancery Office, 424 N. Broadway, Wichita, KS 67202. Tel. (316)269-3900

Wilmington, Bishop Robert E. Mulvee; Chancellor, Rev. Msgr. Joseph F. Rebman. Chancery Office, P.O. Box 2030, 1925 Delaware Ave., Ste 1A, Wilmington, DE 19899. Tel. (302)573-3100. Fax (302)573-3128

Winona, Bishop John G. Vlazny; Chancellor, Rev. Edward F. McGrath. Chancery Office, 55 W. Sanborn, P.O. Box 588, Winona, MN 55987. Tel. (507)454-4643. Fax (507)454-8106

Worcester, Bishop Timothy J. Harrington; Auxiliary Bishop George E. Rueger. Chancery Office, 49 Elm St., Worcester, MA 01609. Tel. (508)791-7171. Fax (508)753-7180

Yakima, Bishop Francis E. George; Vicar General, V. Rev. Perron J. Auve. Chancery Office, 5301-A Tieton Dr., Yakima, WA 98908. Tel. (509)965-7117

Youngstown, Bishop James W. Malone; Auxiliary Bishop Benedict C. Franzetta; Chancellor, Rev. Robert J. Siffrin. Chancery Office, 144 W. Wood St., Youngstown, OH 44503. Tel. (216)744-8451

PERIODICALS

Our Sunday Visitor; The New World; The Criterion; Commonweal; Maryknoll; Columbia; Clarion Herald; The Evangelist; Catholic Universe Bulletin; The Catholic World; Catholic Worker; The Catholic Transcript; Catholic Standard and Times; Liguorian; The Catholic Review; Catholic Light; Homiletic and Pastoral Review; Catholic Herald; Extension; Catholic Digest; Catholic Chronicle; New Oxford Review; The Long Island Catholic; America; Pastoral Life; Columban Mission; Salt; The Pilot; Praying; Providence Visitor; The Tidings; Worship; Saint Anthony Messenger; Review for Religious; The Tablet; Theology Digest; U.S. Catholic

The Romanian Orthodox Church in America

The Romanian Orthodox Church in America is an autonomous Archdiocese chartered under the name of "Romanian Orthodox Archdiocese in America."

The diocese was founded in 1929 and approved by the Holy Synod of the Romanian Orthodox Church in Romania in 1934. The Holy Synod of the Romanian Orthodox Church of July 12, 1950, granted it ecclesiastical autonomy in America, continuing to hold only dogmatical and canonical ties with the Holy Synod and the Romanian Orthodox Patriarchate of Romania.

In 1951, approximately 40 parishes with their clergy from the United States and Canada separated from this church. In 1960, they joined the Russian Orthodox Greek Catholic Metropolia, now called the Orthodox Church in America, which reordained for these parishes a bishop with the title "Bishop of Detroit and Michigan."

The Holy Synod of the Romanian Orthodox Church, on June 11, 1973, elevated the Bishop of Romanian Orthodox Missionary Episcopate in America to the rank of Archbishop.

HEADQUARTERS

19959 Riopelle, Detroit, MI 48203 Tel. (313)893-8390

Media Contact, Archdiocesan Dean & Secretary, V. Rev. Fr. Nicholas Apostola, 44 Midland St., Worcester, MA 01602-4217 Tel. (508)799-0040 Fax (508)756-9866

OFFICERS

Archbishop, His Eminence Victorin Ursache, 19959 Riopelle St., Detroit, MI 48203 Tel. (313)893-8390

Vicar, V. Rev. Archim. Dr. Vasile Vasilachi, 45-03 48th Ave., Woodside, Queens, NY 11377 Tel. (718)784-4453

Inter-Church Relations, Dir., Rev. Fr. Nicholas Apostola, 14 Hammond St., Worcester, MA 01610 Tel. (617)799-0040

Sec., V. Archim. Rev. Felix Dubneae, 19959 Riopelle St., Detroit, MI 48203 Tel. (313)892-2402

PERIODICAL

Credinta—The Faith

The Romanian Orthodox Episcopate of America

This body of Eastern Orthodox Christians of Romanian descent was organized in 1929 as an autonomous Diocese under the jurisdiction of the Romanian Patriarchate. In 1951 it severed all relations with the Orthodox Church of Romania. Now under the canonical jurisdiction of the autocephalous Orthodox Church in America, it enjoys full administrative autonomy and is headed by its own Bishop.

HEADQUARTERS

P.O. Box 309, Grass Lake, MI 49240 Tel. (517)522-4800 Fax (517)522-5907

Mailing Address, P.O. Box 309, Grass Lake, MI 49240

Media Contact, Ed./Sec., Dept. of Publications, David Oancea, P.O. Box 185, Grass Lake, MI 49240-0185 Tel. (517)522-3656 Fax (517)522-5907

OFFICERS

Ruling Bishop, His Grace Bishop Nathaniel Popp

Dean of all Canada, V. Rev. Nicolae Marioncu, Box 995, Ste. 1, 709 First St., W., Assiniboia, SK S0H 0B0

OTHER ORGANIZATIONS

The American Romanian Orthodox Youth, Pres., Nicholas Gibb, 6972 N. Sheridan, Apt. 2, Chicago, IL 60626

Assoc. of Romanian Orthodox Ladies' Aux., Pres., Dr. Eleanor Bujea, P.O. Box 1341, Regina, SK S4P 3B8

Orthodox Brotherhood U.S.A., Pres., John Stanitz, 1908 Doncaster Ct., Wheaton, IL 60187

Orthodox Brotherhood of Canada, Pres., Robert Buchanan, 26 Mill Bay, Regina, SK S4N 1L6

PERIODICALS

Solia/The Herald; Lumina Lina; The Joyous Light

The Russian Orthodox Church Outside of Russia

This group was organized in 1920 to unite in one body of dioceses the missions and parishes of the Russian Orthodox Church outside of Russia. The governing body, set up in Constantinople, was sponsored by the Ecumenical Patriarchate. In November, 1950, it came to the United States. The Russian Orthodox Church Outside of Russia emphasizes being true to the old traditions of the Russian Church. It is not in communion with the Moscow Patriarchate.

HEADQUARTERS

75 E. 93rd St., New York, NY 10128 Tel. (212)534-1601 Fax (212)534-1798

Media Contact, Dep. Sec., Bishop Hilarion

SYNOD OF BISHOPS

Pres., His Eminence Metropolitan Vitaly

Sec., Archbishop of Syracuse and Trinity, Laurus

Dep. Sec., Bishop of Manhattan, Hilarion, Tel. (212)722-6577

Dir. of Public & Foreign Relations Dept., Archbishop Laurus of Syracuse and Trinity

PERIODICALS

Living Orthodoxy; Orthodox America; Orthodox Family; Orthodox Russia (Russian); Orthodox Life (English); Orthodox Voices

The Salvation Army

The Salvation Army, founded in 1865 by William Booth (1829-1912) in London, England, and introduced into America in 1880, is an international religious and charitable movement organized and operated on a paramilitary pattern and is a branch of the Christian church. To carry out its purposes, The Salvation Army has established a widely diversified program of religious and social welfare services which are designed to meet the needs of children, youth and adults in all age groups.

HEADQUARTERS

615 Slaters La., Alexandria, VA 22313 Tel. (703)684-5500 Fax (703)684-5538

Media Contact, Natl. Communications Dir., Col. Leon R. Ferraez, Tel. (703)684-5521 Fax (703)684-5538

OFFICERS

Natl. Commander, Commissioner Kenneth L. Hodder

Natl. Chief Sec., Col. Robert A. Watson

Natl. Communications Dept., Dir., Col. Leon R. Ferraez

TERRITORIAL ORGANIZATIONS

Eastern Territory: 440 W. Nyack Rd., P.O. Box C-635, West Nyack, NY 10994 Tel. (914)623-4700 Fax (914)620-7466; Territorial Commander, Commissioner Ronald G. Irwin

Central Territory: 10 W. Algonquin Rd., Des Plaines, IL 60016 Tel. (708)294-2000 Fax (708)294-2299; Territorial Commander, Commissioner Harold E. Shoults

Western Territory: 30840 Hawthorne Blvd., Ranchos Palos Verdes, CA 90274 Tel. (310)541-4721 Fax (310)544-1674; Territorial Commander, Commissioner Paul A. Rader

Southern Territory: 1424 Northeast Expressway, Atlanta, GA 30329 Tel. (404)728-1300 Fax (404)728-1331; Territorial Commander, Commissioner Kenneth Hood

PERIODICAL

The War Cry

The Schwenkfelder Church

The Schwenkfelders are the spiritual descendants of the Silesian nobleman Caspar Schwenkfeld von Ossig (1489-1561), a scholar, reformer, preacher and prolific writer who endeavored to aid in the cause of the Protestant Reformation. A contemporary of Martin Luther, John Calvin, Ulrich Zwingli and Phillip Melanchthon, Schwenkfeld sought no following, formulated no creed and did not attempt to organize a church based on his beliefs. He labored for liberty of religious belief, for a fellowship of all believers and for one united Christian church.

He and his cobelievers supported a movement known as the Reformation by the Middle Way. Persecuted by state churches, ultimately 180 Schwenkfelders exiled from Silesia emigrated to Pennsylvania. They landed at Philadelphia Sept. 22, 1734. In 1882, the Society of Schwenkfelders, the forerunner of the present Schwenkfelder Church, was formed. The church was incorporated in 1909.

The General Conference of the Schwenkfelder Church is a voluntary association for the Schwenkfelder Churches at Palm, Worcester, Lansdale, Norristown and Philadelphia, Pa.

They practice adult baptism and dedication of children, and observe the Lord's Supper regularly with open Communion. In theology, they are Christo-centric; in polity, congregational; in missions, world-minded; in ecclesiastical organization, ecumenical.

The ministry is recruited from graduates of colleges, universities and accredited theological seminaries. The churches take leadership in ecumenical concerns through ministerial associations, community service and action groups, councils of Christian education and other agencies.

HEADQUARTERS

1 Seminary St., Pennsburg, PA 18073 Tel. (215)679-3103

OFFICERS

Mod., Kenneth D. Slough, Jr., 197 N. Whitehall Rd., Norristown, PA 19403

Sec., Frances Witte, Central Schwenkfelder Church, Worcester, PA 19490

Treas., Syl Rittenhouse, 1614 Kriebel Rd., Lansdale, PA 19446

PERIODICAL

The Schwenkfeldian

Separate Baptists in Christ

The Separate Baptists in Christ are a group of Baptists found in Indiana, Ohio, Kentucky, Tennessee, Virginia, West Virginia, Florida and North Carolina dating back to an association formed in 1758 in North Carolina and Virginia.

Today this group consists of approximately 100 churches. They believe in the infallibility of the Bible, the divine ordinances of the Lord's Supper, feetwashing, baptism and that those who endureth to the end shall be saved.

The Separate Baptists are Arminian in doctrine, rejecting both the doctrines of predestination and eternal security of the believer.

At the 1991 General Association, an additional article of doctrine was adopted. "We believe that at Christ's return in the clouds of heaven all Christians will meet the Lord in the air, and time shall be no more," thus leaving no time for a literal one thousand year reign. Seven associations comprise the General Association of Separate Baptists.

HEADQUARTERS

Media Contact, Clk., Rev. Mark Polston, 787 Kitchen Rd., Mooresville, IN 46158 Tel. (317)834-0286

OFFICERS

Mod., Rev. Jim Goff, 1020 Gagel Ave., Louisville, KY 40216

Asst. Mod., Rev. Jimmy Polston, 785 Kitchen Rd., Mooresville, IN 46158 Tel. (317)831-6745

Clk., Rev. Mark Polston

Asst. Clk., Bro. Randy Polston, 3105 N. Elmhurst Dr., Indianapolis, IN 46226 Tel. (317)549-3782

Serbian Orthodox Church in the U.S.A. and Canada

The Serbian Orthodox Church is an organic part of the Eastern Orthodox Church. As a local church it received its autocephaly from Constantinople in 1219 A.D. The Patriarchal seat of the church today is in Belgrade, Yugoslavia.

In 1921, a Serbian Orthodox Diocese in the United States of America and Canada was organized. In 1963, it was reorganized into three dioceses, and in 1983 a fourth diocese was created for the Canadian part of the church. The Serbian Orthodox Church in the USA and Canada received its administrative autonomy in 1982. The Serbian Orthodox Church is in absolute doctrinal unity with all other local Orthodox Churches.

HEADQUARTERS

St. Sava Monastery, P.O. Box 519, Libertyville, IL 60048 Tel. (708)362-2440

BISHOPS

Metropolitan of Midwestern America, Most Rev. Metropolitan Christopher, Tel. (708)367-0698

Administrator of Canada, Bishop of Milesevo, Georgije, 5A Stockbridge Ave., Toronto, ON M8Z 4M6 Tel. (416)231-4009

Diocese of Western America, Administrator Metropolitan Christopher, 2541 Crestline Terr., Alhambra, CA 91803 Tel. (818)264-6825

Bishop of Eastern America, Rt. Rev. Bishop Mitrophan, P.O. Box 368, Sewickley, PA 15143 Tel. (412)741-5686

OTHER ORGANIZATIONS

Brotherhood of Serbian Orth. Clergy in U.S.A. & Canada, Pres., V. Rev. Branko Skaljac, Lorain, OH

Federation of Circles of Serbian Sisters

Serbian Singing Federation

PERIODICAL

The Path of Orthodoxy

119

Seventh-day Adventist Church

The Seventh-day Adventist Church grew out of a worldwide religious revival in the mid-19th century. People of many religious persuasions believed Bible prophecies indicated that the second coming or advent of Christ was imminent.

When Christ did not come in the 1840s, a group of these disappointed Adventists in the United States continued their Bible studies and concluded they had misinterpreted prophetic events and that the second coming of Christ was still in the future. This same group of Adventists later accepted the teaching of the seventh-day Sabbath and became known as Seventh-day Adventists. The denomination organized formally in 1863.

The church was largely confined to North America until 1874, when its first missionary was sent to Europe. Today over 35,000 congregations meet in 204 countries. Membership exceeds 7.5 million and increases between six and seven percent each year.

In addition to a mission program, the church has the largest worldwide Protestant parochial school system with more than 5,500 schools with more than 775,000 students on elementary through college and university levels.

The Adventist Development and Relief Agency (ADRA) helps victims of war and natural disasters, and many local congregations have community service facilities to help those in need close to home.

The church also has a worldwide publishing ministry with more than 50 printing facilities producing magazines and other publications in over 190 languages and dialects. In the United States and Canada, the church sponsors a variety of radio and television programs, including "Christian Lifestyle Magazine," "It Is Written," "Breath of Life," "Ayer, Hoy, y Mañana," "Voice of Prophecy," and "La Voz de la Esperanza."

The North American Division of Seventh-day Adventist includes 158 Conferences which are grouped together into 9 organized Union Conferences. The various Conferences work under the general direction of these Union Conferences.

HEADQUARTERS

12501 Old Columbia Pike, Silver Spring, MD 20904-6600 Tel. (301)680-6000

Media Contact, Asst. Dir., Archives & Statistics, Evelyn D. Osborn

WORLD-WIDE OFFICERS

Pres., Robert S. Folkenberg
Sec., G. Ralph Thompson
Treas., Donald F. Gilbert

WORLD-WIDE DEPARTMENTS

Church Ministries, Dir., Ronald M. Flowers
Communication, Dir., Shirley Burton
Education, Dir., Humberto M. Rasi
Health & Temperance, Dir., Albert S. Whiting
Ministerial Assoc., Sec., James A. Cress
Public Affairs & Religious Liberty, Dir., B. B. Beach
Publishing, Dir., Ronald E. Appenzeller

NORTH AMERICAN OFFICERS

Pres., Alfred C. McClure
Vice Pres.: Robert L. Dale; Manuel Vasquez
Admn. Asst. to Pres., Gary B. Patterson
Sec., Harold W. Baptiste
Assoc. Sec., Rosa T. Banks
Treas., George H. Crumley

Assoc. Treas.: Donald R. Pierson; Meade C. Van-Puttern

NORTH AMERICAN ORGANIZATIONS

Atlantic Union Conf.: P.O. Box 1189, South Lancaster, MA 01561-1189; Pres., David L. Taylor
Canada: Seventh-day Adventist Church in Canada (see Ch. 4)
Columbia Union Conf.: 5427 Twin Knolls Rd., Columbia, MD 21045; Pres., Ron M. Wisbey
Lake Union Conf.: P.O. Box C, Berrien Springs, MI 49103; Pres., R. H. Carter
Mid-America Union Conf.: P.O. Box 6128, Lincoln, NE 68506; Pres., Joel O. Tompkins
North Pacific Union Conf.: P.O. Box 16677, Portland, OR 97216; Pres., Bruce Johnston
Pacific Union Conf.: P.O. Box 5005, Westlake Village, CA 91359; Pres., Thomas J. Mostert, Jr
Southern Union Conf.: P.O. Box 849, Decatur, GA 30031; Pres., M. D. Gordon
Southwestern Union Conf.: P.O. Box 4000, Burleson, TX 76097; Pres., Cyril Miller

PERIODICALS

Celebration; Adventist Review; Christian Record; Cornerstone Connections; Guide; Insight; Journal of Adventist Education; Liberty; Listen; Message; Ministry; Adult and Junior-Teen Mission; Our Little Friend; Primary Treasure; Shabbat Shalom; Signs of the Times; Vibrant Life; Youth Ministry Accent

Seventh Day Baptist General Conference, USA and Canada

Seventh Day Baptists emerged during the English Reformation, organizing their first churches in the mid-1600s. The first Seventh Day Baptists of record in America were Stephen and Ann Mumford, who emigrated from England in 1664. Beginning in 1665 several members of the First Baptist Church at Newport, R.I. began observing the seventh day Sabbath, or Saturday. In 1671, five members, together with the Mumfords, formed the first Seventh Day Baptist Church in America at Newport.

Beginning about 1700, other Seventh Day Baptist churches were established in New Jersey and Pennsylvania. From these three centers, the denomination grew and expanded westward. They founded the Seventh Day Baptist General Conference in 1802.

The organization of the denomination reflects an interest in home and foreign missions, publications and education. Women have been encouraged to participate. From the earliest years religious freedom has been championed for all and the separation of church and state advocated.

Seventh Day Baptists are members of the Baptist World Alliance. The Seventh Day Baptist World Federation has 17 member conferences on six continents.

HEADQUARTERS

Seventh Day Baptist Center, 3120 Kennedy Rd., P.O. Box 1678, Janesville, WI 53547-1678 Tel. (608)752-5055 Fax (608)752-7711
Media Contact, Gen. Services Admn., Calvin Babcock

OTHER ORGANIZATIONS

Seventh Day Baptist Missionary Society, Exec. Vice-Pres., Mr. Kirk Looper, 119 Main St., Westerly, RI 02891

Seventh Day Bapt. Bd. of Christian Ed., Exec. Dir., Rev. Ernest K. Bee, Jr., Box 115, Alfred Station, NY 14803

Women's Soc. of the Gen. Conference, Pres., Mrs. Donna Bond, RFD 1, Box 426, Bridgeton, NJ 08302

American Sabbath Tract & Comm. Council, Dir. of Communications, Rev. Kevin J. Butler, 3120 Kennedy Rd., P.O. Box 1678, Janesville, WI 53547

Seventh Day Baptist Historical Society, Historian, Don A. Sanford, 3120 Kennedy Rd., P.O. Box 1678, Janesville, WI 53547

Seventh Day Baptist Center on Ministry, Dir. of Pastoral Services, Rev. Rodney L. Henry, 3120 Kennedy Rd., P.O. Box 1678, Janesville, WI 53547

PERIODICAL

Sabbath Recorder

Social Brethren

The Social Brethren were organized in 1867 among members of various evangelical bodies. Its confession of faith has nine articles.

OFFICERS

General Assembly, Mod., Rev. Earl Vaughn, RR #2, Flora, IL 62839 Tel. (618)662-4373

Union Association, Mod., Rev. Herbert Tarleton, 420 S. Mill, Harrisburg, IL 62946 Tel. (618)252-7196

Illinois Association, Mod., Rev. Norman Cozart, Rt. 1, Stonefort, IL 62987

Midwestern Association, Mod., Rev. Edward Darnell, 53 E. Newport, Pontiac, MI 48055 Tel. (313)335-9125

Southern Baptist Convention

The Southern Baptist Convention was organized on May 10, 1845, in Augusta, GA.

Cooperating Baptist churches are located in all 50 states, the District of Columbia, Puerto Rico, American Samoa and the Virgin Islands. The members of the churches work together through 1,208 district associations and 39 state conventions and/or fellowships. The Southern Baptist Convention has an Executive Committee and 20 national agencies — four boards, six seminaries, seven commissions, a foundation and two associated organizations.

The purpose of the Southern Baptist Convention is "to provide a general organization for Baptists in the United States and its territories for the promotion of Christian missions at home and abroad and any other objects such as Christian education, benevolent enterprises, and social services which it may deem proper and advisable for the furtherance of the Kingdom of God." (Constitution, Article II)

The Convention exists in order to help the churches lead people to God through Jesus Christ.

From the beginning, there has been a mission desire to share the Gospel with the peoples of the world. The Cooperative Program is the basic channel of mission support. In addition, the Lottie Moon Christmas Offering for Foreign Missions and the Annie Armstrong Easter Offering for Home Missions support Southern Baptists' world mission programs.

In 1992, there were 3,958 foreign missionaries serving in 131 foreign countries and 4,922 home missionaries serving within the United States.

In 1987, the Southern Baptist Convention adopted themes and goals for the major denominational emphasis of Bold Mission Thrust for 1990-2000. Bold Mission Thrust is an effort to enable every person in the world to have opportunity to hear and to respond to the Gospel of Christ by the year 2000.

HEADQUARTERS

901 Commerce St., Ste. 750, Nashville, TN 37203 Tel. (615)244-2355

Media Contact, Vice-Pres. for Convention Relations, Mark T. Coppenger, Tel. (615)244-2355 Fax (615)742-8919

OFFICERS

Pres., H. Edwin Young, Second Baptist Church, 6400 Woodway, Houston, TX 77057

Recording Sec., David W. Atchison, P.O. Box 1543, Brentwood, TN 37027

Executive Committee: Pres., Morris M. Chapman; Exec. Vice-Pres., Ernest E. Mosley; Vice-Pres., Business & Finance, Jack Wilkerson; Vice-Pres., Convention Relations, Mark Coppenger; Vice-Pres., Convention News, Herb V. Hollinger

GENERAL BOARDS AND COMMISSIONS

Foreign Mission Board: Pres., Jerry A. Rankin, Box 6767, Richmond, VA 23230

Home Mission Board: Pres., Larry L. Lewis, 1350 Spring St., NW, Atlanta, GA 30367 Tel. (404)898-7700

Annuity Board: Pres., Paul W. Powell, P.O. Box 2190, Dallas, TX 75221 Tel. (214)720-0511

Sunday School Board: Pres., James T. Draper, Jr., 127 Ninth Ave., N., Nashville, TN 37234 Tel. (615)251-2000

Brotherhood Commission: Pres., James D. Williams, 1548 Poplar Ave., Memphis, TN 38104 Tel. (901)272-2461

SB Comm. on the Am. Bapt. Theol. Sem.: Exec. Sec.-Treas., Arthur L. Walker, Jr.; Pres. of the Seminary, Odell McGlothian, Sr.

Christian Life Commission: Exec. Dir., Richard D. Land, 901 Commerce St., Nashville, TN 37203 Tel. (615)244-2495

Education Commission: Exec. Sec.-Treas., Stephen P. Carlton, 901 Commerce St., Nashville, TN 37203 Tel. (615)244-2362

Historical Commission: Exec. Dir., Treas., Lynn E. May, Jr., 901 Commerce Street, Nashville, TN 37203 Tel. (615)244-0344

The Radio & TV Commission: Pres., Jack Johnson, 6350 West Freeway, Ft. Worth, TX 76150 Tel. (817)737-4011

Stewardship Commission: Pres., A. R. Fagan, 901 Commerce St., Nashville, TN 37203 Tel. (615)244-2303

STATE CONVENTIONS

Alabama, Troy L. Morrison, 2001 E. South Blvd., Montgomery, AL 36198 Tel. (205)288-2460

Alaska, Bill G. Duncan, 1750 O'Malley Rd., Anchorage, AK 99516 Tel. (907)344-9627

Arizona, Dan C. Stringer, 4520 N. Central Ave., Ste. 550, Phoenix, AZ 85013 Tel. (602)264-9421

Arkansas, Don Moore, P.O. Box 552, Little Rock, AR 72203 Tel. (501)376-4791

California, C. B. Hogue, 678 E. Shaw Ave., Fresno, CA 93710 Tel. (209)229-9533

Colorado, Curtis Griffis, Interim, 7393 So. Alton Way, Englewood, CO 80112 Tel. (303)771-2480

District of Columbia, W. Jere Allen, 1628 16th St. NW, Washington, DC 20009 Tel. (202)265-1526

Florida, John Sullivan, 1230 Hendricks Ave., Jacksonville, FL 32207 Tel. (904)396-2351

Georgia, Dr. J. Robert White, 2930 Flowers Rd., S, Atlanta, GA 30341 Tel. (404)455-0404

Hawaii, O. W. Efurd, 2042 Vancouver Dr., Honolulu, HI 96822 Tel. (808)946-9581

Illinois, Gene Wilson, P.O. Box 19247, Springfield, IL 62794 Tel. (217)786-2600

Indiana, Charles Sullivan, 900 N. High School Rd., Indianapolis, IN 46224 Tel. (317)241-9317

Kansas-Nebraska, R. Rex Lindsay, 5410 W. Seventh St., Topeka, KS 66606 Tel. (913)273-4880

Kentucky, William W. Marshall, P.O. Box 43433, Middletown, KY 40243 Tel. (502)245-4101

Louisiana, Mark Short, Box 311, Alexandria, LA 71301 Tel. (318)448-3402

Maryland-Delaware, Charles R. Barnes, Interim, 10255 S. Columbia Rd., Columbia, MD 21064 Tel. (301)290-5290

Michigan, Robert Wilson, 15635 W. 12 Mile Rd., Southfield, MI 48076 Tel. (313)557-4200

Minnesota-Wisconsin, Dr. William C. Tinsley, 519 16th St. SE, Rochester, MN 55904 Tel. (507)282-3636

Mississippi, William W. Causey, P.O. Box 530, Jackson, MS 39205 Tel. (601)968-3800

Missouri, Donald V. Wideman, 400 E. High, Jefferson City, MO 65101 Tel. (314)635-7931

Nevada, David Meacham, 406 California Ave., Reno, NV 89509 Tel. (702)786-0406

New England, Kenneth R. Lyle, Box 688, 5 Oak Ave., Northboro, MA 01532 Tel. (508)393-6013

New Mexico, Claude Cone, P.O. Box 485, Albuquerque, NM 87103 Tel. (505)247-0586

New York, R. Quinn Pugh, 6538 Collamer Dr., East Syracuse, NY 13057 Tel. (315)475-6173

North Carolina, Roy J. Smith, 205 Convention Dr., Cary, NC 27511 Tel. (919)467-5100

Ohio, Exec. Dir., Orville H. Griffin, 1680 E. Broad St., Columbus, OH 43203 Tel. (614)258-8491

Northwest Baptist Convention, Cecil Sims, 1033 N.E. 6th Ave., Portland, OR 97232 Tel. (503)238-4545

Oklahoma, William G. Tanner, 3800 N. May Ave., Oklahoma City, OK 73112 Tel. (405)942-3800

Pennsylvania-South Jersey, David C. Waltz, 4620 Fritchey St., Harrisburg, PA 17109 Tel. (717)652-5856

South Carolina, B. Carlisle Driggers, 907 Richland St., Columbia, SC 29201 Tel. (803)765-0030

Tennessee, Dr. James M. Porch, P.O. Box 728, Brentwood, TN 37024 Tel. (615)373-2255

Texas, William M. Pinson, Jr., 333 N. Washington, Dallas, TX 75246 Tel. (214)828-5100

Utah-Idaho, Sec., C. Clyde Billingsley, P.O. Box 1039, Sandy, UT 84091 Tel. (801)255-3565

Virginia, Reginald M. McDonough, P.O. Box 8568, Richmond, VA 23226 Tel. (804)672-2100

West Virginia, Don R. Mathis, Number One Mission Way, Scott Depot, WV 25560 Tel. (304)757-0944

Wyoming, John W. Thomason, Box 3074, Casper, WY 82602 Tel. (307)472-4087

FELLOWSHIPS

Dakota Southern Baptist Fellowship, Dewey W. Hickey, P.O. Box 7187, Bismark, ND 58502 Tel. (701)255-3765

Iowa Southern Baptist Fellowship, O. Wyndell Jones, Westview #27, 2400 86th St., Des Moines, IA 50322 Tel. (515)278-1516

Montana Southern Baptist Fellowship, James Nelson, P.O. Box 99, Billings, MT 59103 Tel. (406)252-7537

Canadian Convention of Southern Baptists, Allen E. Schmidt, Postal Bag 300, Cochrane, AL T0L 0W0 Tel. (403)932-5688

PERIODICALS

The Commission; SBC Life; MissionsUSA; Contempo

Southern Methodist Church

Organized in 1939, this body is composed of congregations desirous of continuing in true Biblical Methodism and preserving the fundamental doctrines and beliefs of the Methodist Episcopal Church, South. These congregations declined to be a party to the merger of the Methodist Episcopal Church, The Methodist Episcopal Church, South and the Methodist Protestant Church into The Methodist Church.

HEADQUARTERS

P.O. Box 39, Orangeburg, SC 29116-0039 Tel. (803)536-1378 Fax (803)534-7827

Media Contact, Pres., Rev. Dr. Richard G. Blank

OFFICERS

Pres., Rev. Dr. Richard G. Blank

Admn. Asst. to Pres., Philip A. Rorabaugh

Vice-Pres.: The Carolinas-Virginia Conf., Rev. E. Legrand Adams, Rt. 2, Box 1050, Laurens, SC 29360; Alabama-Florida-Georgia Conf., Rev. John Courson, RD2, Box 280, Madison, FL 32340; Mid-South Conf., Rev. Bedford F. Landers, 1307 Walnut St., Waynesboro, MS 39367; South-Western Conf., Rev. John H. Price, 108 Oak Cir., Monroe, LA 71203

Gen. Conf., Treas., Rev. Philip A. Rorabaugh, P.O. Drawer A, Orangeburg, SC 29116-0039

PERIODICAL

The Southern Methodist

Sovereign Grace Baptists

The Sovereign Grace Baptists are a contemporary movement which began its stirrings in the mid-1950s when some pastors in traditional Baptist churches returned to a Calvinist-theological perspective.

The first "Sovereign Grace" conference was held in Ashland, Ky., in 1954 and since then, conferences of this sort have been sponsored by various local churches on the West Coast, Southern and Northern states and Canada. This movement is a spontaneous phenomenon concerning reformation at the local church level. Consequently, there is no interest in establishing a Reformed Baptist "Convention" or "Denomination." Each local church is to administer the keys to the kingdom.

Most Sovereign Grace Baptists formally or informally relate to the "First London" (1646), "Second London" (1689) or "Philadelphia" (1742) Confessions.

There is a wide variety of local church government in this movement. Many Calvinist Baptists have a plurality of elders in each assembly. Other Sovereign Grace Baptists, however, prefer to function with one pastor and several deacons.

Membership procedures vary from church to church but all require a credible profession of faith in Christ, and proper baptism as a basis for membership.

Calvinistic Baptists financially support gospel

efforts (missionaries, pastors of small churches at home and abroad, literature publication and distribution, radio programs, etc.) in various parts of the world.

HEADQUARTERS

Media Contact, Corres., Jon Zens, P.O. Box 548, St. Croix Falls, WI 54024 Tel. (715)755-3560 Fax (612)465-7373

PERIODICALS

Reformation Today; Searching Together

The Swedenborgian Church

Founded in North America in 1792 as the Church of the New Jerusalem, the Swedenborgian Church was organized as a national body in 1817 and incorporated in Illinois in 1861. Its biblically-based theology is derived from the spiritual, or mystical, experiences and exhaustive biblical studies of the Swedish scientist and philosopher Emanuel Swedenborg (1688-1772).

The church centers its worship and teachings on the historical life and the risen and glorified present reality of the Lord Jesus Christ. It looks with an ecumenical vision toward the establishment of the kingdom of God in the form of a universal Church, active in the lives of all people of good will who desire and strive for freedom, peace and justice for all. It is a member of the NCCC and active in many local councils of churches.

With churches and groups throughout the United States and Canada, the denomination's central administrative offices and its seminary — Swedenborg School of Religion — are located in Newton, Mass. Affiliated churches are found in Africa, Asia, Australia, Canada, Europe, the United Kingdom, Japan and South America. Many philosophers and writers have acknowledged their appreciation of Swedenborg's teachings.

HEADQUARTERS

48 Sargent St., Newton, MA 02158 Tel. (617)969-4240 Fax (617)964-3258
Media Contact, Central Ofc. Mgr., Martha Bauer

OFFICERS

Pres., Rev. Edwin G. Capon, 170 Virginia St., St. Paul, MN 55102

PERIODICALS

The Messenger; Our Daily Bread

Syrian Orthodox Church of Antioch (Archdiocese of the United States and Canada)

An archdiocese in North America of the Syrian Orthodox Church of Antioch, the church traces its origin to the Patriarchate established in Antioch by St. Peter the Apostle. It is under the supreme ecclesiastical jurisdiction of His Holiness the Syrian Orthodox Patriarch of Antioch and All the East, now residing in Damascus, Syria. The Syrian Orthodox Church — composed of several archdioceses, numerous parishes, schools and seminaries - professes the faith of the first three Ecumenical Councils of Nicaea, Constantinople and Ephesus, and numbers faithful in the Middle East, India, the Americas, Europe and Australia.

The first Syrian Orthodox faithful came to North America during the late 1800s, and by 1907 the first Syrian Orthodox priest was ordained to tend to the community's spiritual needs. In 1949, His Emi-

nence Archbishop Mar Athanasius Y. Samuel came to America and was soon appointed Patriarchal Vicar. The Archdiocese was officially established in 1957.

There are 16 official archdiocesan parishes in the United States, located in California, Illinois, Massachusetts, Michigan, New Jersey, New York, Oregon, Rhode Island and Texas. In Canada, there are four official parishes: two in the Province of Ontario and two in the Province of Quebec.

HEADQUARTERS

Archdiocese of the U.S. and Canada, 49 Kipp Ave., Lodi, NJ 07644 Tel. (201)778-0638 Fax (201)773-7506
Media Contact, Archdiocesan Gen. Sec., V. Rev. Chorepiscopus John Meno, 45 Fairmount Ave., Hackensack, NJ 07061 Tel. (201)646-9443 Fax (201)773-7506

OFFICERS

Primate, Archbishop Mar Athanasius Y. Samuel
Archdiocesan Gen. Sec., V. Rev. Chorepiscopus John Meno

Triumph the Church and Kingdom of God in Christ Inc. (International)

This church was given through the wisdom and knowledge of God to the Late Apostle Elias Dempsey Smith on Oct. 20, 1897, in Issaquena County, Miss., while he was pastor of a Methodist church.

The Triumph Church, as this body is more commonly known, was founded in 1902. Its doors opened in 1904 and it was confirmed in Birmingham, Ala., with 225 members in 1915. It was incorporated in Washington, D.C., in 1918 and currently operates in 31 states and overseas. The General Church is divided into 18 districts, including the Africa District.

Triumphant doctrine and philosophy are based on the principles of life, truth and knowledge; the understanding that God is in man and expressed through man; the belief in manifested wisdom and the hope for constant new revelations. Its concepts and methods of teaching the second coming of Christ are based on these and all other attributes of goodness.

Triumphians emphasize that God is the God of the living, not the God of the dead.

HEADQUARTERS

213 Farrington Ave. S.E., Atlanta, GA 30315

OFFICERS

Chief Bishop, Rt. Rev. A. J. Scott, 1323 N.E. 36th St., Savannah, GA 31404 Tel. (912)236-2877
Asst. Chief Apostle, Bishop C. W. Drummond, 7114 Idlewild, Pittsburgh, PA 15208 Tel. (412)731-2286
Gen. Bd of Trustees, Chmn., Bishop Leon Simon, 1028 59th St., Oakland, CA 94608 Tel. (415)652-9576
Gen. Treas., Bishop Hosea Lewis, 1713 Needlewood Ln., Orlando, FL 32818 Tel. (407)295-5488
Gen. Rec. Sec., Bishop Zephaniah Swindle, Box 1927, Shelbyville, TX 75973 Tel. (409)598-3082

PERIODICAL

Mouth and Voice of God

True Orthodox Ch. of Greece (Synod of Metropolitan Cyprian), American Exarchate

The American Exarchate of the True (Old Calendar) Orthodox Church of Greece adheres to the tenets of the Eastern Orthodox Church, which considers itself the legitimate heir of the historical Apostolic Church.

When the Orthodox Church of Greece adopted the New or Gregorian Calendar in 1924, many felt that this breach with tradition compromised the church's festal calendar, based on the Old or Julian calendar, and its unity with world Orthodoxy. In 1935, three State Church Bishops returned to the Old Calendar and established a Synod in Resistance, The True Orthodox Church of Greece. When the last of these Bishops died, the Russian Orthodox Church Abroad consecrated a new hierarchy for the Greek Old Calendarists and, in 1969, declared them a sister church.

In the face of persecution by the state church, some Old Calendarists denied the validity of the Mother Church of Greece and formed two synods, now under the direction of Archbishop Chrysostomos of Athens and Archbishop Andreas of Athens. A moderate faction under Metropolitan Cyprian of Oropos and Fili does not maintain communion with the Mother Church of Greece, but recognizes its validity and seeks a restoration of unity by a return to the Julian Calendar and traditional ecclesiastical polity by the state church. About 1.5 million Orthodox Greeks belong to the Old Calendar Church.

The first Old Calendarist communities in the United States were formed in the 1930s. The Exarchate under Metropolitan Cyprian was established in 1986. Placing emphasis on clergy education, youth programs and recognition of the Old Calendarist minority in American Orthodoxy, the Exarchate has encouraged the establishment of monastic communities and missions. Cordial contacts with the New Calendarist and other Orthodox communities are encouraged. A center for theological training and Patristic studies has been established at the Exarchate headquarters in Etna, Calif.

HEADQUARTERS

St. Gregory Palamas Monastery, P.O. Box 398, Etna, CA 96027 Tel. (916)467-3228 Fax (916)467-3996

Media Contact, Exarch in America, His Eminence Bishop Chrysostomos

OFFICERS

Synodal Exarch in America, His Eminence Bishop Chrysostomos

Asst. to the Exarch, His Grace Bishop Auxentios

Dean of Exarchate, The Rev. James P. Thornton, P.O. Box 2833, Garden Grove, CA 92642

PERIODICAL

Orthodox Tradition

Ukrainian Orthodox Church of America (Ecumenical Patriarchate)

This body was organized in the United States in 1928, when the first convention was held. In 1932, Dr. Joseph Zuk was consecrated as first Bishop. His successor was the Most Rev. Bishop Bohdan, Primate, who was consecrated by the order of the Ecumenical Patriarchate of Constantinople in 1937, in New York City. He was succeeded by the Most Rev. Metropolitan Andrei Kuschak, consecrated by the blessing of Ecumenical Patriarch by Archbishop Iakovos, Metropolitan Germanos and Bishop Silas of Greek-Orthodox Church, in 1967. His successor is Bishop Vsevolod, ordained in 1987 by Archbishop Iakovos, Metropolitan Silas and Bishops Philip and Athenagoras.

HEADQUARTERS

Ukrainian Orthodox Church of America, 90-34 139th St., Jamaica, NY 11435 Tel. (718)297-2407 Fax (718)291-8308

Media Contact, Primate, Bishop Vsevolod

OFFICERS

Primate, Rt. Rev. Bishop Vsevolod

Administrator for Canada, Rev. Michael Pawlyshyn

Chancellor, Rev. W. Czekaluk

PERIODICAL

Ukrainian Orthodox Herald

Ukrainian Orthodox Church of the U.S.A.

The church was formally organized in the United States in 1919. Archbishop John Theodorovich arrived from Ukraine in 1924.

HEADQUARTERS

P.O. Box 495, South Bound Brook, NJ 08880 Tel. (908)356-0090 Fax (908)356-5556

Media Contact, Consistory Sec., Fr. Frank Estocin

OFFICERS

Metropolitan, Most Rev. Constantine Buggan, Archbishop of Chicago & Philadelphia, P.O. Box 495, South Bound Brook, NJ 08880

Archbishop, His Grace Archbishop Antony, Archbishop of New York & Washington, 4 Von Steuben La., South Bound Brook, NJ 08880

Consistory: Pres., V. Rev. William Diakiw; Vice-Pres., V. Rev. Bohdan Zelechiwsky; Sec., V. Rev. Frank Estocin; Treas., V. Rev. Taras Chubenko

PERIODICAL

Ukrainian Orthodox Word

United Brethren in Christ

The Church of the United Brethren in Christ had its beginning with Philip William Otterbein and Martin Boehm, who were leaders in the revivalistic movement in Pennsylvania and Maryland from the late 1760s into the early 1800s.

On Sept. 25, 1800, they and others associated with them formed a society under the name of United Brethren in Christ. Subsequent conferences adopted a Confession of Faith in 1815 and a constitution in 1841. The Church of the United Brethren in Christ adheres to the original constitution as amended in 1957, 1961 and 1977.

HEADQUARTERS

302 Lake St., Huntington, IN 46750 Tel. (219)356-2312 Fax (219)356-4730

Media Contact, Bishop, Dr. Ray A. Seilhamer

OFFICERS

Bishop, Dr. Ray A. Seilhamer

Bishops: Clarence A. Kopp, Jr.; Jerry Datema

Gen. Treas./Office Mgr., Marda J. Hoffman

Dept. of Education, Dir., Dr. G. Blair Dowden

Dept. of Church Services, Dir., Rev. Paul Hirschy

PERIODICAL

UB

United Christian Church

The United Christian Church originated about 1864. There were some ministers and laymen in the United Brethren in Christ Church who disagreed with the position and practice of the church on infant baptism, voluntary bearing of arms and belonging to oath-bound secret combinations. This group developed into United Christian Church, organized at a conference held in Campbelltown, Pa., on May 9, 1877. The principal founders of the denomination were George Hoffman, John Stamn and Thomas Lesher. Before they were organized, they were called Hoffmanites.

The United Christian Church has district conferences, a yearly general conference, a general board of trustees, a mission board, a board of directors of the United Christian Church Home, a camp meeting board, a young peoples' board and local organized congregations.

It believes in the Holy Trinity and the inspired Holy Scriptures with the doctrines they teach. The church practices the ordinances of Baptism, Holy Communion and Foot Washing.

It welcomes all into its fold who are born again, believe in Jesus Christ as Savior and Lord and have received the Holy Spirit.

HEADQUARTERS

c/o John P. Ludwig, Jr., 523 W. Walnut St., Cleona, PA 17042 Tel. (717)273-9629
Media Contact, Presiding Elder, John P. Ludwig, Jr.

OFFICERS

Mod. & Presiding Elder, Elder John P. Ludwig, Jr.
Conf. Sec., Mr. Lee Wenger, 1625 Thompson Ave., Annville, PA 17003

OTHER ORGANIZATIONS

Mission Board: Pres., Elder John P. Ludwig, Jr.; Sec., Elder Walter Knight, Jr., Rt. #3, Box 98, Palmyra, PA 17078; Treas., Elder Henry C. Heagy, 2080 S. White Oak St., Lebanon, PA 17042

United Church of Christ

The United Church of Christ was constituted on June 25, 1957 by representatives of the Congregational Christian Churches and of the Evangelical and Reformed Church, in Cleveland, Ohio.

The Preamble to the Constitution states: "The United Church of Christ acknowledges as its sole head, Jesus Christ ... It acknowledges as kindred in Christ all who share in this confession. It looks to the Word of God in the Scriptures, and to the presence and power of the Holy Spirit ... It claims ... the faith of the historic Church expressed in the ancient creeds and reclaimed in the basic insights of the Protestant Reformers. It affirms the responsibility of the Church in each generation to make this faith its own in ... worship, in honesty of thought and expression, and in purity of heart before God.

The creation of the United Church of Christ brought together four unique traditions:

(1) Groundwork for the Congregational Way was laid by Calvinist Puritans and Separatists during the late 16th-early 17th centuries, then achieved prominence among English Protestants during the civil war of the 1640s. Opposition to state control prompted followers to emigrate to the United States, where they helped colonize New England in the 17th century. Congregationalists have been self-consciously a denomination from the mid-19th century.

(2) The Christian Churches, an 18th-century American restorationist movement emphasized Christ as the only head of the church, the New Testament as their only rule of faith, and "Christian" as their sole name. This loosely organized denomination found in the Congregational Churches a like disposition. In 1931, the two bodies formally united as the Congregational Christian Churches.

(3) The German Reformed Church comprised an irenic aspect of the Protestant Reformation, as a second generation of Reformers drew on the insights of Zwingli, Luther and Calvin to formulate the Heidelberg Catechism of 1563. People of the German Reformed Church began immigrating to the New World early in the 18th century, the heaviest concentration in Pennsylvania. Formal organization of the American denomination was completed in 1793. The church spread across the country. In the Mercersburg Movement, a strong emphasis on evangelical catholicity and Christian unity was developed.

(4) In 19th-century in Germany, Enlightenment criticism and Pietist inwardness decreased long-standing conflicts between religious groups. In Prussia, a royal proclamation merged Lutheran and Reformed people into one United Evangelical Church (1817). Members of this new church way migrated to America. The Evangelicals settled in large numbers in Missouri and Illinois, emphasizing pietistic devotion and unionism; in 1840 they formed the German Evangelical Church Society in the West. After union with other Evangelical church associations, in 1877 it took the name of the German Evangelical Synod of North America.

On June 25, 1934, this Synod and the Reformed Church in the U.S. (formerly the German Reformed Church) united to form the Evangelical and Reformed Church. They blended the Reformed tradition's passion for the unity of the church and the Evangelical tradition's commitment to the liberty of conscience inherent in the gospel.

HEADQUARTERS

700 Prospect Ave., Cleveland, OH 44115 Tel. (216)736-2100 Fax (216)736-2120
Media Contact, UCC-Sec., Edith A. Guffey, Tel. (216)736-2110

OFFICERS

Pres., Rev. Paul H. Sherry
Sec., Ms. Edith A. Guffey
Dir. of Fin. & Treas., Rev. Doris R. Powell
Asst. to Pres. for Ecumenical Concerns, Rev. John H. Thomas
Asst. to Pres., Ms. Marilyn Dubasak
Affirmative Action Officer, Rev. Hollis Wilson
Chpsn. Exec. Council, Rev. William A. Dalke
Vice-Chpsn., Rev. Lorain R. Giles
Mod., Mr. Victor Mendez
Asst. Mod.: Ms. Donna J. Debney; Rev. Anthony L. Taylor

ORGANIZATIONS

United Church Board for World Min.: Tel. (216)736-3200; 475 Riverside Dr., New York, NY 10115 Tel. (212)870-2637; 14 Beacon St., Boston, MA 02108; Exec. Vice-Pres., Rev. Scott S. Libbey; Mission Program Unit, Gen. Sec.,

Rev. Daniel F. Romero; Support Services Unit, Treas., Mr. Bruce Foresman

United Church Board for Homeland Min.: Tel. (216)736-3800 Fax (216)736-3803; Office of Exec. Vice-Pres., Exec. Vice-Pres., Rev. Thomas E. Dipko; Gen. Sec., Rev. Robert P. Noble, Jr.; Office of the Treasurer, Treas., Rev. Robert P. Noble, Jr.; Div. of Evangelism & Local Church Dev., Gen. Sec., Rev. Robert L. Burt; Div. of Education & Publication, Gen. Sec., Rev. Ansley Coe Throckmorton; Div. of American Missionary Association, Co-Gen. Secs., Rev. B. Ann Eichhorn

Commission for Racial Justice: Ofc. for Urban & Natl. Racial Justice, 5113 Georgia Ave. NW, Washington, DC 20011 Tel. (202)291-1593; Ofc. for Constituency Dev./Rural Racial Justice, Franklinton Center, P.O. Box 187, Enfield, NC 27823 Tel. (919)437-1723; Ofc. for Ecumenical Racial Justice, 475 Riverside Dr., Room 1948, New York, NY 10115 Tel. (212)870-2077; Exec. Dir., Ms. Bernice Powell Jackson

Council for American Indian Ministry: 122 W. Franklin Ave., Rm. 304, Minneapolis, MN 55405 Tel. (612)870-3679; Exec. Dir., Rev. Armin L. Schmidt

Council for Health & Human Service Min.: Tel. (216)736-2250; Exec. Dir., Rev. Bryan Sickbert

Coord. Center for Women in Church & Soc.: Tel. (216)736-2150; Exec. Dir., Rev. Mary Sue Gast

Office for Church in Society: 110 Maryland Ave. NE, Washington, DC 20002; Exec. Dir., Ms. Valerie E. Russell, (OH) Dir., Washington Ofc., Rev. Jay E. Lintner

Office for Church Life & Leadership: Exec. Dir., Rev. William A. Hulteen, Jr. (OH)

Office of Communication: 475 Riverside Dr., 16th Fl., New York, NY 10115 Tel. (212)870-2137; Dir., Dr. Beverly J. Chain

Stewardship Council: 1400 N. Seventh St., St. Louis, MO 63106; 409 Prospect St., Box 304, New Haven, CT 06511; 475 Riverside Dr., 16th Fl., New York, NY 10115; Exec. Dir., Rev. Ronald G. Kurtz

Commission on Development: Dir. Planned Giving, Rev. Donald G. Stoner

Historical Council: Office of Archivist, Philip Schaff Library, Lancaster Theological Seminary, 555 W. James St., Lancaster, PA 17603

Pension Boards: 475 Riverside Dr., New York, NY 10115; Exec. Vice-Pres., Dr. John Ordway

United Church Foundation, Inc.: 475 Riverside Dr., New York, NY 10115; Financial Vice-Pres. & Treas., Mr. Donald G. Hart

CONFERENCES

Western Region

California, Nevada, Northern, Rev. David J. Jamieson, 20 Woodside Ave., San Francisco, CA 94127

California, Southern, Rev. Davida Foy Crabtree, 466 E. Walnut St., Pasadena, CA 91101

Hawaii, Rev. Norman Jackson, 15 Craigside Pl., Honolulu, HI 96817

Montana-Northern Wyoming, Rev. John M. Schaeffer, 2016 Alderson Ave., Billings, MT 59102

Central Pacific, Rev. Donald J. Sevetson, 0245 SW Bancroft St., Ste. E, Portland, OR 97201

Rocky Mountain, Rev. William A. Dalke, 7000 Broadway, Ste. 420, ABS Bldg., Denver, CO 80221

Southwest, Rev. Carole G. Keim, 4423 N. 24th St., Ste. 600, Phoenix, AZ 85016

Washington-North Idaho, Rev. Lynne S. Fitch, 720 14th Ave. E., Seattle, WA 98102

Washington-North Idaho, Rev. David J. Brown, 12 N. Chelan, Wenatchee, WA 98801

West Central Region

Iowa, Rev. Donald A. Gall, 600 42nd St., Des Moines, IA 50312

Kansas-Oklahoma, Rev. John H. Krueger, 1248 Fabrique, Wichita, KS 67218

Minnesota, Rev. Jeffrey N. Stinehelfer, 122 W. Franklin Ave., Rm. 323, Minneapolis, MN 55404

Missouri, Rev. A. Gayle Engel, 461 E. Lockwood Ave., St. Louis, MO 63119

Nebraska, Rev. Clarence M. Higgins, Jr., 825 M St., Lincoln, NE 68508

North Dakota, Rev. Jack J. Seville, Jr., 227 W. Broadway, Bismarck, ND 58501

South Dakota, Rev. Ed Mehlhaff, 3500 S. Phillips Ave., #121, Sioux Falls, SD 57105-6864

Great Lakes Region

Illinois, Rev. W. Sterling Cary, 1840 Westchester Blvd., Westchester, IL 60154

Illinois South, Rev. Martha Ann Baumer, Box 325, 1312 Broadway, Highland, IL 62249

Indiana-Kentucky, Rev. Carla J. Bailey, 1100 W. 42nd St., Indianapolis, IN 46208

Michigan, Rev. Herman Haller, P.O. Box 1006, East Lansing, MI 48826

Ohio, Rev. Ralph C. Quellhorst, 4041 N. High St., Ste. 301, Columbus, OH 43214

Wisconsin, Rev. Frederick R. Trost, 4459 Gray Rd., Box 495, De Forest, WI 53532-0495

Southern Region

Florida, Rev. Charles L. Burns, Jr., 222 E. Welbourne Ave., Winter Park, FL 32789

South Central, Rev. James Tomasek, Jr., 6633 E. Hwy. 290, #200, Austin, TX 78723-1157

Southeast, Rev. Roger Knight, 756 W. Peachtree St., NW, Atlanta, GA 30308

Southern, Rev. Rollin O. Russell, 217 N. Main St., Box 658, Graham, NC 27253

Middle Atlantic Region

Central Atlantic, Rev. John R. Deckenback, 916 S. Rolling Rd., Baltimore, MD 21228

New York, Rev. William Briggs, The Church Center, Rm. 260, 3049 E. Genesee St., Syracuse, NY 13224

Penn Central, Rev. Lyle J. Weible, The United Church Center, Rm. 126, 900 S. Arlington Ave., Harrisburg, PA 17109

Penn Northeast, Rev. Donald E. Overlock, 431 Delaware Ave., P.O. Box 177, Palmerton, PA 18071

Penn Southeast, Rev. Franklin R. Mittman, Jr., 505 Second Ave., P.O. Box 400, Collegeville, PA 19426

Penn West, Rev. Paul L. Westcoat, Jr., 320 South Maple Ave., Greensburg, PA 15601

Puerto Rico, Rev. Jaime Rivera-Solero, Box 5427, Hato Rey, PR 00919

New England Region

Connecticut, Rev. David Y. Hirano, 125 Sherman St., Hartford, CT 06105

Maine, Rev. Otto E. Sommer, 68 Main St., P.O. Box 966, Yarmouth, ME 04096

Massachusetts, Rev. Bennie E. Whiten, Jr., P.O. Box 2246, Salem & Badger Rds., Framingham, MA 01701

New Hampshire: Rev. Carole C. Carlson; Rev. Benjamin C. L. Crosby; Rev. Philip Joseph Mayher, Jr.; Rev. Robert D. Witham, 314 S. Main, P.O. Box 465, Concord, NH 03302

Rhode Island, Rev. H. Dahler Hayes, 56 Walcott St., Pawtucket, RI 02860
Vermont, Rev. D. Curtis Minter, 285 Maple St., Burlington, VT 05401
Nongeographic
Calvin Synod, Rev. Francis Vitez, 493 Amboy Ave., Perth Amboy, NJ 08861

PERIODICALS
United Church News; Courage in the Struggle for Justic and Peace

United Holy Church of America, Inc.

The United Holy Church of America, Inc. is an outgrowth of the great revival that began with the outpouring of the Holy Ghost on the Day of Pentecost. The church is built upon the foundation of the Apostles and Prophets, Jesus Christ being the cornerstone.

During a revival of repentence, regeneration and holiness of heart and life that swept through the South and West, the United Holy Church was born. The founding fathers had no desire to establish a denomination but were pushed out of organized churches because of this experience of holiness and testimony of the Spirit-filled life.

On the first Sunday in May 1886, in Method, N.C., what is today known as the United Holy Church of America, Inc. was born. The church was incorporated on Sept. 25, 1918.

Baptism by immersion, the Lord's Supper and feet washing are observed. The premillennial teaching of the Second Coming of Christ, Divine healing, justification by faith, sanctification as a second work of grace and Spirit baptism are accepted.

HEADQUARTERS
5104 Dunstan Rd., Greensboro, NC 27405 Tel. (919)621-0669
Mailing Address, Bishop Thomas E. Talley, P.O. Box 1035, Portsmouth, VA 23705
Media Contact, Gen. Rec. Sec., Rev. A. Thomas Godfrey, P.O. Box 7940, Chicago, IL 60680 Tel. (312)849-2525

PERIODICAL
The Holiness Union

The United Methodist Church

The United Methodist Church was formed April 23, 1968, in Dallas by the union of The Methodist Church and The Evangelical United Brethren Church. The two churches shared a common historical and spiritual heritage. The Methodist Church resulted in 1939 from the unification of three branches of Methodism — the Methodist Episcopal Church, the Methodist Episcopal Church, South, and the Methodist Protestant Church.

The Methodist movement began in 18th-century England under the preaching of John Wesley, but the Christmas Conference of 1784 in Baltimore is regarded as the date on which the organized Methodist Church was founded as an ecclesiastical organization. It was there that Francis Asbury was elected the first bishop in this country.

The Evangelical United Brethren Church was formed in 1946 with the merger of the Evangelical Church and the Church of the United Brethren in Christ, both of which had their beginnings in Pennsylvania in the evangelistic movement of the 18th and early 19th centuries. Philip William Otterbein and Jacob Albright were early leaders of this movement among the German-speaking settlers of the Middle Colonies.

HEADQUARTERS
Media Contact, Dir., United Methodist News Service, Thomas S. McAnally, P.O. Box 320, Nashville, TN 37202 Tel. (615)742-5470 Fax (615)742-5469

OFFICERS
Gen. Conference, Sec., Carolyn M. Marshall, 204 N. Newlin St., Veedersburg, IN 47987
Council of Bishops: Pres., Bishop J. Woodrow Hearn, 5215 S. Main St., Houston, TX 77002 Tel. (713)528-6881; Sec., Bishop Melvin G. Talbert, P.O. Box 467, San Francisco, CA 94101 Tel. (415)474-3101

BISHOPS AND CONFERENCE COUNCIL DIRECTORS
North Central Jurisdiction
Central Illinois: Bishop David J. Lawson, Tel. (217)544-4604; Larry L. Lawler, P.O. Box 515, Bloomington, IL 61702 Tel. (309)828-5092 Fax (309)829-8369
Detroit: Bishop Donald A. Ott, Tel. (313)559-7000; ——, 21700 Northwestern Hwy., Southfield, MI 48075 Tel. (313)559-7000 Fax (313)569-4380
East Ohio: Bishop Edwin C. Boulton, Tel. (216)499-3972; Judith A. Olin, 8800 Cleveland Ave. NW, North Canton, OH 44720 Tel. (216)499-3972 Fax (216)499-3279
Iowa: Bishop Charles W. Jordan, Tel. (515)283-1991; Don Mendenhall, 1019 Chestnut St., Des Moines, IA 50309 Tel. (515)283-1991 Fax (515)288-1906
Minnesota: Bishop Sharon Brown Christopher, Tel. (612)870-4007; Patricia Hinker, 122 W. Franklin Ave., Room 400, Minneapolis, MN 55404 Tel. (612)870-0058 Fax (612)870-1260
North Dakota: Bishop William B. Lewis, Tel. (701)232-2241; Ray Wagner, 2410 12th St. N., Fargo, ND 58102 Tel. (701)232-2241 Fax (701)232-2615
North Indiana: Bishop Woodie W. White, 1100 W. 42nd St., Indianapolis, IN 46208 Tel. (317)924-1321; Louis E. Haskell, P.O. Box 869, Marion, IN 46952 Tel. (317)664-5138 Fax (317)664-2307
Northern Illinois: Bishop R. Sheldon Duecker, Tel. (312)380-5060; Bonnie Ogie-Kristianson, 8765 W. Higgins Rd., Ste. 650, Chicago, IL 60631 Tel. (312)380-5060 Fax (312)380-5067
South Dakota: Bishop William B. Lewis, Tel. (701)232-2241; Richard Fisher, P.O. Box 460, Mitchell, SD 57301 Tel. (605)996-6552 Fax (605)996-1766
South Indiana: Bishop Woodie W. White, Tel. (317)924-1321; Robert Coleman, Box 5008, Bloomington, IN 47407 Tel. (812)336-0186 Fax (812)336-0216
Southern Illinois: Bishop David J. Lawson, Tel. (217)544-4604; William Frazier, 1919 Broadway, Mt. Vernon, IL 62864 Tel. (618)242-4070 Fax (618)242-9227
West Michigan: Bishop Donald A. Ott, Tel. (313)559-7000; David B. Nelson, P.O. Box 6287, Grand Rapids, MI 49516 Tel. (616)459-4503 Fax (616)459-0191

West Ohio: Bishop Judith Craig, Tel. (614)228-6784; Vance Summers, 471 E. Broad St., Ste. 1106, Columbus, OH 43215 Tel. (614)228-6784 Fax (614)222-0612

Wisconsin: Bishop Sharon Z. Rader, Tel. (608)837-8526; Billy F. Bross, P.O. Box 220, Sun Prairie, WI 53590 Tel. (608)837-7328 Fax (608)837-8547

Northeastern Jurisdiction

Baltimore-Washington: Bishop Joseph H. Yeakel, Tel. (301)587-9226; Marcus Matthews, 5124 Greenwich Ave., Baltimore, MD 21229 Tel. (301)233-7300

Central Pennsylvania: Bishop Felton E. May, Tel. (717)652-6705; Bruce Fisher, 900 S. Arlington Ave., #112, Harrisburg, PA 17109 Tel. (717)652-0460

Eastern Pennsylvania: Bishop Susan M. Morrison, Tel. (215)666-9090; Robert Daughtery, P.O. Box 820, P.O. Box 820, Valley Forge, PA 19482 Tel. (215)666-9090

New England: Bishop F. Herbert Skeete, Tel. (617)266-3900; ——, 566 Commonwealth Ave., Boston, MA 02115 Tel. (617)266-3900

New York: Bishop Forrest C. Stith, Tel. (914)684-6922; Wilson Boots, 252 Bryant Ave., White Plains, NY 10605 Tel. (914)997-1570

North Central New York: Bishop Hae-Jong Kim, Tel. (716)271-3400; Garrie F. Stevens, P.O. Box 1515, Cicero, NY 13039 Tel. (315)699-5506

Northern New Jersey: Bishop Neil L. Irons, Tel. (609)737-3940; Barrie T. Smith, P.O. Box 546, Madison, NJ 07940 Tel. (201)377-3800

Peninsula-Delaware: Bishop Susan M. Morrison, Tel. (212)666-9090; Harvey Manchester, 139 N. State St., Dover, DE 19901 Tel. (302)674-2626

Southern New Jersey: Bishop Neil F. Irons, Tel. (609)737-3940; George T. Wang, 1995 E. Marlton Pike, Cherry Hill, NJ 08003 Tel. (609)424-1701

Troy: Bishop William B. Grove, Tel. (518)426-0386; James M. Perry, P.O. Box 560, Saratoga Springs, NY 12866 Tel. (518)584-8214

West Virginia: Bishop S. Clifton Ives, Tel. ((304)344-8330; Thomas E. Dunlap, Sr., P.O. Box 2313, Charleston, WV 25328 Tel. (304)344-8331

Western New York: Bishop Hae-Jong Kim, Tel. (716)271-3400; J. Fay Cleveland, 8499 Main St., Buffalo, NY 14221 Tel. (716)633-8558

Western Pennsylvania: Bishop George W. Bashore, Tel. (412)776-2300; John Ross Thompson, 1204 Freedom Rd., Mars, PA 16046 Tel. (412)776-2300

Wyoming: Bishop William B. Grove, Tel. (518)426-0386; Charles F. Gommer, Jr., 1700 Monroe St., Endicott, NY 13760 Tel. (607)757-0608

South Central Jurisdiction

Exec. Dir.: L. Ray Branton, 5646 Milton St., #240, Dallas, TX 75228 Tel. (214)692-9081

Central Texas: Bishop Joe A. Wilson, Tel. (817)877-5222; Michael Patison, 464 Bailey, Ft. Worth, TX 76107 Tel. (817)877-5222

Kansas East: Bishop A. F. Mutti, Tel. (913)272-0587; H. Sharon Howell, P.O. Box 4187, Topeka, KS 66604 Tel. (913)272-9111

Kansas West: Bishop A. F. Mutti, Tel. (913)272-0587; Wayne D. Findley, Sr., 9440 E. Boston, #150, Wichita, KS 67207 Tel. (316)684-0266

Little Rock: Bishop Richard B. Wilke, Tel. (501)324-8019; Jay Lofton, 715 Center St., Ste. 202, Little Rock, AR 72201 Tel. (501)374-5027

Louisiana: Bishop William B. Oden, Tel. (504)346-1646; Donald C. Cottrill, 527 North Blvd., Baton Rouge, LA 70802 Tel. (504)346-1646

Missouri East: Bishop Ann B. Sherer, Tel. (314)891-8001; Duane Van Giesen, 870 Woods Mill Rd., #400, Ballwin, MO 63011 Tel. (314)891-1207

Missouri West: Bishop Ann B. Sherer, Jr., Tel. (314)891-8001; Keith T. Berry, 1512 Van Brunt Blvd., Kansas City, MO 64127 Tel. (816)241-7650

Nebraska: Bishop Joel L. Martinez, Tel. (402)464-5994; Richard D. Turner, P.O. Box 4553, Lincoln, NE 68504 Tel. (402)464-5994

New Mexico: Bishop Alfred L. Norris, Tel. (505)255-8786; Milton Chester, 8100 Mountain Rd. NE, Albuquerque, NM 87110 Tel. (505)255-8786

North Arkansas: Bishop Richard B. Wilke, Tel. (501)324-8019; Jim Beal, 715 Center St., Little Rock, AR 72201 Tel. (501)753-8946

North Texas: Bishop Bruce Blake, Tel. (214)522-6741; Gary E. Mueller, P.O. Box 516069, Dallas, TX 75251 Tel. (214)490-3438

Northwest Texas: Bishop Alfred L. Norris, Tel. (505)255-8786; Louise Schock, 1415 Ave. M, Lubbock, TX 79401 Tel. (806)762-0201

Oklahoma: Bishop Dan E. Solomon, Tel. (405)525-2252; David Severe, 2420 N. Blackwelder, Oklahoma City, OK 73106 Tel. (405)525-2252

Oklahoma Indian Missionary: Bishop Dan E. Solomon, Tel. (405)525-2252; Becky Thompson, 3020 S. Harvey, Oklahoma City, OK 73109 Tel. (405)632-2006

Rio Grande: Bishop Raymond Owen, Tel. (512)432-0401; Arturo Mariscal, Jr., P.O. Box 28098, San Antonio, TX 78284 Tel. (512)432-2534

Southwest Texas: Bishop Raymond Owen, Tel. (210)431-6400; Harry G. Kahl, P.O. Box 28098, San Antonio, TX 78284 Tel. (512)432-4680

Texas: Bishop J. Woodrow Hearn, Tel. (713)528-6881; Asbury Lenox, 5215 S. Main St., Houston, TX 77002 Tel. (713)521-9383

Southeastern Jurisdiction

Exec. Dir.: Gordon C. Goodgame, P.O. Box 67, Lake Junaluska, NC 28745 Tel. (704)452-2881

Alabama-West Florida: Bishop William W. Morris, Tel. (205)277-1787; William Calhoun, P.O. Box 700, Andalusia, AL 36420 Tel. (205)222-3127

Florida: Bishop H. Hasbrock Hughes, Jr., Tel. (813)688-4427; Robert Bledsoe, P.O. Box 3767, Lakeland, FL 33802 Tel. (813)688-5563

Holston: Bishop Clay F. Lee, Tel. (615)525-1809; Peyton L. Rowlett, Jr., P.O. Box 1178, Johnson City, TN 37605 Tel. (615)928-2156

Kentucky: Bishop Robert C. Morgan, Tel. (502)893-6715; Larry B. Gardner, P.O. Box 55107, Lexington, KY 40555 Tel. (606)254-7388

Louisville: Bishop Robert C. Morgan, Tel. (502)893-6715; Rhoda Peters, 1115 S. Fourth St., Louisville, KY 40203 Tel. (502)584-3838

Memphis: Bishop Kenneth L. Carder, Tel. (615)831-0710; James H. Holmes, St., 575 Lambuth Blvd., Jackson, TN 38301 Tel. (901)427-8589

Mississippi: Bishop M. L. Meadows, Jr., Tel. (601)948-4561; Jack Loflin, P.O. Box 1147, Jackson, MS 39215 Tel. (601)354-0515

North Alabama: Bishop Robert E. Fannin, Tel. (205)322-8665; C. Phillip Huckaby, 898 Arkadelphia Rd., Birmingham, AL 35204 Tel. (205)226-7950

North Carolina: Bishop C. P. Minnick, Jr., Tel. (919)832-9560; Robert L. Baldridge, P.O. Box 10955, Raleigh, NC 27605 Tel. (919)832-9560

North Georgia: Bishop J. Lloyd Knox, Tel. (404)659-0002; Rudolph R. Baker, Jr., 159 Ralph McGill Blvd. NE, Atlanta, GA 30365 Tel. (404)659-0002

Red Bird Missionary: Bishop Robert C. Morgan, Tel. (502)893-6715; Ruth Wiertzema, Queendale Ctr., Box 3, Beverly, KY 40913 Tel. (606)598-5915

South Carolina: Bishop Joseph B. Bethea, Tel. (803)786-9486; Lemuel C. Carter, 4908 Colonial Dr., Ste. 101, Columbia, SC 29203 Tel. (803)754-0297

South Georgia: Bishop Richard C. Looney, Tel. (912)738-0048; William E. McTier, Jr., P.O. Box 408, St. Simons Island, GA 31522 Tel. (912)638-8626

Tennessee: Bishop Kenneth L. Carder, Tel. (615)831-0710; Charles F. Armistead, P.O. Box 120607, Nashville, TN 37212 Tel. (615)329-1177

Virginia: Bishop Thomas B. Stockton, Tel. (804)359-9451; Lee B. Sheaffer, P.O. 11367, Richmond, VA 23230 Tel. (804)359-9451

Western North Carolina: Bishop L. Bevel Jones, Tel. (704)535-2260; Harold K. Bales, P.O. Box 18005, PO Box 18005, Charlotte, NC 28218 Tel. (704)535-2260

Western Jurisdiction

Alaska Missionary: Bishop William W. Dew, Jr., Tel. (503)226-7931; James Campbell, Box 182, Willow, AK 99508 Tel. (907)333-5050

California-Nevada: Bishop Melvin G. Talbert, Tel. (415)474-3101; James H. Corson, P.O. Box 420467, San Francisco, CA 94142-0467 Tel. (415)474-3101

California-Pacific: Bishop Roy I. Sano, Tel. (818)568-7300; J. Delton Pickering, P.O. Box 6006, Pasadena, CA 91102 Tel. (818)568-7300

Desert Southwest: Bishop Elias Galvin, Tel. (602)956-4472; Lawrence A. Hinshaw, 2933 E. Indian School Rd., #402, Phoenix, AZ 85016 Tel. (602)496-9446

Oregon-Idaho: Bishop William A. Dew, Jr., Tel. (503)226-7931; Thomas Rannells, 1505 SW 18th Ave., Portland, OR 97201 Tel. (503)226-7931

Pacific Northwest: Bishop Calvin D. McConnell, Tel. (206)728-7674; W. F. Summerour, 2112 Third Ave., Ste. 300, Seattle, WA 98121 Tel. (206)728-7462

Rocky Mountain: Bishop Mary Ann Swenson, Tel. (303)733-5035; Janet Forbes, 2200 S. University Blvd., Denver, CO 80210 Tel. (303)733-3736

Yellowstone: Bishop Mary Ann Swenson, Tel. (303)733-5035; Gary Keene, 335 Broadwater Ave., Billings, MT 59101 Tel. (406)256-1385

AGENCIES

Judicial Council: Pres., Tom Matheny; Sec., Wayne Coffin, 2420 N. Blackwelder, Oklahoma City, OK 73106 Tel. (405)721-5528

Council on Finance & Administration: Pres., Bishop Forrest C. Stith; Gen. Sec., Clifford Droke, 1200 Davis St., Evanston, IL 60201 Tel. (708)869-3345

Council on Ministries: Pres., Bishop William W. Dew, Jr.; Gen. Sec., C. David Lundquist, 601 W. Riverview Ave., Dayton, OH 45406 Tel. (513)227-9400

Board of Church & Society: Pres., Bishop Joseph H. Yeakel; Gen. Sec., Thom White Wolf Fasset, 100 Maryland Ave. NE, Washington, DC 20002 Tel. (202)488-5600

Board of Discipleship: Pres., Bishop David J. Lawson; Gen. Sec., Ezra Earl Jones, P.O. Box 840, Nashville, TN 37202 Tel. (615)340-7200

Board of Global Ministries: Pres., Bishop F. Herbert Skeete; Gen. Sec., Randolph Nugent, 475 Riverside Dr., New York, NY 10115 Tel. (212)870-3600

Board of Higher Education & Ministry: Pres., Bishop Calvin D. McConnell; Gen. Sec., Roger Ireson, P.O. Box 871, Nashville, TN 37202 Tel. (615)340-7000 Fax (615)340-7048

Board of Pensions: Pres., Bishop Clay F. Lee; Gen. Sec., ——, 1200 Davis St., Evanston, IL 60201 Tel. (708)869-4550

Board of Publications: Chpsn., William Deel; United Methodist Publishing House, Pres. & Publisher, Robert K. Feaster, P.O. Box 801, Nashville, TN 37202 Tel. (615)749-6000

Commission on Archives & History: Pres., Bishop Emilio de Carvalho; Gen. Sec., Charles Yrigoyen, P.O. Box 127, Madison, NJ 07940 Tel. (201)822-2787

Comm. Christian Unity/Interrel. Concerns: Pres., Bishop William B. Grove; Gen. Sec., Bruce Robbins, 475 Riverside Dr., Rm. 1300, New York, NY 10115 Tel. (212)749-3553

Comm. on Communication/UM Communications: Pres., Bishop L. Bevel Jones, III; Gen. Sec., ——, P.O. Box 320, 810 12th Ave. S., Nashville, TN 37202 Tel. (615)742-5400

Commission on Religion & Race: Pres., Bishop Joseph B. Bethea; Gen. Sec., Barbara R. Thompson, 100 Maryland Ave. NE, Washington, DC 20002 Tel. (202)547-4270

Commission on the Status & Role of Women: Pres., Bishop Ann B. Sherer; Gen. Secretariat, Stephanie Anna Hixon; Cecelia M. Long, 1200 Davis St., Evanston, IL 60201 Tel. (312)869-7330

PERIODICALS

Mature Years; El Interprete; New World Outlook; Newscope; Interpreter; Methodist History; Christian Social Action; Pockets; Response; The United Methodist Reporter; United Methodist Review; United Methodist Record; Quarterly Review; alive now!; youth!; Circuit Rider; El Aposento Alto; weavings; The Upper Room

United Pentecostal Church International

The United Pentecostal Church International came into being through the merger of two oneness Pentecostal organizations — the Pentecostal Church, Inc., and the Pentecostal Assemblies of Jesus Christ. The first of these was known as the Pentecostal Ministerial Alliance from its inception in 1925 until 1932. The second was formed in 1931 by a merger of the Apostolic Church of Jesus Christ with the Pentecostal Assemblies of the World.

The church contends that the Bible teaches that there is one God who manifested himself as the Father in creation, in the Son in redemption and as the Holy Spirit in regeneration; that Jesus is the name of this absolute deity and that water baptism should be administered in his name, not in the titles Father, Son and Holy Ghost (Acts 2:38, 8:16, and 19:6).

The Fundamental Doctrine of the United Pentecostal Church International, as stated in its *Articles of Faith,* is "the Bible standard of full salvation, which is repentance, baptism in water by immersion in the name of the Lord Jesus Christ for the remission of sins, and the baptism of the Holy Ghost with the initial sign of speaking with other tongues as the Spirit gives utterance."

Further doctrinal teachings concern of a life of holiness and separation, the operation of the gifts of the Spirit within the church, the second coming of the Lord and the church's obligation to take the gospel to the whole world.

HEADQUARTERS

8855 Dunn Rd., Hazelwood, MO 63042 Tel. (314)837-7300 Fax (314)837-4503
Media Contact, Gen. Sec.-Treas., Rev. C. M. Becton

OFFICERS

Gen. Supt., Rev. Nathaniel A. Urshan
Asst. Gen. Supts.: Rev. James Kilgore, Box 15175, Houston, TX 77020; Jesse Williams, P.O. Box 64277, Fayetteville, NC 28306
Gen. Sec.-Treas., Rev. C. M. Becton
Dir. of Foreign Missions, Rev. Harry Scism
Gen. Dir. of Home Missions, Rev. Jack Cunningham
Editor-in-Chief, Rev. J. L. Hall
Gen. Sunday School Dir., Rev. E. J. McClintock

OTHER ORGANIZATIONS

Pentecostal Publishing House, Mgr., Rev. Marvin Curry
Youth Division (Pentecostal Conquerors), Pres., Darrell Johns, Hazelwood, MO 63042
Ladies Auxiliary, Pres., Gwyn Oakes, P.O. Box 247, Bald Knob, AR 72010
Harvestime Radio Broadcast, Dir., Rev. J. Hugh Rose, 698 Kerr Ave., Cadiz, OH 43907
Stewardship Dept., Contact Church Division, Hazelwood, MO 63042
Education Division, Supt., Rev. Arless Glass, 4502 Aztec, Pasadena, TX 77504
Public Relations Division, Contact Church Division, Hazelwood, MO 63042
Historical Society & Archives

PERIODICALS

The Pentecostal Herald; The Global Witness; The Outreach; Homelife; Conqueror; Reflections; Forward

United Zion Church

A branch of the Brethren in Christ which settled in Lancaster County, Pa., the United Zion Church was organized under the leadership of Matthias Brinser in 1855.

HEADQUARTERS

United Zion Home, 722 Furnace Hills Pk, Lititz, PA 17543
Media Contact, Bishop, Carl Eberly, 270 Clay School Rd., Ephrata, PA 17522 Tel. (717)733-3932

OFFICERS

Gen. Conf. Mod., Bishop Carl Eberly, 270 Clay School Rd., Ephrata, PA 17522 Tel. (717)733-3932

Asst. Mod., Rev. Donald Martzall, 287 Radio Rd., Elizabethtown, PA 17022 Tel. (717)361-8982
Gen. Conf. Sec., Rev. Melvin Horst, 2021 Main St., Rothsville, PA 17573 Tel. (717)626-0677
Gen. Conf. Treas., Kenneth Kleinfelter, 919 Sycamore Lane, Lebanon, PA 17042

PERIODICAL

Zion's Herald

Unity of the Brethren

Czech and Moravian immigrants in Texas (beginning about 1855) established congregations which grew into an Evangelical Union in 1903, and with the accession of other Brethren in Texas, into the Evangelical Unity of the Czech-Moravian Brethren in North America. In 1959, it shortened the name to the original name used in 1457, the Unity of the Brethren (Unitas Fratrum, or Jednota Bratrska).

HEADQUARTERS

3829 Sandstone, San Angelo, TX 76904
Media Contact, Sec. of Exec. Committee, Adelle Morehead, Rt. 2 Box 32A, Caldwell, TX 77836 Tel. (409)272-2300

OFFICERS

Pres., Rev. Tommy Tallas
1st Vice Pres., Rev. James D. Heil, 209 Cherrywood Cir., Taylor, TX 76574 Tel. (512)352-6890
Sec., Adelle Morehead, Rt. 2 Box 32A, Caldwell, TX 77836 Tel. (409)272-2300
Fin. Sec., Roy Vajdak, 920 Malone, Houston, TX 77007
Treas., Ron Sulak, 1217 Christine, Troy, TX 76579

PERIODICAL

Brethren Journal

Universal Fellowship of Metropolitan Community Churches

The Universal Fellowship of Metropolitan Community Churches was founded Oct. 6, 1968 by the Rev. Troy D. Perry in Los Angeles, with a particular but not exclusive outreach to the gay community. Since that time, the Fellowship has grown to include congregations throughout the world.

The group is trinitarian and accepts the Bible as the divinely inspired Word of God. The Fellowship has two sacraments, baptism and holy communion, as well as a number of traditionally recognized rites such as ordination.

This Fellowship acknowledges "the Holy Scriptures interpreted by the Holy Spirit in conscience and faith, as its guide in faith, discipline, and government." The government of this Fellowship is vested in its General Council (consisting of Elders and District Coordinators), clergy and church delegates, who exert the right of control in all of its affairs, subject to the provisions of its Articles of Incorporation and By-Laws.

HEADQUARTERS

5300 Santa Monica Blvd. #304, Los Angeles, CA 90029 Tel. (213)464-5100 Fax (213)464-2123
Media Contact, PR Rep., Rev. Kittridge Cherry

OFFICERS

Mod., Rev. Elder Troy D. Perry
Vice-Mod., Rev. Elder Nancy L. Wilson
Treas., Rev. Elder Donald Eastman

Clk., Elder Larry Rodriguez
Rev. Elder Darlene Garner, 7245 Lee Hwy., Falls Church, VA 22046
Rev. Elder Willem A. Hein, P.O. Box 68-437, Newton, Auckland, New Zealand
Rev. Elder Hong Kia Tan, 72 Fleet Rd., Hampstead, London, NW3 2QT England
Dir. of Admn., Mr. Ravi Verma

DISTRICT COORDINATORS

Australian District, Rev. Greg Smith, MCC Sydney, P.O. Box 1237, Darlinghurst NSW 2012, Australia
Eastern Canadian District, Ms. Lydia Segal, 409-64 Wellesley St., E., Toronto, ON M4Y 1G6
European North Sea District, Rev. Mia Anderson, P.O. Box 1023, Kobenhavn, 1007, Denmark
Great Lakes District, Judy Dale, 1300 Ambridge Dr., Louisville, KY 40207 Tel. (502)897-3821
Gulf Lower Atlantic District, Mr. Jay Neely, P.O. Box 8356, Atlanta, GA 30306
Mid-Central District, Rev. L. Robert Arthur, P.O. Box 8291, Omaha, NE 68103
Mid-Atlantic District, Rev. Arlene Ackerman, P.O. Box 552, Mountville, PA 17554
Northeast District, Rev. Jeff Pulling, 2006 Mill Pond Dr., S. Windsor, CT 06074
Northwest District, Rev. Scott Phipps, 604 I St., Petaluma, CA 94952
South Central District, Clarke Friesen, P.O. Box 7441, Houston, TX 44248-7441
Southeast District, Rev. Judy Davenport, P.O. Box 12768, St. Petersburg, FL 33733
Southwest District, Rev. Don Pederson, 11012 Ventura Blvd., #1254, Studio City, CA 91604
Western Canadian District, Rev. Bev Baptiste, 3531-3rd Ave., Edmonton, AB T6L 4N6

OTHER COMMISSIONS & COMMITTEES

Bd. of World Church Extension, Field Dir., Rev. Louis Kavar
Commission on Faith, Fellowship & Order, Chpsn., Rev. Steven Torrence, 1215 Petronia St., Key West, FL 33040
Dept. of People of Colors, Exec. Dir., Bernard Barbour, 1744 Michigan, Houston, TX 77006
Commission on the Laity, Chpsn., JoNee Shelton, 7624 Kingsmill Terr., Ft. Worth, TX 76112
Clergy Credentials & Concerns, Admn. Asst., Gene Van Horn
Bd. of Pensions, Admn., Ms. Lois Luneburg, P.O. Box 107, Arnold, CA 95223
Ecumenical Witness & Ministry: Dir., Rev. Kittridge Cherry
UFMCC AIDS Ministry: Field Dir., Rev. A. Stephen Pieters
Women's Secretariat, Chpsn., Rev. Coni Staff, 354 Irwin St., San Rafael, CA 94901

PERIODICALS
Keeping in Touch; ALERT; Global Outreach

Volunteers of America

Volunteers of America, founded in 1896 by Ballington and Maud Booth, provides spiritual and material aid for those in need in more than 300 communities across the United States. As one of the nation's largest and most diversified human-service agencies, VOA offers more than 400 programs for the elderly, families, youth, alcoholics, drug abusers, offenders and the disabled.

HEADQUARTERS
3939 N. Causeway Blvd., Metairie, LA 70002 Tel. (504)837-2652 Fax (504)837-4200
Media Contact, Dir. of Publ. Relations, Arthur Smith

OFFICERS
Chpsn., Walter Faster
Pres., J. Clint Cheveallier
Vice-Pres.: Alex Brodrick; David Cheveallier; Thomas Clark; Charles Gould; Dianna Kunz; Margaret Ratcliff; John Hood

PERIODICALS
Spirit; Gazette

The Wesleyan Church

The Wesleyan Church was formed on June 26, 1968, through the union of the Wesleyan Methodist Church of America (1843) and the Pilgrim Holiness Church (1897). The headquarters was established at Marion, Ind., and relocated to Indianapolis in 1987.

The Wesleyan movement centers around the beliefs, based on Scripture, that the atonement in Christ provides for the regeneration of sinners and the entire sanctification of believers. John Wesley led a revival of these beliefs in the 18th century.

When a group of New England Methodist ministers led by Orange Scott began to crusade for the abolition of slavery, the bishops and others sought to silence them. This led to a series of withdrawals from the Methodist Episcopal Church. In 1843, the Wesleyan Methodist Connection of America was organized and led by Scott, Jotham Horton, LaRoy Sunderland, Luther Lee and Lucius C. Matlack.

During the holiness revival in the last half of the 19th century, holiness replaced social reform as the major tenet of the Connection. In 1947 the name was changed from Connection to Church and a central supervisory authority was set up.

The Pilgrim Holiness Church was one of many independent holiness churches which came into existence as a result of the holiness revival. Led by Martin Wells Knapp and Seth C. Rees, the International Holiness Union and Prayer League was inaugurated in 1897 in Cincinnati. Its purpose was to promote worldwide holiness evangelism and the Union had a strong missionary emphasis from the beginning. It developed into a church by 1913.

The Wesleyan Church is now spread across most of the United States and Canada and 37 other countries. The Wesleyan World Fellowship was organized in 1972 to unite Wesleyan mission bodies developing into mature churches. The Wesleyan Church is a member of the Christian Holiness Association, the National Association of Evangelicals and the World Methodist Council.

HEADQUARTERS
P.O. Box 50434, Indianapolis, IN 46250 Tel. (317)842-0444
Media Contact, Gen. Sec., Dr. Ronald R. Brannon, Tel. (317)576-8154 Fax (317)577-4397

OFFICERS
Gen. Supts.: Dr. Earle L. Wilson; Dr. Lee M. Haines; Dr. H. C. Wilson
Gen. Sec., Dr. Ronald R. Brannon
Gen. Treas., Mr. Daniel D. Busby
Gen. Director of Communications, Dr. Norman G. Wilson
Gen. Publisher, Rev. Nathan Birky
Evangelism & Church Growth, Gen. Dir., Dr. B. Marlin Mull

World Missions, Gen. Dir., Dr. Donald L. Bray
Local Church Educ., Gen. Dir., Dr. Keith Drury
Youth, Gen. Dir., Dr. Thomas E. Armiger
Education & the Ministry, Gen. Dir., Dr. Kenneth R. Heer
Estate Planning, Gen. Dir., Rev. Howard B. Castle
Wesleyan Pension Fund, Gen. Dir., Mr. Bobby L. Temple
Wesleyan Investment Foundation, Gen. Dir., Dr. John A. Dunn

PERIODICALS

Wesleyan Woman; The Wesleyan Advocate; Wesleyan World

Wesleyan Holiness Association of Churches

This body was founded Aug. 4, 1959 near Muncie, Ind. by a group of ministers and laymen who were drawn together for the purpose of spreading and conserving sweet, radical, scriptural holiness. These men came from various church bodies. This group is Wesleyan in doctrine and standards.

HEADQUARTERS

108 Carter Ave., Dayton, OH 45405 Tel. (513)278-3770
Media Contact, Gen. Sec.-Treas., Rev. Robert W. Wilson, P.O. Box 381, Middleburg, PA 17842

OFFICERS

Gen. Supt., Rev. J. Stevan Manley
Asst. Gen. Supt., Rev. Jack W. Dulin, Rt. 2, Box 309, Milton, KY 40045 Tel. (502)268-5826
Gen. Sec.-Treas., Rev. Robert W. Wilson, P.O. Box 381, Middleburg, PA 17842 Tel. (717)966-4147
Gen. Youth Pres., Rev. John Brewer, 504 W. Tyrell St., St. Louis, MI 48880 Tel. (517)681-2591

PERIODICAL

Eleventh Hour Messenger

Wisconsin Evangelical Lutheran Synod

Organized in 1850 at Milwaukee, Wisc. by three pastors sent to America by a German mission society, the Wisconsin Evangelical Lutheran Synod still reflects its origins, although it now has congregations in 50 states and three Canadian provinces.

The Wisconsin Synod federated with the Michigan and Minnesota Synods in 1892 in order to more effectively carry on education and mission enterprises. A merger of these three Synods followed in 1917 to give the Wisconsin Evangelical Lutheran Synod its present form.

Although at its organization in 1850 the Synod turned away from conservative Lutheran theology, today it is ranked as one of the most conservative Lutheran bodies in the United States. The Synod confesses that the Bible is the verbally inspired, infallible Word of God and subscribes without reservation to the confessional writings of the Lutheran Church. Its interchurch relations are determined by a firm commitment to the principle that unity of doctrine and practice are the prerequisites of pulpit and altar fellowship and ecclesiastical cooperation. It does not hold membership in ecumenical organizations.

HEADQUARTERS

2929 N. Mayfair Rd., Milwaukee, WI 53222 Tel. (414)256-3888 Fax (414)256-3899

OFFICERS

Pres., Rev. Karl R. Gurgel
1st Vice-Pres., Rev. Richard E. Lauersdorf, 105 Aztalan Ct., Jefferson, WI 53549
2nd Vice-Pres., Rev. Robert J. Zink, S68 W14329 Gaulke Ct., Muskego, WI 53150
Sec., Rev. Douglas L. Bode, 1005 E. Broadway, Prairie du Chien, WI 53821

OTHER ORGANIZATIONS

Bd. of Trustees, Admn., Mr. Clair V. Ochs
Bd. for Worker Trng., Admn., Rev. Wayne Borgwardt
Bd. for Parish Services, Admn., Rev. Wayne Mueller
Bd. for Home Missions, Admn., Rev. Harold J. Hagedorn
Bd. for World Missions, Admn., Rev. Duane K. Tomhave

PERIODICALS

Wisconsin Lutheran Quarterly; Northwestern Lutheran; The Lutheran Educator

RELIGIOUS BODIES IN THE UNITED STATES ARRANGED BY FAMILIES

The following list of religious bodies appearing in the Directory Section of this yearbook shows the "families," or related clusters into which American religious bodies can be grouped. For example, there are many communions that can be grouped under the heading "Baptist" for historical and theological reasons. It is not to be assumed, however, that all denominations under one family heading are similar in belief or practice. Often, any similarity is purely coincidental. The family clusters tend to represent historical factors more often than theological or practical ones. The family categories provided one of the major pitfalls of church statistics because of the tendency to combine the statistics by "families" for analytical and comparative purposes. Such combined totals are almost meaningless, although often used as variables for sociological analysis.

Religious bodies not grouped under family headings appear alphabetically and are not indented in the following list.

Adventist Bodies

Advent Christian Church
Church of God General Conference (Oregon IL.)
Primitive Advent Christian Church
Seventh-day Adventists

Amana Church Society

American Evangelical Christian Churches

American Rescue Workers

Apostolic Christian Church (Nazarene)

Apostolic Christian Churches of America

The Anglican Orthodox Church

Baptist Bodies

American Baptist Association
American Baptist Churches in the U.S.A.
Baptist Bible Fellowship International
Baptist General Conference
Baptist Missionary Association of America
Conservative Baptist Association of America
General Association of Regular Baptist Churches
General Association of General Baptists
General Conference of the Evangelical Baptist Church, Inc.
Liberty Baptist Fellowship
National Association of Free Will Baptists
National Baptist Convention of America
National Baptist Convention, U.S.A., Inc.
National Missionary Baptist Convention of America
National Primitive Baptist Convention, Inc.
North American Baptist Conference
Primitive Baptists
Progressive National Baptist Convention, Inc.
Separate Baptists in Christ
Seventh Day Baptist General Conference, USA and Canada
Southern Baptist Convention
Sovereign Grace Baptists

Berean Fundamental Church

Brethren (German Baptists)

Brethren Church (Ashland, Ohio)
Church of the Brethren
Fellowship of Grace Brethren Churches
Old German Baptist Brethren

Brethren, River

Brethren in Christ Church
United Zion Church

Christadelphians

The Christian and Missionary Alliance

Christian Brethren (also known as Plymouth Brethren)

Christian Catholic Church (Evangelical-Protestant)

The Christian Congregation, Inc.

Christian Nation Church U.S.A.

Christian Union

Church of Christ, Scientist

Church of Daniel's Band

The Church of Illumination

Church of the Living God (Motto: Christian Workers for Fellowship)

Church of the Nazarene

Churches of Christ in Christian Union

Churches of Christ-Christian Churches

Christian Church (Disciples of Christ)
Christian Churches and Churches of Christ
Churches of Christ

Churches Of God

Church of God (Anderson, Ind.)
Church of God by Faith, Inc.
The Church of God (Seventh Day), Denver, Colo.,
Church of God (Which He Purchased With His Own Blood)
Churches of God, General Conference

Churches of the New Jerusalem

General Church of the New Jerusalem
The Swedenborgian Church

Conservative Congregational Christian Conference

Eastern Churches

Albanian Orthodox Archdiocese in America
Albanian Orthodox Diocese of America
The American Carpatho-Russian Orthodox Greek Catholic Church
The Antiochian Orthodox Christian Archdiocese of North America

Apostolic Catholic Assyrian Church of the East, North American Dioceses
Armenian Apostolic Church of America
Bulgarian Eastern Orthodox Church
Coptic Orthodox Church
Diocese of the Armenian Church of America
Greek Orthodox Archdiocese of North and South America
Holy Ukrainian Autocephalic Orthodox Church in Exile
The Orthodox Church in America
Romanian Orthodox Church in America
The Romanian Orthodox Episcopate of America
Patriarchal Parishes of the Russian Orthodox Church in the U.S.A.,
The Russian Orthodox Church Outside Russia
Serbian Orthodox Church in the U.S.A. and Canada
Syrian Orthodox Church of Antioch (Archdiocese of the United States and Canada)
True Orthodox Church of Greece (Synod of Metropolitan Cyprian), American Exarchate
Ukrainian Orthodox Church of the U.S.A.
Ukrainian Orthodox Church in America (Ecumenical Patriarchate)

The Episcopal Church
The Evangelical Church
Evangelical Congregational Church
The Evangelical Covenant Church
The Evangelical Free Church of America
Fellowship of Fundamental Bible Churches
The Fire Baptized Holiness Church (Wesleyan)
Free Christian Zion Church of Christ

Friends

Evangelical Friends International—North America Region
Friends General Conference
Friends United Meeting
Religious Society of Friends (Conservative)
Religious Society of Friends (Unaffiliated Meetings)

Grace Gospel Fellowship
The Holiness Church of God, Inc.
House of God, Which is the Church of the Living God, the Pillar and Ground of the Truth, Inc.
Independent Fundamental Churches of America
International Council of Community Churches
Israelite House of David
Jehovah's Witnesses
Kodesh Church of Immanuel

Latter Day Saints

Church of Christ
The Church of Jesus Christ (Bickertonites)
The Church of Jesus Christ of Latter-day Saints
Reorganized Church of Jesus Christ of Latter Day Saints

The Liberal Catholic Church-Province of the United States of America

Lutherans

The American Association of Lutheran Churches

RSN PHOTO/Reuters

REMEMBERING KING

Marchers gather at the Reflecting Pool near the Washington Monument August 28 during the 30th anniversary celebrations of Martin Luther King Jr.' "I Have a Dream" speech.

Apostolic Lutheran Church of America
The Association of Free Lutheran Congregations
Church of the Lutheran Brethren of America
Church of the Lutheran Confession
Conservative Lutheran Association
Estonian Evangelical Lutheran Church
Evangelical Lutheran Church in America
Evangelical Lutheran Synod

Latvian Evangelical Lutheran Church in
America
The Lutheran Church—Missouri Synod
The Protes'tant Conference (Lutheran), Inc.
Wisconsin Evangelical Lutheran Synod

Mennonite Bodies

Beachy Amish Mennonite Churches
Church of God in Christ (Mennonite)
The Conference of Mennonite Brethren
Churches
Evangelical Mennonite Church
Fellowship of Evangelical Bible Churches
Hutterian Brethren
Mennonite Church
Mennonite Church, The General Conference
Old Order Amish Church
Old Order (Wisler) Mennonite Church
Reformed Mennonite Church

Methodist Bodies

African Methodist Episcopal Church
African Methodist Episcopal Zion Church
Allegheny Wesleyan Methodist Connection
(Original Allegheny Conference)
Christian Methodist Episcopal Church
Evangelical Methodist Church
Free Methodist Church of North America
Fundamental Methodist Church, Inc.
Primitive Methodist Church in the U.S.A.
Reformed Methodist Union Episcopal Church
Reformed Zion Union Apostolic Church
Southern Methodist Church
The United Methodist Church
The Wesleyan Church

The Metropolitan Church Association, Inc.
The Missionary Church

Moravian Bodies

Moravian Church in America (Unitas Fratrum)
Unity of the Brethren

National Association of Congregational Chris-
tian Churches
National Organization of the New Apostolic
Church of North America
National Spiritualist Association of Churches
North American Old Roman Catholic Church
(Archdiocese of New York)

Old Catholic Churches

Christ Catholic Church
North American Old Roman Catholic Church

Pentecostal Bodies

Apostolic Faith Mission of Portland, Oregon
Apostolic Faith Mission Church of God
Apostolic Overcoming Holy Church of God,
Inc.
Assemblies of God
Assemblies of God International Fellowship
(Independent/Not Affiliated)
The Bible Church of Christ, Inc.
Bible Way Church of Our Lord Jesus Christ,
World Wide, Inc.
Christian Church of North America, General
Council
The Church of God

Church of God (Cleveland, Tenn.)
The Church of God in Christ
Church of God in Christ, International
The Church of God of Prophecy
The Church of God, Mountain Assembly, Inc.
Church of Our Lord Jesus Christ of the Apos-
tolic Faith, Inc.
Congregational Holiness Church
Elim Fellowship
Full Gospel Assemblies International
Full Gospel Fellowship of Churches and Min-
isters International
International Church of the Foursquare Gos-
pel
The International Pentecostal Church of
Christ
International Pentecostal Holiness Church
Open Bible Standard Churches, Inc.
The (Original) Church of God, Inc.
Pentecostal Assemblies of the World, Inc.
Pentecostal Church of God
Pentecostal Fire-Baptized Holiness Church
Pentecostal Free Will Baptist Church, Inc.
United Holy Church of America, Inc.
United Pentecostal Church International

Pillar of Fire
Polish National Catholic Church of America

Presbyterian Bodies

Associate Reformed Presbyterian Church
(General Synod)
Cumberland Presbyterian Church
Cumberland Presbyterian Church in America
Evangelical Presbyterian Church
Korean Presbyterian Church in America, Gen-
eral Assembly of the
The Orthodox Presbyterian Church
Presbyterian Church in America
Presbyterian Church (U.S.A.)
Reformed Presbyterian Church of North Amer-
ica

Reformed Bodies

Christian Reformed Church in North America
Hungarian Reformed Church in America
Netherlands Reformed Congregations
Protestant Reformed Churches in America
Reformed Church in America
Reformed Church in the United States
United Church of Christ

Reformed Episcopal Church
The Roman Catholic Church
The Salvation Army
The Schwenkfelder Church
Social Brethren
Triumph the Church and Kingdom of God in
Christ Inc. (International)
Unitarian Universalist Association
Universal Fellowship of Metropolitan Commu-
nity Churches

United Brethren Bodies

United Brethren in Christ
United Christian Church

Volunteers of America
Wesleyan Holiness Association of Churches

4. RELIGIOUS BODIES IN CANADA

A large number of Canadian religious bodies were organized by immigrants from Europe and elsewhere, and a smaller number sprang up originally on Canadian soil. In the case of Canada, moreover, many denominations that overlap the U.S.-Canada border have headquarters in the United States.

If you have difficulty finding a particular denomination, check the index of organizations. In some cases alternative names for denominations are listed there. A final section lists denominations according to denominational families. This can be a helpful tool in finding a particular denomination.

Complete statistics for Canadian denominations are found in the table "Canadian Current and Non-current Statistics" in the statistical section of the *Yearbook*.

Addresses for periodicals are found in the listing of Canadian Religious Periodicals. Information about finances for some of the denominations is in the Church Finance section.

The Anglican Church of Canada

Anglicanism came to Canada with the early explorers such as Martin Frobisher and Henry Hudson. Continuous services began in Newfoundland about 1700 and in Nova Scotia in 1710. The first Bishop, Charles Inglis, was appointed to Nova Scotia in 1787. The numerical strength of Anglicanism was increased by the coming of American Loyalists and by massive immigration both after the Napoleonic wars and in the later 19th and early 20th centuries.

The Anglican Church of Canada has enjoyed self-government for over a century and is an autonomous member of the worldwide Anglican Communion. The General Synod, which normally meets triennially, consists of the Archbishops, Bishops and elected clerical and lay representatives of the 30 dioceses. Each of the Ecclesiastical Provinces—Canada, Ontario, Rupert's Land and British Columbia—is organized under a Metropolitan and has its own Provincial Synod and Executive Council. Each diocese has its own Diocesan Synod.

HEADQUARTERS
Church House, 600 Jarvis St., Toronto, ON M4Y 2J6 Tel. (416)924-9192 Fax (416)968-7983
Media Contact, Dir. of Communications, Mr. Douglas Tindal

GENERAL SYNOD OFFICERS
Primate of the Anglican Church of Canada, Most Rev. Michael G. Peers
Prolocutor, Mrs. Amy Newell, RR #1, Fitzroy Harbor, ON K0A 1X0
Gen. Sec., Ven. James B. Boyles
Treas., Gen. Synod, Mr. Robert G. Armstrong
Exec. Dir. of Program, Ms. Suzanne Lawson

DEPARTMENTS AND DIVISIONS
Anglican Book Centre, Dir. & Publ., Rev. M. J. Lloyd
Missionary Society, Exec. Sec., Rev. J. S. Barton
Div. of Pensions, Dir., Mrs. Jenny Mason
Dir. of Admn. & Fin., Mr. Robert G. Armstrong
Dir. of Communications, Mr. Douglas Tindal
Dir. of Ministries in Church & Society, Rev. Peter Elliott
Dir. of Stewardship & Financial Development, Rev. Canon James Dugan
Dir. of World Mission, Rev. J. S. Barton

METROPOLITANS (ARCHBISHOPS)
Ecclesiastical Province of: Canada, The Most Rev.

Stewart S. Payne, 25 Main St., Corner Brook, NF A2H 1C2 Tel. (709)639-8712 Fax (709)639-1636; Rupert's Land, —, 935 Nesbitt Bay, Winnipeg, MB R3T 1W6 Tel. (204)453-6130 Fax (204)452-3915; British Columbia, —, 302-814 Richards St., Vancouver, BC V6B 3A7 Tel. (604)684-6306 Fax (604)684-7017; Ontario, The Most Rev. Perry R. O'Driscoll, 4-220 Dundas St., London, ON N6A 1H3 Tel. (519)434-6893 Fax (519)673-4151

DIOCESAN BISHOPS
Algoma: The Rt. Rev. Leslie Peterson, 619 Wellington St. E, Box 1168, Sault Ste. Marie, ON P6A 5N7 Tel. (705)256-5061 Fax (705)946-1860
Arctic: The Rt. Rev. Christopher Williams, 1055 Avenue Rd., Toronto, ON M5N 2C8 Tel. (416)481-2263 Fax (416)487-4948
Athabasca: The Right Rev. John R. Clarke, P.O. Box 6868, Peace River, AB T8S 1S6 Tel. (403)624-2767 Fax (403)624-2365
Brandon: The Rt. Rev. Malcolm Harding, 341-13th St., Brandon, MB R7A 4P8 Tel. (204)727-7550 Fax (204)727-4135
British Columbia: The Rt. Rev. Barry Jenks, 912 Vancouver St., Victoria, BC V8V 3V7 Tel. (604)386-7781 Fax (604)386-4013
Caledonia: The Rt. Rev. John E. Hannen, Box 278, Prince Rupert, BC V8J 3P6 Tel. (604)624-6013 Fax (604)624-4299
Calgary: The Rt. Rev. Barry Curtis, 3015 Glencoe Rd. SW, Calgary, AB T2S 2L9 Tel. (403)243-3673 Fax (403)243-2182
Cariboo: The Right Rev. James D. Cruickshank, 5-618 Tranquille Rd., Ste. 5, Kamloops, BC V2B 3H6 Tel. (604)376-0112 Fax (604)376-1984
Central Newfoundland: The Rt. Rev. Edward Marsh, 34 Fraser Rd., Gander, NF A1V 2E8 Tel. (709)256-2372 Fax (709)256-2396
Eastern Newfoundland and Labrador: The Rt. Rev. Donald F. Harvey, 19 King's Bridge Rd., St. John's, NF A1C 3K4 Tel. (709)576-6697 Fax (709)576-7122
Edmonton: The Rt. Rev. Kenneth Genge, 10033 - 84 Ave., Edmonton, AB T6E 2G6 Tel. (403)439-7344 Fax (403)439-6549
Fredericton: The Rt. Rev. George C. Lemmon, 115 Church St., Fredericton, NB E3B 4C8 Tel. (506)459-1801 Fax (506)459-8475
Huron: The Most Rev. Perry R. O'Driscoll, 4-220 Dundas St., London, ON N6A 1H3 Tel. (519)434-6893 Fax (519)673-4151

Keewatin: The Rt. Rev. Thomas W. R. Collings, 915 Ottawa St., Keewatin, ON P0X 1C0 Tel. (807)547-3353 Fax (807)547-3356

Kootenay: The Rt. Rev. David P. Crawley, 201-1636 Pandosy St., Kelowna, BC V1Y 1P7 Tel. (604)762-3306 Fax (604)762-4150

Montreal: The Rt. Rev. Andrew S. Hutchison, 1444 Union Ave., Montreal, QC H3A 2B8 Tel. (514)843-6577 Fax (514)843-3221

Moosonee: The Rt. Rev. Caleb J. Lawrence, Box 841, Schumacher, ON P0N 1G0 Tel. (705)360-1129 Fax (705)360-1120

New Westminster: The Rt. Rev. Michael C. Ingham, 302-814 Richards St., Vancouver, BC V6B 3A7 Tel. (604)684-6306 Fax (604)684-7017

Niagara: The Right Rev. Walter Asbil, 67 Victoria Ave. S, Hamilton, ON L8N 2S8 Tel. (416)527-1278 Fax (416)527-1281

Nova Scotia: The Rt. Rev. Arthur G. Peters, 5732 College St., Halifax, NS B3H 1X3 Tel. (902)420-0717 Fax (902)425-0717

Ontario: The Rt. Rev. Peter Mason, 90 Johnson St., Kingston, ON K7L 1X7 Tel. (613)544-4774 Fax (613)547-3745

Ottawa: The Rt. Rev. John A. Baycroft, 71 Bronson Ave., Ottawa, ON K1R 6G6 Tel. (613)232-7124 Fax (613)232-7088

Qu'Appelle: The Rt. Rev. Eric Bays, 1501 College Ave., Regina, SK S4P 1B8 Tel. (306)522-1608 Fax (306)352-6808

Quebec: The Rt. Rev. Bruce Stavert, 36 rue des Jardins, Quebec, QC G1R 4L5 Tel. (418)692-3858 Fax (418)692-3876

Rupert's Land: —, 935 Nesbitt Bay, Winnipeg, MB R3T 1W6 Tel. (204)453-6130 Fax (204)452-3915

Saskatchewan: The Rt. Rev. Anthony Burton, Box 1088, Prince Albert, SK S6V 5S6 Tel. (306)763-2455 Fax (306)764-5172

Saskatoon: The Rt. Rev. Thomas O. Morgan, Box 1965, Saskatoon, SK S7K 3S5 Tel. (306)244-5651 Fax (306)933-4606

Toronto: The Most Rev. Terence E. Finlay, 135 Adelaide St. East, Toronto, ON M5C 1L8 Tel. (416)363-6021 Fax (416)363-3683

Western Newfoundland: Archbishop, The Most Rev. Stewart S. Payne, 25 Main St., Corner Brook, NF A2H 1C2 Tel. (709)639-8712 Fax (709)639-1636

Yukon: The Rt. Rev. Ronald C. Ferris, Box 4247, Whitehorse, YT Y1A 3T3 Tel. (403)667-7746 Fax (403)667-6125

PERIODICALS

Anglican Montreal Anglican; The Anglican; Huron Church News; Newfoundland Churchmen; Rupert's Land News; Saskatchewan Anglican; Topic

The Antiochian Orthodox Christian Archdiocese of North America

The approximately 100,000 members of the Antiochian Orthodox community in Canada are under the jurisdiction of the Antiochian Orthodox Christian Archdiocese of North America with headquarters in Englewood, N.J. There are churches in Edmonton, Winnipeg, Halifax, London, Ottawa, Toronto, Windsor, Montreal and Saskatoon.

HEADQUARTERS

Metropolitan Philip Saliba, 358 Mountain Rd., Englewood, NJ 07631 Tel. (201)871-1355 Fax (201)871-7954

Media Contact, Vicar, The V. Rev. George S. Corey, 52 78th St., Brooklyn, NY 11209 Tel. (718)748-7940 Fax (718)855-3608

Apostolic Christian Church (Nazarene)

This church was formed in Canada as a result of immigration from various European countries. The body began as a movement originated by the Rev. S. H. Froehlich, a Swiss pastor, whose followers are still found in Switzerland and Central Europe.

HEADQUARTERS

Apostolic Christian Church Foundation, 1135 Sholey Rd., Richmond, VA 23231 Tel. (804)222-1943

OFFICER

Exec. Dir., James Hodges

The Apostolic Church in Canada

The Apostolic Church in Canada is affiliated with the worldwide organization of the Apostolic Church with headquarters in Great Britain. A product of the Welsh Revival (1904 to 1908), its Canadian beginnings originated in Nova Scotia in 1927. Today its main centers are in Nova Scotia, Ontario and Quebec. This church is evangelical, fundamental and Pentecostal, with special emphasis on the ministry gifts listed in Ephesians 4:11-12.

HEADQUARTERS

27 Castlefield Ave., Toronto, ON M4R 1G3

Media Contact, Natl. Sec., Rev. John Kristensen, 388 Gerald St., La Salle, QC H8P 2A5 Tel. (514)366-8356

OFFICERS

Pres., Rev. D. S. Morris, 685 Park St. S., Peterborough, ON K9J 3S9 Tel. (705)743-3418

Natl. Sec., Rev. John Kristensen, 388 Gerald St., Ville LaSalle, QC H8P 2A5

Apostolic Church of Pentecost of Canada Inc.

This body was founded in 1921 at Winnipeg, Manitoba, by Pastor Frank Small. Doctrines include belief in eternal salvation by the grace of God, baptism of the Holy Spirit with the evidence of speaking in tongues, water baptism by immersion in the name of the Lord Jesus Christ.

HEADQUARTERS

200-809 Manning Rd. NE, Calgary, AB T2E 7M9

Media Contact, Clk./Admn., Leonard K. Larsen, Tel. (403)273-5777 Fax (403)273-8102

OFFICERS

Mod., Rev. G. Killam

Clk., Leonard K. Larsen

PERIODICAL

A.C.O.P. Messenger

The Armenian Church of North America, Diocese of Canada

The Canadian branch of the ancient Church of Armenia founded in A.D. 301 by St. Gregory the Illuminator was established in Canada at St. Catherines, Ontario, in 1930. The diocesan organization is under the jurisdiction of the Holy See of Etchmiadzin, Armenia. The Diocese has churches in St. Catherine, Hamilton, Toronto, Scarborough, Ottawa, Vancouver, Mississauga and Montreal.

HEADQUARTERS

Diocesan Offices: Primate, Canadian Diocese, Archbishop Hovnan Derderian, 615 Stuart Ave., Outremont, QC H2V 3H2 Tel. (514)276-9479 Fax (514)276-9960
Media Contact, Exec. Dir., Arminé Keuchgerian

PERIODICALS

Nor Serount; Pourastan

Armenian Evangelical Church

Founded in 1960 by immigrant Armenian evangelical families from the Middle East, this body is conservative doctrinally, with an evangelical, biblical emphasis. The polity of churches within the group differ with congregationalism being dominant, but there are presbyterian Armenian Evangelical churches as well. Most of the local churches have joined main-line denominations. All of the remaining Armenian Evangelical (congregational or presbyterian) local churches in the United States and Canada have joined with the Armenian Evangelical Union of North America.

HEADQUARTERS

Armenian Evangelical Church of Toronto, 34 Glenforest Rd., Toronto, ON M4N 1Z8
Media Contact, Chief Editor, Rev. Yessayi Sarmazian, 42 Glenforest Rd., Toronto, ON M4N 1Z8 Tel. (416)489-3188 Fax (416)485-4336

A.E.U.N.A. OFFICERS

Min. to the Union, Rev. Karl Avakian, 1789 E. Frederick Ave., Fresno, CA 93720
Mod., Rev. Ronald Tovmassian, 32 Bigelow, Watertown, MA 02171

OFFICER

Min., Rev. Yessayi Sarmazian, 42 Glenforest Rd., Toronto, ON M4N 1Z8 Tel. (416)489-3188

PERIODICAL

Canada Armenian Press

Associated Gospel Churches

The Associated Gospel Churches (A.G.C.) body traces its historical roots to the early years of the 20th century, which were marked by the growth of liberal theology in many established denominations. Individuals and whole congregations, seeking to uphold the final authority of the Scriptures in all matters of faith and conduct, withdrew from those denominations and established churches with an evangelical ministry under the inspired Word of God. These churches defended the belief that "all Scripture is given by inspiration of God" and also declared that the Holy Spirit "gave the identical words of sacred writings of holy men of old, chosen by Him to be the channel of His revelation to man."

In 1922, four churches of similar background in Ontario banded together in fellowship for counsel and cooperation. Known as The Christian Workers' Church in Canada, the group consisted of the Gospel Tabernacle, Hamilton; the Winona Gospel Tabernacle; the Missionary Tabernacle, Toronto; and West Hamilton Gospel Mission. The principal organizers were Dr. P. W. Philpott of Hamilton and H. E. Irwin, K. C., of Toronto.

In 1925 the name was changed to Associated Gospel Churches under a new Dominion Charter. Since that time the A.G.C. has grown steadily.

HEADQUARTERS

3430 South Service Rd., Burlington, ON L7N 3T9 Tel. (416)634-8184 Fax (416) 634-6283
Media Contact, Pres., D. G. Hamilton

OFFICERS

Pres., Rev. D. G. Hamilton
Vice-Pres., ——
Mod., Rev. S. R. Sadlier, Box 55, King City, ON L0G 1K0 Tel. (416)833-5104
Sec.-Treas., Stan Dorey

PERIODICAL

Advance

Association of Regular Baptist Churches (Canada)

The Association of Regular Baptist Churches was organized in 1957 by a group of churches for the purpose of mutual cooperation in missionary activities. The Association believes the Bible to be God's word, stands for historic Baptist principles and opposes modern ecumenism.

HEADQUARTERS

130 Gerrard St. E., Toronto, ON M5A 3T4 Tel. (416)925-3261
Media Contact, Sec., Rev. W. P. Bauman, Tel. (416)925-3263 Fax (416)925-8305

OFFICERS

Chmn., Pastor D. Brehart, Box 149, Petitcodiac, NB E0A 2H0
Sec., Rev. W. P. Bauman

PERIODICAL

The Gospel Witness

Baptist General Conference of Canada

The Baptist General Conference was founded in Canada by missionaries from the United States. Originally a Swedish body, BGC Canada now includes people of many nationalities and is conservative and evangelical in doctrine and practice.

HEADQUARTERS

4306-97 St., Edmonton, AB T6E 5R9 Tel. (403)438-9127 Fax (403)435-2478
Media Contact, Exec. Dir., Rev. Abe Funk

OFFICERS

Exec. Dir., Rev. Abe Funk, 11635-51st. Ave., Edmonton, AB T6H 0M4 Tel. (403)435-4403
Bd. Chpsn., Rev. Ed Stuckey, 851 Lee Ridge Rd., Edmonton, AB T6K 0R1

PERIODICAL

BGC Canada News

The Central Canada Baptist Conference

Central Baptist Conference, originally a Scandinavian group, is one of three districts of the Baptist

General Conference of Canada. In 1907, churches from Winnipeg—Grant Memorial, Teulon, Kenora, Port Arthur, Sprague, Erickson and Midale—organized under the leadership of Fred Palmberg. Immigration from Sweden declined, and in 1947 only nine churches remained. In 1948 the group dropped the Swedish language, withdrew from the Baptist Union and city churches were started. Today the CCBC has 37 functioning churches.

An evangelical Baptist association holding to the inerrancy of the Bible, CCBC seeks to reach Central Canada for Christ by establishing local gospel-preaching churches.

CCBC offers pastoral aid to new churches and recommendations as to pastoral supply, counsel and fellowship. It encourages contributions to the CCBC and BGC of Canada budgets, support of the Conference BATT program (contributions to special needs of churches) and other projects to assist needy churches and pastors.

HEADQUARTERS
Box 135, Stonewall, MB R0C 2Z0 Tel. (204)467-2169
Media Contact, Exec. Min., Dr. Dave Selness

OFFICERS
Exec. Min., Dr. Dave Selness

Baptist General Conference of Alberta

HEADQUARTERS
5011 122nd A St., Edmonton, AB T6H 3S8 Tel. (403)438-9126
Media Contact, Exec. Sec., Virgil Olson

OFFICER
Exec. Sec., Virgil Olson

PERIODICAL
The Alberta Alert

British Columbia Baptist Conference

British Columbia Baptist Conference is a district of the Baptist General Conference of Canada, with roots in Sweden, where Christians began to read the Bible in their homes. One convert, F.O. Nilsson, saw the significance of baptism subsequent to a personal commitment to Christ; he went to Hamburg, Germany, where he was baptized in the Elbe River by Rev. John Oncken. When Nilsson returned to Sweden, five of his converts were baptized in the North Sea and, with him, formed the first Swedish Baptist Church. Nilsson was imprisoned by the local government for violation of state church regulations and later, when exiled from Sweden, went to the United States. As Swedish Baptists came to the United States to escape persecution, they formed churches in Illinois, Iowa, Minnesota and Wisconsin and carried on aggressive evangelism among other immigrating Swedes. In 1879 they formed the Swedish Baptist General Conference of America, later named The Baptist General Conference.

The Mission Statement of British Columbia Baptist Conference reads "To aggressively plant and grow worshiping, caring churches through evangelism and discipleship."

HEADQUARTERS
7600 Glover Rd., Langley, BC V3A 6H4 Tel. (604)888-2246 Fax (604)888-1905
Media Contact, District Exec. Min., Rev. Walter W. Wieser

OFFICER
Dist. Exec. Min., Rev. Walter W. Wieser

PERIODICAL
B.C. Conference Call

The Bible Holiness Movement
The Bible Holiness Movement, organized in 1949 as an outgrowth of the city mission work of the late Pastor William James Elijah Wakefield, an early-day Salvation Army officer, has been headed since its inception by his son, Evangelist Wesley H. Wakefield, its bishop-general.

It derives its emphasis on the original Methodist faith of salvation and scriptural holiness from the late Bishop R. C. Horner. It adheres to the common evangelical faith in the Bible, the Deity and the atonement of Christ. It stresses a personal experience of salvation for the repentant sinner, of being wholly sanctified for the believer and of the fullness of the Holy Spirit for effective witness.

Membership involves a life of Christian love and evangelistic and social activism. Members are required to totally abstain from liquor and tobacco. They may not attend popular amusements or join secret societies. Divorce and remarriage are forbidden. Similar to Wesley's Methodism, members are, under some circumstances, allowed to retain membership in other evangelical church fellowships. Interchurch affiliations are maintained with a number of Wesleyan-Arminian Holiness denominations.

Year-round evangelistic outreach is maintained through open-air meetings, visitation, literature and other media. Noninstitutional welfare work, including addiction counseling, is conducted among minorities. There is direct overseas famine relief, civil rights action, environment protection and antinuclearism. The movement sponsors a permanent committee on religious freedom and an active promotion of Christian racial equality.

The movement has a world outreach with branches in the United States, India, Nigeria, Philippines, Ghana, Liberia, Cameroon, Kenya, Zambia, South Korea and Haiti. It ministers to 89 countries in 42 languages through literature, radio and audiocassettes.

HEADQUARTERS
Box 223, Postal Stn. A, Vancouver, BC V6C 2M3 Tel. (604)498-3895
Media Contact, Bishop-General, Evangelist Wesley H. Wakefield, P.O. Box 223, Postal Station A, Vancouver, BC V6C 2M3 Tel. (604)498-3895

DIRECTORS
Bishop-General, Evangelist Wesley H. Wakefield, (Intl. Leader)
Evangelist M. J. Wakefield, Oliver, BC
Mrs. W. Sneed, Dalhousie Rd., N.W., Calgary, AB
Pastor Vincente Hernando, Phillipines
Pastor Morasol Hernando, Phillipines
Pastor & Mrs. Daniel Stinnett, 1425 Mountain View W., Phoenix, AZ 85021
Pastor A. Sanon, Port-au-Prince, Haiti
Evangelist I. S. Udoh, Abak, Akwalbom, Nigeria, West Africa
Pastor Augustus Theo Seongbae, Sr., Monrovia, Liberia
Pastor Choe Chong Dee, Cha Pa Puk, S. Korea

PERIODICAL

Hallelujah

Brethren in Christ Church, Canadian Conference

The Brethren in Christ, formerly known as Tunkers in Canada, arose out of a religious awakening in Lancaster County, Pa. late in the 18th century. Representatives of the new denomination reached Ontario in 1788 and established the church in the southern part of the present province. Presently the conference has congregations in Ontario, Alberta, Quebec and Saskatchewan. In theology they have accents of the Pietist, Anabaptist, Wesleyan and Evangelical movements.

HEADQUARTERS

Brethren in Christ Church, Gen. Ofc., P.O. Box 290, Grantham, PA 17027-0290 Tel. (717)697-2634 Fax (717)697-7714

Canadian Headquarters, Bishop's Ofc., 2619 Niagara Pkwy., Ft. Erie, ON L2A 5M4 Tel. (416)871-9991

Media Contact, Mod., Harvey R. Sider, Brethren in Christ Church Gen. Ofc.

OFFICERS

Mod., Bishop R. Dale Shaw, 2619 Niagara Pkwy., Ft. Erie, ON L2A 5M4 Tel. (416)871-9991

Sec., Rev. Darrell Winger, RR 4, Stayner, ON L0M 1S0

British Methodist Episcopal Church of Canada

The British Methodist Episcopal Church was organized in 1856 in Chatham, Ontario and incorporated in 1913. It has congregations across the Province of Ontario.

HEADQUARTERS

460 Shaw St., Toronto, ON M6G 3L3 Tel. (416)534-3831

Media Contact, Editor, Rev. Jean Markham, 1413-145 Hillcrest, Mississauga, ON L5B 3Z1 Tel. (416)272-8207

OFFICERS

Gen. Supt., Rev. Dr. D. D. Rupwate, 66 Golfwood Dr., Hamilton, ON L9C 6W3 Tel. (416)383-6856

Asst. Gen. Supt., Rev. Livingston Yearwood, 16 Lynvalley Cres., Scarborough, ON M1R 2V3 Tel. (416)445-2646

Gen. Sec., Rev. Maurice M. Hicks, 3 Boxdene Ave., Scarborough, ON M1V 3C9 Tel. (416)298-5715

Gen. Treas., Helen Smith, 60 Parkview Rd., St. Catharines, ON L2M 5S4 Tel. (416)934-4175

Canadian and American Reformed Churches

The Canadian and American Reformed Churches accept the Bible as the infallible Word of God, as summarized in The Belgic Confession of Faith (1561), The Heidelberg Cathechism(1563) and The Canons of Dordt (1618-1619). The denomination was founded in Canada in 1950 and in the United States in 1955.

HEADQUARTERS

Synod: P.O. Box 62053, Burlington, ON L7R 4K2

Canadian Reformed Churches: Ebenezer Canadian Reformed Church, P. O. Box 62053, Burlington Mall Postal Outlet, Burlington, ON L7R 4K2

American Reformed Churches: American Reformed Church, Rev. P. Kingma, 3167-68th St. S.E., Caledonia, MI 46316

Media Contact, Rev. G. Nederveen, 3089 Woodward Ave., Burlington, ON L7N 2M3 Tel. (416)681-9837 Fax (416)681-9837

PERIODICALS

Reformed Perspective: A Magazine for the Christian Fam.; In Holy Array; Clarion: The Canadian Reformed Magazine

Canadian Baptist Federation

The Canadian Baptist Federation has four federated member bodies: (1) Baptist Convention of Ontario and Quebec, (2) Baptist Union of Western Canada, (3) the United Baptist Convention of the Atlantic Provinces, (4) Union d'Églises Baptistes Françaises au Canada (French Baptist Union). Its main purpose is to act as a coordinating agency for the four groups.

HEADQUARTERS

7185 Millcreek Dr., Mississauga, ON L5N 5R4 Tel. (905)826-0191 Fax (905)826-3441

Media Contact, Gen. Sec.-Treas., Dr. Richard C. Coffin

OFFICERS

Pres., Rev. Nelson W. Hooper, 45 Applewood Cres., Cambridge, ON N1S 4K1

Vice-Pres.: Dr. Bruce Milne, 2937 West 16 Ave., Vancouver, BC V6K 3C7; Dr. Joyce Boillat, 2565 Montmartre, Brossard, QC J4Y 1N7; Mrs. Mary Price, P.O. Box 1486, Wolfville, NS B0P 1X0

Gen. Sec.-Treas., Dr. Richard C. Coffin

Canadian Baptist Overseas Mission Bd., Gen. Sec., Rev. R. Berry

PERIODICALS

The Canadian Baptist; Enterprise

Baptist Convention of Ontario and Quebec

The Baptist Convention of Ontario and Quebec is a family of 372 churches in Ontario and Quebec, united for mutual support and encouragement and united in missions in Canada and the world.

The Convention was formally organized in 1888. It has two educational institutions—McMaster University, founded in 1887, and the Baptist Leadership Education Centre at Whitby. The Convention works through the all-Canada missionary agency, Canadian Baptist International Ministries. The churches also support the Sharing Way, the relief and development arm of the Canadian Baptist Federation.

HEADQUARTERS

195 The West Mall, Ste. 414, Etobicoke, ON M9C 5K1 Tel. (416)922-5163 Fax (416)922-3254

Media Contact, Exec. Min., Rev. John Wilton

OFFICERS

Pres., Mrs. Barbara Bell

1st Vice-Pres., Mr. Merlyn Neal

2nd Vice-Pres., Mr. Vince Judge

Treas./Bus. Admn., Mrs. Nancy Bell

Exec. Min., Rev. John Wilton

Baptist Union of Western Canada

HEADQUARTERS
202, 838-11th Ave. S.W., Calgary, AB T2R 0E5
Tel. (403)234-9044 Fax (403)269-6755
Media Contact, Exec. Min., Rev. William Cram

OFFICERS
Pres., Ron Basky
Exec. Min., Rev. William Cram
Assoc. Exec. Min./Resourcing, Rev. Gerald
Fisher, 14 Milford Cr., Sherwood Park, AB T8A
3V4
Area Min., Alberta, ——
Area Min., British Columbia, Dr. Don Anderson,
201-7 St., New Westminster, BC V3M 3K2
Area Min., Saskatchewan, Rev. Wayne Larson,
3542 Burns Rd., Regina, SK S4V 2G3
Carey Theological College, Principal & Field
Educ. Dir., Rev. Philip Collins, 5920 Iona Dr.,
Vancouver, BC V6T 1J6
Baptist Leadership Training School (Lay), Acting
Principal, Rev. Myrna R. Sears, 4330-16 Street
SW, Calgary, AB T2T 4H9

United Baptist Convention of the Atlantic Provinces

The United Baptist Convention of the Atlantic
Provinces is the largest Baptist Convention in
Canada. Through the Canadian Baptist Federation,
it is a member of the Baptist World Alliance.

In 1763 two Baptist churches were organized in
Atlantic Canada, one in Sackville, New Brunswick
and the other in Wolfville, Nova Scotia. Although
both these churches experienced crises and lost
continuity, they recovered and stand today as the
beginning of organized Baptist work in Canada.

Nine Baptist churches met in Lower Granville,
Nova Scotia in 1800 and formed the first Baptist
Association in Canada. By 1846 the Maritime
Baptist Convention was organized consisting of
169 churches. Two streams of Baptist life merged
in 1905 to form the United Baptist Convention.
This is how the unique term "United Baptist" was
derived. Today there are 546 churches within 21
associations across the Convention.

The Convention has two educational institutions: Atlantic Baptist College in Moncton, New
Brunswick, a Christian Liberal Arts University,
and Acadia Divinity College in Wolfville, Nova
Scotia, a Graduate School of Theology. The Convention engages in world mission through Canadian Baptist International Ministries, the
all-Canada mission agency. In addition to an active
program of home mission, evangelism, training,
social action and stewardship, the Convention
operates ten senior citizen complexes and a Christian bookstore.

HEADQUARTERS
1655 Manawagonish Rd., Saint John, NB E2M
3Y2 Tel. (506)635-1922 Fax (506)635-0366
Media Contact, Dir. of Communications, Rev.
Douglas Hapeman

OFFICERS
Pres., Rev. Fred Smith
Exec. Min., Dr. Eugene Thompson
Dir. of Admn. & Treas., Mr. Daryl MacKenzie
Dir. of Home Missions & Church Planting, Dr.
Harry Gardner
Dir. of Evangelism, Rev. Malcolm Beckett
Dir. of Training, Ms. Marilyn McCormick
Dir. of Communications, Rev. Douglas Hapeman

PERIODICALS
The Atlantic Baptist; Tidings

Union d'Eglises Baptistes Françaises au Canada

Baptist churches in French Canada first came
into being through the labors of two missionaries
from Switzerland, Rev. Louis Roussy and Mme.
Henriette Feller, who arrived in Canada in 1835.
The earliest church was organized in Grande Ligne
(now St.-Blaise), Quebec in 1838.

By 1900 there were 7 churches in the province of
Quebec and 13 French-language Baptist churches
in the New England states. The leadership was
totally French Canadian.

By 1960, the process of Americanization had
caused the disappearance of the French Baptist
churches. During the 1960s, Quebec as a society,
began rapidly changing in all its facets: education,
politics, social values and structures. Mission,
evangelism and church growth once again flourished. In 1969, in response to the new conditions,
the Grande Ligne Mission passed control of its
work to the newly formed Union of French Baptist
Churches in Canada, which then included 8
churches. By 1990 the French Canadian Baptist
movement had grown to include 25 congregations.

The Union d'Églises Baptistes Françaises au
Canada is a member body of the Canadian Baptist
Federation and thus is affiliated with the Baptist
World Alliance.

HEADQUARTERS
2285 avenue Papineau, Montreal, QC H2K 4J5 Tel.
(514)526-6643
Media Contact, Sec. Gen., John S. Gilmour

OFFICERS
Sec. Gen., ——

PERIODICAL
Le Trait D'Union

Canadian Conference of Mennonite Brethren Churches

The conference was incorporated Nov. 22, 1945.

HEADQUARTERS
3-169 Riverton Ave., Winnipeg, MB R2L 2E5 Tel.
(204)669-6575 Fax (204)654-1865
Media Contact, Conf. Min., Ike Bergen

OFFICERS
Mod., Abe Konrad, 12404-40 Ave., Edmonton,
AB T6J 0S5 Tel. (403)435-1074
Asst. Mod., Roland Marsch, 1420 Portage Ave.,
Winnipeg, MB R3G 0W2 Tel. (204)774-4414
Sec., Peter Enns, 34676 Skyline Dr., Abbotsford,
BC V2S 1H8 Tel. (604)859-5097

PERIODICALS
Mennonite Brethren Herald; Mennonitische Rundschau; IdeaBank; Le Lien; Expression

Canadian Convention of Southern Baptists

The Canadian Convention of Southern Baptists was formed at the Annual Meeting, May 7-9, 1985, in Kelowna, British Columbia. It was formerly known as the Canadian Baptist Conference, founded in Kamloops, British Columbia, in 1959 by pastors of existing churches.

HEADQUARTERS
Postal Bag 300, Cochrane, AB T0L 0W0 Tel. (403)932-5688 Fax (403)932-4937
Media Contact, Exec. Dir.-Treas., Rev. Allen E. Schmidt

OFFICERS
Exec. Dir.-Treas., Allen E. Schmidt, Box 7, Site 4, R.R. 1, Cochrane, AB T0L 0W0
Pres., Rev. Robert Shelton, Garden Park Baptist Church, Box 9, Group 256, RR 2, Winnipeg, MB R3C 2E6

PERIODICAL
The Baptist Horizon

Canadian District of the Moravian Church in America, Northern Province

The work in Canada is under the general oversight and rules of the Moravian Church, Northern Province, general offices for which are located in Bethlehem, PA. For complete information, see "Religious Bodies in the United States" section of the *Yearbook*.

HEADQUARTERS
1021 Center St., P.O. Box 1245, Bethlehem, PA 18016-1245
Media Contact, Ed., *The Moravian*, The Rev. Hermann I. Weinlick

OFFICER
Pres., Rev. Allen L. Bergmann, 2304 38th St., Edmonton, AB T6L 4K9 Tel. (403)463-7084

Canadian Yearly Meeting of the Religious Society of Friends

The Canadian Yearly Meeting of the Religious Society of Friends was founded in Canada as an offshoot of the Quaker movement in Great Britain and colonial America. Genesee Yearly Meeting, founded 1834, Canada Yearly Meeting (Orthodox), founded in 1867, and Canada Yearly Meeting, founded in 1881, united in 1955 to form the Canadian Yearly Meeting. The Canadian Yearly Meeting is affiliated with the Friends United Meeting and the Friends General Conference. It is also a member of Friends World Committee for Consultation.

HEADQUARTERS
91A Fourth Ave., Ottawa, ON K1S 2L1 Tel. (613)235-8553 Fax (613)235-8553
Media Contact, Gen. Sec.-Treas., Anne Thomas

OFFICERS
Gen. Sec./Treas., Anne Thomas
Clk., Elaine Bishop
Archivist, Jane Zavitz Bond

Archives, Arthur G. Dorland, Pickering College, 389 Bayview St., Newmarket, ON L3Y 4X2 Tel. (416)895-1700

PERIODICALS
The Canadian Friend; Quaker Concern

Christ Catholic Church

The Christ Catholic Church, with cathedrals, churches and missions in both Canada and the United States, is a catholic communion established in 1968 to minister to the growing number of people seeking an experiential relationship with God. In 1992 the Christ Catholic Church merged with the Liberal Catholic Church of Ontario. It is working to bring together various branches of Old Catholicism into one united church.

HEADQUARTERS
5165 Palmer Ave., Niagara Falls, ON L2E 3T9 Tel. (905)354-2329 Fax (905)354-9934

OFFICERS
Presiding Bishop, The Most Rev. Donald W. Mullan

PERIODICAL
St. Luke Magazine

Christadelphians in Canada

For a description of the Christadelphians, see the chapter "Religious Bodies in the United States." Free literature on Bible topics is available on request.

HEADQUARTERS
P.O. Box 57513, Weston, ON M9P 3V5

Christian and Missionary Alliance in Canada

A Canadian movement, dedicated to the teaching of Jesus Christ the Saviour, Sanctifier, Healer and Coming King, commenced in Toronto in 1887 under the leadership of the Rev. John Salmon. Two years later, the movement united with The Christian Alliance of New York, founded by Rev. A. B. Simpson, becoming the Dominion Auxiliary of the Christian Alliance, Toronto, under the presidency of the Hon. William H. Howland. Its four founding branches were Toronto, Hamilton, Montreal, and Quebec. By Dec. 31, 1992, there were 348 churches across Canada, with 1099 official workers, including a worldwide missionary force of 258.

In 1980, the Christian and Missionary Alliance in Canada became autonomous. Its General Assembly is held every two years.

HEADQUARTERS
Natl. Office, #510-105 Gordon Baker Rd., North York, ON M2H 3P8 Tel. (416)492-8775 Fax (416)492-7708
Media Contact, Dir. of Communications, Myrna McCombs

OFFICERS
Pres., Dr. Arnold Cook, Box 7900, Postal Sta. B, Willowdale, ON M2K 2R6
Vice-Pres./Personnel & Missions, Rev. Wallace C.E. Albrecht
Vice-Pres./Fin., Mr. Milton H. Quigg
Vice-Pres./Canadian Ministries, Rev. C. Stuart Lightbody
Vice-Pres./Gen. Services, Mr. Kenneth Paton

DISTRICT SUPERINTENDENTS

Canadian Pacific: Rev. Gordon R. Fowler
Western Canadian: Rev. Arnold Downey
Canadian Midwest: Rev. Arnold Reimer
Eastern and Central: Rev. Robert J. Gould
St. Lawrence: Rev. Jesse D. Jespersen

Christian Brethren (also known as Plymouth Brethren)

This orthodox and evangelical movement, which began in the British Isles in the 1820s, is now worldwide. For more detail on the history and theology, see "Religious Bodies in the United States" section of this *Yearbook*.

In the 1840s the movement divided. The "exclusive" branch, led by John Darby, stressed the interdependence of congregations. Canadian congregations number approximately 150, with an inclusive membership estimated at 11,000. The "open" branch of the movement, stressing evangelism and foreign missions, followed the leadership of George Muller in rejecting the "exclusive" principle of binding discipline and has escaped large-scale division.

Canadian congregations number approximately 450, with an inclusive membership estimated at 41,000. There are 250 "commended" full-time ministers, not including foreign missionaries.

HEADQUARTERS

Quebec: C.B.C. in the Province of Quebec, Sec., Norman R. Buchanan, 222 Alexander St., Sherbrooke, QC J1H 4S7
North America: Interest Ministries, Pres., Bruce R. McNicol, P.O. Box 190, Wheaton, IL 60189 Tel. (708)653-6573 Fax (708)653-6595
Media Contact, Editorial Asst., Naomi Bauman, P.O. Box 190, Wheaton, IL 60189 Tel. (708)653-6573 Fax (708)653-6595

OTHER ORGANIZATIONS

Missionary Service Comm., Exec. Dir., Claude Loney, 1562A Danforth Ave., Toronto, ON M4J 1N4 Tel. (416)469-2012
Vision Ontario, Dir., Gord Martin, P.O. Box 28032, Waterloo, ON N2L 6J8 Tel. (519)725-1212 Fax (519)725-9421

PERIODICAL

News of Quebec

Christian Church (Disciples of Christ) in Canada

Disciples have been in Canada since 1810 but were organized nationally in 1922 when the All-Canada Committee was formed. It seeks to serve the Canadian context as part of the whole Christian Church (Disciples of Christ) in the United States and Canada.

HEADQUARTERS

128 Woolwich St., #202, P.O. Box 64, Guelph, ON N1H 6J6 Tel. (519)823-5190 Fax (519)823-5190
Media Contact, Exec. Min., Robert W. Steffer

OFFICERS

Mod., Rev. Robert Dees, 6 Jedburgh, Toronto, ON M5M 3J6
Vice-Mod., Mrs. A. Elizabeth Manthorne, P.O. Box 156, Milton, NS B0T 1P0

Exec. Min., Rev. Dr. Robert W. Steffer, 7 Lynwood Dr., Guelph, ON N1G 1P8

PERIODICAL

Canadian Disciple

Christian Reformed Church in North America

Canadian congregations of the Christian Reformed Church in North America have been formed since 1908. For detailed information about this denomination, please refer to the listing for the Christian Reformed Church in North America in Chapter 3, "Religious Bodies in the United States."

HEADQUARTERS

United States Office: 2850 Kalamazoo Ave., S.E., Grand Rapids, MI 49560 Tel. (616)246-0744 Fax (616)246-0834
Canadian Office: 3475 Mainway, P.O. Box 5070, Burlington, ON L7R 3Y8 Tel. (416)336-2920 Fax (416)336-8344
Media Contact, Gen. Sec., Leonard J. Hofman, U.S. Office

OFFICERS

Gen. Sec., Rev. Leonard J. Hofman, U.S. Office
Exec. Dir./Ministries, Dr. Peter Borgdorff, U.S.Office
Fin. Coord., Harry J. Vander Meer, U.S. Office
Coun. of Christian Ref. Churches in Can., Exec. Sec., Arie G. Van Eek, Canadian Office

Church of God (Anderson, Ind.)

This body is one of the largest of the groups which have taken the name "Church of God." Its headquarters are at Anderson, Ind. It originated about 1880 and emphasizes Christian unity.

HEADQUARTERS

Western Canada Assembly, Chpsn., Jack Wagner, 4717 56th St., Camrose, AB T4V 2C4 Tel. (403)672-0772 Fax (403)672-6888
Eastern Canada Assembly, Chpsn., Jim Wiebe, 38 James St., Dundas, ON L9H 2J6
Media Contact for Western Canada, Church Service/Mission Coordinator, John D. Campbell

PERIODICALS

College News & Updates; The Gospel Contact; The Messenger

Church of God (Cleveland, Tenn.)

This body began in the United States in 1886 as the outgrowth of the holiness revival under the name Christian Union, and in 1902 it was reorganized as the Holiness Church. In 1907, the church adopted the name Church of God. Its doctrine is fundamental and Pentecostal, and it maintains a centralized form of government and an evangelistic and missionary program.

The first church in Canada was established in 1919 in Scotland Farm, Manitoba. Paul H. Walker became the first overseer of Canada in 1931.

HEADQUARTERS

Intl. Offices: 2490 Keith St., NW, Cleveland, TN 37311 Tel. (615)472-3361
Media Contact, Dir. of Publ. Relations, Michael L. Baker, P.O. Box 2430, Cleveland, TN 37320-2430 Tel. (615)472-7112 Fax (615)478-7066

OFFICERS

Exec. Office in Canada, Rev. Paul Clawson, P.O. Box 2036, Brampton, ON L6T 3T0 Tel. (416)793-2213

Western Canada, Rev. Philip F. Siggelkow, Box 54055, 2640 52 St. NE, Calgary, AB T1Y 6S6 Tel. (403)293-8817 Fax (403)293-8832

Church of God in Christ (Mennonite)

The Church of God in Christ, Mennonite was organized by the evangelist-reformer John Holdeman in Ohio. The church unites with the faith of the Waldenses, Anabaptists and other such groups throughout history. Emphasis is placed on obedience to the teachings of the Bible, including the doctrine of the new birth and spiritual life, noninvolvement in government or the military, a head-covering for women, beards for men and separation from the world shown by simplicity in clothing, homes, possessions and lifestyle. The church has a worldwide membership of about 15,000, largely concentrated in the United States and Canada.

HEADQUARTERS

P.O. Box 313, 420 N. Wedel Ave., Moundridge, KS 67107 Tel. (316)345-2532 Fax (316)345-2582

PERIODICAL

Messenger of Truth

The Church of God of Prophecy in Canada

In the late 19th century, people seeking God's eternal plan as they followed the Reformation spirit began to delve further for scriptural light concerning Christ and his church. A small group emerged which dedicated and covenanted themselves to God and one another to be the Church of God. On June 13, 1903, A.J. Tomlinson joined them during a period of intense prayer and Bible study. Under Tomlinson's dynamic leadership, the church enjoyed tremendous growth.

In 1923 two churches emerged. Those that opposed Tomlinson's leadership are known today in Canada as the New Testament Church of God. Tomlinson's followers are called the Church of God of Prophecy.

In Canada, the first Church of God of Prophecy congregation was organized in Swan River, Manitoba, in 1937. Churches are now established in British Columbia, Manitoba, Alberta, Saskatchewan, Ontario, Quebec and all 50 states.

The church accepts the whole Bible rightly divided, with the New Testament as the rule of faith and practice, government and discipline. The membership upholds the Bible as the inspired Word of God and believes that its truths are known by the illumination of the Holy Spirit. The Trinity is recognized as one supreme God in three persons—Father, Son and Holy Ghost. It is believed that Jesus Christ, the virgin-born Son of God, lived a sinless life, fulfilled his ministry on earth, was crucified, resurrected and later ascended to the right hand of God. Believers now await Christ's return to earth and the establishment of the millenial kingdom.

HEADQUARTERS

Canadian Headquarters: 1st Line East, RR #2, Brampton, ON L6V 1A1 Tel. (416)843-2379

World Headquarters: Bible Place, P.O. Box 2910, Cleveland, TN 37320-2910

Media Contact, Natl. Overseer, Bishop Wade H. Phillips, P.O. Box 457, Brampton, ON L6V 1A1 Tel. (416)843-2379

OFFICERS

Canada East, Natl. Overseer, Bishop Wade H. Phillips, P.O. Box 457, Brampton, ON L6V 2L4 Tel. (416)843-2379

Canada West, Natl. Overseer, Bishop Vernon Van Deventer, Box 952, Strathmore, AB T0J 3H0 Tel. (403)934-4787

BOARD OF DIRECTORS

Pres., Bishop Wade H. Phillips

Vice-Pres., Bishop Vernon Van Deventer

Sec., John Anderson

Members: Bishop Billy Murray; Bishop Adrian Varlack; Bishop A. R. Morrison; Bishop Leroy V. Greenaway

PERIODICAL

Canadian Trumpeter Canada-West

The Church of Jesus Christ of Latter-day Saints in Canada

This body has only stake and mission offices in Canada. Elders Cree-L Kofford, Yoshihiko Kikuchi and Durrell Woolsey of the Quorum of the Seventy oversee the church's activities in Canada. They reside in Salt Lake City, Utah. All General Authorities may be reached at the headquarters. [See U.S. Directory, "Religious Bodies in the United States" in this edition for further details.] In Canada there are 34 stakes, 6 missions, 9 districts and 391 wards/branches (congregations).

HEADQUARTERS

50 East North Temple St., Salt Lake City, UT 84150

Media Contact, Public Affairs Dir., William & Donna Smart, 91 Scenic Millway, North York, ON M2L 1S9 Tel. (416)441-0452 Fax (416)441-0457

PERIODICALS

Church News; The Ensign

Church of the Lutheran Brethren

Organized in Milwaukee, Wis. in 1900, the Church of the Lutheran Brethren adheres to the Lutheran Confessions and accepts into membership those who profess a personal faith in Jesus Christ.

For detailed information, see listing in "Religious Bodies in the United States" in this edition.

HEADQUARTERS

1007 Westside Dr., P.O. Box 655, Fergus Falls, MN 56538 Tel. (218)739-3336 Fax (218)739-5514

Media Contact, Pres., Rev. Robert M. Overgaard

Church of the Nazarene

The first Church of the Nazarene in Canada was organized in November, 1902, by Dr. H. F. Reynolds. It was in Oxford, Nova Scotia. The Church of the Nazarene is Wesleyan Arminian in theology, representative in church government and warmly evangelistic.

73800-19 St., N.E., Calgary, AB T2E 6V2
Media Contact, Gen. Sec., Dr. Jack Stone, 6401
The Paseo, Kansas City, MO 64131 Tel.
(816)333-7000

Exec. Admn., Neil Hightower, Tel. (403)247-3193
Chmn., Rev. William Stewart, 14 Hollywood Dr.,
Moncton, NB E1E 2R5
Vice-Chmn., Charles Muxworthy, Ste. 205, 1255
56th St., Delta, BC V4L 2B9
Sec., Murray Sandell, Box 2610, Windsor, NS B0N
T2O

Churches of Christ in Canada

Churches of Christ are autonomous congregations, whose members appeal to the Bible alone to determine matters of faith and practice. There are no central offices or officers. Publications and institutions related to the churches are either under local congregational control or independent of any one congregation.

Churches of Christ shared a common fellowship in the 19th century with the Christian Churches/Churches of Christ and the Christian Church (Disciples of Christ). Fellowship was broken after the introduction of instrumental music in worship and centralization of church-wide activities through a missionary society. Churches of Christ began in Canada soon after 1800, largely in the middle provinces. The few pioneer congregations were greatly strengthened in the mid-1800s, growing in size and number.

Members of Churches of Christ believe in the inspiration of the Scriptures, the divinity of Jesus Christ, and immersion into Christ for the remission of sins. The New Testament pattern is followed in worship and church organization.

Media Contact, Man. Ed., Gospel Herald, Eugene
C. Perry, 4904 King St., Beansville, ON L0R 1B6
Tel. (416)563-7503 Fax (416)563-7503

Gospel Herald; Good News West

Conference of Mennonites in Canada

The Conference of Mennonites in Canada began in 1902 as an organized fellowship of Mennonite immigrants from Russia clustered in southern Manitoba and around Rosthern, Saskatchewan. The first annual sessions were held in July, 1903. Its members hold to traditional Christian beliefs, believer's baptism and congregational polity. They emphasize practical Christianity: opposition to war, service to others and personal ethics. Further immigration from Russia in the 1920s and 1940s increased the group which is now located in all provinces from New Brunswick to British Columbia. This conference is affiliated with the General Conference Mennonite Church whose offices are at Newton, Kan.

600 Shaftesbury Blvd., Winnipeg, MB R3P 0M4
Tel. (204)888-6781 Fax (204)831-5675
Media Contact, Gen. Sec., Helmut Harder

Chpsn., Menno Epp, 78 Oak St. E., Leamington,
ON N8H 2C6
Vice-Chpsn., Gerd Bartel, 62500 49 Ave., Delta, BC
V4K 4S5
Sec., Mary Anne Loeppky, Box 973, Altona, MB
R0G 0B0
Gen. Sec., Helmut Harder

Mennonite Reporter

Congregational Christian Churches in Canada

This body originated in the early 18th century when devout Christians within several denominations in the northern and eastern United States, dissatisfied with sectarian controversy, broke away from their own denominations and took the simple title "Christians." First organized in 1821 at Keswick, Ontario, the Congregational Christian Churches in Canada was incorporated on Dec. 4, 1989, as a national organization. In doctrine the body is evangelical, being governed by the Bible as the final authority in faith and practice. It believes that Christian character must be expressed in daily living; it aims at the unity of all true believers in Christ that others may believe in Him and be saved. In church polity, the body is democratic and autonomous. It is also a member of The World Evangelical Congregational Fellowship.

P.O. Box 4688, Brantford, ON N3T 6H2 Tel.
(519)751-0606
Media Contact, Pres., Rev. John Tweedie, 48 Sky
Acres Dr., Brantford, ON N3R 1P3 Tel.
(519)759-4692

Pres., Rev. John Tweedie
Exec. Dir., Rev. Walter Riegert
Sec., Mr. Garth McMillan

The Coptic Church in Canada

The Coptic Church in North America was begun in Canada in 1964 and was registered in the province of Ontario in 1965. The Coptic Church has spread since then to a number of locations in North America.

The governing body of each local church is an elected Board of Deacons. The Diocesan Council is the national governing body and meets at least once a year.

Archpriest, Fr. M. A. Marcos, St. Mark's Coptic
Orthodox Church, 41 Glendinning Ave., Agincourt, ON M1W 3E2 Tel. (416)494-4449

Elim Fellowship of Evangelical Churches and Ministers

The Elim Fellowship of Evangelical Churches and Ministers, a Pentecostal body, was established in 1984 as a sister organization of Elim Fellowship in the United States.

This is an association of churches, ministers and missionaries seeking to serve the whole body of Christ. It is Pentecostal and has a charismatic orientation.

30 Amelia St., Paris, ON N3L 3V5 Tel. (519)442-3288 Fax (519)442-1487
Ofc. Mgr., Larry Jones
Sec., Debbie Jones

OFFICERS
Pres., Errol Alchin
Vice-Pres., Winston Nunes, 4 Palamino Cres., Willowdale, ON M2K 1W1
Sec., Paul Heidt, 123 Woodlawn Ave., Brantford, ON N3V 1B4
Treas., Aubrey Phillips, 267 Steeple Chase Dr., Exton, PA 19341
President Emeritus, Carlton Spencer

COUNCIL OF ELDERS
Errol Alchin, Tel. (519)442-1310
Paul Heidt, Tel. (519)758-1335
Henk Katerberg, Tel. (519)821-2082
Winston Nunes, Tel. (416)225-4824
Aubrey Phillips, Tel. (706)745-3304
L. Dayton Reynolds, Tel. (716)624-2253

The Estonian Evangelical Lutheran Church
The Estonian Evangelical Lutheran Church (EELC) was founded in 1917 in Estonia and reorganized in Sweden in 1944. The teachings of the EELC are based on the Old and New Testaments, explained through the Apostolic, Nicean and Athanasian confessions, the unaltered Confession of Augsburg and other teachings found in the Book of Concord.

HEADQUARTERS
383 Jarvis St., Toronto, ON M5B 2C7 Tel. (416)925-5465
Media Contact, Archbishop, Rev. Udo Petersoo

OFFICERS
Archbishop, The Rev. Udo Petersoo
Bishop, ——
Gen. Sec., Dean Edgar Heinsoo

PERIODICAL
Eesti Kirik

The Evangelical Covenant Church of Canada
A Canadian denomination organized in Canada at Winnipeg in 1904 which is affiliated with the Evangelical Covenant Church of America and with the International Federation of Free Evangelical Churches, which includes churches in 11 European countries.

This body believes in the one triune God as confessed in the Apostles' Creed, that salvation is received through faith in Christ as Saviour, that the Bible is the authoritative guide in all matters of faith and practice. Christian Baptism and the Lord's Supper are accepted as divinely ordained sacraments of the church. As descendants of the 19th century northern European pietistic awakening, the group believes in the need of a personal experience of commitment to Christ, the development of a virtuous life and the urgency of spreading the gospel to the "ends of the world."

HEADQUARTERS
245 21st St. E., Prince Albert, SK S6V 1L9 Tel. (306)922-3449 Fax (306)922-5414

Media Contact, Supt., Rev. Jerome Johnson, 8-7224 Neal St., Vancouver, BC V6P 3N7 Tel. (604)321-7004 Fax (604)321-7004

OFFICERS
Supt., Rev. Jerome Johnson
Chpsn., Marlowe Hanson, Ste 209, 13910 101 Ave., Surrey, BC V3T 1L6
Sec., Elnice Doell, RR #2, Wetaskiwin, AB T9A 1W9
Treas., Grace McKenzie, 60 Bowerman Cres., Prince Albert, SK S6V 6G4

PERIODICAL
The Covenant Messenger

Evangelical Free Church of Canada
The Evangelical Free Churches in Canada celebrated 50 years of Free Church work under the American Evangelical Free Church by becoming incorporated as a Canadian organization on March 21, 1967. On July 8, 1984, the Evangelical Free Church of Canada was given its autonomy as a self-governing Canadian denomination.

HEADQUARTERS
Mailing Address, Box 56109, Valley Centre P.O., Langley, BC V3A 8B3 Tel. (604)888-8668 Fax (604)888-3108
Locational Address, 7600 Glover Rd., Langley, BC
Media Contact, Admn. Asst., Lily Moore

OFFICERS
Pres., Rev. Rick Penner
Mod., Mr. Dave Enns, 23 Watercress Rd., Winnipeg, MB R2J 2W2
Vice-Mod., Rev. Tim Seim, S.S. 1-3-131, Lethbridge, AB T1J 4B3
Fin. Chpsn., Mrs. Donna Pippus

Evangelical Lutheran Church in Canada
The Evangelical Lutheran Church in Canada was organized in 1985 through a merger of The Evangelical Lutheran Church of Canada (ELCC) and the Lutheran Church in America—Canada Section.

The merger is a result of an invitation issued in 1972 by the ELCC to the Lutheran Church in America—Canada Section and the Lutheran Church—Canada. Three-way merger discussions took place until 1978 when it was decided that only a two-way merger was possible. The ELCC was the Canada District of the ALC until autonomy in 1967.

The Lutheran Church in Canada traces its history back more than 200 years. Congregations were organized by German Lutherans in Halifax and Lunenburg County in Nova Scotia in 174⌐ German Lutherans, including many United ⌐mpire Loyalists, also settled in large numbers along the St. Lawrence and in Upper Canada. In the late 19th century, immigrants arrived from Scandinavia, Germany and central European countries, many via the United States. The Lutheran synods in the United States have provided the pastoral support and help for the Canadian church.

HEADQUARTERS
1512 St. James St., Winnipeg, MB R3H 0L2 Tel. (204)786-6707 Fax (204)783-7548
Media Contact, Bishop, Rev. Donald W. Sjoberg

OFFICERS

Bishop, Rev. Telmor G. Sartison
Vice-Pres., Janet Morley
Sec., Rev. Leon C. Gilbertson
Treas., Don Rosten

DIVISIONS AND OFFICES

Div. for Canadian Mission, Exec. Dir., Rev. James A. Chell
Div. for Church & Society, Exec. Dir., Rev. Dr. Kenneth C. Kuhn
Div. for College & Univ. Services, Exec. Dir., Rev. Dr. Lawrence Denef
Div. for Parish Life, Exec. Dir., Rev. Dr. Rolf Nosterud
Div. for Theological Educ. & Leadership, Exec. Dir., Rev. Dr. Lawrence Denef
Div. for World Mission, Exec. Dir., Rev. Peter E. Mathiasen
Ofc. for Communication, ——
Dept. of Fin. & Admn., Dir., Joan E. Nolting
Ofc. for Resource Dev., Exec. Dir., ——
Evangelical Lutheran Women, Pres., Marquise Sopher
Exec. Dir., Diane Doth Rehbein

SYNODS

Alberta and the Territories: Bishop, Rev. J. Robert Jacobson, 10014-81 Ave., Edmonton, AB T6E 1W8 Tel. (403)439-2636 Fax (403)433-6623
Eastern: Bishop, Rev. Dr. William D. Huras, 50 Queen St. N., Kitchener, ON N2H 6P4 Tel. (519)743-1461 Fax (519)743-4291
British Columbia: Bishop, Rev. Dr. Marlin Aadland, 80-10th Ave., E., New Westminster, BC V3L 4R5 Tel. (604)524-1318 Fax (604)524-9255
Manitoba/Northwestern Ontario: Bishop, Rev. Dr. G. W. Luetkeholelter, 201-3657 Roblin Blvd., Winnipeg, MB R3G 0E2 Tel. (204)889-3760 Fax (204)869-0272
Saskatchewan: Bishop, Rev. Allan A. Grundahl, Bessborough Towers, Rm. 707, 601 Spadina Cres. E., Saskatoon, SK S7K 3G8 Tel. (306)244-2474 Fax (306)664-8677

PERIODICALS

CLBI-Cross Roads; Canada Lutheran; Esprit

The Evangelical Mennonite Conference

The Evangelical Mennonite Conference came about as the result of a renewal movement among a small group of Mennonites in Southern Russia in 1812. Klaas Reimer, a Mennonite minister, had become concerned about the apparent decline of spiritual life in the church, lack of discipline and the church's backing of the Russian government in the Napoleonic War. Around 1812, Reimer and several others began separate worship services, emphasizing a more strict discipline and separation from the world. By 1814, they were organized as a separate group, called the Kleinegemeinde (small church).

Increasing pressure from the Russian government, particularly in the area of military conscription, finally led to a migration (1874 to 1875) of the entire group to North America. Fifty families settled in Manitoba and 36 families settled in Nebraska. Ties between the two segments gradually weakened, and eventually the U.S. group gave up its EMC identity.

The conference has passed through numerous difficult times and survived several schisms and migrations. Beginning in the 1940s, a growing vision for missions and concern for others fostered a new vitality and growth, reaching people from a variety of cultural backgrounds. Thirty-two of the 51 congregations are in Manitoba. In 1991 its membership passed 6,000. The conference has some 150 mission workers in 23 countries of the world.

HEADQUARTERS

Box 1268, 440 Main St., Steinbach, MB R0A 2A0 Tel. (204)326-6401 Fax (204)326-1613
Media Contact, Conf. Sec., Don Thiessen

OFFICERS

Conf. Mod., John Koop, Box 129, Kleefeld, MB R0A 0V0
Bd. of Missions, Exec. Sec., Henry Klassen

PERIODICAL

The Messenger

Evangelical Mennonite Mission Conference

This group was founded in 1936 as the Rudnerweider Mennonite Church in Southern Manitoba and organized as the Evangelical Mennonite Mission Conference in 1959. It was incorporated in 1962. The Annual Conference meeting is held in July.

HEADQUARTERS

Box 52059, Niakwa P.O., Winnipeg, MB R2M 5P9 Tel. (204)253-7929 Fax (204)256-7384
Media Contact, David Penner, 635 Dalhousie Dr., Winnipeg, MB R3T 3R4

OFFICERS

Mod., Mr. David Penner, 635 Dalhousie Dr., Winnipeg, MB R3T 3R4
Vice-Mod., Frank Zacharias, 14-214 South St. W., Aylmer, ON N5H 3E6
Sec., Wes Hildebrand, 216-1660 Henderson Hwy., Winnipeg, MB R2G 1H7
Exec. Sec., Henry Dueck

OTHER ORGANIZATIONS

Missions Dir., Rev. Leonard Sawatzky
The Gospel Message: Box 1622, Saskatoon, SK S7K 3R8 Tel. (306)242-5001 Fax (306)242-6115; 210-401-33rd St. W., Saskatoon, SK S7L 0V5 Tel. (306)242-5001; Radio Pastor, Rev. Ed Martens; Radio Admn., Ernest Friessen
Aylmer Bible School: Principal, Abe Harms, Box 246, Aylmer, ON N5H 2R9 Tel. (519)773-5095

PERIODICAL

EMMC Recorder

The Evangelical Missionary Church of Canada

This denomination in Canada is affiliated with the worldwide body of the Missionary Church. Historically part of the Anabaptist, Mennonite movement, it changed its name to the United Missionary Church in 1947 and in 1969 it merged with the Missionary Church Association of Fort Wayne, Indiana. It is an evangelical, missionary church and became an autonomous national church in Canada in 1987.

147

HEADQUARTERS

Media Contact, Asst. to the Pres., Mr. C. Murray Bennett, 89 Centre Ave., North York, ON M2M 2L7 Tel. (416)223-3019 Fax (416)229-4017

OFFICERS

Pres., Rev. David Crouse, 89 Centre Ave., North York, ON M2M 2L7 Tel. (416)223-3019 Fax (416)229-4017

Canada East District: Dist. Supt., Rev. Lloyd Fretz, 130 Fergus Ave., Kitchener, ON N2A 2H2

Canada West District: Dist. Supt., Rev. David Crouse, #309, 259 Midpark Way S.E., Calgary, AB T2X 1M2

The Fellowship of Evangelical Baptist Churches in Canada

This organization was founded in 1953 by the merging of the Union of Regular Baptist Churches of Ontario and Quebec with the Fellowship of Independent Baptist Churches of Canada.

HEADQUARTERS

679 Southgate Dr., Guelph, ON N1G 4S2 Tel. (519)821-4830 Fax (519)821-9829

Media Contact, Pres., Rev. Terry D. Cuthbert

OFFICERS

Pres., Rev. Terry D. Cuthbert
Chmn., Mr. Gordon Johnson

PERIODICALS

B.C. Fellowship Baptist; Intercom; Evangelical Baptist Magazine

Foursquare Gospel Church of Canada

The Western Canada District was formed in 1964 with the Rev. Roy Hicks as supervisor. Prior to 1964 it had been a part of the Northwest District of the International Church of the Foursquare Gospel with headquarters in Portland, Oregon.

A Provincial Society, The Church of the Foursquare Gospel of Western Canada, was formed in 1976; a Federal corporation, the Foursquare Gospel Church of Canada, was incorporated in 1981 and a national church formed.

HEADQUARTERS

#200-3965 Kingsway, Burnaby, BC V5H 1Y7

Media Contact, Pres. & Gen. Supervisor, Timothy J. Peterson, Tel. (604)439-9567 Fax (604)439-1451

OFFICERS

Pres. & Gen. Supervisor, Timothy J. Peterson

Free Methodist Church in Canada

The Free Methodist Church was founded in New York in 1860 and expanded to Canada in 1880. It is Methodist in doctrine, evangelical in ministry and emphasizes the teaching of holiness of life through faith in Jesus Christ.

The Free Methodist Church in Canada was incorporated in 1927 after the establishment of a Canadian Executive Board. In 1959 the Holiness Movement Church merged with the Free Methodist Church. Full autonomy for the Canadian church was realized in 1990 with the formation of a Canadian General Conference. Mississauga, Ontario, continues to be the location of the Canadian Headquarters.

The Free Methodist Church ministers in 28 countries through its World Ministries Center in Indianapolis, Indiana. Aldersgate College in Moose Jaw, Saskatchewan, is the church's Canadian college.

HEADQUARTERS

4315 Village Centre Ct., Mississauga, ON L4Z 1S2 Tel. (905)848-2600 Fax (905)848-2603

Media Contact, Rev. Paul G. Johnston

OFFICERS

Pres., Bishop Gary R. Walsh
Exec. Dir.-Treas., Rev. Paul G. Johnston
Stewardship Dir., Rev. Keith E. Lohnes
Canada East Conference Supt., Rev. Robert J. Buchanan, Box 670 (101-3 Applewood Dr.), Belleville, ON K8N 5B3 Tel. (613)968-8511 Fax (613)968-6190
Canada Great Lakes Conference Supt., Rev. Laverne W. Bates, 30 King St., Brantford, ON N3T 3C5 Tel. (519)753-7390
Canada West Conference Supt., Rev. Dennis H. Camplin, 7-3012 Louise St., Saskatoon, SK S7J 3L8 Tel. (306)955-3320

PERIODICAL

The Free Methodist Herald

Free Will Baptists

As revival fires burned throughout New England in the mid- and late 1700s, Benjamin Randall proclaimed his doctrine of Free Will to large crowds of seekers. In due time, a number of Randall's converts moved to Nova Scotia. One such believer was Asa McGray, who was to become instrumental in the establishment of several Free Baptist churches. Local congregations were organized in New Brunswick. After several years of numerical and geographic gains, disagreements surfaced over the question of music, Sunday school, church offerings, salaried clergy and other issues. Adherents of the more progressive element decided to form their own fellowship. Led by George Orser, they became known as Free Christian Baptists.

The new group faithfully adhered to the truths and doctrines which embodied the theological basis of Free Will Baptists. Largely through Archibald Hatfield, contact was made with Free Will Baptists in the United States in the 1960s. The association was officially welcomed into the Free Will Baptist family in July 1981, by the National Association.

HEADQUARTERS

RR 6, Woodstock, NB E0J 2B0 Tel. (506)325-9381

Media Contact, Oral McAffee

OFFICER

Mod., Mr. Oral McAffee

General Church of the New Jerusalem

The Church of the New Jerusalem is founded on the Writings of Emanuel Swedenborg (1688-1772). These were first brought to Ontario in 1835 by Christian Enslin.

HEADQUARTERS

40 Chapel Hill Dr., Kitchener, ON N2G 3W5 Tel. (519)748-5802

Media Contact, Exec. Vice-Pres., Rev. Louis D. Synnestvedt

Pres., Rt. Rev. P. M. Buss, Bryn Athyn, PA 19009
Exec. Vice-Pres., Rev. Louis D. Synnestvedt
Sec., Penny Orr, 208-21 Richgrove Dr., Weston, ON M9R 2L2
Treas., Peter Bailey, 36 Moffat Ave., Brampton, ON L6Y 2M8

New Church Canadian

Greek Orthodox Diocese of Toronto (Canada)

Greek Orthodox Christians in Canada are under the jurisdiction of the Ecumenical Patriarchate of Constantinople (Istanbul).

27 Teddington Park Ave., Toronto, ON M4N 2C4 Tel. (416)322-5055
Media Contact, Sec. to the Bishop, Fr. Stavros Moschos, Tel. (416)485-5929

Primate of the Archdiocese of North & South America, The Most Rev. Iakovos
Bishop of the Diocese of Toronto, The Rt. Rev. Bishop Sotirios

Independent Assemblies of God—Canada

This fellowship of churches has been operating in Canada for over 25 years. It is a branch of the Pentecostal Church in Sweden. Each church within the fellowship is completely independent.

1211 Lancaster St., London, ON N5V 2L4 Tel. (519)451-1751
Media Contact, Gen. Sec., Rev. Harry Wuerch

Gen. Sec., Rev. Harry Wuerch

The Mantle

Independent Holiness Church

The former Holiness Movement of Canada merged with the Free Methodist Church in 1958. Some churches remained independent of this merger and they formed the Independent Holiness Church in 1960, in Kingston, Ontario. The doctrines are Methodist and Wesleyan. The General Conference is every three years, next meeting in 1995.

Rev. R. E. Votary, Box 194, Sydenham, ON K0H 2T0 Tel. (613)376-3114
Media Contact, Gen. Sec., Dwayne Reaney, 5025 River Rd. RR #1, Manotick, ON K4M 1B2 Tel. (613)692-3237

Gen. Supt., Rev. R. E. Votary, Sydenham, ON K0H 2T0 Tel. (613)376-3114
Gen. Sec., Mr. Dwayne Reaney
Additional Officers: E. Brown, 104-610 Pesehud-off Cresc., Saskatoon, SK S7N 4G7; D. Wallace, RR #3, Metcalfe, ON K0A 2P0

Gospel Tidings

The Italian Pentecostal Church of Canada

This body had its beginnings in Hamilton, Ontario, in 1912 when a few people of an Italian Presbyterian Church banded themselves together for prayer and received a Pentecostal experience of the baptism in the Holy Spirit. Since 1912, there has been a close association with the teachings and practices of the Pentecostal Assemblies of Canada.

The work spread to Toronto, then to Montreal, where it also flourished. In 1959, the church was incorporated in the province of Quebec. The early leaders of this body were the Rev. Luigi Ippolito and the Rev. Ferdinand Zaffuto. The churches carry on their ministry in both the English and Italian languages.

6724 Fabre St., Montreal, QC H2G 2Z6 Tel. (514)593-1944
Media Contact, Gen. Sec., Rev. John DellaForesta, 6550 Maurice Duplesis, Montreal North, QC H1G 6K9 Tel. (514)323-3087

Gen. Supt., Rev. Alberico De Vito, 7685 Tremblay St., Brossard, QC J4W 2W2 Tel. (514)465-2846
Gen. Sec., Rev. John DellaForesta, 6550 Maurice Duplesis, Montreal North, QC H1G 6K9 Tel. (514)323-3087
Gen. Treas., Mr. Joseph Manafò, Tel. (514)593-1833
Overseer, Rev. Mario Spiridigliozz, 505 Nanaimo St., Vancouver, BC V5L 4S2 Tel. (604)255-0423
Overseer, Rev. Daniel Ippolito, 384 Sunnyside, Toronto, ON M6R 2S1 Tel. (416)766-6692 Fax (416)766-8014

Voce Evangelica/Evangel Voice

Jehovah's Witnesses

For details on Jehovah's Witnesses see "Religious Bodies in United States" in this edition of the *Yearbook*.

25 Columbia Heights, Brooklyn, NY 11201 Tel. (718)625-3600
Canadian Branch Office: Box 4100, Halton Hills, ON L7G 4Y4
Media Contact, Robert P. Johnson

The Latvian Evangelical Lutheran Church in America

This body was organized into a denomination on Aug. 22, 1975, after having existed as the Federation of Latvian Evangelical Lutheran Churches in America since 1955. This church is a regional constituent part of the Lutheran Church of Latvia in Exile, a member of the Lutheran World Federation and the World Council of Churches.

The Latvian Evangelical Lutheran Church in America works to foster religious life, tradition and customs in its congregations in harmony with the Holy Scriptures, the Apostles', Nicene and Athanasian Creeds, the unaltered Augsburg Confession, Martin Luther's Small and Large Catechisms and other documents of the Book of Concord.

The LELCA is ordered by its Synod, executive board, auditing committee and district conferences.

HEADQUARTERS

6551 W. Montrose Ave., Chicago, IL 60634-1499
Tel. (312)725-3820 Fax (312)725-3835
Media Contact, Pres., Rev. Vilis Varsbergs

Lutheran Church—Canada

The Lutheran Church was established in 1959 at Edmonton, Alberta, as a federation of Canadian districts of the Lutheran Church, Missouri Synod; it was constituted in 1988 at Winnipeg, Manitoba, as an autonomous church.

The church confesses the Bible as both inspired and infallible, the only source and norm of doctrine and life and subscribes without reservation to the Lutheran Confessions as contained in the Book of Concord of 1580.

HEADQUARTERS

200-1625 Dublin Ave., Winnipeg, MB R3H 0W3
Tel. (204)772-0676 Fax (204)772-1090
Media Contact, Pres., Dr. Edwin Lehman

OFFICERS

Pres., Rev. Edwin Lehman
Vice-Pres., Rev. Karl Koslowsky, 871 Cavalier Dr., Winnipeg, MB R2Y 1C7
2nd Vice-Pres., Rev. Dennis Putzman, 24 Valencia Dr., St. Catharines, ON L2T 3X8
3rd Vice-Pres., Rev. Ralph Mayan, 8631 Wagner Dr., Richmond, BC V7A 4N2
Sec., Rev. William Ney, 7100 Ada Blvd., Edmonton, AB T5B 4E4
Treas., Mr. Ken Werschler

DISTRICT OFFICES

Alberta-British Columbia: Pres., Rev. H. Ruf, 7100 Ada Blvd., Edmonton, AB T5B 4E4 Tel. (403)474-0063 Fax (403)477-9829
Central: Pres., Dr. R. Holm, 1927 Grant Dr., Regina, SK S4S 4V6 Tel. (306)586-4434 Fax (306)586-0656
East: Pres., Dr. R. Winger, 275 Lawrence Ave., Kitchener, ON N2M 1Y3 Tel. (519)578-6500 Fax (519)578-3369

PERIODICALS

Update; Canadian Lutheran

Netherlands Reformed Congregations of North America

The Netherlands Reformed Congregations, presently numbering 162 congregations in the Netherlands (90,000 members), 25 congregations in North America (10,000 members) and a handful of congregations in various other countries, organized denominationally in 1907. The so-called Churches Under the Cross (established in 1839 after breaking away from the 1834 secession congregations) and the so-called Ledeboerian churches (established in 1841 under the leadership of Rev. Ledeboer who seceded from the Reformed state church), united in 1907 under the leadership of the then 25-year-old Rev. G. H. Kersten to form the Netherlands Reformed Congregations (Gereformeerde Gemeenten).

Many of the North American congregations left the Christian Reformed Church to join the Netherlands Reformed Congregations after the Kuyperian presupposed regeneration doctrine began making serious inroads into that denomination.

All Netherlands Reformed congregations, office bearers and members subscribe to three Reformed Forms of Unity: the Belgic Confession of Faith (by DeBres), the Heidelberg Catechism and the Canons of Dordt. The Belgic Confession and Canons of Dordt are read regularly at worship services, and the Heidelberg Catechism is preached weekly except on church feast days.

The NRC stresses the traditional Reformed doctrines of grace, such as the sovereignty of God, responsibility of humankind, the necessity of the new birth and the experience of God's sanctifying grace.

HEADQUARTERS

Media Contact, Clk. of Synod, Dr. Joel R. Beeke, 2115 Romence Ave., NE, Grand Rapids, MI 49503 Tel. (616)459-6565 Fax (616)459-7709

OFFICERS

Clk. of Synod, Dr. Joel R. Beeke

PERIODICAL

Insight Into

North American Baptist Conference

Churches belonging to this conference emanated from German Baptist immigrants of more than a century ago. Although scattered across Canada and the U.S., they are bound together by a common heritage, a strong spiritual unity, a Bible-centered faith and a deep interest in missions.

Note: The details of general organization, officers, and periodicals of this body will be found in the North American Baptist Conference directory in the "Religious Bodies in the United States" section of this *Yearbook*.

HEADQUARTERS

1 S. 210 Summit Ave., Oakbrook Terrace, IL 60181 Tel. (708)495-2000 Fax (708)495-3301
Media Contact, Dev. Dept. Dir., Dr. Lewis Petrie

OFFICER

Exec. Dir., Dr. John Binder

The Old Catholic Church of Canada

The church was founded in 1948 in Hamilton, Ontario. The first bishop was the Rt. Rev. George Davis. The Old Catholic Church of Canada accepts all the doctrines of the Eastern Orthodox Churches and, therefore, not Papal Infallibility or the Immaculate Conception. The ritual is Western (Latin Rite) and is in the vernacular language. Celibacy is optional. The Old Catholic Church of Canada is affiliated with the North American Old Roman Catholic Church, whose Presiding Bishop is Most Rev. Theodore Rematt of Chicago (see the directory in the "Religious Bodies in the United States" section of this *Yearbook*).

HEADQUARTERS

RR #1, Midland, ON L4R 4K3 Tel. (705)835-6940
Media Contact, Bishop, The Most Rev. David Thomson

OFFICER

Bishop, The Most Rev. David Thomson

Old Order Amish Church

This is the most conservative branch of the Mennonite Church and direct descendants of Swiss Brethren (Anabaptists) who emerged from the Reformation in Switzerland in 1525. The Amish, followers of Bishop Jacob Ammann, became a distinct group in 1693. They began migrating to North America about 1720; all of them still reside in the United States or Canada. They first migrated to Ontario in 1824 directly from Bavaria, Germany and also from Pennsylvania and Alsace-Lorraine. Since 1953 some Amish have migrated to Ontario from Ohio, Indiana and Iowa.

In 1992 there were 17 congregations in Ontario, each being autonomous. No membership figures are kept by this group, and there is no central headquarters. Each congregation is served by a bishop, two ministers and a deacon, all of whom are chosen from among the male members by lot for life.

CORRESPONDENT
Pathway Publishers, David Luthy, Rt. 4, Aylmer, ON N5H 2R3

PERIODICALS
Blackboard Bulletin; The Budget; The Diary; Die Botschaft; Family Life; Herold der Wahrheit; Young Companion

The Open Bible Standard Churches of Canada

This is the Canadian branch of the Open Bible Standard Churches, Inc., USA of Des Moines, Iowa. It is an evangelical, full gospel denomination emphasizing evangelism, missions and the message of the Open Bible. The Canadian Branch was chartered Jan. 7, 1982.

HEADQUARTERS
Bramalea Christian Fellowship, Lot 17, RR #4, Bramalea Rd. N., Bramalea, ON L6T 3S1 Tel. (905)799-2400
Media Contact, Gen. Overseer, Dr. Peter Morgan

Orthodox Church in America (Canada Section)

The Archdiocese of Canada of the Orthodox Church in America was established in 1926. First organized by St. Tikhon, martyr Patriarch of Moscow, previously Archbishop of North America, it is part of the Russian Metropolia and its successor, the autocephalous Orthodox Church in America.

The Archdiocesan Council meets twice yearly, the General Assembly of the Archdiocese takes place every three years.

HEADQUARTERS
P.O. Box 179, Spencerville, ON K0E 1X0 Tel. (613)925-5226 Fax (613)925-1521

OFFICERS
Bishop of Ottawa & Canada, The Rt. Rev. Seraphim
Chancellor, V. Rev. John Tkachuk, P.O. Box 1390, Place Bonaventure, Montreal, QC H5A 1H3 Tel. (514)481-5093 Fax same
Treas., Mr. Nikita Lopoukhine, 55 Clarey Ave., Ottawa, ON K1S 2R6
Eastern Sec., Olga Jurgens

Western Sec., Deacon Andrew Piasta, Box 25, Site 5, RR #2, Winterburn, AB T0E 2N0 Tel. (403)987-4500 Fax same

ARCHDIOCESAN COUNCIL
Clergy Members: V. Rev. Nicolas Boldireff; V. Rev. Orest Olekshy; Rev. Andrew Morbey; Rev. Dennis Pihach; Rev. Larry Reinheimer; Protodeacon Cyprian Hutcheon
Lay Members: Audrey Ewanchuk; Yves Drolet; Nicholas Ignatieff; David Grier; John Hadjinicolaou; Rhoda Zion
Ex Officio: Chancellor; Treas.; Eastern Sec.; Western Sec.

REPRESENTATIVES TO METROPOLITAN COUNCIL
Rev. Andrew Morbey
Mary Ann Lopoukhine

PERIODICAL
Canadian Orthodox Messenger

Patriarchal Parishes of the Russian Orthodox Church in Canada

This is the diocese of Canada of the former Exarchate of North and South America of the Russian Orthodox Church. It was originally founded in 1897 by the Russian Orthodox Archdiocese in North America.

HEADQUARTERS
St. Barbara's Russian Orthodox Cathedral, 10105 96th St., Edmonton, AB T5H 2G3
Media Contact, Sec.-Treas., Victor Lopushinsky, #303 9566-101 Ave., Edmonton, AB T5H 0B4 Tel. (403)455-9071

OFFICER
Admn., Bishop of Zaraisk, Most Rev. Pavel, 10812-108 St., Edmonton, AB T5H 3A6

The Pentecostal Assemblies of Canada

This body is incorporated under the Dominion Charter of 1919 and is also recognized in the Province of Quebec as an ecclesiastical corporation. Its beginnings are to be found in the revivals at the turn of the century, and most of the first Canadian Pentecostal leaders came from a religious background rooted in the Holiness movements.

The original incorporation of 1919 was implemented among churches of eastern Canada only. In the same year, a conference was called in Moose Jaw, Saskatchewan, to which the late Rev. J. M. Welch, general superintendent of the then-organized Assemblies of God in the U.S., was invited. The churches of Manitoba and Saskatchewan were organized as the Western District Council of the Assemblies of God. They were joined later by Alberta and British Columbia. In 1921, a conference was held in Montreal, to which the general chairman of the Assemblies of God was invited. Eastern Canada also became a district of the Assemblies of God, joining Eastern and Western Canada as two districts in a single organizational union.

In 1920, at Kitchener, Ontario, eastern and western churches agreed to dissolve the Canadian District of the Assemblies of God and unite under the name The Pentecostal Assemblies of Canada.

Today the Pentecostal Assemblies of Canada operate throughout the nation, and religious services are conducted in more than 27 languages in more than 200 ethnic churches. There are 109 native churches.

HEADQUARTERS

6745 Century Ave., Mississauga, ON L5N 6P7 Tel. (905) 542-7400 Fax (905) 542-7313
Media Contact, Gen. Supt., Rev. James M. MacKnight

OFFICERS

Gen. Supt., Rev. James M. MacKnight
Gen. Sec., Rev. William A. Griffin
Gen. Treas., Rev. Reuben L. Schmunk
Overseas Missions, Exec. Dir., Rev. Lester E. Markham
Church Ministries, Exec. Dir., Rev. Keith H. Parks
Home Missions & Bible Colleges, Exec. Dir., Rev. Kenneth B. Birch
Women's Ministries, Dir., Mrs. Eileen Stewart
Full Gospel Publishing House, Mgr., Mr. Harry E. Anderson

DISTRICT SUPERINTENDENTS

British Columbia: Rev. William R. Gibson, 5641 176 A St., Surrey, BC V3S 4G8 Tel. (604) 576-9421 Fax (604) 576-1499
Alberta: Rev. John A. Keys, 10585-111 St., #101, Edmonton, AB T5H 3E8 Tel. (403) 426-0084 Fax (403) 420-1318
Saskatchewan: Rev. L. Calvin King, 119-C Cardinal Cres., Saskatoon, SK S7L 6H5 Tel. (306) 652-6088 Fax (306) 652-0199
Manitoba: Rev. Gordon V. Peters, 187 Henlow Bay, Winnipeg, MB R3Y 1G4 Tel. (204) 488-6800 Fax (204) 489-0499
Western Ontario: Rev. W. D. Morrow, 3214 S. Service Rd., Burlington, ON L7M 3J2 Tel. (905) 637-5566 Fax (905) 637-7558
Eastern Ontario and Quebec: Rev. E. Stewart Hunter, Box 1600, Belleville, ON K8N 5J3 Tel. (613) 968-3422 Fax (613) 968-8715
Maritime Provinces: Rev. David C. Slauenwhite, Box 1184, Truro, NS B2N 5H1 Tel. (902) 895-4212 Fax (902) 897-0705

CONFERENCES

German Conference: Rev. Philip F. Kniesel, #310, 684 Belmont Ave., W, Kitchener, ON N2M 1N6
French Conference: Rev. Raymond Lemaire, 4975 Sir Wilfred Laurier Blvd., St. Hubert, QC J3Y 7R6
Slavic Conferences: Eastern District, Rev. Walter Senko, RR 1, Wilsonville, ON N0E 1Z0; Western District, Rev. Michael Brandebura, 4108-134 Ave., Edmonton, AB T5A 3M2
Finnish Conference: Rev. A. Wirkkala, 1920 Argyle Dr., Vancouver, BC V5P 2A8

PERIODICALS

Pentecostal Testimony; Resource: The National Leadership Magazine

Pentecostal Assemblies of Newfoundland

This body began in 1910 and held its first assembly at the Bethesda Pentecostal Mission at St. John's. It was incorporated in 1925 as the Bethesda Pentecostal Assemblies and changed its name in 1930 to the Pentecostal Assemblies of Newfoundland.

HEADQUARTERS

57 Thorburn Rd., St. John's, NF A1B 3N4 Tel. (709) 753-6314 Fax (709) 753-4945
Media Contact, Gen. Sec.-Treas., Clarence Buckle, P.O. Box 8895, Stn. A, St. John's, NF A1B 3T2 Tel. (709) 753-6314 Fax (709) 753-4945

OFFICERS

Pres. & Gen. Supt., Roy D. King, 50 Brownsdale St., St. John's, NF A1E 4R2
First Asst. Supt., B. Q. Grimes, 14 Chamberlain St., Grand Falls, NF A2A 2G4
Second Asst. Supt., H. E. Perry, P.O. Box 449, Lewisporte, NF A0G 3A0
Gen. Sec.-Treas., Clarence Buckle, P.O. Box 8895, Stn. A, St. John's, NF A1B 3T2

DEPARTMENTS

Youth & Sunday School, Dir., Robert H. Dewling, 26 Wicklow St., St. John's, NF A1B 3H2
Literature, Gen. Mgr., Clarence Buckle, P.O. Box 8895, Stn. A, St. John's, NF A1B 3T2
Women's Ministries, Dir., Mrs. Sylvia Purchase, Box 64, R.R. #3, Botwood, NF A0H 1E0
Men's Fellowship, Dir., Gordon W. Young, 7 Stamp's Ln., St. John's, NF A1E 3C9

PERIODICAL

Good Tidings

Pentecostal Holiness Church of Canada

The first General Conference convened in May, 1971 in Toronto. Prior to this, the Canadian churches were under the leadership of the Pentecostal Holiness Church in the U.S.A. The General Conference meets every four years. The next meeting is in 1994.

HEADQUARTERS

Box 442, Waterloo, ON N2J 4A9 Tel. (519) 746-1310

OFFICERS

Gen. Supt., Rev. Wayne Longard
Asst. Supt., Rev. Nicholas Murray
Asst. Supt., Rev. Vincent Brufatto
Asst. Supt., Rev. Ward Rowan

Presbyterian Church in America (Canadian Section)

Canadian congregations of the Reformed Presbyterian Church, Evangelical Synod, became a part of the Presbyterian Church in America when the RPCES joined PCA in June 1982. Some of the churches were in predecessor bodies of the RPCES, which was the product of a 1965 merger of the Reformed Presbyterian Church in North America, General Synod and the Evangelical Presbyterian Church. Others came into existence later as a part of the home missions work of RPCES. Congregations are located in six provinces, and the PCA is continuing church extension work in Canada. The denomination is committed to world evangelization and to a continuation of historic Presbyterianism. Its officers are required to subscribe to the Reformed faith as set forth in the Westminster Confession of Faith and Catechisms.

Media Contact, Correspondent, Doug Codling, Faith Reformed Presbyterian Church, 2581 E. 45th St., Vancouver, BC V5R 3B9 Tel. (604)438-8755

PERIODICAL
Coast to Coast

The Presbyterian Church in Canada

This is the nonconcurring portion of the Presbyterian Church in Canada that did not become a part of The United Church of Canada in 1925.

HEADQUARTERS
50 Wynford Dr., Don Mills, ON M3C 1J7 Tel. (416)441-1111 Fax (416)441-2825
Media Contact, Principal Clk., Rev. Thomas Gemmell

OFFICERS
Mod., Rev. Earle F. Roberts
Clks. of Assembly: Principal Clk., Rev. Thomas Gemmell; Dep. Clk., Dr. T. Plomp; Dep. Clk., Mrs. B. McLean
Assembly Council: Sec., Rev. Thomas Gemmell; Treas., Mr. G. Jones

NATIONAL BOARDS
Life & Mission Agency: Gen. Sec., Rev. Glen Davis; Sec. for Ministry, Rev. Jean Armstrong; Sec. for Educ. & Discipleship, Rev. John Bannerman; Sec. for Educ. & Discipleship, Mrs. Joyce Hodgson; Sec. for Educ. & Discipleship, Rev. Diane Strickland; Justice Ministries, Rev. Dr. Ray Hodgson; Canada Ministries, Rev. Ian Morrison; Intl. Ministries, Dr. Marjorie Ross; Presbyterian World Service & Dev., Dir., Rev. Richard Fee
Presbyterian Church Building Corp.: Dir., Rev. F. R. Kendall
Service Agency: Gen. Sec., Rev. Karen A. Hincke; Sec. for Resource Production, Rev. Glenn Cooper; Comp., D. A. Taylor
Women's Missionary Society (WD): Pres., Mrs. Kay Cowper, Hamilton, ON; Exec. Dir., Mrs. Tamiko Corbett
Atlantic Missionary Society (ED): Pres., Mrs. Dorothy Creighton, Chatham, NB

PERIODICALS
Channels; The Presbyterian Message; Presbyterian Record; Glad Tidings; La Vie Chrétienne

Reformed Church in Canada

The Canadian branch of the Reformed Church in America consists of 42 churches organized under the Council of the Reformed Church in Canada and within the classis of Ontario (24 churches), British Columbia (11 churches), Canadian Prairies (7 churches). The Reformed Church in America was established in 1628 by the earliest Dutch settlers in America as the Reformed Protestant Dutch Church. It is evangelical in theology and presbyterian in government.

HEADQUARTERS
Gen. Sec., Rev. Edwin G. Mulder, 475 Riverside Dr., Rm. 1811, New York, NY 10115 Tel. (212)870-2841 Fax (212)870-2499

Council of the Reformed Church in Canada, Exec. Sec., Rev. Dr. Jonathan N. Gerstner, Reformed Church Center, RR #4, Cambridge, ON N1R 5S5 Tel. (519)622-1777
Media Contact, Dir., Stewardship & Communications Services, Rev. E. Wayne Antworth, 475 Riverside Dr., New York, NY 10115 Tel. (212)870-2954 Fax (212)870-2499

The Reformed Episcopal Church

The Reformed Episcopal Church is a separate entity. It was established in Canada by an act of incorporation given royal assent on June 2, 1886. It maintains the founding principles of episcopacy (in historic succession from the apostles), Anglican liturgy and Reformed doctrine and evangelical zeal. In practice it continues to recognize the validity of certain nonepiscopal orders of evangelical ministry.

HEADQUARTERS
Office of the Secretary, 7822 Langley St., Burnaby, BC V3N 3Z8 Tel. (604)521-3580
Media Contact, Sec., Miss Eleanor R. MacQueen

OFFICERS
Pres., Rt. Rev. Wilbur W. Lyle, 1544 Broadview Cres., Coquitlam, BC V3J 5X9
Vice-Pres., Rt. Rev. E. A. Follows, Church of Our Lord, 626 Blanchard St., Victoria, BC V8W 3G6
Sec., Miss Eleanor R. MacQueen
Treas., Mr. Lorne Saxon, #307, 3330 Glasgow Ave., Victoria, BC V8X 1M6

Reinland Mennonite Church

This group was founded in 1958 when 10 ministers and approximately 600 members separated from the Sommerfelder Mennonite Church. In 1968, four ministers and about 200 members migrated to Bolivia. The church has work in six communities in Manitoba and one in Ontario.

HEADQUARTERS
Bishop William H. Friesen, P.O. Box 96, Rosenfeld, MB R0G 1X0 Tel. (204)324-6339
Media Contact, Deacon, Henry Wiebe, Box 2587, Winkler, MB R6W 4C3 Tel. (204)325-8487

Reorganized Church of Jesus Christ of Latter Day Saints

Founded April 6, 1830, by Joseph Smith, Jr., the church was reorganized under the leadership of the founder's son, Joseph Smith III, in 1860. The Church is established in 38 countries including the United States and Canada, with nearly a quarter of a million members. A biennial world conference is held in Independence, Missouri. The current president is Wallace B. Smith, great-grandson of the founder.

HEADQUARTERS
World Headquarters Complex: The Temple, P.O. Box 1059, Independence, MO 64051 Tel. (816)833-1000 Fax (816)521-3095
Ontario Regional Ofc.: 390 Speedvale Ave. E., Guelph, ON N1E 1N5
Media Contact, Public Relations Commissioner, Stephanie Kelley, World Headquarters

CANADIAN REGIONS AND DISTRICTS

North Plains & Prairie Provinces Region: Regional Admn., Alvin Mogg, 119 MacEwan Pack Heights NW, Calgary, AB T3K 3W6; Alberta District, John Nichol, 31 Croydon Rd., NW, Calgary, AB T2K 1S5; Saskatchewan District, Charles J. Lester, 629 East Place, Saskatoon, SK S7J 2Z1

Pacific Northwest Region: Regional Admn., Raymond Peter, P.O. Box 18469, 4820 Morgan, Seattle, WA 98118; British Columbia District, Dennis L. McKelvie, 207-25 Richmond St., New Westminster, BC V3L 5P9

Ontario Region: Regional Admn., Donald H. Comer, 390 Speedvale Ave. E., Guelph, ON N1E 1N5; Chatham District, David R. Wood, 127 Mount Pleasant Crescent, Wallaceburg, ON N8A 5A3; Grand River District, Douglas A. Robinson, 7 Kennedy Drive, Breslau, ON N0B 1M0; London District, John H. German, 354 Erie St., Port Stanley, ON N0L 2A0; Niagara District, Dennis Jones, P.O. Box 93001, Headon Postal Outlet, Burlington, ON L7M 4A3; Northern Ontario District, Donald Males, P.O. Box 662, New Liskeard, ON P0J 1P0; Ottawa District, Marion Smith, 70 Mayburry St., Hull, QC J9A 2E9; Owen Sound District, Robin M. Duff, P.O. Box 52, Owen Sound, ON N1K 5P1; Toronto Metropole, Larry D. Windland, 8142 Islington Ave. N., Woodridge, ON L4L 1B7

PERIODICAL

Saints Herald

The Roman Catholic Church in Canada

The largest single body of Christians in Canada, the Roman Catholic Church is under the spiritual leadership of His Holiness the Pope. Catholicism in Canada dates back to 1534, when the first Mass was celebrated on the Gaspé Peninsula on July 7, by a priest accompanying Jacques Cartier. Catholicism had been implanted earlier by fishermen and sailors from Europe. Priests came to Acadia as early as 1604. Traces of a regular colony go back to 1608 when Champlain settled in Quebec City. The Recollets (1615), followed by the Jesuits (1625) and the Sulpicians (1657), began the missions among the native population. The first official Roman document relative to the Canadian missions dates from March 20, 1618. Bishop François de Montmorency-Laval, the first bishop, arrived in Quebec in 1659. The church developed in the East, but not until 1818 did systematic missionary work begin in western Canada.

In the latter 1700s, English-speaking Roman Catholics, mainly from Ireland and Scotland, began to arrive in Canada's Atlantic provinces. After 1815 Irish Catholics settled in large numbers in what is now Quebec. The Irish potato famine of 1847 greatly increased that population in all parts of eastern Canada.

By the 1850s the Catholic Church in both English- and French-speaking Canada had begun to erect new dioceses and found many religious communities. These communities did educational, medical and charitable work among their own people as well as among Canada's native peoples. By the 1890s large numbers of non-English and non-French-speaking Catholics had settled in Canada, especially in the Western provinces.

In the 20th century the pastoral horizons have continued to expand to meet the needs of what has now become a very multiracial church.

HEADQUARTERS

Media Contact, Dir. of Information, Mr. Dennis Gruending, 90 Parent St., Ottawa, ON K1N 7B1

OFFICERS

General Secretariat of the Episcopacy
Secrétaire général (French Sector), Père Alexandre Taché
General Secretary (English Sector), Rev. V. James Weisgerber
Assistant General Secretary (English Sector), Mr. Bede Martin Hubbard
Secrétaire général adjoint (French Sector), Mr. M. J. Fernand Tanguay

CANADIAN ORGANIZATION

Canadian Conference of Catholic Bishops: (Conférence des évêques cath. du Canada), 90 Parent Ave., Ottawa, ON K1N 7B1 Tel. (613)236-9461 Fax (613)236-8117

EXECUTIVE COMMITTEE

National Level
Pres., Msgr. Jean-Guy Hamelin, (Rouyn-Noranda)
Vice-Pres., Most Rev. Francis J. Spence, (Kingston)
Co-Treas.: Most Rev. Austin Burke, (Halilfax); Msgr. Jean-Claude Turcotte, (Montréal)

EPISCOPAL COMMISSIONS

National Level
Social Affairs, Most Rev. Joseph Faber MacDonald
Canon Law—Inter-rite, Msgr. Jean-Guy Couture
Relations with Assoc. of Priests, Religious, & Laity, Most Rev. Jacques Berthelet
Missions, Most Rev. Joseph N. MacNeil
Ecumenism, Msgr. Bertrand Blanchet
Theology, Most Rev. Adam Exner
Sector Level
Comm. sociales, Msgr. Roger Ebacher
Social Comm., Most Rev. John A. O'Mara
Éducation chrétienne, Msgr. Gilles Cazabon
Christian Education, Most Rev. Anthony F. Tonnos
Liturgie, Msgr. Raymond Saint-Gelais
Liturgy, Most Rev. James M. Hayes

OFFICES

Secteur français
Office des Missions, Dir., Père Lucien Casterman, O.M.I.
Office des communications sociales, Dir. général, L'abbé Jacques Paquette, 1340 est, boul. St. Joseph, Montréal, QC H2J 1M3 Tel. (514)524-8223 Fax (514)524-8522
Office national de liturgie, coordonnateur, M. l'abbé Paul Boily, 3530, rue Adam, Montréal, QC H1W 1Y8 Tel. (514)522-4930
Service incroyance et foi, Dir., Père Giles Langevin, s.j., 7400, boulevard Saint-Laurent, Montréal, QC H2R 2Y1 Tel. (514)948-3186
Centre canadien d'oecuménisme, Rev. Thomas Ryan, C.S.P., 2065 ouest, rue Sherbrooke, Montréal, QC H3H 1G6 Tel. (514)937-9176 Fax (514)935-5497
Services des relations publiques, Dir., M. Gerald Baril
Service des Editions, Dir., Mlle Claire Dubé
Affaires sociales, Dir., M. Bernard Dufresne

English Sector

Natl. Liturgical Ofc., Dir., Rev. John Hibbard

Natl. Ofc. of Religious Educ., Dir., Mrs. Bernadette Tourangeau

Ofc. for Missions, Dir., Fr. Lucien Casterman, O.M.I.

Public Information Ofc., Dir., Mr. Dennis Gruending

Social Affairs, Dir., Mr. Tony Clarke

REGIONAL EPISCOPAL ASSEMBLIES

Atlantic Episcopal Assembly: Pres., Msgr. Gérard Dionne; Vice-Pres., Most Rev. J. Edward Troy, C.S.C.; Sec., Rev. Guy Léger, C.S.C., Site 1 Boîte 389, R.R. 1, St. Joseph, NB E0A 2Y0 Tel. (506)758-2531 Fax (506)758-1187

Assemblée des évêques du Que: Prés., Mgr. Bernard Hubert; Vice-Pres., Mgr. Maurice Couture; Sécretaire général, L'abbé Clément Vigneault; Secrétariat, 1225 Boulevard Saint Joseph est, Montréal, QC H2J 1L7 Tel. (514)274-4323 Fax (514)274-4383

Ontario Conference of Catholic Bishops: Pres., Most Rev. John A. O'Mara; Vice-Pres., Msgr. Eugene P. LaRocque; Sec., Rev. Angus J. Macdougall, S.J.; Secretariat, 67 Bond St., Ste. 304, Toronto, ON M5B 1X5 Tel. (416)368-1804 Fax (416)368-6687

Western Catholic Conference: Pres., Msgr. Antoine Hacault; Vice-Pres., Most Rev. Maxim Hermaniuk; Sec., Msgr. Peter-Alfred Sutton, 108-1st St., West, P.O. Box 270, Le Pas, MB R9A 1K4 Tel. (204)623-6152 Fax (204)623-6121

MILITARY ORDINARIATE

Ordinaire aux forces canadiennes: Msgr. André Vallée, P.M.É., National Defense Headquarters, Ottawa, ON K1A 0k2 Tel. (613)992-1261

Canadian Religious Conference: Sec. Gen., Sr. Colette Tardif, SGM, 324 Laurier Ave. East, Ottawa, ON K1N 6P6 Tel. (613)236-0824 Fax (613)236-0825

LATIN RITE

Alexandria-Cornwall: Msgr. Eugene P. LaRocque, Centre diocésain, 220 Chemin Montréal, C. P. 1388, Cornwall, ON K6H 5V4 Tel. (613)933-1138

Amos: Evêché, Msgr. Gérard Drainville, 450, Principale Nord, Amos, QC J9T 2M1 Tel. (819)732-6515

Antigonish: Bishop Colin Campbell, Chancery Office, 155 Main St., P.O. Box 1330, Antigonish, NS B2G 2L7 Tel. (902)863-4818

Baie-Comeau: Evêché, Msgr. Pierre Morissette, 639 Rue de Bretagne, Baie-Comeau, QC G5C 1X2 Tel. (418)589-5744

Bathurst: Evêché, Msgr. André Richard, 645, avenue Murray, C.P. 460, Bathurst, NB E2A 3Z4 Tel. (506)546-3493

Calgary: Bishop Paul J. O'Byrne, Bishop's Office, 1916 Second St. S.W., Calgary, AB T2S 1S3 Tel. (403)228-4501

Charlottetown: Most Rev. Joseph Vernon Fougère, D.D., P.O. Box 907, Charlottetown, PE C1A 7L9 Tel. (902)368-8005

Chicoutimi: Evêché, Msgr. Jean-Guy Couture, 602 est, rue Racine, C.P. 278, Chicoutimi, QC G7H 6J6 Tel. (418)543-0783

Churchill-Baie D'Hudson: Evêché, Msgr. Reynald Rouleau, O.M.I., C.P. 10, Churchill, MB R0B 0E0 Tel. (204)675-2541

Archdiocese of Edmonton: Archbishop, Joseph N. MacNeil, Archdiocesan Office, 8421-101st Ave., Edmonton, AB T6A 0L1 Tel. (403)469-1010

Edmundson: Evêché, Msgr. Gérard Dionne, Centre diocésain, Edmundston, NB E3V 3K1 Tel. (506)735-5578

Gaspé: Evêché, —— C.P. 440, Gaspé, QC G0C 1R0 Tel. (418)368-2274

Gatineau-Hull: Archévêché, Msgr. Roger Ebacher, 180, boulevard Mont-Bleu, Hull, QC J8X 3J5 Tel. (819)771-8391

Grand Falls: Bishop, Joseph Faber MacDonald, Chancery Office, P.O. Box 397, Grand Falls, NF A2A 2J8 Tel. (709)489-4019

Gravelbourg: Secrétariat, Msgr. Noel Delaquis, C.P. 690, Gravelbourg, SK S0H 1X0 Tel. (306)648-2615

Archidiocèse de Grouard-McLennan: Archévêché, Msgr. Henri Légaré, C.P. 388, McLennan, AB T0H 2L0 Tel. (403)324-3002

Archdiocese of Halifax: Archbishop, Austin E. Burke, Archbishop's Residence, 6541 Coburg Rd., P.O. Box 1527, Halifax, NS B3J 2Y3 Tel. (902)429-9388

Hamilton: Bishop, Anthony F. Tonnos, 700 King St. W., Hamilton, ON L8P 1C7 Tel. (416)528-7988

Hearst: Evêché, ——, 76, 7 rue C.P. 1330, Hearst, ON P0L 1N0 Tel. (705)362-4903

Joliette: Evêché, Msgr. Gilles Lussier, 2 rue St.-Charles Borromée, Nord. C.P. 470, Joliette, QC J6E 6H6 Tel. (514)753-7596

Kamloops: Bishop, Lawrence Sabatini, Bishop's Residence, 635A Tranquile Rd., Kamloops, BC V2B 3H5 Tel. (604)376-3351

Archidiocèse de Keewatin-LePas: Archbishop, Peter-Alfred Sutton, Résidence, 108 1st St. W., C.P. 270, Le Pas, MB R9A 1K4 Tel. (204)623-3529

Archdiocese of Kingston: Archbishop, Francis J. Spence, 390 Palace Rd., Kingston, ON K7L 4X3 Tel. (613)548-4461

Labrador City-Schefferville: Evêché, Msgr. Henri Goudreault, 318 Ave. Elizabeth, Labrador City, Labrador, NF A2V 2K7 Tel. (709)944-2046

London: Bishop, John M. Sherlock, Chancery Office, 1070 Waterloo St., London, ON N6A 3Y2 Tel. (519)433-0658

Mackenzie-Fort Smith (T.No.O.): Evêché, Msgr. Denis Croteau, 5117, 52 rue, Yellowknife, T.N.O., X1A 1T7 Tel. (403)920-2129

Archidiocèse de Moncton: Archévêché, Msgr. Donat Chiasson, C.P. 248, Moncton, NB E1C 8K9 Tel. (506)857-9531

Mont-Laurier: Evêché, Msgr. Jean Gratton, 435 rue de la Madone, C.P. 1290, Mont Laurier, QC J9L 1S1 Tel. (819)623-5530

Archidiocèse de Montréal: Archévêché, Msgr. Jean-Claude Turcotte, 2000 ouest rue Sherbrooke, Montréal, QC H3H 1G4 Tel. (514)931-7311

Monsonee: Msgr. Vincent Cadieux, Résidence, C.P. 40, Moosonee, ON P0L 1Y0 Tel. (705)336-2908

Abbatia Mullius of Muenster: Rt. Rev. Peter Novecosky, OSB, Abbot's Residence, St. Peter's Abbey, Muenster, SK S0K 2Y0 Tel. (306)682-5521

Nelson: Bishop Peter Mallon, Chancery Office, 813 Ward St., Nelson, BC V1L 1T4 Tel. (604)352-6921

Nicolet: Evêché, Msgr. Raymond Saint-Gelais, C.P. 820, Nicolet, QC J0G 1E0 Tel. (819)293-4234

Archidiocèse D'Ottawa: Chancellerie, Msgr. Marcel A.J. Gervais, 1247, avenue Kilborn, Ottawa, ON K1H 6K9 Tel. (613)738-5025

Pembroke: Bishop, Brendon M. O'Brien, Bishop's Residence, 188 Renfrew St., P.O. Box 7, Pembroke, ON K8A 6X1 Tel. (613)732-3895

Peterborough: Bishop, James L. Doyle, Bishop's Residence, 350 Hunter St. W., Peterborough, ON K9J 6Y8 Tel. (705)745-5123

Prince-Albert: Evêché, Msgr. Blaise Morand, 1415-ouest, 4e Ave. West, Prince-Albert, SK S6V 5H1 Tel. (306)922-4747

Prince-George: Most Rev. Gerald Wisner, Chancery Office, 2935 Highway 16 West, P.O. Box 7000, Prince George, BC V2N 3Z2 Tel. (604)964-4424

Archidiocèse de Québec: Archévêché, Msgr. Maurice Couture, 2 rue Port Dauphin, C.P. 459, Québec, QC G1R 4R6 Tel. (418)692-3935

Archdiocese of Regina: Archbishop, Charles A. Halpin, Chancery Office, 455 Broad St. North, Regina, SK S4R 2X8 Tel. (306)352-1651

Archidiocèse de Rimouski: Archévêché, Msgr. Bertrand Blanchet, 34 ouest, rue de L'évêché, ouest C.P. 730, Rimouski, QC G5L 7C7 Tel. (418)723-3320

Rouyn-Noranda: Evêché, Msgr. Jean-Guy Hamelin, 515 avenue Cuddihy, C.P. 1060, Rouyn-Noranda, QC J9X 5W9 Tel. (819)764-4660

Ste-Anne de la Pocatière: Evêché, Msgr. André Gaumond, C.P. 430 La Pocatière, Pocatière, QC G0R 1Z0 Tel. (418)856-1811

Archidiocèse de Saint-Boniface: Archévêché, Msgr. Antoine Hacault, 151 ave de la Cathédrale, St-Boniface, MB R2H 0H6 Tel. (204)237-9851

St. Catharine's: Bishop, Thomas B. Fulton, Bishop's Residence, 122 Riverdale Ave., St. Catharines, ON L2R 4C2 Tel. (416)684-0154

St. George's: Bishop, Raymond J. Lahey, Bishop's Residence, 16 Hammond Dr., Corner Brook, NF A2H 2W2 Tel. (709)639-7073

Saint Hyacinthe: Evêché, Msgr. Louis-de-Gonzaque Langevin, 1900 ouest Girouard, C. P. 190, Saint-Hyacinthe, QC J2S 7B4 Tel. (514)773-8581

Saint-Jean-de-Longueuil: Evêché, Msgr. Bernard Hubert, 740 boul. Ste-Foy, C.P. 40, Longueuil, QC J4K 4X8 Tel. (514)679-1100

Saint-Jérome: Evêché, Msgr. Charles Valois, 355 rue St-Georges, C.P. 580, Saint-Jérome, QC J7Z 5V3 Tel. (514)432-9741

Saint John: Bishop, J. Edward Troy, Chancery Office, 1 Bayard Dr., Saint John, NB E2L 3L5 Tel. (506)632-9222

Archdiocese of St. John's: Archbishop, James H. MacDonald, Archbishop's Residence, P.O. Box 37, Basilica Residence, St. John's, NF A1C 5H5 Tel. (709)726-3660

Saint-Paul: Evêché, Msgr. Raymond Roy, 4410 51e Ave., St-Paul, AB T0A 3A2 Tel. (403)645-3277

Saskatoon: Bishop, James P. Mahoney, Chancery Office, 106 - 5th Ave. N., Saskatoon, SK S7K 2N7 Tel. (306)242-1500

Sault Ste. Marie: Bishop, Jean-Louis Plouffe, Bishop's Residence, 480 McIntyre St., W., P.O. Box 510, North Bay, ON P1B 8J1 Tel. (705)476-1300

Archidiocèse de Sherbrooke: Archévêché, Msgr. Jean-Marie Fortier, 130 rue de la Cathedrale, C.P. 430, Sherbrooke, QC J1H 5K1 Tel. (819)563-9934

Thunder Bay: Bishop, John A. O'Mara, Bishop's Residence, P.O. Box 756, Thunder Bay, ON P7C 4W6 Tel. (807)622-8144

Timmins: Most Rev. Gilles Cazabon, O.M.I., 65, avenue Jubilee est, Timmins, ON P4N 5W4 Tel. (705)267-6224

Archdiocese of Toronto: Archbishop, Aloysius M. Ambrozic, Chancery Office, 355 Church St., Toronto, ON M5B 1Z8 Tel. (416)977-1500

Trois-Rivières: Evêché, Msgr. Laurent Noël, 362 rue Bonaventure, C.P. 879, Trois-Rivièrès, QC G9A 5J9 Tel. (819)374-9847

Valleyfield: Evêché, Msgr. Robert Lebel, 11 rue de l'Eglise, Valleyfield, QC J6T 1J5 Tel. (514)373-8122

Archdiocese of Vancouver: Archbishop, Adam Exner, Chancery Office, 150 Robson St., Vancouver, BC V6B 2A7 Tel. (604)683-0281

Victoria: Bishop, Remi J. De Roo, Bishop's Office, 1 - 4044 Nelthorpe St., Victoria, BC V8X 2A1 Tel. (604)479-1331

Whitehorse (Yukon): Bishop, Thomas Lobsinger, O.M.I. Bishop's Residence, 5119 5th Ave., Whitehorse, YT Y1A 1L5 Tel. (403)667-2052

Archdiocese of Winnipeg: Most Rev. Leonard J. Wall, 1495 Pembina Hwy, Winnipeg, ON R3T 2C6 Tel. (204)452-2227

Yarmouth: Most Rev. James Wingle, 53 rue Park, Yarmouth, NS B5A 4B2 Tel. (902)742-7163

EASTERN RITES

Eparchy of Edmonton Eparch: Most Rev. Myron Daciuk, V Eparch's Residence, 6240 Ada Blvd., Edmonton, AB T5W 4P1 Tel. (403)479-0381

Eparchy of New Westminster: Eparch, ——— Eparch's Residence, 502 5th Ave., New Westminster, BC V3L 1S2 Tel. (604)521-8015

Eparchy of Saskatoon: Eparch, Most Rev. Basil Filevich, Eparch's Residence, 866 Saskatchewan. Crescent East, Saskatoon, SK S7N 0L4 Tel. (306)653-0138

Ukrainian Eparchy of Toronto: Eparch, Most Rev. Isidore Borecky, Eparch's Residence, 61 Glen Edyth Dr., Toronto, ON M4V 2V8 Tel. (416)924-2381

Toronto, Ontario Eparchy: For Slovaks, Eparch, Most Rev. Michael Rusnak, Chancery Office, 223 Carlton Rd., Unionville, ON L3R 3M2 Tel. (416)477-4867

Ukrainian Archeparchy of Winnipeg: Archeparchy, Most Rev. Michael Bzdel, Archiparch's Residence, 235 Scotia St., Winnipeg, MB R2V 1V7 Tel. (204)339-7457

Montréal (Qué) Archéparchie: Pour Les Grecs-Melkites, Archéparque, Msgr. Michel Hakim, Chancelerie: 34 Maplewood, Montréal, QC H2V 2M1 Tel. (514)272-6430

Archéparchie de Montréal: Pour les Maronites, Archéparque, Msgr. Georges Abi-Saber, 12475, rue Grenet, Montréal, QC H4J 2K4 Tel. (514)331-2807

PERIODICALS

Catholic New Times; The Catholic Times; Dimanche et Fête; Companion Magazine; Global Village Voice; Discover the Bible; L'Église Canadienne; The Monitor; National Bulletin on Liturgy; The New Freeman; Messenger (of the Sacred Heart); Foi et Culture (Bulletin natl. de liturgie) Liturgie; Prairie Messenger; La Vie des Communautés religieuses; Relations; Caravan: A Resource for Adult Religious Education; Insight: A Resource for Adult Religious Education; Présence; The Communicator; Scarboro Missions

Romanian Orthodox Church in America (Canadian Parishes)

The first Romanian Orthodox immigrants in Canada called for Orthodox priests from their native country of Romania. Between 1902 and 1914, they organized the first Romanian parish communities and built Orthodox churches in different cities and farming regions of western Canada (Alberta, Saskatchewan, Manitoba) as well as in the eastern part (Ontario and Quebec).

In 1929, the Romanian Orthodox parishes from Canada joined with those of the United States in a Congress held in Detroit, Michigan, and asked the Holy Synod of the Romanian Orthodox Church of Romania to establish a Romanian Orthodox Missionary Episcopate in America. The first Bishop, Policarp (Morushca), was elected and consecrated by the Holy Synod of the Romanian Orthodox Church and came to the United States in 1935. He established his headquarters in Detroit with jurisdiction over all the Romanian Orthodox parishes in the United States and Canada.

In 1950, the Romanian Orthodox Church in America (i.e. the Romanian Orthodox Missionary Episcopate in America) was granted administrative autonomy by the Holy Synod of the Romanian Orthodox Church of Romania, and only doctrinal and canonical ties remain with this latter body.

In 1974 the Holy Synod of the Romanian Orthodox Church of Romania recognized and approved the elevation of the Episcopate to the rank of the Romanian Orthodox Archdiocese in America and Canada.

HEADQUARTERS

Canadian Office: St. Demetrios Romanian Orthodox Church, 103 Furby St., Winnipeg, MB R3C 2A4 Tel. (204)775-6472

Media Contact, Most Rev. Archbishop Victorin, 19959 Riopelle St., Detroit, MI 48203 Tel. (313)893-8390

OFFICERS

Archbishop, Most Rev. Archbishop Victorin, 19959 Riopelle St., Detroit, MI 48203 Tel. (313)893-8390

The Romanian Orthodox Episcopate of America (Jackson, MI)

This body of Eastern Orthodox Christians of Romanian descent is fully autonomous. For complete description and listing of officers, please see chapter 3, "Religious Bodies in the United States."

HEADQUARTERS

2522 Grey Tower Rd., Jackson, MI 49201 Tel. (517)522-4800 Fax (517)522-5907

Mailing Address, P.O. Box 309, Grass Lake, MI 49240

Media Contact, Ed./Sec., David Oancea, P.O. Box 185, Grass Lake, MI 49240-0185 Tel. (517)522-4800 Fax (517)522-5907

OFFICERS

Dean of all Canada, Very Rev. Nicolae Marioncu, Box 995, Ste. 1, 709 First St., W, Assiniboia, SK S0H 0B0

The Salvation Army in Canada

The Salvation Army, an evangelical branch of the Christian Church, is an international movement founded in 1865 in London, England. The ministry of Salvationists, consisting of clergy (officers) and laity, comes from a commitment to Jesus Christ and is revealed in practical service, regardless of race, color, creed, sex or age.

The goals of The Salvation Army are to preach the gospel, disseminate Christian truths, instill Christian values, enrich family life and improve the quality of all life.

To attain these goals, The Salvation Army operates local congregations, provides counseling, supplies basic human needs and undertakes spiritual and moral rehabilitation of any needy people who come within its influence.

A quasi-military system of government was set up in 1878, by General William Booth, founder (1829-1912). Converts from England started Salvation Army work in London, Ontario, in 1882. Two years later, Canada was recognized as a Territorial Command, and since 1933 it has included Bermuda. An act to incorporate the Governing Council of The Salvation Army in Canada received royal assent on May 19, 1909.

HEADQUARTERS

Salvation Square, P.O. Box 4021, Postal Sta. A, Toronto, ON M5W 2B1 Tel. (416)598-2071

Media Contact, Asst. Public Rel. Sec. for Comm. & Spec. Events, Major Gary Venables, P.O. Box 4021, Stn. A, Toronto, ON M5W 2B1 Tel. (416)340-2162 Fax (416)598-1672

OFFICERS

Territorial Commander, Commissioner Roy J. Calvert

Territorial Pres., Women's Organizations, Mrs. Commissioner Ruth Calvert

Chief Sec., Lt.Col. John Busby

Field Sec. for Personnel, Lt.Col. John Carew

Bus. Adm. Sec., Lt. Col. Clyde Moore

Fin. Sec., Lt. Col. Douglas Kerr

Public Rel. Sec., Lt. Col. Mel W. Bond

Property Sec., Major Boyde Goulding

Program Sec., Lt. Col. Ralph Stanley

PERIODICALS

The War Cry; En Evant!; The Young Soldier; The Edge; Sally Ann; The Ministry to Women Sketch; Horizons

Serbian Orthodox Church in the U.S.A. and Canada, Diocese of Canada

The Serbian Orthodox Church is an organic part of the Eastern Orthodox Church. As a local church it received its autocephaly from Constantinople in A.D. 1219. The Patriarchal seat of the church today is in Belgrade, Yugoslavia. In 1921, a Serbian Orthodox Diocese in the United States of America and Canada was organized. In 1963, it was reorganized into three dioceses, and in 1983 a fourth diocese was created for the Canadian part of the church. The Serbian Orthodox Church is in absolute doctrinal unity with all other local Orthodox Churches.

HEADQUARTERS

5a Stockbridge Ave., Toronto, ON M8Z 4M6 Tel. (416)231-4409 Fax (416)231-5008
Media Contact, Branko Dopalovic

Seventh-day Adventist Church in Canada

The Seventh-day Adventist Church in Canada is part of the worldwide Seventh-day Adventist Church with headquarters in Washington, D.C. (See "Religious Bodies in the United States" section of this *Yearbook* for a fuller description.) The Seventh-day Adventist Church in Canada was organized in 1901 and reorganized in 1932.

HEADQUARTERS

1148 King St., E., Oshawa, ON L1H 1H8 Tel. (416)433-0011 Fax (416)433-0982
Media Contact, G. Willis

OFFICERS

Pres., D. D. Devnich
Treas., Robert E. Lemon
Sec., Orville D. Parchment

DEPARTMENTS

Under Treas., Brian Christenson
Asst. Treas., Clareleen Ivany
Computer Services, Brian Ford
Communications, ——
Coord. of Ministries, Claude Sabot
Education, Jan Saliba
Ministerial Assoc., ——
Public Affairs/Religious Liberty Trust, Karnik Doukmetzian
Publishing, George Dronen

PERIODICAL

Canadian Adventist Messenger

Syrian Orthodox Church of Antioch (Archdiocese of the United States and Canada)

An archdiocese of the Syrian Orthodox Church of Antioch in North America, the Syrian Orthodox Church professes the faith of the first three ecumenical councils of Nicaea, Constantinople and Ephesus and numbers faithful in the Middle East, India, the Americas, Europe and Australia. It traces its origin to the Patriarchate established in Antioch by St. Peter the Apostle and is under the supreme ecclesiastical jurisdiction of His Holiness the Syrian Orthodox Patriarch of Antioch and All the East, now residing in Damascus, Syria.

The Archdiocese of the Syrian Orthodox Church in the U.S. and Canada was formally established in 1957. The first Syrian Orthodox faithful came to Canada in the 1890s and formed the first Canadian parish in Sherbrooke, Quebec. Today four official parishes of the Archdiocese exist in Canada—two in Quebec and two in Ontario. There is also an official congregation in Calgary, Alberta.

HEADQUARTERS

Archdiocese of the U.S. & Canada, 49 Kipp Ave., Lodi, NJ 07644 Tel. (201)778-0638 Fax (201)773-7506
Media Contact, Archdiocesan Gen. Sec., V.Rev. Chorepiscopus John Meno, 45 Fairmount Ave., Hackensack, NJ 07601 Tel. (201)646-9443 Fax (201)773-7506

OFFICERS

Primate, Archbishop Mar Athanasius Y. Samuel
Archdiocesan Gen. Sec., Very Rev. Chorepiscopus John Meno, 45 Fairmount Ave., Hackensack, NJ 07601 Tel. (201)646-9443

Ukrainian Orthodox Church of Canada

Toward the end of the 19th century many Ukrainian immigrants settled in Canada—1991 marked the centenary of this immigration. In 1918, these pioneers established the Ukrainian Orthodox Church of Canada, today the largest Ukrainian Orthodox Church beyond the borders of Ukraine.

HEADQUARTERS

Consistory of the Ukrainian Orthodox Church of Canada, 9 St. John's Ave., Winnipeg, MB R2W 1G8 Tel. (204)586-3093 Fax (204)582-5241
Media Contact, V. Rev. Dr. Ihor Kutash, 6270-12th Ave., Montreal, QC H1X 3A5 Tel. (514)727-2236 Fax (514)728-9834

OFFICERS

Presidium, Chpsn., Very Rev. William Makarenko
Primate, Most Rev. Metropolitan Wasyly, 174 Seven Oaks Ave., Winnipeg, MB R2V 0K8

PERIODICAL

Visnyk: The Herald

Union of Spiritual Communities of Christ (Orthodox Doukhobors in Canada)

The Doukhobors are groups of Canadians of Russian origin living in the western provinces of Canada, but their beginnings in Russia are unknown. The name "Doukhobors," or "Spirit Wrestlers," was given in derision by the Russian Orthodox clergy in Russia as far back as 1785. Victims of decades of persecution in Russia, about 7,500 Doukhobors arrived in Canada in 1899.

The teaching of the Doukhobors is penetrated with the Gospel spirit of love. Worshiping God in the spirit, they affirm that the outward church and all that is performed in it and concerns it has no importance for them; the church is where two or three are gathered together, united in the name of Christ. Their teaching is founded on tradition, which they call the "Book of Life," because it lives in their memory and hearts. In this book are sacred songs or chants, partly composed independently, partly formed out of the contents of the Bible, and these are committed to memory by each succeeding generation. Doukhobors observe complete pacifism and non-violence.

The Doukhobors were reorganized in 1938 by their leader, Peter P. Verigin, shortly before his death, into the Union of Spiritual Communities of Christ, commonly called Orthodox Doukhobors. It is headed by a democratically elected Executive Committee which executes the will and protects the interests of the people.

HEADQUARTERS

USCC Central Office, Box 760, Grand Forks, BC V0H 1H0 Tel. (604)442-8252 Fax (604)442-3433
Media Contact, John J. Verigin

OFFICERS

Hon. Chpsn. of the Exec. Comm., John J. Verigin

Chpsn., Andrew Evin
Admn., S. W. Babakaiff

PERIODICAL
Iskra

Unitarian Universalist Association

Three of the 23 districts of the Unitarian Universalist Association are located partly or wholly in Canada, as are 40 of the 1,020 congregations. Conseil Unitaire Canadien handles matters of particular concern to Canadian churches and fellowships. See "Religious Bodies in the United States" section of this *Yearbook* for a fuller description of the history and theology.

HEADQUARTERS

Headquarters: 25 Beacon St., Boston, MA 02108 Tel. (617)742-2100 Fax (617)367-3237
Conseil Unitaire Canadien: 600 Eglinton Ave. E., Toronto, ON M4P 1P3 Fax (416)489-4121
Media Contact, Dir. of Public Rel. & Marketing, Deborah Weiner, Fax (617)523-4123

DISTRICTS AND OFFICERS

Pacific Northwest: Rod Stewart, 370 Mathers Ave., West Vancouver, BC V7S 1H3
St. Lawrence: Rev. Wendy Colby, 695 Elmwood Ave., Buffalo, NY 14222
Western Canada: Stefan Jonasson, 408 Amhurst St., Winnipeg, MB R3J 1Y9
Northeast: Rev. Glenn Turner, 125 Auburn St., Portland, ME 04103
Trustee-at-Large from Canada: Dr. Sheilah Thompson, 930 Whitchurch St., North Vancouver, BC V7L 2A6

United Brethren Church in Canada

Founded in 1767 in Lancaster County, Pa., missionaries came to Canada about 1850. The first class was held in Kitchener in 1855, and the first building was erected in Port Elgin in 1867.

The Church of the United Brethren in Christ had its beginning with Philip William Otterbein and Martin Boehm, who were leaders in the revivalistic movement in Pennsylvania and Maryland during the late 1760s.

HEADQUARTERS

302 Lake St., Huntington, IN 46750 Tel. (219)356-2312 Fax (219)356-4730

GENERAL OFFICERS

Pres., Rev. Brian Magnus, 120 Fife Rd., Guelph, ON N1H 6Y2 Tel. (519)836-0180
Treas., Mr. Brian Winger, 2233 Hurontario St., Apt. 916, Mississauga, ON L5A 2E9

The United Church of Canada

The United Church of Canada was formed on June 10, 1925, through the union of the Methodist Church, Canada, the Congregational Union of Canada, the Council of Local Union Churches and 70 percent of the Presbyterian Church in Canada. The union culminated years of negotiation between the churches, all of which had integral associations with the development and history of the nation.

In fulfillment of its mandate to be a uniting as well as a United Church, the denomination has been enriched by other unions during its history. The Wesleyan Methodist Church of Bermuda joined in 1930. On January 1, 1968, the Canada Conference of the Evangelical United Brethren became part of The United Church of Canada. At various times, congregations of other Christian communions have also become congregations of the United Church.

The United Church of Canada is a full member of the World Methodist Council, the World Alliance of Reformed Churches (Presbyterian and Congregational), and the Canadian and World Councils of Churches.

The United Church is the largest Protestant denomination in Canada.

NATIONAL OFFICES

The United Church House, 85 St. Clair Ave. E., Toronto, ON M4T 1M8 Tel. (416)925-5931 Fax (416)925-3394
Media Contact, Publicist, Mary-Frances Denis

GENERAL COUNCIL

Mod., Rev. Dr. Stanley J. McKay
Gen. Sec., Rev. Dr. Howard M. Mills
Management & Personnel, Sec., Barbara M. Copp
Theology, Faith & Ecumenism, Sec., ——
Personnel Dir., Margaret C. Scriven
Archivist, Jean E. Dryden, 73 Queen's Park Cr., E., Toronto, ON M5C 1K7 Tel. (416)585-4563 Fax (416)585-4584

ADMINISTRATIVE DIVISIONS

Communication: Gen. Sec., Rev. Randolph L. Naylor
Finance: Gen. Sec., Melanie A. Macdonald
Ministry Personnel & Education: Gen. Sec., Gordon D. MacBeth
Mission in Canada: Gen. Sec., ——
World Outreach: Gen. Sec., Rhea Whitehead

CONFERENCE EXECUTIVE SECRETARIES

Alberta and Northwest: (Acting), Helen Stover-Scott, 9911-48 Ave., Edmonton, AB T6E 5V6 Tel. (403)435-3995 Fax (403)434-0597
All Native Circle: Speaker, Rev. Grafton Antone, 18-399 Berry St., Winnipeg, MB R3J 1N6 Tel. (204)831-0740 Fax (204)837-9703
Bay of Quinte: Rev. David M. Iverson, 218 Barrie St., Kingston, ON K7L 3K3 Tel. (613)549-2503 Fax (613)549-1050
British Columbia: (Acting), Pearl Griffin, 1955 W. 4th Ave., Vancouver, BC V6J 1M7 Tel. (604)734-0434 Fax (604)734-7024
Hamilton: K. Virginia Coleman, Box 100, Carlisle, ON L0R 1H0 Tel. (416)659-3343 Fax (416)659-7766
London: Rev. W. Peter Scott, 359 Windermere Rd., London, ON N6G 2K3 Tel. (519)672-1930 Fax (519)439-2800
Manitoba and Northwestern Ontario: H. Dianne Cooper, 120 Maryland St., Winnipeg, MB R3G 1L1 Tel. (204)786-8911 Fax (204)774-0159
Manitou: Rev. J. Stewart Bell, 1402 Regina St., North Bay, ON P1B 2L5 Tel. (705)474-3350 Fax (705)497-3597
Maritime: Rev. Robert H. Mills, Box 1560, Sackville, NS E0A 3C0 Tel. (506)536-1334 Fax (506)536-2900
Montreal and Ottawa: Rev. Tadashi Mitsui, 225-50 Ave., Lachine, QC H8T 2T7 Tel. (514)634-7015 Fax (514)634-2489

Newfoundland and Labrador: Rev. Boyd L. Hiscock, 320 Elizabeth Ave., St. John's, NF A1B 1T9 Tel. (709)754-0386 Fax (709)754-8336

Saskatchewan: Rev. Wilbert R. Wall, 418 A. McDonald St., Regina, SK S4N 6E1 Tel. (306)721-3311 Fax (306)721-3171

Toronto: Dr. Helga Kutz-Harder, Rm. 404, 85 St. Clair Ave., E., Toronto, ON M4T 1L8 Tel. (416)967-1880 Fax (416)925-3394

PERIODICALS

United Church Observer; Mandate; Aujourd'hui Credo

United Pentecostal Church in Canada

This body, which is affiliated with the United Pentecostal Church, International, with headquarters in Hazelwood, Mo., accepts the Bible standard of full salvation, which is repentance, baptism by immersion in the name of the Lord Jesus Christ for the remission of sins and the baptism of the Holy Ghost, with the initial signs of speaking in tongues as the Spirit gives utterance. Other tenets of faith include the Oneness of God in Christ, holiness, divine healing and the second coming of Jesus Christ.

HEADQUARTERS

United Pentecostal Church Intl., 8855 Dunn Rd., Hazelwood, MO 63042 Tel. (314)837-7300 Fax (314)837-4503

Media Contact, Gen. Sec.-Treas., Rev. C. M. Becton

DISTRICT SUPERINTENDENTS

Atlantic: Rev. R. A. Beesley, Box 965, Sussex, NB E0E 1P0

British Columbia: Rev. Paul V. Reynolds, 13447-112th Ave., Surrey, BC V3R 2E7

Canadian Plains: Rev. Johnny King, 615 Northmount Dr., NW, Calgary, AB T2K 3J6

Central Canadian: Rev. Clifford Heaslip, 4215 Roblin Blvd., Winnipeg, MB R3R 0E8

Nova Scotia-Newfoundland: Rev. John D. Mean, P.O. Box 2183, D.E.P.S., Dartmouth, NS B2W 3Y2

Ontario: Rev. Carl H. Stephenson, 63 Castlegrove Blvd., Don Mills, ON M3A 1L3

Universal Fellowship of Metropolitan Community Churches

The Universal Fellowship of Metropolitan Community Churches is a Christian church which directs a special ministry within, and on behalf of, the gay and lesbian community. Involvement, however, is not exclusively limited to gays and lesbians; U.F.M.C.C. tries to stress its openness to all people and does not call itself a "gay church."

Founded in 1968 in Los Angeles by the Rev. Troy Perry, the U.F.M.C.C. has 250 member congregations worldwide. Sixteen congregations are in Canada, in Victoria, Vancouver, Edmonton, Calgary,

Windsor, London, Toronto, Kingston, Ottawa, Maple Ridge, Winnipeg, Halifax, Mississauga and Belleville.

Theologically, the Metropolitan Community Churches stand within the mainstream of Christian doctrine, being "ecumenical" or "interdenominational" in stance (albeit a "denomination" in their own right).

The Metropolitan Community Churches are characterized by their belief that the love of God is a gift, freely offered to all people, regardless of sexual orientation and that no incompatibility exists between human sexuality and the Christian faith.

The Metropolitan Community Churches in Canada were founded in Toronto in 1973 by the Rev. Robert Wolfe.

HEADQUARTERS

Media Contact, Marrie Wexler, 33 Holly St., #1117, Toronto, ON M4S 2G8 Tel. (416)487-8429

OFFICERS

Western Canada District: Rev. Bev Baptiste, 270 Simcoe St., Winnipeg, MB R3G 1W1 Tel. (403)490-0478

Eastern Canada District: Rev. Marrie Wexler, 33 Holly St., #1117, Toronto, ON M4S 2G8 Tel. (416)487-8429

The Wesleyan Church of Canada

This group is the Canadian portion of The Wesleyan Church which consists of the Atlantic and Central Canada districts. The Central Canada District of the former Wesleyan Methodist Church of America was organized at Winchester, Ontario, in 1889 and the Atlantic District was founded in 1888 as the Alliance of the Reformed Baptist Church, which merged with the Wesleyan Methodist Church in July, 1966.

The Wesleyan Methodist Church and the Pilgrim Holiness Church merged in June, 1968, to become The Wesleyan Church. The doctrine is evangelical and Arminian and stresses holiness beliefs. For more details, consult the U.S. listing under The Wesleyan Church.

HEADQUARTERS

The Wesleyan Church Intl. Center, P.O. Box 50434, Indianapolis, IN 46250-0434

Media Contact, Dist. Supt., Central Canada, Rev. S. Allan Summers, 3 Applewood Dr., Ste. 102, Belleville, ON K8P 4E3 Tel. (613)966-7527 Fax (613)968-6190

DISTRICT SUPERINTENDENTS

Central Canada: Rev. S. Allan Summers

Atlantic: Rev. Ray E. Barnwell, P.O. Box 20, 41 Summit Ave., Sussex, NB E0E 1P0 Tel. (506)433-1007

PERIODICALS

Atlantic Wesleyan; Central Canada Clarion

RELIGIOUS BODIES IN CANADA
ARRANGED BY FAMILIES

The following list of religious bodies appearing in the preceding directory, "Religious Bodies in Canada," shows the "families" or related clusters into which Canadian religious bodies can be grouped. For example, there are many bodies that can be grouped under the heading "Baptist" for historical and theological reasons. It is not to be assumed, however, that all denominations under one family heading are necessarily similar in belief or practice. Often any similarity is purely coincidental since ethnicity, theological divergence and even political and personality factors have shaped the directions denominational groups have taken.

Family categories provide one of the major pitfalls of church statistics because of the tendency to combine statistics by "families" for analytical and comparative purposes. Such combined totals are almost meaningless, although often used as variables for sociological analysis.

Religious bodies not grouped under family headings appear alphabetically and are not indented in the following list.

The Anglican Church of Canada
Apostolic Christian Church (Nazarene)
Armenian Evangelical Church
Associated Gospel Churches

Baptist Bodies

The Association of Regular Baptist Churches
(Canada)
Baptist General Conference of Canada
The Central Canada Baptist Conference
Baptist General Conference of Alberta
British Columbia Baptist Conference
Canadian Baptist Federation
Baptist Convention of Ontario and Québec
Baptist Union of Western Canada
Union d'Églises Baptistes Françaises au
Canada
United Baptist Convention of the Atlantic
Provinces
Canadian Convention of Southern Baptists
*Fellowship of Evangelical Baptist Churches in
Canada*
Free Will Baptists
North American Baptist Conference

Bible Holiness Movement
Brethren in Christ Church, Canadian Conference
Canadian Province of the Moravian Church in America, Northern Province
The Canadian Yearly Meeting of the Religious Society of Friends
Christadelphians in Canada
The Christian and Missionary Alliance in Canada
Christian Brethren (aka Plymouth Brethren)
Church of God, (Anderson, Ind.)
Church of the Nazarene

Churches of Christ—Christian Churches

*Christian Church (Disciples of Christ) in
Canada*
*Christian Churches and Churches of Christ in
Canada*
Churches of Christ in Canada
Congregational Christian Churches in Canada

Doukhobors

Union of Spiritual Communities of Christ (Orthodox Doukhobors in Canada)

Eastern Churches

The Antiochian Orthodox Christian Archdiocese of North America
The Armenian Church of North America, Diocese of Canada
The Coptic Church in Canada
Greek Orthodox Diocese of Toronto (Canada)
Orthodox Church in America (Canada Section)
*Patriarchal Parishes of the Russian Orthodox
Church in Canada*
Romanian Orthodox Church in America (Canadian Parishes)
The Romanian Orthodox Episcopate of America (Jackson, MI)
*Serbian Orthodox Church in the U.S.A. and
Canada, Diocese of Canada*
Syrian Orthodox Church of Antioch (Archdiocese of the United States and Canada)
Ukrainian Orthodox Church of Canada

The Evangelical Covenant Church of Canada
Evangelical Free Church of Canada
General Church of the New Jerusalem
Independent Holiness Church
Jehovah's Witnesses

Latter Day Saints

*The Church of Jesus Christ of Latter-day
Saints in Canada*
*Reorganized Church of Jesus Christ of Latter
Day Saints*

Lutherans

Church of the Lutheran Brethren
The Estonian Evangelical Lutheran Church
The Evangelical Lutheran Church in Canada
*The Latvian Evangelical Lutheran Church in
America*
Lutheran Church—Canada

Mennonite Bodies

Church of God in Christ, Mennonite
*Canadian Conference of Mennonite Brethren
Churches*
Conference of Mennonites in Canada
The Evangelical Mennonite Conference
Evangelical Mennonite Mission Conference
Old Order Amish Church
Reinland Mennonite Church

Methodist Bodies

British Methodist Episcopal Church of Canada
The Evangelical Missionary Church of Canada
Free Methodist Church in Canada
The Wesleyan Church of Canada

The Old Catholic Church of Canada

Pentecostal Bodies

The Apostolic Church in Canada
Apostolic Church of Pentecost of Canada, Inc.
Church of God (Cleveland, Tenn.)
The Church of God of Prophecy in Canada
Elim Felowship of Evangelical Churches and Ministers
Foursquare Gospel Church of Canada
Independent Assemblies of God—Canada
The Italian Pentecostal Church of Canada
The Open Bible Standard Churches of Canada
The Pentecostal Assemblies of Canada
Pentecostal Assemblies of Newfoundland
Pentecostal Holiness Church of Canada

United Pentecostal Church in Canada

Polish National Catholic Church of Canada

Presbyterian Bodies

Presbyterian Church in America (Canadian Section)
The Presbyterian Church in Canada

Reformed Bodies

Canadian and American Reformed Churches
Christian Reformed Church in North America
Netherlands Reformed Congregations of North America
Reformed Church in Canada
The United Church of Canada
The Reformed Episcopal Church
The Roman Catholic Church in Canada
The Salvation Army in Canada
Seventh-day Adventist Church in Canada
United Brethren Church in Canada
Universal Fellowship of Metropolitan Community Churches

THE YEAR IN IMAGES

Des Moine Register PHOTO

MISSISSIPPI RIVER FLOODS

An Amish woman takes a break from filling sand bags used to hold back the Mississippi River. Churches from across the country responded to the needs of victims of the flooding. Suprisingly few church buildings were damaged as water rolled into fields and villages.

5. OTHER RELIGIONS IN CANADA AND THE UNITED STATES

People in Canada and the United States participate in a wide variety of religious organizations. Some of those that do not claim to be Christian are listed below.

Bahá'í Faith

The Bahá'í Faith is an independent world religion with adherents in virtually every country. Bahá'ís are followers of Bahá'u'lláh (1817-1892). The religion upholds the basic principles of the oneness of God, the oneness of religion, and the oneness of humankind.

The Bahá'í administrative order consists of elected local Spiritual Assemblies, National Spiritual Assemblies and the Universal House of Justice. The Local and National Spiritual Assemblies are elected annually. The Universal House of Justice, located in Haifa, Israel, is elected every five years. There are 165 National Assemblies and approximately 20,000 local Spiritual Assemblies worldwide. Literature of the Bahá'í Faith has been published in 802 languages.

U.S. HEADQUARTERS

National Spiritual Assembly, 536 Sheridan Rd., Wilmette, IL 60091 Tel. (708)869-9039 Fax (708)869-0247

Media Contact, Natl. Public Information Officer, 866 U.N. Plaza, Ste. 120, New York, NY 10017 Tel. (212)756-3500

CANADIAN HEADQUARTERS

Bahá'í National Centre of Canada, 7200 Leslie St., Thornhill, ON L3T 6L8 Tel. (416)889-8168 Fax (416)889-8184

Media Contact, Dir., Dept. of Public Affairs, Dr. Gerald Filson

Buddhist Churches of America

Founded in 1899, organized in 1914 as the Buddhist Mission of North America, this body was incorporated in 1944 under the present name and represents the Jodo Shinshu Sect of Buddhism affiliated with the Hongwanji-ha Hongwanji denomination in the continental United States. It is a school of Buddhism which believes in becoming aware of the ignorant self and relying upon the infinite wisdom and compassion of Amida Buddha, which is expressed in sincere gratitude through the recitation of the Nembutsu, Namu Amida Butsu.

In Canada, the Buddhist Churches were first established in 1904. This body is the Mahayana division of Buddhism, and its sectarian belief is the Pure Land School based on the Three Canonical Scriptures with emphasis on pure faith.

U.S. HEADQUARTERS

1710 Octavia St., San Francisco, CA 94109 Tel. (415)776-5600 Fax (415)771-6293

Media Contact, Admn. Ofc., Henry N. Shibata

CANADIAN HEADQUARTERS

4860 Garry St., Richmond, BC V7E 2V2 Tel. (604)272-6640

Media Contact, Bishop, Y. Matsubayashi

Jewish Organizations

There are organized Jewish communities throughout the U.S. and Canada. Jews arrived in the American colonies before 1650. The first congregation, the Shearith Israel (Remnant of Israel), is recorded in New York City in 1654. In Canada, the first synagogue was organized in 1768 in Quebec.

US HEADQUARTERS

Synagogue Council of America, Pres., Rabbi Haskel Lookstein 327 Lexington Ave., New York, NY 10016 Tel. (212)686-8670

CANADIAN HEADQUARTERS

Media Contact, Dir., Communications, Jack Samuel, 3101 Bathurst St. #400, Toronto, ON M6A 2A6 Tel. (416)789-3351 Fax (416)789-9436

US PERIODICALS

American Jewish History; Conservative Judaism; Jewish Action; Journal of Reform Judaism; Judaism; Reconstructionism Today; Reform Judaism; Tradition: A Journal of Orthodox Jewish Thought; United Synagogue Review

CANADIAN PERIODICALS

Canadian Jewish News; Canadian Jewish Outlook; Jewish Post and News; Jewish Standard; Journal of Psychology and Judaism

Muslims

Islam claims several million adherents in the United States and Canada. Some are immigrants who represent almost every part of the world. Others are Americans and Canadians who have converted to Islam. There are also many who come to North America temporarily as diplomats, students and employees of international businesses.

Many Islamic organizations exist under such titles as Islamic Society, Islamic Center or Muslim Mosque. All the groups hold the same beliefs and aspire to practice the same rituals—namely prayers, fasting, almsgiving and pilgrimage to Makkah Almukarramah (Mecca). Black organizations may mix civil rights aspirations with Islamic objectives and may, therefore, follow a rigid discipline for their members.

REGIONAL AND NATIONAL GROUPS

The Islamic Center of Washington, 2551 Massachusetts Ave. NW, Washington, DC 20008 Tel. (202)332-8343

Fed. of Islamic Assn. in the US & Canada, Sec. Gen., Nihad Hamed, 25351 Five Mile Rd., Redford Twp., MI 48239 Tel. (313)535-0014 Fax (313)534-1474

Council of Muslim Communities of Canada, Dir., Dr. Mir Iqbal Ali, 1250 Ramsey View Ct., Ste. 504, Sudbury, ON P3E 2E7 Tel. (705)522-2948

Sikh

Sikhism was born in the northwestern part of the Indo-Pakistan sub-continent in Punjab province about 500 years ago. The Sikh Holy Book, known as the Guru Granth, contains writings of the Sikh Gurus and some Hindu and Muslim saints.

Sikhs started migrating from India more than 50 years ago. Sikhs are now found in all major cities of the United States and Canada.

Unitarian Universalist Association

The Unitarian Universalist Association is the consolidated body of the former American Unitarian Association and the Universalist Church of America.

The Unitarian movement arose in congregationalism in the 18th century, producing the American Unitarian Association in 1825. In 1865 a national conference was organized. The philosophy of Universalism originated with the doctrine of universal salvation in the first century and was brought to America in the 18th century. Universalists were first formally organized in 1793.

In May, 1961, the Unitarian and Universalist bodies were consolidated to become the Unitarian Universalist Association. The movement is noncreedal. The UUA has observer status with the National Council of Churches.

HEADQUARTERS

25 Beacon St., Boston, MA 02108 Tel. (617)742-2100 Fax (617)367-3237
Media Contact, Dir. of Publ. Info., Deborah Weiner

US PERIODICAL

The World

Vedanta Societies

These societies are followers of the Vedas, the scriptures of the Indo-Aryans, doctrines expounded by Swami Vivekananda at the Parliament of Religions, Chicago, 1893. There are 13 such Centers in the United States and one in Canada. All are under the spiritual guidance of the Ramakrishna Mission, organized by Swami Vivekananda in India.

HEADQUARTERS

34 W. 71st St., New York, NY 10023 Tel. (212)877-9197

6. UNITED STATES REGIONAL AND LOCAL ECUMENICAL AGENCIES

One of the many ways Christians and Christian churches relate to one another locally and regionally is through ecumenical agencies. The membership in these ecumenical organizations is diverse. Historically, councils of churches were formed primarily by Protestants, but many local and regional organizations now include Orthodox and Roman Catholics. Many are made up of congregations or judicatory units of churches. Some have a membership-base of individuals. Others foster cooperation between ministerial groups, community ministries, coalitions or church agencies. While Councils of Churches is a term still commonly used to describe this form of cooperation, other terms such as "conference of churches," "ecumenical councils," "churches united," "metropolitan ministries," are coming into use.

Ecumenical organizations that are national in scope are listed in section 1, "Cooperative Organizations."

An increasing number of ecumenical agencies have been exploring ways to strengthen the interreligious aspect of life in the context of religious pluralism in the U.S. today. Some organizations in this listing are interfaith agencies primarily through the inclusion of Jewish congregations in their membership. Other organizations nurture partnerships with a broader base of religious groups in their communities, especially in the areas of public policy and interreligious dialogue.

This list does not include all local and regional ecumenical and interfaith organizations in existence today. For information about other groups contact the Ecumenical Networks Working Group of the National Council of the Churches of Christ in the U.S.A., Director, Dr. Kathleen S. Hurty, Room 868, New York, NY 10115-0050. Tel. (212)870-2155. Fax (212)870-2158.

The terms regional and local are relative, making identification somewhat ambiguous. Regional councils may cover sections of large states or cross state borders. Local councils may be made up of several counties, towns or clusters of congregations. State councils or state-level ecumenical contacts exist in 47 of the 50 states. These state-level or multi-state organizations are marked with a "*" and are the first listing for each state. Other listings are in alphabetical order under the state. Consult the index to find organizations if the state is not known.

ALABAMA

Greater Birmingham Ministries
1205 N. 25th St., Birmingham, AL 35234-3197
  Tel. (205)326-6821 Fax (205)326-6823
Media Contact, Scott Douglas
Exec. Dir., Scott Douglas
Economic Justice, Co-Chpsn.: Hattie Belle Lester; Scott Douglas
Direct Services, Chpsn., Janine Hagan
Finance & Fund-Raising, Chpsn., Dick Sales
Pres., Richard Johnson
Sec., Della Huber
Treas., Chris Hamlin
Major activities: Direct Service Ministries (Food, Utilities, Rent and Nutrition Education, Shelter); Alabama Arise (Statewide legislative network focusing on low income issues); Economic Justice Issues (Low Income Housing and Advocacy, Health Care, Community Development, Jobs Creation); Faith in Community Ministries (Interchurch Forum, Interpreting and Organizing, Bible Study)

Interfaith Mission Service
411-B Holmes Ave. NE, Huntsville, AL 35801 Tel. (205)536-2401 Fax (205)536-2402
Exec. Min., Rev. Robert Loshuertos
Pres., Karen Neir
Major activities: Food Pantry and Emergency Funds; Interfaith Dialogue; Harvest of Food; Ministry Development; Clergy Luncheon; Workshops; Evaluation of Member Ministries; Response to Community Needs; Information and Referral; Police Department Chaplains; Interfaith Understanding

ALASKA

*Alaska Christian Conference
1375 E. Bogard Rd., Wasilla, AK 99687 Tel. (907)376-5053
Media Contact, Pres., Rev. Gene Straatmeyer
Pres., Rev. Gene Straatmeyer
Vice-Pres., Barbara Block, 3840 O'Malley Rd., Anchorage, AK 99516
Sec., Rev. Linda Jean P. Myers, 1980 Black Bear Dr., Wasilla, AK 99687
Treas., Mary Kron, 9650 Arlene Dr., Anchorage, AK 99515
Major activities: Legislative & Social Concerns; Resources and Continuing Education; New Ecumenical Ministries; Communication; Alcoholism (Education & Prevention); Family Violence (Education & Prevention); Native Issues; Ecumenical/Theological Dialogue; HIV/AIDS Education and Ministry; Criminal Justice

ARIZONA

*Arizona Ecumenical Council
4423 N. 24th St., Ste. 750, Phoenix, AZ 85016 Tel. (602)468-3818 Fax (602)955-4540
Media Contact, Pres., Dr. Carl Wallen, 525 E. Alameda Dr., Tempe, AZ 85282 Tel. (602)967-6040 Fax (602)955-4540
Admn., Dr. Arlo Nau
Pres., Dr. Carl Wallen, 525 E. Alameda Dr., Tempe, AZ 85282
Major activities: Donohoe Ecumenical Forum Series; Political Action Team; Legislative Workshop; Arizona Ecumenical Indian Concerns Committee; Mexican/American Border Issues; VISN-TV; Disaster Relief

ARKANSAS

*Arkansas Interfaith Conference
16th & Louisiana, P.O. Box 164073, Little Rock, AR 72216 Tel. (501)375-1553
Media Contact, Conf. Exec., Mimi Dortch, Tel. (501)375-2865
Conf. Exec., Mimi Dortch
Pres., Rev. Bryan Fulwider, P.O. Box 6594, Sherwood, AR 72116
Sec., Rev. James Lupton, P.O. Box 726, Stuttgart, AR 72160
Treas., Mr. Jim Davis, Box 7239, Little Rock, AR 72217
Major activities: Task Force on Hunger; Institutional Ministry; Interfaith Executives' Advisory Council; Drug Abuse, Interfaith Relations; Church Women United; IMPACT; AIDS Task Force; Our House-Shelter; Governor's Task Force on Education; Statewide Fair Trial Committee Legislation; Ecumenical Choir Camp; Interreligious Health Care

CALIFORNIA

*California Council of Churches, Office for State Affairs
1300 N. St., Sacramento, CA 95814 Tel. (916)442-5447 Fax (916)442-3036
Media Contact, Exec. Dir., Patricia Whitney-Wise
Exec. Dir., Patricia Whitney-Wise
Major activities: Monitoring State Legislation; Calif. IMPACT Network; Legislative Principles; Food Policy Advocacy; Family Welfare Issues; Health; Church/State Issues

*Northern California Ecumenical Council
942 Market St., No. 301, San Francisco, CA 94102 Tel. (415)434-0670 Fax (415)434-3110
Media Contact, Rev. Ben Fraticelli
Exec. Dir., Rev. Ben Fraticelli
Pres., Rev. Phillip Lawson
Vice-Pres., Nancy Nielsen
Sec., Rev. Michael Cooper-White
Treas., Paul Stang
Admn. Asst., Juliet Twomey
Major activities: Peace with Justice; Faith and Witness; Refugee Services; Health Care Education; Public Policy Advocacy

*Southern California Ecumenical Council
1010 S. Flower, Ste. 403, Los Angeles, CA 90015 Tel. (213)746-7677 Fax (213)765-5418
Exec. Dir., David Bremer
Admn. Coord., Magaly Sevillano
Pres., Rev. J. Delton Pickering
Ed. Hope Publishing, Ms. Faith Sand
Interfaith Hunger Coalition, Dir., Ms. Elizabeth Riley
Interfaith Taskforce on Central America, Dir., Ms. Mary Brent Wehrli
Witness for Peace, Dir., ——
Peace with Justice, Dir., Rev. Ignacio Custuera
Witness Life, Dir., Rev. Al Cowen
Faith & Order, Dir., Rev. Barbara Mudge
Ecology Task Force, Dir., Rev. Gary Herbertson

L.A.N.D., Dir., Mr. Bruce Young
Interfaith Taskforce on South America, Dir., ——

Major activities: Communications Div. (*Ecumedia*, Hope Publ. House, *Ecunews*); Faith and Order; Witness Life (Clergy and Laity Concerned, Disaster Response, Econ. Devel., Ecology Task Force, Interfaith Hunger; Peace with Justice (Southern Calif. Interfaith Task Force on Central America; Southern Calif. Ecumenical Task Force on South Africa; Witness for Peace

Council of Churches of Contra Costa County
1543 Sunnyvale Ave., Walnut Creek, CA 94596 Tel. (510)933-6030
Media Contact, Dir., Rev. Machrina L. Blasdell
Dir., Rev. Machrina L. Blasdell
Chaplains: Rev. Keith Spooner; Rev. Jana L. Johnsen; Rev. Duane Woida; Rev. Harold Wright
Pres., Rev. Tim Tiffany
Treas., Mr. Bertram Sturm
Major activities: Institutional Chaplaincies, Community Education

The Council of Churches of Santa Clara County
1229 Naglee Ave., San Jose, CA 95126 Tel. (408)297-2660 Fax (408)297-2661
Media Contact, Assoc. Dir., Nina McCrory
Exec. Dir., Rev. Hugh Wire
Affordable Housing, James McCullough
Interpretation & Dev., Paul Burks
Pres., Rev. John L. Freesemann
Assoc. Dir., Nina McCrory
Food Proj. Coord., Gini Leport
Major activities: Social Education/Action; Ecumenical and Interfaith Witness; Affordable Housing; Emergency Food Supply

The Ecumenical Council of the Pasadena Area Churches
P.O. Box 41125, Pasadena, CA 91114-8125 Tel. (818)797-2402
Media Contact, Exec. Dir., Donald R. Locher
Exec. Dir., Rev. Dr. Donald R. Locher
Pres., Tobias English
Major activities: Christian Education; Community Worship; Community Concerns; Christian Unity; Ethnic Ministries; Hunger; Peace; Food, Clothing Assistance for the Poor; Emergency Shelter Line

Ecumenical Ministries of Northern California
1645 Fulton St., San Francisco, CA 94117 Tel. (415)923-1140
Exec. Dir., Neil Housewright
NIL

Fresno Metropolitan Ministry
1055 N. Van Ness, Ste. H, Fresno, CA 93728 Tel. (209)485-1416 Fax (209)233-3626
Media Contact, Exec. Dir., Rev. Walter P. Parry
Exec. Dir., Rev. Walter P. Parry
Admn. Asst., Sandy Sheldon
Pres., Rev. Michael Rogers
Major activities: Hunger Relief Advocacy; Homelessness, Human Relations and Anti-Racism; Cross Cultural Mental Health; Health Care Ad-

vocacy; Public Education Concerns; Children's Needs; Biblical and Theological Education For Laity; Refugee Advocacy; Ecumenical & Interfaith Celebrations & Cooperation; Youth Needs; Community Network Building

Interfaith Service Bureau
3720 Folsom Blvd., Sacramento, CA 95816 Tel. (916)456-3815
Media Contact, Interim Dir., Dexter McNamara
Interim Dir., Dexter McNamara
Co-Pres.: Rev. Lloyd Hansen; Rev. Lewis Knight
Major activities: Chaplaincy; Interfaith Food Closet Network; Clergy Concerns Committee; Religious Cable Television; Brown Bag Network (ages 60 & up); Faith in Crisis; Interfaith Hospitality Network

Marin Interfaith Council
35 Mitchell Blvd., Ste. 13, San Rafael, CA 94903 Tel. (415)492-1052
Exec. Dir., Rev. Linda Compton
Major activities: Interfaith Dialogue; Education; Advocacy; Convening; Interfaith Worship Services & Commemorations; Three Commissions: Basic Human Needs; Values & the Public Good; Religious Leadership Development for Lay & Clergy

Pacific and Asian American Center for Theology and Strategies (PACTS)
Graduate Theological Union, 1798 Scenic Ave., Berkeley, CA 94709 Tel. (510)849-0653
Media Contacts: Admn. Asst., Ruby Okazaki; Lilia Lopez-Karu
Dir., Julia K. Estrella
Pres., Dr. Tevita Puloka
Fin. Sec., Rev. Daniel Maedjaja
Major activities: Collect and Disseminate Resource Materials; Training Conferences; Public Seminars; Women in Ministry; Racial and Ethnic Minority Concerns; Journal and Newsletter; Hawaii & Greater Pacific Programme; Sale of Sadao Watanabe Calendars

Pomona Valley Council of Churches
1753 N. Park Ave., Pomona, CA 91768 Tel. (714)622-3806 Fax (714)622-0484
Media Contact, Dir. of Development, Holly Eichinger
Pres., Rev. Ricky Porter
Exec. Dir., Ms. Pat Irish
Sec., Ms. Mary Anne Parrot
Treas., Ms. Dorothy Becker
Major activities: Advocacy and Education for Social Justice; Ecumenical Celebrations; Hunger Advocacy; Emergency Food and Shelter Assistance; Farmer's Market; Affordable Housing; Transitional Housing

San Diego County Ecumenical Conference
4075 Park Bldg., San Diego, CA 92103
Media Contact, Exec. Dir., Rev. E. Vaughan Lyons, P.O. Box 3628, San Diego, CA 92163 Tel. (619)296-4557
Exec. Dir., Rev. E. Vaughan Lyons
Admn., Patricia R. Munley
Pres., Rev. Glenn Allison

Treas., Joseph Ramsey
Major activities: Interfaith Shelter Network/Transitional Housing for the Homeless; Emerging Issues; Communications; Faith Order & Witness; Worship & Celebration; Ecumenical Tribute Dinner; Advent Prayer Breakfast; AIDS Chaplaincy Program; Third World Opportunies; Seafarer's Mission; Seminars and Workshops; Called to Dance Assn.; S.D. Names Project *Quilt*

San Fernando Valley Interfaith Council
10824 Topanga Canyon Blvd., No. 7, Chatsworth, CA 91311 Tel. (818)718-6460 Fax (818)718-8694
Media Contact, Dir., Public Relations, Arlene C. Landon
Exec. Dir., Barry Smedberg
Pres., Rev. Allyn D. Axelton
Major activities: Seniors Multi-Purpose Centers; Nutrition & Services; Meals to Homebound; Meals on Wheels; Interfaith Reporter; Interfaith Relations; Interfaith AIDS Committee; Social Adult Day Care; Hunger/Homelessness; Volunteer Care-Givers; Clergy Gatherings; Food Pantries and Outreach; Peace and Justice; Aging; Hunger; Human Relations; Child Abuse Program; Medical Service; Homeless Program

South Coast Ecumenical Council
3326 Magnolia Ave., Long Beach, CA 90806 Tel. (310)595-0268 Fax (310)595-0268
Media Contact, Exec. Dir., Rev. Ginny Wagener
Exec. Dir., Rev. Ginny Wagener
Interfaith Action for the Aging, Cathy Trott
Centro Shalom, Olivia Herrera
Counseling Ministries, Dr. Lester Kim
Farmers' Markets, Rev. Dale Whitney
Peninsula Harbor Adult Day Care., Bernelle Harbert
Pres., Fr. Tom Hall
Major activities: Homeless Support Services; Interfaith Action for Aging; Farmers' Markets; Hunger Projects; Lay Academy of Religion; Church Athletic Leagues; Community Action; Hunger Walks; Christian Unity Worships; Interreligious Dialogue; Justice Advocacy

Westside Interfaith Conference
P.O. Box 1402, Santa Monica, CA 90406 Tel. (310)394-1518 Fax (310)576-1895
Media Contact, Rev. Gregory Garland
Exec. Dir., Rev. Gregory Garland
Major activities: Convalescent Hospital Visiting; Meals on Wheels; Community Religious Services; Convalescent Hospital Chaplaincy; Shelter Coordinator

COLORADO

*Colorado Council of Churches
1234 Bannock St., Denver, CO 80204-3631 Tel. (303)825-4910
Media Contact, Interim Dir., Cynthia Buschagen
Pres., Elder Beverly Webber
Major activities: Ecumenical Witness and Religious Dialogue; Institutional Ministries; Human Needs and Economic Issues (Includes Home-

lessness, Migrant Ministry, Justice in the Workplace); World Peace and Global Affairs; Communication, Media and the Arts; Interfaith Child Care Network

Interfaith Council of Boulder
3700 Baseline Rd., Boulder, CO 80303 Tel. (303)499-1444
Media Contact, Pres., Mark Peterson
Pres., Mark Peterson
Major activities: Interfaith Dialogue and Programs; Thanksgiving Worship Services; Food for the Hungry; Share-A-Gift; Quarterly Newsletter

CONNECTICUT

*Christian Conference of Connecticut (CHRISCON)
60 Lorraine St., Hartford, CT 06105 Tel. (203)236-4281 Fax (203)236-9977
Media Contact, Exec. Dir., Rev. Stephen J. Sidorak, Jr., Tel. (203)236-9977
Exec. Dir., Rev. Stephen J. Sidorak, Jr.
Exec. Asst., Sharon Anderson
Admn. Asst., Mildred Robertson
Pres., Rev. Geroge B. Elia
Vice-Pres., Ms. Elisabeth C. Miller
Sec., Rev Walter M. Elwood
Treas., Mr. Thomas F. Sarubbi
Major activities: Communications; Institutional Ministries; Conn. Bible Society; Conn. Council on Alcohol Problems; Ecumenical Forum; Faith & Order; Social Concerns; Public Policy

Association of Religious Communities
213 Main St., Danbury, CT 06810 Tel. (203)792-9450
Media Contact, Exec. Dir., Samuel E. Deibler, Jr.
Exec. Dir., Samuel E. Deibler, Jr.
Pres., The Rev. Dr. Mark A. Horton
Major activities: Refugee Resettlement, Family Counseling; Family Violence Prevention; Affordable Housing

The Capital Region Conference of Churches
30 Arbor St., Hartford, CT 06106 Tel. (203)236-1295
Media Contact, Exec. Dir., Rev. Roger W. Floyd
Exec. Dir., Rev. Roger W. Floyd
Pastoral Care & Training, Dir., Rev. John Swift
Aging Project, Dir., Rev. Robert Feldmann
Community Organizer, Mr. Joseph Wasserman
Broadcast Ministry Consultant, Ivor T. Hugh
Pres., Rev. Arthur Murphy
Major activities: Organizing for Peace and Justice; Aging; Legislative Action; Cooperative Broadcast Ministry; Ecumenical Cooperation; Interfaith Reconciliation; Chaplaincies; Low-Income Senior Empowerment; Anti-Racism Education

Center City Churches
170 Main St., Hartford, CT 06106 Tel. (203)728-3201
Media Contact, Exec. Dir., Paul C. Christie
Exec. Dir., Paul C. Christie
Pres., Rev. Hopeton Scott
Sec., Jon Luopa

Treas., Maggie Alston Claud
Major activities: Senior Services; Family Support Center; Energy Bank; Crisis Intervention; After-School Tutoring; Summer Day Camp; Housing for Persons with AIDS; Mental Health Residence; Community Soup Kitchen

Christian Community Action
98 S. Main St., South Norwalk, CT 06854 Tel. (203)854-1811
Dir., Jacquelyn P. Miller
Major activities: Emergency Food Program; Used Furniture; Loans for Emergencies; Loans for Rent, Security and Fuel

Christian Community Action
168 Davenport Ave., New Haven, CT 06519 Tel. (203)777-7848 Fax (203)777-7923
Media Contact, Bruce Blair
Exec. Dir., The Rev. Bonita Grubbs
Major activities: Emergency Food Program; Used Furniture & Clothing; Loans for Rent, Security and Fuel; Emergency Housing for Families; Advocacy

Council of Churches and Synagogues of Lower Fairfield County
628 Main St., Stamford, CT 06901 Tel. (203)348-2800 Fax (203)358-0627
Media Contact, Communications Ofc., Dorene LeMoult
Major activities: Prison Visitation; Senior Neighborhood Support Services; Ecumenical Services; Interfaith Dialogue; Food Bank; Fuel Assistance; Interfaith AIDS Ministry; Elderly Visitation Programs; Adopt-A-House; Friendship House; Homeless Planning

Council of Churches of Greater Bridgeport, Inc.
126 Washington Ave., Bridgeport, CT 06604 Tel. (203)334-1121 Fax (203)367-8113
Media Contact, Exec. Dir., Rev. John S. Kidd
Exec. Dir., Rev. John S. Kidd
Pres., Gilbert Mott
Sec., Mrs. Dorothy Allsop
Treas., Lynne Quido
Major activities: Youth in Crisis; Youth Shelter; Criminal Justice; Hospital, Nursing Home and Jail Ministries; Local Hunger; Ecumenical Relations, Prayer and Celebration; Covenantal Ministries; Homework Help

The Downtown Cooperative Ministry in New Haven
57 Olive St., New Haven, CT 06511 Tel. (203)776-9526
Media Contact, Coord., Rev. Samuel N. Slie
Coord., Rev. Samuel N. Slie
Pres., V. Rev. F. Aaron Laushway, O.P., 5 Hillhouse Ave., New Haven, CT 06511
Treas., Murray Harrison, 264 Curtis St., Meriden, CT 06450
Major activities: Mission to Poor and Dispossessed; Criminal Justice; Elderly; Sheltering Homeless; Soup Kitchen; Low Income Housing; AIDS Residence; Summer Children's Program; Pastoral Counseling Center

Manchester Area Conference of Churches

736 East Middle Tpke., P.O. Box 773, Manchester, CT 06045 Tel. (203)649-2093
Media Contact, Exec. Dir., Denise Cabana
Exec. Dir., Denise Cabana
Dir. of Human Ministries, Joseph Piescik
Dept. of Human Needs, Dir., Elizabeth Harlow
Pres., Wayne Mantz
Treas., Florence Noyes
Major activities: Provision of Basic Needs (Food, Fuel, Clothing, Furniture); Emergency Aid Assistance; Emergency Shelter; Soup Kitchen; Reentry Assistance to Ex-Offenders; Pastoral Care in Local Institutions; Interfaith Day Camp; Advocacy for the Poor; Ecumenical Education and Worship

New Britain Area Conference of Churches (NEWBRACC)

19 Chestnut St., New Britain, CT 06051 Tel. (203)229-3751
Media Contact, Exec. Dir., Michael Gorzoch
Exec. Dir., Michael Gorzoch
Pastoral Care/Chaplaincy: Rev. Susan Gregory-Davis; Rev. Ron Smith; Rev. Will Baumgartner; Diane Cardinal
Pres., Ernie Groth
Treas., Jacqueline Maddy
Ofc. Mgr., Judy Briggs
Major activities: Worship; Social Concerns; Emergency Food Bank Support; Communications-Mass Media; Hospital and Nursing Home Chaplaincy; Elderly Programming; Homelessness and Hunger Programs; Telephone Ministry; Urban Sisters Center; Thanksgiving Vouchers

Waterbury Area Council of Churches

24 Central Ave., Waterbury, CT 06702 Tel. (203)756-7831
Media Contact, Coord., Susan Girdwood
Coord., Susan Girdwood
Pres., Rev. Dennis Calhoun
Admn. Asst., Judith Juraschka
Major activities: Emergency Food Program; Emergency Fuel Program; Soup Kitchens; Ecumenical Worship; Christmas Toy Sale

DELAWARE

*The Christian Council of Delaware and Maryland's Eastern Shore

1626 N. Union St., Wilmington, DE 19806 Tel. (302)655-6151 Fax (302)573-2393
Media Contact, Exec. Dir., Rev. Elizabeth Doty
Exec. Dir., Rev. Elizabeth Doty
Interfaith Resource Center, Dir., Mrs. Elaine B. Stout
Pres., Rev. Harvey Manchester
Major activities: Ecumenical Work in: Public Policy; Faith and Order; Religious Education; Supporting Local Efforts

DISTRICT OF COLUMBIA

The Council of Churches of Greater Washington

5 Thomas Circle NW, Washington, DC 20005 Tel. (202)722-9240
Media Contact, Exec. Dir., Rev. Rodney L. Young
Exec. Dir., Rev. Rodney L. Young
Asst. Dir. for Prog., City, Mr. Daniel Thompson
D.C. Communities Ministries, Rev. George N. Bolden
Prog. Coord., Hope Valley Camp, Mr. Daniel Thompson
Pres., Rev. Lincoln S. Dring
Major activities: Development of Group and Community Ministries; Church Development and Redevelopment; Liaison with Public Agencies; In-school Youth Employment; Summer Youth Employment; Hope Valley Camp; Institutional Ministry; Hunger Relief; Vision to Action—Community Revitalization; Health Ministries; Cluster of Store Front Churches

Interfaith Conference of Metropolitan Washington

1419 V St. NW, Washington, DC 20009 Tel. (202)234-6300
Media Contact, Exec. Dir., Rev. Dr. Clark Lobenstine, Fax (202)234-6303
Exec. Dir., Rev. Dr. Clark Lobenstine
Asst. Dir., Rev. Ruth Bersin
Ofc. Mgr., Ms. Kadija Ash
Staff Assoc., Ms. Susan Burton
Sec., Najla Robinson
Pres., Bishop J. Clinton Hoggard
1st Vice-Pres., Bishop E. Harold Jansen
Vice-Pres.: Elder Raul McQuivey; Imam Yusuf Saleem; James Cardinal Hickey; Dr. Amrit Kaur
Sec., Rev. Dr. Rena Karefa-Smart
Treas., Simeon Kriesberg, Esq.
Major activities: Interfaith Dialogue; Interfaith Concert; Racial and Ethnic Polarization; Drugs; AIDS; Hunger; Homelessness

FLORIDA

*Florida Council of Churches

924 N. Magnolia Ave., Ste. 236, Orlando, FL 32803 Tel. (407)839-3454 Fax (407)246-0019
Media Contact, Pres., Dr. Edwin Albright, Jr., 1937 University Blvd., Jacksonville, FL 32217 Tel. (904)733-6658 Fax (904)733-6658
Exec. Dir., Walter F. Horlander
Admn. Asst., Carletta Stewart
Refugee Services, Orlando Ofc., Staff Assoc., Mildred Barnes
Refugee Services, Tallahassee Ofc., Staff Assoc., Thomas Frederick
Disaster Response, Staff Assoc., William Nix
Haitian Issues, Assoc., Jean Claude Picard
Major activities: Faith and Order; Education and Renewal; Evangelism and Mission; Justice and Peace Refugee Resettlement; Disaster Response; Legislation & Public Policy

Christian Service Center for Central Florida, Inc.

808 W. Central Blvd., Orlando, FL 32805-1809 Tel. (407)425-2523
Media Contact, Exec. Dir., ——, Tel. (407)425-2524 Fax (407)849-1495

Exec. Dir., ——
Family Emergency Services, Dir., Andrea Evans
Marriage & Family Therapy Center, Dir., Dr. Gloria Lobnitz
Alzheimers Respite, Dir., Mary Ellen Ort-Marvin
Fresh Start, Interim Dir., Rev. Homer Marigna
Dir. of Mktg., Margaret Ruffier-Farris
Pres., W. Marvin Hardy, III
Treas., Brenda de Treville
Sec., Bethany Mott
Major activities: Provision of Basic Needs (food, clothing, shelter); Emergency Assistance; Professional Counseling. Noon-time Meals; Sunday Church Services at Walt Disney World; Collection and Distribution of Used Clothing; Shelter & Training for Homeless; Respite for caregivers of Alzheimers

GEORGIA

*Georgia Christian Council
P.O. Box 7193, Macon, GA 31209-7193 Tel. (912)474-3906
Media Contact, Exec. Dir., ——
Exec. Dir., ——
Pres., Rev. Gordon Reinertsen, 3264 Northside Pkwy. NW, Atlanta, GA 30327
Treas., Rev. William K. Bagwell, P.O. Box 61, Ocilla, GA 31774
Major activities: Local Ecumenical Support and Resourcing; Legislation (GRAIN); Rural Development; Racial Justice; Networking for Migrant Coalition and Aging Coalition

Christian Council of Metropolitan Atlanta
465 Boulevard, S.E., Atlanta, GA 30312 Tel. (404)622-2235 Fax (404)627-6626
Media Contact, Exec. Dir., Dr. Robert P. Reno
Exec. Dir., Dr. Robert P. Reno
Assoc. Dir., Mr. Neal P. Ponder, Jr.
Pres., Marie Cofer
Treas., Ms. June B. Debatin
Major activities: Refugee Services; Emergency Assistance; Voluntary Service; Employment; Racism; Homeless; Ecumenical and Interreligious Events; Interchurch Ministry Planning; Persons with Handicapping Conditions; Women's Concerns; Seminary Student Internship Program

HAWAII

*Hawaii Council of Churches
1300 Kailua Rd., B-1, Kailua, HI 96734 Tel. (808)263-9788 Fax (808)262-8915
Exec. Dir., ——
Program Dir., Charles Berkstresser
Major activities: Laity and Clergy Education; Ecumenical Worship; Legislative Concerns; Interfaith TV and Radio Ministry; Social Action; AIDS Education; Advocacy for Peace with Justice and Hawaiian Self-Determination; Disaster Response

IDAHO

The Regional Council for Christian Ministry, Inc.
1100 S. Lee, Idaho Falls, ID 83403 Tel. (208)524-9935

Exec. Sec., Wendy Schoonmaker
Major activities: Island Park Ministry; Community Food Bank; Community Observances; Community Information and Referral Service; F.I.S.H.

ILLINOIS

*Illinois Conference of Churches
615 S. 5th St., Springfield, IL 62703 Tel. (217)544-3423
Media Contact, Gen. Sec., Rev. Dr. Carol M. Worthing, Fax (217)544-9307
Gen. Sec., Rev. Dr. Carol M. Worthing
Impact, Dir., Rev. Dr. George Ogle
Farm Worker Min., Dir., Rev. George Ogle
Domestic Violence Prog., Dir., Mrs. Nancy Tegtmeier
Human Services Min., Dir., Mrs. Nancy Tegtmeier
Unity & Relationships, Dir., Rev. Dr. Carol M. Worthing
Pres., Dr. David MacDonna, 1360 W. Main, Decatur, IL 62522 Tel. (217)423-1396
Treas., Mrs. Jacque Moore, 821 S. 2nd St., Springfield, IL 62704 Tel. (217)525-1876
Major activities: Migrant & Farm Worker Ministry; Chaplaincy in Institutions; Governmental Concerns and Illinois Impact; Ecumenical Courier; Ministry to Developmentally Disabled; Ministry with Aging; Domestic Violence; Semi-annual Assemblies on Ecumenical/Ecclesial Themes

Churches United of the Quad City Area
630 - 9th St., Rock Island, IL 61201 Tel. (309)786-6494
Media Contact, Exec. Dir., Charles R. Landon, Jr, 630 9th St., Rock Island, IL 61201 Tel. (309)786-6494
Exec. Dir., Charles R. Landon, Jr.
Assoc. Exec. Dir., Sheila D. Fitts
Pres., Dortha Hoy
Treas., Betty Bull
Major activities: Jail Ministry; Hunger Projects; Minority Enablement; Criminal Justice; Radio-TV; Peace; Local Church Development

Contact Ministries of Springfield
1100 E. Adams, Springfield, IL 62703 Tel. (217)753-3939
Media Contact, Exec. Dir., Ethel Butcher
Exec. Dir., Ethel Butcher
Major activities: Information; Referral and Advocacy; Ecumenical Coordination; Low Income Housing Referral; Food Pantry Coordination; Low Income Budget Counseling; 24 hours on call; Emergency On-site Overnight Shelter

Evanston Ecumenical Action Council
P.O. Box 1414, Evanston, IL 60204 Tel. (708)475-1150
Media Contact, Comm. Chpsn., Rev. Steve Durham, 2515 Central Park Ave., Evanston, IL 60201 Tel. (708)869-9210
Dir. Hospitality Cntr. for the Homeless, Patricia Johnson
Pres., Sandy Hubbard
Treas., Prentis A. Bryson

Major activities: Interchurch Communication and Education; Peace and Justice Ministries; Coordinated Social Action; Soup Kitchens; Multi-Purpose Hospitality Center for the Homeless; Worship and Renewal

Greater Chicago Broadcast Ministries
112 E. Chestnut St., Chicago, IL 60611-2014 Tel. (312)988-9001
Media Contact, Exec. Dir., Lydia Talbot
Pres., Bd. of Dir., John M. Buchanan
Exec. Dir., Lydia Talbot
Admn. Asst., Margaret Early
Major activities: Television, Cable, Interfaith/Ecumenical Development; Social/Justice Concerns

The Hyde Park & Kenwood Interfaith Council
1448 East 53rd St., Chicago, IL 60615 Tel. (312)363-1620
Media Contact, Exec. Dir., Mr. Werner H. Heymann, 1448 E. 53rd St., Chicago, IL 60615 Tel. (312)363-1620
Exec. Dir., Mr. Werner H. Heymann
Pres., Rabbi Elliot B. Gertel
Treas., Ms. Barbara Krell
Major activities: Interfaith Work; Hunger Projects; Community Development

Oak Park-River Forest Community of Congregations
P.O. Box 3365, Oak Park, IL 60303-3365 Tel. (708)386-8802
Media Contact, Patricia C. Koko
Admn. Sec., Patricia C. Koko
Vice-Pres., Rev. Edward Bergstraesser
Pres., Rev. Thomas Cross
Major activities: Community Affairs; Ecumenical/Interfaith Affairs; Youth Education; Food Pantry; Senior Citizens Worship Services; Interfaith Thanksgiving Services; Good Friday Services; UNICEF Children's Fund Drive; ASSIST (Network); Blood Drive; Literacy Training; Christian Unity Week Pulpit Exchange; CROP/CWS Hunger Walkathon; Austin Community Table (feeding hungry); Work with Homeless Commission; Unemployed Task Force; Economic & Health Bridgemaking to Chicago Westside

Peoria Friendship House of Christian Service
800 N.E. Madison Ave., Peoria, IL 61603 Tel. (309)671-5200
Media Contact, Exec. Dir., Rev. Arthur J. Campbell, Fax (309)671-5206
Exec. Dir., Rev. Arthur J. Campbell
Community Outreach, Dir., Ms. M. Lee Shaw
Prog. & Spiritual Nurture, Dir., Rev. Beth Hennessey
Pres. of Bd., Ms. Nora Sullivan

Major activities: Children's After-School; Teen Programs; Parenting Groups; Recreational Leagues; Senior Citizens Activities; Emergency Food/Clothing Distribution; Emergency Payments for Prescriptions, Rent, Utilities, Transportation; Community Outreach/Housing Advocacy; Economic Development; Grassroots Community Organizing; Crime Prevention; Neighborhood Empowerment

INDIANA

*Indiana Council of Churches
1100 W. 42nd St., Rm. 355, Indianapolis, IN 46208-3383 Tel. (317)923-3674 Fax (317)924-4859
Pres., Edith M. Jones
Vice Pres., Bishop Ralph A. Kempski
Sec., Rev. Bryon Rose
Treas., David F. Rees
Peace with Justice Facilitator, Rev. John E. Gaus
Major activities: Educational Ministries; Communications and Public Media; Social Ministries; Peace and Justice; Farmworker Ministries; Institutional Ministries; Ecumenical Concerns; Indiana Rural Justice Network; Refugee Resettlement; NAESNET; IMPACT

The Associated Churches of Fort Wayne & Allen County, Inc.
602 E. Wayne St., Fort Wayne, IN 46802 Tel. (219)422-3528
Media Contact, Exec. Dir., Rev. Vernon R. Graham
Exec. Dir., Rev. Vernon R. Graham
Sec., Linda Elliot
Foodbank: Ellen Graham; Mark Burris
WRE Coord., Maxine Bandemer
Prog. Development, Ellen Graham
Pres., Lewis Griffin, 4310 River Bluff Dr., Fort Wayne, IN 46835
Treas., Jean Streicher, 436 Downing Ave., Fort Wayne, IN 46807
Major activities: Weekday Religious Ed.; Radio & TV; Church Clusters; Church and Society Commission; Ed. for Christian Life Division; Clergy United for Action; Faith and Order Commission; Christian Ed.; Widowed-to-Widowed; CROP; Campus Ministry; Feeding the Babies; Food Bank System; Peace Education; Welfare Reform; Endowment Development; Habitat for Humanity; Child Care Advocacy; Project 25; Ecumenical Dialogue; Feeding Children; Vincent House (Homeless); A Learning Journey (Literacy); Reaching Out in Love

Christian Ministries of Delaware County
404 E. Main, Muncie, IN 47305 Tel. (317)288-0601
Media Contact, Exec. Dir., Sallie Maish
Exec. Dir., Sallie Maish
Pres., Barbara Eidson
Treas., Dr. J. B. Black
Major activities: Feed-the-Baby Program; Youth Ministry at Detention Center; Community Church Festivals; Community Pantry; Commu-

nity Assistance Fund; CROP Walk; Social Justice; Family Life Education; Combined Clergy

Church Community Services
1703 Benham Ave., Elkhart, IN 46516 Tel. (219)295-3673
Media Contact, Dir., Mary Jane Carpenter
Exec. Dir., Mary Jane Carpenter
Major activities: Advocacy for Low Income Persons; Emergency Housing, Financial Assistance; Transportation; Educational Programs; Food Pantry

The Church Federation of Greater Indianapolis, Inc.
1100 W. 42nd St., Ste. 345, Indianapolis, IN 46208 Tel. (317)926-5371 Fax (317)926-5373
Media Contact, Dir., Development, Carol J. Blinzinger, 1100 W. 42nd. St., Ste. 345, Indianapolis, IN 46208 Tel. (317)926-5371
Interim Exec. Dir., Rev. Angelique Walker-Smith
Social Min., Dir., Rosalyn Gurnell
Development & Communications, Dir., Carol J. Blinzinger
Pres., Priscilla Savage
Treas., Wayne R. Reynolds
Major activities: Celebrations and Unity; Ministries in Media; Ministries in Specialized Settings; Ministries in Society; Education and Training

Evansville Area Council of Churches, Inc.
414 N.W. Sixth St., Evansville, IN 47708-1332 Tel. (812)425-3524
Media Contact, Exec. Dir., Joseph N. Peacock, 414 NW Sixth St., Evansville, IN 47708 Tel. (812)425-3524
Exec. Dir., Rev. Joseph N. Peacock
Weekday Supervisor, Ms. Linda M. Schenk
Office Mgr., Ms. Barbara Gaisser
Pres., Rev. Conrad Grosenick
Sec., Ms. Sue Woodson
Fin. Chpsn., Rev. Will Jewsbury
Major activities: Christian Education; Community Responsibility & Service; Public Relations; Interpretation; Church Women United; Institutional Ministries; Interfaith Dialogue; Earth Care Ethics; Public Education Support; Disaster Preparedness

Indiana Interreligious Commission on Human Equality
1100 W. 42nd St., Ste. 365, Indianapolis, IN 46208 Tel. (317)924-4226 Fax (317)923-3658
Media Contact, Exec. Dir., Cathy J. Cox-Overby
Exec. Dir., Cathy J. Cox-Overby
Pres., Dr. Hamilton F. Niss
Treas., Rev. Norman L. Morford
Major activities: Human Rights; Anti-Racism Training; Racism/Sexism Inventory; Cultural and Religious Intolerance; South Africa Consultations; Interfaith Dialogue

Interfaith Community Council, Inc.
702 E. Market St., New Albany, IN 47150 Tel. (812)948-9248
Media Contact, Fin. Dir., Mary Ann Sodrel
Exec. Dir., Rev. Dr. David Bos

Fin. Dir., Mary Ann Sodrel
Child Dev. Center, Dir., Carol Welsh
Programs/Emergency Assistance, Jane Alcorn
Hedden House, Dir., Hope LaChance
RSVP, Dir., Matie Watts
Major activities: Child Development Center; Emergency Assistance; Hedden House (Half Way Home for Recovering Alcoholic Women); Retired Senior Volunteer Program; New Clothing and Toy Drives; Convalescent Sitter & Mother's Aides; Senior Day College; Emergency Food Distribution; Homeless Prevention

Lafayette Urban Ministry
12 North 8th St., Lafayette, IN 47901 Tel. (317)423-2691
Media Contact, Exec. Dir., Joseph Micon, 12 N. 8th St., Lafayette, IN 47901 Tel. (317)423-2691 Fax (317)742-2721
Exec. Dir., Joseph Micon
Advocate Coord., Jean Stearns
Public Policy Coord., Jo Johannsan
Pres., John Dahl
Major activities: Social Justice Ministries with and among the Poor

United Religious Community of St. Joseph County
2015 Western Ave., South Bend, IN 46629 Tel. (219)282-2397
Media Contact, Exec. Dir., Dr. James J. Fisko, Tel. (219)282-2387
Exec. Dir., Dr. James J. Fisko
Pres., Lawrence H. Dwyer
State Prison Visitation, Coord., Sr. Susan Kinzele, CSC
Victim Offender Reconciliation Prog., Coord., Neil Horsburgh
Volunteer Advocacy Project, Coord., Sara Goetz
Major activities: Religious Understanding; Social and Pastoral Ministries; Congregational Ministries

West Central Neighborhood Ministry, Inc.
1210 Broadway, Fort Wayne, IN 46802-3304 Tel. (219)422-9319
Media Contact, Exec. Dir., Andrea S. Thomas
Exec. Dir., Andrea S. Thomas
Ofc. Mgr., Joseph L. Falk
Food Bank Coord., Doras Bailey
Neighborhood Services Dir., Linnea Bartling
Neighborhood Services Coord., Carol Salge
Senior Citizens Dir., Gayle Mann
Major activities: After-school Program; Teen Drop-In Center; Church League Basketball; Summer Day Camp; Summer Overnight Camps; Information and Referral Services; Food Pantry; Nutrition Program for Senior Citizens; Senior Citizens Activities; Vocational Development for Teens/Young Adults; Developmental Services for Families, Senior Citizens and Disabled

IOWA

*Ecumenical Ministries of Iowa (EMI)
3816 - 36th St., Ste. 202, Des Moines, IA 50310 Tel. (515)255-5905 Fax (515)255-1421
Media Contact, Exec. Dir., Dr. James R. Ryan, 3816-36th St., Ste. 202, Des Moines, IA 50310

Exec. Dir., Dr. James R. Ryan
Office Mgr., Martha E. Jungck
Major activities: Facilitating the denominations' cooperative agenda of resourcing local expression of the church; Assess needs & develop responses through Global, Justice and Unity Commissions

Churches United, Inc.
866 4th Ave. SE, Cedar Rapids, IA 52403 Tel. (319)366-7163
Media Contact, Admn. Sec., Marcey Luxa
Admn. Sec., Mrs. Marcey Luxa
Pres., Rev. Lloyd Brockmeyer
Finance Chair, Rev. Robert Nelson, 2895 14th Ave., Marion, IA 52302 Tel. (319)377-3275
Major activities: Community Food Bank; LEAF (Local Emergency Assistance Fund; CROP; Co-operative Low Income Store (ONE Store); Community Information and Referral; Jail Chaplaincy; World Hunger; Nursing Home Ministry; Radio and TV Ministry; Ecumenical City-Wide Celebrations

Des Moines Area Religious Council
3816 - 36th St., Des Moines, IA 50310 Tel. (515)277-6969 Fax (515)255-1421
Media Contact, Exec. Dir., Forrest Harms
Exec. Dir., Forrest Harms
Pres., Michelle Parker
Treas., Tim Diebel
Major activities: Outreach and Nurture; Education; Social Concerns; Mission; Worship; Emergency Food Pantry; Ministry to Widowed; Child Care Assistance

KANSAS

*Kansas Ecumenical Ministries
5942 SW 29th St., Ste. D, Topeka, KS 66614-2539 Tel. (913)272-9531 Fax (913)272-9533
Media Contact, Exec. Dir., Rev. Alden Hickman
Exec. Dir., Rev. Alden Hickman
Pres., Rev. Kathy Timpany
Vice-Pres., Mrs. Winnie Crapson
Sec., Rev. George Harvey
Major activities: Legislative Activities; Program Facilitation and Coordination; World Hunger; Higher Education Concerns; Interfaith Rural Life Committee; Education; Mother-to-Mother Program; Peacemaking; Rural Development; Housing; Health Care

Cross-Lines Cooperative Council
736 Shawnee Ave., Kansas City, KS 66105 Tel. (913)281-3388
Media Contact, Dir. of Dev., Michael Greene, Tel. (913)281-2344
Exec. Dir., David Schmidt Shulman
Dir. of Programs, Rev. Robert L. Moore

Major activities: Emergency Assistance; Family Support Advocacy; Crisis Heating/Plumbing Repair; Thrift Store; Workcamp Experiences;

Adult Education (GED and Basic English Literacy Skills); School Supplies; Christmas Store; Institute for Poverty and Empowerment Studies (Education on poverty for the non-poor); Business Incubator (Entrepeneurial assistance for the poor)

Inter-Faith Ministries—Wichita
334 N. Topeka, Wichita, KS 67202-2410 Tel. (316)264-9303 Fax (316)264-2233
Media Contact, Dev./Communications Dir., Tina Lott
Exec. Dir., Rev. Sam Muyskens
Ofc. Mgr., Virginia Courtright
Community Ministry, Pat Cameron
Racia Justice Ministries, Rose Mburu
Inter-Faith Inn (Homeless Shelter), Dir., Sandy Swank
Operation Holiday, Dir., Sally Dewey
Dev./Communications, Dir., Christina Lott
Pres., Carolyn Benefiel
Major activities: Communications; Urban Education; Inter-religious Understanding; Community Needs and Issues; Theology and Worship; Hunger; Advocacy

KENTUCKY

*Kentucky Council of Churches
1039 Goodwin Dr., Lexington, KY 40505 Tel. (606)253-3027 Fax (606)231-5028
Media Contact, Exec. Dir., Nancy Jo Kemper
Exec. Dir., Rev. Nancy Jo Kemper
Disaster Recovery Prog., Coord., ——
Ed., *Intercom*, Dr. David Berg
Pres., Rev. William Brown, P.O. Box 12350, Lexington, KY 40582-2350
Major activities: Christian Unity; Hunger; Church and Government; Disaster Response; Peace Issues; Racism; Health Care Issues; Local Ecumenism; Rural Land/Farm Issues

Fern Creek/Highview United Ministries
P.O. Box 91372, Louisvlle, KY 40291 Tel. (502)239-4967
Exec. Dir., Darla A. Bailey
Pres., Elizabeth A. Sneed
Major activities: Ecumenically supported social service agency providing services to the community, including Emergency Financial Assistance, Food/Clothes Closet, Health Aid Equipment Loans, Information/Referral, Advocacy, Monthly Blood-Pressure Checks; Holiday Programs, Adult Day-Care Program, Life Skills Training and Intensive Care Management

Hazard-Perry County Community Ministries, Inc.
P.O. Box 1506, Hazard, KY 41702 Tel. (606)436-5043
Media Contact, Gerry Feamster-Martin
Exec. Dir., Ms. Gerry Feamster-Martin
Chpsn., Richard Mobawed
Treas., Ralph Ed Miller
Major activities: Food Pantry/Crisis Aid Program; Day Care; Summer Day Camp; After-school Program; Christmas Tree

Highlands Community Ministries

1140 Cherokee Rd., Louisville, KY 40204 Tel. (502)451-3695
Media Contact, Exec. Dir., Stan Esterle
Exec. Dir., Stan Esterle
Pres., Rev. Jack Oliver
Vice-Pres., Sandy Hoover
Sec./Treas., Larry Carr
Major activities: Welfare Assistance; Day Care; Counseling with Youth, Parents and Adults; Adult Day Care; Social Services for Elderly; Housing for Elderly and Handicapped; Ecumenical Programs; Community Classes; Activities for Children; Neighborhood and Business

Kentuckiana Interfaith Community

1115 South 4th St., Louisville, KY 40203 Tel. (502)587-6265
Media Contact, Exec. Dir., Rev. Dr. Gregory C. Wingenbach, 1115 S. 4th St., Louisville, KY 40203 Tel. (502)587-6265
Exec. Dir., Rev. Dr. Gregory C. Wingenbach
Pres., Rev. Dr. William E. Summers, III
Vice-Pres., Ms. Sara Klein Wagner
Sec., Sr. Gayle Brabec
Treas., Rev. Dr. Jim Holladay
Hunger/Racial Justice, Coord., Ed Koffenberger
Admn. Sec., Mrs. Sue Weatherford
Major activities: Christian/Jewish Ministries in Kentucky, Southern Indiana; Consensus Advocacy; Interfaith Dialogue; Ministry Support; Education & Racial Justice Forums; Network for Neighborhood-based Ministries; Community Winterhelp; Interfaith Caregivers; LUAH/Hunger & Racial Justice Commission; Intermedia: Radio and Cable TV, *Horizon* Newspaper; Ecumenical Research & Planning; Chaplaincy Support; Networking with Seminaries & Religious-Affiliated Colleges

Northern Kentucky Interfaith Commission, Inc.

601 Greenup St., Covington, KY 41011 Tel. (606)581-2237
Media Contact, Admin. Asst., Karen Yates, 218 Wallace Ave., Covington, KY 41011 Tel. (606)261-7834
Exec. Dir., Rev. William C. Neuroth
Major activities: Understanding Faiths; Meeting Spiritual and Human Needs; Enabling Churches to Greater Ministry

Paducah Cooperative Ministry

1359 S. 6th St., Paducah, KY 42003 Tel. (502)442-6795
Media Contact, Dir., Jo Ann Ross
Dir., Jo Ann Ross
Chpsn., Rev. Brian Cope
Major activities: Programs for: Hungry, Elderly, Poor, Homeless, Handicapped, Undereducated

South East Associated Ministries (SEAM)

2125 Goldsmith Ln., Bldg. #5, Louisville, KY 40218 Tel. (502)454-0380
Media Contact, Mary Beth Helton
Exec. Dir., Mary Beth Helton
Life Skills Center, Dir., Kay Sanders
Youth Services, Dir., Tracey Frazier

Pres., Era Boone Ferguson
Treas., Joe Hays
Major activities: Emergency Food and Financial Assistance; Life Skills Center (Programs of Prevention and Self-Sufficiency Through Education, Empowerment, Support Groups, etc.); Juvenile Court Diversion Program; Bloodmobile; Ecumenical Education and Worship; Family Counseling

South Louisville Community Ministries

Peterson Social Services Center, 204 Seneca Trail, Louisville, KY 40214 Tel. (502)367-6445
Media Contact, Exec. Dir., J. Michael Jupin
Exec. Dir., J. Michael Jupin
Bd. Chair., Rev. Lloyd Spencer
Bd. Vice-Chair., ——
Bd. Treas., Eugene Wells
Major activities: Food, Clothing & Financial Assistance; Home Delivered Meals, Transportation, Refugee Resettlement; Ecumenical Worship; Juvenile Diversion Program; Affordable Housing; Adult Day Care

St. Matthews Area Ministries

319 Browns Ln., Louisville, KY 40207 Tel. (502)893-0205
Exec. Dir., ——
Exec. Dir., ——
Emergency Fin. Assistance, Dir., Linda Leeser
After-School Care Centers, Dir., Janet Hennessey
Major activities: After-School Care; Youth Services; Interchurch Worship and Education; Emergency Financial Assistance; Housing Development

LOUISIANA

*Louisiana Interchurch Conference

660 N. Foster Dr., Ste. A-225, Baton Rouge, LA 70806 Tel. (504)924-0213
Media Contact, Exec. Dir., Rev. C. Dana Krutz
Exec. Dir., Rev. C. Dana Krutz
Pres., Bishop Marshall Gilmore
Major activities: Ministries to Aging; Prison Reform; Liason with State Agencies; Ecumenical Dialogue; Institutional Chaplains; Racism

Greater Baton Rouge Federation of Churches and Synagogues

P.O. Box 626, Baton Rouge, LA 70821 Tel. (504)925-3414
Media Contact, Exec. Dir., Rev. Jeff Day
Exec. Dir., Rev. Jeff Day
Admn. Asst., Mrs. Marion Zachary
Pres., Dr. William Staats
Vice-Pres., Mr. Richard K. Goldberger
Treas., Mr. E. Cole Thornton
Major activities: Combating Hunger; Housing (Helpers for Housing); Lay Academy of Religion (training); Interfaith Relations

Greater New Orleans Federation of Churches

4545 Magnolia St., #206, New Orleans, LA 70115 Tel. (504)897-4488 Fax (504)897-4208
Exec. Dir., Rev. J. Richard Randels

Major activities: Radio-TV Programs; Central Business District Ministries; Regional Suburban Network; Leadership Training; Senior Citizens; Social Action; Public Information; Religious Census and Survey; Literacy; Counseling Coordination; Cable TV Channel; Emergency

MAINE

*Maine Council of Churches
15 Pleasant Ave., Portland, ME 04103 Tel. (207)772-1918 Fax (207)772-2947
Media Contact, Communications Director, Sarah Campbell
Pres., Marc Mutty
Exec. Dir., Thomas C. Ewell
Major activities: Legislative Issues; Criminal Justice; Adult Education; Environmental Issues

MARYLAND

*Central Maryland Ecumenical Council
Cathedral House, 4 E. University Pkwy., Baltimore, MD 21218 Tel. (410)467-6194 Fax (410)554-6387
Media Contact, Ofc. Mgr., Martha Young
Pres., Rev. Barbara Sands
Major activities: Interchurch Communicationis and Collaboration; Information Systems; Ecumenical Relations; Urban Mission and Advocacy; Staff Judicatory Leadership Council; Commission on Dialogue; Commission on Church & Society; Commission on Admin. & Dev.; Annual Ecumenical Choral Concert; Annual Ecumenical Service

Community Ministries of Rockville
114 West Montgomery Ave., Rockville, MD 20850 Tel. (301)762-8682 Fax (301)762-2939
Media Contact, Newsletter Editor, Sylvia George
Exec. Dir. & Comm. Min., Mansfield M. Kaseman
Assoc. Dir., Dr. June R. Allred
Major activities: Shelter Care; Emergency Assistance; Elderly Home Care; Affordable Housing; Political Advocacy; Community Education

Community Ministry of Montgomery County
114 West Montgomery Ave., Rockville, MD 20850 Tel. (301)762-8682 Fax (301)762-2939
Media Contact, Exec. Dir., Lincoln S. Dring, Jr.
Exec. Dir., Lincoln S. Dring, Jr.
Major activities: Interfaith Clothing Center; Grant Assistance Program; Manna Food Center; The Advocacy Function; Thanksgiving in February; Information and Referral Services; Friends in Action; The Thanksgiving Hunger Drive; Montgomery Habitat for Humanity

MASSACHUSETTS

*Massachusetts Council of Churches
14 Beacon St., Rm. 416, Boston, MA 02108 Tel. (617)523-2771
Media Contact, Exec. Dir., Rev. Diane C. Kessler, Fax (617)523-2771
Exec. Dir., Rev. Diane C. Kessler

Public Policy, Assoc. Dir., Dr. Ruy Costa
Ecumenical Dev., Assoc. Dir., Rev. David A. Anderson
Major activities: Christian Unity; Education and Evangelism; Defend Social Justice & Individual Rights; Ecumenical Worship; Services and Resources for Individuals and Churches

Attleboro Area Council of Churches, Inc.
505 N. Main St., Attleboro, MA 02703 Tel. (508)222-2933
Media Contact, Executive Director, Carolyn L. Bronkar
Exec. Dir., Carolyn L. Bronkar
Admn. Sec., Joan H. Lindstrom
Ofc. Asst., Roberta Kohler
Hosp. Chpln. (Interim), Rev. John Crandall
Pres., Rev. Carole Baker, P.O. Box 1319, Attleboro Falls, MA 02760
Treas., David Quinlan, 20 Everett St., Plainville, MA 02762
Major activities: Hospital Chaplaincy; Personal Growth/Skill Workshops; Ecumenical Worship; Media Resource Center; Referral Center; Communications/Publications; Community Social Action; Food'n Friends Kitchens; Emergency Food and Shelter Fund; Nursing Home Volunteer Visitation Program

The Cape Cod Council of Churches, Inc.
142 Corporation Rd., Hyannis, MA 02601 Tel. (508)775-5073
Media Contact, Exec. Dir., Rev. Ellen C. Chahey
Exec. Dir., Rev. Ellen C. Chahey
Admn. Asst., Muriel L. Eggers
Pres., Ms. Elizabeth Bishop
Chaplain, Cape Cod Hospital, Rev. William Wilcox
Chaplain, Barnstable County Hospital, Elizabeth Stommel
Chaplain, Falmouth Hospital, Rev. Allen Page
Chaplain, House of Correction & Jail, Rev. Thomas Shepherd
Service Center & Thrift Shop: Dir., Joan McCurdy, P.O. Box 125, Dennisport, MA 02639 Tel. (508)394-6361; Asst. to Dir., Merilyn Lansing
Major activities: Pastoral Care; Social Concerns; Religious Education; Emergency Distribution of Food, Clothing, Furniture; Referral and Information; Church World Service; Interfaith Relations; Media Presence; Hospital & Jail Chaplaincy

Cooperative Metropolitan Ministries
474 Centre St., Newton, MA 02158 Tel. (617)244-3650
Media Contact, Exec. Dir., Claire Kashuck, 474 Centre S., Newton, MA 01258 Tel. (617)244-3650
Exec. Dir., Claire Kashuck
Bd. Pres., Thayer Morgan
Treas., James Blanchflower
Clk., Rev. Donna Sloan
Major activities: Low Income, Elderly, Affordable Housing; Legislative Advocacy; Hunger; Networking; Volunteerism; Publications & Worksops on Elder Housing Options

Council of Churches of Greater Springfield

32 Ridgewood Pl., Springfield, MA 01105 Tel. (413)733-2149

Media Contact, Asst. to Dir., Sr. John Bridgid, 152 Sumner Ave., Springfield, MA 01108 Tel. (413)733-2149 Fax (413)733-9817

Exec. Dir., Rev. Ann Geer

Community Min., Dir., Rev. L. Edgar Depaz

Pres., The Rev. Dr. Rolf Hedburg

Treas., Mr. Jerre Hoffman

Major activities: Christian Education Resource Center; Advocacy; Emergency Fuel Fund; Peace and Justice Division; Community Ministry; Task Force on Aging; Hospital and Jail Chaplaincies; Pastoral Service; Crisis Counseling; Christian Social Relations; Relief Collections; Ecumenical and Interfaith Relations; Ecumenical Dialogue with Roman Catholic Diocese; Mass Media; Church/Community Projects and Dialogue

Greater Lawrence Council of Churches

117A S. Broadway, Lawrence, MA 01843 Tel. (508)686-4012

Media Contact, Exec. Dir., David Edwards

Exec. Dir., David Edwards

Major activities: Ecumenical Worship; Radio Ministry; Hospital and Nursing Home Chaplancy; ; Church Women United; Afterschool Children's Program; Vacation Bible School

Inter-Church Council of Greater New Bedford

412 County St., New Bedford, MA 02740 Tel. (508)993-6242 Fax (508)991-3158

Media Contact, Exec. Min., Rev. Dr. John Douhan

Exec. Min., Rev. Dr. John Douhan

Pres., Rev. Nehemiah Boynton, III

Treas., Ms. Adra Cook

Major activities: Pastoral Counseling; Chaplaincy; Housing for Elderly; Urban Affairs; Parent-Child Center; Social Rehabilitation Club

Massachusetts Commission on Christian Unity

82 Luce St., Lowell, MA 01852 Tel. (508)453-5423

Media Contact, Exec. Dir., Rev. K. Gordon White

Exec. Sec., Rev. K. Gordon White

Major activities: Faith and Order Dialogue with Church Judicatories

Worcester County Ecumenical Council

25 Crescent St., Worcester, MA 01605 Tel. (508)757-8385

Media Contact, Sec., Eleanor G. Bird

Exec. Dir., Rev. Richard A. Hennigar

Program Mgr., Rev. Mary Jane O'Connor

Pres., Rev. Clifford Gerber

Major activities: Clusters of Churches; Electronic Media; Youth Ministries; Ecumenical Worship and Dialogue; Interfaith Activities; Nursing Home Chaplaincies; Assistance to Churches; Peace; Hunger Ministries; AIDS Pastoral Care Network; Mental Illness; Group Purchasing Consortium; Alcohol & Other Drug Abuse Prevention

MICHIGAN

*Michigan Ecumenical Forum

809 Center St., Ste. 7-B, Lansing, MI 48906 Tel. (517)485-4395

Media Contact, Coord./Exec. Dir., Rev. Steven L. Johns-Boehme, 809 Centre St., Ste. 7-B, Lansing, MI 48906 Tel. (517)485-4395

Coord./Exec. Dir., Rev. Steven L. Johns-Boehme

Major activities: Communication and Coordination; Support and Development of Regional Ecumenical Fora; Ecumenical Studies; Fellowship and Celebration; Church and Society Issues; Continuing Education

ACCORD—Area Churches Together . . .Serving

312 Capital Ave., NE, Battle Creek, MI 49017 Tel. (616)966-2500

Media Contact, Exec. Dir., Patricia A. Staib

Exec. Dir., Patricia A. Staib

Pres., Rev. David Morton

Vice-Pres./Church, Rev. Charles Sandum

Vice-Pres./Admn., David Lucas

Vice-Pres./Community, Rev. Joseph Bistayi

Major activities: CROP Walk; Thanksgiving International Student Homestay; Food Closet; Christian Sports; Week of Prayer for Christian Unity; Nursing Home Vesper Services; Ecumenical Worship

Bay Area Ecumenical Forum

P.O. Box 2061, Bay City, MI 48707-2061 Tel. (517)892-1200

Media Contact, Rev. Jim Orford

Jim Orford

Major activities: Ecumenical Worship; Community Issues; Christian Unity; Education; CROP Walk

Berrien County Association of Churches

275 Pipestone, Benton Harbor, MI 49022 Tel. (616)926-0030

Media Contact, Sec., Leona Ross

Pres., Rev. William Payne

Dir., Street Ministry, Rev. James Atterberry

Major activities: Street Ministry; CROP Walk; Community Issues; Fellowship; Christian Unity; Camp Program

Christian Communication Council of Metropolitan Detroit Churches

1300 Mutual Building, 28 W. Adams, Detroit, MI 48226 Tel. (313)962-0340

Exec. Dir., Rev. Edward Willingham, Jr.

Assoc. Dir., Mrs. Angie Willingham

Media Assoc., Mrs. Tawnya Bender

Meals for Shut-ins, Prog. Dir., Mr. John Simpson

Summer Feeding Prog., Coord., Mrs. Michelle Ballard

Major activities: Theological and Social Concerns; Ecumenical Worship; Educational Services; Electronic Media; Print Media; Meals for Shut-Ins; Summer Feeding Program

Grand Rapids Area Center for Ecumenism (GRACE)

38 W. Fulton, Grand Rapids, MI 49503 Tel. (616)774-2042

Media Contact, Exec. Dir., Rev. David P. Baak

Exec. Dir., Rev. David P. Baak

Prog. Dir., Ms. Betty Zylstra

Major activities: Hunger Walk; November Hunger and Shelter Awareness Week; Shelter Forum; AIDS Pastoral Care Network; Clergy Interracial Forum; Annual Week of Prayer for Christian Unity; Ecumenical Eucharist and Pentecost Services, Educational Forums.; Affiliates: AC-CESS (All County Churches Emergency Support System); FISH for My People (Transportation); Habitat for Humanity/GR; *Grace Notes*

Greater Flint Council of Churches

314 1/2 W. Third Ave., Flint, MI 48503-2522 Tel. (313)238-3691

Media Contact, Pres., Tom Brown, II

Pres., Tom Brown, II

Major activities: Christian Education; Christian Unity; Christian Missions; Hospital and Nursing Home Visitors; Church in Society; American Bible Society Materials; Interfaith Dialogue; Church Teacher Exchange Sunday; Directory of Area Faiths and Clergy; Operation Brush-up; Thanksgiving & Easter Sunrise Services

The Jackson County Interfaith Council

425 Oakwood, P.O. Box 156, Clarklake, MI 49234-0156

Media Contact, Exec. Dir., Rev. Loyal H. Wiemer, Box 156, Clarklake, MI 49234 Tel. (517)529-9721

Exec. Dir., Rev. Loyal H. Wiemer

Major activities: Chaplaincy at Institutions and Senior Citizens Residences; Martin L. King, Jr. Day Celebrations; Ecumenical Council Representation; Radio and TV Programs; Food Pantry; Interreligious Events; Clergy Directory

Muskegon County Cooperating Churches

315 W. Webster Ave., Muskegon, MI 49440 Tel. (616)725-8556

Media Contact, Admn. Asst., Sally Funkhauser

Exec. Dir., Mrs. Jeanette Bytwerk

Major activities: Dispute Resolution; Habitat for Humanity; Prison Ministry; CROP Walk; Ecumenical Worship; Education; Jewish-Christian Dialogue; AIDS Ministry; Community Issues

MINNESOTA

*Minnesota Council of Churches

122 W. Franklin Ave., Rm. 100, Minneapolis, MN 55404 Tel. (612)870-3600 Fax (612)870-3622

Media Contact, Exec. Dir., Rev. Dr. Margaret J. Thomas

Exec. Dir., Rev. Dr. Margaret J. Thomas

Life & Work, Dir., Louis S. Schoen

Hispanic Min., Dir., Carlos Mariani-Rosa

Unity & Relationships, Dir., Rev. Molly M. Cox

Refugee Services, Dir., Tatiana Pigoreva

Caseworker, Ge Cheuthang Yang

Indian Ministry, Dir., Mary Ann Walt

Facilities, Dir., Cynthia Darrington-Ottinger

Twin Cities Metropolitan Church Comm., Dir., Rev. Sally L. Hill

Joint Religious Legislative Coalition, Dir., Brian Rusche

Pres., Rev. Dean Larson

Major activities: Minnesota Church Center; Local Ecumenism; Life & Work: Anti-Racism; Hispanic Ministry, Indian Ministry; Legislative Advocacy; Refugee Services; Service to Newly Legalized/Undocumented Persons; Sexual Exploitation within the Religious Community; Unity & Relationships: Clergy Support; Consultation on Church Union; Ecumenical Study & Dialogue; Jewish-Christian Relations; Muslim-Christian Relations; Spirituality; State Fair Ministry

Arrowhead Council of Churches

230 E. Skyline Pkwy., Duluth, MN 55811 Tel. (218)727-5020

Media Contact, Exec. Dir., Ava M. Calbreath, 230 E. Skyline Parkway, Duluth, MN 55811 Tel. (218)727-5022 Fax (218)727-5022

Exec. Dir., Ava M. Calbreath

Pres., Joel Huenemann

Major activities: Inter-Church Evangelism; Community Concerns; Joint Religious Legislative Coalition; Downtown Ecumenical Good Friday Service; Corrections Chaplaincy; CROP Hunger Walk; Forum for Interfaith Dialogue; Community Seminars; Children's Concerns

Community Emergency Assistance Program (CEAP)

7231 Brooklyn Blvd., Brooklyn Center, MN 55429 Tel. (612)566-9600 Fax (612)566-9604

Media Contact, Exec. Dir., Edward T. Eide

Exec. Dir., Edward T. Eide

Major activities: Provision of Basic Needs (Food, Clothing, Furniture); Emergency Financial Assistance for Shelter; Home Delivered Meals; Chore Services and Homemaking Assistance; Single Parent Loan Program; Volunteer Services

Greater Minneapolis Council of Churches

122 W. Franklin Ave., Ste. 218, Minneapolis, MN 55404 Tel. (612)870-3660 Fax (612)870-3663

Media Contact, Dir. of Public Relations, Gay Gonnerman

Exec. Dir., Rev. Dr. Gary B. Reierson

Pres., Phyllis Sutton

Treas., Mike McCarthy

Indian Work, Assoc. Exec. Dir., Mary Ellen Dumas

Twin Cities Metropolitan Church Comm., Dir., Rev. Sally L. Hill

Meals on Wheels, Dir., Barbara Green

Minnesota FoodShare, Dir., Rev. Peg Chemberlin

Correctional Chaplains: Rev. Norman Menke; Rev. Susan Allers Hatlie; Rev. Thomas Van Leer

Congregations Concerned for Children, Dir., Carolyn Hendrixson

Shared Ministries Tutorial Program, Dir., Rev. Belinda Green

Metro Paint-A-Thon, Dir., Jodi Young

HandyWorks, Dir., DeLaine Brown

Div. of Indian Work: Emerg. Asst. Prog., Dir., George McCauley; Family Violence Prog., Dir., Don Bibeau; Teen Parents Prog., Dir., Noya Woodrich; Youth Leadership Dev. Prog., Dir., Margaret Thunder

Finance & Admn., Dir., Philip J. A. Hatlie

Dev., Church Relations & Communications, Dir., Gay Gonnerman

Major activities: Indian Work (Emergency Assistance, Youth Leadership, Teen Indian Parents Program, and Family Violence Program); Minnesota FoodShare; Metro Paint-A-Thon; Meals on Wheels; Shared Ministries Tutorial Program; Congregations Concerned for Children; Correctional Chaplaincy Program; HandyWorks; Education and Celebration

The Joint Religious Legislative Coalition

122 West Franklin Ave., Rm. 315, Minneapolis, MN 55404 Tel. (612)870-3670

Media Contact, Executive Director, Brian Rusche, 122 W. Franklin, Rm. 315, Minneapolis, MN 55404 Tel. (612)870-3670

Exec. Dir., Brian Rusche

Research Dir., Jim Casebolt

Major activities: Lobbying at State Legislature; Researching Social Justice Issues and Preparing Position Statements; Organizing Grassroots Citizen's Lobby

St. Paul Area Council of Churches

1671 Summit Ave., St. Paul, MN 55105 Tel. (612)646-8805 Fax (612)646-6866

Media Contact, Admin. Asst., Ella Snyder

Exec. Dir., Rev. Thomas Duke

Chaplaincy, Dr. Fred A. Hueners

Ecumenical Relations, Rev. Sally L. Hill

Congregations Concerned for Children, Ms. Peg Wangensteen

Volunteer Care Ministries, Ms. Pat Argyros

Dept. of Indian Work, Ms. Sheila WhiteEagle

Pres., Rev. George Weinman

Treas., Bert Neinaber

Sec., Ms. Kay Tellekson-Andrews

Major activities: Chaplaincy at Detention and Corrections Authority Institutions; Police Chaplaincy; Education and Advocacy Regarding Children and Poverty; Assistance to Churches Developing Children's/Parenting Care Services; Ecumenical Encounters and Activities; Indian Ministries; Leadership in Forming Cooperative Ministries for Children and Youth; Parent Befriender Ministry

Twin Cities Metropolitan Church Commission

122 W. Franklin, Rm. 100, Minneapolis, MN 55404 Tel. (612)870-3600 Fax (612)870-3663

Media Contact, Exec. Dir., Rev. Sally L. Hill

Exec. Dir., Rev. Sally L. Hill

Pres., Rev. Thomas Duke, 1671 Summit Ave., St. Paul, MN 55105

Major activities: Education; Peace Education Project; Interreligious Committee on Central America; Ecumenical Decade; Churches in Solidarity with Women; International Religious Exchanges; Sexism; Ecumenical Worship/Festival/Concert

MISSISSIPPI

*Mississippi Religious Leadership Conference

P.O. Box 68123, Jackson, MS 39286-8123 Tel. (601)948-5954 Fax (601)354-3401

Media Contact, Exec. Dir., Rev. Canon Thomas E. Tiller

Exec. Dir., Rev. Canon Thomas E. Tiller, Jr.

Chair, Rev. Rayford Woodrick

Treas., Mrs. Barbara Barnes

Co-Treas., Rev. Tom Clark

Major activities: Cooperation among Religious Leaders; Lay/Clergy Retreats; Social Concerns Seminars; Disaster Task Force; Advocacy for Disadvantaged

MISSOURI

Council of Churches of the Ozarks

P.O. Box 3947, Springfield, MO 65808-3947 Tel. (417)862-3586 Fax (417)862-2129

Media Contact, Comm. Dir., Jeanne Rudloff

Exec. Dir., Dr. Dorsey E. Levell

Major activities: Ministerial Alliance; Hospital Chaplains' Fellowship; Retired Sr. Volunteer Prog.; Treatment Center for Alcohol and Drug Abuse; Helping Elderly Live More Productively; Daybreak Adult Day Care Services; Ombudsman for Nursing Homes; Homesharing; Family Day Care Homes; USDA Food Program; Youth Ministry; Disaster Aid and Counseling; Homebound Shoppers; Alternatives to Incarceration; Food and Clothing Pantry; Ozarks Food Harvest; Spiritual Care Chaplains; Parenting Life Family Skills

Ecumenical Ministries

#2 St. Louis Ave., Fulton, MO 65251 Tel. (314)642-6065

Media Contact, Ofc. Mgr., Karen Luebbert

Exec. Dir., Rev. Jonelle Loehnis

Pres., William Jessop

Major activities: Kingdom Hospice; CROP Hunger Walk; Little Brother and Sister; Christmas Bookmobile; Unity Service; Family Ministry; Community Pastor Study; Senior Center Bible Study; Senior Advocacy and Study Seminars; F.I.S.H.; Habitat for Humanity

Interfaith Community Services

200 Cherokee St., P.O. Box 4038, St. Joseph, MO 64504-0038 Tel. (816)238-4511

Media Contact, Exec. Dir., David G. Berger, P.O. Box 4038, St. Joseph, MO 64504-0038 Tel. (816)238-4511

Exec. Dir., David G. Berger

Major activities: Child Development; Neighborhood Family Services; Group Home for Girls; Retired Senior Volunteer Program; Nutrition Program; Mobile Meals; Southside Youth Program; Church and Community; Housing Development

MONTANA

*Montana Association of Churches

Andrew Square, Ste. G, 100 24th St. W., Billings, MT 59102 Tel. (406)656-9779
Media Contact, Exec. Dir., Margaret E. McDonald, Andrew Square, Ste. G., 100 24th St. W., MT 59102 Tel. (406)656-9779
Exec. Dir., Margaret E. MacDonald
Admn. Asst., Larry D. Drane
Pres., Catherine D. Day, 3013 8th Ave., S., Great Falls, MT 59405
Treas., Don Patterson, East Lake Shore Rd., Big Fork, MT 59911
Legislative Liaison, ——
Campus Ministries Program Assoc., Rev. Kent Elliot, P.O. Box 389, Boulder, MT 59632
Major activities: Christian Education; Montana Religious Legislative Coalition; Christian Unity; Junior Citizen Camp; Public Information; Ministries Development; Social Ministry

NEBRASKA

*Interchurch Ministries of Nebraska

215 Centennial Mall S., Rm. 411, Lincoln, NE 68508-1888 Tel. (402)476-3391 Fax (402)476-9310
Media Contact, Exec. Sec., Rev. Daniel J. Davis, Sr.
Exec. Sec., Rev. Daniel J. Davis, Sr.
Admin. Asst., Sharon K. Kalcik
Pres., Rev. Dr. Roger Harp
Treas., Bishop James E. Krotz
Major activities: Interchurch Planning and Development; Comity; Indian Ministry; Rural Church Strategy; Hunger; Refugee Resettlement Coordination; United Ministries in Higher Education; Disaster Response; Christian in Society Forum; Clergy Consultations; Farm Families Crisis Response Network; Interim Ministry Network; Pantry Network; Farm Mediation Services; Hispanic Ministry; the Church & Mental Illness Program; Conflict Management; Rural Health

Lincoln Interfaith Council

215 Centennial Mall South, Rm. 408, Lincoln, NE 68508-1888 Tel. (402)474-3017 Fax (402)476-9310
Media Contact, Mr. David Hancock, Tel. (402)475-3262
Exec. Dir., Rev. Dr. Norman E. Leach
Pres., Cantor Michael Weisser
Treas., Ms. Nancy Glaesemann
Media Specialist, Mr. David Hancock
Urban Ministires, Rev. Dr. Norman E. Leach
Admn. Asst., Jean Burkhart
Fiscal Mgr., Jean Burkhart
Jail Chaplain, Cantor Michael Weisser
Communities of Hope, Rev. Otto Schultz
Major activities: Media Ministry; Emergency Food Pantry; Communites of Hope; Jail Chaplaincy; Clergy Connection for Non-Lincoln Patients; Prayer Breakfast; Refugee Work; Week of Prayer for Christian Unity; Torch of Understanding Award; Interfaith Leadership Award; Anti-Drug & Gang Activities; Boy-Girl Scouts/Campfire/4-H Religious Awards Programs; HS Baccalaureate; UNICEF; Festival of Faith; Holocaust Memorial Observance; Dr.

Martin Luther King, Jr. Observance; Asian Cultural Center for State of Nebraska

NEW HAMPSHIRE

*New Hampshire Council of Churches

24 Warren St., P.O. Box 1107, Concord, NH 03302 Tel. (603)224-1352 Fax (603)224-9161
Media Contact, Exec. Sec., Mr. David Lamarre-Vincent
Exec. Sec., Mr. David Lamarre-Vincent
Pres., Rev. Robert D. Witham, P.O. Box 465, Concord, NH 03302
Treas., Richard Edmunds, P.O. Box 136, Concord, NH 03302
Major activities: Ecumenical Work

NEW JERSEY

*New Jersey Council of Churches

116 N. Oraton Pkwy., East Orange, NJ 07017 Tel. (201)675-8600 Fax (201)675-0620
176 W. State St., Trenton, NJ 08608 Tel. (609)396-9546
Media Contact, Interim Exec. Dir., Jeffry H. Kittros
Commission on Impact & Public Witness, Rev. Steven C. Case
Commission on Mission Planning & Strategy, Rev. Robert K. Stuhlmann
Commission on Theology & Interreligious Relations, Rev. John Beardslee
Dir., IMPACT, Ms. Joan Diefenbach
Pres., Rev. James H. Chesnutt
Major activities: Racial Justice; AIDS Education; Ethics Public Forums; Advocacy; Economic Justice

Bergen County Council of Churches

165 Burton Ave., Hasbrouck Hts., NJ 07604 Tel. (201)288-3784
Media Contact, Pres., Rev. Stephen Giordano, Clinton Avenue Reformed Church, Clinton Ave. & James St., Bergenfield, NJ 07621 Tel. (201)384-2454
Exec. Sec., Neila Vander Vliet
Major activities: Ecumenical and Religious Institute; Brotherhood/Sisterhood Breakfast; Center for Food Action; Homeless Aid; Operation Santa Claus; Aging Services; Boy & Girl Scouts; Easter Dawn Services; Music; Youth; Ecumenical Representation; Support of Chaplains in Jails & Hospitals

Council of Churches of Greater Camden

P.O. Box 1208, Merchantville, NJ 08109 Tel. (609)985-5162
Media Contact, Exec. Sec., Rev. Dr. Samuel A. Jeanes, Braddock Bldg., 205 Tuckerton Road, Medford, NJ 08055 Tel. (609)985-7724
Exec. Sec., Rev. Dr. Samuel A. Jeanes
Pres., Rev. Lawrence L. Dunn
Treas., Mr. William G. Mason
Major activities: Radio & T.V.; Hospital Chaplaincy; United Services; Good Friday Breakfast; Mayors' Prayer Breakfast; Public Affairs; Easter Sunrise Service

Metropolitan Ecumenical Ministry

525 Orange St., Newark, NJ 07107 Tel. (201)481-6650
Exec. Dir., C. Stephen Jones
Major activities: Community Advocacy (education, housing, environment); Church Mission Assistance; Community and Clergy Leadership Development

Trenton Ecumenical Area Ministry (TEAM)

2 Propsect St., Trenton, NJ 08618
Media Contact, Exec. Dir., Rev. David A. Gibbons, 2 Prospect St., Trenton, NJ 08618 Tel. (609)396-9166
Exec. Dir., Rev. David A. Gibbons
Chpsn., Rev. Joanne B. Bullock
Hospital Chaplains: Rev. Leo Forsberg; Ms. Lee Carol S. Hollendonner; Rev. Jessie L. Irvin
Campus Chaplains: Rev. Wayne Griffith; Rev. Nancy Schulter; Rev. Jana Purkis-Brash
Sec., Ms. Tina Swan
Major activities: Racial Justice; Children & Youth Ministries; Advocacy; CROP Walk; Ecumenical Worship; Hospital Chaplaincy; Church Women United; Campus Chaplaincy; Congregational Empowerment; Prison Chaplaincy; Substance Abuse Ministry Training

NEW MEXICO

*New Mexico Conference of Churches

124 Hermosa SE, Albuquerque, NM 87108-2610 Tel. (505)255-1509 Fax (505)256-0071
Media Contact, Exec. Sec., Dr. Wallace Ford
Pres., Rev. James Smith, 10453 Springwood Dr., El Paso, TX 79925-7645
Treas., Rev. Norm Scrimshire
Exec. Sec., Dr. Wallace Ford
Major activities: State Task Forces: Peace With Justice, Poverty, Disability Concerns, Legislative Concerns/Impact, Faith and Order, AIDS, Correctional Ministries, Public Education, Eco-Justice, Ecumenical Continuing Education; Regional Task Forces: Aging, Ecumenical Worship, Refugees, Emergency Care, Alcoholism; Church's Solidarity with Women

Inter-Faith Council of Santa Fe, New Mexico

818 Camino Sierra Vista #6, Santa Fe, NM 87501 Tel. (505)983-2892
Media Contact, Secretary, Barbara A. Robinson, Fax (505)473-5637
Pres., Har Har Singh Khalsa
Chpsn., Barbara A. Robinson
Peace with Justice Task Force, Chpsn., Marjorie Schuckman
Major activities: Faith Community Assistance Center; Hunger Walk, Interfaith Dialogues/Celebrations/Visitations; Peace Projects; Understanding Hispanic Heritage; Newsletter

NEW YORK

*New York State Council of Churches, Inc.

Program Ofc.: 362 State St., Albany, NY 12210 Tel. (518)436-9319 Fax (518)427-6705
Administrative Ofc.: 3049 E. Genesee St., Syracuse, NY 13224-1699 Tel. (315)446-6151 Fax (315)446-5789
Media Contact, Assoc. for Admn. & Communications, Thila A. Bell
Exec. Dir., Rev. Dr. Arleon L. Kelley
Mod., Rev. J. Fay Cleveland
1st Vice-Mod., Rev. Allen A. Stanley
2nd Vice-Mod., The Ven. Michael S. Kendall
Sec., Isabel Morrison
Treas., Dr. George H. DeHority
New York State Interfaith IMPACT, Edward J. Bloch
Chaplaincy, Program Assoc., Rev. Frank Snow
Admn. Asst., Sylvenia Cochran
Consultant for Resource Dev., Mary Lu Brown
Finance & Personnel, Helen Vault
Communications Consultant, Thila A. Bell
Issues Research & Advocacy, Progam Assoc.,
———
Major activities: Public Policy and Ecumenical Ministries; Chaplaincy in State Institutions; Rural Poor and Migrants; Homeless; AIDS; Universal Health Care; Life and Law; U.S.-Canadian Border Concerns; Single Parent Families; Faith and Order; Environmental Issues; The Family, Education, Violence; Covenanting Congregations

Allied Christians of Tioga

228 Main Street, Owego, NY 13827 Tel. (607)687-6919
Exec. Dir., Mr. Alfred Smith, Jr.
Pres., Jack Checchia
Major activities: Jail Ministry; Soup Kitchen; Food Pantry; Coordinate Special Events

Bronx Division of the Council of Churches of the City of New York

39 W. 190th St., P.O. Box 144, Bronx, NY 10468 Tel. (718)367-0612
Media Contact, Gregory Groover
Pres., Rev. Robert L. Foley, Sr.
Exec. Dir., Gregory Groover
Major activities: Pastoral Care; Christian Education & Youth Ministry; Welfare & Advocacy; Substance Abuse

Brooklyn Council of Churches

125 Ft. Greene Pl, Brooklyn, NY 11217 Tel. (718)625-5851
Media Contact, Dir., Charles Henze
Dir., Mr. Charles Henze
Pres., Rev. Harvey P. Jamison
Treas., Rev. Albert J. Berube
Major activities: Education Workshops; Food Pantries; Welfare Advocacy; Hospital and Nursing Home Chaplaincy; Church Women United; Legislative Concerns

Broome County Council of Churches, Inc.

81 Main St., Binghamton, NY 13905 Tel. (607)724-9130

Media Contact, Exec. Dir., Mr. William H. Stanton, Fax (607)724-9148
Exec. Dir., Mr. William H. Stanton
Admn. Asst., Ms. Joyce M. Kirby
Hospital Chaplains: Rev. LeRoy Flohr; Mrs. Betty Pomeroy
Jail Chaplain, Rev. Philip Singer
Aging Ministry Coord., Mrs. Dorothy Myers
CHOW Prog. Coord., Mrs. Billie L. Briggs
Pres., Mr. Ray A. Hull
Treas., Mrs. Rachel Light
Major activities: Hospital and Jail Chaplains; Youth and Aging Ministries; CHOW (Emergency Hunger Program); Christian Education; Ecumenical Worship and Fellowship; Media; Community Affairs; Peace

Buffalo Area Council of Churches
1272 Delaware Ave., Buffalo, NY 14209-2401 Tel. (716)882-4793
Media Contact, Exec. Dir., Rev. Dr. G. Stanford Bratton
Exec. Dir., Rev. Dr. G. Stanford Bratton
Pres., Rev. Dr. Robert L. Graham
1st Vice-Pres., Charles Banks
2nd Vice-Pres., Rev. Donald Garrett
Sec., Dolores Gibbs
Treas., Mr. Gerald Richardson
Chpsn. of Trustees, Mr. Charles Leonard
Church Women United: Coord., Sally Giordano; Pres., Bobbie Campbell
Community Witness & Ministry, Chpsn., Ms. Sheila Nickson
Spirituality & Community Bldg., Chpsn., Rev. Paul Robinson
Public Policy, Chpsn., Father Julius Jackson
Radio & TV: Coord., Linda Velazquez; Chpsn., Rev. Robert Hutchinson
Major activities: Radio-TV; Social Services; Chaplains; Church Women United; Ecumenical Relations; Refugees; Public Policy; Community Development; Lay/Clergy Education; Interracial Dialogue; Police/Community Relations; Buffalo Coalition for Common Ground

Buffalo Area Metropolitan Ministries, Inc.
775 Main St., Ste. 203, Buffalo, NY 14203-1310 Tel. (716)854-0822 Fax (716)856-1480
Media Contact, Exec. Dir., Rev. Cynthia L. Bronson
Exec. Dir., Rev. Cynthia L. Bronson
Pres., Rabbi Joshua Aaronson
Vice-Pres. for Plng. & Prog., Ms. Brenda Easley
Vice-Pres. for Admn. & Fin., Rev. Lloyd Noyes
Sec., Sr. Marita Lannan
Treas., Rev. Carl Thitchener
Chair, Food for All Prog., Maureen Gensler
Major activities: An association of religious communities in Western New York with Jewish, Muslim, Christian, Unitarian, Univeralist, Hindu, and Jain membership providing a united religious witness through these major activities: Shelter; Hunger; Economic Issues; Interreligious Dialogue; Interfaith AIDS Network

Capital Area Council of Churches, Inc.
646 State St., Albany, NY 12203 Tel. (518)462-5450
Media Contact, Admn. Asst., Renee Kemp

Exec. Dir., Rev. Dr. Robert C. Lamar
Admn. Asst., Renee Kemp
Pres., Rev. Fred Shilling
Treas., Mr. Alan Spencer
Major activities: Hospital Chaplaincy; Food Pantries; CROP Walk; Jail and Nursing Home Ministries; Martin Luther King Memorial Service and Scholarship Fund; Emergency Shelter for the Homeless; Campus Ministry; Ecumenical Dialogue; Forums on Social Concerns; Peace and Justice Education; Inter-Faith Programs; Legislative Concerns; Half-Way House for Ex-Offenders; Annual Ecumenical Musical Celebration

Chautauqua County Rural Ministry
127 Central Ave., P.O. Box 362, Dunkirk, NY 14048 Tel. (716)366-1787
Media Contact, Acting Exec. Dir., Mrs. Kathleen Peterson
Acting Exec. Dir., Mrs. Kathleen Peterson
Major activities: Chautauqua County Food Bank; Collection/Distribution of Furniture, Clothing, & Appliances; Homeless Services; Building & Refurbishing Housing; Summer Work Camps

Christians United in Mission, Inc.
224 Mohawk Ave., Box 2199, Scotia, NY 12302 Tel. (518)382-7505
Media Contact, Coord., Jim Murphy
Coord., Jim Murphy
Major activities: Promote Cooperation/Coordination Among Member Judicatories in Urban Ministries, Social Action

Concerned Ecumenical Ministry to the Upper West Side
286 LaFayette Ave., Buffalo, NY 14213 Tel. (716)882-2442
Media Contact, Exec. Dir., Cliff Whitman
Exec. Dir., Mr. Cliff Whitman
Pres., Carl Henzelman, Jr.
Major activities: Community center serving youth, young families, seniors and the hungry

Cortland County Council of Churches, Inc.
7 Calvert St., Cortland, NY 13045 Tel. (607)753-1002
Media Contact, Office Mgr., Joy Niswender
Exec. Dir., Rev. Donald M. Wilcox
Major activities: College Campus Ministry; Hospital Chaplaincy; Nursing Home Ministry; Newspaper Column; Interfaith Relationships; Hunger Relief; CWS; Crop Walk; Leadership Education; Community Issues; Mental Health Chaplaincy, Grief Support

Council of Churches of Chemung County, Inc.
330 W. Church St., Elmira, NY 14901 Tel. (607)734-7622
Media Contact, Exec. Dir., Joan Geldmacher
Exec. Dir., Mrs. Joan Geldmacher
Pres., Rev. Curtis Coley
Chaplain, Rev. Nancy Lane, Tel. (607)732-0027
Major activities: CWS Clothing Collection; CROP

Walk; UNICEF; Institutional Chaplaincies; Radio, Easter Dawn Service; Communications Network; Representation on Community Boards and Agencies; Meals on Wheels; Campus Ministry; Food Cupboards; Ecumenical Services; Amerasian Resettlement

Council of Churches of the City of New York

475 Riverside Dr., Rm. 439, New York, NY 10015 Tel. (212)870-2120 Fax (212)870-2025
Media Contact, Exec. Dir., Rev. Patricia A. Reeberg
Exec. Dir., Rev. Patricia A. Reeberg
Pres., Dr. Spencer C. Gibbs
1st Vice-Pres., Rev. N. J. L'Heureux, Jr.
2nd Vice-Pres., Rev. Robert L. Foley, Sr.
3rd. Vice-Pres., Rev. Edward Earl Johnson
Sec., Ms. Paule Alexander
Treas., Dr. John E. Carrington
Major activities: Radio & TV; Pastoral Care; Protestant Chapel, Kennedy International Airport; Coordination and Strategic Planning; Religious Conferences; Referral & Advocacy; Youth Development; Women's Interfaith Network

Dutchess Interfaith Council, Inc.

9 Vassar St., Poughkeepsie, NY 12601 Tel. (914)471-7333
Media Contact, Exec. Dir., Rev. Gail A. Burger
Exec. Dir., Rev. Gail A. Burger
Pres., Margaret O. Kelland
Treas., Elizabeth M. DiStefano
Major activities: CROP Hunger Walk; Interfaith Music Festival; Public Worship Events; Interfaith Dialog; Christian Unity; Interfaith Youth Evening; Oil Purchase Group; Interfaith Volunteer Caregivers Program; County Jail Chaplaincy; Radio

East Harlem Interfaith

2050 - 2nd Ave., New York, NY 10029 Tel. (212)427-1500 Fax (212)427-1636
Media Contact, Chpsn., Rev. Robert V. Lott, 1356 96th St., New York, NY 10128 Tel. (212)289-0425 Fax (212)996-2028
Exec. Dir., ——
Bd. Chmn., Rev. Robert V. Lott
Major activities: Ecumenical Worship; Welfare and Hunger Advocacy; AIDS Advocacy; Community Organizing; Economic Development (Community Reinvestment)

Genesee County Churches United, Inc.

P.O. Box 547, Batavia, NY 14021 Tel. (716)343-6763
Media Contact, Pres., Glenn Bloom, 5614 Burns Rd., Medina, NY 14103 Tel. (716)343-6763
Pres., Glenn Bloom
Exec. Sec., Helen H. Mullen
Chaplain, Rev. Ellison Elmer
Major activities: Jail Ministry.; Food Pantries; Serve Needy Families; Radio Ministry; Pulpit Exchange; Community Thanksgiving; Ecumenical Services at County Fair

Genesee-Orleans Ministry of Concern

118 S. Main St., Box 245, Albion, NY 14411

Media Contact, Exec. Dir., Marian M. Adrian, GNSH, Tel. (716)589-9210
Exec. Dir., Marian M. Adrian, G.N.S.H., P.O. Box 245, Albion, NY 14411 Tel. (716)589-9210
Advocates: Jeannette Winiarz; Robert Fleming
Pres., Kevin Kennedy
Chaplains: Orleans County Jail, Rev. Wilford Moss; Orleans Albion Correctional Facility, Sr. Dolores O'Dowd
Major activities: Advocacy Services for the Disadvantaged, Homeless, Ill, Incarcerated and Victims of Family Violence; Emergency Food, Shelter, Utilities, Medicines

Greater Rochester Community of Churches

17 S. Fitzhugh St., Rochester, NY 14614-1488 Tel. (716)232-6530
Media Contact, Exec. Dir., Rev. Lawrence E. Witmer
Exec. Dir., Rev. Lawrence E. Witmer
Admn. Asst., Marie E. Gibson
Fin. Admn., Ilse Kearney
Pres., Rev. J. Paul Womack
Treas., Stanley Grenn
Major activities: Mission Education & Training; Refugee Resettlement; Hospital Chaplaincies; Evangelism; Church Unity; Social Ministries; Commission on Christian-Jewish Relations; Commission on Christian-Muslim Relations; Community Economic Development

InterReligious Council of Central New York

910 Madison St., Syracuse, NY 13210 Tel. (315)476-2001
Media Contact, Development Assoc., Marianne Valone
Exec. Dir., Dorothy F. Rose
Pres., Marilyn L. Pinsky
Assoc. Dir.: Rev. Dale Hindmarsh; Rev. Robert Stoppert
Refugee Resettlement, Dir., Nona Stewart
Senior Companion Prog., Dir., Virginia Frey
Hunger Outreach Services, Dir., ——
Project Exodus Re-entry Program, Dir., Sr. Judith Falk
Covenant Housing, Dir., Anne Peterson
Interreligious Relations, Mary Keller
Community & Cong. Concerned for Children, Dir., Joan Bordett
Bus. Mgr., Arthur A. West
Major activities: Interreligious Relations; Education, Worship; Institutional Pastoral Care; Children/Youth Ministry; Low Cost Housing Program; Community Advocacy and Planning

Livingston County Coalition of Churches

P.O. Box 548, Lakeville, NY 14480 Tel. (716)658-2122
Coord., Rev. Robert Booher
Pres., Rev. Richard Clough
Major activities: Hospice Program; Jail Ministry; Visitors' Center at Groveland Correctional Facility; Food Pantries; Gateways Family Service; Parents Anonymous; Alternative Sentencing Program; Coordinate Services for Aging and Rural Poor; Christian Education Learning Fair; Lecture Series and Chaplain at SUNY Geneseo

The Long Island Council of Churches

1644 Denton Green, Hempstead, NY 11550 Tel. (516)565-0290
Eastern Office, 235 Sweezy Ave., Riverhead, NY 11901
Media Contact, Admn. Asst., Ms. Barbara McLaughlin, Fax Call for inst
Exec. Dir., Rev. Robert L. Pierce
Exec. Asst., Rev. Ruth Phillips
Admn. Asst., Ms. Barbara McLaughlin
Pastoral Care, Dir., Rev. Dr. Kai Borner
Clinical Pastoral Educ., Dir., Rev. Dr. Kai Borner
Social Services, Dir., Mrs. Lillian Sharik, Tel. (516)565-0390
Project REAL, Dir., Mr. Stephen Gervais
Counseling Services, Dir., Rev. S. Bruce Wagner
Nassau County Ofc., Social Services Sec., Ms. Mildred McMahon
Suffolk County Ofc., Family Support, Ms. Carolyn Gumbs
Food Prog., Mrs. Millie McSteen
Blood Prog. Coord.: Ms. Leila Truman; Ms. Audry Wolf
Training in Caring Ministry, Coord., Ms. Barbara Mathews
Major activities: Pastoral Care in Hospitals and Jails; Clinical Pastoral Education; Emergency Food; Family Support & Advocacy; Advocacy for Domestic and International Peace & Justice; Blood Donor Coordination; Church World Service; Interfaith Cooperation; Clergy/Laity Training; Newsletter; Church Directory; Counseling Service; Community Residences for Adults with Psychiatric Disabilities (Project REAL); HIV Education Projects; Special Projects

The Niagara Council of Churches Inc.

Rainbow Blvd. at Second St., Niagara Falls, NY 14303 Tel. (716)285-7505
Media Contact, Pres., Nessie S. Bloomquist, 7120 Laur Rd., Niagara Falls, NY 14304 Tel. (716)297-0698 Fax (716)298-1193
Exec. Dir., Caroline C. Latham
Pres., Nessie S. Bloomquist, 7120 Laur Rd., Niagara Falls, NY 14304
Treas., Edward Weber, 1306 Maple Ave., Niagara Falls, NY 14305
Trustees Chpsn., Rev. Robert Bellingham, 1889 Pierce Ave., Niagara Falls, NY 14301
Major activities: Ecumenical Worship; Bible Study; Christian Ed. & Social Concerns; Church Women United; Evangelism & Mission; Institutional Min. Youth Activities; Hymn Festival; Week of Prayer for Christian Unity; CWS Projects; Audio-Visual Library; UNICEF; Food Pantries and Kitchens; Community Missions, Inc.; Political Refugees; Eco-Justice Task Force; Migrant/rural Ministries; Interfaith Coalition on Energy

Niagara County Migrant Rural Ministry

5465 Upper Mountain Rd., Lockport, NY 14094 Tel. (716)433-4070
Media Contact, Exec. Dir., Ms. Barbara Meeks, 5465 Upper Mountain Road, (716)439-0477
Chpsn., Beverly Farnham
1st Vice-Chpsn., David Dickinson
2nd Vice-Chpsn., Rev. Patricia Ludwig
Sec., Anne Eifert

Treas., Betty Stimson
Major activities: Migrant Farm Worker Program; Primary Health Clinic; Assist with immigration problems and application process for social services; Emergency Food Pantry; "Rummage Room" for clothing and household goods; Monitor Housing Conditions; Assist Rural Poor; Referrals to appropriate service agencies

Queens Federation of Churches

86-17 105th St., Richmond Hill, NY 11418-1597 Tel. (718)847-6764 Fax (718)847-7392
Media Contact, Rev. N. J. L'Heureux, Jr.
Exec. Dir., Rev. N. J. L'Heureux, Jr.
Exec. Asst., Kevin Murphy
York College Chaplain, Rev. Dr. Hortense Merritt
Pres., Rev. Dr. Hortense Merritt
Treas., Lloyd W. Patterson, Jr.
Major activities: Emergency Food Service; York College Campus Ministry; Blood Bank; Scouting; Christian Education Workshops; Planning and Strategy; Church Women United; Community Consultations; Seminars for Church Leaders; Directory of Churches and Synagogues; Christian Relations (Prot/RC); Chaplancies; Public Policy Issues; N.Y.S. Interfaith Commission on Landmarking of Religious Property; Queens Interfaith Hunger Network

Rural Migrant Ministry

P.O. Box 4757, Poughkeepsie, NY 12601 Tel. (914)485-8627
Media Contact, Exec., Richard Witt
Exec., Richard Witt
Pres., Mary Sherwig
Major activities: Serving the rural poor and migrants through a ministry of advocacy & emposerment; Women's Support Group; Youth Program; Latino Committee; Organization and Advocacy with and for Rural Poor

Schenectady Inner City Ministry

5 Catherine St., Schenectady, NY 12307 Tel. (518)374-2683
Media Contact, Urban Agent, Rev. Phillip N. Grigsby
Urban Agent, Rev. Phillip N. Grigsby
Admn. Asst., Ms. Elaine MacKinnon
Emergency Food Liaison, Ms. Patricia Obrecht
Nutrition Dir., Diane Solomon
Project SAFE/Safehouse Dir., Ms. Delores Edmonds-McIntosh
Church/Community Worker, Jim Murphy
Learning Tree Nursery, Dir., Victoria Filiaci
Pres., Sr. Stella Dillon
Bethesda House, Rev. Paul Fraser
Save and Share, Nilda Colon
Major activities: Emergency Food; Advocacy; Housing; Child Care; Alternatives to Prostitution for Runaway and At-Risk Youth; Shelter for Runaway/Homeless Youth; Neighborhood and Economic Issues; Ecumenical Worship and Fellowship; Community Research; Education in Churches on Faith Responses to Social Concerns; Legislative Advocacy; Nutrition Outreach Program; Hispanic Community Ministry; Food Buying Club; Day Shelter; CROP Walk

Southeast Ecumenical Ministries

25 Westminister Rd., Rochester, NY 14607 Tel. (716)271-5350
Dir., Laura Julien
Pres., Rev. F. Wilson Brown
Major activities: Food Cupboard; Transportation of Elderly

Staten Island Council of Churches

2187 Victory Blvd., Staten Island, NY 10314 Tel. (718)761-6782
Media Contact, Exec. Sec., Mrs. Mildred J. Saderholm, 94 Russell St., Staten Island, NY 10308 Tel. (718)761-6782
Pres., Rev. James A. Martin
Vice-Pres., Rev. Debra Jameson
Exec. Sec., Mrs. Mildred J. Saderholm
Major activities: Support; Christian Education; Pastoral Care; Congregational Concerns; Urban Affairs

Troy Area United Ministries

17 First St., #2, Troy, NY 12180 Tel. (518)274-5920
Media Contact, Exec. Dir., Margaret T. Stoner
Exec. Dir., Mrs. Margaret T. Stoner
Pres., Brian O'Shaughnessy
Chaplain, R.P.I., Rev. Donald Stroud
Chaplain, Russell Sage College, Cheryl Donkin
Major activities: Community Dispute Settlement (mediation) Program; College Ministry; Nursing Home Ministry; CROP Walk; Homeless and Housing Concerns; Weekend Meals Program at Homeless Shelter; Community Worship Celebrations; Racial Relations; and Bias Awareness

Wainwright House Interfaith Center

260 Stuyvesant Ave., Rye, NY 10580 Tel. (914)967-6080 Fax (914)967-6114
Media Contact, Gen. Mgr., James Wall
Gen. Mgr., James Wall
Major activities: Educational Program and Conference Center; Intellectual, Psychological, Physical and Spiritual Growth

NORTH CAROLINA

*North Carolina Council of Churches

Methodist Bldg., 1307 Glenwood Ave., Ste. 162, Raleigh, NC 27605-3258 Tel. (919)828-6501
Media Contact, Exec. Dir., Rev. S. Collins Kilburn
Exec. Dir., Rev. S. Collins Kilburn
Program Assoc., Jimmy Creech
Pres., Rev. Ann Calvin Rogers-Witte, 814 Dixie Tr., Raleigh, NC 27607
Treas., Dr. James W. Ferree, P.O. Box 11772, Winston-Salem, NC 27116
Major activities: Children and Families; Health Care Justice; Christian Unity; Equal Rights; Legislative Program; Criminal Justice; Farmworker Ministry; Peace; Rural Crisis; Racial Justice; Disaster Response; CaringProgram for Children; AIDS Ministry; Workplace Safety

Asheville-Buncombe Community Christian Ministry (ABCCM)

24 Cumberland Ave., Asheville, NC 28801 Tel. (704)259-5300 Fax (704)259-5316
Media Contact, Exec. Dir., Rev. Scott Rogers
Exec. Dir., Rev. Scott Rogers
Pres., Mr. James A. Lee
Major activities: Crisis Ministry; Jail/Prison Ministry; Shelter Ministry; Medical Ministry

Greensboro Urban Ministry

305 West Lee St., Greensboro, NC 27406 Tel. (919)271-5959 Fax (919)271-5920
Media Contact, Exec. Dir., Rev. Mike Aiken
Exec. Dir., Rev. Mike Aiken
Major activities: Emergency Financial Assistance; Housing; Hunger Relief; Inter-Faith and Inter-Racial Understanding; Justice Ministry; Indigent Health Care

NORTH DAKOTA

*North Dakota Conference of Churches

227 W. Broadway, Bismarck, ND 58501 Tel. (701)255-0604 Fax (701)222-8543
Media Contact, Office Mgr., Eunice Brinckerhoff
Pres., Paula Ringuette, PBVM
Treas., Rev. Randall Phillips
Ofc. Mgr., Eunice Brinckerhoff
Major activities: Prison Chaplaincy; Rural Life Ministry; Interfaith Dialogue; BEM Study; Faith and Order

OHIO

*Ohio Council of Churches

89 E. Wilson Bridge Rd., Columbus, OH 43085-2391 Tel. (614)885-9590 Fax (614)885-6097
Exec. Dir., Rev. Debra L. Moody-Vaughn
Public Policy, Dir., Rev. David O. McCoy
Church & Community Issues, Dir., Mr. Raymond S. Blanks
Pres., Mrs. Violet Retzer
Treas., Mrs. Catherine Childs
Vice Pres., Rev. Charles W. Loveless
Sec., Rev. Joseph J. Witmer
Major activities: Agricultural Issues; Economic & Social Justice; Ecumenical Relations; Health Care Reform; Public Policy Issues; Criminal Justice Issues

Akron Area Association of Churches

750 Work Dr., Akron, OH 44320 Tel. (216)535-3112
Media Contact, Admin. Asst., Chloe Ann Kriska
Exec. Dir., Rev. Harry Eberts, Jr.
Bd. of Trustees, Pres., Rev. Jan Walker
Vice-Pres.: Rev. David Frees; Mary Ann Boland
Sec., Rev. Curtis Walker
Treas., Dr. Stephen Laning
Program Dir., Elsbeth Fritz
Christian Ed., Dir., Mrs. Kimberly Porter
Major activities: Messiah Sing; Interfaith Council; Newsletters; Resource Center; Community Worship; Training of Local Church Leadership; Radio Programs; Clergy and Lay Fellowship Breakfasts; Cable TV; Interfaith Caregivers;

Neighborhood Development; Community Outreach

Alliance of Churches
470 E. Broadway, Alliance, OH 44601 Tel. (216)821-6648
Media Contact, Dir., Richard A. Duro
Dir., Richard A. Duro
Pres., Rev. Robert Stewart
Treas., Betty Rush
Major activities: Christian Education; Community Relations & Service; Ecumenical Worship; Community Ministry; Peacemaking; Medical Transportation for Anyone Needing It

Churchpeople for Change and Reconciliation
326 W. McKibben, Box 488, Lima, OH 45802 Tel. (419)229-6949
Media Contact, Exec. Dir., Richard Keller
Exec. Dir., Richard Keller
Major activities: Developing Agencies for Minorities, Poor, Alienated and Despairing; Community Kitchens

Council of Christian Communions of Greater Cincinnati
2439 Auburn Ave., Cincinnati, OH 45219-2701 Tel. (513)579-0099
Media Contact, Exec. Dir., Joellen W. Grady
Exec. Dir., Joellen W. Grady
Justice Chaplaincy, Assoc. Dir., Rev. Jack Marsh
Educ., Assoc., Sharon D. Jones
Communication, Asst. Dir., John H. Gassett
Pres., Mattie Henderson
Major activities: Christian Unity & Interfaith Cooperation; Justice Chaplaincies; Police-Clergy Team; Adult and Juvenile Jail Chaplains; Religious Education; Broadcasting and Communications; Information Service; Social Concerns

Ecumenical Communications Commission of Northwestern Ohio, Inc.
1011 Sandusky, Ste. M, P.O. Box 351, Perrysburg, OH 43551 Tel. (409)874-3932
Media Contact, Dir., Margaret Hoepfl
Dir., Ms. Margaret Hoepfl
Major activities: Electronic Media Production; Media Education

Greater Dayton Christian Council
212 Belmonte Park E., Dayton, OH 45405 Tel. (513)222-8654
Media Contact, Exec. Dir., Robert B. Peiffer, Fax (513)222-8656
Exec. Dir., Rev. Robert B. Peiffer
Volunteer Jail Chaplaincy Program, Coord., Nancy Haas
Race Relations, Dir., James Burton
Pres., Rev. Don Dixon
Major activities: Communications: Service to Churches and Community; Housing Advocacy; Race Relations Advocacy; Substance Abuse Prevention; Jail Chaplaincy

Inner City Renewal Society
2230 Euclid Ave., Cleveland, OH 44115 Tel. (216)781-3913
Media Contact, Exec. Dir., Myrtle L. Mitchell
Exec. Dir., Myrtle L. Mitchell
Major activities: Friendly Town; Urban Ministries Training and Community Development Center; Drug and Alcohol Education; Project Chore; Scholarship; Burial Aid

Interchurch Council of Greater Cleveland
2230 Euclid Ave., Cleveland, OH 44115-2499 Tel. (216)621-5925 Fax (216)621-0588
Media Contact, Janice Giering
Exec. Dir., Rev. Thomas Olcott, Tel. (216)621-5925
Church & Society, Dir., Ms. Mylion Waite
Communications, Dir., Ms. Janice Giering
Pres., Rev. James Roberson
Chmn. of the Assembly, Bert Moyer
Major activities: Church and Society; Communications; Hunger; Christian Education; Legislation; Faith and Order; Public Education; Interchurch News; Tutoring; Parent-Child First Teachers Program; Shelter for Homeless Women and Children; Radio & T.V.; Interracial Cooperation; Interfaith Cooperation; Adopt-A-School; Women of Hope; Leadership Development; Religious Education; Center for Peace & Reconciliation—Youth and the Courts

Mahoning Valley Association of Churches
631 Wick Ave., Youngstown, OH 44502 Tel. (216)744-8946
Media Contact, Exec. Dir., Elsie L. Dursi
Exec. Dir., Elsie L. Dursi
Pres., Mrs. June Ewing, 456 Bradley La., Youngstown, OH 44504
Treas., Mr. Paul Fryman, 42 Venloe Dr., Poland, OH 44514
Major activities: Communications; Christian Education; Ecumenism; Social Action; Advocacy

Metropolitan Area Church Council
760 E. Broad St., Columbus, OH 43205 Tel. (614)461-7103
Media Contact, Exec. Dir., Rev. Burton Cantrell
Exec. Dir., Rev. Burton Cantrell
Chpsn. of Bd., Rev. Ron Botts
Sec., Mrs. Juanita Bridges
Treas., Alvin Hadley
Major activities: Newspaper; Liaison with Community Organizations; Assembly; Week of Prayer for Christian Unity; Support for Ministerial Associations and Church Councils; Seminars for Church Leaders; Prayer Groups; CROP Walk; Social Concerns Hearings

Metropolitan Area Religious Coalition of Cincinnati
1035 Enquirer Bldg., 617 Vine St., Cincinnati, OH 45202 Tel. (513)721-4843 Fax (513)721-4844
Media Contact, Dir., Rev. Duane Holm
Dir., Rev. Duane Holm
Pres., Ms. Alice Skirtz
Major activities: Children-At-Risk; Food & Welfare; Housing; Public Education

Pike County Outreach Council
122 E. Second St., Waverly, OH 45690 Tel. (614)947-7151
Dir., Judy Dixon

Toledo Ecumenical Area Ministries
444 Floyd St., Toledo, OH 43620 Tel. (419)242-7401 Fax (419)242-7404
Media Contact, Admn., Nancy Lee Atkins
Metro-Toledo Churches United, Admn., Nancy Lee Atkins
Toledo Campus Ministry, Exec. Dir., Rev. Glenn B. Hosman, Jr.
Toledo Metropolitan Mission, Exec. Dir., Nancy Lee Atkins
Major activities: Ecumenical Relations; Interfaith Relations; Food Program; Campus Ministry; Social Action (Public Education; Health Care; Urban Ministry; Employment; Community Organization; Welfare Rights; Housing; Refugee Assistance; Mental Retardation; Voter Registration/Education)

Tuscarawas County Council for Church and Community
120 First Dr. SE, New Philadelphia, OH 44663 Tel. (216)343-6012
Exec. Dir., Barbara E. Lauer
Pres., Mr. Thomas L. Kane, Jr., 1221 Crater Ave., Dover, OH 44622
Treas., Mr. James Barnhouse, 120 N. Broadway, New Phladelphia, OH 44663
Office Mgr., Shirley Dinger
Major activities: Human Services; Health; Family Life; Child Abuse; Housing; Educational Programs; Emergency Assistance; Legislative Concerns; Juvenile Prevention Program; Teen Pregnancy Prevention Program; Prevention Program for High Risk Children; Bimonthly newsletter *The Pilot*

West Side Ecumenical Ministry
4315 Bridge Ave, Cleveland, OH 44113 Tel. (216)651-2037 Fax (216)651-4145
Media Contact, Exec. Dir., Elving F. Otero
Exec. Dir., Elving F. Otero
Assoc. Dir., Sister Madeline Shemo
Major activities: Emergency Food Centers; Senior Meals Programs; Youth Services; Advocacy; Empowerment Programs; Church Clusters; Drug Rehabilitation Program; Head Start Centers; Theatre

OKLAHOMA

*Oklahoma Conference of Churches
P.O. Box 60288, 2901 Classen Blvd., Ste. 260, Oklahoma City, OK 73146-0288 Tel. (405)525-2928 Fax (405)524-9310
Media Contact, Exec. Dir., The Rev. Dr. William B. Moorer
Exec. Dir., The Rev. Dr. William B. Moorer
Pres., Rev. John A. Petuskey, P.O. Box 510, Edmond, OK 73083
Treas., Mrs. Ann Fent
Major activities: Christian Unity Issues; COCU

Covenanting; Community Building Among Members; Farm Crisis; Ecumenical Decade with Women ; Children's Advocacy; Day at the Legislature; Interfaith Relations; Public Education

Tulsa Metropolitan Ministry
221 S. Nogales, Tulsa, OK 74127 Tel. (918)582-3147 Fax (918)582-3159
Exec. Dir., Sr. Sylvia Schmidt, S.C.C.
Assoc. Dir., Rev. Adam Kittrell
Resident Service Dir., Carolyn Kusler
Day Center for the Homeless, Dir., Marcia Sharp
Housing Outreach Services of Tulsa, Dir., Rev. Charles Boyle
Advocacy Program Dir., Rev. Larry Cowan
Pres., Sylvia Tuers
Vice-Pres., Maynard Ungerman
Sec., William Moore
Treas., M. C. Potter
Major activities: Corrections Ministry; Jewish-Christian Understanding; Police-Community Relations; Shelter for the Homeless; Women's Issues; Shelter for Mentally Ill; Outreach and Advocacy for Public Housing; Spirituality and Aging; Legislative Issues; Interfaith Dialogue TV Series; Christian Issues/Justice and Peace Issues; Central America Concerns & Events; Eco-Spirituality; Environmental Concerns; Communications; Racism Task Force

OREGON

*Ecumenical Ministries of Oregon
0245 S.W. Bancroft St., Ste. B, Portland, OR 97201 Tel. (503)221-1054 Fax (503)223-7007
Media Contact, Exec. Dir., Rev. Rodney I. Page
Exec. Dir., Rev. Rodney I. Page
Dep. Dir., Barbara J. George
Fin. Services Mgr., Sandy Johnson
Fin. Dev. & Publicity, Bill Deiz
Center for Urban Education, Dir., Rodney I. Page
Legis. & Govt. Ofc., Dir., Ellen C. Lowe
Grants & Contracts Specialist, Gary B. Logsdon
Clinical Services, Dir., Cindy Klug
Med. Dir., Neal Rendleman, M.D.
Hopewell House Dir., Judith Kenning
HopeHaven, Dir., Meg Oleson
Hemophilia NW, Dirs.: Larkey DeNeffe; Beth Weinstein
Drug Educ. Proj., Bob McNeil
Alcohol & Drug Min., Nancy Anderson
Police Chaplain, Rev. Greg Kammann
Sponsors Organized to Assist Refugees, Gary Gamer, Fax (503)284-6445
Emergency Food, Dir., Jack Kennedy
Folk-Time (Soc. Prog. for Mentally Ill), Dir., Maggie Austin
Job Opportunity Bank, Dir., Karen Quitt, Fax (503)249-2857
HIV Day Center, Dir., Tina Tommaso-Jennings
Camp Odyssey, Eric Massanari
12 Step Haven, Holly Hale
Cult Resource Center, Bernie Muller
Common Ground, Jane Harper
Pres., The Rev. William Creevey
Treas., Ron Means
Major activities: Educational Ministries; Legislation; Urban Ministries; Refugees; Chaplaincy; Social Concerns; Jewish-Christian Relations; Farm\Rural Ministry; Alcohol\Drug Ministry; Welfare Advocacy; Faith & Order; Peace Ministries; IMPACT; Diversity Training; Communi-

cations; AIDS Ministry; HIV Day Center; Prostitution Ministry; Racism; Religious Education; Health & Human Ministries; Medical Clinic; Cult Resource Center; Emergency Food; Job Search; Computer Training; Mental Illness Support

PENNSYLVANIA

*Pennsylvania Conference on Interchurch Cooperation

P.O. Box 2835, 223 North St., Harrisburg, PA 17105 Tel. (717)545-4761 Fax (717)238-1473
900 S. Arlington Ave., Harrisburg, PA 17109
Media Contact, Dr. Howard Fetterhoff
Co-Staff: Dr. Howard Fetterhoff; Rev. Albert E. Myers
Co-Chpsns.: Bishop Nicholas C. Datillo; Bishop Guy S. Edmiston, Jr.
Major activities: Theological Consultation; Social Concerns; Inter-Church Planning; Conferences and Seminars; Disaster Response Preparedness

*The Pennsylvania Council of Churches

900 S. Arlington Ave., Ste. 100, Harrisburg, PA 17109 Tel. (717)545-4761
Media Contact, Exec. Dir., Rev. Albert E. Myers, Fax (717)545-4765
Exec. Dir., Rev. Albert E. Myers
Soc. Min., Asst. Exec. Dir., Rev. Paul D. Gehris
Pres., Bishop Charlie F. McNutt, Jr., 221 N. Front St., P.O. Box 11937, Harrisburg, PA 17108
Vice-Pres., Mrs. Pattee Miller, Jr.
Sec., Rev. Jack Rothenberger
Treas., Robert Ziegler
Bus. Mgr., Janet Gollick
Major activities: Institutional Ministry; Migrant Ministry; Truck Stop Chaplaincy; Social Ministry; Park Ministry; Inter-Church Planning and Dialog; Conferences; Disaster Response; Trade Association Activities; Church Education; Ethnic Cooperation

Allegheny Valley Association of Churches

1333 Freeport Rd., Natrona Heights, PA 15065 Tel. (412)226-0606
Media Contact, Exec. Dir., Luella H. Barrage
Exec. Dir., Luella H. Barrage
Pres., Rev. Dr. W. James Legge, RR #4, Box 186, Tarentum, PA 15084
Treas., Mrs. Libby Grimm, RR #2, Box 36, Tarentum, PA 15084
Major activities: Education Evangelism Workshops; Ecumenical Services; Dial-a-Devotion; Youth Activities; CROP Walk; Food Bank; Super Cupboard; Emergency Aid; Cross-on-the-Hill; AVAC Interfaith Hospitality Network for Homeless Families

Christian Associates of Southwest Pennsylvania

239 Fourth Ave., #1817, Pittsburgh, PA 15222-1769 Tel. (412)288-4020 Fax (412)288-4023
Media Contact, Exec. Dir., Rev. Donald E. Leiter
Exec. Dir., Rev. Donald E. Leiter
Assoc. Exec. Dir., Rev. Bruce H. Swenson
Cable TV Coord., Mr. Earl C. Hartman, Jr.
Admn. Asst., Mrs. Barbara Irwin
Pres., Dr. Andrew C. Harvey

Treas., Rev. David Zubik
Communications Coord., Mr. Bruce J. Randolph
Major activities: Communications; Planning; Church and Community; Leadership Development; Theological Dialogue; Evangelism/Church Growth; Racism

Christian Churches United of the Tri-County Area

900 S. Arlington Ave., Rm. 128, Harrisburg, PA 17109 Tel. (717)652-2771 Fax (717)545-7777
Media Contact, Interim Exec. Dir., Rev. Driss Knickerbocker
Interim Exec. Dir., Rev. Driss Knickerbocker
Pres., Rev. K. Joy Kaufman
Treas., Rev. Lawrence Jones
Vice-Pres., Geraldine Brown
Sec., Doris Frysinger
HELP, Dir., Jacqueline Rucker, 201 Locust St., Harrisburg, PA 17101 Tel. (717)238-5670 Fax (717)238-1916
La Casa, Dir., Maria Davila, 1312 Derry St., Harrisburg, PA 17104 Tel. (717)236-3279
Major activities: Volunteer Ministries to Prisons; Hospitals; Mental Health; Aging; Christian Education; HELP (Housing, Rent, Food, Medication, Transportation, Home Heating, Clothing); La Casa de Amistad (The House of Friendship) Social Services; AIDS Outreach; Prison Chaplaincy; Disaster Rebuilding

Christians United in Beaver County

1098 Third St., Beaver, PA 15009 Tel. (412)774-1446
Media Contact, Exec. Sec., Mrs. Lois L. Smith
Exec. Sec., Mrs. Lois L. Smith
Chaplains: Rev. Samuel Ward; Mrs. Erika Bruner; Rev. Anthony Massey; Rev. Frank Churchill; Mr. Jack Kirkpatrick
Pres., Mrs. Erika Bruner, 1320 Third St., Beaver, PA 15009 Tel. (412)774-1446
Treas., Mrs. Jane Mine, 2601-19th St., Beaver Falls, PA 15010
Major activities: Christian Education; Evangelism; Radio; Social Action; Church Women United; United Church Men; Ecumenism; Hospital, Detention Home and Jail Ministry

Delaware Valley Media Ministry

1501 Cherry St., Philadelphia, PA 19102 Tel. (215)563-7854 Fax (215)563-6849
Media Contact, Exec. Dir., Ms. Nancy Nolde
Exec. Dir., Ms. Nancy Nolde
Major activities: Interfaith Communication and Television Production Agency

East End Cooperative Ministry

250 N. Highland Ave., Pittsburgh, PA 15206 Tel. (412)361-5549 Fax (412)361-0151
Media Contact, Nancy Paul
Exec. Dir., Mrs. Judith Marker
Major activities: Food Pantry; Soup Kitchen; Men's Emergency Shelter; Drop-In Shelter for Homeless; Meals on Wheels; Casework and Supportive Services for Elderly; Information and Referral; Program for Children and Youth; Bridge Housing Program for Men and Women in Recovery and their Children

Ecumenical Conference of Greater Altoona

1208 - 13th St., P.O. Box 305, Altoona, PA 16603 Tel. (814)942-0512
Media Contact, Exec. Dir., Mrs. Eileen Becker
Exec. Dir., Mrs. Eileen Becker
Major activities: Religious Education; Workshops; Ecumenical Activities; Religious Christmas Parade; Campus Ministry; Community Concerns; Peace Forum; Religious Education for Mentally Handicapped; Inter-faith Committee

Greater Bethlehem Area Council of Churches

520 E. Broad St., Bethlehem, PA 18018 Tel. (215)867-8671
Media Contact, Exec. Dir., Rev. Dr. Catherine A. Ziel
Exec. Dir., Rev. Dr. Catherine A. Ziel
Pres., Dr. Richard W. Cost, Moravian College, 1200 Main St., Bethlehem, PA 18018
Treas., Mrs. Polly McClure, 7 W. Washington Ave., Bethlehem, PA 18018
Major activities: Support Ministry; Institutional Ministry to Elderly and Infirm; Family Concerns; Scripture Center; Social Concerns; World Local Hunger Projects; Elderly Ministry

Hanover Area Council of Churches

120 York St., Hanover, PA 17331 Tel. (717)633-6353
Media Contact, Exec. Dir., Rev. Nancy M. Hewitt
Exec. Dir., Rev. Nancy M. Hewitt
Major activities: Meals on Wheels, Provide a Lunch Program, Fresh Air Program, Clothing Bank, Hospital Chaplaincy Services Congregational & Interfaith Relations, Public Ecumenical Programs and Services, State Park Chaplaincy Services & Children's Program

Inter-Church Ministries of Erie County

252 W. 7th St., Erie, PA 16501 Tel. (814)454-2411
Media Contact, Exec. Dir., The Rev. Willis J. Merriman, 252 West 7th Street, Erie, PA 16501 Tel. (814)454-2411
Exec. Dir., Rev. Willis J. Merriman
Adjunct Staff: Pastoral Counseling, Dr. David J. Sullivan; Aging Prog., Ms. Carolyn A. DiMattio
Pres., Thomas A. Tupitza, 120 W. 10th St., Erie, PA 16501
Treas., The Rev. Victoria Wood Parrish, 538 E. 10th St., Erie, PA 16503
Major activities: Local Ecumenism; Ministry with Aging; Social Ministry; Pastoral Counseling; Continuing Education; N.W. Pa. Conf. of Bishops and Judicatory Execs.; Institute of Pastoral Care; Theological Dialogue; AIDS Ministry; Walking in Black History; Coats for Kids

Lancaster County Council of Churches

447 E. King St., Lancaster, PA 17602 Tel. (717)291-2261
Media Contact, Publ. Chpsn., Peg Wentworth, 909 Larchmont La., Lancaster, PA 17601 Tel. (717)397-4841
Pres., Rev. Robert Bailey
Interim Exec. Dir., Rev. Robert Bistline

Prescott House, Dir., Casey Jones
Asst. Admn., Kim Y. Wittel
Child Abuse, Dir., Ursula Wanner
CONTACT, Dir., Rhoda Mull
Service Ministry, Dir., Adela Dohner
Major activities: Social Ministry; Residential Ministry to Youthful Offenders; CONTACT; Advocacy; Child Abuse Prevention

Lebanon County Christian Ministries

818 Water St., P.O. Box 654, Lebanon, PA 17042 Tel. (717)274-2601
Media Contact, Exec. Dir., P. Richard Forney
Exec. Dir., P. Richard Forney
Food & Clothing Bank Dir., Lillian Morales
H.O.P.E. Services, P. Richard Forney
Noon Meals Coord., Mrs. Glenda Wenger
Major activities: H.O.P.E. (Helping Our People in Emergencies); Food & Clothing Bank; Free Meal Program; Commodity Distribution Program; Ecumenical Events; Chaplaincy and Support Services

Lehigh County Conference of Churches

534 Chew St., Allentown, PA 18102 Tel. (215)433-6421 Fax (215)437-8799
Media Contact, Exec. Dir., Rev. William A. Seaman
Exec. Dir., Rev. William A. Seaman
Pres., Mr. Watson Skinner
1st Vice-Pres., Rev. Richard Guhl
2nd Vice-Pres., Msgr. John Murphy
Treas., Mr. George Nichols
Major activities: Chaplaincy Program; Migrant Ministry; Social Concerns and Action; Clergy Dialogues; Drop-In-Center for De-Institutionalized Adults; Ecumenical Food Kitchen; Housing Advocacy Program; Pathways (Reference to Social Services), Street Contact

Metropolitan Christian Council of Philadelphia

1501 Cherry St., Philadelphia, PA 19102 Tel. (215)563-7854 Fax (215)563-6849
Media Contact, Assoc. Communications, Ms. Nancy Nolde
Exec. Dir., Rev. C. Edward Geiger
Assoc. Communications, Ms. Nancy Nolde
Admn. Asst., Mrs. Joan G. Shipman
Pres., Rev. Gus Roman
Vice-Pres., Rt. Rev. Allen L. Bartlett, Jr.
Treas., A. Louis Denton, Esq.
Major activities: Congregational Clusters; Public Policy Advocacy; Communication; Interfaith Dialogue

North Hills Youth Ministry

802 McKnight Park Dr., Pittsburgh, PA 15237 Tel. (412)366-1300
Media Contact, Exec. Dir., Rev. Ronald B. Barnes
Exec. Dir., Ronald B. Barnes
Major activities: Junior and Senior High School Family and Individual Counseling; Elementary Age Youth Early Intervention Counseling; Educational Programming for Churches and Schools; Youth Advocacy

Northside Common Ministries

P.O. Box 99861, Pittsburgh, PA 15233 Tel. (412)323-1163
Media Contact, Exec. Dir., Roy J. Banner
Exec. Dir., Roy J. Banner
Pres., Rev. Richard L. Merkner
Major activities: Pleasant Valley Shelter for Homeless Men; Advocacy around Hunger, Housing, Poverty, and Racial Issues; Community Food Pantry and Service Center; Transitional Housing

Northwest Interfaith Movement

6757 Greene St., Philadelphia, PA 19119 Tel. (215)843-5600 Fax (215)843-2755
Media Contact, Exec. Dir., Rev. Richard R. Fernandez
Exec. Dir., Rev. Richard R. Fernandez
Chpsn., Pat Schogel
Long Term Care Connection, Dir., Valerie Pogozelski
Philadelphia Rel. Leadership Dev. Fund, Dir., Dyan Gwynn
Neighborhood Child Care Resource Prog., Dir, Amy Gendall
Major activities: Community Development & Community Reinvestment; Older Adult Concerns; Nursing Home Program; Unemployment; Economic Issues; Public Education; Peace; Racism; Poverty Issues

ProJeCt of Easton, Inc.

330 Ferry St., Easton, PA 18042 Tel. (215)258-4361
Pres., John Updegrove
Vice-Pres., Nelson Nkabinde
Sec., Lynn D. Klein
Treas., Rev. John Deisinger
Exec. Dir., Maryellen Shuman
Major activities: Food Bank; Adult Literacy Program; English as a Second Language; Tutor Bank for School Children; Parents as Student Support; CROP Walk; Interfaith Council

Reading Berks Conference of Churches

54 N. 8th St., Reading, PA 19601 Tel. (215)375-6108
Media Contact, Exec. Dir., Rev. Dr. Larry T. Nallo
Exec. Dir., Rev. Dr. Larry T. Nallo
Pres., Rev. Edward Ward
Treas., Mr. Lee M. LeVan
Major activities: Institutional Ministry; Social Action; Migrant Ministry; CWS; CROP Walk for Hunger; Emergency Assistance; Furniture Bank; Prison Chaplaincy; AIDS Hospice Development; Hospital Chaplaincy

Reading Urban Ministry

134 N. Fifth St., Reading, PA 19601 Tel. (215)374-6917
Media Contact, Beth Bitler
Exec. Dir., Beth Bitler
Pres., Mark C. Potts
Vice-Pres., William Wenrich
Sec., Sarah Boyd
Treas., Raymond Drain
Major activities: Community Clothing Center; Friendly Visitor Program to Elderly; Summer Youth Program; Family Action Support Team (For Single-Parent Families)

South Hills Interfaith Ministries

393 Vanadium Rd., Pittsburgh, PA 15243 Tel. (412)279-9942 Fax (412)279-9957
Media Contact, Publ. Rel. Dir., Ms. Marcy Suroucak
Exec. Dir., James Craig Yearsley
Psychological Services, Mr. Don Zandier
Community Services, Sherry Kotz
Volunteer Services Admn., Ms. Georgia Smith
Chpsn., Rev. Dan Merry
Treas., Mr. Jack Kelly
Major activities: Basic Human Needs; Unemployment; Community Organization and Development; Inter-Faith Cooperation; Family Hospice; Personal Growth

United Churches of Williamsport and Lycoming County

202 E. Third St., Williamsport, PA 17701 Tel. (717)322-1110
Media Contact, Exec. Dir., Mrs. Gwen Nelson Bernstine
Exec. Dir., Mrs. Gwen Nelson Bernstine
Ofc. Sec., Mrs. Linda Winter
Pres., Msgr. William J. Fleming, 410 Walnut St., Williamsport, PA 17701
Treas., Mr. Russell E. Tingue, 1987 Yale Ave., Williamsport, PA 17701
Shepherd of the Streets, Rev. Joseph L. Walker, 130 E. 3rd St., Williamsport, PA 17701
Ecumenism, Dir., Rev. Robert L. Driesen, 324 Howard St., South Williamsport, PA 17701
Educ. Ministries, Dir., Rev. George E. Doran, Jr., 122 S. Main St., Hughesville, PA 17737
Institutional Ministry, Dir., Rev. Kenneth L. Lynn, 220 High St., Jersey Shore, PA 17740
Radio-TV, Dir., Rev. Max W. Furman, RD 1, Box 199, Allenwood, PA 17810
Prison Ministry, Dir., Rev. John N. Mostoller, 1200 Almond St., Williamsport, PA 17701
Major activities: Ecumenism; Educational Ministries; Church Women United; Church World Service and CROP; Prison Ministry; Radio-TV; Nursing Homes; Fuel Bank; Food Pantry; Family Life; Shepherd of the Streets Urban Ministry; Peace Concerns; Housing Initiative

Willkinsburg Community Ministry

710 Mulberry St., Pittsburgh, PA 15221 Tel. (412)241-8072 Fax (412)241-8315
Media Contact, Dir., Rev. Vivian Lovingood
Dir., Rev. Vivian Lovingood
Pres. of Bd., Rev. Walter Pietschmann
Major activities: Hunger Ministry; After School Youth Programs; Child Care for Working Parents; Summer Bible School; Teen-Moms Infant Care; Meals on Wheels; Tape Ministry

Wyoming Valley Council of Churches

35 S. Franklin St., Wilkes-Barre, PA 18701 Tel. (717)825-8543
Media Contact, Exec. Dir., Rev. Lynn P. Lampman
Exec. Dir., Rev. Lynn P. Lampman
Ofc. Sec., Mrs. Sandra Karrott
Pres., Rev. Donald Lyon
Treas., Ronald Honeywell
Major activities: Hospital and Nursing Home

Chaplaincy; Church Women United; High Rise Apartment Ministry; Hospital Referral Service; Emergency Response; Food Bank; Migrant Ministry; Meals on Wheels; Dial-A-Driver; Radio and TV; Leadership Schools; Interfaith Programs; Night Chaplain Ministry; Area Hospitals; CROP Hunger Walks; Pastoral Care Ministries

York County Council of Churches

104 Lafayette St., York, PA 17403 Tel. (717)854-9504
Media Contact, Exec. Dir., Rev. Patrick B. Walker
Exec. Dir., Rev. Patrick B. Walker
Ofc. Mgr., Rebecca A. McClune
Pres., Rev. Henry Korinth
Treas., Rev. Pamela Cianciosi-Kinter
Major activities: Educational Development; Spiritual Growth and Renewal; Worship and Witness; Congregational Resourcing; Outreach and Mission

RHODE ISLAND

*The Rhode Island State Council of Churches

734 Hope St., Providence, RI 02906 Tel. (401)861-1700 Fax (401)331-3080
Media Contact, Exec. Minister, Rev. James C. Miller
Exec. Minister, Rev. James C. Miller
Admn. Asst., Ms. Peggy Macnie
Pres., Mr. George Weavill, Jr.
Treas., Mr. Robert A. Mitchell
Major activities: Urban Ministries; TV; Institutional Chaplaincy; Advocacy/Justice & Service; Legislative Liaison; Faith & Order; Leadership Development; Campus Ministries

SOUTH CAROLINA

*South Carolina Christian Action Council, Inc.

P.O. Box 3663, Columbia, SC 29230 Tel. (803)786-7115 Fax (803)786-7116
Media Contact, Exec. Minister, Dr. L. Wayne Bryan
Exec. Minister, Dr. L. Wayne Bryan
Pres., Ms. Betty Park
Major activities: Advocacy and Ecumenism; Continuing Education; Interfaith Dialogue; Citizenship and Public Affairs; Publications

United Ministries

606 Pendleton St., Greenville, SC 29601 Tel. (803)232-6463 Fax (803)370-3518
Media Contact, Exec. Dir., Rev. Beth Templeton
Exec. Dir., Rev. Beth Templeton
Pres., Rev. Bob Coon
Vice-Pres., Mr. Curt Elmore
Sec., Ms. Mack Pazdan
Treas., Mr. Bill Kellett
Major activities: Volunteer Programs; Adopt-A-House; Spend a Day; Building Wheelchair Ramps; Emergency Assistance with Rent, Utilities, Medication, Heating, Food, Shelter Referrals; Homeless Programs: Place of Hope Day Shelter for Homeless; Employment Readiness; Travelers Aid; Magdalene Project; Case Management

SOUTH DAKOTA

*Association of Christian Churches

1320 S. Minnesota Ave., Ste. 210, Sioux Falls, SD 57105 Tel. (605)334-1980
Media Contact, Pres., Rev. Howard Carroll, 3000 W. 41st St., Sioux Falls, SD 57105 Tel. (605)333-3366
Pres., Rev. Howard Carroll
Ofc. Mgr., Pat Willard
Major activities: Ecumenical Forums; Continuing Education for Clergy; Legislative Information; Resourcing Local Ecumenism; Native American Issues; Ecumenical Fields Ministries; Rural Economic Development

TENNESSEE

*Tennessee Association of Churches

103 Oak St., Ashland City, TN 37015 Tel. (615)792-4631
Media Contact, Ecumenidal Admn., Dr. David Davis
Ecumenical Admn., Dr. David Davis
Major activities: Faith and Order; Christian Unity; Social Concern Ministries; Legislative Concerns

Metropolitan Inter Faith Association (MIFA)

P.O. Box 3130, Memphis, TN 38173-0130 Tel. (901)527-0208 Fax (901)527-3202
Media Contact, Dir., Media Relations, Kim Gaskill
Exec. Dir., Mr. Allie Prescott
Urban Ministries, Dir., Sara Holmes
Major activities: Emergency Housing; Emergency Services (Rent, Utility, Food, Clothing Assistance); Home-Delivered Meals and Senior Support Services; Youth Services

Volunteer Ministry Center

113 South Gay St., Knoxville, TN 37902 Tel. (615)524-3926
Exec. Dir., Richard Evans
Pres., Dr. Jack Kiger
Vice-Pres., John Hanes
Treas., Charles Finn
NIL

TEXAS

*Texas Conference of Churches

6633 Hwy. 290 East, Ste. 200, Austin, TX 78723-1157 Tel. (512)451-0991 Fax (512)451-2904
Media Contact, Exec. Dir., Rev. Dr. Frank H. Dietz
Exec. Dir., Rev. Dr. Frank H. Dietz
Church & Society Asst., Mary Berwick
Dir., Addictions Min., Ms. Trish Merrill
Pres., Mr. Hernan Gonzalez
Major activities: Church and Society; Ecumenism; Christian-Jewish Relations; Domestic Violence; Peace; Disaster Response; BARCA; Texas Church World Service/CROP; Alcoholism-Addiction Education; Church Woman United In Texas; Central American Issues; Texas IMPACT; AIDS

Austin Metropolitan Ministries

2026 Guadalupe, Ste. 226, Austin, TX 78705 Tel. (512)472-7627
Media Contact, Exec. Dir., Patrick Flood, Fax (512)472-5274
Exec. Dir., Patrick Flood
Pres., Gail Miller
Treas., Rev. T. James Bethell
Chaplains: Travis Co. Jails, Rev. Charles I. Fay; Travis Co. Jails, Rev. Tommy MacIntosh; Gardner-Betts Juvenile Home, Rev. Floyd Vick
Program Staff, Rev. Don Bobb
Office Admn., Carole Hatfield
Major activities: Pastoral Care in Jails; Broadcast Ministry; Emergency Assistance; Older Persons Task Force; Housing Task Force; Peace and Justice Commission; Youth at Risk; AIDS Service; Commission on Racism; Interfaith Dialogues; Economy and Jobs Issues

Border Association for Refugees from Central America (BARCA), Inc.

P.O. Box 715, Edinburg, TX 78540 Tel. (512)631-7447 Fax (512)687-9266
Media Contact, Exec. Dir., Ninfa Ochoa-Krueger
Exec. Dir, Ninfa Ochoa-Krueger
Refugee Children Serv., Dir., Bertha de la Rosa
Major activities: Food, Shelter, Clothing to Central Americans; Medical and Other Emergency Aid; Legal Advocacy; Special Services to Children; Speakers on Refugee Concerns for Church Groups

Corpus Christi Metro Ministries

1919 Leopard St., P.O. Box 4899, Corpus Christi, TX 78469-4899 Tel. (512)887-0151
Media Contact, Exec. Dir., Rev. Edward B. Seeger, P.O. Box 4899, Corpus Christi, TX 78469-4899 Tel. (512)887-0151 Fax (512)887-7900
Exec. Dir., Rev. Edward B. Seeger
Admn., Dir., Daniel D. Scott
Volunteers, Dir., Ann Schiro
Fin. Coord., Sue McCown
Loaves & Fishes, Dir., Ray Gomez
Counseling, Dir., Amie Harrell
Rustic House, Dir., Amie Harrell
Employment, Dir., Curtis Blevins
Bethany House, Dir., Stanley Neely
Rainbow House, Dir., Alicia Ruiz
Child Abuse Prevention, Dir., Jo Flindt
Health Clinic, Dir., Ann Schiro
Major activities: Free Cafeteria; Shelters; Counseling; Job Readiness; Job Placement; Abuse Prevention and Intervention; Adult Day Care; Primary Health Care; Community Service Restitution

East Dallas Cooperative Parish

P.O. Box 720305, Dallas, TX 75372-0305 Tel. (214)823-9149 Fax (214)823-2015
Media Contact, Ofc. Mgr., Elizabeth Blessing
Pres., Rev. Jimmie Mobley
Sec., Ms. Corinne Bryan

Major activities: Emergency Food, Clothing, Job Bank; Medical Clinic; Legal Clinic, Tutorial Education; Home Companion Service; Pre-School Education; Developmental Learning Center; Asian Ministry; Hispanic Ministry; Activity Center for Low Income Older Adults; Pastoral Counseling

Greater Dallas Community of Churches

2800 Swiss Ave., Dallas, TX 75204 Tel. (214)824-8680 Fax (214)824-8726
Media Contact, Exec. Asst., Colleen Townsley Hager
Exec. Dir., Rev. Thomas H. Quigley
Church & Community, Assoc. Dirs.: Rev. Holsey Hickman; John Stoesz
Community College Min., Dir., Dr. Philip del Rosario
Development Dir., Carole Rylander
Pres., Frank Jackson
Treas., Gilbert Hernandez
Child Advocacy, Program Assoc., Rev. Carolyn Bullard-Zerweck
Major activities: Hospital Chaplaincy; Community College Ministry; Housing; Hunger; Peacemaking; Faith and Life; Jewish-Christian Relations; Racial Ethnic Justice; Child Advocacy

Interfaith Ministries for Greater Houston

3217 Montrose Blvd., Houston, TX 77006 Tel. (713)522-3955 Fax (713)520-4663
Media Contact, Exec. Dir., Betty K. Mathis, Tel. (713)520-4603
Exec. Dir., Betty K. Mathis
Assoc. Exec. Dir., David A. Leslie
Finance, Assoc. Dir., Douglass L. Simmons
Programs, Assoc. Dir., Larry Norton
Development, Dir., Lisa Estes
Family Connection, Dir., Larry Norton
Foster Grandparent Program, Dir., Vicki Hopkins
Hunger Coalition, Dir., Judy Durand
Meals on Wheels, Dir., Evelyn Velasquez
Refugee Services, Dir., David Deming
Retired Senior Volunteer Services, Dir., Candice Twyman
Youth Victim/Witness, Dir., Pamela Hobbs
Pres., Jo Ann Swinney
Treas., Everett A. Marley, Jr.
Major activities: Community Concerns: Hunger; Older Adults; Families; Youth; Child Abuse; Refugee Services; Jail Chaplaincy; Congregational and Interfaith Development

North Dallas Shared Ministries

2530 Glenda Ln., #500, Dallas, TX 75229 Tel. (214)620-8696 Fax (214)620-0433
Media Contact, Exec. Dir., Rev. Matt English
Exec. Dir., Rev. Matt English
Pres., Edward St. John
Major activities: Emergency Assistance; Job Counseling; Advocacy for Homeless; ESL

Northside Inter-Church Agency (NICA)

506 N.W. 15th St., Fort Worth, TX 76106 Tel. (817)626-1102
Dir., Francine Esposito Pratt

San Antonio Community of Churches

1101 W. Woodlawn, San Antonio, TX 78201 Tel. (210)733-9159
Media Contact, Exec. Dir., Dr. Kenneth Thompson
Exec. Dir., Dr. Kenneth Thompson
Pres., Dr. Dan McLendon
Major activities: Christian Educ.; Missions; Radio-TV; Resource Center Infant Formula and Medical Prescriptions for Children of Indigent Families; Continuing Education For Clergy; Media Resource Center; Social Issues; Aging Concerns; Youth Concerns; Family, Congregation and Community Life Resource Center

San Antonio Urban Ministries

2002 W. Olmos Dr., San Antonio, TX 78201 Tel. (210)733-5080 Fax (210)733-5408
Media Contact, Sue Kelly
Exec. Dir., Sue Kelly
Pres., Troy Warwick
Major activities: Homes for Discharged Mental Patients; After School Care for Latch Key Children; Christian Based Community Ministry; San Antonio Legalization Education Coalition

Southeast Area Churches (SEARCH)

P.O. Box 51256, Fort Worth, TX 76105 Tel. (817)531-2211
Media Contact, Exec. Dir., Ms. Dorothy Anderson-Develrow
Dir., Ms. Dorothy Anderson-Develrow
Major activities: Emergency Assistance; Advocacy; Information and Referral; Community Worship

Southside Area Ministries (SAM)

305 W. Broadway, Fort Worth, TX 76104 Tel. (817)332-3778
Exec. Dir., Diane Smiley
Major activities: Assisting those for whom English is a second language; Tutoring grades K-12; Mentoring Grades 6-9; Programs for Senior Citizens and Refugees

Tarrant Area Community of Churches

801 Texas St., Fort Worth, TX 76102 Tel. (817)335-9341
Media Contact, Pres., Elizabeth F. Lambert
Pres., Rev. Dr. John Tietjen
Treas., Mr. Luther Atkinson
Acting Exec. Dir., Rev. Elizabeth F. Lambert
Major activities: Councils: Church, Community-based, Interfaith, Pastoral Ministry. Sponsor: Jail and elderly ministry

United Board of Missions

1701 Bluebonnet Ave., P.O. Box 3856, Port Arthur, TX 77643-3856 Tel. (409)982-9412 Fax (409)985-3668

Media Contact, Admn. Asst., Carolyn Schwarr, P.O.Box 3856, Port Arthur, TX 77643 Tel. (409)982-9412 Fax (409)985-3668
Exec. Dir., Clark Moore
Pres., Charlie Harris
Major activities: Emergency Assistance (Food and Clothing, Rent and Utility, Medical, Dental, Transportation); Share a Toy at Christmas; Counseling; Back to School Clothing Assistance; Information and Referral; Hearing Aid Bank; Meals on Wheels; Super Pantry; Energy Conservation Programs; Job Bank

UTAH

The Shared Ministry

175 W. 200 S., Ste. 3006, Salt Lake City, UT 84101 Tel. (801)355-0168 Fax (801)355-5512
Exec. Min., Rev. Dr. Max E. Glenn
Major activities: Poverty, Hunger and Homelessness; Legislation Concerns; Family Counseling; Peacemaking; Prison Youth and Singles Ministries

VERMONT

*Vermont Ecumenical Council and Bible Society

285 Maple St., Burlington, VT 05401 Tel. (802)864-7723
Media Contact, Admn. Asst., Carolyn Carpenter
Exec. Sec., Rev. John E. Nutting
Pres., Rev. Marcheta Townsend
Vice-Pres., Barr Swennerfelt
Treas., Rev. Louis Drew, Jr.
Major activities: Christian Unity; Bible Distribution; Social Justice; Committees on Peace, Life and Work, Faith and Order, and Bible

VIRGINIA

*Virginia Council of Churches, Inc.

1214 W. Graham Rd., Richmond, VA 23220-1409 Tel. (804)321-3300 Fax (804)329-5066
Media Contact, Gen. Min., Rev. James F. McDonald
Gen. Min., Rev. James F. McDonald
Prog. Assoc., Rev. Judith Bennett
Migrant Head Start, Dir., Richard D. Cagnan
Refugee Resettlement, Dir., Rev. David Montanye
Weekday Rel. Educ., Coord., Ms. Evelyn W. Simmons, P.O. Box 245, Clifton Forge, VA 24422
Campus Ministry Forum, Coord., Rev. Robert Thomason, 5000 Echols Ave., Alexandria, VA 22304
Major activities: Faith and Order; Network Building & Coordination; Ecumenical Communications; Justice and Legislative Concerns; Educational Development; Rural Concerns; Refugee Resettlement; Migrant Ministries and Migrant Day Care; Disaster Coordination

Community Ministry of Fairfax County

1920 Association Dr., Rm. 116, Reston, VA 22091 Tel. (703)620-5014 Fax (703)860-2903
Media Contact, Exec. Dir., Frederick S. Lowry
Exec. Dir., Rev. Frederick S. Lowry
Newsletter Ed., James Vining

Chpsn., Nancy Wormeli
Sec., Marge DeBlaay
Treas., Robert Hunt
Major activities: Ecumenical Social Ministry; Elderly; Criminal Justice; Housing; Public Education

WASHINGTON

*Washington Association of Churches
4759 - 15th Ave. N.E., Seattle, WA 98105 Tel. (206)525-1988 Fax (206)524-5886
Exec. Min., Rev. John C. Boonstra
Legislative, Dir., Tony Lee
Pres., Rev. Paul Bartling
Treas., Rev. David T. Alger
Major activities: Faith and Order; Justice Advocacy; Hunger Action; Legislation; Denominational Ecumenical Coordination; Theological Formation; Leadership Development; Refugee Advocacy; Racial Justice Advocacy; International Solidarity

Associated Ministries of Tacoma-Pierce County
1224 South "I" St., Tacoma, WA 98405 Tel. (206)383-3056 Fax (206)572-3193
Media Contact, Exec. Dir., Rev. David T. Alger
Exec. Dir., Rev. David T. Alger, 4510 Defiance, Tacoma, WA 98407
Assoc. Dir., Janet Leng, 1809 N. Lexington, Tacoma, WA 98406
Pres., Virginia Gilmore
Sec., Betty Tober
Treas., Mr. Richard Stender
Vice-Pres., Danna Clancy
Major activities: FISH/Food Banks; Hunger Awareness; Economic Justice; Christian Education; Shalom (Peacemaking) Resource Center; Social Service Program Advocacy; Communication and Networking of Churches; Housing; Paint Tacoma/Pierce Beautiful; Interfaith Task Force on Safe Streets; Mental Health Chaplaincy; Interfaith Hospitality Network; Theological Dialogue

Associated Ministries of Thurston County
P.O. Box 895, Olympia, WA 98507 Tel. (206)357-7224 Fax (206)943-1258
Media Contact, Exec. Dir., Ken Schwilk
Exec. Dir., Ken Schwilk
Pres., Richard S. Smith
Treas., Carroll Dick
Major activities: Church Information and Referral; Interfaith Worship; Workshops; Social and Health Concerns;

Center for the Prevention of Sexual and Domestic Violence
1914 N. 34th St., Ste. 105, Seattle, WA 98103 Tel. (206)634-1903 Fax (206)634-0115
Media Contact, Exec. Dir., Rev. Dr. Marie M. Fortune
Exec. Dir., Rev. Marie M. Fortune
Admn. Asst., Alex McGee
Video Project Coord., Jean Anton
Program Specialist, Rev. Thelma B. Burgonio-Watson
Program Assoc., Sandra Barone

Devel. Assoc., Lennie Ziontz
Program Specialist, Elizabeth A. Stellas, M.Div.
Finance & Dev., Dir., Nan Stoops
Marketing Asst., Dinah Hall
Major activities: Educational Ministry; Clergy and Lay Training; Social Action.

Church Council of Greater Seattle
4759 - 15th Ave., NE, Seattle, WA 98105 Tel. (206)525-1213 Fax (206)525-1218
Media Contact, Assoc. Dir., Alice M. Woldt, 4759 15th Ave. NE, Seattle, WA 98105 Tel. (206)525-1213 Fax (206)525-1218
Pres./Dir., Rev. Elaine J. W. Stanovsky
Urban Min., Assoc. Dir., Rev. David C. Bloom
Admn., Assoc. Dir., Alice M. Woldt
Exec. Asst., Angela W. Ford
Emergency Feeding Prog., Dir., Arthur Lee
Friend-to-Friend, Dir., Marilyn Soderquist
Youth Service Chaplaincy, Dir., Terrie Ward
Mental Health Chaplaincy, Dir., Rev. Craig Rennebohm
Native American Task Force, Dir., Ron Adams
The Sharehouse, Dir., Mike Buchman
Homelessness Project, Dir., Nancy Dorman
Mission for Music & Healing, Dir., Esther "Little Dove" John
Seattle Displacement Coalition, Dir., John Fox
Task Force on Aging, Dir., Mary Liz Chaffee
Interfaith Relations, Coord., Rev. Joyce Manson
Housing & Homelessness Task Force, Dir., Josephine Archuleta
Academy of Religious Broadcasting, Dir., Rev. J. Graley Taylor
Vice-Pres., Rev. Rodney Romney
Treas., Dorothy Eley
Ed., *Source*, Marge Lueders
Major activities: Racial Justice; Peace Action; Pastoral Ministry; Hunger; Mental Health; Gay Rights; Aging; Latin America; Asia Pacific; South Africa; Native Americans; Jewish-Christian Relations; Ecology; Homelessness; Labor & Economic Justice; Children, Youth & Families; Race Relations; International Relations

Northwest Harvest/Ecumenical Metropolitan Ministry
P.O. Box 12272, Seattle, WA 98102 Tel. (206)625-0755 Fax (206)625-7518
Media Contact, Devel. Officer, Mel Matteson
Exec. Dir., Ruth M. Velozo
Chpsn., The Rev. Henry F. Seaman
Major activities: Northwest Harvest (Statewide Hunger Response); Cherry Street Food Bank (Community Hunger Response); Northwest Infants Corner (Special Nutritional Products for Infants and Babies); E.M.M. (Advocacy, Education, Communications Relative to Programs and Economic Justice); Northwest Caring Ministry (Individuals and Family Crisis Intervention and Advocacy)

North Snohomish County Association of Churches
2301 Hoyt, P.O. Box 7101, Everett, WA 98201 Tel. (206)252-6672
Media Contact, Exec. Dir., Rev. Lisa Jankanish, 2301 Hoyt, P.O. Box 7101, Everett, WA 98201 Tel. (206)252-6672
Exec. Dir., Rev. Lisa Jankanish

Pres., Ralph H. Quaas
Major activities: Housing and Shelter; Economic Justice; Hunger; Family Life; Interfaith Worship

Spokane Council of Ecumenical Ministries
E. 245-13th Ave., Spokane, WA 99202 Tel. (509)624-5156
Media Contact, Admn. Coord. & Editor, Mary Stamp, Tel. (509)535-1813
Exec. Dir., Rev. John A. Olson
Pres., Rev. Jim Burford
Treas., Rev. Samuel Vaughn
Admn. Coord. & Ed., Mary Stamp
Major activities: Greater Spokane Coalition Against Poverty; Multi-Cultural Human Relations Camp for High School Youth; Night Walk Ministry; Calling and Caring Training; *Fig Tree* Newspaper; Solidarity with Women Task Force; Dir. of Churches & Community Agencies; Interfaith Thanksgiving Worship; Community Easter Sunrise Service; Forums on Issues; Friend to Friend Visitation with Nursing Home Patients; Interstate Task Force on Human Relations

WEST VIRGINIA

*West Virginia Council of Churches
1608 Virginia St. E., Charleston, WV 25311 Tel. (304)344-3141
Media Contact, Exec. Dir., Rev. James M. Kerr, 1608 Virginia St., E., Charleston, WV 25311 Tel. (304)344-3141 Fax (304)343-3295
Exec. Dir., Rev. James M. Kerr
Pres., Bishop L. Alexander Black, ELCA Synod of WV-MD, 503 Morgantown Ave., Atrium Mall, Ste. 100, Fairmont, WV 26554
Vice-Pres., Mary Virginia DeRoo, 2006 Northwood Rd., Charleston, WV 25314
Sec., Sr. Marguerite St. Amand, 63 Elk River Rd., Clendinin, WV 25045
Treas., Rev. Richard Flowers, P.O. Box 667, Scott Depot, WV 25560
Major activities: Leisure Ministry; Disaster Response; Faith and Order; Family Concerns; Inter-Faith Relations; Peace and Justice; Government Concerns; Support Sevices Network

Greater Fairmont Council of Churches
P.O. Box 108, Fairmont, WV 26554 Tel. (304)366-8126
Media Contact, Exec. Sec., Nancy Hoffman
Exec. Sec., Nancy Hoffman
Major activities: Community Ecumenical Services; Youth and Adult Sports Leagues; CROP Walk Sponsor; Weekly Radio Broadcasts

The Greater Wheeling Council of Churches
110 Methodist Bldg., Wheeling, WV 26003 Tel. (304)232-5315
Exec. Dir., Kathy J. Burley
Hospital Notification Sec., Mrs. Ruth Fletcher
Pres., Rev. Charles Ellwood
Treas., Mrs. Naoma Boram
Major activities: Christian Education; Evangelism; Summer Vespers; Television; Institutional Ministry; Religious Film Library; Church

Women United; Volunteer Pastor Care at OVMC Hospital; School of Religion; Hospital Notification; Hymn Sing in the Park; Flood Relief Network; Pentecost Celebration; Clergy Council, Easter Sunrise Service; Community Seder

WISCONSIN

*Wisconsin Conference of Churches
1955 W. Broadway, Ste. 104, Madison, WI 53713 Tel. (608)222-9779 Fax (608)222-2854
Media Contact, Communications Coord., Ms. Linda Spilde
Exec. Dir., Rev. John D. Fischer
Ofc. Mgr./Communications Coord., Ms. Linda Spilde
Social Min., Assoc. Dir., Ms. Bonnee Voss
Broadcasting, Assoc. Dir., Rev. Robert P. Seater, 2717 E. Hampshire, Milwaukee, WI 53211 Tel. (414)332-2133
Peace & Justice Ecumenical Partnership: Co-Dir., Jane Hammatt-Kavaloski, Rt. #3, Box 228E, Dodgeville, WI 53533; Co-Dir., Vincent Kavaloski, Rt. #3, Box 228E, Dodgeville, WI 53533
Chaplaincy Coord., Rev. M. Charles Davis, 1221 Jackson St., Oshkosh, WI 54901
Commission on Aging, Coord., Mr. A. Rowland Todd
Pres., Bishop Robert H. Herder
Treas., Mr. Chester Spangler, 625 Crandall, Madison, WI 53711
Major activities: Church and Society; Migrant Ministry; Broadcasting Ministry; Aging; IMPACT; Institutional Chaplaincy; Peace and Justice; Faith and Order; Rural Concerns Forum; American Indian Ministries Council; Park Ministry

Center for Community Concerns
1501 Villa St., Racine, WI 53403 Tel. (414)637-9176
Media Contact, Exec. Dir., Jean Mandli
Exec. Dir., Mrs. Jean Mandli
Skillbank Coord., Eleanor Sorenson
Volunteer Prog. Coord., Chris Udell-Solberg
RSVP (Retired Senior Volunteer Program), Kay Larson
Admn. Asst., Bonnie Wrixton
Major activities: Advocacy; Direct Services; Research; Community Consultant; Criminal Justice; Volunteerism; Senior Citizen Services

Christian Youth Council
1715-52nd St., Kenosha, WI 53140 Tel. (414)652-9543
Exec. Dir., Ron Stevens
Sports Dir., Kris Jensen
Outreach Dir., Linda Osborne
Class Dir., Karin Carbone
Pres., Keith Bosman
Major activities: Leisure Time Ministry; Institutional Ministries; Ecumenical Committee; Social Concerns

Interfaith Conference of Greater Milwaukee
1442 N. Farwell Ave., Ste. 200, Milwaukee, WI 53202 Tel. (414)276-9050 Fax (414)224-0243

Media Contact, Exec. Dir., Jack Murtaugh, 1442 N. Farwell, Ste. 200, Milwaukee, WI 53202 Tel. (414)276-9050 Fax (414)224-0243

Exec. Dir., Mr. Jack Murtaugh

First Vice-Chair, Archbishop Rembert G. Weakland

Second Vice-Chair, Rev. Quentin Meracle

Sec., Rev. Paul Bodine, Jr.

Treas., Rev. Mary Ann Neevel

Poverty Issues, Program Coord., Mr. Marcus White

Ofc. Admn., Mrs. Frankie Mason-McCain

Public Educ., Prog. Coord., Mrs. Charlotte Holloman

Consultant in Communications, Rev. Robert P. Seater

Chpsn., Rev. Robert Horst

Beyond Racism Program, Mrs. Charlotte Holloman

Major activities: Economic Issues; Racism; CROP Walk; Public Policy; Religion and Labor Committee; Public Education Committee; TV Programming; Peace and International Issues Committee; Annual Membership Luncheon

Madison Urban Ministry

1127 University Ave., Madison, WI 53715 Tel. (608)256-0906

Media Contact, Office/Program Mgrs., Cheryl Wade

Exec. Dir., Charles Pfeifer

Ofc./Program Mgrs.: Margaret Tanaka; Cheryl Wade

Admn. Asst., Dorothy Miller

Major activities: Community Projects; Race Relations; Affordable Housing Coalition; Tutoring/Mentoring Network

WYOMING

*Wyoming Church Coalition

P.O. Box 990, Laramie, WY 82070 Tel. (307)745-6000

Media Contact, Chair, Rev. Michael Parr, Lander United Methodist Church, 262 N. 3rd, Lander, WY 82520-2811 Tel. (307)332-3188

Admn. Coord., Melissa Sanders

Chair, Rev. Michael Parr, 262 N. 3rd, Lander, WY 82520-2811 Tel. (307)332-3188

Penitentiary Chaplain, Rev. Lynn Schumacher, P.O. Box 400, Rawlins, WY 82301

Major activities: Death Penalty; Empowering the Poor and Oppressed; Peace and Justice; Prison Ministry

7. CANADIAN REGIONAL AND LOCAL ECUMENICAL AGENCIES

Most of the organizations listed below are councils of churches in which churches participate officially, whether at the parish or judicatory level. They operate at either the city, metropolitan area, or county level. Parish clusters within urban areas are not included.

Canadian local ecumenical bodies operate without paid staff, with the exception of a few which have part-time staff. In most cases the name and address of the president or chairperson is listed. As these offices change from year to year, some of this information may be out of date by the time the *Yearbook of American and Canadian Churches* is published. Up-to-date information may be secured from the Canadian Council of Churches, 40 St. Clair Ave., E., Toronto, Ontario M4T 1M9.

ALBERTA

Calgary Council of Churches
Treas., Stephen Kendall, 1009-15 Ave. SW, Calgary, AB T2R 0S5 Tel. (403)249-2599

The Micah Institute of Southern Alberta
Dir., Caroline Brown, 240-15 Ave. SW, Calgary, AB T2R 0P7 Tel. (403)262-5111 Fax (403)264-8366

BRITISH COLUMBIA

Canadian Ecumenical Action
2040 West 12th Ave., Vancouver, BC V6J 2J2 Tel. (604)736-1613 Fax (604)875-1433

MANITOBA

Association of Christian Churches in Manitoba
Pres., Rev. Cliff McMillan, 622 Tache Ave., Winnipeg, MB R2H 2B4

NEW BRUNSWICK

Moncton Area Council of Churches
Rev. Yvon Berrieau, Visitation Ministry, Grande Digue, NB E0A 1S0
Pres., Rev. David Luker, 211 Peck Dr., Riverview, NB E1B 1M9 Tel. (506)386-3481

NOVA SCOTIA

Amherst and Area Council of Churches
Treas., Shirley MacTavish, 38 Kent Dr., Amherst, NS B4H 4L5 Tel. (902)667-3128
Rev. John Tonks, 18 Elmwood Dr., Amherst, NS B4H 2H1

Annapolis Royal Council of Churches
Rev. Derrick Marshall, Riverview Dr., Annapolis Royal, NS B0S 1A0

Bridgewater Inter-Church Council
Pres., Wilson Jones, 30 Parkdale Ave., Bridgewater, NS B4V 1L8

Halifax-Dartmouth Council of Churches
Rep., Mr. Lorne White, 18 Winston Cres., Halifax, NS B3M 1Z1

Industrial Cape Breton Council of Churches
Valerie Hunt, 76 Lynch Dr., Sydney, NS B1S 1V2 Tel. (902)564-6992

Kentville Council of Churches
Rev. Canon S.J.P. Davies, 325-325 Main St., Kentville, NS B4N 1C5

Mahone Bay Council of Churches
Rev. Dale Rose, Box 902, Mahone Bay, NS B0J 2E0

Pictou Council of Churches
Sec., Rev. D. J. Murphy, P.O. Box 70, Pictou, NS B0K 1H0

Queens County Association of Churches
Rev. Bruce Ward, P.O. Box 1369, Liverpool, NS B0T 1K0

Wolfville Area Council of Churches
Dr. R. Forsman, Box 574, RR #2, Wolfville, NS B0P 1X0

Wolfville Interchurch Council
Rev. Roger Prentice, Office of the Chaplain, Acadia Univ., Wolfville, NS B0P 1X0

ONTARIO

Christian Council of the Capital Area
Bernard Barrett, All Saints Church, 347 Richmond Rd., Ottawa, ON K2A 0E7 Tel. (613)725-9487

Christian Leadership Council of Downtown Toronto
Chair, Ken Bhagan, 40 Homewood Ave. #509, Toronto, ON M4Y 2K2

Ecumenical Committee
Rev. William B. Kidd, 76 Eastern Ave., Sault Ste. Marie, ON P6A 4R2

Glengarry-Prescott-Russell Christian Council
Pres., Rev. Gerald Labrosse, St. Eugene's Parish, C.P. 70 St. Eugene's, Prescott, ON K0B 1P0

Hamilton & District Christian Association
Rev. Dr. John Johnston, 147 Chedoke Ave., Hamilton, ON L8P 4P2 Tel. (905)529-6896 Fax (905)521-2539

Hemmingford Ecumenical Committee
Sec.-Treas., Catherine Priest, 434 Route 202, P.O. Box 213, Hemmingford, QC J0L 1H0

Ignace Council of Churches
Box 5, 205 Pine St., Ignace, ON P0T 1H0

Inter Church Council of Burlington
Michael Biggle, Box 62120, Burlington Mall RPO, Burlington, ON L7R 4K2 Tel. (905)526-1523

Kitchener-Waterloo Council of Churches
Rev. Clarence Hauser, CR, 53 Allen St. E, Waterloo, ON N2J 1J3

Lay Ecumenical Council of Aurora
c/o 53 Cambridge Cres., Bradford, ON L3Z 1E2

London Inter-Faith Team
Chair, David Carouthers, United Church, 711 Colbourne St., London, ON N6A 3Z4

Massey Inter-Church Committee
Sec., Eva Fraser, Box 238, Massey, ON P0P 1P0

Spadina-Bloor Interchurch Council
Chair, Rev. Frances Combes, Bathurst St. United Church, 427 Bloor St. W, Toronto, ON M5S 1X7

St. Catharines & District Clergy Fellowship
Rev. Victor Munro, 663 Vince 4 St., St. Catherines, ON L2M 3V8

Stratford & District Council of Churches
Chair, Rev. Ted Heinze, 202 Erie St., Stratford, ON N5A 2M8

Thorold Inter-Faith Council
1 Dunn St., St. Catharines, ON L2T 1P3

Thunder Bay Council of Churches
Rev. Richard Darling, 1800 Moodie St. E, Thunder Bay, ON P7E 4Z2

PRINCE EDWARD ISLAND
Charlottetown Christian Council
Ms. Eunice D. Wonnacott, 45 Roper Dr., Charlottetown, PE C1A 6J1 Tel. (902)894-4363

Summerside Christian Council
Sec., P.O. Box 1527, Summerside, PE C1N 2Z8

QUEBEC
The Ecumenical Group
Mrs. C. Haten, 1185 Ste. Foy, St. Bruno, QC J3V 3C3

Montreal Council of Churches
Rev. Ralph Watson, 3500 Connaugh Ave., Montreal, QC H4B 1X3

SASKATCHEWAN
Humboldt Clergy Council
Fr. Leo Hinz, OSB, Box 1989, Humboldt, SK S0K 2A0

Melville Association of Churches
Catherine Gaw, Box 878, Melville, SK S0A 2P0

Saskatoon Centre for Ecumenism
1006 Broadway Ave., Saskatoon, SK S7N 1B9

Saskatoon Council of Churches
816 Spadina Cres. E, Saskatoon, SK S7K 3H4 Tel. (306)242-5146

8. THEOLOGICAL SEMINARIES AND BIBLE COLLEGES IN THE UNITED STATES

The following list includes theological seminaries and departments in colleges and universities in which ministerial training is given. Many denominations have additional programs. The lists of Religious Bodies in the United States should be consulted for the address of denominational headquarters.

Inclusion in or exclusion from this list implies no judgment about the quality or accreditation of any institution. Those schools that are members (both accredited and affiliated) of the Association of Theological Schools are marked with a "*." Additional information about enrollment in ATS member schools can be found in the statistical section.

The listing includes the institution name, denominational sponsor when appropriate, location, head, telephone number and fax number when known.

Abilene Christian University, (Churches of Christ), ACU Station, Box 7000, Abilene, TX 79699. Royce Money. Tel. (915)674-2412. Fax (915)674-2958

Academy of the New Church (Theology School), (General Church of the New Jerusalem), 2815 Huntingdon Pk., Box 717, Bryn Athyn, PA 19009. Brian W. Keith. Tel. (215)938-2525. Fax (215)938-2616

Alaska Bible College, (Nondenominational), P.O. Box 289, Glennallen, AK 99588. Gary J. Ridley. Tel. (907)822-3201. Fax (907)822-5027

Alliance Theological Seminary,* (The Christian and Missionary Alliance), 122 S. Highland Ave., Nyack, NY 10960-4121. Paul F. Bubna. Tel. (914)358-1710. Fax (914)358-2651

American Baptist College, (Interdenominational Baptist), 1800 Baptist World Center Dr., Nashville, TN 37207. Bernard Lafayette. Tel. (615)262-1369. Fax (615)262-1369

American Baptist Seminary of the West,* (American Baptist Churches in the U.S.A.), 2606 Dwight Way, Berkeley, CA 94704. Theodore Keaton. Tel. (510)841-1905

Anderson University School of Theology,* (Church of God (Anderson, Ind.)), Anderson University, Anderson, IN 46012-3462. James Earl Massey. Tel. (317)641-4032. Fax (317)641-3851

Andover Newton Theological School,* (American Bapt.; United Church of Christ), 210 Herrick Rd., Newton Centre, MA 02159. David T. Shannon. Tel. (617)964-1100. Fax (617)965-9756

Appalachian Bible College, (Nondenominational), P.O. Box ABC, Bradley, WV 25818. Daniel L. Anderson. Tel. (304)877-6428. Fax (304)877-6423

Aquinas Institute of Theology,* (The Roman Catholic Church), 3642 Lindell Blvd., St. Louis, MO 63108. Charles E. Bouchard. Tel. (314)658-3882. Fax (314)652-0935

Arizona College of the Bible, (Nondenominational), 2045 W. Northern Ave., Phoenix, AZ 85021. Robert W. Benton. Tel. (602)995-2670

Arlington Baptist College, 3001 W. Division, Arlington, TX 76012. David Bryant. Tel. (817)461-8741. Fax (817)274-1138

Asbury Theological Seminary,* (Interdenominational), 204 N. Lexington Ave., Wilmore, KY 40390-1199. David McKenna. Tel. (606)858-3581

Ashland Theological Seminary,* (Brethren Church (Ashland, Ohio)), 910 Center St., Ashland, OH 44805. Frederick J. Finks. Tel. (419)289-5161. Fax (419)289-5969

Assemblies of God Theological Seminary,* (Assemblies of God), 1445 Boonville Ave., Springfield, MO 65802. Del Tarr. Tel. (417)862-3344. Fax (417)862-3214

Associated Mennonite Biblical Seminary,* (Mennonite Church), 3003 Benham Ave., Elkhart, IN 46517-1999. Marlin E. Miller. Tel. (219)295-3726. Fax (219)295-0092

Athenaeum of Ohio,* (The Roman Catholic Church), 6616 Beechmont Ave., Cincinnati, OH 45230-2091. Robert J. Mooney. Tel. (513)231-2223. Fax (513)231-3245

Atlanta Christian College, (Christian Churches and Churches of Christ), 2605 Ben Hill Rd., East Point, GA 30344. R. Edwin Groover. Tel. (404)761-8861. Fax (404)669-2024

Austin Presbyterian Theological Seminary,* (Presbyterian Church (U.S.A.)), 100 E. 27th St., Austin, TX 78705. Jack L. Stotts. Tel. (512)472-6736. Fax (512)479-0738

Azusa Pacific University,* (Interdenominational), 901 E. Alosta, P.O. Box APU, Azusa, CA 91702. Richard Felix. Tel. (818)969-3434. Fax (818)969-7180

Bangor Theological Seminary,* (United Church of Christ), 300 Union St., Bangor, ME 04401. Malcolm Warford. Tel. (207)942-6781. Fax (207)942-4914

Baptist Bible College, (Baptist Bible Fellowship International), 628 E. Kearney, Springfield, MO 65803. Leland Kennedy. Tel. (417)869-9811. Fax (417)831-8029

Baptist Bible College and Seminary, (Interdenominational-Baptist), 538 Venard Rd., Clarks Summit, PA 18411. Milo Thompson. Tel. (717)587-1172. Fax (717)586-1753

Baptist Missionary Association Theological Seminary, (Baptist Missionary Association of America), 1530 E. Pine St., Jacksonville, TX 75766. Philip R. Bryan. Tel. (903)586-2501. Fax (903)586-0378

Barclay College, (Evangelical Friends International—North America Region), P.O. Box 288, Haviland, KS 67059. Robin W. Johnston. Tel. (316)862-5252. Fax (316)862-5403

Bay Ridge Christian College, (Church of God (Anderson, Ind.)), P.O. Box 726, Kendleton, TX 77451. Percy L. Lewis. Tel. (409)532-3982. Fax (409)532-4352

Berean Christian College, 5549-A N. Union Blvd., Colorado Springs, CO 80918. Adelia Bachman. Tel. (719)531-5914

Berkeley Divinity School at Yale,* (Episcopal Church), 363 St. Ronan St., New Haven, CT 06511. Dean Philip Turner. Tel. (203)432-6106. Fax (203)432-6110

Bethany College, (Assemblies of God), 800 Bethany Dr., Scotts Valley, CA 95066. Tom Duncan. Tel. (408)438-3800. Fax (408)438-4517

Bethany Lutheran Theological Seminary, (Evangelical Lutheran Synod), 447 N. Division St., Mankato, MN 56001. W. W. Petersen. Tel. (507)625-2977. Fax (507)625-1849

Bethany Theological Seminary,* (Church of the Brethren), Butterfield and Meyers Rd., Oak Brook, IL 60521. Eugene F. Roop. Tel. (708)620-2200. Fax (708)620-9014

Bethel Theological Seminary,* (Baptist General Conference), 3949 Bethel Dr., St. Paul, MN 55112. George K. Brushaber. Tel. (612)638-6230. Fax (612)638-6002

Beulah Heights Bible College, (The International Pentecostal Church of Christ), 892 Berne St. SE, Atlanta, GA 30316. Samuel R. Chand. Tel. (404)627-2681. Fax (404)627-0702

Biblical Theological Seminary, (Interdenominational), 200 N. Main St., Hatfield, PA 19440. David G. Dunbar. Tel. (215)368-5000. Fax (215)368-7002

Boise Bible College, (Nondenominational), 8695 Marigold St., Boise, ID 83714. Charles A. Crane. Tel. (208)376-7731

Boston University (School of Theology),* (The United Methodist Church), 745 Commonwealth Ave., Boston, MA 02215. Robert C. Neville. Tel. (617)353-3050. Fax (617)353-3061

Brite Divinity School, Texas Christian University,* (Christian Church (Disciples of Christ)), P.O. Box 32923, TCU, Ft. Worth, TX 76129. Leo G. Perdue. Tel. (817)921-7575. Fax (817)921-7333

Calvary Bible College and Theological Seminary, (Nondenominational), 15800 Calvary Rd., Kansas City, MO 64147-1341. Donald A. Urey. Tel. (800)326-3960. Fax (816)331-4474

Calvin Theological Seminary,* (Christian Reformed Church in North America), 3233 Burton St. SE, Grand Rapids, MI 49546. J. A. DeJong. Tel. (616)957-6036. Fax (616)957-8621

Candler School of Theology, Emory University,* (The United Methodist Church), Bishops Hall 202, Emory University, Atlanta, GA 30322. R. Kevin LaGree. Tel. (404)727-6324. Fax (404)727-2915

Catholic Theological Union,* (The Roman Catholic Church), 5401 S. Cornell Ave., Chicago, IL 60615. Donald Senior. Tel. (312)324-8000

Catholic University of America, Dept. of Theology,* (The Roman Catholic Church), 620 Michigan Ave., NE, Washington, DC 20064. Raymond Collins. Tel. (202)319-5481. Fax (202)319-4967

Central Baptist College, (Baptist Missionary Association of America), 1501 College Ave., Conway, AR 72032. Charles Attebery. Tel. (501)329-6872. Fax (501)329-2941

POPE VISITS

Pope John Paul II greets thousands of cheering youth at Mile High Stadium, August 12. The Pope visited Denver for World Youth Day activities. Here he is seen riding in what is known as his popemobile.

Central Baptist Theological Seminary,*
(American Baptist Churches in the U.S.A.), 741 N. 31st St., Kansas City, KS 66102-3964. Thomas E. Clifton. Tel. (913)371-5313. Fax (913)371-8110

Central Baptist Theological Seminary in Indiana, (National Baptist Convention, U.S.A., Inc.), 1535 Dr. A. J. Brown Ave. N, Indianapolis, IN 46202. F. Benjamin Davis. Tel. (317)636-6622

Central Bible College, (Assemblies of God), 3000 N. Grant Ave., Springfield, MO 65803. H. Maurice Lednicky. Tel. (417)833-2551. Fax (417)833-5141

Central Christian College of the Bible, (Christian Churches and Churches of Christ), 911 E. Urbandale, Moberly, MO 65270. Lloyd M. Pelfrey. Tel. (816)263-3900. Fax (816)263-3936

Central Indian Bible College, (Assemblies of God), P.O. Box 550, Mobridge, SD 57601. M. George Kallappa. Tel. (605)845-7801. Fax (605)845-7744

Central Wesleyan College, (The Wesleyan Church), One Wesleyan Dr., P.O. Box 1020, Central, SC 29630. John Newby. Tel. (803)639-2453. Fax (803)639-0826

Chicago Theological Seminary,* (United Church of Christ), 5757 South University Ave., Chicago, IL 60637. Kenneth B. Smith. Tel. (312)752-5757. Fax (312)752-5925

Christ the King Seminary,* (The Roman Catholic Church), 711 Knox Rd., P.O. Box 607, East Aurora, NY 14052. Frederick D. Leising. Tel. (716)652-8900. Fax (716)652-8903

Christ the Savior Seminary, (The American Carpatho-Russian Orthodox Greek Catholic Church), 225 Chandler Ave., Johnstown, PA 15906. Nicholas Smisko. Tel. (814)539-8086. Fax (814)536-4699

Christian Theological Seminary,* (Christian Church (Disciples of Christ)), 1000 W. 42nd St., Indianapolis, IN 46208. Richard D. N. Dickinson. Tel. (317)924-1331. Fax (317)923-1961

Church Divinity School of the Pacific,* (Episcopal Church), 2451 Ridge Rd., Berkeley, CA 94709. Charles A. Perry. Tel. (510)204-0700. Fax (510)644-0712

Church of God School of Theology,*
(Church of God (Cleveland, Tenn.)),
P.O. Box 3330, Cleveland, TN 37320-
3330. Cecil B. Knight. Tel. (615)478-
1131. Fax (615)478-7711

Cincinnati Bible College and Seminary,
(Christian Churches and Churches of
Christ), 2700 Glenway Ave., Cincinnati,
OH 45204. J. Edward Rauch. Tel.
(513)244-8100. Fax (513)244-8140

Circleville Bible College, (Churches of
Christ in Christian Union), P.O. Box
458, Circleville, OH 43113. David Van
Hoose. Tel. (614)474-8896. Fax
(614)477-7755

Clear Creek Baptist Bible College,
(Southern Baptist Convention), 300
Clear Creek Rd., Pineville, KY 40977.
Bill Whittaker. Tel. (606)337-3196. Fax
(606)337-2372

**Colegio Biblico Pentecostal de Puerto
Rico,** (Church of God (Cleveland,
Tenn.)), P.O. Box 901, Saint Just, PR
00978. Ismael López-Borrero. Tel.
(809)761-0640

Colgate Rochester/Bexley Hall/Crozer,*
(Interdenominational), 1100 S. Goodman St., Rochester, NY 14620. James H.
Evans. Tel. (716)271-1320. Fax
(716)271-2166

Colorado Christian University, (Nondenominational), 180 S. Garrison St.,
Lakewood, CO 80226. Ronald R.
Schmidt. Tel. (303)238-5386. Fax
(303)233-2735

**Columbia Biblical Seminary and Gradu-
ate School of Missions,*** (Interdenominational), P.O. Box 3122, Columbia, SC
29230-3122. Johnny Miller. Tel.
(803)754-4100. Fax (803)786-4209

Columbia Theological Seminary,* (Presbyterian Church (U.S.A.)), P.O. Box
520, Decatur, GA 30031. Douglas Old-
enburg. Tel. (404)378-8821. Fax
(404)377-9696

Concordia Seminary,* (The Lutheran
Church—Missouri Synod), 801 De Mun
Ave., St. Louis, MO 63105. John F.
Johnson. Tel. (314)721-5934. Fax
(314)721-5902

Concordia Theological Seminary,* (The
Lutheran Church—Missouri Synod),
6600 N. Clinton St., Ft. Wayne, IN
46825. David G. Schmiel. Tel.
(219)481-2100. Fax (219)481-2121

Covenant Theological Seminary,* (Presbyterian Church in America), 12330
Conway Rd., St. Louis, MO 63141. Paul
Kooistra. Tel. (314)434-4044. Fax
(314)434-4819

Cranmer Seminary, (The Anglican Ortho-
dox Church), P.O. Box 329, 323 Walnut
St., Statesville, NC 28677. James P.
Dees. Tel. (704)873-8365

Criswell Center for Biblical Studies, 4010
Gaston Ave., Dallas, TX 75246. Richard
R. Melick. Tel. (214)818-1300. Fax
(214)818-1320

Criswell College, 4010 Gaston Ave., Dallas, TX 75246. Richard R. Melick. Tel.
(214)818-1300. Fax (214)818-1320

Crown College, (The Christian and Missionary Alliance), 6425 County Rd. 30,
St. Bonifacius, MN 55375. Bill W. Lan-
pher. Tel. (612)446-4100. Fax
(612)446-4149

Dallas Christian College, (Christian
Churches and Churches of Christ), 2700
Christian Pky., Dallas, TX 75234. Gene
Shepherd. Tel. (214)241-3371. Fax
(214)241-8021

Dallas Theological Seminary,* (Interdenominational), 3909 Swiss Ave., Dallas,
TX 75204. Donald K. Campbell. Tel.
(214)841-3614. Fax (214)841-3625

De Sales School of Theology,* (The Roman
Catholic Church), 721 Lawrence St. NE,
Washington, DC 20017. John W.
Crossin. Tel. (202)269-9412

Denver Conservative Baptist Seminary,*
(Conservative Baptist Association of
America), Box 10,000, Denver, CO
80250-0100. Edward L. Hayes. Tel.
(303)761-2482. Fax (303)761-8060

**Disciples Divinity House, University of
Chicago,** (Christian Church (Disciples
of Christ)), 1156 E. 57th St., Chicago, IL
60637. Kristine A. Culp. Tel. (312)643-
4411

Dominican House of Studies,* (The Roman Catholic Church), 487 Michigan
Ave. NE, Washington, DC 20017-1585.
Philip Smith. Tel. (202)529-5300. Fax
(202)636-4460

**Dominican School of Philosophy and The-
ology,*** (The Roman Catholic Church),
2401 Ridge Road, Berkeley, CA 94709.
Allen Duston. Tel. (510)849-2030

Drew University (Theological School),*
(The United Methodist Church), 36
Madison Ave., Madison, NJ 07940-
4010. Robin Warren Lovin. Tel.
(201)408-3258. Fax (201)408-3808

Duke University (Divinity School),* (The
United Methodist Church), Duke U. Divinity School, Box 90968, Durham, NC
27708. Dennis M. Campbell. Tel.
(919)660-3400. Fax (919)660-3473

Earlham School of Religion,* (Interdenominational-Friends), 228 College Ave., Richmond, IN 47374. Andrew P. Grannell. Tel. (800)432-1377. Fax (317)983-1688

East Coast Bible College, (Church of God (Cleveland, Tenn.)), 6900 Wilkinson Blvd., Charlotte, NC 28214. Ronald Martin. Tel. (704)394-2307. Fax (704)394-2308

Eastern Baptist Theological Seminary,* (American Baptist Churches in the U.S.A.), P.O. Box 12438, Philadelphia, PA 19151-0438. Manfred T. Brauch. Tel. (215)896-5000. Fax (215)649-3834

Eastern Mennonite Seminary,* (Mennonite Church), Eastern Mennonite Seminary, Harrisonburg, VA 22801. George R. Brunk. Tel. (703)432-4260. Fax (703)432-4444

Eden Theological Seminary,* (United Church of Christ), 475 E. Lockwood Ave., St. Louis, MO 63119. Charles R. Kniker. Tel. (314)961-3627. Fax (314)961-9063

Emmanuel School of Religion,* (Christian Churches and Churches of Christ), One Walker Dr., Johnson City, TN 37601. Calvin L. Phillips. Tel. (615)926-1186. Fax (615)461-1556

Emmaus Bible College, (Nondenominational), 2570 Asbury Rd., Dubuque, IA 52001. Daniel Smith. Tel. (319)588-8000. Fax (319)588-1216

Episcopal Divinity School,* (Episcopal Church), 99 Brattle St., Cambridge, MA 02138. William Rankin. Tel. (617)868-3450. Fax (617)864-5385

Episcopal Theological Seminary of the Southwest,* (Episcopal Church), P.O. Box 2247, Austin, TX 78768-2247. Durstan R. McDonald. Tel. (512)472-4133. Fax (512)472-3098

Erskine Theological Seminary,* (Associate Reformed Presbyterian Church, General Synod), Drawer 668, Due West, SC 29639. R. T. Ruble. Tel. (803)379-8885. Fax (803)379-8759

Eugene Bible College, (Open Bible Standard Churches, Inc.), 2155 Bailey Hill Rd., Eugene, OR 97405. Jeffrey E. Farmer. Tel. (503)485-1780. Fax (503)343-5801

Evangelical School of Theology,* (The Evangelical Congregational Church), 121 S. College St., Myerstown, PA 17067. Kirby N. Keller. Tel. (717)866-5775. Fax (717)866-4667

Faith Baptist Bible College and Seminary, (General Association of Regular Baptist Churches), 1900 NW 4th St., Ankeny, IA 50021. David Boylan. Tel. (515)964-0601. Fax (515)964-1638

Faith Evangelical Lutheran Seminary, 3504 N. Pearl St., Tacoma, WA 98407. R. H. Redal. Tel. (206)752-2020

Florida Bible College, (Independent Fundamental Churches of America), 1701 N. Poinciana Blvd., Kissimmee, FL 34758. Warren Eck. Tel. (407)933-4500. Fax (407)933-4500

Florida Christian College, (Christian Churches and Churches of Christ), 1011 Bill Beck Blvd., Kissimmee, FL 34744. A. Wayne Lowen. Tel. (407)847-8966. Fax (407)847-8966

Franciscan School of Theology,* (The Roman Catholic Church), 1712 Euclid Ave., Berkeley, CA 94709. William M. Cieslak. Tel. (510)848-5232. Fax (510)549-9466

Free Will Baptist Bible College, (National Association of Free Will Baptists), 3606 West End Ave., Nashville, TN 37205. Tom Malone. Tel. (615)383-1340. Fax (615)269-6028

Fuller Theological Seminary,* (Interdenominational), 135 N. Oakland Ave., Pasadena, CA 91182. Richard J. Mouw. Tel. (818)584-5200. Fax (818)795-8767

Garrett-Evangelical Theological Seminary,* (The United Methodist Church), 2121 Sheridan Rd., Evanston, IL 60201. Neal F. Fisher. Tel. (708)866-3900. Fax (708)866-3957

General Theological Seminary, The,* (Episcopal Church), 175 Ninth Ave., New York, NY 10011-4977. Craig B. Anderson. Tel. (212)243-5150. Fax (212)727-3907

George Mercer, Jr. Memorial School of Theology, (Episcopal Church), 65 Fourth St., Garden City, NY 11530. Lloyd A. Lewis. Tel. (516)248-4800. Fax (516)248-4883

God's Bible School and College, (Nondenominational), 1810 Young St., Cincinnati, OH 45210. Bence Miller. Tel. (513)721-7944. Fax (513)721-3971

Golden Gate Baptist Theological Seminary,* (Southern Baptist Convention), Strawberry Point, Mill Valley, CA 94941. William O. Crews. Tel. (415)388-8080. Fax (415)383-0723

Gordon-Conwell Theological Seminary,* (Interdenominational), 130 Essex St., South Hamilton, MA 01982. Robert E. Cooley. Tel. (508)468-7111. Fax (508)468-6691

Grace Bible College, (Grace Gospel Fellowship), P.O. Box 910, Grand Rapids, MI 49509. E. Bruce Kemper. Tel. (616)538-2330. Fax (616)538-0599

Grace College of the Bible, (Nondenominational), Ninth and William, Omaha, NE 68108. Neal F. McBride. Tel. (402)449-2800

Grace Theological Seminary, (Fellowship of Grace Brethren Churches), 200 Seminary Dr., Winona Lake, IN 46590. Ronald E. Manahan. Tel. (219)372-5100. Fax (219)372-5265

Graduate Theological Union,* (Nondenominational), 2400 Ridge Rd., Berkeley, CA 94709. Glenn R. Bucher. Tel. (510)649-2410. Fax (510)649-1417

Great Lakes Christian College, (Christian Churches and Churches of Christ), 6211 W. Willow Hwy., Lansing, MI 48917. Kenneth E. Henes. Tel. (517)321-0242. Fax (517)321-5902

Greenville College, (Free Methodist Church of North America), 315 E. College Ave., P.O. Box 159, Greenville, IL 62246. Robert E. Smith. Tel. (618)664-1840. Fax (618)664-1748

Hartford Seminary,* (Interdenominational), 77 Sherman St., Hartford, CT 06105. Barbara Brown Zikmund. Tel. (203)232-4451. Fax (203)236-8570

Harvard Divinity School,* (Nondenominational), 45 Francis Ave., Cambridge, MA 02138. Ronald F. Thiemann. Tel. (617)495-5761. Fax (617)495-9489

Hebrew Union College—Jewish Inst. of Religion, (Jewish Organizations), 1 W. 4th St., New York, NY 10012. Alfred Gottschalk. Tel. (212)674-5300. Fax (212)533-0129

Hebrew Union College—Jewish Inst. of Religion, (Jewish Organizations), 3077 University, Los Angeles, CA 90007. Uri Herscher. Tel. (213)749-3424. Fax (213)747-6128

Hebrew Union College—Jewish Institute of Religion, (Jewish Organizations), 3101 Clifton Ave., Cincinnati, OH 45215. Alfred Gottschalk. Tel. (513)221-1875. Fax (513)221-2810

Hobe Sound Bible College, (Nondenominational), P.O. Box 1065, Hobe Sound, FL 33475. Robert E. Whitaker. Tel. (407)546-5534. Fax (407)545-1422

Holy Cross Gk. Orthodox School of Theology(Hellenic College),* (Greek Orthodox Archdiocese of North and South America), 50 Goddard Ave., Brookline, MA 02146. Methodios of Boston. Tel. (617)731-3500. Fax (617)738-9169

Holy Trinity Orthodox Seminary, (The Russian Orthodox Church Outside of Russia), P.O. Box 36, Jordanville, NY 13361. Archbishop Laurus. Tel. (315)858-0940. Fax (315)858-0505

Hood Theological Seminary, (African Methodist Episcopal Zion Church), 800 W. Thomas St., Salisbury, NC 28144. James R. Samuel. Tel. (704)638-5643

Howard University School of Divinity,* (Interdenominational), 1400 Shepherd St. NE, Washington, DC 20017. Clarence G. Newsome. Tel. (202)806-0500. Fax (202)806-0711

Huntington College, Graduate School of Christian Ministries, (United Brethren in Christ), 2303 College Ave., Huntington, IN 46750. Paul R. Fetters. Tel. (800)642-6493. Fax (219)356-9448

Iliff School of Theology,* (The United Methodist Church), 2201 S. University Blvd., Denver, CO 80210. Donald E. Messer. Tel. (303)744-1287. Fax (303)744-3387

Immaculate Conception Seminary School of Theology,* (The Roman Catholic Church), 400 S. Orange Ave., South Orange, NJ 07079. Robert E. Harahan. Tel. (201)761-9575. Fax (201)761-9577

Indiana Wesleyan University, (The Wesleyan Church), 4201 S. Washington, Marion, IN 46953. Joseph W. Seaborn. Tel. (317)677-2241. Fax (317)677-2499

Interdenominational Theological Center,* (Interdenominational), 671 Beckwith St. SW, Atlanta, GA 30314. James H. Costen. Tel. (404)527-7702. Fax (404)527-0901

Jesuit School of Theology at Berkeley,* (The Roman Catholic Church), 1735 LeRoy Ave., Berkeley, CA 94709. Thomas F. Gleeson. Tel. (510)841-8804. Fax (510)841-8536

Jewish Theological Seminary of America, (Jewish Organizations), 3080 Broadway, New York, NY 10027-4649. Ismar Schorsch. Tel. (212)678-8000. Fax (212)678-8947

John Wesley College, (Interdenominational), 2314 N. Centennial St., High Point, NC 27265. Brian C. Donley. Tel. (919)889-2262. Fax (919)889-2261

Johnson Bible College, (Christian Churches and Churches of Christ), 7900 Johnson Dr., Knoxville, TN 37998. David L. Eubanks. Tel. (615)573-4517. Fax (615)579-2336

Kansas City College and Bible School, (The Holiness Church of God, Inc.), 7401 Metcalf Ave., Overland Park, KS 66204. Noel Scott. Tel. (913)722-0272. Fax (913)722-0351

Kenrick-Glennon Seminary,* (The Roman Catholic Church), 5200 Glennon Dr., St. Louis, MO 63119. Ronald W. Ramson. Tel. (314)644-0266. Fax (314)644-3079

Kentucky Christian College, 617 N. Carol Malone Blvd., Grayson, KY 41143-1199. Keith P. Keeran. Tel. (606)474-6613. Fax (606)474-3155

Kentucky Mountain Bible College, (Interdenominational), Box 10, Vancleve, KY 41385. Philip Speas. Tel. (606)666-5000. Fax (606)666-7744

L.I.F.E. Bible College, (International Church of the Foursquare Gospel), 1100 Covina Blvd., San Dimas, CA 91773. Ron Mehl. Tel. (909)599-5433. Fax (909)599-6690

La Sierra University, (Seventh-day Adventist Church), 4700 Pierce St., Riverside, CA 92515-8247. Lawrence T. Geraky. Tel. (714)785-2000. Fax (714)785-2901

Lancaster Bible College, (Nondenominational), 901 Eden Rd., Lancaster, PA 17601. Gilbert A. Peterson. Tel. (717)569-7071. Fax (717)560-8213

Lancaster Theological Sem. of the United Church of Christ,* (United Church of Christ), 555 W. James St., Lancaster, PA 17603-2897. Peter Schmiechen. Tel. (717)393-0654. Fax (717)393-4254

Lexington Theological Seminary,* (Christian Church (Disciples of Christ)), 631 S. Limestone St., Lexington, KY 40508. Richard L. Harrison. Tel. (606)252-0361. Fax (606)281-6042

Lincoln Christian College and Seminary,* (Christian Churches and Churches of Christ), 100 Campus View Dr., Lincoln, IL 62656. Charles A. McNeely. Tel. (217)732-3168. Fax (217)732-5914

Louisville Presbyterian Theological Seminary,* (Presbyterian Church (U.S.A.)), 1044 Alta Vista Rd., Louisville, KY 40205. John M. Mulder. Tel. (502)895-3411. Fax (502)895-1096

Luther Northwestern Theological Seminary,* (Evangelical Lutheran Church in America), 2481 Como Ave., St. Paul, MN 55108. David L. Tiede. Tel. (612)641-3456. Fax (612)641-3425

Lutheran Bible Institute in California, (Interdenominational Lutheran), 641 S. Western Ave., Anaheim, CA 92804. Clifton Pederson. Tel. (714)827-1940. Fax (714)995-6020

Lutheran Bible Institute of Seattle, (Interdenominational Lutheran), 4221 - 228th Ave. SE, Issaquah, WA 98027. Trygve R. Skarsten. Tel. (206)392-0400. Fax (206)392-0404

Lutheran Brethren Seminary, (Church of the Lutheran Brethren of America), 815 W. Vernon, Fergus Falls, MN 56537. Joel Egge. Tel. (218)739-3375. Fax (218)739-3372

Lutheran Center for Christian Learning, (Church of the Lutheran Brethren of America), 815 W. Vernon, Fergus Falls, MN 56537. Joel Egge. Tel. (218)739-3375. Fax (218)739-3372

Lutheran School of Theology at Chicago,* (Evangelical Lutheran Church in America), 1100 E. 55th St., Chicago, IL 60615-5199. William E. Lesher. Tel. (312)753-0700. Fax (312)753-0782

Lutheran Theological Seminary,* (Evangelical Lutheran Church in America), 61 NW Confederate Ave., Gettysburg, PA 17325. Darold H. Beekmann. Tel. (717)334-6286. Fax (717)334-3469

Lutheran Theological Seminary at Philadelphia,* (Evangelical Lutheran Church in America), 7301 Germantown Ave., Philadelphia, PA 19119. Robert G. Hughes. Tel. (215)248-4616. Fax (215)248-4577

Lutheran Theological Southern Seminary,* (Evangelical Lutheran Church in America), Lutheran Theological Southern Seminary, Columbia, SC 29203. H. Frederick Reisz. Tel. (803)786-5150

Magnolia Bible College, (Churches of Christ), P.O. Box 1109, Kosciusko, MS 39090. Cecil May. Tel. (601)289-2896. Fax (601)289-1850

Manhattan Christian College, (Christian Churches and Churches of Christ), 1415 Anderson Ave., Manhattan, KS 66502. Kenneth Cable. Tel. (913)539-3571. Fax (913)539-0832

Manna Bible Institute, (Nondenominational), 700 E. Church La., Philadelphia, PA 19144. Arvelle C. Jones. Tel. (215)843-3600

Mary Immaculate Seminary, (The Roman Catholic Church), 300 Cherryville Rd., Box 27, Northampton, PA 18067. William W. Sheldon. Tel. (215)262-7866. Fax (215)262-6766

Maryknoll School of Theology,* (The Roman Catholic Church), P.O. Box 305, Maryknoll, NY 10545. John K. Halbert. Tel. (914)941-7590. Fax (914)941-5753

McCormick Theological Seminary,* (Presbyterian Church (U.S.A.)), 5555 S. Woodlawn Ave., Chicago, IL 60637. G. Daniel Little. Tel. (312)947-6300. Fax (312)947-0376

Meadville/Lombard Theological School,* (Unitarian Universalist Association), 5701 S. Woodlawn Ave., Chicago, IL 60637. Spencer Lavan. Tel. (312)753-3195. Fax (312)753-1323

Memphis Theol. Sem. of the Cumberland Presbyterian Church,* (Cumberland Presbyterian Church), 168 E. Parkway S, Memphis, TN 38104. J. David Hester. Tel. (901)458-8232. Fax (901)452-4051

Mennonite Brethren Biblical Seminary,* (The General Conference of Mennonite Brethren Churches), 4824 E. Butler Ave. (at Chestnut Ave.), Fresno, CA 93727. Henry J. Schmidt. Tel. (209)251-8628. Fax (209)251-7212

Methodist Theological School in Ohio,* (The United Methodist Church), 3081 Columbus Pk., P.O. Box 1204, Delaware, OH 43015-0931. Norman E. Dewire. Tel. (614)363-1146. Fax (614)362-3135

Mid-America Bible College, (The Church of God), 3500 SW 119th St., Oklahoma City, OK 73170. Forrest R. Robinson. Tel. (405)691-3800. Fax (405)692-3165

Midwestern Baptist Theological Seminary,* (Southern Baptist Convention), 5001 N. Oak St. Trafficway, Kansas City, MO 64118. Milton Ferguson. Tel. (816)453-4600. Fax (816)455-3528

Minnesota Bible College, (Christian Churches and Churches of Christ), 920 Mayowood Rd. SW, Rochester, MN 55902. Donald Lloyd. Tel. (507)288-4563. Fax (507)288-9046

Moody Bible Institute, (Interdenominational), 820 N. La Salle Blvd., Chicago, IL 60610. Joseph M. Stowell. Tel. (312)329-4000

Moravian Theological Seminary,* (Moravian Church in America, Unitas Fratrum), 1200 Main St., Bethlehem, PA 18018. David A. Schattschneider. Tel. (215)861-1516. Fax (215)861-1569

Moreau Seminary (Holy Cross Fathers), (The Roman Catholic Church), Moreau Seminary, Notre Dame, IN 46556. Thomas K. Zurcher. Tel. (219)239-7735. Fax (219)631-9233

Morehouse School of Religion, (Interdenominational Baptist), 645 Beckwith St. SW, Atlanta, GA 30314. William T. Perkins. Tel. (404)527-7777. Fax (404)527-0901

Mount Angel Seminary,* (The Roman Catholic Church), St. Benedict, OR 97373. Patrick S. Brennan. Tel. (503)845-3951. Fax (503)845-3126

Mt. St. Mary's Seminary,* (The Roman Catholic Church), Emmitsburg, MD 21727-7797. Kenneth W. Roeltgen. Tel. (301)447-5295. Fax (301)447-5636

Mt. St. Mary's Seminary of the West, (The Roman Catholic Church), 6616 Beechmont Ave., Cincinnati, OH 45230. Robert J. Mooney. Tel. (513)231-2223. Fax (513)231-3254

Multnomah Bible College and Biblical Seminary,* (Interdenominational), 8435 NE Glisan St., Portland, OR 97220. Joseph C. Aldrich. Tel. (503)255-0332. Fax (503)254-1268

Mundelein Seminary of the Univ. of St. Mary-of-the-Lake,* (The Roman Catholic Church), Mundelein, IL 60060. Gerald F. Kicanas. Tel. (708)566-6401. Fax (708)566-7330

Nashotah House (Theological Seminary),* (Episcopal Church), 2777 Mission Rd., Nashotah, WI 53058-9793. Gary W. Kriss. Tel. (414)646-3371. Fax (414)646-2215

Nazarene Bible College, (Church of the Nazarene), 1111 Chapman Dr., Box 15749, Colorado Springs, CO 80916. Jerry Lambert. Tel. (719)596-5110. Fax (719)550-9437

Nazarene Theological Seminary,* (Church of the Nazarene), 1700 E. Meyer Blvd., Kansas City, MO 64131. A. Gordon Wetmore. Tel. (816)333-6254. Fax (816)822-9025

Nebraska Christian College, (Christian Churches and Churches of Christ), 1800 Syracuse Ave., Norfolk, NE 68701. Ray D. Stites. Tel. (402)371-5960. Fax (402)371-5967

New Brunswick Theological Seminary,* (Reformed Church in America), 17 Seminary Pl., New Brunswick, NJ 08901-1107. Norman J. Kansfield. Tel. (908)247-5241. Fax (908)249-5412

New Orleans Baptist Theological Seminary,* (Southern Baptist Convention), 3939 Gentilly Blvd., New Orleans, LA 70126. Landrum P. Leavell. Tel. (504)282-4455. Fax (504)944-4455

New York Theological Seminary,* (Interdenominational), Five W. 29th St., 9th Floor, New York, NY 10001. M. William Howard. Tel. (212)532-4012. Fax (212)684-0757

North American Baptist Seminary,* (North American Baptist Conference), 1321 W. 22nd St., Sioux Falls, SD 57105. Charles M. Hiatt. Tel. (605)336-6588. Fax (605)355-9090

North Central Bible College, (Assemblies of God), 910 Elliot Ave. S, Minneapolis, MN 55404. Don Argue. Tel. (612)332-3491. Fax (612)343-4778

North Park Theological Seminary, * (The Evangelical Covenant Church), 3225 W. Foster Ave., Chicago, IL 60625. David G. Horner. Tel. (312)583-2700. Fax (312)583-0858

Northern Baptist Theological Seminary,* (American Baptist Churches in the U.S.A.), 660 E. Butterfield Rd., Lombard, IL 60148. Ian M. Chapman. Tel. (708)620-2100. Fax (708)620-2194

Northwest College of the Assemblies of God, (Assemblies of God), 5520 108th Ave. NE, P.O. Box 579, Kirkland, WA 98083-0579. Dennis A. Davis. Tel. (206)822-8266. Fax (206)827-0148

Notre Dame Seminary,* (The Roman Catholic Church), 2901 S. Carrollton Ave., New Orleans, LA 70118. Gregory M. Aymond. Tel. (504)866-7426

Oak Hills Bible College, (Interdenominational), 1600 Oak Hills Rd. SW, Bemidji, MN 56601. Mark Hovestol. Tel. (218)751-8670. Fax (218)751-8825

Oblate College,* (The Roman Catholic Church), 391 Michigan Ave. NE, Washington, DC 20017. George F. Kirwin. Tel. (202)529-6544

Oblate School of Theology,* (The Roman Catholic Church), 285 Oblate Dr., San Antonio, TX 78216-6693. Patrick Guidon. Tel. (210)341-1366. Fax (210)341-4519

Oral Roberts University School of Theology,* (Interdenominational), 7777 South Lewis Ave., Tulsa, OK 74171. Paul G. Chappell. Tel. (918)495-6096. Fax (918)495-6033

Ozark Christian College, (Christian Churches and Churches of Christ), 1111 N. Main St., Joplin, MO 64801. Ken Idleman. Tel. (417)624-2518

Pacific Christian College, (Christian Churches and Churches of Christ), 2500 E. Nutwood Ave., Fullerton, CA 92631. E. Leroy Lawson. Tel. (714)879-3901. Fax (714)526-0231

Pacific Lutheran Theological Seminary,* (Evangelical Lutheran Church in America), 2770 Marin Ave., Berkeley, CA 94708. Jerry L. Schmalenberger. Tel. (510)524-5264. Fax (510)524-2408

Pacific School of Religion,* (Interdenominational), 1798 Scenic Ave., Berkeley, CA 94709. Eleanor Scott Meyers. Tel. (510)848-0528. Fax (510)845-8948

Payne Theological Seminary,* (African Methodist Episcopal Church), P.O. Box 474, Wilberforce, OH 45384. Louis-Charles Harvey. Tel. (513)376-2946. Fax (513)376-3330

Pepperdine University, (Churches of Christ), Religion Division, Malibu, CA 90263. Thomas H. Olbricht. Tel. (310)456-4352. Fax (310)456-4314

Perkins School of Theology (Southern Methodist University),* (The United Methodist Church), Kirby Hall, Dallas, TX 75275-0133. James E. Kirby. Tel. (214)768-2138. Fax (214)768-2117

Philadelphia College of Bible, (Nondenominational), 200 Manor Ave., Langhorne, PA 19047-2990. W. Sherrill Babb. Tel. (215)752-5800. Fax (215)752-5812

Philadelphia Theological Seminary, (Reformed Episcopal Church), 7372 Henry Ave., Philadelphia, PA 19128. Ray R. Sutton. Tel. (215)483-2480. Fax (215)483-2484

Phillips Graduate Seminary,* (Christian Church (Disciples of Christ)), Box 2335, University Sta., Enid, OK 73702. William Tabbernee. Tel. (405)548-2238. Fax (405)237-1607

Piedmont Bible College, 716 Franklin St., Winston-Salem, NC 27101. Howard L. Wilburn. Tel. (919)725-8344

Pittsburgh Theological Seminary,* (Presbyterian Church (U.S.A.)), 616 N. Highland Ave., Pittsburgh, PA 15206. Carnegie Samuel Calian. Tel. (412)362-5610. Fax (412)363-3260

Point Loma Nazarene College, (Church of the Nazarene), 3900 Lomaland Dr., San Diego, CA 92106. Jim Bond. Tel. (619)221-2200. Fax (619)221-2579

Pontifical College Josephinum,* (The Roman Catholic Church), 7625 N. High St., Columbus, OH 43235. Blase J. Cupich. Tel. (614)885-5585. Fax (614)885-2307

Pope John XXIII National Seminary,* (The Roman Catholic Church), 558 South Ave., Weston, MA 02193. Cornelius M. McRae. Tel. (617)899-5500. Fax (617)899-9057

Practical Bible Training School, (Independent Baptist), Box 601, Bible School Park, NY 13737. Dale E. Linebaugh. Tel. (607)729-1581. Fax (607)729-2962

Presbyterian School of Christian Education,* (Presbyterian Church (U.S.A.)), 1205 Palmyra Ave., Richmond, VA 23227. Wayne G. Boulton. Tel. (804)359-5031. Fax (804)254-8060

Princeton Theological Seminary,* (Presbyterian Church (U.S.A.)), P.O. Box 821, Princeton, NJ 08542-0803. Thomas W. Gillespie. Tel. (609)921-8300. Fax (609)924-2973

Protestant Episcopal Theological Seminary in Virginia,* (Episcopal Church), 3737 Seminary Rd., Alexandria, VA 22304. Richard Reid. Tel. (703)370-6600. Fax (703)370-6234

Puget Sound Christian College, (Christian Churches and Churches of Christ), 410 Fourth Ave. N, Edmonds, WA 98020-3171. Glen R. Basey. Tel. (206)775-8686

Rabbi Isaac Elchanan Theological Seminary, (Jewish Organizations), 2540 Amsterdam Ave., New York, NY 10033. Zevulun Charlop. Tel. (212)960-5344. Fax (212)960-0061

Reconstructionist Rabbinical College, (Jewish Organizations), Church Rd. and Greenwood Ave., Wyncote, PA 19095. David A. Teutsch. Tel. (215)576-0800. Fax (215)576-6143

Reformed Bible College, (Interdenominational), 3333 East Beltline NE, Grand Rapids, MI 49505. Edwin D. Roels. Tel. (616)363-2050. Fax (616)363-9771

Reformed Presbyterian Theological Seminary,* (Reformed Presbyterian Church of North America), 7418 Penn Ave., Pittsburgh, PA 15208. Bruce C. Stewart. Tel. (412)731-8690

Reformed Theological Seminary,* (Nondenominational), 5422 Clinton Blvd., Jackson, MS 39209. Luder G. Whitlock. Tel. (601)922-4988. Fax (601)922-1153

Regent University School of Theology,* (Interdenominational), 1000 Centerville Tpks., Virginia Beach, VA 23464-5041. Terry Lindvall. Tel. (804)523-7063. Fax (804)424-7051

Roanoke Bible College, (Christian Churches and Churches of Christ), 714 First St., Elizabeth City, NC 27909. William A. Griffin. Tel. (919)338-5191. Fax (919)338-0801

SS. Cyril and Methodius Seminary, (The Roman Catholic Church), Orchard Lake, MI 48324. Francis B. Koper. Tel. (313)682-1885. Fax (313)683-0402

Sacred Heart Major Seminary,* (The Roman Catholic Church), 2701 Chicago Blvd., Detroit, MI 48206. John Nienstedt. Tel. (313)883-8500. Fax (313)868-6440

Sacred Heart School of Theology,* (The Roman Catholic Church), P.O. Box 429, Hales Corners, WI 53130-0429. John A. Kasparek. Tel. (414)425-8300. Fax (414)529-6999

Saint Bernard's Institute,* (The Roman Catholic Church), 1100 S. Goodman St., Rochester, NY 14620. Sebastian A. Falcone. Tel. (716)271-1320. Fax (716)271-2166

St. Charles Borromeo Seminary,* (The Roman Catholic Church), 1000 East Wynnewood Rd., Overbrook, PA 19096. Daniel A. Murray. Tel. (215)667-3394. Fax (215)667-7635

St. Francis Seminary,* (The Roman Catholic Church), 3257 S. Lake Dr., St. Francis, WI 53235. David A. Lichter. Tel. (414)747-6400. Fax (414)747-6442

St. John's Seminary,* (The Roman Catholic Church), 127 Lake St., Brighton, MA 02135. Timothy Moran. Tel. (617)254-2610. Fax (617)787-2336

St. John's Seminary College,* (The Roman Catholic Church), 5118 Seminary Rd., Camarillo, CA 93012-2599. Rafael Luévano. Tel. (805)482-2755. Fax (805)987-5097

St. John's University, School of Theology,* (The Roman Catholic Church), Collegeville, MN 56321. Dale Launderville. Tel. (612)363-2100. Fax (616)363-2504

St. Joseph's Seminary,* (The Roman Catholic Church), 201 Seminary Ave., (Dunwoodie) Yonkers, NY 10704. Raymond T. Powers. Tel. (914)968-6200. Fax (914)968-7912

St. Louis Christian College, (Christian Churches and Churches of Christ), 1360 Grandview Dr., Florissant, MO 63033. Thomas W. McGee. Tel. (314)837-6777. Fax (314)837-8291

St. Mary Seminary,* (The Roman Catholic Church), 28700 Euclid Ave., Wickliffe, OH 44092. Allan R. Laubenthal. Tel. (216)943-7600. Fax (216)585-3528

St. Mary's Seminary, (The Roman Catholic Church), 9845 Memorial Dr., Houston, TX 77024-3498. Chester L. Borski. Tel. (713)686-4345. Fax (713)681-7550

St. Mary's Seminary and University,* (The Roman Catholic Church), 5400 Roland Ave., Baltimore, MD 21210. Robert F. Leavitt. Tel. (301)323-3200. Fax (301)323-3554

St. Meinrad School of Theology,* (The Roman Catholic Church), St. Meinrad, IN 47577. Eugene Hensell. Tel. (812)357-6611. Fax (812)357-6964

St. Patrick's Seminary,* (The Roman Catholic Church), 320 Middlefield Rd., Menlo Park, CA 94025. Gerald D. Coleman. Tel. (415)325-5621. Fax (415)322-0997

Saint Paul School of Theology,* (The United Methodist Church), 5123 Truman Rd., Kansas City, MO 64127. Lovett H. Weems. Tel. (816)483-9600. Fax (816)483-9605

St. Paul Seminary School of Divinity,* (The Roman Catholic Church), 2260 Summit Ave., St. Paul, MN 55105. Phillip J. Rask. Tel. (612)962-5050. Fax (612)962-5790

Saint Thomas Theological Seminary,* (The Roman Catholic Church), 1300 S. Steele St., Denver, CO 80210. J. Dennis Martin. Tel. (303)722-4687. Fax (303)722-7422

St. Tikhon's Orthodox Theological Seminary, (The Orthodox Church in America), P.O. Box 130, South Canaan, PA 18459-0121. Herman. Tel. (717)937-4686. Fax (717)937-4939

St. Vincent Seminary,* (The Roman Catholic Church), Latrobe, PA 15650. Thomas Acklin. Tel. (412)537-4592. Fax (412)537-4554

St. Vincent de Paul Regional Seminary,* (The Roman Catholic Church), 10701 S. Military Trail, Boynton Beach, FL 33436. Pablo Navarro. Tel. (407)732-4424. Fax (407)737-2205

St. Vladimir's Orthodox Theological Seminary,* (The Orthodox Church in America), 575 Scarsdale Rd., Crestwood, NY 10707. Thomas Hopko. Tel. (914)961-8313. Fax (914)961-4507

San Francisco Theological Seminary,* (Presbyterian Church (U.S.A.)), 2 Kensington Rd., San Anselmo, CA 94960. J. Randolph Taylor. Tel. (415)258-6500. Fax (415)454-2493

San Jose Christian College, (Nondenominational), 790 S. 12th St., P.O. Box 1090, San Jose, CA 95108. Bryce L. Jessup. Tel. (408)293-9058. Fax (408)293-7352

Savonarola Theological Seminary, (Polish National Catholic Church of America), 1031 Cedar Ave., Scranton, PA 18505. John F. Swantek. Tel. (717)343-0100

School of Theology at Claremont,* (The United Methodist Church), 1325 N. College Ave., Claremont, CA 91711. Robert W. Edgar. Tel. (800)626-7821. Fax (909)626-7062

Seabury-Western Theological Seminary,* (Episcopal Church), 2122 Sheridan Rd., Evanston, IL 60201. Mark S. Sisk. Tel. (708)328-9300. Fax (708)328-9624

Seattle University Institute for Theological Studies,* (The Roman Catholic Church), Broadway & Madison, Seattle, WA 98122. Loretta Jancoski. Tel. (206)296-5330

Seminario Evangelico de Puerto Rico,* (Interdenominational), 776 Ponce de Leon Ave., San Juan, PR 00925. Luis Fidel Mercado. Tel. (809)751-6483. Fax (809)751-0847

Seminary of the Immaculate Conception,* (The Roman Catholic Church), 440 West Neck Rd., Huntington, NY 11743. John J. Strynkowski. Tel. (516)423-0483. Fax (516)423-2346

Seventh Day Baptist School of Ministry, (Seventh Day Baptist General Conference, USA and Canada), 3120 Kennedy Rd., P.O. Box 1678, Janesville, WI 53547. Rodney L. Henry. Tel. (608)752-5055. Fax (608)752-7711

Seventh-day Adventist Theological Seminary, Andrews Univ.,* (Seventh-day Adventist Church), Berrien Springs, MI 49104. Werner Vyhmeister. Tel. (616)471-3536. Fax (616)471-6202

Shaw Divinity School, P.O. Box 2090, Raleigh, NC 27102. Talbert O. Shaw. Tel. (919)832-1701. Fax (919)832-6082

Simpson College, (The Christian and Missionary Alliance), 2211 College View Dr., Redding, CA 96003. James M. Grant. Tel. (916)224-5600. Fax (916)224-5608

Southeastern Baptist College, (Baptist Missionary Association of America), Highway 15N, Laurel, MS 39441. Gerald D. Kellar. Tel. (601)426-6346

Southeastern Baptist Theological Seminary,* (Southern Baptist Convention), 222 N. Wingate, P.O. Box 1889, Wake Forest, NC 27588-1889. Paige Patterson. Tel. (919)556-3101. Fax (919)556-0998

Southeastern Bible College, (Interdenomational), 3001 Highway 280 E, Birmingham, AL 35243. John D. Talley. Tel. (205)969-0880. Fax (205)969-0880

Southeastern College of the Assemblies of God, (Assemblies of God), 1000 Longfellow Blvd., Lakeland, FL 33801. James L. Hennesy. Tel. (813)665-4404. Fax (813)666-8103

Southern Baptist Theological Seminary,* (Southern Baptist Convention), 2825 Lexington Rd., Louisville, KY 40280. R. Albert Mohler. Tel. (502)897-4011. Fax (502)897-4202

Southern Christian University, (Churches of Christ), 1200 Taylor Rd., P.O. Box 240240, Montgomery, AL 36124-0240. Rex A. Turner. Tel. (205)277-2277. Fax (205)271-0002

Southwestern Assemblies of God College, (Assemblies of God), 1200 Sycamore St., Waxahachie, TX 75165. Delmer R. Guynes. Tel. (214)937-4010. Fax (214)923-0488

Southwestern Baptist Theological Seminary,* (Southern Baptist Convention), P.O. Box 22000, Fort Worth, TX 76122. Russell H. Dilday. Tel. (817)923-1921. Fax (817)923-0610

Southwestern College, (Conservative Baptist Association of America), 2625 E. Cactus Rd., Phoenix, AZ 85032. Donald R. Engram. Tel. (602)992-6101. Fax (602)404-2159

Starr King School for the Ministry,* (Unitarian Universalist Association), 2441 LeConte Ave., Berkeley, CA 94709. Rebecca Parker. Tel. (510)845-6232. Fax (510)845-6232

Swedenborg School of Religion, (The Swedenborgian Church), 48 Sargent St., Newton, MA 02158. Mary Kay Klein. Tel. (617)244-0504. Fax (617)964-3258

Talbot School of Theology,* (Nondenominational), 13800 Biola Ave., La Mirada, CA 90639. Dennis H. Dirks. Tel. (310)903-4816. Fax (310)903-4759

Temple Baptist Seminary, (Interdenominational Baptist), 1815 Union Ave., Chattanooga, TN 37404. Barkev Trachian. Tel. (615)493-4221. Fax (615)493-4141

Theological College of America,* (The Roman Catholic Church), 401 Michigan Ave. NE, Washington, DC 20017. Howard P. Bleichner. Tel. (202)319-5900. Fax (202)319-5909

Theological School of the Protestant Reformed Churches, (Protestant Reformed Churches in America), 4949 Ivanrest Ave., Grandville, MI 49418. Robert D. Decker. Tel. (616)531-1490. Fax (616)531-3033

Toccoa Falls College, (The Christian and Missionary Alliance), Toccoa Falls, GA 30598. Paul L. Alford. Tel. (706)886-6831. Fax (706)886-0210

Trevecca Nazarene College (Religion Dept.), (Church of the Nazarene), 333 Murfreesboro Rd., Nashville, TN 37210. Timothy M. Green. Tel. (615)248-1200. Fax (615)248-7728

Trinity Bible College, (Assemblies of God), Ellendale, ND 58436. Steven C. Tvedt. Tel. (701)349-3621. Fax (701)349-5443

Trinity College at Miami, (The Evangelical Free Church of America), 500 NE 1st Ave., P.O. Box 019674, Miami, FL 33101-9674. Kenneth Meyer. Tel. (305)577-4600. Fax (305)577-4612

Trinity College of Florida/Tampa Bay Seminary, (Nondenominational), 2430 Trinity Oaks Blvd., New Port Richey, FL 34655. Glenn Speed. Tel. (813)376-6911. Fax (813)376-0781

Trinity Episcopal School for Ministry,* (Episcopal Church), 311 Eleventh St., Ambridge, PA 15003. William C. Frey. Tel. (412)266-3838. Fax (412)266-4617

Trinity Evangelical Divinity School,* (The Evangelical Free Church of America), 2065 Half Day Rd., Deerfield, IL 60015. Kenneth Meyer. Tel. (708)945-8800. Fax (708)317-8090

Trinity Lutheran Seminary,* (Evangelical Lutheran Church in America), 2199 E. Main St., Columbus, OH 43209-2334. Dennis A. Anderson. Tel. (614)235-4136. Fax (614)238-0263

Union Theological Seminary,* (Interdenominational), 3041 Broadway, New York, NY 10027. Holland L. Hendrix. Tel. (212)662-7100. Fax (212)280-1416

Union Theological Seminary in Virginia,* (Presbyterian Church (U.S.A.)), 3401 Brook Rd., Richmond, VA 23227. T. Hartley Hall. Tel. (804)355-0671. Fax (804)355-3919

United Theological Seminary,* (The United Methodist Church), 1810 Harvard Blvd., Dayton, OH 45406. Leonard I. Sweet. Tel. (513)278-5817. Fax (513)278-1218

United Theological Seminary of the Twin Cities,* (United Church of Christ), 3000 Fifth St. NW, New Brighton, MN 55112. Benjamin Griffin. Tel. (612)633-4311. Fax (612)633-4315

University of Chicago (Divinity School),* (Interdenominational), 1025 E. 58th St., Chicago, IL 60637. W. Clark Gilpin. Tel. (312)702-8221. Fax (312)702-6048

University of Dubuque Theological Seminary,* (Presbyterian Church (U.S.A.)), 2000 University Ave., Dubuque, IA 52001. J. David Pierce. Tel. (319)589-3118. Fax (319)589-3682

University of Notre Dame, Dept. of Theology,* (The Roman Catholic Church), Notre Dame, IN 46556. Laurence S. Cunningham. Tel. (219)631-7811. Fax (219)631-4268

University of St. Thomas School of Theology,* (The Roman Catholic Church), 9845 Memorial Drive, Houston, TX 77024. John Gallagher. Tel. (713)686-4345. Fax (713)683-8673

University of the South, Sewanee (School of Theology),* (Episcopal Church), 335 Tennessee Ave., Sewanee, TN 37383-1000. Guy Fitch Lytle. Tel. (615)598-1288. Fax (615)598-1165

Valley Forge Christian College, (Assemblies of God), Charlestown Rd., Phoenixville, PA 19460. Wesley W. Smith. Tel. (215)935-0450. Fax (215)935-9353

Vanderbilt University (Divinity School),* (Interdenominational), Nashville, TN 37240. Joseph C. Hough. Tel. (615)322-2776. Fax (615)343-9957

Vennard College, (Interdenominational), Box 29, University Park, IA 52595. Blake J. Neff. Tel. (515)673-8391. Fax (515)673-8365

Virginia Union University (School of Theology),* (Interdenominational Baptist), 1601 W. Leigh St., Richmond, VA 23220. John W. Kinney. Tel. (804)257-5715. Fax (804)257-5784

Walla Walla College (School of Theology), (Seventh-day Adventist Church), 204 S. College Ave., College Place, WA 99324. Douglas Clark. Tel. (509)527-2194. Fax (509)527-2253

Wartburg Theological Seminary,* (Evangelical Lutheran Church in America), 333 Wartburg Pl., Dubuque, IA 52003-7797. Roger Fjeld. Tel. (319)589-0200. Fax (319)589-0333

Wash. Theological Consortium & Washington Inst. of Ecumenics, 487 Michigan Ave. NE, Washington, DC 20017. David Trickett. Tel. (202)832-2675. Fax (202)526-0818

Washington Bible College/Capital Bible Seminary, (Nondenominational), 6511 Princess Garden Pkwy., Lanham, MD 20706. John A. Sproule. Tel. (301)552-1400. Fax (301)552-2775

Washington Theological Union,* (The Roman Catholic Church), 9001 New Hampshire Ave., Silver Spring, MD 20903. Vincent D. Cushing. Tel. (301)439-0551. Fax (301)445-4929

Wesley Biblical Seminary,* (Interdenominational), P.O. Box 9938, Jackson, MS 39286-0938. Harold Spann. Tel. (601)957-1314

Wesley Theological Seminary,* (The United Methodist Church), 4500 Massachusetts Ave. NW, Washington, DC 20016. G. Douglass Lewis. Tel. (202)885-8600. Fax (202)885-8605

Western Evangelical Seminary,* (Interdenominational), P.O. Box 23939, Portland, OR 97281. David LeShana. Tel. (503)639-0559. Fax (503)598-4338

Western Evangelical Theological Seminary,* (Interdenominational), 4200 Southeast Jennings Ave., Portland, OR 97267. David Le Shana. Tel. (503)639-0559. Fax (503)598-4338

Western Seminary, (Conservative Baptist Association of America), 5511 SE Hawthorne Blvd., Portland, OR 97215. Lawrence W. Ayers. Tel. (503)233-8561. Fax (503)239-4216

Western Theological Seminary,* (Reformed Church in America), 101 E. 13th St., Holland, MI 49423. Marvin D. Hoff. Tel. (616)392-8555. Fax (616)392-7717

Westminster Theological Seminary,* (Nondenominational), Chestnut Hill, P.O. Box 27009, Philadelphia, PA 19118. Samuel T. Logan. Tel. (215)887-5511. Fax (215)887-5404

Weston School of Theology,* (The Roman Catholic Church), 3 Phillips Pl., Cambridge, MA 02138. Robert Wild. Tel. (617)492-1960. Fax (617)492-5833

William Tyndale College, (Interdenominational), 35700 W. Twelve Mile Rd., Farmington Hills, MI 48331. James C. McHann. Tel. (313)553-7200. Fax (313)553-5963

Winebrenner Theological Seminary,* (Churches of God, General Conference), 701 E. Melrose Ave., P.O. Box 478, Findlay, OH 45839. David E. Draper. Tel. (419)422-4824. Fax (419)424-3433

Wisconsin Lutheran Seminary, (Wisconsin Evangelical Lutheran Synod), 11831 N. Seminary Dr., 65W, Mequon, WI 53092. Armin Panning. Tel. (414)242-7200. Fax (414)242-7255

Yale University (Divinity School),* (Nondenominational), 409 Prospect St., New Haven, CT 06511-2167. Thomas Ogletree. Tel. (203)432-5303. Fax (203)432-5756

9. THEOLOGICAL SEMINARIES AND BIBLE SCHOOLS IN CANADA

The following list includes theological seminaries and departments in colleges and universities in which ministerial training is given. Many denominations have additional programs. The lists of Religious Bodies in Canada should be consulted for the address of denominational headquarters.

The list has been developed from direct correspondence with the institutions. Inclusion in or exclusion from this list implies no judgment about the quality or accreditation of any institution. A "*" after the name of the institution indicates that it is either an accredited or affiliated member of the Association of Theological Schools. Information about total enrollment in ATS schools can be found in the statistical section.

The listing includes the institution name, denominational sponsor when appropriate, location, head, telephone number and fax number when known.

Acadia Divinity College,* (United Baptist Convention of the Atlantic Provinces), Acadia University, Wolfville, NS B0P 1X0. Andrew D. MacRae. Tel. (902)542-2285. Fax (902)542-7527

Alberta Bible College, (Christian Churches and Churches of Christ in Canada), 599 Northmount Dr. N.W., Calgary, AB T2K 3J6. Ronald A. Fraser. Tel. (403)282-2994. Fax (403)282-3084

Aldersgate College, (Free Methodist Church in Canada), Box 460, Moose Jaw, SK S6H 4P1. Joseph F. James. Tel. (306)693-7773. Fax (306)692-8821

Arthur Turner Training School, (The Anglican Church of Canada), Box 378, Pangnirtung, NT X0A 0R0. Roy Bowkett. Tel. (819)473-8375

Associated Can. Theological Schools at Trinity Western Univ.,* (Baptist General Conference of Canada), 7600 Glover Rd., Langley, BC V3A 6H4. Kenneth R. Davis. Tel. (604)888-6158. Fax (604)888-3354

Atlantic Baptist College, (United Baptist Convention of the Atlantic Provinces), Box 6004, Moncton, NB E1C 9L7. W. Ralph Richardson. Tel. (506)858-8970. Fax (506)858-9694

Atlantic School of Theology,* (Interdenominational), 640 Francklyn St., Halifax, NS B3H 3B5. Gordon MacDermid. Tel. (902)423-6801. Fax (902)492-4048

Baptist Leadership Training School, (Canadian Baptist Federation), 4330 16th St. S.W., Calgary, AB T2T 4H9. Myrna R. Sears. Tel. (403)243-3770. Fax (403)287-1930

Bethany Bible College—Canada, (The Wesleyan Church of Canada), 26 Western St., Sussex, NB E0E 1P0. David S. Medders. Tel. (506)432-4400. Fax (506)432-4425

Bethany Bible Institute, (Canadian Conference of Mennonite Brethren Churches), Box 160, Hepburn, SK S0K 1Z0. James Nikkel. Tel. (306)947-2175. Fax (306)947-4229

Briercrest Bible College and Biblical Seminary, (Interdenominational), 510 College Dr., Caronport, SK S0H 0S0. John Barkman. Tel. (306)756-3200. Fax (306)756-3366

Canadian Bible College, (Christian and Missionary Alliance in Canada), 4400-4th Ave., Regina, SK S4T 0H8. Robert A. Rose. Tel. (306)545-1515. Fax (306)545-0210

Canadian Lutheran Bible Institute, (Evangelical Lutheran Church in Canada), 4837 52A St., Camrose, AB T4V 1W5. Ronald B. Mayan. Tel. (403)672-4454

Canadian Nazarene College, (Church of the Nazarene), 1301 Lee Blvd., Winnipeg, MB R3T 2P7. Riley Coulter. Tel. (204)269-2120. Fax (204)269-7772

Canadian Reformed Churches, Theol. College of the, (Reformed Church in Canada), 110 West 27th St., Hamilton, ON L9C 5A1. J. Geertsema. Tel. (416)575-3688. Fax (416)575-0799

Canadian Theological Seminary,* (Christian and Missionary Alliance in Canada), 4400-4th Ave., Regina, SK S4T 0H8. Robert A. Rose. Tel. (306)545-1515. Fax (306)545-0210

Central Pentecostal College, University of Saskatchewan, (The Pentecostal Assemblies of Canada), 1303 Jackson Ave., Saskatoon, SK S7H 2M9. J. H. Faught. Tel. (306)374-6655. Fax (306)373-6968

Centre d'Études Théologiques Évangéliques, (Union d'Eglises Baptistes Françaises au Canada), 2285, avenue Papineau, Montréal, QC H2K 4J5. Amar Djaballah. Tel. (514)526-6643

THE YEAR IN IMAGES

RNS PHOTO/Reuters

WORLD PARLIAMENT OF RELIGIONS

The Dalai Lama, spiritual leader of Tibet, attended the World Parliament of Religions in Chicago, September 2. Several hundred religious leaders gathered for the Parliament that was last held 100 years ago.

Centre for Christian Studies, (The Anglican Church of Canada), 77 Charles St. W., Toronto, ON M5S 1K5. Gertrude Lebans. Tel. (416)923-1168. Fax (416)923-5496

Church Army College of Evangelism, (The Anglican Church of Canada), 397 Brunswick Ave., Toronto, ON M5R 2Z2. Roy E. Dickson. Tel. (416)924-9279. Fax (416)924-2931

Collège Dominicain de Philosophie et de Théologie, (The Roman Catholic Church in Canada), 96 avenue Empress, Ottawa, ON K1R 7G3. Michel Gourgues. Tel. (613)233-5696. Fax (613)233-6064

College Biblique Québec, (The Pentecostal Assemblies of Canada), 1320 rue St-Paul, ste. 200, Ancienne Lorette, QC G2E 1Z4. Pierre Bergeron. Tel. (418)871-5292

College of Emmanuel and St. Chad, (The Anglican Church of Canada), 1337 College Dr., Saskatoon, SK S7N 0W6. William Niels Christensen. Tel. (306)975-3753. Fax (306)934-2683

Columbia Bible College, (Interdenominational Mennonite), 2940 Clearbrook Rd., Clearbrook, BC V2T 2Z8. Walter Unger. Tel. (604)853-3358. Fax (604)853-3063

Concord College, (Canadian Conference of Mennonite Brethren Churches), 1-169 Riverton Ave., Winnipeg, MB R2L 2E5. James N. Pankratz. Tel. (204)669-6583. Fax (204)654-1865

Concordia Lutheran Seminary,* (Lutheran Church—Canada), 7040 Ada Blvd., Edmonton, AB T5B 4E3. L. Dean Hempelmann. Tel. (403)474-1468. Fax (403)479-3067

Concordia Lutheran Theological Seminary,* (Lutheran Church—Canada), 470 Glenridge Ave., Box 1117, St. Catharines, ON L2R 7A3. Jonathan Grothe. Tel. (416)688-2362. Fax (416)688-9744

Covenant Bible College, (The Evangelical Covenant Church of Canada), 245 21st St. E., Prince Albert, SK S6V 1L9. Neil R. Josephson. Tel. (306)922-3443. Fax (306)922-5414

Eastern Pentecostal Bible College, (The Pentecostal Assemblies of Canada), 780 Argyle St., Peterborough, ON K9H 5T2. Carl F. Verge. Tel. (705)748-9111. Fax (705)748-3931

Edmonton Baptist Seminary,* (North American Baptist Conference), 11525-23 Ave., Edmonton, AB T6J 4T3. Sid Page. Tel. (403)437-1960. Fax (403)436-9416

Emmanuel Bible College, (The Evangelical Missionary Church of Canada), 100 Fergus Ave., Kitchener, ON N2A 2H2. Thomas E. Dow. Tel. (519)894-8900. Fax (519)894-5331

Emmanuel College,* (The United Church of Canada), 75 Queen's Park Crescent, Toronto, ON M5S 1K7. John C. Hoffman. Tel. (416)585-4539. Fax (416)585-4516

Faith Alive Bible College, 637 University Dr., Saskatoon, SK S7N 0H8. David Pierce. Tel. (306)652-2230. Fax (306)665-1125

Full Gospel Bible Institute, (Apostolic Church of Pentecost of Canada Inc.), Box 579, Eston, SK S0L 1A0. Alan B. Mortensen. Tel. (306)962-3621. Fax (306)962-3810

Gardner Bible College, (Church of God (Anderson, Ind.)), 4704 55th St., Camrose, AB T4V 2B6. Bruce Kelly. Tel. (403)672-0171. Fax (403)672-6888

Great Lakes Bible College, (Churches of Christ in Canada), 4875 King St. E., Beamsville, ON L0R 1B0. Dave McMillan. Tel. (416)563-5374. Fax (416)563-0818

Heritage Baptist College/Heritage Theological Seminary, (The Fellowship of Evangelical Baptist Churches in Canada), 30 Grand Ave., London, ON N6C 1K8. Marvin Brubacher. Tel. (519)434-6801. Fax (519)434-4998

Huron College,* (The Anglican Church of Canada), 1349 Western Rd., London, ON N6G 1H3. Charles J. Jago. Tel. (519)438-7224. Fax (519)438-3938

Institut Biblique Beree, (The Pentecostal Assemblies of Canada), 1711 Henri-Bourassa Est, Montréal, QC H2C 1J5. Raymond Lemaire. Tel. (514)385-4238. Fax (514)462-1789

Institut Biblique Laval, (Canadian Conference of Mennonite Brethren Churches), 1775, boul. Édouard-Laurin, Ville Saint-Laurent, QC H4L 2B9. Jean Théorêt. Tel. (514)331-0878. Fax (514)331-0879

Institut Biblique Word of Life - Bethel, (Nondenominational), 1175 Chemin Woodward Hill, RR1, Lennoxville, QC J1M 2A2. Wayne Lewis. Tel. (819)823-8435. Fax (819)823-2468

Institute for Christian Studies, (Nondenominational), 229 College St., Toronto, ON M5T 1R4. Harry Fernhout. Tel. (416)979-2331. Fax (416)979-2332

International Bible College, (Church of God (Cleveland, Tenn.)), 401 Trinity La., Moose Jaw, SK S6H 0E3. Lyndon Cramer. Tel. (306)692-4041

Key-Way-Tin Bible Institute, (Interdenominational), Box 540, Lac La Biche, AB T0A 2C0. Leigh Wolverton. Tel. (403)623-4565. Fax (403)623-1788

Knox College,* (The Presbyterian Church in Canada), 59 St. George St., Toronto, ON M5S 2E6. Arthur Van Seters. Tel. (416)978-4500. Fax (416)971-2133

Living Faith Bible College, Box 100, Caroline, AB T0M 0M0. Cliff A. Stalwick. Tel. (403)722-2225. Fax (403)722-3400

Lutheran Theological Seminary,* (Evangelical Lutheran Church in Canada), 114 Seminary Crescent, Saskatoon, SK S7N 0X3. Roger Nostbakken. Tel. (306)975-7004. Fax (306)975-0084

Maritime Christian College, (Christian Churches and Churches of Christ in Canada), P.O. Box 1145, 503 University Ave., Charlottetown, PE C1A 7M8. Stewart J. Lewis. Tel. (902)628-8887. Fax (902)892-3959

McGill University Faculty of Religious Studies,* (Interdenominational), 3520 University St., Montreal, QC H3A 2A7. Donna R. Runnalls. Tel. (514)398-4125. Fax (514)398-6665

McMaster Divinity College,* (Baptist Convention of Ontario and Quebec), McMaster Divinity College, Hamilton, ON L8S 4K1. William H. Brackney. Tel. (905)525-9140. Fax (905)577-4782

Millar College of the Bible, (Interdenominational), Box 25, Pambrun, SK S0N 1W0. Bob Peters. Tel. (306)582-2033. Fax (306)582-2027

Montreal Diocesan Theological College,* (The Anglican Church of Canada), 3473 University St., Montreal, QC H3A 2A8. John Simons. Tel. (514)849-3004

Mount Carmel Bible School, (Christian Brethren (also known as Plymouth Brethren)), 4725 106 Ave., Edmonton, AB T6A 1E7. Jay Gurnett. Tel. (403)465-3015. Fax (403)466-2485

National Native Bible College, (Elim Fellowship of Evangelical Churches and Ministers), Box 478, Deseronto, ON K0K 1X0. Ross W. Maracle. Tel. (613)396-2311. Fax (613)396-2555

Newman Theological College,* (The Roman Catholic Church in Canada), 15611 St. Albert Trail, Edmonton, AB T5L 4H8. K. Carr. Tel. (403)447-2993. Fax (403)447-2685

Nipawin Bible Institute, (Interdenominational), Box 1986, Nipawin, SK S0E 1E0. Mark Leppington. Tel. (306)862-5095. Fax (306)862-3651

North American Baptist College/Edmonton Baptist Seminary, (North American Baptist Conference), 11525-23rd Ave., Edmonton, AB T6J 4T3. Paul H. Siewert. Tel. (403)437-1960. Fax (403)436-9416

Northwest Baptist Theological College and Seminary, (The Fellowship of Evangelical Baptist Churches in Canada), 22606 76A Ave., P.O. Box 790, Langley, BC V3A 8B8. Doug Harris. Tel. (604)888-3310. Fax (604)888-3354

Northwest Bible College, (The Pentecostal Assemblies of Canada), 11617-106 Ave., Edmonton, AB T5H 0S1. G. K. Franklin. Tel. (403)452-0808. Fax (403)452-5803

Okanagan Bible College, (Interdenominational), Box 407, Kelowna, BC V1Y 7N8. Henry Esau. Tel. (604)768-4410. Fax (604)768-0631

Ontario Christian Seminary, (Christian Churches and Churches of Christ in Canada), P.O. Box 324, Stn. D; 260 High Park Ave., Toronto, ON M6P 3J9. Nelson L. Deuitch. Tel. (416)769-7115. Fax (416)769-7115

Ontario Theological Seminary,* (Interdenominational), 25 Ballyconnor Ct., North York, ON M2M 4B3. Bruce E. Gordon. Tel. (416)226-6380. Fax (416)226-6746

Pacific Bible College, (Interdenominational), 15100 66 A Ave., Surrey, BC V3S 2A6. Mel D. Davis. Tel. (604)597-9331. Fax (604)597-9090

Peace River Bible Institute, (Interdenominational), Box 99, Sexsmith, AB T0H 3C0. Reuben Kvill. Tel. (403)568-3962. Fax (403)568-4931

Prairie Graduate School, (Interdenominational), Box 4000, Three Hills, AB T0M 2A0. Paul Ferris. Tel. (403)443-5511. Fax (403)443-5540

Presbyterian College, (The Presbyterian Church in Canada), 3495 University St., Montreal, QC H3A 2A8. W. J. Klempa. Tel. (514)288-5256. Fax (514)398-6665

Providence College and Theological Seminary,* (Interdenominational), General Delivery, Otterburne, MB R0A 1G0. Larry J. McKinney. Tel. (204)433-7488. Fax (204)433-7158

Queen's College,* (The Anglican Church of Canada), Queen's College, St. John's, NF A1B 3R6. Frank Cluett. Tel. (709)753-0640. Fax (709)753-1214

Queen's Theological College,* (The United Church of Canada), Queen's Theological College, Kingston, ON K7L 3N6. Hallett E. Llewellyn. Tel. (613)545-2110. Fax (613)545-6879

Regent College,* (Interdenominational), 5800 University Blvd., Vancouver, BC V6T 2E4. Walter C. Wright. Tel. (800)663-8664. Fax (604)224-3097

Regis College,* (The Roman Catholic Church in Canada), 15 St. Mary St., Toronto, ON M4Y 2R5. John E. Costello. Tel. (416)922-5474. Fax (416)922-2898

Rocky Mountain College: Centre for Biblical Studies, 4039 Brentwood Rd. NW, Calgary, AB T4L 1L1. Randy L. Steinwand. Tel. (403)284-5100. Fax (403)220-9567

St. Andrew's Theological College,* (The United Church of Canada), 1121 College Dr., Saskatoon, SK S7N 0W3. Charlotte Caron. Tel. (306)966-8970. Fax (306)966-6575

St. Augustine's Seminary of Toronto,* (The Roman Catholic Church in Canada), 2661 Kingston Rd., Scarborough, ON M1M 1M3. John A. Boissonneau. Tel. (416)261-7207. Fax (416)261-2529

St. John's College, Univ. of Manitoba, Faculty of Theology, (The Anglican Church of Canada), St. John's College, Univ. of Manitoba, Winnipeg, MB R3T 2M5. Bradley McLean. Tel. (204)474-6852. Fax (204)275-1498

Saint Paul University, Faculty of Theology, (The Roman Catholic Church in Canada), 223 Main St., Ottawa, ON K1S 1C4. M. Hubert Doucet. Tel. (613)236-1393. Fax (613)236-4108

St. Peter's Seminary,* (The Roman Catholic Church in Canada), 1040 Waterloo St., London, ON N6A 3Y1. Patrick W. Fuerth. Tel. (519)432-1824. Fax (519)432-0964

St. Stephen's College, Grad. & Continuing Theological Educ.,* (The United Church of Canada), 8810 112th St., Edmonton, AB T6G 2J6. Garth I. Mundle. Tel. (403)439-7311. Fax (403)433-8875

The Salvation Army Catherine Booth Bible College, (The Salvation Army in Canada), 447 Webb Pl., Winnipeg, MB R3B 2P2. Lloyd Hetherington. Tel. (204)947-6701. Fax (204)942-3856

Salvation Army College for Officer Training, (The Salvation Army in Canada), 2130 Bayview Ave., Toronto, ON M4N 3K6. K. Douglas Moore. Tel. (416)481-6131. Fax (416)481-6810

Steinbach Bible College, (Interdenominational-Mennonite), Box 1420, Steinbach, MB R0A 2A0. Stan Plett. Tel. (204)326-6451. Fax (204)326-6908

Swift Current Bible Institute, (Conference of Mennonites in Canada), Box 1268, Swift Current, SK S9H 3X4. Ray Friesen. Tel. (306)773-0604. Fax (306)773-9250

Toronto Baptist Seminary and Bible College, (Association of Regular Baptist Churches (Canada)), 130 Gerrard St., E., Toronto, ON M5A 3T4. G. A. Adams. Tel. (416)925-3263. Fax (416)925-8305

Toronto School of Theology,* (Interdenominational), 47 Queens Park Crescent E., Toronto, ON M5S 2C3. Jean-Marc Laporte. Tel. (416)978-4039. Fax (416)978-7821

Trinity College, Faculty of Divinity,* (The Anglican Church of Canada), 6 Hoskin Ave., Toronto, ON M5S 1H8. R. H. Painter. Tel. (416)978-2370. Fax (416)978-2797

United Theological College/Le Séminaire Uni, (The United Church of Canada), 3521 rue Université, Montréal, QC H3A 2A9. Pierre Goldberger. Tel. (514)849-2042. Fax (514)398-6665

Université Laval, Faculté de théologie, (The Roman Catholic Church in Canada), Cité Universitaire Ste-Foy, Ste-Foy, QC G1K 7P4. René Michael Roberge. Tel. (418)656-7823. Fax (418)656-2809

Université de Montréal, Faculté de théologie, (The Roman Catholic Church in Canada), C. P. 6128 Succ.A, Montréal, QC H3C 3J7. Laval Letourneau. Tel. (514)343-7160. Fax (514)343-5738

Université de Sherbrooke, Faculté de théologie,, (The Roman Catholic Church in Canada), 2500 boul. Université, Sherbrooke, QC J1K 2R1. Lucien Vachon. Tel. (819)821-7600

University of St. Michael's College, Faculty of Theology,* (The Roman Catholic Church in Canada), 81 St. Mary St., Toronto, ON M5S 1J4. Michael A. Fahey. Tel. (416)926-7140. Fax (416)926-7276

University of Winnipeg, Faculty of Theology,* (Interdenominational), 515 Portage Ave., Winnipeg, MB R3B 2E9. Harold J. King. Tel. (204)786-9390. Fax (204)786-1824

Vancouver School of Theology,* (Interdenominational), 6000 Iona Dr., Vancouver, BC V6T 1L4. W. J. Phillips. Tel. (604)228-9031. Fax (604)228-0189

Victory Bible College, (Nondenominational), Box 1780, Lethbridge, AB T1J 4K4. Jim Craig. Tel. (403)320-1565. Fax (403)327-9013

Waterloo Lutheran Seminary,* (Evangelical Lutheran Church in Canada), 75 University Ave. W., Waterloo, ON N2L 3C5. Richard C. Crossman. Tel. (519)884-1970. Fax (519)725-2434

Western Christian College, (Churches of Christ in Canada), Box 5000, Dauphin, MB R7N 2V5. John V. McMillan. Tel. (204)638-8801

Western Pentecostal Bible College, (The Pentecostal Assemblies of Canada), Box 1700, Abbotsford, BC V2S 7E7. James G. Richards. Tel. (604)853-7491. Fax (604)853-8951

Winkler Bible Institute, (Canadian Conference of Mennonite Brethren Churches), 121 7 St. S., Winkler, MB R6W 2N4. Eldon DeFehr. Tel. (204)325-4242. Fax (204)325-9028

Wycliffe College,* (The Anglican Church of Canada), 5 Hoskin Ave., Toronto, ON M5S 1H7. Harry Hilchey. Tel. (416)979-2870. Fax (416)979-0471

10. RELIGIOUS PERIODICALS IN THE UNITED STATES

This list of religious periodicals contains two types of periodicals. First, there are official national publications of denominations. Regional publications and newsletters are not included. The denominational listings in sections 3 and 4 include the names of periodicals found in this listing.

The second type of periodical listed here is independent national religious publications.

Probably the most inclusive list of religious periodicals published in the United States can be found in *Gale Directory of Publications and Broadcast Media, 1992*, (Gale Research, Inc., P.O. Box 33477, Detroit MI 48232-5477).

Each entry lists the title of the periodical, frequency of publication, religious affiliation, editor's name, address, telephone number and fax number when known.

21st Century Christian, (m) Churches of Christ, M. Norvel Young, Box 40304, Nashville, TN 37204. Tel. 800-331-5991

A.M.E. Review, African Methodist Episcopal Church, Paulette Coleman, PhD, 500 Eighth Ave., S., Nashville, TN 37203-4181. Tel. (615)256-7020. Fax (615)256-7020

ALERT, (m) Universal Fellowship of Metropolitan Community Churches, A. Stephen Pieters, 5300 Santa Monica Blvd., Ste. 304, Los Angeles, CA 90029. Tel. (213)464-5100. Fax (213)464-2123

Action, (10/yr) Churches of Christ, Tex Williams, Box 9346, Austin, TX 78766. Tel. (512)345-8191. Fax (512)345-6634

Adult Quarterly, The, (q) Associate Reformed Presbyterian Church (General Synod), W. H. F. Kuykendall, PhD., One Cleveland St., Greenville, SC 29601. Tel. (803)232-8297

Advance, (m) Assemblies of God, Harris Jansen, 1445 Boonville Ave., Springfield, MO 65802. Tel. (417)862-2781. Fax (417)862-8558

Advent Christian News, (m) Advent Christian Church, Robert Mayer, P.O. Box 23152, Charlotte, NC 28227. Tel. (704)545-6161. Fax (704)573-0712

Advent Christian Witness, The, (m) Advent Christian Church, Robert Mayer, P.O. Box 23152, Charlotte, NC 28227. Tel. (704)545-6161. Fax (704)573-0712

Adventist Review, (w) Seventh-day Adventist Church, W. G. Johnsson, 12501 Old Columbia Pike, Silver Spring, MD 20904-6600. Tel. (301)680-6560. Fax (301)680-6638

Advocate, (m) Churches of Christ in Christian Union, Daniel L. Tipton, P.O. Box 30, Circleville, OH 43113.

Advocate, The, (m) Baptist Missionary Association of America, Ronald J. Beasley, 8101 Joffree Dr., Jacksonville, FL 32210.

Again, The Antiochian Orthodox Christian Archdiocese of North America, Peter Gillquist, 6884 Pasado Rd., Santa Barbara, CA 93117. Tel. (805)968-4014. Fax (805)968-8767

alive now!, (6/yr) The United Methodist Church, George Graham, P.O. Box 189, Nashville, TN 37202. Tel. (615)340-7218

Allegheny Wesleyan Methodist, The, (m) Allegheny Wesleyan Methodist Connection (Original Allegheny Conference), John Englant, 1827 Allen Dr., Salem, OH 44460. Tel. (216)337-9376. Fax (216)337-9376

Alliance Life, (bi-w) The Christian and Missionary Alliance, Maurice Irvin, P.O. Box 35000, Colorado Springs, CO 80935. Tel. (719)599-5999. Fax (719)593-8692

America, (W) The Roman Catholic Church, George W. Hunt, 106 W. 56th St., New York, NY 10019. Tel. (212)581-4640. Fax (212)399-3596

American Baptist Quarterly, (q) American Baptist Churches in the U.S.A., William R. Millar, P.O. Box 851, Valley Forge, PA 19482. Tel. (215)768-2378

American Baptists in Mission, (6/yr) American Baptist Churches in the U.S.A., Richard W. Schramm, P.O. Box 851, Valley Forge, PA 19482-0851. Tel. (215)768-2077. Fax (215)768-2320

American Bible Society Record, (10/yr) Nondenominational, Clifford P. Macdonald, 1865 Broadway, New York, NY 10023. Tel. (212)408-1480. Fax (212)408-1456

American Jewish History, (q) Jewish Organizations, Marc Lee Raphael, 2 Thornton Rd., Waltham, MA 02154. Tel. (617)891-8110. Fax (617)899-9208

American Presbyterians: Journal of Presbyterian History, (q) Presbyterian Church (U.S.A.), James H. Smylie, 425 Lombard St., Philadelphia, PA 19147. Tel. (215)627-1852. Fax (215)627-0509

Armenian Church, The, (10/yr) Diocese of the Armenian Church of America, Michael A. Zeytodnian, 630 Second Ave., New York, NY 10016. Tel. (212)686-0710

Associate Reformed Presbyterian, The, (m) Associate Reformed Presbyterian Church (General Synod), Ben Johnston, One Cleveland St., Greenville, SC 29601. Tel. (803)232-8297

At Ease, (bi-m) Assemblies of God, Lemuel McElyea, Gospel Publishing House, 1445 Boonville Ave., Springfield, MO 65802. Tel. (417)862-2781. Fax (417)863-7276

Attack, A Magazine for Christian Men, (q) National Association of Free Will Baptists, James Vallance, P.O. Box 5002, Antioch, TN 37011-5002. Tel. (615)731-6812

Awake!, Jehovah's Witnesses, Watchtower Society, 25 Columbia Heights, Brooklyn, NY 11201. Tel. (718)625-3600. Fax (718)624-8030

Banner of Truth, The, (m) Netherlands Reformed Congregations, Joel R. Beeke, 2115 Romence Ave., N.E., Grand Rapids, MI 29503.

Banner, The, (w) Christian Reformed Church in North America, John Suk and John H. Kromminga, 2850 Kalamazoo Ave., SE, Grand Rapids, MI 49560. Tel. (616)246-0791. Fax (616)246-0834

Baptist Bible Tribune, The, (m) Baptist Bible Fellowship International, James O. Combs, P.O. Box 309 HSJ, Springfield, MO 65801. Tel. (417)831-3996. Fax (417)865-0794

Baptist Bulletin, (m) General Association of Regular Baptist Churches, Vernon D. Miller, 1300 N. Meacham Rd., Schaumburg, IL 60173-4888. Tel. (708)843-1600. Fax (708)843-3757

Baptist Herald, (10/yr) North American Baptist Conference, Barbara J. Binder, 1 S. 210 Summit Ave., Oakbrook Terrace, IL 60181. Tel. (708)495-2000. Fax (708)495-3301

Baptist Herald, (m) Baptist Missionary Association of America, Jerry Derfelt, P.O. Box 218, Galena, KS 66739. Tel. (316)783-1371. Fax (316)783-4236

Baptist History and Heritage, (q) Southern Baptist, Lynn E. May, 901 Commerce St., Ste. 400, Nashville, TN 37203-3630. Tel. (615)244-0344. Fax (615)242-2153

Baptist Leader, (q) American Baptist Churches in the U.S.A., Linda Isham, P.O. Box 851, Valley Forge, PA 19842-0851. Tel. (215)768-2153. Fax (215)768-2056

Baptist Progress, (w) Baptist Missionary Association of America, Danny Pope, P.O. Box 2085, Waxahachie, TX 85165. Tel. (214)923-0756. Fax (214)923-2679

Baptist Trumpet, (w) Baptist Missionary Association of America, David Tidwell, P.O. Box 192208, Little Rock, AR 72219. Tel. (501)565-4601

Baptist Witness, (m) Primitive Baptists, Lasserre Bradley, Jr., Box 17037, Cincinnati, OH 45217. Tel. (513)821-7289

Being In Touch, (q) Mennonite Church, The General Conference, David Linscheid, Box 347, 722 Main St., Newton, KS 67114. Tel. (316)283-5100. Fax (316)283-0454

Bible Advocate, The, (m) The Church of God (Seventh Day), Denver, Colo., Roy Marrs, P.O. Box 33677, Denver, CO 80233.

Brethren Evangelist, The, (m) Brethren Church (Ashland, Ohio), Richard C. Winfield, 524 College Ave., Ashland, OH 44805. Tel. (419)289-1708. Fax (419)281-0450

Brethren Journal, (m) Unity of the Brethren, Milton Maly, Rte. 3, Box 558N, Brenham, TX 77833. Tel. (409)830-8762

Brethren Missionary Herald, Fellowship of Grace Brethren Churches, Jeffry Carroll, P.O. Box 544, Winona Lake, IN 46590. Tel. (219)267-7158. Fax (219)267-4745

Bridegroom's Messenger, The, The International Pentecostal Church of Christ, Janice Boyce, 121 W. Hunters Tr., Elizabeth City, NC 27909. Tel. (919)338-3003

Builder, (m) Mennonite Church, David R. Hiebert, 616 Walnut Ave., Scottdale, PA 15683. Tel. (412)887-8500. Fax (412)887-3111

Burning Bush, The, (bi-m) The Metropolitan Church Association, Inc., E. L. Adams, The Metropolitan Church Association, 323 Broad St., Lake Geneva, WI 53147. Tel. (414)248-6786

Calvary Messenger, The, (m) Beachy Amish Mennonite Churches, Ervin N. Hershberger, Rt. 1, Box 176, Meyersdale, PA 15552. Tel. (814)662-2483

Campus Life, (10/yr) Nondenominational, Harold B. Smith, 465 Gunderson Dr., Carol Stream, IL 60188. Tel. (708)260-6200. Fax (708)260-0114

Capsule, (m) General Association of General Baptists, Charles Carr, 100 Stinson Dr., Poplar Bluff, MO 63901. Tel. (314)785-7746. Fax (314)785-0564

Caring, (9/yr) Assemblies of God, Owen Wilkie, Gospel Publishing House, 1445 Boonville Ave., Springfield, MO 65802. Tel. (417)862-2781. Fax (417)862-8558

Catholic Chronicle, (bi-w) The Roman Catholic Church, Richard S. Meek, Jr., P.O. Box 1866, 2130 Madison Ave., Toledo, OH 43624. Tel. (419)243-4178. Fax (419)243-4235

Catholic Digest, (m) The Roman Catholic Church, Henry Lexau, P. O. Box 64090, St. Paul, MN 55164. Tel. (612)647-5296. Fax (612)647-4346

Catholic Herald, (w) The Roman Catholic Church, Ethel M. Gintoft, 3501 S. Lake Dr., St. Francis, WI 53235-0913. Tel. (414)769-3500. Fax (414)769-3468

Catholic Light, (bi-w) The Roman Catholic Church, James B. Earley, 300 Wyoming Ave., Scranton, PA 18503. Tel. (717)346-8915. Fax (717)346-8917

Catholic Review, The, (w) The Roman Catholic Church, Daniel L. Medinger, P.O. Box 777, Baltimore, MD 21203. Tel. (410)547-5327. Fax (410)385-0113

Catholic Standard and Times, (w) The Roman Catholic Church, Paul S. Quinter, 222 N. 17th St., Philadelphia, PA 19103. Tel. (215)587-3660. Fax (215)587-3979

Catholic Transcript, The, (w) The Roman Catholic Church, Janet L. Alampi, 785 Asylum Ave., Hartford, CT 06105-2886. Tel. (203)527-1175. Fax (203)947-6397

Catholic Universe Bulletin, (bi-w) The Roman Catholic Church, Patrick Hyland, 1027 Superior Ave., Cleveland, OH 44114-2556. Tel. (216)696-6525. Fax (216)696-6519

Catholic Worker, (8/yr) The Roman Catholic Church, Jo Roberts, 36 E. First St., New York, NY 10003. Tel. (212)777-9617

Catholic World, The, (bi-m) The Roman Catholic Church, Laurie Felknor, 997 Macarthur Blvd., Mahwah, NJ 07430. Tel. (201)825-7300. Fax (201)825-8345

Cela Biedrs, (10/yr) The Latvian Evangelical Lutheran Church in America, Eduards Putnins, 1468 Hemlock St., Napa, CA 94559. Tel. (707)252-1809

Celebration, (m) Seventh-day Adventist Church, John R. Calkins, 55 W. Oak Ridge Dr., Hagerstown, MD 21740.

Celebration: An Ecumenical Worship Resource, (m) Interdenominational, William Freburger, P.O. Box 419493, Kansas City, MO 64141. Tel. (816)531-0538. Fax (816)531-7466

Cerkovnyj Vistnik—Church Messenger, (bi-w) The American Carpatho-Russian Orthodox Greek Catholic Church, James S. Dutko, 280 Clinton St., Binghamton, NY 13905.

Charisma Courier, The, Nondenominational, John Archer, 600 Rinehart Rd., Lake Mary, FL 32746. Tel. (407)333-0600. Fax (407)333-9753

Childlife, (q) Nondenominational, Terry Madison, 919 W. Huntington Dr., Monrovia, CA 91016. Tel. (818)357-7979. Fax (818)357-0915

Christadelphian Advocate, Christadelphians, Alex T. Kay, Jr. and Edward W. Farrar, 4 Mountain Park Ave., Hamilton, ON L9A 1A2. Tel. (416)383-1817

Christadelphian Tidings, (m) Christadelphians, Donald H. Styles, 30480 Oakleaf Ln., Franklin, MI 48025. Tel. (317)851-3028. Fax same

Christadelphian Watchman, (m) Christadelphians, George Booker, 2500 Berwyn Cir., Austin, TX 78745. Tel. (512)447-8882

Christian Baptist, The, (m) Primitive Baptists, S. T. Tolley, P.O. Box 68, Atwood, TN 38220. Tel. (901)662-7417

Christian Bible Teacher, (m) Churches of Christ, J. J. Turner, Box 1060, Abilene, TX 79604. Tel. (915)677-6262. Fax (915)677-1511

Christian Century, The, (38/yr) Nondenominational, James M. Wall, 407 S. Dearborn St., Chicago, IL 60605. Tel. (312)427-5380. Fax (312)427-1302

Christian Chronicle, The, (m) Churches of Christ, Howard W. Norton, Box 11000, Oklahoma City, OK 73136. Tel. (405)425-5070. Fax (405)425-5076

Christian Community, The, (m) International Council of Community Churches, Jeffrey R. Newhall, 19715 S. LaGrange Rd., Ste. C, Mokena, IL 60448. Tel. (708)479-8400. Fax (708)479-8402

Christian Contender, The, (q) Interdenominational Mennonite, Kenneth Mast and Robert Zimmerman, P.O. Box 3, Hwy. 172, Crockett, KY 41413. Tel. (606)522-4348. Fax (606)522-4896

Christian Echo, The, (m) Churches of Christ, R. N. Hogan, Box 37266, Los Angeles, CA 90037.

Christian Education Counselor, (m) Assemblies of God, Sylvia Lee, Sunday School Promotion and Training, 1445 Boonville Ave., Springfield, MO 65802-1894. Tel. (417)862-2781. Fax (417)862-8558

Christian Endeavor World, The, (q) Nondenominational, David G. Jackson, 3575 Valley Rd., P.O. Box 820, Liberty Corner, NJ 07938-0820. Tel. (908)604-9440

Christian Index, The, (bi-m) Christian Methodist Episcopal Church, Lawrence L. Reddick, III, P.O. Box 665, Memphis, TN 38101-0665. Tel. (901)345-1173

Christian Living, (8/yr) Mennonite Church, David Graybill, 616 Walnut Ave., Scottdale, PA 15683. Tel. (412)887-8500. Fax (412)887-3111

Christian Ministry, The, (6/yr) Nondenominational, James M. Wall, 407 S. Dearborn St., Chicago, IL 60605. Tel. (312)427-5380. Fax (312)427-1302

Christian Monthly, (m) Apostolic Lutheran Church of America, Alvar Helmes, Apostolic Lutheran Book Concern, P.O. Box 537, Brush Prairie, WA 98606. Tel. (206)687-7088

Christian Outlook, (m) Pentecostal Assemblies of the World, Inc., Johnna E. Hampton, 3939 Meadow Dr., Indianapolis, IN 46208. Tel. (317)547-9541. Fax (317)543-0512

Christian Reader, The, (bi-m) Nondenominational, Bonne Steffen, 465 Gundersen Dr., Carol Stream, IL 60188. Tel. (708)260-6200. Fax (708)260-0114

Christian Record, (m) Seventh-day Adventist Church, R. J. Kaiser, P.O. Box 6097, Lincoln, NE 68506. Tel. (402)488-0981. Fax (402)488-7582

Christian Recorder, The, (bi-w) African Methodist Episcopal Church, Robert H. Reid, Jr., 500 8th Ave., S., Nashville, TN 37203. Tel. (615)256-8548

Christian Science Journal, The, (m) Church of Christ, Scientist, William E. Moody, One Norway St., Boston, MA 02115. Tel. (617)450-2000

Christian Science Monitor, The, (d & w) Church of Christ, Scientist, Richard Cattani, One Norway St., Boston, MA 02115.

Christian Science Quarterly, (q) Church of Christ, Scientist, William E. Moody, One Norway St., Boston, MA 02115.

Christian Science Sentinel, (w) Church of Christ, Scientist, William E. Moody, One Norway St., Boston, MA 02115. Tel. (617)450-2000

Christian Social Action, (m) The United Methodist Church, Lee Ranck, 100 Maryland Ave. NE, Washington, DC 20002. Tel. (202)488-5621. Fax (202)488-5619

Christian Standard, (w) Christian Churches and Churches of Christ, Sam E. Stone, 8121 Hamilton Ave., Cincinnati, OH 45231. Tel. (513)931-4050. Fax (513)931-0904

Church & Society Magazine, (bi-m) Presbyterian Church (U.S.A.), Kathy Lancaster, 100 Witherspoon St., Louisville, KY 40202-1396. Tel. (502)569-5810. Fax (502)569-8116

Church Advocate, The, (m) Churches of God, General Conference, Linda M. Draper, P.O. Box 926, 700 E. Melrose Ave., Findlay, OH 45839. Tel. (419)424-1961. Fax (419)424-3433

Church Bytes, (8/yr) Nondenominational, Neil B. Houk, 562 Brightleaf Square No. 9, 905 West Main St., Durham, NC 27701. Tel. (919)490-8927

Church Herald, The, (11/yr) Reformed Church in America, Jeffrey Japinga, 4500 60th St. SE, Grand Rapids, MI 49512. Tel. (616)698-7071

Church History, (q) Nondenominational, Martin E. Marty and Jerald C. Brauer, The Univ. of Chicago, 1025 E. 58th St., Chicago, IL 60637. Tel. (312)702-8215. Fax (312)702-6048

Church School Herald, (q) African Methodist Episcopal Zion Church, Mary A. Love, P.O. Box 32305, Charlotte, NC 28232-2305. Tel. (704)332-9873. Fax (704)333-1769

Church of God Evangel, (m) Church of God (Cleveland, Tenn.), Homer G. Rhea, P.O. Box 2250, Cleveland, TN 37320. Tel. (615)478-7592. Fax (615)478-7521

Church of God Missions, (m) Church of God (Anderson, Ind.), Dondeena Caldwell, Box 2498, Anderson, IN 46018-2498. Tel. (317)642-0256. Fax (317)642-4279

Church of God Progress Journal, (bi-m) Church of God General Conference (Oregon, IL and Morrow, GA), David Krogh, Box 100,000, Morrow, GA 30260. Tel. (404)362-0052. Fax (404)362-9307

Church of God Quarterly; COG Newsletter, The, (q) The Church of God, Voy M. Bullen, Box 13036, 1207 Willow Brook, Apt. #2, Huntsville, AL 35802. Tel. (205)881-9629

Churchman's Human Quest, The, (bi-m) Nondenominational, Edna Ruth Johnson, 1074 23rd Ave. N., St. Petersburg, FL 33704. Tel. (813)894-0097

Churchwoman, (bi-m) Interdenominational, Martha M. Cruz, 475 Riverside Dr., Rm. 812, New York, NY 10115. Tel. (212)870-2344. Fax (212)870-2338

Circuit Rider, (m) The United Methodist Church, J. Richard Peck, 201 Eighth Ave. S., Nashville, TN 37203. Tel. (615)749-6488

Clarion Herald, (bi-w) The Roman Catholic Church, Peter P. Finney, Jr., P. O. Box 53247, 1000 Howard Ave., Suite 400, New Orleans, LA 70153. Tel. (504)596-3030. Fax (504)596-3020

Clergy Journal, The, (10/yr) Nondenominational, Sharilyn Figueroa, P.O. Box 240, South St. Paul, MN 55075. Tel. (800)328-0200. Fax (612)457-4617

Co-Laborer, (bi-m) National Association of Free Will Baptists, Melissa L. Riddle, Women Nationally Active for Christ, P.O. Box 5002, Antioch, TN 37011-5002. Tel. (615)731-6812. Fax (615)731-0049

Columbia, (m) The Roman Catholic Church, Richard McMunn, One Columbus Plaza, New Haven, CT 06510. Tel. (203)772-2130. Fax (203)777-0114

Commission, The, (6/yr) Southern Baptist Convention, Leland F. Webb, Box 6767, Richmond, VA 23230. Tel. (804)353-0151. Fax (804)358-0504

Commonweal, (bi-w) The Roman Catholic Church, Margaret O'Brien Steinfels, 15 Dutch St., Rm. 502, New York, NY 10038-3760. Tel. (212)732-0800

Congregationalist, The, (bi-m) National Association of Congregational Christian Churches, Joseph B. Polhemus, 1105 Briarwood Rd., Mansfield, OH 44907. Tel. (419)756-5526. Fax (419)524-2621

Conqueror, (bi-m) United Pentecostal Church International, Darrell Johns, 8855 Dunn Rd., Hazelwood, MO 63042. Tel. (314)837-7300. Fax (314)837-7403

Conservative Judaism, (q) Jewish Organizations, Benjamin Scolnic, 3080 Broadway, New York, NY 10027. Tel. (212)678-8060. Fax (212)749-9166

Contact, (m) National Association of Free Will Baptists, Jack Williams, P.O. Box 5002, Antioch, TN 37011-5002. Tel. (615)731-6812. Fax (615)731-0049

Contempo, (m) Southern Baptist Convention, Cindy Lewis Dake, P.O. Box 830010, Birmingham, AL 35283. Tel. (205)991-8100. Fax (205)995-4841

Cornerstone Connections, (q) Seventh-day Adventist Church, Gary B. Swanson, 12501 Old Columbia Pike, Silver Spring, MD 20904. Tel. (301)680-6160. Fax (301)680-6155

Courage in the Struggle for Justice and Peace, (10/yr) United Church of Christ, Rubin Tendai, 110 Maryland Ave., NE, Washington, DC 20002. Tel. (202)543-1517. Fax (202)543-5994

Covenant Companion, (m) The Evangelical Covenant Church, James R. Hawkinson, 5101 N. Francisco Ave., Chicago, IL 60625. Tel. (312)784-3000. Fax (312)784-4366

Covenant Home Altar, (q) The Evangelical Covenant Church, James R. Hawkinson, 5101 N. Francisco Ave., Chicago, IL 60625. Tel. (312)784-3000. Fax (312)784-4366

Covenant Quarterly, (q) The Evangelical Covenant Church, Wayne C. Weld, 3225 W. Foster Ave., Chicago, IL 60625-4895. Tel. (312)478-2696. Fax (312)583-0858

Covenanter Witness, The, (m) Reformed Presbyterian Church of North America, Drew Gordon and Lynne Gordon, 7408 Penn Ave., Pittsburgh, PA 15208. Tel. (412)241-0436

Credinta—The Faith, (m) The Romanian Orthodox Church in America, Vasile Vasilachi, 19959 Riopelle St., Detroit, MI 48203. Tel. (313)893-8390

Criterion, The, (w) The Roman Catholic Church, John F. Fink, P.O. Box 1717, 1400 N. Meridian, Indianapolis, IN 46206. Tel. (317)236-1570

Crosswalk, (w) Church of the Nazarene, Carol Wight Gritton, Word Action Publishing, Box 419527, Kansas City, MO 64141. Tel. (816)333-7000. Fax (816)333-4315

Cumberland Flag, The, (m) Cumberland Presbyterian Church in America, Robert Stanley Wood, 226 Church St., Huntsville, AL 35801. Tel. (205)536-7481. Fax (205)536-7482

Cumberland Presbyterian, The, (m) Cumberland Presbyterian Church, M. Jacqueline DeBerry Warren, 1978 Union Ave., Memphis, TN 38104. Tel. (901)276-4572. Fax (901)276-4578

Currents in Theology and Mission, (6/yr) Evangelical Lutheran Church in America, Ralph W. Klein, 1100 E. 55th St., Chicago, IL 60615. Tel. (312)753-0751. Fax (312)753-0782

Decision, (11/yr) Nondenominational, Roger C. Palms, 1300 Harmon Pl., Minneapolis, MN 55403. Tel. (612)338-0500. Fax (612)335-1299

Disciple, The, (m) Christian Church (Disciples of Christ), Robert L. Friedly, Box 1986, Indianapolis, IN 46206. Tel. (317)353-1491. Fax (317)359-7546

EMC Today, (bi-m) Evangelical Mennonite Church, Donald W. Roth, 1420 Kerrway Ct., Fort Wayne, IN 46805. Tel. (219)423-3649. Fax (219)420-1905

Ecumenical Trends, (m) Nondenominational, William Carpe, P.O. Box 16136, Ludlow, KY 41016. Tel. (606)581-6216

El Aposento Alto, (6/yr) The United Methodist Church, Hector R. de la Cerda, P.O. Box 189, Nashville, TN 37202. Tel. (615)340-7246

El Interprete, (6/yr) The United Methodist Church, Edith LaFontaine, P.O. Box 320, Nashville, TN 37202. Tel. (615)742-5115. Fax (615)742-5460

Eleventh Hour Messenger, (bi-m) Wesleyan Holiness Association of Churches, J. Stevan Manley, 108 Carter Ave., Dayton, OH 45405. Tel. (513)278-3770

Elim Herald, (q) Elim Fellowship, L. Dayton Reynolds, 7245 College St., Lima, NY 14485. Tel. (716)582-2790. Fax (716)624-1229

Emphasis on Faith and Living, (bi-m) The Missionary Church, Robert Ransom, P.O. Box 9127, Ft. Wayne, IN 46899. Tel. (219)747-2027. Fax (219)747-5331

Ensign, The, (m) The Church of Jesus Christ of Latter-day Saints, Rex D. Pinegar, 50 E. North Temple St., Salt Lake City, UT 84150. Tel. (801)240-2950. Fax (801)240-1727

Evangel, The, (m) The American Association of Lutheran Churches, Christopher Barnekov, P.O. Box 17097, Minneapolis, MN 55420. Tel. (612)884-7784

Evangelical Beacon, (8/yr) The Evangelical Free Church of America, Carol Madison, 901 East 78th St., Minneapolis, MN 55420-1300.

Evangelical Friend, (6/yr) Evangelical Friends International—North America Region, Paul Anderson, P.O. Box 232, Newberg, OR 97132. Tel. (503)538-7345. Fax (503)538-7033

Evangelical Visitor, (m) Brethren in Christ Church, Glen A. Pierce, P.O. Box 166, Nappanee, IN 46550. Tel. (219)773-3164

Evangelist, The, (w) The Roman Catholic Church, James Breig, 40 N. Main Ave., Albany, NY 12203. Tel. (518)453-6688. Fax (518)453-6793

Extension, (9/yr) The Roman Catholic Church, Bradley Collins, 35 East Wacker Dr., Rm. 400, Chicago, IL 60601-2105. Tel. (312)236-7240. Fax (312)236-5276

Faith & Fellowship, (17/yr) Church of the Lutheran Brethren of America, David Rinden, P.O. Box 655, Fergus Falls, MN 56538. Tel. (218)736-7357. Fax (218)736-2200

Faith and Truth, (m) Pentecostal Fire-Baptized Holiness Church, Edgar Vollrath, 593 Harris-Lord Rd., Commerce, GA 30529.

Faith-Life, (bi-m) The Protes'tant Conference (Lutheran), Inc., Marcus Albrecht, P.O. Box 2141, LaCrosse, WI 54601. Tel. (414)733-1839

Fellowship Magazine, The, (6/yr) Assemblies of God International Fellowship (Independent/Not affiliated), T. A. Lanes, 8504 Commerce Ave., San Diego, CA 92121. Tel. (619)530-1727. Fax (619)530-1543

Fellowship Tidings, (q) Full Gospel Fellowship of Churches and Ministers International, Chester P. Jenkins, 4325 W. Ledbetter Dr., Dallas, TX 75233. Tel. (214)339-1200. Fax (214)339-8790

Firm Foundation, (m) Churches of Christ, H. A. Dobbs, P.O. Box 690192, Houston, TX 77269-0192.

First Things: A Monthly Journal of Religion and Public, (m) Interdenominational, Richard J. Neuhaus, 156 Fifth Ave., Ste. 400, New York, NY 10010. Tel. (212)627-2288. Fax (212)627-2184

Flaming Sword, The, (m) The Fire Baptized Holiness Church (Wesleyan), Susan Davolt, 10th St. & College Ave., Independence, KS 67301.

For the Poor, (m) Primitive Baptists, W. H. Cayce, P.O. Box 38, Thornton, AR 71766. Tel. (501)352-3694

Foresee, (bi-m) Conservative Congregational Christian Conference, Wanda Evans, 7582 Currell Blvd., #108, St. Paul, MN 55125. Tel. (612)739-1474

Forum Letter, (m) Interdenominational Lutheran, Russell E. Saltzman, P.O. Box 327, Delhi, NY 13753. Tel. (607)746-7511

Forward, (q) United Pentecostal Church International, J. L. Hall, 8855 Dunn Rd., Hazelwood, MO 63042. Tel. (314)837-7300. Fax (314)837-4503

Foursquare World Advance, (6/yr) International Church of the Foursquare Gospel, Ron Williams, 1910 W. Sunset Blvd., Ste 200, Los Angeles, CA 90026. Tel. (213)484-2400. Fax (213)413-3824

Free Will Baptist Gem, (m) National Association of Free Will Baptists, Nathan Ruble, P.O. Box 991, Lebanon, MO 65536.

Free Will Baptist, The, (m) Original Free Will Baptist Church, Janie Jones Sowers, P.O. Box 159, Ayden, NC 28513. Tel. (919)746-6128. Fax (919)746-9248

Free Will Bible College Bulletin, (6/yr) National Association of Free Will Baptists, Bert Tippett, 3606 West End Ave., Nashville, TN 37205. Tel. (615)383-1340. Fax same

Friend, The, (m) The Church of Jesus Christ of Latter-day Saints, Vivian Paulsen, 50 E. North Temple St., Salt Lake City, UT 84150. Tel. (801)240-2210. Fax (801)240-1727

Friends Journal, (m) Friends General Conference, Vinton Deming, 1501 Cherry St., Philadelphia, PA 19102-1497. Tel. (215)241-7277. Fax (215)568-1377

Front Line, (q) Conservative Baptist Association of America, Walter Fricke and Robert Rummel, P.O. Box 66, Wheaton, IL 60189. Tel. (708)653-5350. Fax (708)653-5387

Full Gospel Ministries Mission Outreach Report, (q) Full Gospel Assemblies International, Simeon Strauser, P.O. Box 1230, Coatesville, PA 19320. Tel. (610)857-2357

Gazette, (m) Volunteers of America, Leslie Hornich, 3939 N. Causeway Blvd., Metairie, LA 70002. Tel. (504)837-2652. Fax (504)837-4200

Gem, The, (w) Churches of God, General Conference, Evelyn J. Sloat, P.O. Box 926, Findlay, OH 45839.

General Baptist Messenger, (m) General Association of General Baptists, Samuel S. Ramdial, 100 Stinson Dr., Poplar Bluff, MO 63901. Tel. (314)686-9051. Fax (314)686-6011

Gleaner, The, (m) Baptist Missionary Association of America, F. Donald Collins, P.O. Box 193920, Little Rock, AR 72219-3920.

Global Outreach, (m) Universal Fellowship of Metropolitan Community Churches, Louis Kavar, 5300 Santa Monica Blvd., #304, Los Angeles, CA 90029. Tel. (213)464-5100

Global Witness, The, United Pentecostal Church International, Mervyn Miller, 8855 Dunn Rd., Hazelwood, MO 63042.

God's Field, (bi-w) Polish National Catholic Church of America, Anthony M. Rysz, 1002 Pittston Ave., Scranton, PA 18505. Tel. (717)346-9131

Gospel Advocate, (m) Churches of Christ, F. Furman Kearley, Box 150, Nashville, TN 37202. Tel. (615)254-8781. Fax (615)254-7411

Gospel Herald, (w) Mennonite Church, J. Lorne Peachey, 616 Walnut Ave., Scottdale, PA 15683. Tel. (412)887-8500. Fax (412)887-3111

Gospel Herald, The, Church of God, Mountain Assembly, Inc., Dennis McClanahan, P.O. Box 157, Jellico, TN 37762.

Gospel Messenger, The, (m) Congregational Holiness Church, Cullen L. Hicks, P.O. Box 643, Lincolnton, GA 30817. Tel. (706)359-4000

Gospel News, The, (m) The Church of Jesus Christ (Bickertonites), Anthony Scolaro, 20 Byrd Ave., Bloomfield, NJ 07003. Tel. (313)429-5080. Fax (313)429-4714

Gospel Tidings, (bi-m) Fellowship of Evangelical Bible Churches, Robert L. Frey, 5800 S. 14th St., Omaha, NE 68107. Tel. (402)731-4780. Fax (402)731-1173

Gospel Tidings, (m) Churches of Christ, Travis Allen, Box 4355, Englewood, CO 80155. Tel. (303)694-3560. Fax (303)850-0623

Gospel Truth, The, (m) Church of the Living God (Motto: Christian Workers for Fellowship), W. E. Crumes, 430 Forest Ave., Cincinnati, OH 45229. Tel. (513)569-5660

Guardian of Truth, (bi-w) Churches of Christ, Mike Willis, Box 9670, Bowling Green, KY 42101. Tel. (800)428-0121. Fax (317)745-4708

Guide, (w) Seventh-day Adventist Church, Jeannette R. Johnson, 55 W. Oak Ridge Dr., Hagerstown, MD 21740. Tel. (301)791-7000. Fax (301)791-7012

Heartbeat, (bi-m) National Association of Free Will Baptists, Don Robirds, Foreign Missions Office, P.O. Box 5002, Antioch, TN 37011-5002. Tel. (615)731-6812. Fax (615)731-5345

Helping Hand, (bi-m) International Pentecostal Holiness Church, Doris Moore, P.O. Box 12609, Oklahoma City, OK 73157. Tel. (405)787-7110

Herald of Christian Science, The, (m) Church of Christ, Scientist, William E. Moody, One Norway St., Boston, MA 02115. Tel. (617)450-2000

Herald of Holiness, (m) Church of the Nazarene, Wesley D. Tracy, 6401 The Paseo, Kansas City, MO 64131. Tel. (816)333-7000. Fax (816)333-1748

Heritage, (q) Assemblies of God, Wayne E. Warner, 1445 Boonville Ave., Springfield, MO 65802. Tel. (417)862-1447. Fax (417)862-8558

High Adventure, (q) Assemblies of God, Marshall Bruner, Gospel Publishing House, 1445 Boonville Ave., Springfield, MO 65802-1894. Tel. (417)862-2781. Fax (417)862-8558

Holiness Union, The, (m) United Holy Church of America, Inc., Joseph T. Durham, 13102 Morningside La., Silver Spring, MD 20904. Tel. (301)989-9093. Fax (301)559-6732

Homelife, United Pentecostal Church International, Mark Christian, 8855 Dunn Rd., Hazelwood, MO 63042.

Homiletic and Pastoral Review, (m) The Roman Catholic Church, Kenneth Baker, 86 Riverside Dr., New York, NY 10024. Tel. (212)799-2600

Horizons, (bi-m) Presbyterian Church (U.S.A.), Barbara A. Roche, Presbyterian Women, 100 Witherspoon St., Louisville, KY 40202. Tel. (502)569-5367. Fax (502)569-8085

Horizons, (m) Christian Churches and Churches of Christ, Norman L. Weaver, Box 2427, Knoxville, TN 37901. Tel. (615)577-9740. Fax (615)577-9743

Image, Churches of Christ, Danny Boultinghouse, 3117 N. 7th St., West Monroe, LA 71291-2227. Tel. (318)396-4366

Insight, (w) Seventh-day Adventist Church, Lori L. Peckham, 55 W. Oak Ridge Dr., Hagerstown, MD 21740. Tel. (301)791-7000. Fax (301)791-7012

Insight, (q) Advent Christian Church, Millie Griswold, P.O. Box 23152, Charlotte, NC 28227.

Interest, (m) Christian Brethren (also known as Plymouth Brethren), Debra Locklear, P.O. Box 190, Wheaton, IL 60189. Tel. (708)653-6573. Fax (708)653-6595

International Bulletin of Missionary Research, (q) Nondenominational, Gerald H. Anderson, 490 Prospect St., New Haven, CT 06511. Tel. (203)624-6672. Fax (203)865-2857

International Pentecostal Holiness Advocate, The, (m) International Pentecostal Holiness Church, Shirley Spencer, P.O. Box 12609, Oklahoma City, OK 73157. Tel. (405)787-7110. Fax (405)789-3957

Interpretation, (q) Interdenominational, Jack D. Kingsbury, 3401 Brook Rd., Richmond, VA 23227. Tel. (804)355-0671. Fax (804)355-3919

Interpreter, (8/yr) The United Methodist Church, Ralph E. Baker, P.O. Box 320, Nashville, TN 37202-0320. Tel. (615)742-5107. Fax (615)742-5460

Islamic Horizons, Muslims, Kamran Memon, P.O. Box 38, Plainfield, IN 46168. Tel. (317)839-8157. Fax (317)839-1840

Jewish Action, (q) Jewish Organizations, Charlotte Friedland, 333 Seventh Ave., 18th Floor, New York, NY 10001. Tel. (212)563-4000. Fax (212)564-9058

John Three Sixteen, (w) The Fire Baptized Holiness Church (Wesleyan), Mary Cunningham, 10th St. & College Ave., Independence, KS 67301.

Journal of Adventist Education, (5/yr) Seventh-day Adventist Church, Beverly Rumble, 12501 Old Columbia Pike, Silver Spring, MD 20904-6600. Tel. (301)680-5075. Fax (301)622-9627

Journal of Christian Education, (q) African Methodist Episcopal Church, Kenneth H. Hill, 500 Eighth Ave., S., Nashville, TN 37203. Tel. (615)242-1420. Fax (615)726-1866

Journal of Ecumenical Studies, (q) Interdenominational, Leonard Swidler, Temple Univ. (022-38), Philadelphia, PA 19122. Tel. (215)204-7714. Fax (215)204-4569

Journal of Pastoral Care, The, (q) Nondenominational, Orlo Strunk, Jr., 1549 Clairemont Rd., Ste. 103, Decatur, GA 30030-4611.

Journal of Reform Judaism, (q) Jewish Organizations, Henry Bamberger, 192 Lexington Ave., New York, NY 10016. Tel. (212)684-4990. Fax (212)689-1649

Journal of Theology, (4/yr) Church of the Lutheran Confession, John Lau, Immanuel Lutheran College, 501 Grover Road, Eau Claire, WI 54701-7199. Tel. (715)836-6621. Fax (715)836-6634

Journal of the American Academy of Religion, (q) Nondenominational, William Scott Green, Dept. of Religion & Classics, Univ. of Rochester, Rochester, NY 14627. Tel. (716)275-5415

Joyous Light, The, (q) The Romanian Orthodox Episcopate of America, David Oancea, P.O. Box 185, Grass Lake, MI 49240-0185. Tel. (517)522-3656. Fax (517)522-5907

Judaism, (q) Jewish Organizations, Ruth B. Waxman, 15 E. 84th St., New York, NY 10028. Tel. (212)879-4500. Fax (212)249-3672

Keeping in Touch, (m) Universal Fellowship of Metropolitan Community Churches, Kittredge Cherry, 5300 Santa Monica Blvd, #304, Los Angeles, CA 90029. Tel. (213)464-5100. Fax (213)464-2123

Leadership: A Practical Journal for Church Leaders, (q) Nondenominational, Marshall Shelley, 465 Gundersen Dr., Carol Stream, IL 60188. Tel. (708)260-6200. Fax (708)260-0114

Leaves of Healing, (q) Christian Catholic Church (Evangelical-Protestant), Roger W. Ottersen, 2500 Dowie Memorial Dr., Zion, IL 60099. Tel. (708)746-1411. Fax (708)746-1452

Liberty, (bi-m) Seventh-day Adventist Church, Clifford Goldstein, 12501 Old Columbia Pike, Silver Spring, MD 20904. Tel. (301)680-6691. Fax (301)680-6695

Light and Life Magazine, (m) Free Methodist Church of North America, Robert Haslam, P.O. Box 535002, Indianapolis, IN 46253-5002.

Light of Hope, The, (bi-m) Apostolic Faith Mission of Portland, Oregon, Dwight L. Baltzell, 6615 S.E. 52nd Ave., Portland, OR 97206. Tel. (503)777-1741. Fax (503)777-1743

Liguorian, (m) The Roman Catholic Church, Allan J. Weinert, C.SS.R., 1 Liguori Dr., Liguori, MO 63057. Tel. (314)464-2500. Fax (314)464-8449

Listen, (m) Seventh-day Adventist Church, Lincoln E. Steed, 55 W. Oak Ridge Dr., Hagerstown, MD 21740. Tel. (301)791-7000. Fax (301)791-7012

Living Orthodoxy, (bi-m) The Russian Orthodox Church Outside of Russia, Gregory Williams, Rt. 1, Box 205, Liberty, TN 37095. Tel. (615)536-5239

Long Island Catholic, The, (w) The Roman Catholic Church, Elizabeth O'Connor, P. O. Box 9009, 99 North Village Ave., Rockville Centre, NY 11571-9119. Tel. (516)594-1000. Fax (516)594-1092

Lookout, The, (w) Christian Churches and Churches of Christ, Simon J. Dahlman, 8121 Hamilton Ave., Cincinnati, OH 45231. Tel. (513)931-4050. Fax (513)931-0904

Lumina Lina, (q) The Romanian Orthodox Episcopate of America, David Oancea, P.O. Box 185, Grass Lake, MI 49240-0185. Tel. (517)522-3656. Fax (517)522-5907

Lutheran Ambassador, The, (bi-w) The Association of Free Lutheran Congregations, Robert L. Lee, 86286 Pine Grove Rd., Eugene, OR 97402. Tel. (503)687-8643

Lutheran Educator, The, (q) Wisconsin Evangelical Lutheran Synod, John R. Isch, Dr. Martin Luther College, 1884 College Heights, New Ulm, MN 56073. Tel. (507)354-8221. Fax (507)354-8225

Lutheran Forum, (q) Interdenominational Lutheran, Leonard R. Klein, P.O. Box 327, Delhi, NY 13753. Tel. (607)746-7511. Fax (607)829-2158

Lutheran Sentinel, (m) Evangelical Lutheran Synod, P. Madson, 813 S. Willow Ave., Sioux Falls, SD 57104. Tel. (605)334-4225

Lutheran Spokesman, The, (m) Church of the Lutheran Confession, Paul Fleischer, 710 4th Ave., SW, Sleepy Eye, MN 56085. Tel. (507)794-7793

Lutheran Synod Quarterly, (q) Evangelical Lutheran Synod, W. W. Peterson, Bethany Lutheran Theological Seminary, 447 N. Division St., Mankato, MN 56001. Tel. (507)625-2977. Fax (507)625-1849

Lutheran Witness, The, (m) The Lutheran Church—Missouri Synod, David Mahsman, 1333 S. Kirkwood Rd., St. Louis, MO 63122-7295. Tel. (314)965-9917. Fax (314)965-3396

Lutheran, The, (m) Evangelical Lutheran Church in America, Edgar R. Trexler, 8765 W. Higgins Rd., Chicago, IL 60631-4183. Tel. (312)380-2540. Fax (312)380-2751

Magyar Egyhaz, (6/yr) Hungarian Reformed Church in America, Stefan M. Torok, 331 Kirkland Pl., Perth Amboy, NJ 08861. Tel. (908)442-7799

Majallat Al-Masjid, (q) Muslims, Dawud Assad, 99 Woodview Dr., Old Bridge, NJ 08857. Tel. (908)679-8617. Fax (908)679-1260

Maranatha, (q) Advent Christian Church, Robert Mayer, P.O. Box 23152, Charlotte, NC 28227. Tel. (704)545-6161. Fax (704)573-0712

Marriage Partnership, (q) Nondenominational, Ron Lee, 465 Gundersen Dr., Carol Stream, IL 60188. Tel. (708)260-6200. Fax (708)260-0114

Maryknoll, (m) The Roman Catholic Church, Joseph R. Veneroso, M.M., Maryknoll Fathers and Brothers, Maryknoll, NY 10545. Tel. (914)941-7590. Fax (914)945-0670

Mature Years, (q) The United Methodist Church, Marvin W. Cropsey, 201 Eighth Ave. S, Nashville, TN 37203. Tel. (615)749-6292. Fax (615)749-6512

Media&Values, (q) Rosalind Silver, Center for Media and Values, 1962 S. Shenandoah St., Los Angeles, CA 90034. Tel. (310)559-2944. Fax (310)559-9396

Memos: A Magazine for Missionettes Leaders, (q) Assemblies of God, Linda Upton, Gospel Publishing House, 1445 Boonville Ave., Springfield, MO 65802. Tel. (417)862-2781. Fax (417)862-8558

Mennonite Historical Bulletin, (q) Mennonite Church, Levi Miller, 1700 S. Main St., Goshen, IN 46526. Tel. (219)535-7477. Fax (219)535-7293

Mennonite Quarterly Review, (q) Mennonite Church, John D. Roth, 1700 S. Main St., Goshen, IN 46526. Tel. (219)535-7433. Fax (219)535-7438

Mennonite, The, (semi-m) Mennonite Church, The General Conference, Gordon Houser, Box 347, 722 Main St., Newton, KS 67114. Tel. (316)283-5100. Fax (316)283-0454

Message, (bi-m) Seventh-day Adventist Church, Stephen P. Ruff, 55 West Oak Ridge Dr., Hagerstown, MD 21740.

Message of the Open Bible, (10/yr) Open Bible Standard Churches, Inc., Delores A. Winegar, 2020 Bell Ave., Des Moines, IA 50315-1096. Tel. (515)288-6761. Fax (515)288-2510

Messenger, (m) Presbyterian Church in America, Robert G. Sweet, 1852 Century Pl., Ste. 101, Atlanta, GA 30345. Tel. (404)320-3388. Fax (404)329-1280

Messenger, (m) Church of the Brethren, Kermon Thomasson, 1451 Dundee Ave., Elgin, IL 60120. Tel. (708)742-5100. Fax (708)742-6103

Messenger of Truth, (bi-w) Church of God in Christ, Mennonite, Gladwin Koehn, P.O. Box 230, Moundridge, KS 67107. Fax (316)345-2582

Messenger, The, (m) The (Original) Church of God, Inc., Johnny Albertson, 2214 E. 17th St., Chattanooga, TN 37404. Tel. (615)629-4505

Messenger, The, (m) The Swedenborgian Church, Patte LeVan, P.O. Box 985, Julian, CA 92036. Tel. (619)765-2915. Fax (619)765-2915

Messenger, The, (m) The Pentecostal Free Will Baptist Church, Inc., Don Sauls, P.O. Box 1568, Dunn, NC 28335. Tel. (910)892-0297. Fax (910)892-6876

Methodist History, (q) The United Methodist Church, Charles Yrigoyen, Jr., P.O. Box 127, Madison, NJ 07940. Tel. (201)822-2787. Fax (201)408-3909

Mid-Stream: An Ecumenical Journal, (q) Christian Church (Disciples of Christ), Paul A. Crow, Jr., P.O. Box 1986, Indianapolis, IN 46206. Tel. (317)353-1491. Fax (317)359-7546

Midwest Missionary Baptist, (m) Baptist Missionary Association of America, Roy H. Inman, Sr., 4920 E. 26th St., Lake Station, IN 46405. Tel. (219)962-8149

Ministry, (m) Seventh-day Adventist Church, J. David Newman, 12501 Old Columbia Pike, Silver Spring, MD 21029-6600. Tel. (301)680-6510. Fax (301)680-6502

Ministry Today, (bi-m) The Missionary Church, Robert Ransom, P.O. Box 9127, Ft. Wayne, IN 46899. Tel. (219)747-2027. Fax (219)747-5331

Mission Grams, (bi-m) National Association of Free Will Baptists, Roy Thomas, Home Missions Office, P.O. Box 5002, Antioch, TN 37011-5002. Tel. (615)731-6812. Fax (615)731-0049

Mission Herald, (bi-m) National Baptist Convention, U.S.A., Inc., William J. Harvey, III, 701 S. 19th St., Philadelphia, PA 19146. Tel. (215)878-2854. Fax (215)735-1721

Mission, Adult and Junior-Teen, (q) Seventh-day Adventist Church, Charlotte Ishkanian, 12501 Old Columbia Pike, Silver Spring, MD 20904. Tel. (301)680-6167. Fax (301)890-3965

Missionary Messenger, The, (m) Christian Methodist Episcopal Church, P. Ann Pegues, 2309 Bonnie Ave., Bastrop, LA 71220. Tel. (318)281-3044

Missionary Messenger, The, (11/yr) Cumberland Presbyterian Church, Mark Brown, 1978 Union Ave., Memphis, TN 38104. Tel. (901)276-4572. Fax (901)276-4578

Missionary Seer, (m) African Methodist Episcopal Zion Church, Kermit J. De-Graffenreidt, 475 Riverside Dr., Rm. 1935, New York, NY 10115. Tel. (212)870-2952. Fax (212)870-2055

MissionsUSA, (bi-m) Southern Baptist Convention, Phyllis Thompson, 1350 Spring St. NW, Atlanta, GA 30367. Tel. (404)898-7520. Fax (404)898-7542

Moments With God, (q) North American Baptist Conference, Dorothy Ganoung, 1 S. 210 Summit Ave., Oakbrook Terrace, IL 60181. Tel. (708)495-2000. Fax (708)495-3301

Monday Morning, (bi-m) Presbyterian Church (U.S.A.), Kevin Piecuch, 100 Witherspoon St., Louisville, KY 40202. Tel. (502)569-5755. Fax (502)569-5018

Moody Magazine, (11/yr) Nondenominational, Bruce Anderson, 820 N. LaSalle Dr., Chicago, IL 60610. Tel. (312)329-2163. Fax (312)329-2149

Moravian, The, (10/yr) Moravian Church in America (Unitas Fratrum), Hermann I. Weinlick, 1021 Center St., P.O. Box 1245, Bethlehem, PA 18016. Tel. (610)867-0594. Fax (610)866-9223

Mother Church, The, (m) Diocese of the Armenian Church of America, Sipan Mekhsian, 1201 N. Vine St., Hollywood, CA 90038. Tel. (213)466-5265. Fax (213)466-7612

Mountain Movers, (m) Assemblies of God, Joyce Wells Booze, Gospel Publishing House, 1445 Boonville Ave., Springfield, MO 65802. Tel. (417)862-2781. Fax (417)862-0085

Mouth and Voice of God, (bi-a) Triumph the Church and Kingdom of God in Christ Inc. (International), Loreen Webb, 17495 NE 13th Ave., North Miami Beach, FL 33161. Tel. (305)653-4279

Muslim World, The, (q) Muslims, Wadia Haddad and David Kerr and Ibrahim Abu-Rabin, 77 Sherman St., Hartford, CT 06105. Tel. (203)232-4451. Fax (203)231-0348

NBCA Lantern, National Baptist Convention of America, Inc., E. Edward Jones, Pres., 1540 Pierre Ave., Shreveport, LA 71113.

National Catholic Reporter, (44/yr) Independent, Thomas C. Fox, P.O. Box 419281, Kansas City, MO 64141. Tel. (816)531-0538. Fax (816)531-7466

National Christian Reporter, The,, (w) Nondenominational, John A. Lovelace, P.O. Box 222198, Dallas, TX 75222. Tel. (214)630-6495. Fax (214)630-0079

National Spiritualist Summit, The, (m) National Spiritualist Association of Churches, Sandra Pfortmiller, P.O. Box 56039, Phoenix, AZ 85079. Tel. (602)274-3161

New Church Life, (m) General Church of the New Jerusalem, Donald L. Rose, Box 277, Bryn Athyn, PA 19009. Tel. (215)947-6225. Fax (215)947-3078

New Era, The, (m) The Church of Jesus Christ of Latter-day Saints, Richard Romney, 50 E. North Temple St., Salt Lake City, UT 84150. Tel. (801)240-4700. Fax (801)240-1727

New Horizons in the Orthodox Presbyterian Church, (10/yr) The Orthodox Presbyterian Church, Thomas E. Tyson, 303 Horsham Rd., Ste. G, Horsham, PA 19044-2029. Tel. (215)956-0123. Fax (215)957-6286

New Oxford Review, (10/yr) The Roman Catholic Church, Dale Vree, 1069 Kains Ave., Berkeley, CA 94706. Tel. (510)526-5374

New World Outlook, (bi-m) The United Methodist Church, Alma Graham, 475 Riverside Dr., Rm. 1351, New York, NY 10115. Tel. (212)870-3765. Fax (212)870-3940

New World, The, (w) The Roman Catholic Church, Thomas C. Widner, S.J., 1144 W. Jackson Blvd., Chicago, IL 60607. Tel. (312)243-1300. Fax (312)243-1526

News, The, (m) The Anglican Orthodox Church, Margaret D. Lane, Anglican Orthodox Church, P.O. Box 128, Statesville, NC 28677. Tel. (704)873-8365

Newscope, (w) The United Methodist Church, J. Richard Peck, P.O. Box 801, Nashville, TN 37202. Tel. (615)749-6488. Fax (615)749-6079

North American Catholic, The, (m) North American Old Roman Catholic Church, Nan Simpson, 4200 N. Kedvale Ave., Chicago, IL 60641. Tel. (312)685-0461

Northwest Profile, (m) Baptist Missionary Association of America, Leo Hornaday, 5575 Barger St., Eugene, OR 97402. Tel. (503)689-6874

Northwestern Lutheran, (m) Wisconsin Evangelical Lutheran Synod, Gary P. Baumler, 2929 N. Mayfair Rd., Milwaukee, WI 53222. Tel. (414)256-3888. Fax (414)256-3899

On Course, Assemblies of God, Melinda Booze, Gospel Publishing House, 1445 Boonville Ave., Springfield, MO 65802. Tel. (417)862-2781. Fax (417)866-1146

On the Line, (w) Mennonite Church, Mary C. Meyer, 616 Walnut Ave., Scottdale, PA 15683. Tel. (412)887-8500. Fax (412)887-3111

One Church, (bi-m) Patriarchal Parishes of the Russian Orthodox Church in the U.S.A., Feodor Kovalchuk, 727 Miller Ave., Youngstown, OH 44502. Tel. (216)788-0151. Fax (216)788-9361

Orthodox America, (8/yr) The Russian Orthodox Church Outside of Russia, Mary Mansur, P.O. Box 992132, Redding, CA 96099.

Orthodox Church, The, (m) The Orthodox Church in America, Leonid Kishkovsky, P.O. Box 675, Syosset, NY 11791.

Orthodox Family, (q) The Russian Orthodox Church Outside of Russia, Deborah Johnson, P.O. Box 45, Beltsville, MD 20705. Tel. (301)890-3552

Orthodox Life (English), (bi-m) The Russian Orthodox Church Outside of Russia, Fr. Luke, Holy Trinity Monastery, P.O. Box 36, Jordanville, NY 13361-0036. Tel. (315)858-0840

Orthodox Observer, The, (m) Greek Orthodox Archdiocese of North and South America, Jim Golding, 8 E. 79th St., New York, NY 10021. Tel. (212)628-2590

Orthodox Russia (Russian), (26/yr) The Russian Orthodox Church Outside of Russia, Abp. Laurus, Holy Trinity Monastery, P.O. Box 36, Jordanville, NY 13361.

Orthodox Tradition, (4/yr) True Orthodox Ch. of Greece (Synod of Metropolitan Cyprian), American Exarchate, James Thornton and Bishop Auxentios, St. Gregory Palamas Monastery, Etna, CA 96027. Fax (916)467-3996

Orthodox Voices, The Russian Orthodox Church Outside of Russia, Thomas Webb and Ellen Webb, P.O. Box 23644, Lexington, KY 40523. Tel. (606)271-3877

Our Daily Bread, (m) The Swedenborgian Church, Richard H. Tafel, Jr., 8065 Lagoon Rd., Ft. Myers Beach, FL 33931. Tel. (813)463-5030

Our Little Friend, (w) Seventh-day Adventist Church, Aileen Andres Sox, P.O. Box 7000, Boise, ID 83707. Tel. (208)465-2500. Fax (208)465-2531

Our Sunday Visitor, (w) The Roman Catholic Church, David Scott, 200 Noll Plaza, Huntington, IN 46750. Tel. (219)356-8400. Fax (219)356-8472

Outreach, (m) Armenian Apostolic Church of America, Iris Papazian, 138 E. 39th St., New York, NY 10016. Tel. (212)689-7810. Fax (212)689-7168

Outreach, The, (q) United Pentecostal Church International, J. L. Fiorino, 8855 Dunn Rd., Hazelwood, MO 63042. Tel. (314)837-7300. Fax (314)837-2387

Paraclete, (q) Assemblies of God, David Bundrick, Gospel Publishing House, 1445 Boonville Ave., Springfield, MO 65802. Tel. (417)862-2781. Fax (417)866-1146

Pastor's Journal, The, (q) International Council of Community Churches, Robert Puckett, 19715 S. LaGrange Rd., Ste. C, Mokena, IL 60448. Tel. (708)479-8400. Fax (708)479-8402

Pastoral Life, (m) The Roman Catholic Church, Anthony Chenevey, Box 595, Canfield, OH 44406-0595. Tel. (216)533-5503. Fax (216)533-1076

Path of Orthodoxy, The, (English, m) Serbian Orthodox Church in the U.S.A. and Canada, Rade Merick and Mirko Dobrijevich, P.O. Box 36, Leetsdale, PA 15056. Tel. (412)741-8660. Fax (412)741-9235

Path of Orthodoxy, The, (Serbian, m) Serbian Orthodox Church in the U.S.A. and Canada, Nedeljko Lunich, 300 Striker Ave., Joliet, IL 60436. Tel. (815)741-1023

Pentecost Today, (q) Full Gospel Assemblies International, AnnaMae Strauser, P.O. Box 1230, Coatesville, PA 19320. Tel. (610)857-2357

Pentecostal Evangel, (w) Assemblies of God, Richard G. Champion, Gospel Publishing House, 1445 Boonville Ave., Springfield, MO 65802. Tel. (417)862-2781. Fax (417)862-0416

Pentecostal Herald, The, (m) United Pentecostal Church International, J. L. Hall, 8855 Dunn Rd., Hazelwood, MO 63042. Tel. (314)837-7300. Fax (314)837-4503

Pentecostal Interpreter, The, The Church Of God In Christ, H. Jenkins Bell, P.O. Box 320, Memphis, TN 38101.

Pentecostal Leader, The International Pentecostal Church of Christ, Lorraine Roberts, P.O. Box 739, London, OH 43140. Tel. (614)852-0348

Pentecostal Messenger, The, (m) Pentecostal Church of God, Donald K. Allen, P.O. Box 850, Joplin, MO 64802. Tel. (417)624-7050. Fax (417)624-7102

People's Mouthpiece, The, (q) Apostolic Overcoming Holy Church of God, Inc., Juanita R. Arrington, PhD, 1120 North 24th St., Birmingham, AL 35234. Tel. (205)324-2202

Perspectives on Science & Christian Faith, (q) Nondenominational, J. W. Haas, Jr., P.O. Box 668, Ipswich, MA 01938. Tel. (508)356-5656. Fax (508)356-4375

Pilot, The, (w) The Roman Catholic Church, Peter V. Conley, 49 Franklin St., Boston, MA 02110. Tel. (617)482-4316. Fax (617)482-5647

Pockets, (m) The United Methodist Church, Janet R. McNish, P.O. Box 189, Nashville, TN 37202. Tel. (615)340-7333. Fax (615)340-7006

Polka, (q) Polish National Catholic Church of America, Cecelia Lallo, 1002 Pittston Ave., Scranton, PA 18505.

Power for Today, (q) Churches of Christ, Steven S. Lemley and Emily Y. Lemley, Box 40526, Nashville, TN 37204.

Praying, (bi-m) The Roman Catholic Church, Art Winter, P.O. Box 419335, 115 E. Armour Blvd., Kansas City, MO 64141. Tel. (816)531-0538. Fax (816)531-7466

US PERIODICALS

Preacher's Magazine, (q) Church of the Nazarene, Randal Denny, 10814 E. Broadway, Spokane, WA 99206. Tel. (509)926-1545

Preacher, The, (bi-m) Baptist Bible Fellowship International, James O. Combs, P.O. Box 309 HSJ, Springfield, MO 65801. Tel. (417)831-3996

Presbyterian Outlook, (w) Presbyterian Church (U.S.A.), Robert H. Bullock, Jr., Box 85623, Richmond, VA 23285-5623. Tel. (804)359-8442. Fax (804)353-6369

Presbyterian Survey, (m) Presbyterian Church (U.S.A.), Catherine Cottingham, 100 Witherspoon St., Louisville, KY 40202-1396. Tel. (502)569-5637. Fax (502)569-5018

Primary Treasure, (w) Seventh-day Adventist Church, Aileen Andres Sox, P.O. Box 7000, Boise, ID 83707. Tel. (208)465-2500. Fax (208)465-2531

Primitive Baptist, (m) Primitive Baptists, W. H. Cayce, P.O. Box 38, Thornton, AR 71766. Tel. (501)352-3694

Priority, (m) The Missionary Church, Ken Stucky, P.O. Box 9127, Ft. Wayne, IN 46899. Tel. (219)747-2027. Fax (219)747-5331

Providence Visitor, (w) The Roman Catholic Church, Michael Brown, 184 Broad St., Providence, RI 02903. Tel. (401)272-1010. Fax (401)421-8418

Purpose, (w) Mennonite Church, James E. Horsch, 616 Walnut Ave., Scottdale, PA 15683. Tel. (412)887-8500. Fax (412)887-3111

Pursuit, (q) Nondenominational, Carol Madison, 901 East 78th St., Minneapolis, MN 55420-1300. Tel. (612)853-1750

Qala min M'Dinkha (Voice from the East), (q) Apostolic Catholic Assyrian Church of the East, North American Dioceses, Akhitiar Moshi, Diocesan Offices, 7201 N. Ashland, Chicago, IL 60626. Tel. (312)465-4777. Fax (312)465-0776

Quaker Life, (10/yr) Friends United Meeting, James R. Newby, 101 Quaker Hill Dr., Richmond, IN 47374-1980. Tel. (317)962-7573. Fax (317)966-1293

Quarterly Review, (q) The United Methodist Church, Sharon Hels, Box 871, Nashville, TN 37202. Tel. (615)340-7334. Fax (615)340-7048

Quarterly Review, (q) African Methodist Episcopal Zion Church, James D. Armstrong, P.O. Box 31005, Charlotte, NC 28231.

Reconstructionism Today, (q) Jewish Organizations, Larry Bush, Church Rd. & Greenwood Ave., Wycote, PA 19095. Tel. (215)887-1988. Fax (215)887-5348

Reflections, (bi-m) United Pentecostal Church International, Melissa Anderson, 8855 Dunn Rd., Hazelwood, MO 63402. Tel. (314)837-7300

Reform Judaism, (4/yr) Jewish Organizations, Aron Hirt-Manheimer, 838 Fifth Ave., New York, NY 10021. Tel. (212)249-0100. Fax (212)734-2857

Reformation Today, (bi-m) Sovereign Grace Baptists, Erroll Hulse, c/o Tom Lutz, 3743 Nichol Ave., Anderson, IN 46011-3008. Tel. (317)644-0994. Fax (317)644-0994

Reformed Herald, (m) Reformed Church in the United States, P. Grossmann, Box 362, Sutton, NE 68979. Tel. (402)773-4227

Rejoice!, (q) Interdenominational Mennonite, Katie Funk Wiebe, 836 Amidon, Wichita, KS 67203-3112. Tel. (316)269-9185

Religious Broadcasting, (11/yr) Nondenominational, Ron J. Kopczick, National Religious Broadcasters, 7839 Ashton Ave., Manassas, VA 22110. Tel. (703)330-7000. Fax (703)330-7100

Religious Education, Nondenominational, Jack D. Spiro, Virginia Commonwealth Univ., Richmond, VA 23284.

Reporter, (m) The Lutheran Church—Missouri Synod, David Mahsman, 1333 S. Kirkwood Rd., St. Louis, MO 63122-7295. Tel. (314)965-9917. Fax (314)965-3396

Rescue Herald, The, (q) American Rescue Workers, Robert N. Coles, Sr., 1209 Hamilton Blvd., Hagerstown, MD 21742. Tel. (301)797-0061. Fax (301)797-1480

Response, (m) The United Methodist Church, Dana Jones, 475 Riverside Dr., Room 1363, New York, NY 10115. Tel. (212)870-3755. Fax (212)870-3940

Restitution Herald, The, (bi-m) Church of God General Conference (Oregon, IL and Morrow, GA), Kent Ross, Box 100,000, Morrow, GA 30260. Tel. (404)362-0052. Fax (404)362-9307

Restoration Herald, (m) Christian Churches and Churches of Christ, H. Lee Mason, 5664 Cheviot Rd., Cincinnati, OH 45247-7071. Tel. (513)385-0461. Fax (513)385-0461

Restoration Quarterly, (q) Churches of Christ, James W. Thompson, Box 8227, Abilene, TX 79699-8227. Tel. (915)674-3781

Restoration Witness, (bi-m) Reorganized Church of Jesus Christ of Latter Day Saints, Barbara Howard, P.O. Box 1059, Independence, MO 64051. Tel. (816)252-5010. Fax (816)252-3976

Review for Religious, (bi-m) The Roman Catholic Church, David L. Fleming, S.J., 3601 Lindell Blvd., St. Louis, MO 63108. Tel. (314)535-3048. Fax (314)535-0601

Review of Religious Research, (4/yr) Non-denominational, D. Paul Johnson, Texas Tech. Univ., Dept. of Sociology, Anthropology, & SW, Lubbock, TX 79409. Tel. (806)742-2400. Fax (806)742-1088

Rocky Mountain Christian, Churches of Christ, Jack W. Carter, 2247 Highway 86 E., Castlerock, CO 80104. Tel. (303)646-3521. Fax (303)646-0180

SBC Life, (10/yr) Southern Baptist Convention, Mark T. Coppenger, 901 Commerce St., Nashville, TN 37203. Tel. (615)244-2355. Fax (615)742-8919

Sabbath Recorder, (m) Seventh Day Baptist General Conference, USA and Canada, Kevin J. Butler, 3120 Kennedy Rd., P.O. Box 1678, Janesville, WI 53547. Tel. (608)752-5055. Fax (608)752-7711

Saint Anthony Messenger, (m) The Roman Catholic Church, Norman Perry, 1615 Republic St., Cincinnati, OH 45210. Tel. (513)241-5616. Fax (513)241-0399

St. Luke Magazine, (m) Christ Catholic Church, Donald W. Mullan, P.O. Box 73, Niagara Falls, ON L2E 6S8. Tel. (416)354-2329

St. Willibrord Journal, (q) Christ Catholic Church, Charles E. Harrison, P.O. Box 271751, Houston, TX 77277-1751. Tel. (417)587-3951

Saints Herald, (m) Reorganized Church of Jesus Christ of Latter Day Saints, Roger Yarrington, P.O. Box 1770, Independence, MO 64055. Tel. (816)252-5010. Fax (816)252-3976

Salt, (m) The Roman Catholic Church, Mark J. Brummel, 205 W. Monroe St., Chicago, IL 60606. Tel. (312)236-7782. Fax (312)236-7230

Schwenkfeldian, The, (q) The Schwenkfelder Church, Brittney Pettis, 1 Seminary St., Pennsburg, PA 18073.

Searching Together, (q) Sovereign Grace Baptists, Jon Zens, P.O. Box 548, St. Croix Falls, WI 54024. Tel. (715)755-3560

Secret Chamber, African Methodist Episcopal Church, George L. Champion, 5728 Major Blvd., Orlando, FL 82819. Tel. (407)352-8797. Fax (407)352-6097

Secret Place, The, (q) American Baptist Churches in the U.S.A., Kathleen Hayes, P.O. Box 851, Valley Forge, PA 19482. Tel. (215)768-2240. Fax (215)768-2056

Shabbat Shalom, (q) Seventh-day Adventist Church, Clifford Goldstein, 55 W. Oak Ridge Dr., Hagerstown, MD 21740.

Share, (bi-m) The Evangelical Church, James Lanz, Evangelical Church Board of Missions, 7733 West River Rd., Minneapolis, MN 55444. Tel. (612)561-0174

Sharing, (q) Interdenominational Mennonite, Steve Bowers, P.O. Box 438, Goshen, IN 46526. Tel. (219)533-9511. Fax (219)533-5264

Shiloh's Messenger of Wisdom, (m) Israelite House of David, William Robertson, P.O. Box 1067, Benton Harbor, MI 49023.

Signs of the Times, (m) Seventh-day Adventist Church, Greg Brothers, P.O. Box 7000, Boise, ID 83707. Tel. (208)465-2577. Fax (208)465-2531

Social Questions Bulletin, (bi-m) Nondenonominational, George McClain, 76 Clinton Ave., Shalom House, Staten Island, NY 10301. Tel. (718)273-6372. Fax (718)273-6372

Sojourners, (10/yr) Nondenominational, Jim Wallis, 2401 15th St. NW, Washington, DC 20009. Tel. (202)328-8842. Fax (202)328-8757

Solia/The Herald, (m) The Romanian Orthodox Episcopate of America, David Oancea, P.O. Box 185, Grass Lake, MI 49240-0185. Tel. (517)522-3656. Fax (517)522-5907

Southern Methodist, The, (m) Southern Methodist Church, Thomas M. Owens, Sr., P.O. Box 39, Orangeburg, SC 29116-0039. Tel. (803)534-9853. Fax (803)534-7827

Spectrum, (bi-m) Conservative Baptist Association of America, Dennis N. Baker and Wendy Gill, P.O. Box 66, Wheaton, IL 60189. Tel. (708)653-5350. Fax (708)653-5387

Spirit, (q) Volunteers of America, Arthur Smith, 3939 N. Causeway Blvd., Metairie, LA 70002. Tel. (504)837-2652. Fax (504)837-4200

Spiritual Sword, The, (q) Churches of Christ, Alan E. Highers, 1511 Getwell Rd., Memphis, TN 38111. Tel. (901)743-0464. Fax (901)743-2197

Standard, The, (m) Baptist General Conference, Gary D. Marsh, 2002 S. Arlington Heights Rd., Arlington Heights, IL 60005. Tel. (312)228-0200. Fax (708)228-5376

Star of Zion, (w) African Methodist Episcopal Zion Church, Morgan W. Tann, P.O. Box 31005, Charlotte, NC 28231. Tel. (704)377-4329. Fax (704)333-1769

Stewardship USA, (q) Nondenominational, Raymond Barnett Knudsen, II, P.O. Box 9, Bloomfield Hills, MI 48303-0009. Tel. (313)737-0895. Fax (313)737-0895

Story Friends, (w) Mennonite Church, Marjorie Waybill, 616 Walnut Ave., Scottdale, PA 15683. Tel. (412)887-8500. Fax (412)887-3111

Sunday, (q) Interdenominational, Jack P. Lowndes, 2930 Flowers Rd., S., #16, Atlanta, GA 30341-5532. Tel. (404)936-5376. Fax (404)451-6081

Tablet, The, (w) The Roman Catholic Church, Ed Wilkinson, 653 Hicks St., Brooklyn, NY 11231. Tel. (718)858-3838. Fax (718)858-2112

The Challenge, (m) The Evangelical Church, John F. Sills, 3000 Market St., NE, Ste. 528, Salem, OR 97301. Tel. (503)371-4818. Fax (503)364-5022

Theology Digest, (q) The Roman Catholic Church, Bernhard A. Asen and Rosemary Jermann, 3634 Lindell Blvd., St. Louis, MO 63108. Tel. (314)658-2857

Theology Today, (q) Nondenominational, Patrick D. Miller and Thomas G. Long, P.O. Box 29, Princeton, NJ 08542. Tel. (609)497-7714. Fax (609)924-2973

These Days, (bi-m) Presbyterian Church (U.S.A.), Vic Jameson, 100 Witherspoon St., Louisville, KY 40202. Tel. (502)569-5472. Fax (502)569-5018

Tidings, The, (w) The Roman Catholic Church, Tod M. Tamberg, 1530 W. Ninth St., Los Angeles, CA 90015. Tel. (213)251-3360. Fax (213)386-8667

Today's Christian Woman, (6/yr) Nondenominational, Julie A. Talerico, 465 Gunderson Dr., Carol Stream, IL 60188. Tel. (708)260-6200. Fax (708)260-0114

Tradition: A Journal of Orthodox Jewish Thought, (q) Jewish Organizations, Emanuel Feldman, Rabbinical Council of America, 275 Seventh Ave., New York, NY 10001. Tel. (212)807-7888. Fax (212)727-8452

Truth, (bi-m) Grace Gospel Fellowship, Roger G. Anderson, 2125 Martindale SW, Grand Rapids, MI 49509.

U.S. Catholic, (m) The Roman Catholic Church, Mark J. Brummel, 205 W. Monroe St., Chicago, IL 60606. Tel. (312)236-7782. Fax (312)236-7230

UB, (m) United Brethren in Christ, Steve Dennie, 302 Lake St., Huntington, IN 46750. Tel. (219)356-2312

Ubique, (q) The Liberal Catholic Church—Province of the United States of America, Joseph L. Tisch, P.O. Box 1117, Melbourne, FL 32902. Tel. (407)254-0499

Ukrainian Orthodox Herald, Ukrainian Orthodox Church of America (Ecumenical Patriarchate), Anthony Ugolnik, c/o St. Mary's Church, 1031 Fullerton Ave., Allentown, PA 18102.

Ukrainian Orthodox Word, (m) Ukrainian Orthodox Church of the U.S.A., Archbishop Antony, 4 Von Steuben La., South Bound Brook, NJ 08880. Tel. (908)469-7248

United Church News, (10/yr) United Church of Christ, W. Evan Golder, 700 Prospect Ave., Cleveland, OH 44115.

United Evangelical Action, (bi-m) Interdenominational, Donald R. Brown, 450 E. Gundersen Dr., Carol Stream, IL 60188. Tel. (708)665-0500. Fax (708)665-8575

United Methodist Record, (m) The United Methodist Church, Ronald Patterson, P.O. Box 660275, Dallas, TX 75266-0275. Tel. (214)630-6495. Fax (214)630-0079

United Methodist Reporter, The, (w) The United Methodist Church, Ronald Patterson, P.O. Box 660275, Dallas, TX 75266-0275. Tel. (214)630-6495. Fax (214)630-0079

United Methodist Review, (26/yr) The United Methodist Church, Ronald Patterson, P.O. Box 660275, Dallas, TX 75266-0275. Tel. (214)630-6495. Fax (214)630-0079

United Synagogue Review, (bi-a) Jewish Organizations, Lois Goldrich, 155-5th Ave., New York, NY 10010. Tel. (212)533-7800

Upper Room, The, (6/yr) The United Methodist Church, Janice Grana, P.O. Box 189, Nashville, TN 37202. Tel. (615)340-7266

Upreach, (q) Churches of Christ, Randy Becton, Box 2001, Abilene, TX 79604. Tel. (915)698-4370

VIP Communique, (q) International Church of the Foursquare Gospel, Beverly Brafford, 1910 W. Sunset Blvd., Los Angeles, CA 90026.

Vanguard, (q) Christian Church (Disciples of Christ), Ann Updegraff Spleth, 222 S. Downey Ave., Box 1986, Indianapolis, IN 46206-1986. Tel. (317)353-1491. Fax (317)352-8294

Vibrant Life, (bi-m) Seventh-day Adventist Church, Barbara L. Jackson-Hall, 55 W. Oak Ridge Dr., Hagerstown, MD 21740. Tel. (301)791-7000. Fax (301)791-7012

Victory (Youth Magazine), (m) Church of God of Prophecy, William M. Wilson, P.O. Box 2910, Cleveland, TN 37320-2910. Tel. (615)479-8511

Vindicator, The, (m) Old German Baptist Brethren, M. Keith Skiles, 1876 Beamsville-Union City Rd., Union City, OH 45390. Tel. (513)968-3877

Vista, (bi-m) Christian Church of North America, General Council, David Perrello, 35 Millbrook Dr., Williamsville, NY 14221. Tel. (716)634-7076

Vital Christianity, (m) Church of God (Anderson, Ind.), David C. Schultz, Box 2499, Anderson, IN 46018. Tel. (317)644-7721. Fax (317)622-9511

Voice, (q) General Association of General Baptists, Gene Koker, 100 Stinson Dr., Poplar Bluff, MO 63901. Tel. (314)785-7746. Fax (314)785-0564

Voice, (11/yr) Mennonite Church, Eve MacMaster, 256 Grove St., Bluffton, OH 45817. Tel. (419)358-8230. Fax (219)293-3977

Voice, The, (m) Independent Fundamental Churches of America, Paul J. Dollaske, P.O. Box 810, Grandville, MI 49418. Tel. (616)531-1840. Fax (616)531-1814

Voice, The, The Bible Church of Christ, Inc., Montrose Bushrod, 1358 Morris Ave., Bronx, NY 10456. Tel. (212)588-2284

Voice of Missions, (q) African Methodist Episcopal Church, Anne R. Elliott, 475 Riverside Dr., Rm. 1926, New York, NY 10115. Tel. (212)870-2258. Fax (212)870-2242

Voice of Missions, The, The Church Of God In Christ, Floyd Mayfield, 1932 Dewey Ave., Evanston, IL 60201. Tel. (901)578-3816

War Cry, The, (bi-w) The Salvation Army, Henry Gariepy, 615 Slaters Ln., Alexandria, VA 22313. Tel. (703)684-5500. Fax (703)684-5539

Watchtower, The, Jehovah's Witnesses, Watchtower Society, 25 Columbia Heights, Brooklyn, NY 11201. Tel. (718)625-3600. Fax (718)624-8030

Wave, The, (q) General Association of General Baptists, Sandra Trivitt, 100 Stinson Dr., Poplar Bluff, MO 63901. Tel. (314)785-7746. Fax (314)785-0564

weavings, (6/yr) The United Methodist Church, John Mogabgab, P.O. Box 189, Nashville, TN 37202. Tel. (615)340-7254

Wesleyan Advocate, The, (m) The Wesleyan Church, Jerry Brecheisen, P.O. Box 50434, Indianapolis, IN 46250-0434. Tel. (317)576-8156. Fax (317)577-4397

Wesleyan Woman, (q) The Wesleyan Church, Karen Disharoon, P.O. Box 50434, Indianapolis, IN 46250. Tel. (317)576-8164. Fax (317)573-0679

Wesleyan World, (m) The Wesleyan Church, Wayne MacBeth, P.O. Box 50434, Indianapolis, IN 46250. Tel. (317)576-8172. Fax (317)841-1125

White Wing Messenger, (bi-w) Church of God of Prophecy, Billy Murray, P.O. Box 2910, Cleveland, TN 37320-2910.

Whole Truth, (m) The Church Of God In Christ, David Hall, P.O. Box 2017, Memphis, TN 38101. Tel. (901)578-3841

Window to Mission, (q) Mennonite Church, The General Conference, Bek Linsenmeyer, Box 347, Newton, KS 67114. Tel. (316)283-5100. Fax (316)283-0454

Wineskins, (m) Churches of Christ, Mike Cope and Rubel Shelly, Box 129004, Nashville, TN 37212-9004. Tel. (615)373-5004. Fax (615)373-5006

Winner, The, (9/yr) Nondenominational, Gerald Wheeler, The Health Connection, P.O. Box 859, Hagerstown, MD 21741. Tel. (301)790-9735. Fax (301)790-9733

Wisconsin Lutheran Quarterly, (q) Wisconsin Evangelical Lutheran Synod, John F. Brug, 11831 N. Seminary Dr., 65 W. Mequon, WI 53092. Tel. (414)242-0967. Fax (414)242-7255

With, (8/yr) Interdenominational Mennonite, Eddy Hall and Carol Duerksen, P.O. Box 347, Newton, KS 67114. Tel. (316)283-5100. Fax (316)283-0454

Witness, (m) International Pentecostal Holiness Church, James Leggett, P.O. Box 12609, Oklahoma City, OK 73157. Tel. (405)787-7110. Fax (405)789-3957

Woman's Touch, (bi-m) Assemblies of God, Sandra Clopine, Gospel Publishing House, 1445 Boonville Ave., Springfield, MO 65802. Tel. (417)862-2781. Fax (417)862-8558

Women's Missionary Magazine, African Methodist Episcopal Church, Bertha O. Fordham, 800 Risley Ave., Pleasantville, NJ 08232.

Word and Work, (11/yr) Nondenominational, Alex V. Wilson, 2518 Portland Ave., Louisville, KY 40212. Tel. (502)897-2831

Word, The, (10/yr) The Antiochian Orthodox Christian Archdiocese of North America, George S. Corey, 52 78th St., Brooklyn, NY 11209. Tel. (718)748-7940. Fax (718)855-3608

Workman, The, (q) Churches of God, General Conference, Evelyn J. Sloat, P.O. Box 926, Findlay, OH 45839.

World Mission, (m) Church of the Nazarene, Roy Stults, World Mission Division, 6401 The Paseo, Kansas City, MO 64131. Tel. (816)333-7000. Fax (816)363-3100

World Parish, (s-m) Interdenominational Methodist, Joe Hale, P.O. Box 518, Lake Junaluska, NC 28745. Tel. (704)456-9432. Fax (704)456-9433

World Partners, (bi-m) The Missionary Church, Charles Carpenter, P.O. Box 9127, Ft. Wayne, IN 46899-9127. Tel. (219)747-2027. Fax (219)747-5331

World Vision, (m) Open Bible Standard Churches, Inc., Paul V. Canfield, 2020 Bell Ave., Des Moines, IA 50315-1096. Tel. (515)288-6761. Fax (515)288-2510

World Vision, (bi-m) Nondenominational, Terry Madison, 919 W. Huntington Dr., Monrovia, CA 91016. Tel. (818)357-7979. Fax (818)357-0915

World, The, (6/yr) Unitarian Universalist Association, Linda C. Beyer, 25 Beacon St., Boston, MA 02108. Tel. (617)742-2100. Fax (617)367-3637

Worldorama, (m) International Pentecostal Holiness Church, Jesse Simmons, P.O. Box 12609, Oklahoma City, OK 73157. Tel. (405)787-7110. Fax (405)787-7729

Worship, (6/yr) The Roman Catholic Church, R. Kevin Seasoltz, St. John's Abbey, Collegeville, MN 56321. Tel. (612)363-3883. Fax (612)363-2504

Y.P.W.W. Topics, (q) The Church Of God In Christ, James L. Whitehead, Jr., 67 Tennyson, Highland Park, MI 48203. Tel. (313)342-5595

youth!, (m) The United Methodist Church, Tony Peterson, 201 Eighth Ave. S., Nashville, TN 37203. Tel. (615)749-6319. Fax (615)749-6079

Youth Ministry Accent, (q) Seventh-day Adventist Church, David Wong, 12501 Old Columbia Pike, Silver Spring, MD 20904-6600. Tel. (301)680-6180. Fax (301)680-6155

YouthGuide, (q) Interdenominational Mennonite, Carol Duerksen and Eddy Hall, P.O. Box 347, Newton, KS 67114. Tel. (316)283-5100. Fax (316)283-0454

Zion's Advocate, Church of Christ, Gary Housknecht, P.O. Box 472, Independence, MO 64051. Tel. (816)833-3995

Zion's Herald, United Zion Church, Martha Harting, 75 Hickory Rd., Denver, PA 17517. Tel. (215)267-5849

11. RELIGIOUS PERIODICALS IN CANADA

The religious periodicals below constitute a basic core of important newspapers, journals and periodicals circulated in Canada. Consult the religious bodies in Canada listing (section 4) for the names of periodicals published by each denomination.

Each entry gives the title of the periodical, frequency of publication, religious affiliation, editor's name, address, telephone number and fax number when known.

A.C.O.P. Messenger, (m) Apostolic Church of Pentecost of Canada Inc., Irvin W. Ellis, 200-807 Manning Rd. NE, Calgary, AB T2E 7M9. Tel. (403)273-5777. Fax (403)273-8102

Advance, (q) Associated Gospel Churches, Wayne Foster, 8 Silver St., Paris, ON N3L 1T6. Tel. (519)442-6220

Alberta Alert, The, Baptist General Conference of Alberta, Virgil Olson, 5011 122A St., Edmonton, AB T6H 3S8. Tel. (403)438-9126

Anglican Montreal Anglican, (10/yr) The Anglican Church of Canada, Joan Shanks, 1444 Union Ave., Montreal, QC H3A 2B8. Tel. (514)843-6344. Fax (514)843-6344

Anglican, The, (10/yr) The Anglican Church of Canada, Vivian Snead, 135 Adelaide St. E, Toronto, ON M5C 1L8. Tel. (416)363-6021. Fax (416)363-7678

Atlantic Baptist, The, (m) United Baptist Convention of the Atlantic Provinces, Michael Lipe, Box 756, Kentville, NS B4N 3X9. Tel. (902)681-6868. Fax (902)681-0315

Atlantic Wesleyan, (q) The Wesleyan Church of Canada, Ray E. Barnwell, Sr., P.O. Box 20, Sussex, NB E0E 1P0. Tel. (506)433-1007. Fax (506)432-6668

Aujourd'hui Credo, (French m) The United Church of Canada, Gérard Gautier, 132 Victoria, Greenfield Park, QC J4V 1L8. Tel. (514)466-7733

B.C. Conference Call, (q) British Columbia Baptist Conference, Walter W. Wieser, 7600 Glover Rd., Langley, BC V3A 6H4. Tel. (604)888-2246. Fax (604)888-1905

B.C. Fellowship Baptist, (m) The Fellowship of Evangelical Baptist Churches in Canada, Bruce Christensen, Box 800, Langley, BC V3A 8C9. Tel. (604)888-3616. Fax (604)888-3601

BGC Canada News, (4/yr) Baptist General Conference of Canada, Abe Funk, 4306 97th St., Edmonton, AB T6E 5R9. Tel. (403)438-9127. Fax (403)435-2478

Baptist Horizon, The, (m) Canadian Convention of Southern Baptists, Nancy McGough, Postal Bag 300, Cochrane, AB T0L 0W0. Tel. (403)932-5688.

Blackboard Bulletin, (m) Old Order Amish Church, Elizabeth Wengerd, Rt. 4, Aylmer, ON N5H 2R3.

Budget, The, (w) Old Order Amish Church, George R. Smith, P.O. Box 249, Sugarcreek, OH 44681. Tel. (216)852-4634. Fax (216)852-4421

CLBI-Cross Roads, (bi-m) Evangelical Lutheran Church in Canada, Felicitas Ackermann, 4837-52A St., Camrose, AB T4V 1W5. Tel. (403)672-4454. Fax (403)672-4455

Canada Armenian Press, (q) Armenian Evangelical Church, Yessayi Sarmazian, 42 Glenforest Rd., Toronto, ON M4N 1Z8.

Canada Lutheran, (11/yr) Evangelical Lutheran Church in Canada, Kenn Ward, 1512 St. James St., Winnipeg, MB R3H 0L2. Tel. (204)786-6707. Fax (204)783-7548

Canadian Adventist Messenger, (12/yr) Seventh-day Adventist Church in Canada, June Polishuk, Maracle Press, 1156 King St. E, Oshawa, ON L1H 7N4. Tel. (416)723-3438. Fax (416)428-6024

Canadian Baptist, The, (10/yr) Canadian Baptist Federation, Larry Matthews, 217 St. George St., Toronto, ON M5R 2M2. Tel. (905)922-5163. Fax (905)922-4369

Canadian Disciple, (4/yr) Christian Church (Disciples of Christ) in Canada, Raymond A. Cuthbert, 240 Home St., Winnipeg, MB R3G 1X3. Tel. (204)783-5881

Canadian Friend, The, (bi-m) Canadian Yearly Meeting of the Religious Society of Friends, Dorothy Parshall, General Delivery, Highland Grove, ON K0L 2A0.

Canadian Jewish News, (50/yr) Jewish Organizations in Canada, Patricia Rucker, 10 Gateway Blvd., Ste. 420, Don Mills, ON M3C 3A1. Tel. (416)422-2331. Fax (416)422-3790

Canadian Jewish Outlook, (8/yr) Jewish Organizations in Canada, Henry M. Rosenthal, 6184 Ash St., #3, Vancouver, BC V5Z 3G9. Tel. (604)324-5101. Fax (604)325-2470

Canadian Lutheran, (bi-m) Lutheran Church—Canada, Robert Hallman, 270 Lawrence Ave., Kitchener, ON N2M 1Y4. Tel. (519)578-7420. Fax (519)742-8091

Canadian Orthodox Messenger, (q) Orthodox Church in America (Canada Section), Rhoda Zion, P.O. Box 179, Spencerville, ON K0E 1X0.

Canadian Trumpeter Canada-West, (bi-m) The Church of God of Prophecy in Canada, Vernon Van Deventer, 130 Centre St., Strathmore, AB T1P 1G9. Tel. (403)934-4787. Fax (403)934-4787

Caravan: A Resource for Adult Religious Education, (q) The Roman Catholic Church in Canada, Joanne M. Chafe, 90 Parent Ave., Ottawa, ON K1N 7B1. Tel. (613)241-9461. Fax (613)241-8117

Catalyst, The, (10/yr) Nondenominational, Andrew Brouwer, 229 College St. #311, Toronto, ON M5T 1R4. Tel. (416)979-2443. Fax (416)979-2458

Catholic New Times, (bi-w) The Roman Catholic Church in Canada, Anne O'Brien, 80 Sackville St., Toronto, ON M5A 3E5. Tel. (416)361-0761

Catholic Times, The, (10/yr) The Roman Catholic Church in Canada, Eric Durocher, 2005 St. Marc St., Montreal, QC H3H 2G8. Tel. (514)937-2301. Fax (514)937-5548

Central Canada Clarion, (q) The Wesleyan Church of Canada, S. Allan Summers, 3 Applewood Dr., Ste. 102, Belleville, ON K8P 4E3. Tel. (613)966-7527. Fax (613)968-6190

Channels, (q) The Presbyterian Church in Canada, J. H. Kouwenberg, 5800 University Blvd., Vancouver, BC V6T 2E4. Tel. (604)224-3245. Fax (604)224-3097

China and Ourselves, (q) Interdenominational, Cynthia K. McLean, 129 St. Clair Ave. W., Toronto, ON M4V 1N5. Tel. (416)921-1923. Fax (416)921-3843

Christian Courier, (w) Nondenominational, Bert Witvoet, 261 Martindale Rd., Unit 4, St. Catharines, ON L2W 1A1. Tel. (905)682-8311. Fax (905)682-8313

Church News, (w) The Church of Jesus Christ of Latter-day Saints in Canada, Dell Van Orden, Box 1257, Salt Lake City, UT 84110.

Clarion: The Canadian Reformed Magazine, (bi-w) Canadian and American Reformed Churches, J. Geertsema, One Beghin Ave., Winnipeg, MB R2J 3X5. Tel. (204)663-9000. Fax (204)663-9202

Coast to Coast, (q) Presbyterian Church in America (Canadian Section), J. Cameron Fraser, Box 490, Sechelt, BC V0N 3A0. Tel. (604)885-9707. Fax (604)885-4696

College News & Updates, (6/yr) Church of God (Anderson, Ind.), Bruce Kelly, 4704 - 55 St., Camrose, AB T4V 2B6. Tel. (403)672-0171. Fax (403)672-6888

Communicator, The, (4/yr) The Roman Catholic Church in Canada, Ron Pickersgill, Box 2400, London, ON N6A 4G3. Tel. (519)439-7514. Fax (519)439-0207

Companion Magazine, (m) The Roman Catholic Church in Canada, Philip Kelly, Station F, Toronto, ON M4Y 2L8. Tel. (416)463-5442

Connexions, (4/yr) Interdenominational, Ulli Diemer, P.O. Box 158, Stn. D, Toronto, ON M6P 3J8. Tel. (416)537-3949

Covenant Messenger, The, (m) The Evangelical Covenant Church of Canada, Mark Evinger, RR 2, Wetaskiwin, AB T9A 1W9. Tel. (403)352-2721. Fax (403)352-2721

Crux, (q) Nondenominational, Donald Lewis, Regent College, 5800 University Blvd., Vancouver, BC V6T 2E4. Tel. (604)224-3245. Fax (604)224-3097

Diary, The, Old Order Amish Church, Don Carpenter, P.O. Box 98, Gordonville, PA 17529.

Die Botschaft, Old Order Amish Church, James Weaver, Brookshire Publishing, Inc., 200 Hazel St., Lancaster, PA 17603. Tel. (717)392-1321. Fax (717)392-2078

Dimanche et Fête, (6/yr) The Roman Catholic Church in Canada, La Revue Vie Liturgique, Inc., 1073 boul. René Lévesque Ouest, Sillery, QC G1S 4R5. Tel. (418)688-1211. Fax (418)688-0868

Discover the Bible, (w) The Roman Catholic Church in Canada, Guy Lajoie, P.O. Box 2400, London, ON N6A 4G3. Tel. (519)439-7211. Fax (519)439-0207

EMMC Recorder, (m) Evangelical Mennonite Mission Conference, Henry Dueck, Box 52059, Niakwa P.O., Winnipeg, MB R2M 5P9. Tel. (204)253-7929. Fax (204)256-7384

Ecumenism/Oecuménisme, (q) Interdenominational, Thomas Ryan, 2065 Sherbrooke St. W, Montreal, QC H3H 1G6. Tel. (514)937-9176. Fax (514)935-5497

Edge, The, (m) The Salvation Army in Canada, Bruce Power, 455 N. Service Rd. E, Oakville, ON L6H 1A5. Tel. (416)845-9235. Fax (416)845-1966

Eesti Kirik, (q) The Estonian Evangelical Lutheran Church, Dean Edgar Heinsoo, 383 Jarvis St., Toronto, ON M5B 2C7. Tel. (416)925-5465

En Evant!, (w) The Salvation Army in Canada, David McCann, 455 N. Service Rd. E, Oakville, ON L6H 1A5. Tel. (416)845-9235. Fax (416)845-1966

Ensign, The, (m) The Church of Jesus Christ of Latter-day Saints in Canada, Jay Todd, 50 E. Temple St., Salt Lake City, UT 84110.

Enterprise, (q) Canadian Baptist Federation, Frank M. Byrne, 7185 Millcreek Dr., Mississauga, ON L5N 5R4. Tel. (905)821-3533. Fax (905)826-3441

Esprit, (bi-m) Evangelical Lutheran Church in Canada, Gwen Hawkins, 1512 St. James St., Winnipeg, MB R3H 0L2. Tel. (204)786-6707. Fax (204)783-7548

Evangelical Baptist Magazine, (m) The Fellowship of Evangelical Baptist Churches in Canada, Terry D. Cuthbert, 679 Southgate Dr., Guelph, ON N1G 4S2. Tel. (519)821-4830. Fax (519)821-9829

Expression, (q) Canadian Conference of Mennonite Brethren Churches, Victor Neufeld, 225 Riverton Ave., Winnipeg, MB R2L 0N1. Tel. (204)667-9576. Fax (204)669-6079

Faith Today, (bi-m) Interdenominational, Brian C. Stiller, Box 8800, Sta. B, Willowdale, ON M2K 2R6. Tel. (416)479-5885. Fax (416)479-4742

Family Life, (11/yr) Old Order Amish Church, Joseph Stoll, Rt. 4, Aylmer, ON N5H 2R3.

Fellowship Magazine, (5/yr) Nondenominational, Lori Gwynne, Box 237, Barrie, ON L4M 4T3. Tel. (705)737-0114. Fax (705)726-7160

Free Methodist Herald, The, (m) Free Methodist Church in Canada, Donald G. Bastian, 4315 Village Centre Ct., Mississauga, ON L4Z 1S2. Tel. (905)848-2600. Fax (905)848-2603

Glad Tidings, (10/yr) The Presbyterian Church in Canada, L. June Stevenson, Women's Missionary Society, 50 Wynford Dr., Don Mills, ON M3C 1J7. Tel. (416)441-1111. Fax (416)441-2825

Global Village Voice, (q) The Roman Catholic Church in Canada, Jack J. Panozzo, 3028 Danforth Ave., Toronto, ON M4C 1N2. Tel. (416)698-7770. Fax (416)698-8269

Good News West, (bi-m) Churches of Christ in Canada, Jim Hawkins, 3460 Shelbourne St., Victoria, BC V8P 4G5. Tel. (604)592-4914. Fax (604)592-4945

Good Tidings, (m) Pentecostal Assemblies of Newfoundland, Roy D. King, 57 Thorburn Rd., P.O. Box 8895, Sta. A, St. John's, NF A1B 3T2. Tel. (709)753-6314. Fax (709)753-4945

Gospel Contact, The, (4/yr) Church of God (Anderson, Ind.), John D. Campbell, 4717 56th St., Camrose, AB T4V 2C4. Tel. (403)672-0772. Fax (403)672-6888

Gospel Herald, (m) Churches of Christ in Canada, Eugene C. Perry and Wayne Turner, 4904 King St., Beamsville, ON L0R 1B6. Tel. (416)563-7503. Fax (416)563-7503

Gospel Standard, The, (m) Nondenominational, Perry F. Rockwood, Box 1660, Halifax, NS B3J 3A1. Tel. (902)423-5540

Gospel Tidings, (m) Independent Holiness Church, R. E. Votary, Box 194, Sydenham, ON K0H 2T0. Tel. (613)376-3114

Gospel Witness, The, (18/yr) Association of Regular Baptist Churches (Canada), W. P. Bauman, 130 Gerrard St. E, Toronto, ON M5A 3T4. Tel. (416)925-3261. Fax (416)925-8305

Grail, (q) Interdenominational, Michael W. Higgins, Univ. of St. Jerome's College, Waterloo, ON N2L 3G3. Tel. (519)884-8110. Fax (519)884-5759

Hallelujah, (bi-m) The Bible Holiness Movement, Wesley H. Wakefield, Box 223, Postal Stn. A, Vancouver, BC V6C 2M3. Tel. (604)498-3895

Herold der Wahrheit, (m) Old Order Amish Church, Cephas Kauffman, 1829 110th St., Kalona, IA 52247.

Horizons, (bi-m) The Salvation Army in Canada, Dudley Coles, 455 N. Service Rd. E, Oakville, ON L6H 1A5. Tel. (416)845-9235. Fax (416)845-1966

Huron Church News, (10/yr) The Anglican Church of Canada, Roger McCombe, 220 Dundas St., 4th Fl., London, ON N6A 1H3. Tel. (519)434-6893. Fax (519)673-4151

IdeaBank, (q) Canadian Conference of Mennonite Brethren Churches, David Wiebe, Christian Ed. Office, 3-169 Riverton Ave., Winnipeg, MB R2L 2E5. Tel. (204)669-6575. Fax (204)654-1865

In Holy Array, (9/yr) Canadian and American Reformed Churches, E. Kampen, Canadian Ref. Young Peoples' Societies, 7949-202A St. RR 4, Langley, BC V3A 4P7. Tel. 604-888-1087

Insight Into, (bi-m) Netherlands Reformed Congregations of North America, H. Hofman, 46660 Ramona Dr., Chilliwack, BC V2P 7W6. Tel. (604)792-3755

Insight: A Resource for Adult Religious Education, The Roman Catholic Church in Canada, Joanne M. Chafe, 90 Parent Ave., Ottawa, ON K1N 7B1. Tel. (613)241-9461. Fax (613)241-8117

Intercom, (q) The Fellowship of Evangelical Baptist Churches in Canada, Terry D. Cuthbert, 679 Southgate Dr., Guelph, ON N1G 4S2. Tel. (519)821-4830. Fax (519)821-9829

Iskra, (bi-w) Union of Spiritual Communities of Christ (Orthodox Doukhobors in Canada), Elizabeth Semenoff, Box 760, Grand Forks, BC V0H 1H0. Tel. (604)442-8252. Fax (604)442-3433

Jewish Post and News, (w) Jewish Organizations in Canada, Matt Bellan, 117 Hutchings St., Winnipeg, MB R2X 2V4. Tel. (204)694-3332

Jewish Standard, (semi-m) Jewish Organizations in Canada, Julius Hayman, 77 Mowat Ave., Ste. 016, Toronto, ON M6K 3E3. Tel. (416)537-2696. Fax (416)789-3872

Journal of Psychology and Judaism, (q) Jewish Organizations in Canada, Reuven P. Bulka, 1747 Featherston Dr., Ottawa, ON K1H 6P4. Tel. (613)731-9119. Fax (613)521-0067

L'Église Canadienne, (15/yr) The Roman Catholic Church in Canada, Rolande Parrot, 1073 boul. St-Cyrille ouest, Sillery, QC G1S 4R5. Tel. (418)688-1211. Fax (418)681-0304

Lien, Le, (11/yr) Canadian Conference of Mennonite Brethren Churches, Annie Brosseau, 1775 Édouard-Laurin, St. Laurent, QC H4L 2B9. Tel. (514)331-0878. Fax (514)331-0879

Liturgie, Foi et Culture (Bulletin natl. de liturgie), (4/yr) The Roman Catholic Church in Canada, Service des Éditions de la CECC, Office national de liturgie, 3530 rue Adam, Montréal, QC H1W 1Y8. Tel. (514)522-4930. Fax (514)522-1557

Mandate, (6/yr) The United Church of Canada, Rebekah Chevalier, Div. of Communication, 85 St. Clair Ave. E, Toronto, ON M4T 1M8. Tel. (416)925-5931. Fax (416)925-9692

Mantle, The, (m) Independent Assemblies of God—Canada, A. W. Rassmussen, M.Div., P.O. Box 2130, Laguna Hills, CA 92654-9901. Tel. (714)859-0946. Fax (714)859-0683

Marketplace, The: A Magazine for Christians in Business, (m) Interdenominational Mennonite, Wally Kroeker, 302-280 Smith St., Winnipeg, MB R3C 1K2. Tel. (204)944-1995. Fax (204)942-4001

Mennonite Brethren Herald, (bi-w) Canadian Conference of Mennonite Brethren Churches, Ron Geddert, 3-169 Riverton Ave., Winnipeg, MB R2L 2E5. Tel. (204)669-6575. Fax (204)654-1865

Mennonite Historian, (q) Interdenominational Mennonite, Abe Dueck and Lawrence Klippenstein, Ctr. for Menn. Brethren Studies, 169 Riverton Ave., Winnipeg, MB R2L 2E5. Tel. (204)669-6575. Fax (204)654-1865

Mennonite Reporter, (bi-w) Conference of Mennonites in Canada, Ron Rempel, 3-312 Marsland Dr., Waterloo, ON N2J 3Z1. Tel. (519)884-3810. Fax (519)884-3331

Mennonitische Post, Die, (bi-m) Interdenominational Mennonite, Isbrand Hiebert, Box 1120, 383 Main St., Steinbach, MB R0A 2A0. Tel. (204)326-6790. Fax (204)326-6302

Mennonitische Rundschau, (bi-w) Canadian Conference of Mennonite Brethren Churches, Lorina Marsch, 3-169 Riverton Ave., Winnipeg, MB R2L 2E5. Tel. (204)669-6575. Fax (204)654-1865

Messenger (of the Sacred Heart), (m) The Roman Catholic Church in Canada, F. J. Power, Apostleship of Prayer, 661 Greenwood Ave., Toronto, ON M4J 4B3. Tel. (416)466-1195

Messenger of Truth, Church of God in Christ (Mennonite), Gladwin Koehn, P.O. Box 230, Moundridge, KS 67107. Tel. (316)345-2532. Fax (316)345-2582

Messenger, The, (bi-w) The Evangelical Mennonite Conference, Menno Hamm, Bd. of Church Ministries, Box 1268, Steinbach, MB R0A 2A0. Tel. (204)326-6401. Fax (204)326-1613

Messenger, The, (4/yr) Church of God (Anderson, Ind.), Paul C. Kilburn, 65 Albacore Cres., Scarborough, ON M1H 2L2. Tel. (416)431-9800

Ministry to Women Sketch, The, The Salvation Army in Canada, David E. Hammond, 455 N. Service Rd. E, Oakville, ON L6H 1A5. Tel. (416)845-9235. Fax (416)845-1966

Monitor, The, (m) The Roman Catholic Church in Canada, Patrick J. Kennedy, P.O. Box 986, St. John's, NF A1C 5M8. Tel. (709)739-6553. Fax (709)739-6458

National Bulletin on Liturgy, (4/yr) The Roman Catholic Church in Canada, J. Frank Henderson, Novalis, P.O. Box 990, Outremont, QC H2V 4S7. Tel. (514)948-1222

New Church Canadian, (q) General Church of the New Jerusalem, Glenn Alden, 40 Chapel Hill Dr., Kitchener, ON N2G 3W5. Tel. (519)748-5302

New Freeman, The, (w) The Roman Catholic Church in Canada, Theresa M. Nowlan, One Bayard Dr., Saint John, NB E2L 3L5. Tel. (506)632-9226. Fax (506)632-9272

Newfoundland Churchmen, (m) The Anglican Church of Canada, William Abraham, 28 Woodwynd St., St. John's, NF A1A 3C9. Tel. (709)754-7627. Fax (709)576-7122

News of Quebec, (q) Christian Brethren (also known as Plymouth Brethren), Richard Strout, 222 Alexander St., P.O. Box 1054, Sherbrooke, QC J1H 5L3. Tel. (819)820-1693. Fax (819)821-9287

Nor Serount, (m) The Armenian Church of North America, Diocese of Canada, Antranik Tchilingirian, 20 Progress Ct., Scarborough, ON M1G 3T5. Tel. (416)431-3001. Fax (416)431-0269

PMC: The Practice of Ministry in Canada, (4-5/yr) Interdenominational, Jim Taylor, P.O. Box 700, Winfield, BC V0H 2C0. Tel. (604)766-2778. Fax (604)766-2736

Passport, (q) Interdenominational, Donna Lynne Erickson, Briercrest Schools, 510 College Dr., Caronport, SK S0H 0S0. Tel. (306)756-3200. Fax (306)756-3359

Pentecostal Testimony, (m) The Pentecostal Assemblies of Canada, Richard P. Hiebert, 6745 Century Ave., Mississauga, ON L5N 6P7. Tel. (905)542-7400. Fax (905)542-7313

Peoples Magazine, The, (q) Paul B. Smith, 374 Sheppard Ave. E, Toronto, ON M2N 3B6. Tel. (416)222-3341. Fax (416)222-3344

Pourastan, (m) The Armenian Church of North America, Diocese of Canada, V. Ketli, 615 Stuart Ave., Montreal, QC H2V 3H2. Tel. (514)279-3066. Fax (514)276-9960

Présence, (8/yr) The Roman Catholic Church in Canada, Louis Lesage, Pères Dominicains, 2715 chemin de la Côte St. Catherine, Montréal, QC H3T 1B6. Tel. (514)739-9797. Fax (514)739-1664

Prairie Messenger, (w) The Roman Catholic Church in Canada, Andrew M. Britz, Box 190, Muenster, SK S0K 2Y0. Tel. (306)682-5215. Fax (306)682-5285

Presbyterian Record, (m) The Presbyterian Church in Canada, John Congram, 50 Wynford Dr., North York, ON M3C 1J7. Tel. (416)441-1111. Fax (416)441-2825

Quaker Concern, (q) Canadian Yearly Meeting of the Religious Society of Friends, Canadian Friends Service Committee, 60 Lowther Ave., Toronto, ON M5R 1C7.

Reformed Perspective: A Magazine for the Christian Fam., (m) Canadian and American Reformed Churches, C. L. Stam, Box 12, Transcona Postal Sta., Winnipeg, MB R2C 2Z5. Tel. (204)663-9000. Fax (204)663-9200

Relations, (m) The Roman Catholic Church in Canada, Carolyn Sharp, 25 ouest, Jarry, Montreal, QC H2P 1S6. Tel. (514)387-2541. Fax (514)387-0206

Religion—Communications for Worship, (6/yr) Nondenominational, Wili Liberman, Box 35, 20 Wellington St. E., Aurora, ON L4G 3H1. Tel. (416)830-4300. Fax (416)853-5096

Resource: The National Leadership Magazine, (5/yr) The Pentecostal Assemblies of Canada, Richard P. Hiebert, 6745 Century Ave., Mississauga, ON L5N 6P7. Tel. (905)542-7400. Fax (905)542-7313

Revival Fellowship, (q) Interdenominational, Dan Erickson, Canadian Revival Fellowship, Box 584, Regina, SK S4P 3A3. Tel. (306)522-3685. Fax (306)522-3686

Rupert's Land News, (10/yr) The Anglican Church of Canada, J. D. Caird, 935 Nesbitt Bay, Winnipeg, MB R3T 1W6. Tel. (214)453-6130

SR: Studies in Religion: Sciences religieuses, (q) Nondenominational, Peter Richardson, c/o Wilfrid Laurier University Press, Waterloo, ON N2L 3C5. Tel. (416)978-7149. Fax (416)978-8854

St. Luke Magazine, (m) Christ Catholic Church, Donald W. Mullan, 5165 Palmer Ave., Niagara Falls, ON L2E 3T9. Tel. (905)354-2329

Saints Herald, (m) Reorganized Church of Jesus Christ of Latter Day Saints, Roger Yarrington, Herald House Canada, 390 Speedvale Ave., E., Guelph, ON N1E 1N5.

Sally Ann, (m) The Salvation Army in Canada, Margaret Hammond, 455 N. Service Rd. E, Oakville, ON L6H 1A5. Tel. (416)845-9235. Fax (416)845-1966

Saskatchewan Anglican, (10/yr) The Anglican Church of Canada, W. Patrick Tomalin, 1501 College Ave., Regina, SK S4P 1B8. Tel. (306)522-1608. Fax (306)352-6808

Scarboro Missions, (9/yr) The Roman Catholic Church in Canada, G. Curry, 2685 Kingston Rd., Scarborough, ON M1M 1M4. Tel. (416)261-7135. Fax (416)261-0820

Servant Magazine, (bi-m) Interdenominational, Phil Callaway, Prairie Bible Institute, Box 4000, Three Hills, AB T0M 2N0. Tel. (403)443-5511. Fax (403)443-5540

Servant, The, (q) Interdenominational Mennonite, Doreen Klassen, Steinbach Bible College, Box 1420, Steinbach, MB R0A 2A0. Tel. (204)326-6451. Fax (204)326-6908

Shantyman, The, (bi-m) Nondenominational, Arthur C. Dixon, 6981 Millcreek Dr., Unit 17, Mississauga, ON L5N 6B8. Tel. (416)821-1175. Fax (416)821-8400

Tidings, (10/yr) United Baptist Convention of the Atlantic Provinces, Margaret Ryan, 100 Arlington Dr., Moncton, NB E1E 3J1. Tel. (506)382-5654

Topic, (m) The Anglican Church of Canada, Lorie Chortyk, #302-814 Richards St., Vancouver, BC V6B 3A7. Tel. (604)684-6306. Fax (604)684-7017

Trait D'Union, Le, (4-5/yr) Union d'Eglises Baptistes Françaises au Canada, Franky Narcisse, 2285 Ave. Papineau, Montréal, QC H2K 4J5. Tel. (514)526-6643

United Church Observer, (m) The United Church of Canada, Muriel Duncan, 84 Pleasant Blvd., Toronto, ON M4T 2Z8. Tel. (416)960-8500. Fax (416)960-8477

Update, (bi-m) Lutheran Church—Canada, Robert Hallman, 270 Lawrence Ave., Kitchener, ON N2M 1Y4. Tel. (519)578-7420. Fax (519)742-8091

Vie Chrétienne, La, (French, m) The Presbyterian Church in Canada, Jean Porret, 2302 Goyer, Montréal, QC H3S 1G9. Tel. (514)737-4168

Vie des Communautés religieuses, La, (5/yr) The Roman Catholic Church in Canada, Laurent Boisvert, 5750 boul. Rosemont, Montréal, QC H1T 2H2. Tel. (514)259-6911. Fax (514)259-7407

Visnyk: The Herald, (m) Ukrainian Orthodox Church of Canada, Stephan Jarmus, 9 St. John's Ave., Winnipeg, MB R2W 1G8. Tel. (204)582-0996. Fax (204)582-5241

Voce Evangelica/Evangel Voice, (q) The Italian Pentecostal Church of Canada, Joseph Manafo and Daniel Ippolito, 6724 Fabre St., Montreal, QC H2G 2Z6. Tel. (416)766-6692. Fax (416)766-8014

War Cry, The, (w) The Salvation Army in Canada, David E. Hammond, 455 N. Service Rd. E, Oakville, ON L6H 1A5. Tel. (416)845-9235. Fax (416)845-1966

Word Alive, (5/yr) Nondenominational, Dwayne Janke, Wycliffe Bible Translators of Canada, Box 3068, Stn. B, Calgary, AB T2M 4L6. Tel. (403)250-5411. Fax (403)250-2623

Young Companion, (11/yr) Old Order Amish Church, Joseph Stoll and Christian Stoll, Rt. 4, Aylmer, ON N5H 2R3.

Young Soldier, The, (w) The Salvation Army in Canada, Judy Power, 455 N. Service Rd. E, Oakville, ON L6H 1A5. Tel. (416)845-9235. Fax (416)845-1966

12. INTERNATIONAL CONGREGATIONS

This directory lists International Congregations seeking to serve an international and ecumenical constituency using the English language.

The churches are listed within global regions and then alphabetically by country.

This list was provided by INTERNATIONAL CONGREGATIONS/Christians Abroad, 475 Riverside Dr., 6th Floor, New York, NY 10115-0050. Tel. (212)870-2463. Fax (212)870-3112.

EUROPE

Albania
International Protestant Assembly of Tirana, a/o MAF for Tirana, Wiesenweg 39, 5102 Rupperswil, Switzerland. Tel. (42) 23262 Fax 42-34708

Austria
Vienna Community Church, Schelleingasse #2/6, A-1040 Vienna. Tel. (0222)50 55 233

United Methodist Church, Sechshauser Strasse 56, A-1150 Vienna. Tel. (01)83 62 67

Belgium
American Protestant Church, Kapelsesteenweg 637 B-2180 Ekeren, Antwerp. Tel. (03)665 37 05

International Protestant Church, Kattenberg, 19 (campus of Int'l School), B-1170 Brussels. Tel. (02)673 05 81 or 660 27 10

Denmark
International Church, Gjorlingsvej 10 DK-2900 Hellerup. Tel. (031) 62 47 85

England
American Church in London, Whitefield Memorial Church, Tottenham Court Road, 79A London WIP 9HB. Tel. (071) 580 2791 or 722 58 46 Fax (071)580 5013

St. Anne & St. Agnes Church, 8 Collingham Gardens, London SW5 OHW. Tel. (071) 373 5566 or (081) 769 2677

International Community Church, Vine House, 41 Portsmouth Road, Cobham, Surrey KT11 1QJ. Tel. (0932) 868 283 or 222 781 Fax 932 868 927

Estonia
International Christian Fellowship, Meeting at Puhavaium Church, Tallinn. Tel. (358) (090) 446 776

Finland
International Evangelical Church, Runeberginkatu 39 A 56 SF-00100 Helsinki. Tel. (0) 406 091 or 684 8051

France
Holy Trinity Episcopal Church, 11 rue de la Buffa, F-06000 Nice. Tel. (093) 87 19 83

American Cathedral of the Holy Trinity, 23 Avenue George V, F-75008 Paris. Tel. (01)47 20 17 92

American Church in Paris, 65 Quai d'Orsay, F-75007 Paris. Tel. (01) 47 05 07 99 or 45 55 98 48

Germany
American Church in Berlin, Onkel Tom Strasse 93 D-1000 Berlin 37. Tel. (030) 813 2021

American Protestant Church, c/o American Embassy, Unit 21701, Box 270, APO AE 09080. Tel. (0228) 374 193 or 373 831

Church of Christ the King, Sebastian Rinzstrasse 22, D-6000 Frankfurt am Main 1. Tel. (069) 550 184

Trinity Lutheran Church, Am Schwalbenschwanz 37, D-6000 Frankfort am Main 50. Tel. (069) 599 478, 512 552 or 598 602. Fax (069) 599 845

United Methodist Church, Ministries with Laity Abroad, Kirchenkanzlei, Wilhelm-Leuschner 8, D-6000 Frankfurt (M) 1. Tel. (069) 239 373 or (06192) 41554. Fax (069) 239 375

Kaiserslautern Lutheran Church, Bruchstrasse 10, D-6750 Kaiserslautern. Tel. (0631) 92 210

Church of the Ascension, Seyboth Strasse 4, D-8000 Munich 90. Tel. (089) 648 185

Peace United Methodist Church, Frauenlobstrasse 5, D-80337 Munich. Tel. (089) 265 091 or 300 6100

Greece
St. Andrew's Protestant Church, Xenopoulou 5, GR-15451 New Psychiko, Athens. Tel. (01) 647 9585 or 277 0964 Fax (01) 652 8191

Hungary
International Church, Box 44, Budapest 1525. Tel./Fax (01) 176 4518

Italy
St. James Episcopal Church, Via Bernardo Rucellai 13, Florence, I-50123. Tel. (055) 294 417

All Saints Anglican Church, Via del Babuino 153B, Rome I-00187. Tel. (06) 679 4357

St. Andrew's Church, Via XX Settembre 7, Rome I-00187. Tel. (06) 482 7627

Ponte Sant'Angelo Methodist Church, Via del Banco di Santo Spirito, 3, Rome I-00186. Tel. (06) 475 1627

Rome Baptist Church, Piazza San Lorenzo in Lucina, 35, Rome I-00186. Tel. (06) 892 6487 or 687 6652

St. Paul's Within the Walls, Via Napoli 58, Rome I-00184. Tel. (06) 474 3569 or 463 339

Protestant English Church, Chiesa Evanglica Valdese, Via S. Pio V 15, 17 Turin I-10125. Tel (011) 669 28 38 or 650 26 01 Fax (011) 65 75 42

The Netherlands
Trinity Church Eindhoven, Pensionaat Eikenburg Chapel, c/o Prof. van der Grintenlann, 18 NL-5652 Eindhoven. Tel. (040) 512 580

American Protestant Church, Esther de Boer Van Rijklaan, 20, NL-2597 TJ The Hague. Tel. (070) 324 44 90 or 324 44 91

Norway

American Lutheran Congregation, Postboks 3012, Elisenberg N-0207 Oslo 2. Tel. (02) 22 44 35 84 or 22 53 26 17

Stavanger International Church, Vaisenhusgt 41, 4012 Stavanger. Tel. (0474) 56 48 43 or 52 21 21

Poland

Warsaw International Church, ul. Obserwatorow 13, 02-714 Warszawa. Tel. 43 29 70

Russia

Moscow Protestant Chaplaincy, c/o AmEmbassy, Moscow APO AE 09721. Tel. (095) 143 3562 or 432-1532

Spain

Community Church of Madrid, Los Alamos, Portal 9, 2-A E-28016 Colmenarejo (Madrid). Tel. (01) 302 0176

Sweden

Immanuel International Church, Kungstensgatan 17, S-113 57 Stockholm. Tel. (08) 15 12 25 or 673 68 03 Fax (08) 31 53 25

International Church of Stockholm, Box 2122, S-103 13 Stockholm. Tel. (08) 723 3029 Fax (08) 21 31 09

Switzerland

Emmanuel Episcopal/American Church, 3 rue de Monthoux, CH-1201 Geneva. Tel. (022) 732 8078

Evangelical Lutheran Church, 20 rue Verdaine, CH- 1204 Geneva. Tel. (022) 310 50 89 or 348 75 95 Fax (022) 798 86 16

International Church, Swiss Methodist Ch., Hirtenhofstr. 52, CH-6005 Luzern Tel. (041) 44 39 16

International Protestant Church/Zurich, French Reformed Church, Haringstrasse 20, CH-8001 Zurich. Tel. (01) 262 5525 or (01) 825 6483

MIDDLE EAST

Bahrain

National Evangelical Church, P.O. Box 1, Manama. Tel. 254 508

Egypt

Alexandria Community Church, P.O. Box 258, Saraya, Alexandria E-21411. Tel. (03) 857 525

Heliopolis Community Church, 25 Ramses Street, E-11341 Heliopolis, Cairo. Tel. (02) 290 9885

St. Andrew's United Church, Box 367, Dokki, Cairo. Tel. (02) 759 451 or 360 3527

Maadi Community Church, Box 218 Maadi, Cairo. Tel. (02) 351 2755 or 353 2118

Jerusalem

Church of the Redeemer, P.O. Box 14076, Old City 91140, Jerusalem. Tel. (02) 89 47 50 or 82 84 01 Fax (02) 89 46 10

Kuwait

National Evangelical Church, P.O. Box 80 Safat, 13001. Tel. 243 1087

Libya

Union Church of Tripoli, Box 6397, Tripoli. Tel. (021) 70531

Oman

Protestant Church in Muscat, P.O. Box 4982 Ruwi. Tel. 70 23 72

Salalah English-Speaking Congregation, Salalah Christian Centre, P.O. Box 19742, Salalah. Tel. 23 56 77

Tunisia

Community Church in Tunis, 5 rue des Protestants, 1006 Tunis, Bab Souika. Tel. (01) 24 36 48

Turkey

Union Church of Istanbul, Istiklal Caddesi 485 TR-80050 Beyoglu, Istanbul. Tel. (1) 244 5212 or 244 5763 Fax (1) 293-0509

United Arab Emirates

United Christian Church of Dubai, P.O. Box 8684, Dubai. Tel (04) 697 629

AFRICA

Kenya

Uhuru Hiway Lutheran Church, P.O. Box 44685, Nairobi

Methodist Community Church, P.O. Box 25030, Nairobi

South Africa

St. Peter's by the Lake, P.O. Box 72023 - Parkview 2122, Johannesburg. Tel. (011) 646 5740

Tanzania

International English Congregation, Azania Front Lutheran Church, P.O. Box 1594, Dar es Salaam. Tel. (051) 25127

NORTH AMERICA

Canada

Chalmers-Wesley United Church, 36 rue des Jardins, Quebec City, Quebec, Canada G1R 4L5. Tel. (418)692-2640 or (418)692-0431 Fax (418)692-3876

Illinois

O'Hare Airport Interdenominational Chapel, Mezzanine level/Terminal 2, P.O. Box 66353, Chicago, IL 60666. Tel. (708) 596-3050 or 333-0020

CENTRAL AMERICA/CARIBBEAN

Costa Rica

Escazu Christian Fellowship, Country Day School, Apartado 1462-1250, Escazu. Tel. (506) 31-5444 or 28-1211 Fax 506-28-7214

Union Church of San Jose, Apartado 4456, San Jose

Dominican Republic
Union Church of Santo Domingo with Epiphany Episcopal Church, Apartado 935, Santo Domingo. Tel. (809)689-2070 or (809)687-3707 Fax (809)685-1635 or (809)541-6550

El Salvador
Union Church of San Salvador, VIPSAL No. 238, P. O. Box 52-5364, Miami, FL 33152-5364. Tel. (503) 23 5505

Guatemala
Church Union of Guatemala, Apartado Postal 150-A, Guatemala City 01909. Tel. (502) 2-316904

Honduras
Union Christian Church, Apartado 1869, Tegucigalpa. Tel. (504) 32-3386 or 32-4454

Mexico
Union Evangelical Church, Reforma 1870-Lomas Chapultepec, Mexico City 11000 D.F. Tel. (05)520-0436 or 520-9931
Union Church of Monterrey, Apartado 1317, 64000 Monterrey, N.L. Tel. (083) 46-05-41 or 47-17-27

Panama
Balboa Union Church, Box 3664, Balboa. Tel. (507) 52-2295
Margarita Union Church, Apartado 2401, Cristobel. Tel. (507) 89 39 54 or 46 44 98
Gamboa Union Church, Apartado 44, Gamboa. Tel. (507) 56 64 70 or 56 68 30

Puerto Rico
Wesleyan Community Church, P.O. Box 2906, Guaynabo 00970. Tel.(809)720-2595 or (809)790-4818
Second Union Church of San Juan, Apolo Avenue & Mileto Street, Guaynabo 00969. Tel. (809) 720-4423 or 789-7178 Fax (809) 789-1380
Grace Lutheran Church, Calle del Parque 150, Santurce 00911. Tel. (809) 722-5372 or 722-1137
St. John's Episcopal Cathedral, P.O. Box 9262, Ponce de Leon, Santurce 00908. Tel. (809)722-3254 or 784 7883
Union Church of San Juan, 2310 Lauel Street, Punta Las Marias, Santurce 00913. Tel. (809)726-0280 or (809)726-8697

SOUTH AMERICA

Argentina
United Community Church, Avenida Santa Fe 839, Acassuso (1640), Buenos Aires. Tel. (01) 792 1375

Bolivia
Community Church, Casilla 4718, La Paz. Tel. (02) 78-6515 or 78-6525
Trinity Union Church, Santa Cruz Cooperative School, Casilla 5941, Santa Cruz. Tel. (03) 32-3091

Brazil
Campinas Community Church, Caixa Postal 1114, 13.100 Campinas, Sao Paolo.
Union Church of Rio, Caixa Postal 37154 2600, Rio de Janiero. Tel. (021) 325-8601
Fellowship Community Church, Rua Carlos Sampaio, 107, 01333-021 Bela Vista, Sao Paulo S.P. Tel. (011) 287-2294 or 844-1153

Chile
Santiago Community Church, Avenida Holanda 151, Santiago, 9

Colombia
Union Church of Bogota, Apartado Aereo 52615, Bogota. Tel. (01) 248-5115

Ecuador
Advent-St. Nicholas Lutheran/Episcopal Church, Casilla 17.03-415, Quito. Tel. (02) 23 43 91
English Christian Fellowship, Casilla 691, Quito

Peru
Union Church of Lima, Casilla 18-0298, Miraflores, Lima 18. Tel. (14) 41-1472 or 41-4882

Uruguay
Christ Church, Arocena 1907, Montevideo. Tel. (02) 61 03 00 or 60 27 11

Venezuela
United Christian Church, Apartado 60320, Caracas 1060-A. Tel. (02) 761-3901 or 751-6438 Fax (02) 761-3902
Christ Church, Apartado 10160, Maracaibo. Tel. (061) 77 548
Protestant Church of Puerto Ordaz, Apartado 229, Estado Bolivar, Puerto Ordaz, 8015A. Tel. (086) 22 89 48

ASIA

Bangladesh
Dhaka International Christian Church, American International School, P.O. Box 6010 Gulsha, Dhaka 12

China
Beijing International Christian Fellowship at the International Club, Jianguomenwai Dajie, Beijing
English-Language Christian Fellowship, St. Paul's Church, c/o Amity Foundation, 17 Da Jian Tin Xiang, Nanjing 210029 Tel. (025) 282-569

Hong Kong
Church of All Nations (Lutheran), 8 Repulse Bay, Hong Kong. Tel. 812-0375 or 873-3585 Fax 812-9508
Hong Kong Union Church, 22A Kennedy Road, Victoria. Tel. 522-1515 or 523-7247 Fax 524-0473
Kowloon Union Church, 4 Jordan Road, Kowloon. Tel. 369-3500 or 517-0691
Methodist Church, 271 Queens Road East, Wanchai. Tel. 5-757 817 or 5-849 6632

India

St. Andrew's Church, 15 B.B.D. Bag, Calcutta 700 001. Tel. (033) 20-1994

St. Paul's Cathedral, Cathedral Road, Calcutta 700 001. Tel.(033) 28-2802 or 28-5127

Church of the Redemption, Church Road (North Avenue), New Delhi 110 001. Tel. (011) 301-4458

Centenary Methodist Church, 25, Lodi Road at Flyover, New Delhi 110 003. Tel. (011) 36-5396

Free Church, 10, Sansad Marg, New Delhi 110 001. Tel. (011) 31-1331

Free Church Green Park, A24 Green Park, New Delhi 110 016. Tel. (011) 66-4574

Indonesia

Jakarta Community Church, Jalan Iskandarsyah II/176, Jakarta 12160. Tel. (021) 7723325

Japan

Kobe Union Church, 2-4-4 Nagamindai, Nada-ku, Kobe 657. Tel. (078) 871-6844 Fax (078) 871-3473

All Soul's Episcopal Church, 935 Makiminato, Urasoe City, Okinawa 901-21

Nagoya Union Church, Kinjo Church UCC, Box 170, Higashi P.O., Nagoya 461-91. Tel.(052) 932-1066 or 772-3043 Fax (052) 931-6421

St. Alban's Anglican/Episcopal Church, 6-25 Shiba-koen 3-chome, Minato-ku, Tokyo 105. Tel.(03) 431-8534 or 432-6040 Fax (03) 5472-4766

Tokyo Union Church, 7-7, Jingumae 5-chome, Shibuya-ku, Tokyo 150. Tel.(03) 3400-0047 Fax (03) 3400-1942

West Tokyo Union Church, 6-10-27 Osawa, Mitaka-shi, Tokyo 181. Tel. (0422) 31-9592 Fax (0422) 32 8140

St. Paul International Lutheran Church, 1-2-32. Fujimi, 1-chome, Chiyoda-ku, Tokyo 102. Tel.(03)3 261-3740 or 3262-8623

Yokohama Union Church, 66 Yamate-cho, Naka-ku, Yokohama 231. Tel./Fax (045) 651-5177

Korea

Seoul Union Church, Memorial Chapel at Foreigners' Cemetery Park, 144 Hapchung-Dong, Mapo-ku, Seoul 122-220. Tel. (02) 333-7393 or 333-0838 Fax (02) 333-7493

International Lutheran Church, 726-39 Hannam-2 Dong, Yongsan-ku, Seoul 140-212. Tel.(02) 794-6274 Fax (02)755-4978

Onnuri Presbyterian Church, 241-96 Sobbingo-dong, Yongsan-ku, Seoul 140-240. Tel. 741-43543 or 336-9690 Fax 741-4355

Malaysia

St. Andrew's International Church, 31 Jalan Raja Chulan. 50200 Kuala Lumpur. Tel. (03) 232-5687 Fax 230-2567

Nepal

International Protestant Congregation, Box 654, Box 654, Kathmandu. Tel.(01) 525-176 or 522 687

Pakistan

Protestant International Congregation, No. 8, St 39, F-6/1, Isalamabad. Tel(051) 818 188

International Church of Karachi, P.O. Box 12251, Karachi 75500. Tel. (021) 57 07 76

International Christian Fellowship, P.O. Box 10164, Lahore 54600. Tel. (042) 879955 or 305867

Philippines

Union Church of Manila, MCCPO Box 184, Makati, Metro Manila. Tel. (02) 818-1634 or 817-4474 Fax (01) 818-2888

Singapore

Lutheran Church of Our Redeemer, 28-30 Dukes Road, Singapore 1026. Tel. (65)466-45590 or 467-5093

Orchard Road Presbyterian Church, 3 Orchard Road, Singapore 0923. Tel. (65)337-6681

St. George's Church (Anglican), Minden Road, Tanglin, Singapore 1024. Tel. (65)473-2783

Sri Lanka

St. Andrew's Church, 73 Galle Road, Colombo 3. Tel. (01) 23765

Taiwan

Kaohsiung Community Church, 151 Ren Yi Street, Kasohsiung 80208. Tel. (07) 331-8131

Taipei International Church, Taipei American School, 4F, 438 Chung Shan North Road, Sec. 6, Tienmou, Taipei. Tel. (02) 872-4073

Thailand

International Church of Bangkok, 61/2 Soi Saen Sabai, Sukhumvit 36 (Rama IV Road), Bangkok 10110. Tel. (02) 258-5821 Fax (02) 258-5821

Evangelical Church of Bangkok, 42 Soi 10, Sukhumvit Road, Bangkok, 10110. Tel. (02)270-0693

Chiang Mai Community Church, Cort Hall, P.O. Box 18, Chiang Mai 50000. Tel. (053) 242661

OCEANIA

American Samoa

Community Christian Church, P.O. Box 1016, Pago Pago 96799. Tel. (684) 699-1544 or 699-9184

Guam

Guam United Methodist Church, P.O. Box 20279 GMF, Barrigada 96291. Tel. (761) 734-3251 or 477-8357

Papua New Guinea

Boroko Baptist Church, P.O. Box 1689, Boroko, NCD. Tel. (675) 25-4410

13. DEPOSITORIES OF CHURCH HISTORY MATERIAL

Kenneth E. Rowe
Drew University

Most American denominations have established central archival-manuscript depositories. In addition, many large communions have formed regional (conference, diocesan, synodical or provincial) depositories. Denominations with headquarters in the United States may also have churches in Canada. Historical material on Canadian sections of these denominations will occasionally be found at the various locations cited below. The reader is also referred to the section "In Canada," which follows.

The section for the United States was compiled by Kenneth E. Rowe. Neil Semple and Jean Dryden contributed to the Canadian section.

IN THE UNITED STATES

The most important general guide is *Directory of Archives and Manuscript Repositories* in the United States, 2d edition, compiled by the National Historical Publications and Records Commission. New York : Oryx Press, 1988.

Major Ecumenical Collections:
American Antiquarian Society, 185 Salisbury St., Worcester, MA 01609 Tel (617)755-5221

American Bible Society Library, 1865 Broadway, New York, NY 10023-9980. Tel (212)408-1495 FAX (212)408-1512. Peter Wosh

Amistad Research Center, Old U.S. Mint Building, 400 Esplanade Ave., New Orleans, LA 70116. Tel (504)522-0432

Billy Graham Center Archives, Wheaton College, 510 College Ave., Wheaton, IL 60187-5593. Tel (708)752-5910. Robert Schuster

Boston Public Library, Copley Square, Boston, MA 02117-0286. Tel (617)536-5400 FAX (617)236-4306

Graduate Theological Union Library, 2400 Ridge Road, Berkeley, CA 94709 Tel (415)649-2540 FAX (415)649-1417. Oscar Burdick

Harvard University (Houghton Library) Cambridge, MA 02138 Tel (617)495-2440

Howard University, Moorland-Springarn Research Center, 500 Howard Place, N.W., Washington, DC 20059 Tel (202)636-7480

Huntington Library, 1151 Oxford Road, San Marino, CA 91108 Tel (213)792-6141.

National Council of Churches Archives, in Presbyterian Church USA Office of History Library, 425 Lombard St., Philadelphia, Pa 19147. Tel (215)627-0509. FAX (215)627-0509. Gerald W. Gillette

Newberry Library, 60 W. Walton St., Chicago, IL 60610-3394. Tel (312)943-9090.

New York Public Library, Fifth Ave. & 42nd St. New York, NY 10018. Tel (212)930-0800 FAX (212)921-2546.

Schomburg Center for Research in Black Culture, 515 Malcolm X Blvd., New York, NY 10037. Tel (212)862-4000. Howard Dodson

Union Theological Seminary (Burke Library) 3041 Broadway, New York, NY 10027. Tel (212)280-1505 FAX (212)280-1416. Richard D. Spoor. Includes Missionary Research Library

University of Chicago (Regenstein Library) 1100 E.57th St. Chicago, IL 60637-1502. Tel (312)702-8740 Curtis Bochanyin

University of Texas Libraries, P.O. Box P, Austin, TX 78713-7330. Tel (512)471-3811 FAX (512)471-8901.

Yale Divinity School Library, 409 Prospect St. New Haven, CT 06510 Tel (203)432-5291. Includes Day Missions Library

Yale University (Sterling Memorial Library) 120 High St., P.O. Box 1603A Yale Station, New Haven, CT 06520. Tel (203)432-1775. FAX (203)432-7231 Katharine D. Morton

Adventist:
Andrews University (James White Library), Berrien Springs, MI 49104 Tel (616) 471-3264. Mr. Warren Johns.

Auroro University (Charles B. Phillips Library) 347 S. Gladstone, Aurora, IL 60506 Tel (708) 844-5437. Ken VanAndel. Advent Christian Church archives

Berkshire Christian College (Linden J. Carter Library) Lenox, MA 01240

Seventh Day Adventists General Conference Archives, 6840

Eastern Ave. NW, Washington, DC 20012 Tel (212)722-6000

Baptist:
American Baptist Archives Center, P.O. Box 851, Valley Forge, PA 19482-0851. Tel (215)768-2000. Beverly Carlson, administrator.

American Baptist-Samuel Colgate Historical Library, 1106 S. Goodman St., Rochester, NY 14620-2532. Tel (716)473- 1740. James R. Lynch.

Andover Newton Theological School, (Franklin Trask Library) 169 Herrick Road, Newton Centre, MA 02159 Tel (617) 964-1100. Ms. Sharon A. Taylor. Includes Backus Historical Library.

Bethel Theological Seminary Library, 3949 Bethel Dr., St. Paul, MN 55112 Tel (612)638-6184. Dr. Norris Magnuson. Swedish Baptist collection.

Elon College (Iris Holt McEwen Library) P.O. Box 187, Elon, NC 27244-2010 Tel (919)584-2479. Diane Gill, archivist. Primitive Baptist Archives.

Seventh Day Baptist Historical Society Library, 3120 Kennedy Rd., P.O. Box 1678, Janesville, WI 53547 Tel (608)752-5055. Janet Thorngate.

Southern Baptist Historical Library & Archives, 901 Commerce St., Suite 400, Nashville TN 37203-3620. Tel (615)244-0344. FAX 615-242-2153. Bill Sumner, director of library and archives.

Brethren in Christ:
Messiah College (Murray Learning Resources Center) Grantham, PA 17027-9990 Tel (717)691-6042. E. Morris Sider.

Church of the Brethren:
Bethany Theological Seminary Library, Butterfield and Meyers Roads, Oak Brook, IL 60521. Tel (708) 620-2214. Dr. Helen K. Mainelli.

Brethren Historical Library and Archives, 1451 Dundee Ave., Elgin, IL 60120 Tel (708)742-5100. Kenneth M. Shaffer Jr.

Juniata College (L. A. Beeghly Library) 18th & Moore, Huntingdon, PA 16652. Tel (814)314-6286. Peter Kupersmith.

Churches of Christ:
Abilene Christian University (Brown Library) 1700 Judge Ely Blvd., ACU Station, P.O. Box 8177, Abilene, TX 79699-8177. Tel (915)674-2344. Marsha Harper

Harding Graduate School of Religion (L.M.Graves Memorial Library) 1000 Cherry Rd., Memphis, TN 38117. (901)761-1354. Don Meredith.

Pepperdine University (Payson Library) Malibu, CA 90263. Tel (213)456-4243. Harrold Holland

Churches of God, General Conference:
University of Findlay (Shafer Library) 1000 N. Main St., Findlay, OH 45840-3695. Tel (419)424-4612. FAX (419)424-4757. Robert W. Shirmer. Archives/Museum of the Churches of God in North America.

Congregational: (See United Church of Christ)

Disciples of Christ:
Brite Divinity School Library, Texas Christian University, P.O. Box 32904, Fort Worth, TX 76219. Tel (817)921-7106. FAX (817) 921-7110. Robert Olsen, Jr.

Christian Theological Seminary Library, P.O. Box 88267, 1000 W. 42nd St., Indianapolis, IN 46208. Tel (317)924-1331. David Bundy.

Culver-Stockton College (Johnson Memorial Library) College Hill, Canton, MO 63435. Tel (314)288-5221. FAX (314)288-3984. John Sperry, Jr.

Disciples Divinity House, University of Chicago, 1156 E. 57th St., Chicago, IL 60637 Tel (312)643-4411

Disciples of Christ Historical Society Library, 1101 Nineteenth Ave., S., Nashville, TN 37212-2196. Tel (615)327- 1444. Dr. James Seale.

Lexington Theological Seminary (Bosworth Memorial Linbrary) 631 South Limestone St., Lexington, KY 40508 Tel (606)252-0361 FAX (606)281-6042. Philip N. Dare

Episcopal:
Archives of the Episcopal Church, P.O. Box 2247, 606 Rathervue Pl., Austin, TX 78768 Tel (512)472-6816. V. Nelle Bellamy

Episcopal Divinity School Library, 99 Brattle St. Cambridge, MA 02138 Tel (617)868-3450. James Dunkly

General Theological Seminary (Saint Mark's Library) 175 Ninth Ave., New York, NY 10011. Tel (212)243-5150. David Green.

Nashotah House Library, 2777 Mission Road, Nashotah, WI 53058-9793. Tel (414)646-3371 FAX (414)646-2215 Mike Tolan.

National Council, The Episcopal Church, 815 2nd Ave., New York, NY 10017. Tel (212)867-8400.

Yale Divinity School Library, 409 Prospect Street, New Haven, CT 06510 Tel (203)432-5291. Berkeley Divinity School Collection.

Evangelical and Reformed
Hartford Seminary (Educational Resources Center) 77 Sherman St., Hartford, CT 06105 Tel (203)232-4451. William Peters

Harvard Divinity Schol (Andover Harvard Theological Library) 45 Francis Ave., Cambridge, MA 02138. Tel (617)495-5770. Russell O. Pollard.

Lancaster Theological Seminary, Archives of the United Church of Christ (Philip Schaff Library) Lancaster Theological Seminary, 555 W. James St., Lancaster, PA 17603 Tel (717)393-0654. Richard R. Berg

Yale Divinity School Library, 409 Prospect Street, New Haven, CT 06510. Tel (203)432-5291

Yale University (Sterling Memorial Library) Yale University, 120 high St., Box 1603A Yale Station, New Haven, CT 06520 Tel (203)436-0907

Evangelical United Brethren:
(see United Methodist Church)

Evangelical Congregational Church:
Evangelical School of Theology (Rostad Library), 121 S. College St., Myerstown, PA 17067. Tel (717)866-5775. FAX (717) 866-4667. Terry Heisey. Historical Society Library of the Evangelical Congregational Church

Friends:
Friends' Historical Library, Swarthmore College, 500 College Ave., Swarthmore, PA 19081. Tel (215)328-8557. FAX (215)328-8673. Mary Ellen Chijioke, curator.

Haverford College (Magill Library) Haverford, PA 19041-1392. Tel (215)-896-1175. FAX (215)896-1224. Edwin Bronner

Jewish:
American Jewish Archives, 3101 Clifton Ave., Cincinnati, OH 45220 Tel (513)221-1875. Kevin Proffit.

Friedman Memorial Library, American Jewish Historical Society, 2 Thornton Rd., Waltham, MA 02154 Tel (617)891-8110. FAX (617)899-9208. Bernard Wax, director of special projects.

YIVO Institute for Jewish Research, Library & Archives, 1048 Fifth Ave., New York, NY 10028. Tel (212)535-6700. Zachary Baker, librarian; Marek Weber, archivist.

Latter-Day Saints:

Church of Jesus Christ of the Latter-Day Saints Library-Archives, Historical Department, 50 E. North Temple St., Salt Lake City, UT 84150. Tel (801)240-2745. Steven Sorenson

Family History Library, 35 North West Temple St., Salt Lake City, UT 84150. Tel (801) 240-2331 FAX (801)240-5551 David M. Mayfield.

Lutheran:

Augustana College (Swenson Swedish Immigration History Center) Box 175, Rock Island, IL 61201. Tel (309)794-7221. Kermit Westerberg.

Evangelical Lutheran Church in American Archives, 8765 West Higgins Road, Chicago, IL 60631-4198. Tel 1-800-NET-ELCA or (312)380-2818. Elisabeth Wittman

Region 1 (Alaska, Idaho, Montana, Oregon and Washington) Pacific Lutheran University (Mortvedt Library) Tacoma, WA 98447 Tel (206)535-7587 Kerstin Ringdahl

Region 2 (Arizona, California, Colorado, Hawaii, New Mexico, Nevada, Utah, Wyoming) Pacific Lutheran Theological Seminary, 2770 Marin Ave., Berkeley, CA, 94708; contact Ray Kibler III, 4249 N. LaJunta Drive, Claremont, CA 91711-3199.

Region 3 (Minnesota, North Dakota, South Dakota) Paul Daniels, Region 3 Archives, ELCA, 2481 Como Avenue West, Saint Paul, MN 55108-1445. Tel (612)641-3205

Region 4 (Arkansas, Kansas, Louisiana, Missouri, Nebraksa, Oklahoma, Texas) No archives esablished by 1992.

Region 5 (Illinois, Iowa, Wisconsin, Upper Michigan) Robert C. Wiederaenders, Region 5 Archives, ELCA, 333 Wartburg Place, Dubuque, IA 52001

Region 6 (Indiana, Kentucky, Michigan, Ohio) No archives established by 1992

Region 7 (New York, New Jersey, Eastern Pennsylvania, New England and the non-geographic Slovak-Zion Synod) John E. Peterson, Region 7 Archives, ELCA, 7301 Germantown Ave., Philadelphioa, PA 19119 Tel (215)248-4616. For Metropolitan New York Synod : David Gaise, 32 Neptune Road, Toms River, NJ 08753

Region 8 (Delaware, Maryland, Central and Western Pennsylvania, West Virginia, Washington, DC) Paul A. Mueller, Thiel College, Greenville, PA 16125 Tel (412)588-7000; (Central Pennsylvania, Delaware, Eastern Maryland, and Washington, DC) Lutheran Theological Seminary (Wentz Library) 66 Confederate Ave., Gettysburg, PA 17325 Tel (717)334-6286. Donald Matthews

Region 9 (Alabama, North and South Carolina, Florida, Georgia, Mississippi, Tennessee, Virginia, and the Caribbean Synod) Lutheran Theological Southern Seminary, 4201 N. Main St., Columbia, SC 29203-5898. Tel (803)786-5150. Lynn A. Feider

Concordia Historical Institute (Dept. of Archives and History, Lutheran Church-Missouri Synod) 801 De Mun Ave., St. Louis, MO 63105-3199. Tel (314)721-5934, Ext 320,321. August R. Suelflow

Concordia Seminary (Fuerbringer Hall library) 801 DeMun Avenue, St. Louis, MO 63105. Tel (314) 721-5934. David O. Berger.

Finnish-American Historical Archives, Suomi College, Hancock, MI 49930. Tel (906)482-5300, ext 273.

Luther College (Preus Library) Decorah, IA 52101. Tel (319)387-1191. FAX (319)382-3717. Ted Stark.

Lutheran School of Theology at Chicago (Jesuit/Kraus/ McCormick Library) 1100 East 55th St., Chicago, IL 60615 Tel (312)753-0739. Mary R. Bischoff

Saint Olaf College (Rolvaag Memorial Library) 1510 St. Olaf Ave., Northfield, MN 55057-1097. Tel (507)663-3225 Joan Olson. Norwegian Lutheran collection.

Wisconsin Lutheran Seminary Archives, 11831 N. Seminary Drive, 65W, Mequon, WI 53092. Tel (414)272-7200. Martin Westerhaus

Mennonite:

Archives of the Mennonite Church, 1700 South Main, Goshen, IN 46526. Tel (219)533-3161, Ext 477

Associated Mennonite Biblical Seminaries, Library, 1445 Boonveille Ave, Northwest Dock, Springfield, MO 65802. Tel (417)862-3344. Joseph F Marics, Jr.

Bethel College, Historical Library, P.O. Drawer A, North Newton, KS 67117-9998. Tel (316)283-2500, Ext 366. FAX (316)284-5286. Dale R. Schrag.

Bluffton College (Mennonite Historical Library) Bluffton, OH 45817 Tel (419)358-8015, ext 271.

Center for Mennonite-Brethren Studies, 4824 E. Butler, Fresno, CA 93727 Tel (209)251-7194, Ext 1055.

Eastern Mennonite College (Menno Simons Historical Library and Archives) Eastern Mennonite College, Harrisonburg, VA 22801 Tel (703)433-2771, ext 177

Goshen College (Mennonite Historical Library) Goshen, IN 46526 Tel (219)535-7418

Mennonite Historians of Eastern Pennsylvania Library and Archives, P.O. Box 82, 656 Yoder Road, Harleysville, PA 19438. Tel (215)256-3020. Joel D. Alderfer

Methodist:

Asbury Theological Seminary (B.L.Fisher Library) Wilmore, KY 40390-1199. Tel (606)858-3581. David W. Faupel

Boston University School of Theology (New England Methodist Historical Society Library) 745 Commonwealth Ave., Boston, MA 02215. Tel (617)353-3034. Stephen Pentek.

Cincinnati Historical Society (Nippert German Methodist Collection) The Museum Center, Cincinnati Union Terminal, 1301 Western Ave., Cincinnati, OH 45403. Tel (513)287-7068. Jonathan Dembo

Drew University Library, Madison, NJ 07940. Tel (201) 408-3590. Kenneth E. Rowe, Methodist Librarian.

Duke Divinity School Library, Duke University, Durham, NC 27706. Tel (919)684-3234. Roger Loyd

Emory University, Candler School of Theology (Pitts Theology Library) Atlanta, GA 30322. Tel (404)727-4166. Channing Jeschke

Free Methodist World Headquarters (Marston Memorial Historical Center) Winona Lake, IN 46590. Tel (219)267-7656. Frances Haslam

Garrett-Evangelical Theological Seminary (United Library) 2121 Sheridan Rd, Evanston, IL 60201. Tel (708)866-3900. David Himrod

General Commission on Archives and History, The United Methodist Church, PO Box 127, Madison, NJ 07940. Tel (201) 822-2787 FAX (201)408-3909 Susan M. Eltscher, Asst. Gen. Sec.

Indiana United Methodist Archives, DePauw University (Roy O. West Library) Greencastle, IN 46135. Tel (317)658-4434. FAX (317)658-4789. Wesley Wilson.

Interdenominational Theological Center (Woodruff Library) 6111 James P. Brawley Drive, S.W., Atlanta, GA 30314. Tel (404)522-8980. Joseph E. Troutman. African American Methodist collection

Livingstone College and Hood Theological Seminary (William J. Walls Heritage Center) 701 W. Monroe St., Salisbury, NC 28144 Tel (704)638-5500 A.M.E.Zion archives

Miles College (W.A.Bell Library) 5500 Avenue G., Birmingham, AL 35208 Tel (205)923-2771. C.M.E. collection

Mother Bethel African Methodist Episcopal Church, 419 South 6th St., Philadelphia, PA 19147 Tel (215)925-0616

Office of the Historiographer, African Methodist Episcopal Church, P.O. Box 301, Williamstown, MA 01267. Tel (413)597-2484 (413)458-4994. Dennis C. Dickerson, historiographer.

Paine College (Candler Library) Augusta, GA 30910 Tel (404)722-4471 C.M.E. collection

Perkins School of Theology (Bridwell Library Center for Methodist Studies) Southern Methodist University, Dallas, TX 75275-0476. Tel (214)692-3483. Dr. Richard P. Heitzenrater

United Methodist Historical Library, Beeghley Library, Ohio Wesleyan University, 43 University Ave., Delaware, OH 43015. Tel (614)369-4431, Ext 3245 FAX (614)363-0079.

United Methodist Publishing House Library, Room 122, 201 Eighth Ave., South, Nashville, TN 37202. Tel (615)749-6437. Rosalyn Lewis

United Theological Seminary (Center for Evangelical United Brethren Studies) 1810 Harvard Blvd., Dayton, OH 45406. Tel (513)278-5817. Elmer J. O'Brien

Upper Room Library, 1908 Grand Avenue, P.O. Box 189, Nashville, TN 37202-0189. Tel (615)340-7204. FAX (615)340-7006. Sarah Schaller-Linn.

Vanderbilt University, Divinity Library, 419 21st Avenue, South, Nashville, TN 37240-0007 Tel (615)322-2865. William J. Hook

Wesley Theological Seminary Library, 4500 Massachusetts Ave., NW, Washington, DC 20016 Tel (202)885-8691 Allen Mueller. Methodist Protestant Church collection

Wesleyan Church Archives & Historical Library, International Center Wesleyan Church, P.O. Box 50434, Indianapolis, IN 46250-0434 Tel (317)842-0444. Daniel L. Burnett

Wilberforce University and Payne Theological Seminary (Rembert E. Stokes Learning Resources Center) Wilberforce, OH 45384-1003 Tel (513)376-2911 ext 628 A.M.E. Archives

World Methodist Council Library, P.O. Box 518, Lake Junaluska, NC 28745 Tel (704)456-9432. Evelyn Sutton

For United Methodist annual conference depositories, see *United Methodist Church Archives and History Directory 1989-1992*. Madison, NJ : General Commission on Archives and History, UMC, 1989.

Moravian:

The Archives of the Moravian Church, 41 W. Locust St., Bethlehem, PA 18018 Tel (215)866-3255 Vernon H. Nelson

Moravian Archives, Southern Province of the Moravian Church, 4 East Bank St., Winston-Salem, NC 27101 Tel (919) 722-1742

Nazarene:

Nazarene Archives, International Headquarters, Church of the Nazarene, 6401 The Paseo, Kansas City, MO 64131. Tel (816) 333-7000, Ext 437 Stan Ingersoll

Nazarene Theological Seminary (Broadhurst Library) 1700 East Meyer Blvd., Kansas City, MO 64131. Tel (816)333-6254 William C. Miller

Pentecostal:

Assemblies of God Archives, 1445 Boonville Ave., Springfield, MO 65802.Tel (417)862-2781. Wayne Warner

Oral Roberts University Library, P.O. Box 2187,777 S. Lewis, Tulsa, OK 74171 Tel (918)495-6894. Oon-Chor Khoo

Pentecostal Research Center, Church of God (Cleveland, Tenn.), P. O. Box 3448, Cleveland, TN 37320. Tel (615)472-3361 FAX (615)478-7052. Joseph Byrd

Polish National Catholic:

Commission on History and Archives, Polish National Catholic Church, 1031 Cedar Ave., Scranton, PA 18505. Chmn., Joseph Wielczerzak

Presbyterian:

Department of History, Presbyterian Church (USA) Library, 425 Lombard St., Philadelphia, PA 19147 Tel (215)627-1852 FAX (215)627-0509. Gerald W. Gillette.

Department of History, Presbyterian Church (USA), Historical Foundation Library, P.O. Box 847, Montreat, NC 28757. Tel (704)669-7061 FAX (704)669-5369. Robert Benedetto

McCormick Theological Seminary (Jesuit/Kraus/McCormick Library) 1100 East 55th St., Chicago, IL 60615 (312)753-0739 Mary R.Bischoff

Princeton Theological Seminary (Speer Library) Library Place and Mercer St., P.O. Box 111, Princeton, NJ 08540 Tel (609)497-7940. James S. Irvine

Presbyterian Church in America, Historical Center,12330 Conway Rd., St. Louis, MO 63141

Reformed:

Calvin College and Seminary Library, 3207 Burton St, S.E., Grand Rapids, MI 49546 Tel (616)949-4000. Harry Boonstra (Christian Reformed)

Commission on History, Reformed Church in America, Gardner A. Sage Library, New Brunswick Theological Seminary, 21 Seminary Place, New Brunswick, NJ 08901-1159. Tel (908)247-5243 FAX (908)249-5412 Russell Gassaro

Lancaster Theological Seminary, Evangelical and Reformed Historical Society (Philip Schaff Library) 555 West James St., Lancaster, PA 17603. Tel (717)393-0654. Richard R. Berg. Reformed in the U.S., Evangelical and Reformed)

Roman Catholic:

American Catholic Historical Society, 263 S. Fourth St., Philadelphia, PA 19106 Mrs. John T. Fisher

Archives of the American Catholic Historical Society of Philadelphia, Ryan Memorial Library, St. Charles Boromeo Seminary, 1000 E. Wynnewood Rd., Overbrook, Philadelphia, PA 19096-3012. Tel (215)667-3394. FAX (215)664-7913. Joseph S. Casino

Catholic University of America (Mullen Library) 620 Michigan Ave., NE Washington, DC 20064 Tel (202)319-5055. Carolyn T. Lee.

Georgetown University (Lauinger Library) P.O.Box 37445, Washington, DC 20013-7445. Tel (202)687-7425 Eugene Rooney

St. Louis University (Pius XII Memorial Library) 3650 Lindell Blvd., St. Louis, MO 63108 Tel (314)658-3100 Thomas Tolles

St. Mary's Seminary & University (Knott Library) 5400 Roland Ave, Baltimore, MD 21210-1994. Tel (301)323-3200, Ext 64. David P. Siemsen

University of Notre Dame Archives (Hesburg Library) Box 513, Notre Dame, IN 46556 Tel (219)239-5252. Sophia K. Jordan.

Salvation Army:

The Salvation Army Archives and Research Center, 615 Slaters Lane, Alexandria, VA 22313. Tel (703)684-5500, Ext 669. Connie Nelson

Schwenkfelder:

Schwenkfelder Library, 1 Seminary Ave., Pennsburg, PA 18073. Tel (215)679-3103. Dennis Moyer

Shaker:

Ohio Historical Society, Archives Library, 1982 Velma Ave., Columbus, OH 43211-2497. Tel (614)297-2510. Wendy Greenwood

Western Reserve Historical Society, 10825 E. Blvd. Cleveland, OH 44106-1788. Tel (216)721-5722 FAX (216)721-0645. Kermit J. Pike

Swedenborgian:

Academy of the New Church Library, 2815 Huntingdon Pike, P.O. Box 278-68, Bryn Athyn, PA 19009. Tel (215)938-2547. Carroll C. Odhner

Unitarian and Universalist:

Harvard Divinity School (Andover-Harvard Theological Library) 45 Francis Ave., Cambridge, MA 02138 Tel (617)495-5770. Alan Seaburg

Meadville/Lombard Theological School Library, 5701 S. Woodlawn Ave., Chicago, IL 60637. Tel (312)753-3196 Neil W. Gerdes

Rhode Island Historical Society Library, 121 Hope St., Providence, RI 02906. Tel (401)331-8575. FAX (401)751-7930. Madeleine Telfeyan

Unitarian-Universalist Association Archives Library, 25 Beacon St., Boston, MA 02108 Tel (617)742-2100. Deborah Weiner

The United Church of Christ:

Chicago Theological Seminary (Hammond Library) 5757 University Ave., Chicago, IL 60637 Tel (312)752-5757. Neil W. Gerdes

Congregational Library, 14 Beacon St., Boston, MA 02108 Tel (617)523-0470. Harold Worthley

Eden Archives, 475 E. Lockwood Ave., Webster Groves, MO 63119-3192. Tel (314)961-3627. Lowell H. Zuck.

Wesleyan, see Methodist

STANDARD GUIDES TO CHURCH ARCHIVES

William Henry Allison, *Inventory of Unpublished Material for American Religious History in Protestant Church Archives and other Depositories* (Washington, DC, Carnegie Institution of Washington, 1910) 254 pp.

John Graves Barrow, *A Bibliography of Bibliographies in Religion* (Ann Arbor, Mich., 1955), pp. 185-198.

Edmund L. Binsfield, "Church Archives in the United States and Canada: a Bibliography," in *American Archivist*, V. 21, No. 3 (July 1958) pp. 311-332, 219 entries.

Nelson R. Burr, "Sources for the Study of American Church History in the Library of Congress," 1953. 13 pp. Reprinted from *Church History*, Vol. XXII, No. 3 (Sept. 1953).

Homer L. Calkin, *Catalog of Methodist Archival and Manuscript Collections* (Mont Alto, PA: World Methodist Historical Society, 1982) 4 vols. to date

Church Records Symposium, *American Archivist*, Vol. 24, October 1961, pp. 387-456.

Mable Deutrich, "Supplement to Church Archives in the United States and Canada, a Bibliography," Washington, DC: 1964.

Andrea Hinding, ed. *Women's History Sources: A Guide to Archives and Manuscript Collections in the U.S.* (New York: Bowker, 1979) 2 vols.

E. Kay Kirkham, *A Survey of American Church Records, for the Period Before The Civil War, East of the Mississippi River* (Salt Lake City, 1959-60) 2 vols. Includes the depositories and bibliographies.

Peter G. Mode, *Source Book and Bibliographical Guide for American Church History* (Menasha, Wisc., George Banta Publishing Co., 1921) 735 pp.

Society of American Archivists. *American Archivist*, 1936/37 (continuing). Has articles on church records and depositories.

A. R. Suelflow, *A Preliminary Guide to Church Records Repositories* (Society of American Archivists, Church Archives Committee, 1969) Lists more than 500 historical-archival depositories with denominational and religious history in America.

U. S. National Historical Publications and Records Commission, *Directory of Archives and Manuscript Repositories in the United States.* 2d edition. (New York : Oryx Press, 1988)

United States, Library of Congress, Division of Manuscripts, Manuscripts in Public and Private Collections in the United States (Washington, DC, 1924).

U. S. Library of Congress, Washington, DC: *The National Union Catalog of Manuscript Collections*, A59—22 vols., 1959-1986. Based on reports from American repositories of manuscripts. Contains many entries for collections of church archives. This series is continuing. Extremely valuable collection. Researchers must consult the cumulative indexes.

IN CANADA

A few small Canadian religious bodies have headquarters in the United States, and therefore the reader is advised to consult "Main Depositories of Church History Material and Sources in the United States," which immediately precedes this section for possible sources of information on Canadian religious groups. Another source: *Directory of Canadian Archives*, edited by Marcel Caya.

The use of the term "main" depositories in this section implies that there are some smaller communions with archival collections not listed below and also that practically every judicatory of large religious bodies (e.g., diocese, presbytery, conference) has archives excluded from this listing. For information on these collections, write directly to the denominational headquarters or to the judicatory involved.

Most American Protestant denominational archives have important primary and secondary source material relating to missionary work in Canada during the pioneer era.

Ecumenical:

Canadian Council of Churches Archives, on deposit in National Archives of Canada, 395 Wellington, Ottawa, Ontario K1A 0N3. Some records remain at the Canadian Council of Churches office located at 40 St. Clair Ave. E., Toronto, ON M4T 1M9. The National Archives of Canada also contains a large number of records and personal papers related to the various churches.

Anglican:

General Synod Archives, 600 Jarvis St., Toronto, ON M4Y 2J6. Archivist: Mrs. Terry Thompson (416)924-9192

Baptist:

Canadian Baptist Archives, McMaster Divinity College, Hamilton, ON L8S 4K1. Librarian: Judith Colwell (416)525-9140, ext. 3511

Evangelical Baptist Historical Library, 679 Southgate Dr., Guelph, ON N1G 4S2 (519)821-4830

Baptist Historical Collection, Vaughan Memorial Library, Acadia University, Wolfville, NS B0P 1X0. Archivist: Mrs. Pat Thompson (912) 542-2205

Disciples of Christ:

Canadian Disciples Archives, 39 Arkell Rd., R.R. 2, Guelph, ON N1H 6H8. Archivist: Gordon Reid (519)824-5190

Reuben Butchart Collection, E.J. Pratt Library, Victoria University, Toronto, ON M5S 1K7, (416) 585-4470

Jewish:

Jewish Historical Society of Western Canada, 404-365 Hargrave St., Winnipeg, MB R3B 2K3. Archivist: Bonnie Tregobov (204) 942-4822

Canadian Jewish Congress (Central Region) Archives, 4600 Bathurst St., Toronto, ON M3T 1Y6. Archivist: Stephen A. Speisman (416)635-2883

Lutheran:

Evangelical Lutheran Church in Canada, 1512 St. James St., Winnipeg, MB R3H 0L2. Archivist: Rev. Leon C. Gilbertson (incorporating archives of the Evangelical Lutheran Church of Canada, the Lutheran Church in America—Canada Section's Central Synod Archives and those of the Western Canada Synod) (204)786-6707. The Eastern Synod Archives are housed at Wilfrid Laurier University, Waterloo, ON N2L 3C5. Archivist: Rev. Erich R.W. Schultz (519)745-3505

Lutheran Church in Canada, Eastern Synod, 50 Queen St. N., ON N2H 6P4. Archivist: Rev. Roy Gross (519)743-1461

Concordia College, Edmonton, AB T5B 4E4. Archivist: Mrs. Hilda Robinson (405)479-8481

Mennonite:

Conrad Grebel College, Archives Centre, Waterloo, Ontario N2L 3G6. Archivist: Sam Steiner (519)885-0220

Mennonite Brethren Bible College, Centre for Mennonite Brethren Studies in Canada, 1-169 Riverton Ave., Winnipeg, MB R2L 2E5. Archivist: Kenneth Reddig (204)669-6575

Mennonite Heritage Centre. Archives of the General Conference of Mennonites in Canada, 600 Shaftesbury Blvd., Winnipeg, MB R3P 0M4. Tel (204)888-6781. Historian-archivist: Peter H. Rempel (204)888-6781

Free Methodist:

4315 Village Centre Ct., Mississauga, ON L4Z 1S2 (416)848-2600

Pentecostal:

The Pentecostal Assemblies of Canada, 6745 Century Ave., Streetsville, ON L5N 6P7. Archivist Douglas Rudd (416) 595-1277

Presbyterian:

Presbyterian Archives, 59 St. George St., Toronto, ON M5S 2E6. Archivist: Miss Kim Arnold (416)595-1277

Roman Catholic:

For guides to many Canadian Catholic diocesan religious community and institutional archives, write: Rev. Pierre Hurtubise, O.M.I., Dir. of the Research Center in Religious History in Canada, St. Paul University, 223 Main St., Ottawa, ON K1S 1C4 (613) 236-1393

Salvation Army:

The George Scott Railton Heritage Centre (Salvation Army), 2130 Bayview Ave., Toronto, ON M4N 3K6. Contact: Elayne Dobel (416)481-4441

The United Church of Canada:

Central Archives, Victoria University, Toronto, ON M5S 1K7. (Methodist, Presbyterian, Congregational, Evangelical United Brethren.) Also Regional Conference Archives. Chief Archivist Jean Dryden (416)585-4563

III

STATISTICAL SECTION

GUIDE TO STATISTICAL TABLES

Earl Brewer
World Network of Religious Futurists

Since there are no religious questions in the U.S. census, the *Yearbook of American and Canadian Churches* becomes as near an "official" record of denominational statistics as is available. It is often supplemented by several sample studies, such as Gallup, National Opinion Research Center, and others.

Students, denominational, ecumenical, or congregational policy-makers may use these statistics to gain insights for program planning. Trends in religious adherents and the population of the countries may be related to these statistics.

In spite of these and other values, there are limitations of these statistics which need to be kept in mind by users:

1. The data are not for a single year. Each year the *Yearbook* staff sends questionnaires to appropriate officers of religious bodies in Canada and the United States. The responses are shown in Tables 1-4.

Denominations have different report schedules and some do not report on a regular basis. Only data that has been reported within the last 10 years is included. Denominations that are not listed have not provided data for at least 10 years.

2. The statistics are not comparable in all cases. Definitions of membership and other important characteristics differ from denomination to denomination. In Tables 1-4 of this section, full or confirmed membership refers to those with full, communicant, or confirmed status. Inclusive membership refers to those who are full communicants or confirmed members plus other members baptized, non-confirmed or non-communicant.

3. The data are incomplete. Different methods and times are used in collecting them. Some denominations don't keep or report statistics in some of the categories listed in the tables.

4. This statistical information is based on reports made by denominational leaders rather than "head counts" of the population. In many cases denominations keep careful records. Other denominations only make estimates.

The *Yearbook* staff wants to make every effort to improve the quality and the quantity of the statistics of the vast number of religious bodies. It is hoped that continued cooperation of religious bodies and ecumenical groups will enhance and make more useful this part of the *Yearbook*.

Statistics collected from other sources than the questionnaire are often included in the *Yearbook*.

Tables 1-4 are based largely on the responses to the questionnaires mailed to appropriate officials in all known religious bodies in Canada and the United States. However, in several cases it was impossible to obtain information directly from a denominational official. Wardell Payne from Howard University School of Divinity kindly provided additional information.

The religious bodies are listed alphabetically. The financial data are based on the currency of the country.

TABLE 1: CANADIAN CURRENT STATISTICS

Religious Body	Year Reported	No. of Churches	Full, Communicant or Confirmed Members	Inclusive Membership	No. of Pastors Serving Parishes	Total No. of Clergy	No. of Sunday or Sabbath Schools	Total Enrollment
The Anglican Church in Canada	1990	1,767	529,943	848,256		3,463	1,623	82,022
The Antiochian Orthodox Christian Archdiocese of North America	1992	13	100,000	100,000	20	22	11	1,100
Apostolic Christian Church (Nazarene)	1985	14		830	49	49		
The Apostolic Church in Canada	1992	14	1,200	1,600	14	19	14	350
Apostolic Church of Pentecost of Canada Inc.	1992	129		14,500	144	286	94	6,000
Associated Gospel Churches	1992	126	9,284	9,284	118	239		
Baptist Convention of Ontario and Quebec	1991	372	33,144	44,713	315	564		
Baptist General Conference of Canada	1987	70		6,066	80	84		
Baptist Union of Western Canada	1992	162	15,886	20,660	150	285	140	8,396
The Bible Holiness Movement	1991	14	358	904	6	1		
Brethren in Christ Church, Canadian Conference	1992	39	3,173	3,173	51	61	31	410
British Columbia Baptist Conference	1992	23	2,264	2,264	36	48	23	1,263
Canadian and American Reformed Churches	1992	44	6,940	13,536	32	53		
Canadian Baptist Federation	1992	1,150	131,349	131,349	1,124	1,236		
Canadian Conference of Mennonite Brethren Churches	1992	104	28,250	28,250	302	302	210	24,119
Canadian Convention of Southern Baptists	1992	104	6,743	6,743	78	83	104	7,870
Canadian Dist. of Moravian Church, Northern Province	1992	9	1,436	2,107	9	12	9	692
Can. Yearly Meeting of Religious Society of Friends	1992	23	1,095	1,095			19	125
The Central Canadian Baptist Conference	1992	37						
Christadelphians	1992	50						
Christian and Missionary Alliance in Canada	1992	348	29,282	80,681	572	755	60	35,749
Christian Brethren (also known as Plymouth Brethren)	1992	60			18	42		
Christian Church (Disciples of Christ) in Canada	1992	35	2,322	4,066	95	100	35	963
Christian Churches and Churches of Canada	1989	140		7,500	198	518		
Christian Reformed Church in North America	1992	240	50,026	86,231				
Church of God (Anderson, Ind.)	1992	50	3,421	3,421	42	61	44	2,159
Church of God (Cleveland, Tenn.)	1992	99	6,670	6,670	32	81		

TABLE 1: CANADIAN CURRENT STATISTICS--Continued

Religious Body	Year Reported	No. of Churches	Full, Communicant or Confirmed Members	Inclusive Membership	No. of Pastors Serving Parishes	Total No. of Clergy	No. of Sunday or Sabbath Schools	Total Enrollment
Church of God in Christ Mennonite	1992	36	3,506	3,506	125	125	36	
The Church of God of Prophecy in Canada	1992	28	2,482	4,232	110	127	27	2,335
Church of Jesus Christ of Latter-day Saints in Canada	1992	391	130,000	130,000			391	
Church of the Luthern Brethren	1992	7	328	505	6	6	8	479
Church of the Nazarene	1991	161	10,915	10,915	117	243	159	15,957
Churches of Christ in Canada	1991	147	7,181	7,181	133		108	
Conference of Mennonites in Canada	1992	150	28,648	37,008	211	367	150	29,697
Congregational Christian Churches in Canada	1991	6	762	762	5	14	4	247
The Coptic Church in Canada	1992	12			20		17	
The Estonian Evangelical Lutheran Church	1990	13	6,268	6,478	13	15		
Evangelical Baptist Churches in Can., Fellowship of	1992	500	61,572	61,572	46	79	39	3,431
Evangelical Church in Canada	1990	46	3,688	3,688	16	31	18	1,753
Evangelical Covenant Church in Canada	1991	23	1,278	1,278				
Evangelical Free Church of Canada	1992	133	6,970	13,699	133			
Evangelical Luthern Church in Canada	1992	656	146,365	203,937	483	858	465	25,425
The Evangelical Mennonite Conference	1992	49	6,358	6,358	196	233	49	5,191
The Evangelical Mennonite Mission Conf. of Can.	1992	27	3,389	3,389	39	54	25	3,032
Foursquare Gospel Church of Canada	1992	53		2,354	93	106	43	1,335
Free Methodist Church in Canada	1989	147		7,479	132	235		
Free Will Baptists	1992	15	435	735	5	8	11	595
General Church of the New Jerusalem	1992	3	275	825	4	6	3	185
Greek Orthodox Diocese of Toronto	1984	58		230,000	45	49		
Independent Holiness Church	1987	13		600	13	21		
The Italian Pentecostal Church of Canada	1990	21	3,300	3,300	20	24		
Jehovah's Witnesses	1992	1,312	106,052	106,052				
The Latvian Evangelical Lutheran Church in America	1990	8	2,200	2,380	6	8	5	
Luthern Church—Canada	1992	326	59,141	79,645	241	352	290	13,584
Mennonite Church	1992	109	14,861	14,861	148	242		

TABLE 1: CANADIAN CURRENT STATISTICS--Continued

Religious Body	Year Reported	No. of Churches	Full, Communicant or Confirmed Members	Inclusive Membership	No. of Pastors Serving Parishes	Total No. of Clergy	No. of Sunday or Sabbath Schools	Total Enrollment
Netherlands Reformed Congregations of N. Am.	1992	9	2,172	4,762	1	1		
North American Baptist Conference	1992	127	17,943	17,943	104	174	122	10,029
Old Order Amish Church	1992	17			61	61		
The Open Bible Standard Churches of Canada	1987	4		1,000	5	6	13	
Orthodox Church in America (Canada Section)	1991	59			37	41		
The Pentecostal Assemblies of Canada	1990	976	192,706	194,972	1,372	1,593	159	14,200
Pentecostal Assemblies of Newfoundland	1991	160	16,000	33,700	254	376		
Presbyterian Church in America (Can. Section)	1992	14	527	821	11	22		386
The Presbyterian Church in Canada	1992	998	152,425	233,335	1,169	1,169	612	33,698
Reformed Church in Canada	1992	42	4,128	6,236	50	76	30	1,997
The Reformed Episcopal Church	1992	3	284	325	3	9		
Reinland Mennonite Church	1987	7		800	10	10		
Reorganized Church of Jesus Christ of Latter Day Saints	1992	82	11,111	11,111		1,075		
Roman Catholic Church in Canada	1990	11,286		11,852,350		44,669		
The Romanian Orthodox Episcopate of Am.(Jackson, MI)	1992	13	8,600	8,600	11	12	10	663
Russian Orthodox Ch. in Can., Patriarchal Parishes	1991	24	6,000	7,000	4	5	3	46
The Salvation Army in Canada	1992	402	24,597	99,658	793	2,098	420	16,873
Seventh-day Adventist Church in Canada	1992	328	42,083	42,083	172	304	357	25,619
Syrian Orthodox Church of Antioch (Archdiocese of the US and Can.)	1992	4	2,000	2,000	3	3	3	132
Ukrainian Orthodox Church of Canada	1988	258		120,000	75	91		
Union d'Eglises Baptistes Francaises au Canada	1992	24	1,169	1,169	16	23	24	
United Baptist Convention of the Atlantic Provinces	1992	546	66,484	66,484	259	529	9	23,288
United Brethren Church in Canada	1992	9	835	835	5	12	9	447
The United Church of Canada	1992	4,019	771,548	1,984,307	2,125	3,902	3,353	168,692
United Pentecostal Church in Canada	1992	213			329	329		
Universal Fellowship of Metropolitan Community Churches	1992	12	50	1,500	8	9	1	36
The Wesleyan Church of Canada	1992	82	5,024	5,256	112	155	72	

TABLE 2: UNITED STATES CURRENT STATISTICS

Religious Body	Year Reported	No. of Churches	Full, Communicant or Confirmed Members	Inclusive Membership	No. of Pastors Serving Parishes	Total No. of Clergy	No. of Sunday or Sabbath Schools	Total Enrollment
Advent Christian Church	1992	335	28,000	28,000	267	498	330	15,000
African Methodist Episcopal Church #	1991	8,000		3,500,000				
African Methodist; Episcopal Zion Church	1991	3,000	1,000,000	1,200,000	2,500	2,686	1,556	50,046
Albanian Orthodox Diocese of America	1992	2	1,873	1,873	1	3		128
Allegheny Wesleyan Methodist Connection	1992	122	1,934	2,060	104	183	117	6,461
Amana Church Society	1990	1	400	450			1	44
The American Baptist Association	1986	1,705		250,000	1,740	1,760		
American Baptist Churches in the USA	1992	5,845	1,534,078	1,534,078	4,506	7,515	73	335,711
The Am. Carpatho-Russian Orthodox Greek Catholic Ch.	1992	72	18,611	18,611	66	77		
American Evangelical Christian Churches	1993				72	197		
American Rescue Workers	1992	16	5,000	35,000	70	96	16	880
The Anglican Orthodox Church	1983	40		6,000	8	8		
Antiochian Orthodox Christian Archdiocese of N. Am.	1992	160	250,000	250,000	200	275	160	27,000
Apostolic Christian Church (Nazarene)	1985	48		2,799	178	178		
Apostolic Christian Churches of America	1989	80		11,450	300	340		
Apostolic Faith Mission Church of God	1992	53	12,000	14,000	60	67	53	500
Apostolic Faith Mission of Portland, Oregon.	1992	55	4,500	4,500	80	95	55	6,820
Apostolic Lutheran Church of America	1992	60	7,000	9,500	35	60	50	2,700
Apostolic Overcoming Holy Church of God, Inc.	1992	192	1,463	1,463	20	27	20	809
Armenian Apostolic Church of America	1992	32	30,000	150,000				
Armenian Church of America (Diocese of the)	1991	72	14,000	414,000	49	70		2,370
Assemblies of God	1992	11,689	1,337,321	2,257,846	17,280	30,893	11,249	1,410,579
Associate Reformed Presbyterian Church	1992	196	33,550	38,763	179	254	169	16,525
Baptist Bible Fellowship International	1992	3,500		1,500,000				
Baptist General Conference	1992	821	134,658	134,658	1,200	1,700		81,896
Baptist Missionary Association of America	1992	1,362	236,604	236,604	1,260	2,700	95,468	95,468

253

TABLE 2: UNITED STATES CURRENT STATISTICS--Continued

Religious Body	Year Reported	No. of Churches	Full Communicant or Confirmed Members	Inclusive Membership	No. of Pastors Serving Parishes	Total No. of Clergy	No. of Sunday or Sabbath Schools	Total Enrollment
Beachy Amish Mennonite Churches	1992	95	6,968	6,968	323	323	91	4,063
Berean Fundamental Church	1991	51	2,768	2,768	60	60	51	725
The Bible Church of Christ Inc.	1992	6	4,200	6,700	8	54	6	6,725
The Brethren Church (Ashland, Ohio)	1992	124	13,132	13,132	87	177	121	6,725
Brethren in Christ Church	1992	184	16,697	16,697	252	284	194	9,672
Bulgarian Eastern Orthodox Church	1992	9	900	1,100	10	13	5	149
Christ Catholic Church	1992	12	1,301	1,558	12	13	0	0
The Christian and Missionary Alliance	1992	1,923	142,346	289,391	1,609	2,369	1,709	183,316
Christian Brethren	1984	1,150		98,000	500			
Christian Catholic Church (Evangelical-Protestant)	1992	5		2,000	9	12	5	
Christian Church (Disciples of Christ)	1992	3,996	655,652	1,011,502	3,883	7,018	3,996	300,430
Christian Church of North America, General Council	1985	104		13,500	107	169		
Christian Churches and Churches of Christ	1988	5,579		1,070,616	5,525	6,596		
The Christian Congregation, Inc.	1992	1,437	111,324	111,324	1,431	1,433	1,293	46,892
Christian Methodist Episcopal Church	1983	2,340		718,922	2,340	2,650		
Christian Nation Church U.S.A.	1989	5		200	4	23		
Christian Reformed Church in North America	1992	736	145,911	223,617	668	1,162	240	11,284
Christian Union	1992	240	9,790	9,790	240	558	240	
Church of Christ, Scientist	1992	2,500			0	0	2,500	
Church of God (Anderson, Ind.)	1992	2,330	214,743	214,743	2,153	3,576	2,244	160,305
Church of God by Faith, Inc.	1991	145	6,819	8,235	155	170		
Church of God (Cleveland, Tenn.)	1992	5,776	672,008	672,008	2,301	6,898	5,611	407,009
Church of God General Conference	1992	87	4,085	5,336	63	80	86	3,130
The Church of God in Christ	1991	15,300	5,499,875	5,499,875	28,988	33,593		
Church of God in Christ (Mennonite)	1992	79	10,234	10,234	358	358	79	
Church of God of the Mountain Assembly, Inc.	1992	111	5,000	5,000	132	136	111	10,500

TABLE 2: UNITED STATES CURRENT STATISTICS--Continued

Religious Body	Year Reported	No. of Churches	Full, Communicant or Confirmed Members	Inclusive Membership	No. of Pastors Serving Parishes	Total No. of Clergy	No. of Sunday or Sabbath Schools	Total Enrollment
Church of God of Prophecy	1992	2,072	72,465	72,465	7,911	7,964	1,592	67,421
Church of God (Seventh Day), Denver, Colo.	1990	153			84	132	7	22
Church of God (Which He Purchased with His Own Blood)	1991	7	800	800		16	3	134
Church of Illumination	1992	10	1,200	1,700	12	18		
Church of Jesus Christ (Bickertonites)	1989	63		2,707	183	262		
The Church of Jesus Christ of Latter-Day Saints	1992	9,654	4,430,000	4,430,000	28,962		9,654	3,596,000
Church of the Brethren	1992	1,139	147,912	147,912	837	1,214	894	
Church of the Living God	1985	170		42,000		170		
Church of Lutheran Brethren of America	1992	110	7,684	12,182	113	207	108	11,161
Church of the Lutheran Confession	1992	70	6,418	8,798	56	77	66	1,425
Church of the Nazarene	1991	5,172	572,152	573,834	4,416	9,363	4,945	860,099
Churches of Christ	1992	13,174	1,284,056	1,684,872			12,350	1,100,000
Churches of God, General Conference	1992	359	33,096	33,096	233	423	359	27,013
Community Churches, International Council of	1992	410	500,000	500,000	583	616		
Congregational Christian Churches- National Association	1992	405	90,000	90,000	600	600	370	
Congregational Holiness Church, Inc.	1991	176	7,116	7,116	312	349	176	7,150
Conservative Baptist Association of America	1992	1,084	200,000	200,000				
Conservative Congregational Christian Conference	1992	188	30,387	30,387	294	513	174	12,674
Conservative Lutheran Association	1987	12		1,530	18	27		
Coptic Orthodox Church	1992	85	180,000	180,000	65	68	85	
Cumberland Presbyterian Church	1992	782	92,240	92,240		782		43,662
Elim Fellowship	1992	66			154	322		
Episcopal Church	1991	7,367	1,615,505	2,471,880	8,040	14,878		531,813
The Estonian Evangelical Lutheran Church	1989	24		7,298	17	19		
The Evangelical Church	1992	43	3,336	3,336	46	88	39	2,121
The Evangelical Congregational Church	1990	155	24,437	32,700	141	222	153	17,100

TABLE 2: UNITED STATES CURRENT STATISTICS--Continued

Religious Body	Year Reported	No. of Churches	Full, Communicant or Confirmed Members	Inclusive Membership	No. of Pastors Serving Parishes	Total No. of Clergy	No. of Sunday or Sabbath Schools	Total Enrollment
Evangelical Covenant Church	1992	596	89,648	89,648	542	1,028		77,903
Evangelical Free Church of America	1992	1,173	117,027	214,186	1,434	1,817		
Evangelical Lutheran Church in America	1992	11,055	3,878,055	5,234,568	9,893	17,416	9,549	1,060,606
Evangelical Lutheran Synod	1992	126	15,929	21,525	111	151	125	5,119
Evangelical Mennonite Church	1992	27	4,130	4,130	30	58	27	3,365
The Evangelical Methodist Church	1992	132	8,500	8,500	137			
Evangelical Presbyterian Church	1992	174	51,423	55,008	250	382	174	33,824
Fellowship of Evangelical Bible Churches	1988	14		1,925	18	47		
Fellowship of Fundamental Bible Churches	1992	25	1,436	2,090	47	52	25	1,351
The Fire Baptized Holiness Church (Wesleyan)	1992	49		692		67	49	
Free Lutheran Congregations, The Association of	1992	225	20,945	28,469	129	181	183	6,576
Free Methodist Church of North America	1992	1,055	58,220	74,168	918	1,854		91,657
Friends Gen. Conf. of Religious Societies of Friends	1992	520	31,500	31,500			500	
Friends United Meeting	1991		50,803	50,803	341	637		17,566
Full Gospel Assemblies International	1992	4			152	327	44	
Full Gospel Fellowship of Churches and Ministers International	1992	475			1,243	1,243		
Fundamental Methodist Church, Inc.	1990	12	675	1,075	14	25	12	431
General Association of Regular Baptist Churches	1992	1,532		160,123				
General Baptists (General Association of)	1990	876	74,156	74,156	1,384	1,384		16,250
General Conference Mennonite Church	1991	229	33,937	33,937	212	394		
General Conference of the Church of God (Seventh Day)	1990	153		5,700		130		
Grace Brethren Churches, Fellowship of	1992	308	36,220	36,220		600		
Grace Gospel Fellowship	1992	128		60,000	160	196	128	
Hungarian Reformed Church in America	1989	27		9,780	29	32		
The Hutterian Brethren	1992	95		6,700		195	95	2,455

TABLE 2: UNITED STATES CURRENT STATISTICS--Continued

Religious Body	Year Reported	No. of Churches	Full Communicant or Confirmed Members	Inclusive Membership	No. of Pastors Serving Parishes	Total No. of Clergy	No. of Sunday or Sabbath Schools	Total Enrollment
Independent Fundamental Churches of America	1992	708	71,672	71,672	718	1,369	708	41,143
International Church of the Foursquare Gospel	1992	1,558	203,043	207,455		2,403	1,144	42,459
International Pentecostal Church of Christ	1992	73	2,661	4,593	72	167	73	3,905
International Pentecostal Holiness Church	1990			131,674				
Jehovah's Witnesses	1992	9,890	914,079	914,079	0	0	0	
Korean Presbyterian Church in America	1992	203	21,788	26,988	326	381		
The Latvian Evangelical Lutheran Church in America	1990	56	11,432	12,553	34	48	19	
The Liberal Catholic Church—Province of the U.S.A.	1987	34		2,800	64	127		
Liberty Baptist Fellowship	1992	100			100	110		
The Lutheran Church- Missouri Synod	1992	5,369	1,953,248	2,609,905	5,674	8,799	5,778	658,478
Lutheran Churches, The American Association of	1988	78		15,150	63	80		
Mennonite Brethren Churches, The American Association of	1991	144	16,843	16,843	196	470		11,299
Mennonite Church	1992	1,056	99,446	99,446	1,637	2,784		
Mennonite Church, General Conference	1992	227	34,040	34,040	393	904	227	15,509
Metropolitan Community Churches, Universal Fellowship of	1992	291	14,664	30,000		296		
Missionary Church, Inc.	1992	309	28,196	28,196	462	765	289	27,909
Moravian Church in America, Northern Province	1992	97	22,533	29,469	88	176	96	6,635
Moravian Church in America, Southern Province	1991	56	17,300	21,513	63	95		8,691
National Association of Free Will Baptists	1992	2,495	209,223	209,223	2,800	2,900	2,495	145,870
National Baptist Convention, USA,Inc.	1992	33,000	8,200,000	8,200,000	32,832	32,832		
National Baptist Convention of America	1987	2,500		3,500,000	8,000			
National Missionary Baptist Convention of America	1992			2,500,000				
National Organization of the New Apostolic Church of North America	1992	549	41,201	41,201	819	925	549	2,658
Netherlands Reformed Congregations	1992	15	2,778	5,336	5	9		
North American Baptist Conference	1992	289	43,446	43,446	277	434	278	23,395

STATISTICAL SECTION

TABLE 2: UNITED STATES CURRENT STATISTICS--Continued

Religious Body	Year Reported	No. of Churches	Full, Communicant or Confirmed Members	Inclusive Membership	No. of Pastors Serving Parishes	Total No. of Clergy	No. of Sunday or Sabbath Schools	Total Enrollment
North American Old Roman Catholic Church	1992	5	400	400	9	10		37
Northwest Yearly Meeting of Friends Church	1992	53	4,813	7,422	54	160	53	3,672
Old German Baptist Brethren	1992	56	5,477	5,477	244	244		
Old Order Amish Church	1992	873	78,570	78,570	3,492	3,517	60	
Open Bible Standard Churches	1992	368	33,000	40,000	535	1,004	350	
Orthodox Church In America	1992	700	400,000	600,000	700	945	510	12,500
The Orthodox Presbyterian Church	1991	170	12,265	18,137		315		
Pentecostal Assemblies of the World #	1989	1,005		500,000				
Pentecostal Church of God, Inc.	1992	1,170	42,985	101,786		1,657		
Pentecostal Fire-Baptized Holiness Church	1992	27	234	234	19	26		
Pentecostal Free Will Baptist Church, Inc.	1992	150	15,000	18,000	175	250	150	18,000
Presbyterian Church in America	1992	1,212	194,825	239,500	1,364	2,217		112,285
Presbyterian Church (U.S.A.)	1992	11,456	2,780,406	3,758,085	10,008	20,527	9,823	1,156,381
Primitive Advent Christian Church	1992	10	340	340	8	11	8	291
Primitive Methodist Church in the U.S.A.	1992	81	7,677	7,677	65	98	74	4,435
Progressive National Baptist Convention, Inc.	1991	1,400	2,500,000	2,500,000	1,400	1,400	1,400	
The Protes'tant Conference (Lutheran), Inc.	1992	7	800	1,100	6	8	5	154
Reformed Church in America	1992	927	190,400	274,521	940	1,670	882	97,709
Reformed Church in the United States	1992	37	3,200	4,178	30	36	37	796
Reformed Episcopal Church	1990	83	5,882	6,565	88	147	72	2,938
Reformed Methodist Union Episcopal Church	1983			3,800	24	33		
Reformed Presbyterian Church of North America	1988	68		5,174	59	127		
Religious Society of Friends (Conservative)	1984	28		1,744		17		
Reorganized Church of Jesus Christ of Latter Day Saints	1992	1,001	150,143	150,143		16,742		
The Roman Catholic Church	1992	19,863		59,220,723		50,907		
The Romanian Orthodox Episcopate of America	1992	37	65,000	65,000	37	81	30	1,800

TABLE 2: UNITED STATES CURRENT STATISTICS--Continued

Religious Body	Year Reported	No. of Churches	Full, Communicant or Confirmed Members	Inclusive Membership	No. of Pastors Serving Parishes	Total No. of Clergy	No. of Sunday or Sabbath Schools	Total Enrollment
Russian Orthodox Ch. in U.S.A., Patriarchal Parishes	1985	38		9,780	37	45		
The Salvation Army	1991	1,151	133,214	446,403	2,710	5,241		107,833
The Schwenkfelder Church	1992	5	2,475	2,475	9	10	5	843
Separate Baptists in Christ	1992	100	8,000	8,000	95	140	100	
Serbian Orthodox Church in the U.S.A. and Canada	1986	68		67,000	60	82		
Seventh-Day Adventist Church	1992	4,261	748,687	748,687	2,370	4,355	4,444	377,150
Seventh Day Baptist General Conference, USA and Canada	1992	90	5,250	5,250	48	81	90	
Southern Baptist Convention	1992	38,401	15,358,866	15,358,866	38,417	63,352	36,778	8,256,745
The Southern Methodist Church	1992	133	7,745	7,745	100	139		
Sovereign Grace Baptists	1992	300	3,000	3,000	400	400	300	
The Swedenborgian Church	1988	50		2,423	45	54		
Syrian Orthodox Church of Antioch (Archdiocese of the United States and Canada)	1992	16	33,000	33,000	14	18	12	1,245
True Orthodox Church of Greece (Synod of Metropolitan Cyprian), American Exarchate	1992	7	1,000	1,000	7	23		
Ukrainian Orthodox Church of America	1986	27		5,000	36	37		
United Brethren in Christ	1992	251	26,879	26,879	267	494	251	14,415
United Christian Church	1987	12		420	8	11		
United Church of Christ	1992	6,264	1,555,382	1,555,382	4,512	10,203		407,261
United Methodist Church	1991	37,100	8,789,101	8,789,101	20,369	38,492	3,322,605	3,851,864
United Pentecostal Church International	1992	3,728	550,000	550,000		7,483		
United Zion Church	1987	13		850	19	20		
Unity of the Brethren	1991	26	2,615	3,615	22	28	21	1,444
The Wesleyan Church (USA)	1992	1,612	106,397	114,174	1,755	2,539	1,592	
Wisconson Evangelical Lutheran Synod	1990	1,211	316,813	420,039	1,167	1,607	1,173	49,395

Figures obtained from the Directory of African American Religious Bodies, 1991

Table 3: SOME STATISTICS OF CHURC[

				TOTAL CONTRIBUTIONS		
Communion	Year	Full or Confirmed Members	Inclusive Members	Total Contributions	Per Capita Full or Confirmed Members	Per Cap Inclusi Membe
Baptist Union of Western Can.	1992	15,886	20,660	23,923,585	1,505.95	1,157.
Christain Church (Disciples of Christ) in Can.	1992	2,322	4,066	1,726,182	743.40	424.
Conference of Mennonites in Canada	1992	28,648	37,008	23,392,181	816.54	632.
Evangelical Luthern Church in Canada	1992	146,365	203,937	54,495,622	372.33	267.
Luthern Church—Canada	1992	59,141	79,645	28,198,783	476.81	354.
Mennonite Church	1992	14,861	14,861	11,258,195	757.57	757.
Moravian Church in America, Canadian District	1992	1,436	2,107	1,386,740	965.70	658.
North American Baptist Conference	1992	17,943	17,943	21,210,796	1,182.12	1,182.
Presbyterian Church in America (Can. Section)	1992	527	821	898,448	1,704.83	1,094.
The Presbyterian Church in Canada	1992	152,425	233,335	77,657,833	509.48	332.
Reformed Church in Canada	1992	4,128	6,236	3,805,022	921.76	610.
Union d'Eglises Baptistes Francaises au Canada	1992	1,169	1,169	818,057	699.79	699.
United Baptist Convention of the Atlantic Provinces	1992	66,484	66,484	31,880,449	479.52	479.
United Brethren Church in Can.	1992	835	835	914,849	1,095.63	1,095.
The United Church of Canada	1992	771,548	1,984,307	294,885,209	382.20	148.
The Wesleyan Church of Can.	1992	5,024	5,256	8,519,899	1,695.84	1,620.

Table 4: SOME STATISTICS OF CHURC[

				TOTAL CONTRIBUTIONS		
Communion	Year	Full or Confirmed Members	Inclusive Members	Total Contributions	Per Capita Full or Confirmed Members	Per Cap Inclusi Membe
Albanian Orthodox Diocese of America	1992	1,873	1,873	188,100	100.43	100.
Allegheny Wesleyan Methodist Connection	1992	1,934	2,060	4,319,530	2,233.47	2,096.
American Baptist Churches in the USA	1992	1,534,078	1,534,078	370,914,553	241.78	241.
Apostolic Faith Mission Church of God	1992	12,000	14,000	53,000	4.42	3.
Associate Reformed Presbyterian Church	1992	33,550	38,763	22,840,011	680.78	589.
Baptist General Conference	1992	134,658	134,658	123,112,848	914.26	914.
Baptist Missionary Association of America	1992	236,604	236,604	57,737,680	244.03	244.
Brethren in Christ Church	1992	16,697	16,697	19,233,360	1,151.91	1,151.
The Christian and Missionary Alliance	1992	142,346	289,391	184,060,025	1,293.05	636.
Christian Church (Disciples of Christ)	1992	655,652	1,011,502	380,069,745	579.68	375.
Church of God (Anderson, Ind.)	1992	214,743	214,743	173,615,710	808.48	808.
Church of God General Conference	1992	4,085	5,336	3,157,483	772.95	591.
Church of Illumination	1992	1,200	1,700	353,570	294.64	207.
Church of the Brethren	1992	147,912	147,912	79,703,215	538.86	538.
Church of the Lutheran Confession	1992	6,418	8,798	3,367,455	524.69	382.
Churches of God, General Conference	1992	33,096	33,096	19,777,586	597.58	597.
Conservative Congregational Christian Conference	1992	30,387	30,387	27,291,180	898.12	898.
Cumberland Presbyterian Ch	1992	92,240	92,240	34,310,518	371.97	371.
Evangelical Lutheran Church in America	1992	3,878,055	5,234,568	1,589,025,637	409.75	303.

FINANCES—CANADIAN CHURCHES

	CONGREGATIONAL FINANCES			BENEVOLENCES			
Total Congregational Contributions	Per Capita Full or Confirmed Members	Per Capita Inclusive Members	Total Benevolences	Per Capita Full or Confirmed Members	PerCapita Inclusive Members	Benevolences As a Percentage of Total Contributions
19,330,578	1,216.83	935.65	4,593,007	289.12	222.31	19.20
1,505,378	648.31	370.24	220,804	95.09	54.30	12.79
13,900,827	485.23	375.62	9,491,354	331.31	256.47	40.57
47,042,061	321.40	230.67	7,453,561	50.92	36.55	13.68
23,054,719	389.83	289.47	5,144,064	86.98	64.59	18.24
7,526,254	506.44	506.44	3,731,941	251.12	251.12	33.15
1,159,427	807.40	550.27	227,313	158.30	107.88	16.39
16,392,627	913.59	913.59	4,818,169	268.53	268.53	22.72
696,770	1,322.14	848.68	201,678	382.69	245.65	22.45
65,634,519	430.60	281.29	12,023,314	78.88	51.53	15.48
3,148,396	762.69	504.87	656,626	159.07	105.30	17.26
738,447	631.69	631.69	79,610	68.10	68.10	9.73
28,371,615	426.74	426.74	3,508,834	52.78	52.78	11.01
618,435	740.64	740.64	296,414	354.99	354.99	32.40
253,771,849	328.91	127.89	41,113,360	53.29	20.72	13.94
7,194,689	1,432.06	1,368.85	1,325,210	263.78	252.13	15.55

FINANCES—UNITED STATES CHURCHES

	CONGREGATIONAL FINANCES			BENEVOLENCES			
Total Congregational Contributions	Per Capita Full or Confirmed Members	Per Capita Inclusive Members	Total Benevolences	Per Capita Full or Confirmed Members	PerCapita Inclusive Members	Benevolences As a Percentage of Total Contributions
170,000	90.76	90.76	18,100	9.66	9.66	9.62
3,234,908	1,672.65	1,570.34	1,084,622	560.82	526.52	25.11
318,150,548	207.39	207.39	52,764,005	34.39	34.39	14.23
34,000	2.83	2.43	19,000	1.58	1.36	35.85
16,932,998	504.71	436.83	5,907,013	176.07	152.39	25.86
99,753,153	740.79	740.79	23,359,695	173.47	173.47	18.97
47,907,707	202.48	202.48	9,829,973	41.55	41.55	17.03
15,950,180	955.27	955.27	3,283,180	196.63	196.63	17.07
148,124,531	1,040.59	511.85	35,935,494	252.45	124.18	19.52
333,629,412	508.85	329.84	46,440,333	70.83	45.91	12.22
150,115,497	699.05	699.05	23,500,213	109.43	109.43	13.54
2,648,085	648.25	496.27	509,398	124.70	95.46	16.13
350,000	291.67	205.88	3,570	2.98	2.10	1.01
57,954,895	391.82	391.82	21,748,320	147.04	147.04	27.29
2,773,082	432.08	315.19	594,373	92.61	67.56	17.65
16,527,403	499.38	499.38	3,250,183	98.20	98.20	16.43
22,979,946	756.24	756.24	4,311,234	141.88	141.88	15.80
29,721,914	322.22	322.22	4,588,604	49.75	49.75	13.37
1,399,419,800	360.86	267.34	189,605,837	48.89	36.22	11.93
4,260,307	1,031.55	1,031.55	1,961,623	474.97	474.97	31.53

Table 4: SOME STATISTICS OF CHURCH

Communion	Year	Full or Confirmed Members	Inclusive Members	Total Contributions	Per Capita Full or Confirmed Members	Per Capita Inclusive Members
Evangelical Mennonite Ch	1992	4,130	4,130	6,221,930	1,506.52	1,506.52
Evangelical Presbyterian Ch	1992	51,423	55,008	65,071,833	1,265.42	1,182.95
Fellowship of Fundamental Bible Churches	1992	1,436	2,090	2,017,017	1,404.61	965.08
Free Methodist Church of North America	1992	58,220	74,168	71,175,143	1,222.52	959.65
Independent Fundamental Churches of America	1992	71,672	71,672	96,996,899	1,353.34	1,353.34
International Pentecostal Church of Christ	1992	2,661	4,593	2,200,767	827.05	479.16
The Lutheran Church-Missouri Synod	1992	1,953,248	2,609,905	909,152,393	465.46	348.35
Mennonite Church	1992	99,446	99,446	96,953,941	974.94	974.94
Mennonite Church, General Conference	1992	34,040	34,040	11,744,656	345.03	345.03
Missionary Church, Inc.	1992	28,196	28,196	36,288,958	1,287.03	1,287.03
Moravian Church in America, Northern Province	1992	22,533	29,469	11,359,325	504.12	385.47
National Association of Free Will Baptists	1992	209,223	209,223	60,300,000	288.21	288.21
North American Baptist Conference	1992	43,446	43,446	35,703,541	821.79	821.79
Presbyterian Church in Am.	1992	194,825	239,500	261,178,991	1,340.58	1,090.52
Presbyterian Church (U.S.A.)	1992	2,780,406	3,758,085	2,005,162,498	721.18	533.56
Primitive Methodist Church in the U.S.A.	1992	7,677	7,677	8,857,540	1,153.78	1,153.78
Reformed Church in America	1992	190,400	274,521	147,895,894	776.76	538.74
Reformed Church in the United States	1992	3,200	4,178	2,317,000	724.06	554.57
The Schwenkfelder Church	1992	2,475	2,475	1,036,585	418.82	418.82
Seventh-Day Adventist Church	1992	748,687	748,687	668,265,516	892.58	892.58
Southern Baptist Convention	1992	15,358,866	15,358,866	5,214,281,810	339.50	339.50
United Brethren in Christ	1992	26,879	26,879	17,928,878	667.02	667.02
United Church of Christ	1992	1,555,382	1,555,382	595,096,785	382.60	382.60
United Methodist Church	1991	8,789,101	8,789,101	3,099,522,282	352.66	352.66
The Wesleyan Church (USA)	1992	106,397	114,174	127,603,567	1,199.32	1,117.62

SUMMARY STATISTICS

Communion	Number Reporting	Full or Confirmed Members	Inclusive Members	Total Contributions	Per Capita Full or Confirmed Members	Per Capita Inclusive Members
Canadian Communions	16	1,288,742	2,678,670	584,971,850	453.91	218.38
United States Communions	44	39,521,497	43,191,444	16,647,464,955	421.23	385.43

	CONGREGATIONAL FINANCES			BENEVOLENCES		
Total Congregational Contributions	Per Capita Full or Confirmed Members	Per Capita Inclusive Members	Total Benevolences	Per Capita Full or Confirmed Members	PerCapita Inclusive Members	Benevolences As a Percentage of Total Contributions
57,528,270	1,118.73	1,045.82	7,543,563	146.70	137.14	11.59
1,715,960	1,194.96	821.03	301,057	209.65	144.05	14.93
60,584,079	1,040.61	816.85	10,591,064	181.91	142.80	14.88
78,966,614	1,101.78	1,101.78	18,030,285	251.57	251.57	18.59
1,637,710	615.45	356.57	563,057	211.60	122.59	25.58
777,467,488	398.04	297.89	131,684,905	67.42	50.46	14.48
68,118,222	684.98	684.98	28,835,719	289.96	289.96	29.74
3,478,956	102.20	102.20	8,265,700	242.82	242.82	70.38
27,348,354	969.94	969.94	8,940,604	317.09	317.09	24.64
10,150,953	450.49	344.46	1,208,372	53.63	41.00	10.64
48,000,000	229.42	229.42	12,300,000	58.79	58.79	20.40
28,375,947	653.13	653.13	7,327,594	168.66	168.66	20.52
192,156,341	986.30	802.32	69,022,650	354.28	288.19	26.43
1,696,092,968	610.02	451.32	309,069,530	111.16	82.24	15.41
4,087,804	532.47	532.47	4,769,736	621.30	621.30	53.85
115,628,622	607.29	421.20	32,267,272	169.47	117.54	21.82
1,917,000	599.06	458.83	400,000	125.00	95.74	17.26
832,858	336.51	336.51	203,727	82.31	82.31	19.65
191,362,737	255.60	255.60	476,902,779	636.99	636.99	71.36
4,462,915,112	290.58	290.58	751,366,698	48.92	48.92	14.41
15,092,467	561.50	561.50	2,836,411	105.53	105.53	15.82
521,190,413	335.09	335.09	73,906,372	47.52	47.52	12.42
2,421,078,608	275.46	275.46	678,443,674	77.19	77.19	21.89
109,488,276	1,029.05	958.96	18,115,291	170.26	158.66	14.20

OF CHURCH FINANCES

	CONGREGATIONAL FINANCES			BENEVOLENCES		
Total Congregational Contributions	Per Capita Full or Confirmed Members	Per Capita Inclusive Members	Total Benevolences	Per Capita Full or Confirmed Members	PerCapita Inclusive Members	Benevolences As a Percentage of Total Contributions
490,086,591	380.28	182.96	94,885,259	73.63	35.42	16.22
13,565,854,125	343.25	314.09	3,081,610,830	77.97	71.35	18.51

TABLE 5: CONSTITUENCY OF THE NATIONAL COUNCIL OF THE CHURCHES IN THE U.S.A.

A separate tabulation has been made of the constituent bodies of the National Council of Churches of Christ in the U.S.A.

Religious Body	Year	Number of Churches	Inclusive Membership	Pastors Serving Parishes
African Methodist Episcopal Church.	1991	8,000	3,500,000	2,500
African Methodist; Episcopal Zion Church.	1991	3,000	1,200,000	4,506
American Baptist Churches in the USA.	1992	5,845	1,534,078	200
Antiochian Orthodox Christian Archdiocese of North America.	1992	160	250,000	49
Armenian Church of America (Diocese of the).	1991	72	414,000	3,883
Christian Church (Disciples of Christ).	1992	3,996	1,011,502	2,340
Christian Methodist Episcopal Church.	1983	2,340	718,922	837
Church of the Brethren.	1992	1,139	147,912	583
Community Churches,International Council of.	1992	410	500,000	65
Coptic Orthodox Church.	1992	85	180,000	8,040
Episcopal Church.	1991	7,367	2,471,880	9,893
Evangelical Lutheran Church in America.	1992	11,055	5,234,568	341
Friends United Meeting.	1991		50,803	610
Greek Orthodox Archdioces of North and South America.	1977	535	1,950,000	29
Hungarian Reformed Church in America.	1989	27	9,780	326
Korean Prebyterian Church in America.	1992	203	26,988	88
Moravian Church in America. Northern Province.	1992	97	29,469	63
Moravian Church in America. Southern Province.	1991	56	21,513	32,832
National Baptist Convention, USA,Inc..	1992	33,000	8,200,000	8,000
National Baptist Convention of America.	1990	2,500	3,500,000	700
Orthodox Church In America.	1992	700	600,000	
Philadelphia Yearly Meeting, Society of Friends.	1991	105	12,627	141
Polish National Catholic Church of North America.	1960	162	282,411	10,008
Presbyterian Church (U.S.A.).	1992	11,456	3,758,085	1,400
Progressive National Baptist Convention, Inc..	1991	1,400	2,500,000	940
Reformed Church in America.	1992	927	274,521	37
Russian Orthodox Church in the U.S.A., Patriarchal Parishes of the.	1985	38	9,780	60
Serbian Orthodox Church in the U.S.A. and Canada.	1986	68	67,000	45
The Swedenborgian Church.	1988	50	2,423	14
Syrian Orthodox Church of Antioch (Archdiocese of the U.S. and Can.)..	1992	16	33,000	36
Ukrainian Orthodox Church of America.	1986	27	5,000	
United Church of Christ.	1992	6,264	1,555,382	4,512
United Methodist Church.	1991	37,100	8,789,101	20,369
Totals		138,200	48,840,745	113,447

TRENDS IN SEMINARY EDUCATION

Gail Buchwalter King, Ph.D.
Associate Director, The Association of Theological Schools

Enrollment at schools affiliated with the Association of Theological Schools has increased in most years for the past 15 years.

This increase is partly due to new schools joining the Association. Much of the growth in enrollment can be attributed to increases in the number of women, African-American, Hispanic and Pacific/Asian American students.

Because of publication schedules, new data is not available for this edition of the *Yearbook*. Those interested in historical data of enrollment should consult the *1993 Yearbook*.

FTE indicates full time equivalent. This provides a way to compare enrollment when some students attend part-time.

STATISTICAL SECTION

TABLE 1 Enrollments in ATS Member Schools

	1987	1988	1989	1990	1991	1992
Number of schools	201	202	202	208	208	215
Total enrollment	55,766	55,745	56,171	59,190	60,086	63,171
FTE enrollment	38,329	36,802	38,178	40,847	40,922	46,404
By Nation						
Canada	3,572	4,024	4,113	4,053	4,648	4,831
United States	52,194	51,721	52,058	55,137	55,438	58,430
By Membership						
Accredited	52,464	52,129	52,913	54,235	55,217	55,727
Not Accredited	3,302	3,616	3,258	4,955	4,869	5,444
By Group						
Women	15,310	16,344	16,461	17,571	18,384	19,653
African American	3,379	3,662	3,961	4,303	4,671	5,554
Hispanic	1,385	1,415	1,490	1,904	1,625	1,670
Pacific/Asian	1,645	1,963	2,065	2,439	2,653	3,072

Schools that are members of the Association of Theological Schools are listed in section 7 and 8. A description of the ATS can be found in section 1.

IV
A CALENDAR FOR CHURCH USE
1994-1997

This Calendar presents for a four-year period the major days of religious observance for Christians, Jews, and Muslims; and, within the Christian community, major dates observed by Roman Catholic, Orthodox, Episcopal, and Lutheran churches. Within each of these communions many other days of observance, such as saints' days, exist, but only those regarded major are listed. Thus, for example, for the Roman Catholic Church, mainly the "solemnities" are listed. Dates of interest to many Protestant communions are also included.

In the Orthodox dates, immovable observances are listed in accordance with the Gregorian calendar. Movable dates (those depending on the date of Easter) often will differ from Western dates, since Paschal (Easter) in the Orthodox communions does not always fall on the same day as in the Western churches. For Orthodox churches that use the old Julian calendar, observances are held thirteen days later than listed here. For Jews and Muslims, who follow differing lunar calendars, the dates of major observances are translated into Gregorian dates. Since the actual beginning of a new month in the Islamic calendar is determined by the appearance of the new moon, the corresponding dates given here on the Gregorian calendar may vary slightly.

(Note: "RC" stands for Roman Catholic, "O" for Orthodox, "E" for Episcopal, "L" for Lutheran, "ECU" for Ecumenical.)

Event	1994	1995	1996	1997
New Year's Day (RC-Solemnity of Mary;O-Circumcision of Jesus Christ; E-Feast of the Holy Name;				
L-Name of Jesus	Jan 01	Jan 01	Jan 01	Jan 01
Epiphany (Armenian Christmas)	Jan 06	Jan 06	Jan 06	Jan 06
Feast Day of St. John the Baptist (O)	Jan 07	Jan 07	Jan 07	Jan 07
First Sunday After Epiphany (Feast of the Baptism of Our Lord)	Jan 09	Jan 08	Jan 07	Jan 12
Week of Prayer for Christian Unity (ECU)	Jan 18 to Jan 25	Jan 18 to Jan 25	Jan 18 to Jan 25	Jan 18 to Jan 2
Week of Prayer for Christian Unity, Canada (ECU)	Jan 23 to Jan 30	Jan 22 Jan 29	Jan 21 to Jan 28	Jan 19 to Jan 2
Ecumenical Sunday (ECU)	Jan 23	Jan 22	Jan 21	Jan 19
Presentation of Jesus in the Temple (O-The Meeting of Our Lord and Savior Jesus Christ)	Feb 02	Feb 02	Feb 02	Feb 02
First Day of the Month of Ramadan (M)	Feb 12	Feb 02	Jan 21	Jan 09
Last Sunday After Epiphany (L-Transfiguration)	Feb 13	Feb 26	Feb 18	Feb 09
Ash Wednesday (Western churches)	Feb 16	Mar 01	Feb 21	Feb 12
Brotherhood Week (Interfaith)	Feb 20 to Feb 26	Feb 19 to Feb 25	Feb 18 to Feb 24	Feb 16 to Feb 2
Purim (Jewish)	Feb 25	Mar 16	Mar 05	Mar 23
World Day of Prayer (ECU)	Mar 04	Mar 06	Mar 01	Mar 07
Easter Lent Begins (Eastern Orthodox)	Mar 14	Mar 06	Feb 25	Mar 10
Id al-Fitr (Festival of the End of Ramadan, celebrated on the first day of the month of Shawwal)	Mar 14	Mar 03	Feb 19	Feb 07
Joseph, Husband of Mary (RC,E,L)	Mar 19	Mar 19	Mar 19	Mar 19
The Annunciation (O)	Mar 25	Mar 25	Mar 25	Mar 25
(Apr 01 for L; Apr 08 for RC and E)				
Holy Week (Western Churches)	Mar 27 to Apr 2	Apr 09 to Apr 15	Mar 31 to Apr 07	Mar 23 to Mar
Holy Week (Eastern Orthodox)	Apr 25 to Apr 29	Apr 17 to Apr 21	Apr 08 to Apr 12	Apr 21 to Apr
Palm Sunday (Sunday of the Passion -Western Churches)	Mar 27	Apr 09	Mar 31	Mar 23
Palm Sunday (Eastern Orthodox)	Apr 24	Apr 16	Apr 07	Apr 20
Holy Thursday (Western Churches)	Mar 31	Apr 13	Apr 04	Mar 27
Holy Thursday (Eastern Orthodox)	Apr 28	Apr 20	Apr 11	Apr 24
Good Friday (Friday of the Passion of Our Lord) (Western Churches)	Apr 01	Apr 14	Apr 05	Mar 28
Holy (Good) Friday, Burial of Jesus Christ (Eastern Orthodox)	Apr 29	Apr 21	Apr 12	Apr 25

Event	1994	1995	1996	1997
Easter (Western Churches)	Apr 03	Apr 16	Apr 07	Mar 30
First Day of Passover (Jewish, 8 days)	Mar 27	Apr 15	Apr 04	Apr 22
Pascha (Eastern Orthodox Easter)	May 01	Apr 23	Apr 14	Apr 27
National Day of Prayer (ECU)	May 05	May 04	May 02	May 01
May Fellowship Day (ECU)	May 06	May 05	May 03	May 02
Rural Life Sunday (ECU)	May 08	May 14	May 12	May 11
Ascension Day (Western Churches)	May 13	May 25	May 16	May 08
Ascension Day (Eastern Orthodox)	Jun 09	Jun 01	May 23	Jun 05
First Day of Shavuot (Jewish, 2 days)	May 16	Jun 04	May 24	Jun 11
Id al-Adha (Festival of Sacrifice at time of annual pilgrimage to Mecca	May 21	May 10	Apr 28	Apr 16
Pentecost (Whitsunday) (Western Churches)	May 22	Jun 04	May 26	May 18
Pentecost (Eastern Orthodox)	Jun 19	Jun 11	Jun 02	Jun 15
Visitation of the Blessed Virgin Mary (RC,E,L)	May 31	May 31	May 31	May 31
Holy Trinity (RC,E,L)	Jun 05	Jun 11	Jun 09	May 25
Corpus Christi (RC)	Jun 09	Jun 15	Jun 131	May 29
Sacred Heart of Jesus (RC)	Jun 10	Jun 16	Jun 14	Jun 05
First Day of the Month of Muharram (Beginning of Muslim Liturgical Year)	Jun 10	Jun 23	Jun 14	Jun 05
Nativity of St. John the Baptist (RC,E,L)	Jun 24	Jun 24	Jun 24	Jun 24
Saint Peter and Saint Paul, Apostles (RC,E,L)	Jun 29	Jun 29	Jun 24	Jun 29
Feast Day of the Twelve Apostles of Christ (O)	Jun 30	Jun 30	Jun 30	Jun 30
Transfiguration of the Lord (RC,O,E)	Aug 06	Aug 06	Aug 06	Aug 06
Feast of the Blessed Virgin Mary (E; RC-Assumption of Blessed Mary the Virgin; O-Falling Asleep (Dormition) of the Blessed Virgin Mary; L-Mary, Mother of Our Lord)	Aug 15	Aug 15	Aug 15	Aug 15
Mawlid al-Nabi (Anniversary of Prophet Muhammad's Birthday)	Aug 20	Aug 09	Jul 28	Jul 15
First Day of Rosh Hashanah (Jewish, 2 days)	Sep 06	Sep 25	Sep 14	Oct 02
The Birth of the Blessed Virgin (RC, O)	Sep 08	Sep 08	Sep 08	Sep 08
Holy Cross Day (O-The Adoration of the Holy Cross; RC-Triumph of the Cross)	Sep 14	Sep 14	Sep 14	Sep 14
Yom Kippur (Jewish)	Sep 15	Oct 04	Sep 23	Oct 11
First Day of Sukkot (Jewish, 7 days)	Sep 20	Oct 09	Sep 28	Oct 16
Shemini Atzeret (Jewish)	Sep 27	Oct 16	Oct 05	Oct 23
Simhat Torah (Jewish)	Sep 28	Oct 17	Oct 06	Oct 24
World Communion Sunday (ECU)	Oct 02	Oct 01	Oct 06	Oct 05
Laity Sunday (ECU)	Oct 09	Oct 08	Oct 13	Oct 12
Thanksgiving Day (Canada)	Oct 10	Oct 09	Oct 14	Oct 13
Reformation Sunday (L)	Oct 30	Oct 29	Oct 27	Oct 26
Reformation Day (L)	Oct 31	Oct 31	Oct 31	Oct 31
All Saints (RC,E,L)	Nov 01	Nov 01	Nov 01	Nov 01
World Community Day (ECU)	Nov 04	Nov 03	Nov 01	Nov 07
Stewardship Day (ECU)	Nov 13	Nov 12	Nov 10	Nov 09
Bible Sunday (ECU)	Nov 20	Nov 19	Nov 17	Nov 16
Last Sunday After Pentecost (RC, L-Feast of Christ the King)	Nov 20	Nov 26	Nov 24	Nov 23
Thanksgiving Sunday (U.S.)	Nov 20	Nov 19	Nov 24	Nov 23
Presentation of the Blessed Virgin Mary in the Temple (also Presentation of the Theotokos) (O)	Nov 21	Nov 21	Nov 21	Nov 21
Thanksgiving Day (U.S.)	Nov 24	Nov 23	Nov 28	Nov 27
First Sunday of Advent	Nov 27	Dec 03	Dec 01	Nov 30
First Day of Hanukkah (Jewish, 8 days)	Nov 28	Dec 18	Dec 06	Dec. 24
Feast Day of St. Andrew the Apostle (RC,O,E,L)	Nov 30	Nov 30	Nov 30	Nov 30
Immaculate Conception of the Blessed Virgin Mary (RC)	Dec 08	Dec 08	Dec 08	Dec 08
Fourth Sunday of Advent (Sunday before Christmas)	Dec 18	Dec 24	Dec 22	Dec 21
Christmas (Except Armenian)	Dec 25	Dec 25	Dec 25	Dec 25

IV

INDEXES

ORGANIZATIONS

INDEXES

INDIVIDUALS

This list contains the names of people found in the listings of Cooperative Organizatins, Religious Bodies, Regional Ecumenical Agencies, Seminaries and Bible Schools and Periodicals.

INDEXES

296